Microsoft®

VBScript

Professional Projects

Microsoft®

VBScript

Professional Projects

Jerry Lee Ford, Jr.

Premier Press™

ISBN: 1-59200-056-8

Library of Congress Catalog Card Number: 2003104025

Printed in the United States of America

03 04 05 06 07 BH 10 9 8 7 6 5 4 3 2 1

Premier Press, a division of Course Technology
25 Thomson Place
Boston, MA 02210

SVP, Retail and Strategic Market Group:
Andy Shafran

Publisher:
Stacy L. Hiquet

Senior Marketing Manager:
Sarah O'Donnell

Marketing Manager:
Heather Hurley

Manager of Editorial Services:
Heather Talbot

Acquisitions Editor:
Todd Jensen

Associate Marketing Manager:
Kristin Eisenzopf

Project Editor:
Argosy

Technical Reviewer:
Zac Hester

Retail Market Coordinator:
Sarah Dubois

Copy Editor:
Ginny Kaczmarek

Interior Layout:
Argosy

Cover Designer:
Mike Tanamachi

Indexer:
Elizabeth Hoff

Proofreader:
Christopher Mattison

Dedication

To Alexander, William, Molly, and Mary.

Acknowledgments

There are a number of people who deserve a lot of credit for their hard work on this book. I especially want to thank Todd Jensen for working with me as the book's acquisitions editor on yet another writing project. I also want to thank the book's project editor, Alex Bilsky, as well as its copy editor, Ginny Kaczmarek, for their excellence. Finally, I wish to thank Zac Hester, the book's technical editor, who has now worked with me on four different books.

About the Author

Jerry Lee Ford, Jr., is an author, educator, and IT professional with 15 years of experience in information technology, including roles as an automation analyst, a technical manager, a technical support analyst, an automation engineer, and a security analyst. Jerry is an MCSE and has also earned Microsoft's MCP and MCP + Internet certifications. In addition, he has a master's degree in business administration from Virginia Commonwealth University in Richmond, Virginia. Jerry is also the author of 11 other books, including *Learn JavaScript in a Weekend*, *Learn VBScript in a Weekend*, *Microsoft Windows Shell Scripting and WSH Administrator's Guide*, *Microsoft WSH and VBScript for the Absolute Beginner*, and *Microsoft Windows XP Professional Administrator's Guide*. He has over five years of experience as an adjunct instructor teaching networking courses in information technology. Jerry lives in Richmond, Virginia, with his wife, Mary, and their children, Alexander, William, and Molly.

Contents at a Glance

Contents

Introduction

Goal of This Book

The goal of this book is to provide programmers, power users, and system administrators who have a previous programming background with a project-oriented approach to learning the VBScript (*Visual Basic Scripting*) language. VBScript is a member of the Visual Basic family of programming languages that includes both Visual Basic and VBA (*Visual Basic for Applications*).

VBScript is a scripting language that acts as a tool for rapid application development in a host of different operating environments. VBScript provides the ability to automate tasks on Windows operating systems using the WSH (*Windows Script Host*). The WSH provides VBScripts with access to Windows resources, such as the Windows file system, the desktop, the registry, and network resources. In addition, when combined with HTML and executed within Internet Explorer, VBScript allows the user to create interactive client-side Web content.

The book's opening chapters provide a complete review of VBScript, covering all the elements that make up this scripting language. The bulk of the book focuses on exploring the implementation of four scripting projects, each of which is based on a real-life scenario. In the first project, VBScript and the WSH are used to assist a small team of desktop engineers with the customization and deployment of new computers. The second project demonstrates how VBScript and the WSH can be used to assist a team of programmers analyzing reports generated by a collection of applications for which they are responsible. The third project builds upon the work performed in the second project by demonstrating how to establish a centralized management reporting station where the programmers can view summary reports based on data retrieved from distributed computers. The final project demonstrates how to use VBScript, the WSH, and Internet Explorer to create dynamic Web content that displays information extracted from data generated by the third project.

One of the powerful capabilities provided to VBScript by the WSH is the ability to execute any Windows command. This capability is exploited by the projects presented in this book. Appendix A provides a complete Windows command reference. Appendix B provides a description of the book's companion Web site, where copies of all the scripts presented by the book can be downloaded.

What You Need to Begin

This book covers VBScript within the context of two different execution environments, the WSH and Internet Explorer. In order to be able to effectively use VBScript with the WSH, you will need a number of tools, including:

- A computer running a Windows operating system
- WSH version 5.6, which can be obtained for free at **http://msdn.microsoft.com/scripting**
- A plain text editor, such as the Windows Notepad application, or a script editor that can be used to create plain text files
- Access to one or more computers on a local area network in order to complete the third project

In order to be able to use the information provided in the book for Web page development, you will need access to the following tools:

- A computer running a Windows operating system
- Internet Explorer and copies of any other Internet Explorer compatible browsers that you plan to support in order to test the display of your Web content
- A plain text or script editor

Conventions Used in This Book

This book includes a number of special elements that are designed to make it easier for you to read and work with. These special elements are outlined below:

NOTE

This special element provides additional helpful or interesting information that is not essential to the topic at hand.

TIP

This special element is used to provide suggested techniques and shortcuts that can help you to save time or work more efficiently.

CAUTION

This special element is used to identify situations where extra attention is required in order to prevent a problem from occurring.

Terms are italicized throughout the book the first time that they are referenced in order to highlight and emphasize key information.

PART I

Introducing Microsoft VBScript

Chapter 1

What Is VBScript?

VBScript is a scripting language created by Microsoft. It was originally developed to support client-side Web page development. However, Microsoft has since ported it over to a number of programming environments, including the WSH (*Windows Script Host*). The WSH is an execution environment designed to support script execution on Windows operating systems. By providing the ability to combine VBScript and the WSH, Microsoft has given power users, programmers, and system and network administrators a scripting language that supports rapid application development using the same friendly and easy-to-learn syntax that made Visual Basic famous.

Introducing VBScript

VBScript is an interpreted scripting language. VBScripts require an execution environment in order to run. Examples of VBScript execution environments include both Internet Explorer and the WSH. Within the context of Web page development, VBScripts are embedded and execute inside HTML (*Hypertext Markup Language*) pages. When executed by the WSH, VBScripts are stored as plain text files with a .vbs file extension and run from the Windows command prompt or the Windows desktop.

VBScript is an excellent language for improving client-side Web page development and for developing small scripts that automate tasks on Windows operating systems. It is also a good choice for quickly developing small applications and utilities or for prototyping new applications.

VBScripts are limited by the constraints imposed by their execution environment. This means that while a VBScript embedded within an HTML page can validate form contents and control browser activity, it cannot access local disk drives or other resources on the computer on which it executes. On the other hand, while VBScripts that are executed by the WSH can access local drivers and printers, they cannot work with browser-based resources.

Examples of tasks that VBScripts embedded inside Web pages can perform include the following:

- Creating animation effects

- Displaying messages on the Internet Explorer status bar
- Interacting with Internet and Intranet visitors using pop-up dialog boxes
- Using cookies to collect and store information about visitors
- Redirecting visitors to specify sets of HTML pages based on their detected browser type and version
- Validating HTML forms
- Managing HTML frames

VBScripts designed to execute with the WSH have an entirely different purpose. Examples of tasks that VBScripts run by the WSH can perform include the following:

- Creating new user accounts
- Managing the Windows file system
- Creating shortcuts
- Managing local drives and printers
- Managing network drives and printers
- Reporting system and status information
- Interacting directly with other applications
- Modifying system settings via modifications to the Windows registry
- Managing Windows services and event logs

History of VBScript

As far as programming languages go, VBScript is still relatively new. Microsoft first introduced it in 1996 as a client-side Web page development scripting language for Internet Explorer 3.0. However, VBScript's arrival was preceded by another client-side scripting language, known at the time as LiveScript and later renamed JavaScript. JavaScript's head start, combined with concern over the proprietary nature of VBScript, led to a slow start for Microsoft's new scripting language. In addition, Netscape never added support for VBScript to its browser, making JavaScript the only universally supported client-side scripting language. As a result, while JavaScript was quickly accepted by the Internet community, VBScript's success was slow in coming.

VBScript's popularity began to increase when Microsoft released VBScript version 2.0 and enabled it to provide IIS 3.0 (*Internet Information Server 3.0*) with a server-side Web development scripting language. By embedding VBScripts inside ASPs (*Active Server Pages*), Web developers were able to use VBScript as a means of accessing data stored on server-side databases and to more easily provide dynamic Web content.

VBScript version 3.0 was released as a component supplied with numerous Microsoft products. This list of products included:

- Internet Explorer 4
- IIS 4
- Outlook 98
- WSH

Of all these environments, it was the WSH where VBScript had the greatest impact. Individuals with a Visual Basic background quickly found that they now had a powerful scripting tool that supported rapid application development and task automation.

VBScript version 4.0 was introduced as part of the Microsoft Visual Studio application development suite and given the ability to access the Windows file system. VBScript version 5.0 was released along with Windows 2000. In addition, Microsoft distributed it as a part of WSH 2.0 and Internet Explorer 5.0. When Microsoft released Windows XP and Internet Explorer 6.0 in 2001, it included VBScript 5.6 and WSH 5.6, both of which represent the current releases of these products.

Visual Basic Family of Programming Languages

VBScript is one of three languages that make up the Visual Basic family of programming languages. These three languages include:

- **Visual Basic**. This language is appropriate for developing stand-alone applications and for developing COM components and ActiveX controls.
- **VBA (*Visual Basic for Applications*)**. This language is used to customize VBA-supported desktop applications such as Microsoft Excel or Microsoft Access.
- **VBScript**. This language is best used for client-side Web page development, for the rapid development of scripts that automate Windows tasks, and for the development of small utilities.

While all three of these languages are closely related and share many of the same features, each has been designed to suit a different developmental need. Visual Basic is designed to support the development of new applications, whereas VBA is designed to provide an automation facility for specific applications. VBScript, on the other hand, is designed as a general purpose scripting language for deployment in a number of different environments.

Visual Basic

Visual Basic was introduced in 1991 and was an instant hit. New programmers found it intuitive and easy to learn, whereas experienced programmers found it reliable and powerful. The current version of Visual Basic is called Visual Basic .NET. This name reflects the language's support for Microsoft's .NET framework.

NOTE

.NET is a Microsoft framework that supports the exchange of data over a number of different mediums, including local area networks and the Internet. Visit **www.microsoft.com/net** to learn more about Microsoft's .NET framework.

Visual Basic applications are compiled programs and can execute independently on any Windows operating system. As a compiled program, all the statements that make up a Visual Basic program are converted into and stored as binary code, allowing them to run quickly. In order to create Visual Basic applications, programmers must first learn how to work with Visual Basic's IDE (*Integrated Development Environment*). An IDE is a development tool that assists programmers in creating new programs by supplying a compiler, a debugger, a help system, and project management tools.

Because of its IDE, Visual Basic is not well suited to the development of small automation scripts. Instead, Visual Basic is best suited to developing applications that require stand-alone execution and that justify the time and effort required to create them.

TIP

To find out more about Visual Basic .NET, refer to *Microsoft Visual Basic .NET Professional Projects*, by Pooja Bembey and Kuljit Kaur with NIIT (Premier Press, 2002).

NOTE

You can learn more about Visual Basic at the Microsoft Visual Basic Web site at **http://msdn.microsoft.com/vbasic**.

Visual Basic for Applications

The second member of the Visual Basic family of applications is VBA, which Microsoft introduced in 1993. VBA provides a subset of Visual Basic's functionality for a particular application. VBA is designed to provide the ability to customize a host application such as Microsoft Excel or Access. For example, using VBA for Microsoft Access, a programmer can develop an entire application that uses the Microsoft Access database as its repository. VBA is designed to provide programmers with a foundation from which to begin their application development, rather than requiring them to start from scratch.

The current version of VBA is version 6.3. It was released in 2001 and supports the following list of applications:

- Microsoft Excel
- Microsoft Access
- Microsoft Word
- Microsoft Outlook
- Microsoft FrontPage
- Microsoft PowerPoint

TIP

To find out more about VBA for Microsoft Excel, refer to *Microsoft Excel VBA Professional Projects*, by Duane Birnbaum (Premier Press, 2003).

TIP

To find out more about VBA for Microsoft Access, refer to *Microsoft Access VBA Programming for the Absolute Beginner*, by Michael Vine (Premier Press, 2002).

NOTE

You can learn more about VBA at the Microsoft Visual Basic Web site at **http://msdn.microsoft.com/vba**.

VBScript Execution Environments

Despite VBScript's initial lackluster start, Microsoft maintained a strong commitment to VBScript, continually updating and improving it. Since its inception, Microsoft has ported VBScript over to a number of different environments, demonstrating VBScript's flexibility and adaptability. As a result, VBScript has grown increasingly popular over the years, providing programmers with multiple avenues for exploiting their VBScript skills.

The following list outlines the major execution environments that currently support VBScript:

- **Internet Explorer.** VBScript provides a robust client-side scripting language for Web page development.
- **WSH.** VBScript provides a scripting language for automating mundane or complex system and network tasks.
- **IIS and ASP.** VBScript, when embedded within ASPs, provides dynamic Web content as well as access data stored on local server-side databases.
- **Outlook.** VBScript provides a tool for automating Outlook functions.
- **Microsoft Windows Script Console.** This is a new technology that allows VBScript to be incorporated into third-party applications, thus extending its deployment to a host of new environments.

VBScript Web Page Development

VBScript was originally developed as a client-side Web scripting language, and over the years, Microsoft has continued its commitment to this technology. When used for client-side Web page development, VBScripts are generally embedded inside HTML pages and downloaded into client browsers as part of a Web page.

Like the HTML pages that contain them, VBScripts can be created using any editor that can saves files in plain text. For example, the Microsoft Notepad application makes for an acceptable editor. However, there are plenty of good HTML editors available today that also include support for VBScript development.

TIP

One good example of an HTML and script editor is HomeSite. HomeSite provides numerous features, including:

- Color coding of HTML and VBScript statements
- The ability to test Web page and script execution without leaving the editor
- Code validation
- Templates and wizards

You can learn more about HomeSite by visiting the Macromedia Web site at **www.macromedia.com/software/homesite**.

Compatible Browsers

VBScript is supported by the Microsoft Internet Explorer browser but not by Netscape Communicator. VBScript is also supported by a larger number of third-party browsers, which are based at least in part on Internet Explorer. This provides VBScript with a significantly broader base of support on the Internet than is generally recognized.

For example, it is not surprising that the MSN Explorer browser supplied by Microsoft to its MSN Internet customers supports VBScript. Other examples include both CompuServe and AOL who supply their customers with custom browsers based on Internet Explorer. The following list provides a glimpse at the number of Internet Explorer compatible browsers currently available.

- MSN Explorer
- AOL
- CompuServe
- EarthLink LiteAOL
- UltraBrowser
- Fast Browser Pro
- NeoPlanet
- ExplorerRapidBrowser

- CrystalPort
- SmartExplorer
- Oligo

NOTE

You can learn more about Internet Explorer at the Microsoft Internet Explorer Web site, **www.microsoft.com/windows/ie**.

Adding VBScript to Web Pages

VBScript integration with Web content is usually achieved by embedding VBScripts directly inside HTML pages by placing VBScript statements inside the HTML `<SCRIPT>` and `</SCRIPT>` tags. You can use these tags to embed VBScripts into both the HEAD and BODY sections of any HTML page.

Using the `<SCRIPT>` and `</SCRIPT>` tags, you can add VBScripts to HTML pages in three different ways, as outlined below.

- To automatically run VBScripts when HTML pages are loaded by the browser
- To run VBScripts in response to events, such as visitors clicking on images, buttons, or links
- To run scripts stored externally from the HTML pages that contain the `<SCRIPT>` and `</SCRIPT>` tag references

Loading VBScripts

The syntax required to embed a VBScript into an HTML page so that it automatically runs when the page is loaded is outlined below.

```
<SCRIPT LANGUAGE="ScriptingLanguage" TYPE="TEXT/Language" SRC="url"> </SCRIPT>
```

The `<SCRIPT>` tag marks the beginning of a VBScript. The `LANGUAGE` attribute specifies the scripting language that is being embedded. For VBScript, you may set the `LANGUAGE` attribute using either of the following methods.

```
LANGUAGE="VBScript"
```

or

```
LANGUAGE="VBS"
```

Alternatively, instead of using the LANGUAGE parameter, you can specify the TYPE parameter, which is used in one of the following forms.

```
TYPE="TEXT/VBScript"
```

or

```
TYPE="TEXT/VBS"
```

Using the SRC parameter, you can specify the name and location of a file where an external VBScript is stored. This option is demonstrated later in this chapter.

The </SCRIPT> tag marks the end of the VBScript. Between the opening <SCRIPT> and closing </SCRIPT> tags you may include as many VBScript statements as required. For example, the following HTML page contains two embedded VBScripts, one in the BODY section and another in the HEAD section.

```
<HTML>
  <HEAD>

    <TITLE>Script 1.1.html - A HTML page with two embedded VBScripts</TITLE>
    <SCRIPT LANGUAGE="VBScript">
      Sub DisplayPopup
        MsgBox "This message was displayed by a second VBScript."
      End Sub
    </SCRIPT>
  </HEAD>
  <BODY>
    <H2>VBScript Demonstration</H2>
    <SCRIPT LANGUAGE="VBScript">
      MsgBox "Greetings. Click on OK to run the second VBScript."
      DisplayPopup
    </SCRIPT>
  </BODY>
</HTML>
```

The VBScript in the BODY section is automatically executed when the HTML page is loaded by the browser. It displays a message in a pop-up dialog box, as demonstrated in Figure 1.1. The second VBScript is defined as a subroutine in the HEAD section and is executed when called by the VBScript located in the BODY section, displaying the pop-up dialog box shown in Figure 1.2.

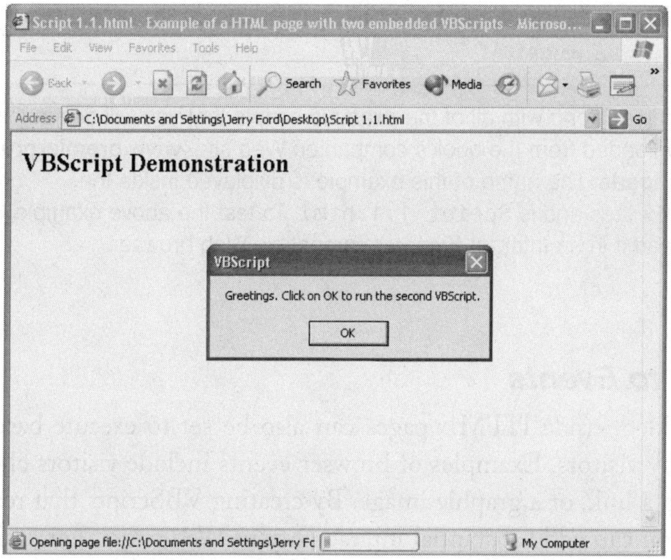

FIGURE 1.1 *A demonstration of a pop-up dialog box displayed when the HTML page that defines it is loaded by Internet Explorer*

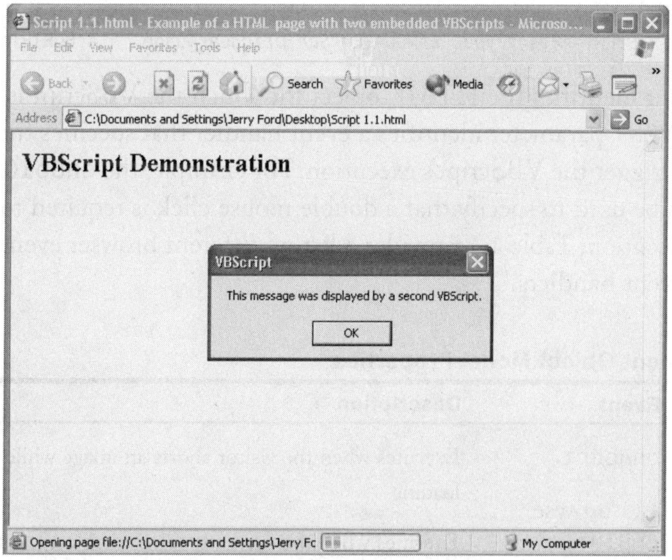

FIGURE 1.2 *Pop-up dialog box generated by a VBScript subroutine called by another VBScript*

NOTE

The previous example, along with all of the example scripts that you will see in this book, can be downloaded from the book's companion Web site, **www.premierpress-books.com/downloads**. The name of this example is displayed inside the `<TITLE></TITLE>` tags and is `Script 1.1.html`. To test the above example, download it and load it in an Internet Explorer compatible Web browser.

Responding to Events

VBScripts embedded inside HTML pages can also be set to execute based on events triggered by visitors. Examples of browser events include visitors clicking on a form button, a link, or a graphic image. By creating VBScripts that react to browser events, you can add substantial interactivity to Web pages. For example, you can ask the visitor for confirmation to continue after clicking on a link where secure information may be stored. You could also trigger a VBScript that performs form validation after the visitor clicks on the Submit button and to provide instructions in the event that the form is not properly filled out.

In order to set up this kind of reference, you must use the following syntax when defining the <SCRIPT> and </SCRIPT> tags.

```
<SCRIPT FOR="Object" EVENT="EventType" LANGUAGE="ScriptingLanguage" > </SCRIPT>
```

The `FOR` parameter identifies the HTML object for which the VBScript is to be associated. The `EVENT` parameter identifies a event handler that specifies the type of event that will trigger the VBScript's execution. For example, the `onDblClick` event handler can be used to specify that a double mouse click is required to trigger the script's execution. Table 1.1 provides a list of different browser events and their associated event handlers.

Table 1.1 Document Object Model Properties

Property	Event	Description
`Abort`	`onAbort`	Executes when the visitor aborts an image while it is loading
`Blur`	`onBlur`	Executes when the currently selected object loses focus
`Change`	`onChange`	Executes when the visitor changes an object

Table 1.1 Document Object Model Properties *(continued)*

Property	Event	Description
`Click`	`onClick`	Executes when the visitor clicks an object
`DblClick`	`onDblClick`	Executes when the visitor double-clicks an object
`DragDrop`	`onDragDrop`	Executes when the visitor drags and drops an object onto a frame or window
`Error`	`onError`	Executes when an error occurs on the HTML page
`Focus`	`onFocus`	Executes when a visitor selects an object
`KeyDown`	`onKeyDown`	Executes when a visitor presses down on a key
`KeyPress`	`onKeyPress`	Executes when a visitor presses and releases a key
`KeyUp`	`onKeyUp`	Executes when a visitor releases a key
`Load`	`onLoad`	Executes when an HTML page or image finishes loading
`MouseDown`	`onMouseDown`	Executes when a visitor presses a mouse button
`MouseMove`	`onMouseMove`	Executes when a visitor moves the pointer
`MouseOut`	`onMouseOut`	Executes when a visitor moves the pointer off of an object
`MouseOver`	`onMouseOver`	Executes when a visitor moves the pointer over an object
`MouseUp`	`onMouseUp`	Executes when a visitor releases a mouse button
`MouseWheel`	`onMouseWheel`	Executes when a mouse wheel is rotated
`Move`	`onMove`	Executes when the visitor moves a frame or window
`Reset`	`onReset`	Executes when a visitor clicks on a reset button
`Resize`	`onResize`	Executes when the visitor resizes a frame or window
`Select`	`onSelect`	Executes when a visitor selects the contents of a form text field
`Submit`	`onSubmit`	Executes when a visitor clicks on a submit button
`Unload`	`onUnload`	Executes when a visitor closes the browser window or frame or loads a different URL

The following example demonstrates how to set up a VBScript inside an HTML page to react when the visitor clicks on a form button.

```
<HTML>
  <HEAD>
    <TITLE>Script 1.2 - Example of a VBScript triggered by a browser event</TITLE>
  </HEAD>
  <BODY>
    <FORM NAME="TestForm">
      <INPUT TYPE=button NAME="TestButton" VALUE="Click on Me">
      <SCRIPT FOR="TestButton" EVENT="onClick" LANGUAGE="VBScript">
      MsgBox "Greetings. Thanks for visiting!"
      </SCRIPT>
    </FORM>
  </BODY>
</HTML>
```

In this example, a form called `TestForm` is defined that contains a single form element, a button called `TestButton` that displays the message `Click on Me`. A VBScript has been added to the HTML page. It has been set up to execute only when the `click` event occurs for `TestButton`, as highlighted in the example. When this occurs, the pop-up dialog box shown in Figure 1.3 is displayed.

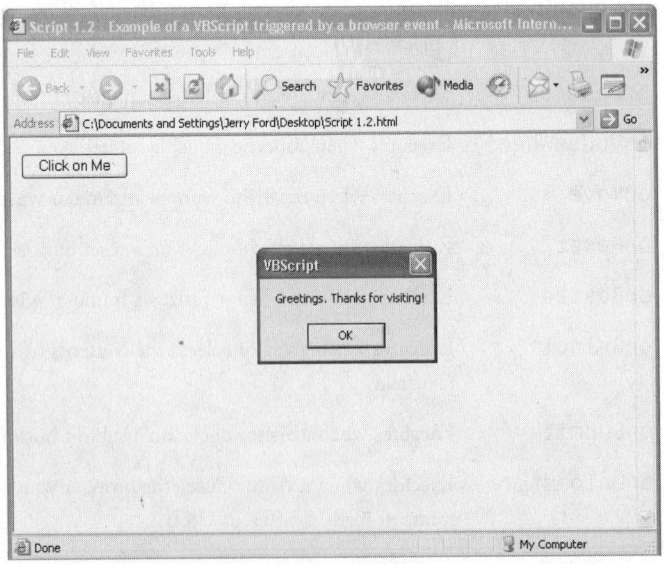

FIGURE 1.3 *A demonstration of a pop-up dialog box triggered by the VBScript* `onClick` *event handler*

Referencing External Scripts

VBScript also provides the ability to separate your VBScripts from your HTML by storing VBScripts as external files with a .vbs file extension and then providing a reference to them. This option keeps your HTML and VBScript code separate, potentially making both more readable and manageable. This option also allows you to create VBScript that can be called upon and shared by any number of HTML pages.

The following example demonstrates how to reference an external script from within an HTML page.

```
<HTML>
  <HEAD>
    <TITLE>Script 1.3 - An example of how to execute an external VBScript</TITLE>
  </HEAD>
  <BODY>
    <SCRIPT SRC="Script 1.4.vbs" LANGUAGE="VBScript"> </SCRIPT>
  </BODY>
</HTML>
```

As you can see, the `SRC="Script 1.4.vbs"` parameter identifies the name of the external VBScript file. The external VBScript file can contain any number of VBScript statements. It must be saved as a plain text file and cannot contain any HTML whatsoever. For example, if the following VBScript statement were saved as `Script 1.4.vbs`, it would display the pop-up dialog box shown in Figure 1.4 when executed by the HTML example.

```
MsgBox "This message is being displayed by an external VBScript."
```

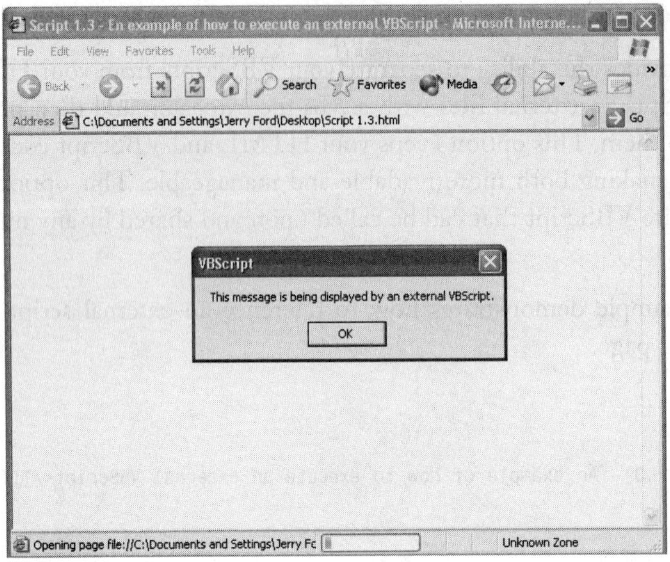

FIGURE 1.4 *A pop-up dialog box displayed by an externally referenced VBScript*

The WSH

The WSH is a programming environment that supports the execution of scripts directly from the Windows desktop or command prompt. By default, the WSH supports both the VBScript and JScript scripting languages, although third-party support for other scripting languages is available. The WSH provides scripts with an environment in which they can execute. In addition, the WSH provides scripts with direct access to a number of Windows resources, including:

- Windows file system
- Windows desktop
- Windows registry
- Windows services
- Printer and disk drives
- Windows Start menu
- Windows Quick Launch toolbar
- Other Windows applications

The current version of the WSH is version 5.6. This version of the WSH was supplied with both versions of the Windows XP operating system. Different versions of the WSH shipped with different versions of Windows, as shown in Table 1.2.

Table 1.2 Microsoft Operating System Support for WSH

Operating System	WSH Supported	Version
Windows 95	Yes	N/A
Windows 98	Yes	1.0
Windows Me	Yes	2.0
Windows NT	Yes	N/A
Windows 2000	Yes	2.0
Windows XP	Yes	5.6

While Windows 95 and NT 4.0 were never shipped with the WSH, these two operating systems do support it. In addition, you can upgrade the WSH to version 5.6 on any Windows operating system starting with Windows 95.

NOTE

To download the most current release of the WSH, visit **http://msdn.microsoft.com/scripting**.

WSH Architecture

The WSH is a 32-bit application. It is composed of three major components. These components include:

- Scripting engines
- Script execution hosts
- A core object model

Scripting engines provide WSH scripts with an interpreter that translates script statements into executable code. The WSH provides two different execution hosts. These hosts provide the ability to run scripts from either the Windows desktop or the Windows command prompt. Finally, the core object model provides scripts with access to Windows resources. Figure 1.5 depicts the relationship of each of these three components to one another.

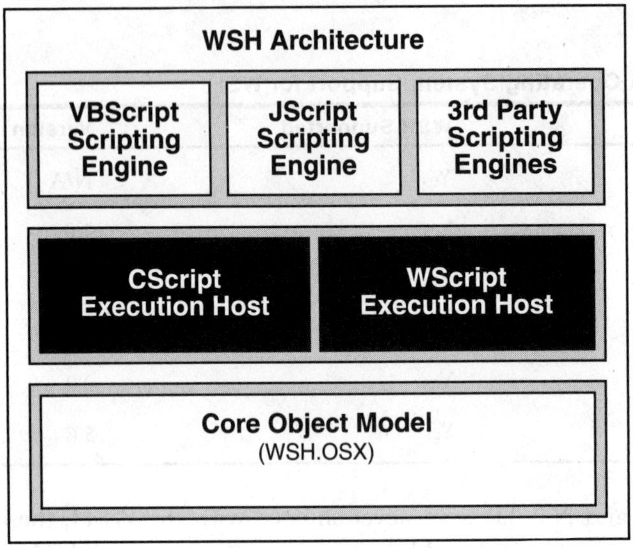

FIGURE 1.5 *The components that comprise the WSH*

Scripting Engines

Scripting engines provide the WSH with the ability to interpret statements written in a particular scripting language to a format that can be executed by an execution host. By default, Microsoft supplies the following scripting engines with the WSH:

- VBScript
- JScript

Microsoft designed the WSH in a modular fashion. This allows Microsoft to update the WSH on a component-by-component basis without having to rework the entire application in order to add new features and capabilities. This same architecture allows third-party software developers to add support for additional scripting engines. This has already been done for a number of different scripting languages, as shown in Table 1.3.

Table 1.3 Third-Party WSH Compatible Script Engines

Language	Name	Web Site
Perl	ActivePerl	**www.activestate.com**
Python	ActivePython	**www.activestate.com**
REXX	Object REXX	**www-3.ibm.com/software/ad/obj-rexx**

The choice of which scripting language to use when automating a Windows task is entirely up to the programmer. However, VBScript has emerged as the most popular scripting language currently supported by the WSH.

Execution Hosts

Once a scripting engine interprets a script, the script is ready to be executed. This is the job of the script execution host. The WSH supplies two different script execution hosts, as outlined below.

- **`CScript.exe`**. Provides for script execution from the Windows command prompt and provides scripts with the ability to display output as text messages within the Windows command console
- **`WScript.exe`**. Provides for script execution from the Windows desktop and provides the ability to display output as text messages inside graphical pop-up dialog boxes

The only difference between the two script execution hosts is the ability of the WScript.exe execution host to display output graphically. Otherwise, both script execution hosts provide equivalent functionality. To run a script from the Windows desktop using the `WScript.exe` execution host, simply locate it and double-click on its icon. Like the `Cscript.exe` execution host, the `WScript.exe` execution host can be used to run scripts from the Windows command prompt. You can run a script from the Windows command prompt using the `WScript.exe` execution host as demonstrated below.

```
WScript scriptname
```

Likewise, you can run a script form the Windows command prompt using the `CScript.exe` execution host, as demonstrated below.

```
CScript scriptname
```

If you have any arguments that you need to pass to the script, type them separated by spaces after the script's name, as demonstrated below.

```
CScript scriptname arg1 arg2 arg3
```

As a general rule, it is typical to use the `CScript.exe` execution host when a script will be run from the Windows command prompt or when it will be run by the Windows scheduling service and no interaction is required with the user. When user interaction is required, it's generally better to do so using pop-up dialog boxes rather than the Windows command prompt, making the `WScript.exe` execution host the better choice.

The Core Object Model

The WSH's core object model provides scripts with the ability to programmatically interact with and manipulate Windows resources, which the object model exposes or represents as objects. The WSH core object model is implemented as an ActiveX control called WSH.OCX. Examples of the objects exposed by the WSH object model include drives, printers, files, and shortcuts. Every object exposed by the WSH object model has a collection of properties and methods. VBScripts can use these properties and methods to interact with and control these resources.

Properties are object-specific attributes that describe or modify a particular feature or component of the object. For example, a desktop shortcut has a file name and a file extension. The values of properties can be viewed and changed, thus having a direct impact on the shortcut. A *method* is a built-in WSH function. Methods can be used to take action on an object. For example, methods exist that allow scripts to create and delete shortcuts.

Using the methods and properties belonging to objects exposed by the WSH core object model, a VBScript can be developed that can automate tasks on any computer running Windows 95 or later where the WSH has been installed.

Writing WSH VBScripts

VBScripts executed by the WSH are saved as plain text files with a .vbs file extension. Unlike Visual Basic or VBA, VBScript does not provide a built-in IDE. You can use any editor to create VBScript files so long as the editor can save the files in plain text. For example, the Notepad application supplied with all versions of Windows suits this purpose.

NOTE

There are a number of third-party VBScript editors that you might want to investigate that will make VBScript development easier when working with the WSH. These editors provide features such as line numbers, color statement coding, and the ability to test scripts without exiting the editor. One such example is VbsEdit, which you will find at **www.adersoft.com**.

For example, the following two VBScript statements represent a small VBScript.

```
UserName = InputBox("What is your name?")
MsgText = MsgBox("Greetings " & UserName)
```

The first statement collects the user's name, and the second statement then uses the user's name to display a custom greeting. Once saved and executed, the VBScript will interact with the user as demonstrated in Figures 1.6 and 1.7.

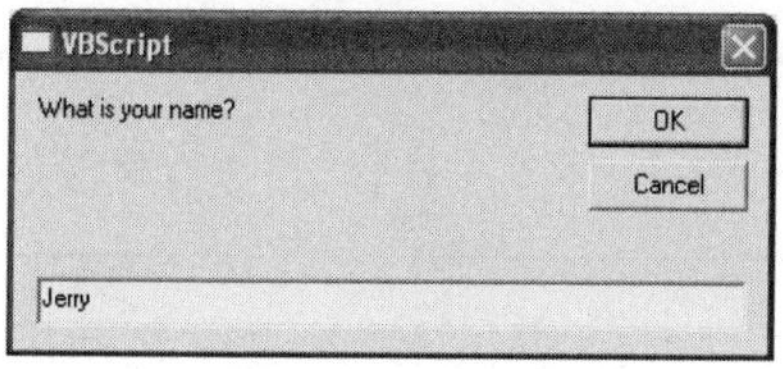

FIGURE 1.6 *Using the WSH to run a VBScript that collects a user's name*

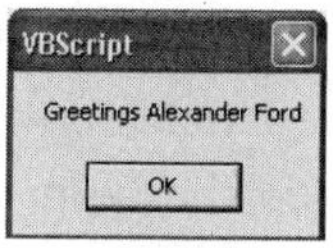

FIGURE 1.7 *Using the user's name to display a custom welcome message*

The Windows Command Prompt

A good understanding of how to work with the Windows command prompt is an important prerequisite for any VBScript programmer. The Windows command prompt is a text-based interface between you and the operating system. It can be used as an effective alternative to working with the Windows GUI (*graphical user interface*).

To access the Windows command prompt on a computer running Windows XP, click on Start, All Programs, Accessories and then Command Prompt. This starts a Windows console, as shown in Figure 1.8.

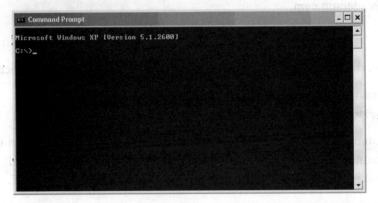

FIGURE 1.8 *To work with the Windows command prompt, you must first open a Windows console*

> **TIP**
>
> To quickly access the Windows command prompt on any Windows computer, click on Start and then Run. This displays the Run dialog box. Next type **CMD** and then click on OK.

By default, the Windows command prompt appears as a drive letter followed by a colon, a backslash, and the greater than (>) character. Just to the right of the command prompt will be a blinking cursor. The blinking cursor indicates that the command prompt is ready to accept a new command. You may now type any Windows command and press the Enter key as demonstrated below.

```
C:\>ver
Microsoft Windows XP [Version 5.1.2600]
C:\>
```

As you can see, the VER command was entered. This command displays information about the version of Windows being run. The output produced by the command was displayed in the Windows console, and then the command prompt was displayed again, along with the blinking cursor indicating that it was ready to accept a new command.

> **NOTE**
>
> For a detailed listing of Windows commands, refer to Appendix A, "Windows Command Reference."

The following VBScript statement represents a one-line VBScript file.

```
WScript.Echo "This message is being displayed by a test VBScript"
```

When executed from the Windows command prompt using the `CScript.exe` execution host, this VBScript displays the output shown in Figure 1.9.

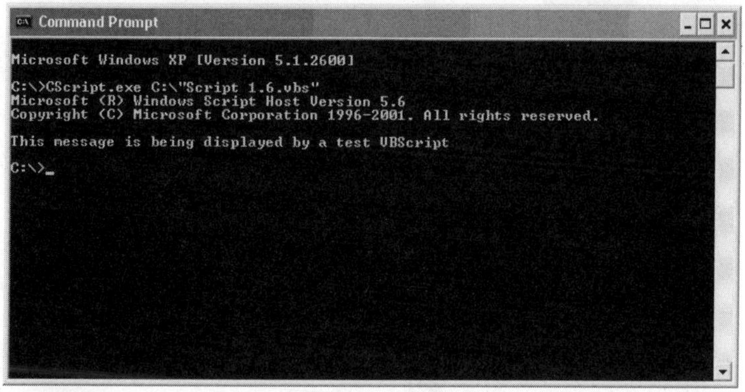
Command Prompt
Microsoft Windows XP [Version 5.1.2600]
C:\>CScript.exe C:\"Script 1.6.vbs"
Microsoft (R) Windows Script Host Version 5.6
Copyright (C) Microsoft Corporation 1996-2001. All rights reserved.
This message is being displayed by a test VBScript
C:\>_

FIGURE 1.9 *Examining the results displayed by a VBScript run using the* `CScript.exe` *execution host*

When done working with the Windows command prompt, you can close the Windows console like any other Windows application. This is done by clicking on the Close icon in the upper right-hand corner of the dialog box or by right-clicking on the command prompt icon in the upper left-hand corner and selecting Close. You may also close the Windows console by typing the `EXIT` command at the Windows command prompt and pressing the Enter key.

Summary

In this chapter, you learned about the origins of VBScript. This included an overview of the Visual Basic family of programming languages as well as an explanation of the various environments to which Microsoft has ported VBScript. In addition, you learned the basic steps involved in integrating VBScripts into HTML pages. You also learned about the basic architecture behind the WSH. Finally, you learned how to create and execute scripts using both the WSH and Internet Explorer.

Chapter 2

Errors, Constants, and Variables

This chapter will cover numerous VBScript topics. It opens with a discussion of VBScript statements and their syntax requirements and then describes how to correct and fix these types of errors. Statements that create VBScript comments and define constants and variables are also reviewed. In addition, the chapter will provide information regarding the use of built-in VBScript constants. Various topics related to variables, including variable naming rules and ways to limit variables' scope, will also be discussed.

VBScript Statements

VBScript is made up of a number of programming statements, each of which performs a specific function. Table 2.1 provides a list of the statements that make up the VBScript programming language. This chapter will cover the VBScript statements that deal with VBScript comments, constants, and variables.

Table 2.1 VBScript Statements

Statement	Description
`Call`	Redirects flow control in the script to a procedure
`Class`	Defines a class name
`Const`	Defines a constant
`Dim`	Defines a VBScript variable
`Do...Loop`	Repeats a group of statements as long as a condition is `True` or until the condition becomes True
`Erase`	Reinitializes the elements in an array
`Execute`	Runs the specified statement
`ExecuteGlobal`	Runs the specified statement in a script's global namespace
`Exit`	Terminates a loop, sub, or function
`For Each...Next`	Iteratively processes the contents of an array or collection
`For...Next`	Repeats a loop a specified number of times

Table 2.1 VBScript Statements (*continued*)

Statement	Description
`Function`	Defines a function name and its arguments
`If...Then...Else`	Performs the execution of one or more statements based on the value of the tested expression
`On Error`	Turns on error handling
`Option Explicit`	Explicitly declares all variables in your script
`Private`	Defines a private variable
`Property Get`	Defines a property name and its arguments and returns its value
`Property Let`	Defines a property procedure's name and arguments
`Property Set`	Defines a property procedure's name and arguments
`Public`	Defines a public variable
`Randomize`	Initializes the random-number generator
`ReDim`	Defines or redefines dynamic-array variables
`Rem`	Used to place comments in scripts
`Select Case`	Defines a collection of tests and executes only one based on the value of an expression
`Set`	Assigns object references to variables
`Sub`	Defines a `Sub` name and its arguments
`While...Wend`	Performs the execution of one or more statements as long the specified condition remains `True`
`With`	Associates a series of statements that are to be executed for a specified object

VBScript Statement Syntax

Every VBScript statement has a unique syntax that must be carefully followed in order to perform a specific task when VBScripts execute. The chapters in this book will outline the specific syntax requirements of individual VBScript statements the first time that the statements are formally introduced and will provide examples of their use.

In addition to the syntax requirements specific to individual VBScript statements, there are a number of general rules that you must follow when writing your VBScript. These rules are outlined below.

- By default, all VBScript statements must be placed on one line.
- You may place two or more statements on a single line by ending each statement with the colon (`:`) character.
- You may spread a single statement over multiple lines by adding the underscore (_) character, known as the continuation character, to the end of each line.
- By default, VBScript is not case sensitive, meaning that different uses of case in the spelling of constants, variables, subroutine names, and function names are permitted.
- Strict enforcement of case sensitivity can be mandated by adding the `Option Explicit` statement to the beginning of a VBScript.

Syntax Errors

There are several types of errors that can occur during the execution of a VBScript. These errors include *logical errors*, in which the script produces unexpected results because of faulty logic on the part of the programmer, and *run-time errors*, which occur when a script attempts to do something that it cannot do. For example, run-time errors occur when scripts attempt to access objects that do not exist or are not available, which can be the case for both local and network disk drives. The third category of error is the *syntax error*, which occurs when programmers fail to use the proper syntax in the formulating of a VBScript statement. Unlike run-time errors, which occur during the execution of the script, syntax errors are flagged by the scripting engine during interpretation, thus preventing the script from even starting.

Run-time errors can be difficult to track down and find because they may be hidden in a seldom used portion of code within the script. On the other hand, a syntax error anywhere in a script will prevent its execution. Therefore, syntax errors should be easily discovered and fixed during initial script development and testing. For example, the following statement will produce the error shown in Figure 2.1 when run by the WSH.

```
MsgBox "Text must be enclosed within a pair of double quotation marks"
```

`MsgBox()` is a built-in VBScript function that can be used to display text in a pop-up dialog box. It requires that the text to be displayed must be enclosed within a matching pair of double quotation marks. In the previous example, the second double quotation mark is missing.

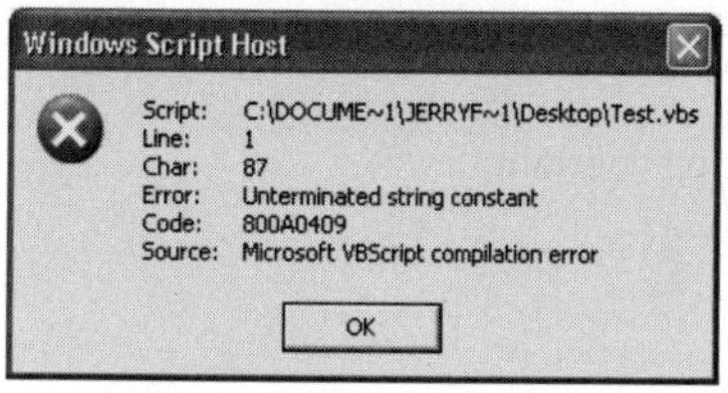

FIGURE 2.1 *Failure to follow a VBScript statement's syntax results in an error that terminates the script's execution*

Table 2.2 provides a list of VBScript errors that can occur as a result of not following the syntax rules for VBScript statements. An error number is assigned to every VBScript syntax error. Depending on the host environment in which VBScripts run, these error messages may be reported in either a hexadecimal or decimal format. Table 2.2 provides both the hexadecimal and decimal error numbers associated with each syntax error message.

Table 2.2 VBScript Syntax Errors

Hexadecimal	Decimal	Description
800A03E9	1001	Out of Memory
800A03EA	1002	Syntax error
800A03ED	1005	Expected ' ('
800A03EE	1006	Expected ') '
800A03F2	1010	Expected identifier
800A03F3	1011	Expected '='
800A03F4	1012	Expected 'If'
800A03F5	1013	Expected 'To'
800A03F5	1013	Invalid number

continues

Table 2.2 VBScript Syntax Errors (*continued*)

Hexadecimal	Decimal	Description
800A03F6	1014	Expected 'End'
800A03F6	1014	Invalid character
800A03F7	1015	Expected 'Function'
800A03F7	1015	Unterminated string constant
800A03F8	1016	Expected 'Sub'
800A03F9	1017	Expected 'Then'
800A03FA	1018	Expected 'Wend'
800A03FB	1019	Expected 'Loop'
800A03FC	1020	Expected 'Next'
800A03FD	1021	Expected 'Case'
800A03FE	1022	Expected 'Select'
800A03FF	1023	Expected expression
800A0400	1024	Expected statement
800A0401	1025	Expected end of statement
800A0402	1026	Expected integer constant
800A0403	1027	Expected 'While' or 'Until'
800A0404	1028	Expected 'While', 'Until', or end of statement
800A0405	1029	Expected 'With'
800A0406	1030	Identifier too long
800A040D	1037	Invalid use of 'Me' keyword
800A040E	1038	'loop' without 'do'
800A040F	1039	Invalid 'exit' statement
800A0410	1040	Invalid 'for' loop control variable
800A0411	1041	Name redefined
800A0412	1042	Must be first statement on the line
800A0414	1044	Cannot use parentheses when calling a Sub

Table 2.2 VBScript Syntax Errors (*continued*)

Hexadecimal	Decimal	Description
800A0415	1045	Expected literal constant
800A0416	1046	Expected 'In'
800A0417	1047	Expected 'Class'
800A0418	1048	Must be defined inside a class
800A0419	1049	Expected Let or Set or Get in property declaration
800A041A	1050	Expected 'Property'
800A041B	1051	Number of arguments must be consistent across properties' specification
800A041C	1052	Cannot have multiple default properties/methods in a class
800A041D	1053	Class initialize or terminate do not have arguments
800A041E	1054	Property Set or Let must have at least one argument
800A041F	1055	Unexpected Next
800A0421	1057	'Default' specification must also specify 'Public'
800A0422	1058	'Default' specification can only be on Property Get

Syntax errors are generally relatively easy to correct. The error messages that appear when syntax errors are discovered identify the error as well as the line number where the error occurred. Usually a quick review of the syntax for the offending statement is all that is required to identify and correct the error.

NOTE

Detailed coverage of run-time errors and how to handle and recover from them is provided in Chapter 6, "Data Collection, Notification, and Error Reporting."

Displaying Syntax Errors within Internet Explorer

The WSH always displays errors when they occur. However, by default, Internet Explorer suppresses the display of error messages. This works well since most users will not understand the error messages or be able to do anything about them anyway. Instead, Internet Explorer displays a small yellow icon in the bottom left-hand corner of the browser's status bar whenever an error occurs.

For example, the following HTML page contains the same type of VBScript error as the previous WSH example did. If you save and run it, you will see that Internet Explorer flags the error as demonstrated in Figure 2.2.

```
<HTML>
  <HEAD>
    <TITLE>Script 2.2 - VBScript syntax error example</TITLE>
  </HEAD>
  <BODY>
    <SCRIPT LANGUAGE="VBScript">
      MsgBox "Text must be enclosed within a pair of double quotation marks
    </SCRIPT>
  </BODY>
</HTML>
```

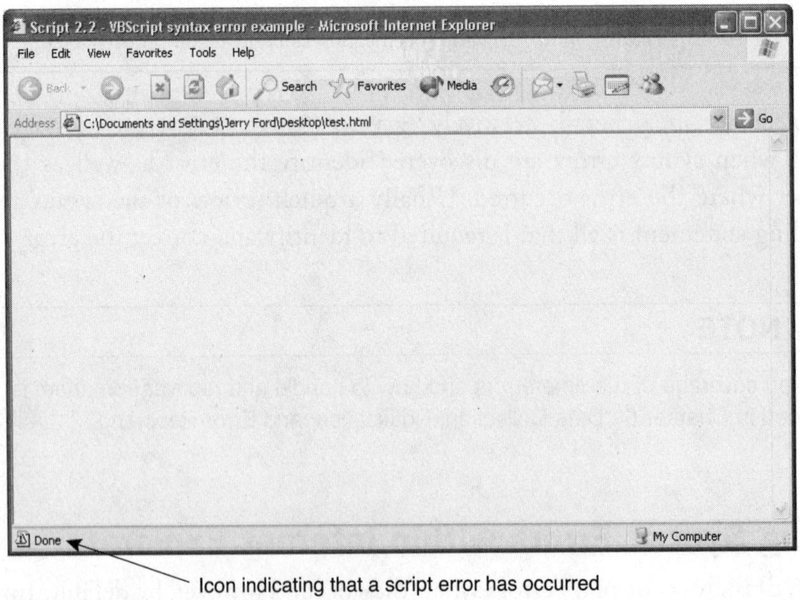

FIGURE 2.2 *Internet Explorer automatically suppresses the display of VBScript error messages*

To view the error message that caused Internet Explorer to display the yellow icon, double-click on the icon and the error will be displayed as demonstrated in Figure 2.3.

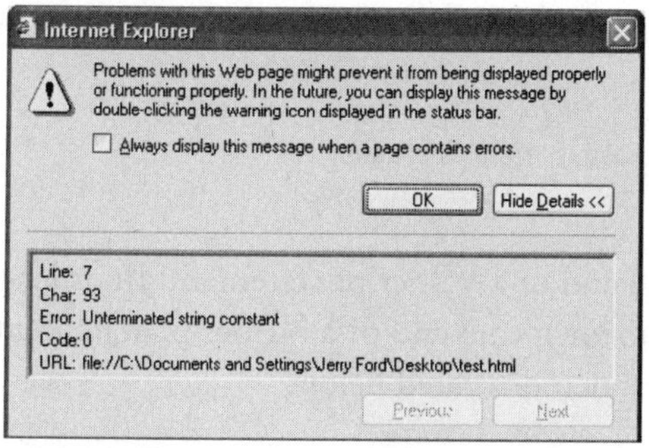

FIGURE 2.3 *Examining a typical script error within Internet Explorer*

TIP

Internet Explorer's suppression of VBScript errors is generally inconvenient for most VBScript programmers because it forces them to search for and display errors. Fortunately, Internet Explorer is flexible enough to allow you to configure it to automatically display script error messages using the following procedure:

1. Open Internet Explorer and select Internet Options from the Tools menu. The Internet Options dialog box appears.
2. Select the Advanced property sheet.
3. Select the Display a notification about every script error option and click OK.

Documenting VBScripts with Comments

Comments provide the ability to make scripts self-documenting, making them easier for others to support. You can add comments to VBScripts using the `Rem` statement. The syntax for the `Rem` statement is shown below.

```
Rem comments
```

For example, the Rem statement can be used as demonstrated below.

```
Rem The VBScript MsgBox() function displays text messages
MsgBox "Greetings!"
```

Alternatively, you can substitute the single quotation mark (') character for the Rem keyword as shown below.

```
' The VBScript MsgBox() function displays text messages
MsgBox "Greetings!"
```

Comments can also be added to the end of a VBScript statement. In order to use the Rem statement to add the comment to the end of a VBScript statement, you must first precede it with a colon, as demonstrated below.

```
MsgBox "Greetings!" :   Rem The VBScript MsgBox() function displays text messages
```

However, if you use the ' character in place of the Rem keyword, you can omit the colon, as shown below.

```
MsgBox "Greetings!"    ' The VBScript MsgBox() function displays text messages
```

Another good use of comments is in the creation of a script template, as demonstrated below.

```
'*************************************************************************
'Script Name: ScriptName.vbs
'Author: Author Name
'Created: mm/dd/yyyy
'Description: Place a brief description of the script here
'*************************************************************************


'Initialization Section


'Main Processing Section


'Procedure Section
```

You will see this template used to document all the WSH scripts that appear in the project sections of this book. The first part of the template provides a place for recording information about the script. The Initialization Section will contain VBScript statements that globally affect the entire script or that define constants, variables, arrays, and objects. The Main Processing Section will contain the VBScript statements that control the overall execution of the script, and the Procedure Section will be used to store all of the procedures that make up the script.

NOTE

Because of the nature and design of HTML pages, it is difficult to design a VBScript template appropriate for that programming environment. However, the liberal use of comments should still be applied to VBScripts embedded inside HTML pages in order to make them easier to understand and support.

Only Internet Explorer and Internet Explorer compatible browsers are able to run VBScripts. Problems will therefore occur when visitors with non-Internet Explorer compatible browsers attempt to access Web pages that contain embedded VBScripts, resulting in the display of the text of the VBScripts statements as if they were part of the Web page's content. The VBScript statements are displayed as text because browsers that do not recognize or support VBScript to not know what else to do with the VBScript statements.

This undesirable behavior can be avoided by simply hiding VBScript statements from non-Internet Explorer compatible browsers. This trick is achieved using the HTML `<!--` and `-->` comment tags along with the VBScript comment statement, as demonstrated below.

```
<SCRIPT LANGUAGE="VBScript">
  <!-- Start hiding VBScript statements
     MsgBox "Greetings!"
  ' End hiding VBScript statements -->
</SCRIPT>
```

Note that the HTML comment tags have been inserted immediately after the first `<SCRIPT>` tag and immediately before the closing `</SCRIPT>` tag. All browsers, even those that do not support VBScript, know not to display text contained in the `<SCRIPT>` and `</SCRIPT>` tags. Browsers that support VBScript will process the VBScript and ignore the first HTML comment. They will also ignore the VBScript comment, thus hiding the last HTML comment. On the other hand, browsers that do not support VBScript will ignore all the VBScript statements between the opening and closing HTML comment tags.

Storing and Retrieving Data from Memory

Like any programming language, VBScript needs to be able to store and retrieve data from memory as it executes. In support of this requirement, VBScript provides three statements that can be used to define constants, variables, and arrays. These statements are outlined in Table 2.3.

Table 2.3 VBScript Statements That Define Data Storage

Statement	Description
`Const`	Defines a VBScript constant
`Dim`	Defines a VBScript variable or array
`ReDim`	Defines a dynamic VBScript array

Using Constants

A *constant* is a value that does not change during the execution of a script. If a script has a known value that will never need to be changed during its execution, it can be stored as a constant. An example of a constant is the value of pi. Constants can be used in two different ways within VBScripts. First, you can define your own custom constants. Second, you can reference built-in VBScript run-time constants.

You cannot change the value assigned to a constant once it has been defined. This protects constants and prevents their accidental modification. Any attempt to change the value of a constant results in an "Illegal assignment xxxxxxxx" error, where xxxxxxxx is the name of the constant that the script attempted to modify.

Defining Constants

Constants are defined using the `Const` statement, which has the following syntax:

```
[Public | Private] Const cCONSTANT = expression
```

`Public` and `Private` are optional keywords. `Public` makes the constant available throughout the entire script. `Private` limits the ability to access a constant to the procedures where it is defined. cCONSTANT is the name assigned to the constant, and expression is the value to be assigned.

TIP

Consider applying a naming convention to all your constants to make them stand out from the rest of your code. In this book, constants are created using the following naming conventions:

- Constant names describe their contents.
- The first letter of the constant name begins with the lowercase letter c.
- The rest of the name is spelled out in all uppercase.
- The underscore character is used to separate the words that make up the constant's name in order to improve readability.

The following example demonstrates how to define a constant and assign it a numeric value.

```
Const cTOTAL_VALUE = 1000
```

To define a string, you must place the value assigned to the constant within quotes, as demonstrated below.

```
Const cCOMPANY_NAME = "XYZ Inc."
```

Similarly, to define a date, place the value inside a pair of matching pound signs, as shown below.

```
Const cPROJECT_DEADLINE = #03-30-03#
```

Constants can be used for a variety of purposes. For example, one use of constants is to establish a common title bar message in pop-up dialog boxes displayed by your scripts, as demonstrated below.

```
Const cTITLEBAR_MSG = "Data Collection Utility"
MsgBox "Click on OK to continue.", , cTITLEBAR_MSG
MsgBox "Click on OK to post saved data.", , cTITLEBAR_MSG
```

When executed, the previous example displays the pop-up dialog boxes shown in Figures 2.4 and 2.5.

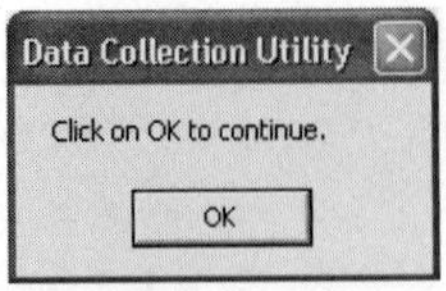

FIGURE 2.4 *Creating a standard title bar message using a constant*

FIGURE 2.5 *Using a constant instead of hard coding data to make scripts easier to maintain*

Referencing VBScript Run-Time Constants

VBScript supplies programmers with a large collection of predefined constants. By adding references to these constants within your scripts, you can save time and simplify your code. For example, the following statement uses the `vbOkCancel` `MsgBox()` constant to display a pop-up dialog box that displays the `OK` and `Cancel` buttons.

```
MsgBox "Do you wish to continue?", vbOkCancel
```

The `MsgBox()` function is a built-in VBScript function that is used to display messages in pop-up dialog boxes. `vbOkCancel` is just one of a number of constants that you can use to specify the appearance of your pop-up dialog boxes. For more information on the constants associated with the `MsgBox()` function, refer to Chapter 6.

VBScript also provides an extensive collection of constants that reference dates and times. Table 2.4 displays a list of these constants.

Table 2.4 VBScript Date and Time Constants

Constant	Value	Description
vbSunday	1	Sunday
vbMonday	2	Monday

Table 2.4 VBScript Date and Time Constants (*continued*º

Constant	Value	Description
vbTuesday	3	Tuesday
vbWednesday	4	Wednesday
vbThursday	5	Thursday
vbFriday	6	Friday
vbSaturday	7	Saturday
vbFirstFourDays	2	First full week with a minimum of four days in the new year
vbFirstFullWeek	3	First full week of the year
vbFirstJan1	1	Week that includes January 1
vbUseSystemDayOfWeek	0	Day of week as specified by the operating system

The date and time constants shown in Table 2.4 can be used as demonstrated below.

```
TodaysDate = Weekday(Date())
If TodaysDate = vbMonday then MsgBox "Please reset time clocks."
```

In this example, a pop-up dialog box is displayed only if the script is executed on a Monday. Another example of built-in constants is VBScript's collection of string constants, shown in Table 2.5.

Table 2.5 VBScript String Constants

Constant	Value	Description
vbCr	Chr(13)	Executes a carriage return
vbCrLf	Chr(13) and Chr(10)	Executes a carriage return and a line feed
vbFormFeed	Chr(12)	Executes a form feed
vbLf	Chr(10)	Executes a line feed
vbNewLine	Chr(13) and Chr(10)	Adds a newline character
vbNullChar	Chr(0)	Creates a 0 or null character

continues

Table 2.5 VBScript String Constants (*continued*)

Constant	Value	Description
`vbNullString`	String with no value	Creates an empty string
`vbTab`	Chr(9)	Executes a horizontal tab
`vbVerticalTab`	Chr(11)	Executes a vertical tab

You can use string constants to format script output, as demonstrated in the following example.

```
Const cTITLEBAR_MSG = "VBScript String Constant Example"
MsgBox "This example demonstrates how to use VBScript" & vbCrLf & _
  "string constants to format text output." & vbCrLf & vbCrLf & _
  vbTab & "End of Example", , cTITLEBAR_MSG
```

As you can see from the previous example, the `vbCrLf` constant can be used to execute a carriage return and a line feed while the `vbTab` constant executes a tab operation.

TIP

Note the use of the ampersand (&) character and the underscore (_) character in the previous example. The & character is a VBScript string concatenation operator. Its purpose is to create a single string by joining two smaller strings. The _ character is used to continue a VBScript statement across another line.

Figure 2.6 shows the pop-up dialog box that is displayed by the previous code.

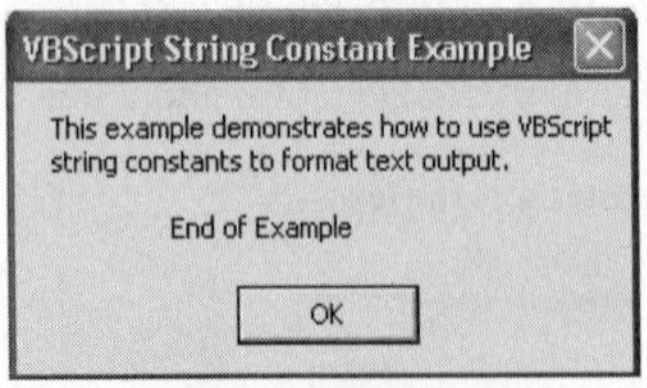

FIGURE 2.6 *Using VBScript string constants to exercise control over the output displayed in pop-up dialog boxes*

Creating Variables

While constants are certainly the right mechanism for storing data that will not change during a script's execution, in most cases, you will find that you need to manipulate the data used by your scripts. In this case, the data should be defined as a variable.

VBScript supports a single type of variable known as a *variant*. However, variants are flexible and can be used to store many different types of data, as listed in Table 2.6.

Table 2.6 VBScript Supported Variant Subtypes

Subtype	Description
`Boolean`	A variant with a value of True or False
`Byte`	An integer whose value is between 0 and 255
`Currency`	A currency value between -922,337,203,685,477.5808 and 922,337,203,685,477.5807
`Date`	A number representing a date between January 1, 100 and December 31, 9999
`Double`	A floating-point number with a range of -1.79769313486232E308 and -4.94065645841247E-324 or 4.94065645841247E-324 and 1.79769313486232E308
`Empty`	A variant that has not been initialized
`Error`	A VBScript error number
`Integer`	An integer with a value that is between -32,768 and 32,767
`Long`	An integer whose value is between -2,147,483,648 and 2,147,483,647
`Null`	A variant set equal to a null value
`Object`	An object
`Single`	A floating-point number whose value is between -3.402823E38 and -1.401298E-45 or 1.401298E-45 and 3.402823E38
`String`	A string up to 2 billion characters long

Variants recognize the type of data assigned to them and behave accordingly. However, you can exercise some control over how VBScript views the data that you assign to variables. For example, you can define a numeric value to a variable as follows:

```
intTotalCount = 100
```

To assign a string to a variable, enclose it inside a matching pair of quotation marks, as demonstrated in both of the following examples.

```
strName = "William Ford"
Age = "4"
```

To explicitly assign data to a variable, place the data inside a pair of matching pound signs, as demonstrated below.

```
dtmDateOfBirth = #03/24/99#
```

You can use built-in VBScript functions to convert data from one type to another, as demonstrated below.

```
varDateOfBirth = #03/24/99#
varDateOfBirth = CStr(varDateOfBirth)
```

In this example, the type of value stored by `varDateOfBirth` is converted from a date to a string.

> **NOTE**
>
> VBScript supplies a number of conversion functions, including `Asc()`, `Cbool()`, `Cbyte()`, `Cbur()`, `Cdate()`, `CDbl()`, `Chr()`, `Cint()`, `CLng()`, `CSng()` and `CStr()`. To find more information about these functions refer to Chapter 4, "Procedures."

Variable Naming Rules

VBScript has a number of rules that must be followed when assigning names to variables. These rules include:

- Variables must be unique within their scope.
- Variable names must be less than 256 characters long.
- Variable names must begin with an alphabetic character.
- Variable names cannot contain spaces.
- Variable names can only consist of alphabetic and numeric characters and the _ character.
- Variable names cannot consist of VBScript reserved words.

Variable names are not case sensitive, meaning the capitalization does not affect the way that VBScript sees a variable's name. Therefore, VBScript sees all three of the following variable names as the same:

```
strUnitColor
strUNITCOLOR
strunitcolor
```

Mixing capitalization styles makes for confusing code and is highly discouraged. Stick with a consistent case throughout your VBScripts and develop a variable naming scheme. For example, many programmers use descriptive words or abbreviations as components of variable names. In addition, capitalizing the first letter of each word or abbreviation helps to make variable names more readable. Another good technique to use when naming variables is to append a three-character prefix identifying the type of data stored in a variable. This is known as Hungarian Notation. Table 2.7 lists prefixes commonly used to name variables.

Table 2.7 Hungarian Prefixes

Prefix	Variable Subtype
Boolean	bln
Byte	byt
Currency	cur
Date	dtm
Double	dbl
Error	err
Integer	int
Long	lng
Object	obj
Single	sng
String	str
Variant	var

The following examples demonstrate the use of variables that follow the conventions stated above.

```
strUserName = "Molly Ford"
intUnitCount = 100
```

Defining Variables

VBScript allows variables to be defined dynamically or formally. To dynamically define a variable, you simply begin using it, as demonstrated below.

```
intTotalCount = intTotalCount + 1
```

Dynamically creating variables is considered to be bad form. Formal variable declaration is strongly preferred. Formal variable declaration makes scripts easier to read and support. VBScript provides the `Dim` statement as a means of formally defining a variable. The syntax of this statement is shown below.

```
Dim variablename
```

`Variablename` is the name of the variable being defined. For example, the following example defines a new variable called `intTotalCount` and then begins working with the variable.

```
Dim intTotalCount
intTotalCount = intTotalCount + 1
```

To reduce the number of lines of code required to define variables, VBScript permits you to define more than one variable at a time using a single `Dim` statement, as demonstrated below.

```
Dim intTotalCount, intAvgCount, intFinalCount
```

Even if you formally define all your variables, there is always the possibility that you may mistype the name of a variable somewhere in your script. When this happens, VBScript simply sees the mistyped variable as a new variable. VBScript allocates memory to it, assigns it a value of empty, and continues running.

For example, take a look at the following script.

```
Dim intUnitCount
intUnitCount = 5
intUnitCount = intUnitCoun + 1
```

```
MsgBox intUnitCount
```

In this example, a variable called `intUnitCount` is defined. It is then assigned a value of 5. The third statement was supposed to add 1 to this value, but a typo was made, creating a new variable called `intUnitCoun`. As a result, when the value of `intUnitCount` is displayed, it shows a value of 1 instead of 6. This is because VBScript assigned a value of 0 to `intUnitCoun`. To prevent this from happening, you can add the `Option Explicit` statement to the beginning of your VBScripts. This statement forces the explicit declaration of all variables within the script. For example, if you modify the previous example as shown below and run it, you'll see the error shown in Figure 2.7 appear.

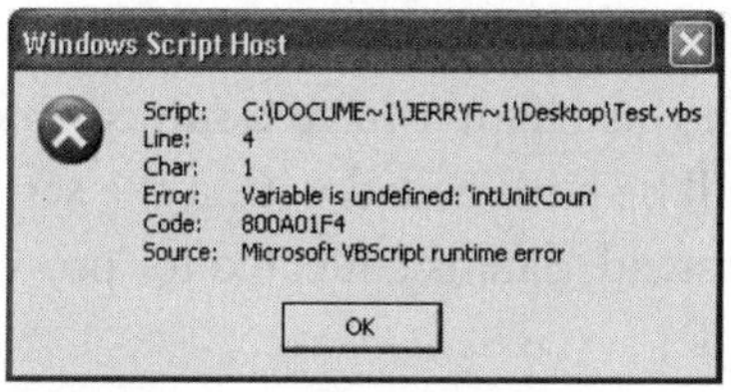

FIGURE 2.7 *The* `Option Explicit` *statement flags all undefined variables, allowing you to fix them during script development*

```
Option Explicit
Dim intUnitCount
intUnitCount = 5
intUnitCount = intUnitCoun + 1
MsgBox intUnitCount
```

NOTE

VBScript imposes a limit of 127 script-level variables per script and 127 procedure-level variables per procedure.

Variable Scope and Lifetime

Variable scope refers to the locations within a script where a variable can be referenced. *Lifetime* refers to the period of time that a variable exists. Any variables defined at the beginning of a script have a global scope, meaning that they can be accessed by any location within the script. In addition, they exist for as long as the script executes.

A variable with a local scope is one that is defined within a procedure. A procedure is a collection of statements that are called and processed as a unit. VBScript supports two types of procedures, subroutines and functions. Procedures are covered in detail in Chapter 4. Variables defined within procedures cannot be accessed from outside of the procedure. In addition, the variable's lifetime is limited to the period of time that the procedure executes.

Other Sources of Data

So far, all the examples that you have seen in this chapter have assumed that any data that the script will need to work with will be hard coded within the script. In reality, scripts are seldom written this way. Instead, data is collected for processing from numerous sources. These sources include:

- **The `InputBox()` function**. This function provides the ability to display a pop-up dialog box that displays an input text field, which the user can use to provide input data to the script. This function is covered in Chapter 6.
- **Data read from input files**. Chapter 17, "Using Configuration Files to Control Script Execution," demonstrates how to collect script input from files.
- **Data read from the Windows registry**. Chapter 22, "Developing the Setup Script," demonstrates the techniques involved in using the registry as a data source.
- **Data passed to the script as arguments**. Chapter 7, "VBScript Objects," describes the process involved in setting up a script to accept arguments passed to it at run time.

Using Operators to Manipulate Variables

To assign a value to a variable or to change the value assigned to a variable, you simply need to assign it a value using the equal sign (=) as follows.

```
intUnitCount = 10
```

Using the equal sign in conjunction with the VBScript arithmetic operators listed in Table 2.8, you can modify the values assigned to variables in a variety of ways. For example, the following script defines a variable named `intUnitCount`, assigns it an initial value of 10, and then proceeds to change its assigned value several times.

```
Dim intUnitCount
intUnitCount = 9  'intUnitCount = 9
intUnitCount = intUnitCount + 1  'intUnitCount = 10
intUnitCount = intUnitCount * 10  'intUnitCount = 100
intUnitCount = intUnitCount / 2  'intUnitCount = 50
intUnitCount = intUnitCount / 2 + 1 * 5  'intUnitCount = 30
MsgBox "intUnitCount = " & intUnitCount
```

When executed, this script displays the results shown in Figure 2.8.

FIGURE 2.8 *Using VBScript operators to manipulate the value assigned to a variable*

Table 2.8 VBScript Arithmetic Operators

Operator	Description
+	Add
-	Subtract
*	Multiply
/	Divide
\	Integer division
Mod	Modulus
-x	Reverses the sign of x
^	Exponentiation

When an expression consists of more than one calculation, VBScript resolves the value of the expression by performing calculations based on a strict order of precedence. Exponentiation is performed first. Then negation occurs, followed by multiplication and division and so on. Table 2.9 outlines VBScript's order of precedence.

Table 2.9 VBScript Order of Precedence

Operators	Description
-	Negation
^	Exponentiation
*, /	Multiplication and division
\	Integer division
Mod	Modulus
+, -	Addition and subtraction

Note: Operators listed at the beginning of the table are evaluated before those that appear later in the table.

You can alter the order in which VBScript performs calculations when resolving an expression by enclosing parts of the expression inside parentheses. For example, examine the following expression:

```
intUnitCount = 10
intUnitCount = intUnitCount / 2 + 1 * 5
```

When resolving this expression, VBScript begins by dividing 10 by 2, getting a result of 5. Next it multiplies 1 by 5, getting a result of 5. Finally, it adds 5 plus 5, getting a final result of 10. Now look at how adding parentheses to the expression changes the results produced when VBScript resolves the value of the expression.

```
intUnitCount = 10
intUnitCount = ((intUnitCount / 2) + 1) * 5
```

In the case of this example, VBScript first divides 10 by 2, getting 5. It then adds 1 to 5, getting 6. Finally it multiplies 5 by 6 for a final result of 30.

VBScript Reserved Words

Like all programming languages, VBScript sets aside a collection of words, called *reserved words*, for its own use. You are not permitted to use these words as variable, procedure, constant, or other type or identifier names. When used, these words must be applied exactly as intended by VBScript, as outlined in its documentation. A list of VBScript's reserved words is displayed in Table 2.10.

Table 2.10 VBScript Reserved Words

And	EndIf	LSet	RSet
As	Enum	Me	Select
Boolean	Eqv	Mod	Set
ByRef	Event	New	Shared
Byte	Exit	Next	Single
ByVal	False	Not	Static
Call	For	Nothing	Stop
Case	Function	Null	Sub
Class	Get	On	Then
Const	GoTo	Option	To
Currency	If	Optional	True
Debug	Imp	Or	Type
Dim	Implements	ParamArray	TypeOf
Do	In	Preserve	Until
Double	Integer	Private	Variant
Each	Is	Public	Wend
Else	Let	RaiseEvent	While
ElseIf	Like	ReDim	With
Empty	Long	Rem	Xor
End	Loop	Resume	

Summary

This chapter reviewed VBScript syntax errors and provided examples of how to identify and correct them. The chapter provided a complete list of VBScript language statements and provided coverage of the statements that define comments, constants, and variables. Also discussed was how to store data in and reference constants and variables. This discussion included a look at built-in VBScript constants and ways to limit the scope of VBScript variables.

Chapter 3

Conditional Logic and Iterative Structures

In this chapter, you will learn how to set up conditional tests within VBScripts using VBScript's `If` and `Select Case` statements. Using these statements, you will be able to perform tests that compare two different values or expressions and alter the logical flow of scripts based on the results of those tests.

In addition, this chapter covers iterative structures. VBScript's iterative statements include the `Do...While`, `Do...Until`, `For...Next`, `While...Wend`, and `For Each...Next` statements. These programming constructs provide you with the ability to iterate (or loop) through a series of object properties or to iterate a specified number of times in order to develop processes capable of manipulating large amounts of data.

Comparison Statements

VBScript provides two different statements that allow you to perform conditional logic tests between two expressions or values. These statements are outlined below.

- **`If`**. A statement that compares two expressions and performs or skips the execution of a portion of the script based on the results of the comparison
- **`Select Case`**. A formal programming construct that allows a programmer to visually organize program execution based on the outcome of a comparison between an expression and a list of possible matching expressions

The `If` and `Select Case` statements provide VBScript with the intelligence required to test data and modify the execution of the logical flow of the scripts in order to accommodate different situations.

The If Statement

The `If` statement performs a comparison between two expressions and then directs the logical execution of the scripts based on the results of that comparison. The syntax of the `If` statement is outlined below.

```
If condition Then
```

```
    statements
ElseIf condition-n Then
    elseifstatements
.
.
.
Else
    elsestatements
End If
```

`condition` is the expression to be tested. `statements` represents one or more statements that are to be executed if the result of the tested condition proves true. `condition-n` is an optional alternative condition to test, and `elseifstatements` are one or more statements that are to be executed if the results of `ElseIf` test prove to be true. `elsestatements` are one or more optional statements to be executed in the event that none of the previous tests prove true.

If Statement Usage

The `If` statement can be used in several forms. To perform a simple comparative test, all that is required is the `If` keyword, the expression to test, and the `Then` keyword followed by a statement to execute if the tested condition proves true. For example, the following statement performs a conditional test to determine whether the value of `intUnitCount` is equal to 100:

```
If intUnitCount = 100 Then MsgBox "Time to place a new inventory order"
```

You can set up an `If` statement to execute more than one statement when the tested condition proves true by adding the `End If` keyword as demonstrated below.

```
If intUnitCount = 100 Then
  MsgBox "Time to place a new inventory order"
  strOrderStatus = "In Progress"
End If
```

Advanced Comparison Operations

In each of the previous `If` statement examples, the equal operator was used to determine whether the value of the two expressions was equal. While this is certainly a useful operation, in many cases you will need to perform conditional tests based on other criteria, such as a not equal to condition or a range of possible conditions. VBScript provides you with a number of different comparison operators, outlined in Table 3.1, that allow you to perform any number of complex conditional tests.

Table 3.1 VBScript Comparison Operators

Operator	Description
=	Equal
<>	Not equal
>	Greater than
<	Less than
>=	Greater than or equal to
<=	Less than or equal to

For example, using the previous example of code, you can modify the `If` statement to determine whether the value of `intUnitCount` is less than or equal to `100`, as shown below.

```
If intUnitCount <= 100 Then
  MsgBox "Time to place a new inventory order"
  strOrderStatus = "In Progress"
End If
```

Alternative Forms of the If Statement

In the previous example, the `If` statement defines which course of action to take if the tested condition proves to be true. To provide an alternative execution path (for example, when the tested condition proves to be false), you need to add the `Else` keyword, as demonstrated below.

```
If intUnitCount < 100 Then
  MsgBox "Time to place a new inventory order"
  strOrderStatus = "In Progress"
Else
  MsgBox "Current inventory levels are within specified limits"
End If
```

You can modify the example above to accommodate alternative tests in the event that the previous comparison proves to be false. This is achieved by adding the `ElseIf` keywords, as follows.

```
If intUnitCount < 100 Then
  MsgBox "Time to place a new inventory order"
  strOrderStatus = "In Progress"
ElseIf intUnitCount < 150 Then
  MsgBox "Inventory levels are within acceptable limits"
  strOrderStatus = "Not in Process"
ElseIf intUnitCount > 200 Then
  MsgBox "Current inventory levels are at maximum"
  strOrderStatus = "Not in process"
End If
```

Nesting Multiple If Statements

VBScripts allow you to embed (or nest) one `If` statement within another in order to perform more complicated logic and to further refine the analysis of tested conditions, as demonstrated below.

```
If intUnitCount < 100 Then
  If Weekday(date()) = 1 Then  'If it is Sunday
    MsgBox "Wait until Monday to place a new inventory order"
  Else
    MsgBox "Time to place a new inventory order"
  End If
Else
  MsgBox "Current inventory levels are within specified limits"
End If
```

These is no limit to the number of layers of embedded `If` statements you can use. However, from a practical standpoint, going more than a few layers deep becomes confusing for most people.

The Select Case Statement

The `If` statements provide an effective mechanism for testing the value of two expressions. However, in situations where you need to compare a single expression against a number of possible matching expressions, VBScript provides the option of using the `Select Case` statement.

The syntax of the `Select Case` statement is shown below.

```
Select Case testexpression
  Case expressionlist-n
    liststatements
      .
      .
      .
  Case Else
    elsestatements
End Select
```

`testexpression` is the expression that will be compared to other expressions specified by one or more `Case` statements. `liststatements` represents one or more VBScript statements that will be executed in the event that one of the expressions specified by one of the `Case` statements equals the value of `testexpression`. `elsestatements` are VBScript statements that will be executed in the event that none of the expressions specified by the `Case` statements prove equal to `testexpression`.

The following example demonstrates how to use the `Select Case` statement.

```
Select Case Weekday(date())
  Case vbSunday
    MsgBox "Today is Sunday"
  Case vbMonday
    MsgBox "Today is Monday"
  Case vbTuesday
    MsgBox "Today is Tuesday"
  Case vbWednesday
    MsgBox "Today is Wednesday"
  Case vbThursday
    MsgBox "Today is Thursday"
  Case vbFriday
    MsgBox "Today is Friday"
  Case vbSaturday
    MsgBox "Today is Saturday"
End Select
```

In this example, the VBScript `Date()` function is used to retrieve the current system date. The result is then fed to the VBScript `Weekday()` function, which returns a value representing the day of the week. The resulting value is then compared to the seven VBScript date constants specified by `Case` statements, each of which represents a different day of the week, to determine which `MsgBox()` statement to execute.

Working with Loops

VBScript provides a number of statements that allow you to establish loops within your scripts. Loops provide the ability to efficiently process large amounts of data using a minimal number of programming statements. These statements are outlined below.

- **`Do...While`**. Sets up a loop that iterates as long as a specified condition remains true
- **`Do...Until`**. Sets up a loop that iterates until a specified condition becomes true
- **`For...Next`**. Sets up a loop that iterates for a specified number of times
- **`While...Wend`**. Sets up a loop that iterates as long as a specified condition remains true
- **`For Each...Next`**. Sets up a loop that iterates through a list of properties belonging to a specified object

Do...While

The `Do...While` statement repeatedly executes a collection of statements as long as a specified condition remains true. VBScript provides two different forms of the `Do...While` statement. In the first version, the `Do...While` loop only begins processing if the tested condition is initially true. Its syntax is shown below.

```
Do While condition
  statements
Loop
```

`condition` is the expression that is to be tested, and `statements` represents one or more VBScript statements to be executed upon each iteration of the loop. For example, the following statements create a loop that will execute until the value of `intCounter` equals 5.

```
strMessageString = "Watch me count!" & vbCrLf & vbCrLf
intCounter = 0
Do While intCounter < 10
  intCounter = intCounter + 1
  strMessageString = strMessageString & intCounter & "    "
Loop
MsgBox strMessageString
```

In this example, a loop is set up to execute while the value of `intCounter`, which is initialized with a value of zero, is less than 10. Each time the loop iterates, it increases the value of `intCounter` by 1 and appends the value of `intCounter` to the end of a string. When the loop finally terminates, the script displays the message string shown in Figure 3.1.

FIGURE 3.1 *Using a* `Do...While` *loop to demonstrate how to count to 10*

Because the `While` keyword was placed at the beginning of the loop, the loop executes only if the tested condition is initially true. The second form of the `Do...While` statement moves the `While` keyword to the end of the loop, forcing the loop to process once, regardless of whether the condition that it is testing is initially true. The syntax for this form of the `Do...While` statement is outlined below.

```
Do
  statements
Loop While condition
```

The following example shows a small VBScript that uses the second form of the `Do...While` loop to collect data from the user. In the case of this example, the script prompts the user to type a name, a part number, and a quantity of a product to be included on a reorder report. Data collection is achieved using the VBScript `InputBox()` function.

NOTE

The `InputBox()` function displays a message in a pop-up dialog box and collects user input, which can then be validated and processed by your scripts. More information on the `InputBox()`, including its syntax and usage, is provided in Chapter 6, "Data Collection, Notification, and Error Reporting."

```
'*************************************************************************
'Script Name: Script 3.1.vbs
'Author: Jerry Ford
'Created: 01/04/2003
'Description: This script demonstrates how to collect user input using a
'Do...While loop
'*************************************************************************

'Initialization Section

Const cTITLEBARMSG = "Inventory Order Report"

Dim intCounter, strInventoryOrder, intPartNumber, intQuantity, strInvReport

intCounter = 0


'Main Processing Section

Do

  intCounter = intCounter + 1

  strInventoryOrder = InputBox("Please type the name of the product to be " & _
    "ordered or type {Quit} when done.", cTITLEBARMSG)

  If Len(strInventoryOrder) = 0 Then
```

```
    MsgBox "Either type a product to be ordered or type Quit", ,cTITLEBARMSG
Else

    If UCase(strInventoryOrder) <> "QUIT" Then
      intPartNumber = InputBox("Please type the part number for " & _
        strInventoryOrder, cTITLEBARMSG)
      intQuantity = InputBox("How many units should of " & strInventoryOrder & _
        " should be ordered?", cTITLEBARMSG)
      strInvReport= strInvReport & intCounter & ".  " & "Item: " & _
        strInventoryOrder & _
        "  Part No: " & intPartNumber & "  Quantity: " & intQuantity & vbCrLf
    End If

  End If
Loop While UCase(strInventoryOrder) <> "QUIT"

If Len(strInvReport) > 0 Then
  MsgBox strInvReport, ,cTITLEBARMSG
End If
```

Each time through the loop, a variable called `intCounter` is incremented. This variable is used to track the number of times that the loop has iterated. It is also used later in the script to help organize the reorder list by assigning a number to each item in the list.

The first thing that this script does is to ask the user to either enter a product name or type **Quit** to exit the script. It stores the user's response in a variable called `strInventoryOrder`. Next, the script checks to see if the length of `strInventoryOrder` is equal to zero. If it is, then the user clicked either on the Cancel button or on the OK button without entering a product name. In this case, the script displays instructions in a pop-up dialog box informing the user how to properly use the script.

If the length of `strInventoryOrder` is not equal to zero, then the script checks to see if the user typed the word **Quit**. The script uses the VBScript `Ucase()` function to convert the user's input to all uppercase to eliminate any confusion over case and then uses a `If` statement to see if the user typed **Quit**. If the user typed **Quit**, then the `Do...While` loop terminates. Another `If` statement follows, which checks the length of the display string used to contain the reorder report. If the length of this string is equal to zero, then the user typed **Quit** without ever entering any data, so there is nothing to display. Otherwise the data entered by the user is displayed in a pop-up dialog box.

If the user did not type **Quit**, then the user is prompted, via two more `InputBox()` statements, as demonstrated in Figure 3.2, to supply a part number and a quantity for each unit to be ordered. The information collected from the user is then concatenated together into a string that will later be used to display the data in report form. The VBScript `vbCrLf` constant is used to format the string by executing a form feed and carriage return at the end of each set of data that is collected as shown in Figure 3.3. This script is relatively simple and performs only a limited amount of validation. However, it serves to demonstrate the power provided by the `Do...While` loop as well as VBScript's ability to collect and process user input.

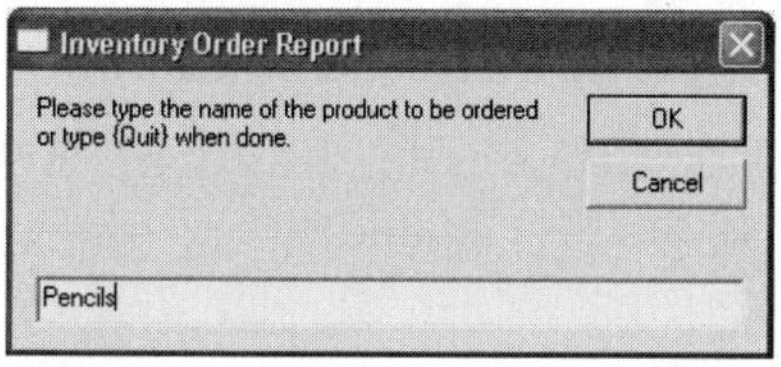

FIGURE 3.2 *Using a* `Do...While` *loop to collect and process user input*

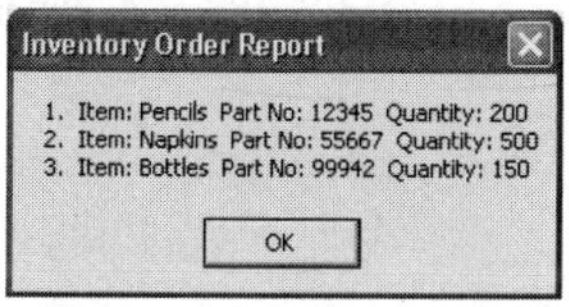

FIGURE 3.3 *An example of the output produced by the script*

Do...Until

Unlike the `Do...While` statement, which executes as long as a condition remains true, the `Do...Until` statement executes until a condition becomes true. Like the `Do...While` statement, the `Do...Until` statement is supported in two forms. In its first form, the `Until` keyword is placed at the beginning of the loop. The syntax for this version of the `Do...Until` loop is shown below.

```
Do Until condition
  statements
Loop
```

`condition` represents the expression to be tested; `statements` represents VBScript statements that will be executed during each iteration of the loop. The following example shows this version of the `Do...Until` loop in action.

```
Dim intCounter, strContactName, strContactList

MsgBox "This script collects the name of up to 5 personal contacts."

intCounter = 0

Do Until intCounter = 5

  strContactName = InputBox("Please enter the name of a personal contact.")

  If Len(strContactName) = 0 Then
    Exit Do
  End If

  intCounter = intCounter + 1

  strContactList = strContactList & intCounter & ".  " & strContactName & vbCrLf

Loop

If Len(strContactList) <> 0 Then
  MsgBox strContactList
End If
```

In this example, a loop is set up that uses the VBScript `InputBox()` to collect the name of up to five personal contacts. The loop runs until the user either types the names of five contacts or terminates loop execution by clicking on Cancel (or by clicking on OK without entering anything).

The second form of the `Do...Until` statement moves the `Until` keyword to the end of the loop. The syntax for this form of the loop is shown below.

```
Do
  statements
Loop Until condition
```

`condition` represents the expression to be tested, and `statements` represents VBScript statements that will be executed during each iteration of the loop. Because the `Until` keyword is now at the end of the loop, the programmer can be assured that the loop will go through at least one iteration.

For...Next

The `For...Next` loop is used to set up a loop that executes for a specific number of iterations. The syntax for the `For...Next` statement is shown below.

```
For counter = begin To end [Step StepValue]
   statements
Next [counter]
```

`counter` is a variable that the loop uses to track the number of times that it has iterated and `statements` represents VBScript statements that will be executed during each iteration of the loop. `begin` specifies the starting value of `counter`. `end` specifies its ending value. `StepValue` specifies the value that `counter` will be incremented by upon each iteration of the loop.

The `For...Next` loop can easily be used to rewrite the previous example, as shown below.

```
Dim intCounter, strContactName, strContactList

MsgBox "This script collects the name of up to 5 personal contacts."

For intCounter = 1 To 5

  strContactName = InputBox("Please enter the name of a personal contact.")

  If Len(strContactName) = 0 Then
    Exit For
  End If

  strContactList = strContactList & intCounter & ".  " & strContactName & vbCrLf
```

```
Next

If Len(strContactList) <> 0 Then
  MsgBox strContactList
End If
```

The nice thing about working with the `For...Next` loop is that it is easy to adjust the loop to change the number of iterations. For example, to enable the previous example to collect 20 personal contacts instead of 5, only one following statement needs to be changed, as shown below.

```
For intCounter = 1 To 20
```

Using the optional `Step` keyword, you can change the value that the `For...Next` loop uses to increment upon each iteration of the loop. For example, the following statements create a `For...Next` loop with a beginning value of 1 and an ending value of 9.

```
Dim intCounter
For intCounter = 1 To 20 Step 3
  WScript.Echo intCounter
Next
```

When saved as a script file with a .VBS file extension and run using the Script.exe execution host, this script displays the following output.

```
C:\>cscript "Script 3.2.vbs"
Microsoft (R) Windows Script Host Version 5.6
Copyright (C) Microsoft Corporation 1996-2001. All rights reserved.

1
4
7
10
13
16
19

C:\>
```

While...Wend

The `While...Wend` statement can be used to create a loop that executes as long as a condition remains true. The syntax for this statement is outlined below.

```
While condition
  statements
Wend
```

`condition` is an expression that is being tested, and `statements` represents VBScript statements that will be executed during each iteration of the loop. The `While...Wend` statement is provided for backward compatibility purposes. Its continued use is discouraged. Its functionality is duplicated by the `Do...While` and `Do...Until` statements, which are more flexible in their application.

For example, the following HTML page includes a VBScript that uses a `While...Wend` loop to build a string that counts from 1 to 10, as demonstrated in Figure 3.4.

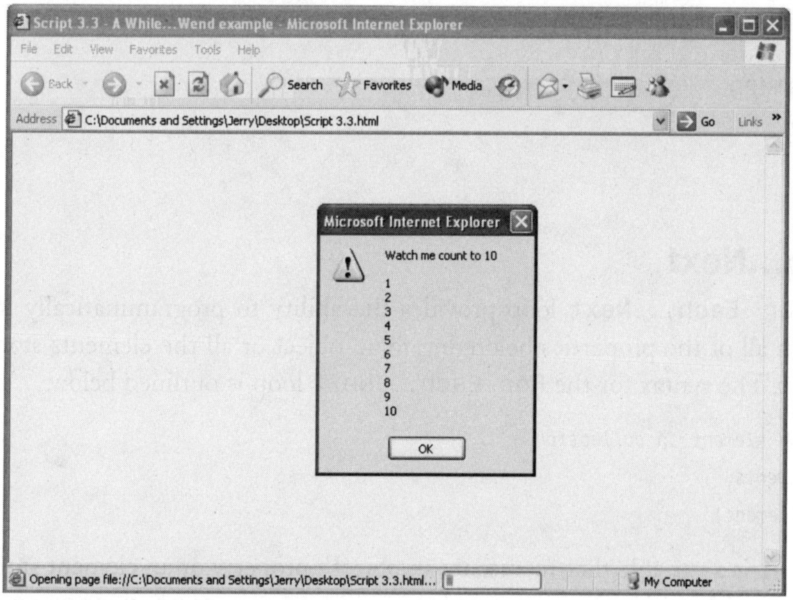

FIGURE 3.4 *Using the* `While...Wend` *loop in a VBScript embedded inside a HTML page*

```
<HTML>
  <HEAD>
    <TITLE>Script 3.3 - A While...Wend example</TITLE>
  </HEAD>
  <BODY>
    <SCRIPT LANGUAGE="VBScript">

      Dim intCounter, strDisplayString

      intCounter = 1
      strDisplayString = "Watch me count to 10" & vbCrLf & vbCrLf

      While intCounter <= 10
        strDisplayString = strDisplayString & intCounter & vbCrLf
        intCounter = intCounter + 1
      Wend

      alert strDisplayString

    </SCRIPT>
  </BODY>
</HTML>
```

For Each...Next

The `For Each...Next` loop provides the ability to programmatically iterate through all of the properties belonging to an object or all the elements stored in an array. The syntax for the `For Each...Next` loop is outlined below.

```
For Each element In collection
  statements
Next [element]
```

`element` is a variable that represents an object's property or an element stored in an array. `collection` is the name of the object or array. `statements` represents the VBScript statements that are executed during each iteration of the loop.

For example, using the `For Each...Next` loop, you can write a WSH VBScript that can process the file contents of any Windows folder, as demonstrated below.

```
'*************************************************************************
'Script Name: Script 3.4.vbs
'Author: Jerry Ford
'Created: 01/04/2003
'Description: This script demonstrates how to use the For Each...Next
'loop to process all the files stored in a folder
'*************************************************************************

'Initialization Section

Option Explicit

Dim FsoObject, FolderName, Member
Dim strFileList, intCounter

Set FsoObject = CreateObject("Scripting.FileSystemObject")
Set FolderName = FsoObject.GetFolder("C:\Temp")

intCounter = 0


'Main Processing Section

For Each Member in FolderName.Files
  intCounter = intCounter + 1
  strFileList =  strFileList & intCounter & ". " & Member.name & vbCrLf
Next

MsgBox strFileList, ,"List of files in " & FolderName
```

In order to complete this script, the VBScript `FileSystemObject` had to be used. This object is a VBScript run-time object that will not be formally introduced in this book until Chapter 17, "Using Configuration Files to Control Script Execution." Therefore, only a minimal explanation will be provided here.

This script begins by defining the variables that it will use. It then instantiates an instance of the `FileSystemObject` and sets up a reference to the location of the target folders using its `GetFolder()` method. Next, a `For Each...Next` loop executes, processing all the files found in the target folder by adding them to a numbered list stored as a string. Finally, the last statement in the script displays the string built by the `For Each...Next` loop, producing the output shown in Figure 3.5.

FIGURE 3.5 *Using a* `For Each...Next` *loop to iterate through the contents of a folder*

`For Each...Next` loops can also be used to process the contents of VBScript arrays. In this situation, you simply specify a variable representing each element in the array and the name of the array, as demonstrated below.

```
For Each Member In TestArray
  statements
Next
```

In this example, the name of the array is `TestArray` and `statements` is used to represent any number of VBScript statements required to process each element stored in the array.

NOTE

To learn more about arrays and how to process them, refer to Chapter 5, "Arrays."

Guarding against Endless Loops

Whenever programmers work with loops, they run the risk of accidentally creating an endless loop. For example, the following `Do...While` loop does exactly this.

```
intCounter = 0
Do While intCounter < 10
  intCounter = intCounter - 1
```

```
Loop
```

Instead of incrementing the value of intCounter each time through the loop, the script is set to decrement its value by 1. Since the value of intCounter will never be greater than 10, a endless loop has been accidentally created. To guard against this predicament, some programmers add an additional counter to their loops as a sort of "safety net," as demonstrated below.

```
intCounter = 0
intNoExecutions = 0
Do While intCounter < 10
  intCounter = intCounter - 1
  intNoExecutions = intNoExecutions + 1
  If intNoExecutions  > 50 Then
  MsgBox "Script execution terminating: Possible Endless Loop!"
    Exit Do
  End If
Loop
```

As you can see, a second variable has been added that tracks the number of iterations that the loop performs and is used to terminate the loop's (not the script's) execution if more than 50 iterations occur. By cutting and pasting a tried and true loop safety net into your scripts during testing and development, you can save time by preventing endless loops that would otherwise crash your computer or force you to take steps to manually terminate runaway scripts. Once your scripts are tested and ready for production, you can always remove the extra code.

NOTE

The previous example introduced the use of the `Exit Do` statement. This statement is used to terminate the execution of a `Do...While` or `Do...Until` loop. It can only be used inside one of these two types of loops. When executed, the `Exit Do` statement switches processing control to the statement immediately following the loop.

The `Exit Do` statement is one of five variations of `Exit` statements. These other statements include:

- `Exit For`
- `Exit Function`
- `Exit Property`
- `Exit Sub`

Summary

In this chapter, you learned about VBScript's decision-making capabilities, which are provided in the form of the `If` and `Select Case` statements. You also examined VBScript's support for iterative processing, including a review of the `Do...While`, `Do...Until`, `For...Next`, `While...Wend`, and `For Each...Next` statements. By combining the capabilities of these two groups of programming statements, you will be able to create VBScripts that can process large amounts of information and alter their own logical execution based on the data that they are presented with.

Chapter 4

Procedures

In this chapter, you will see how VBScript procedures can be used to improve the overall organization and manageability of your scripts. You will learn about the two types of procedures supported by VBScript, subroutines and functions. This chapter will cover how to use procedures to control variable scope by defining local and global variables. You will also learn how to create event handlers that react to browser events and will examine the types of browser events to which VBScript can react. Finally, you will examine VBScript's complete collection of built-in functions.

Organizing VBScript into Procedures

VBScript procedures provide the basic building blocks of VBScript organization. Procedures allow you to create modular scripts that organize statements into logical groups that can be executed as a unit. VBScript supports two different types of procedures:

- **Function**. A type of procedure that can return a result back to its calling statement
- **Subroutine**. A type of procedure that does not return a result back to its calling statement

Procedures have two main benefits: First, they provide a means of organizing VBScripts into a more manageable format. Second, procedures allow you to create reusable code and reduce the overall size of scripts.

Enhanced Script Maintenance

Procedures allow you to create scripts that are easier to maintain by allowing you to group related statements together and to execute them as a unit. Therefore, as a general rule, you should use procedures as the primary organization construct for your VBScripts. By developing modular code using VBScript, you make your scripts easier to read and maintain. For example, by grouping related statements together in a procedure, you make them easier to find. You also make the script easier to update, allowing individual modules or procedures to be updated without having to make substantial changes to other parts of the script.

By making scripts easier to manage, procedures allow you to add more complexity without necessarily making them more difficult for you to work with or maintain. As suggested in Chapter 2, "Errors, Constants, and Variables," when developing scripts that will be run using the WSH, consider developing a VBScript template similar to that in the following example.

```
'*************************************************************************
'Script Name: ScriptName.vbs
'Author: Author Name
'Created: mm/dd/yyyy
'Description: Place a brief description of the script here
'*************************************************************************

'Initialization Section

'Main Processing Section

'Procedure Section
```

Using this template, you would place all subroutines and functions in the Procedure section. This provides a consistent organization to your scripts by providing a predictable location for storing and finding procedures. The important thing is to group your procedures together where you can easily find them in your VBScripts. Most VBScript programmers choose to store their subroutines and procedures at the end of their scripts.

When developing VBScripts that are embedded inside HTML pages, most programmers generally locate their subroutines and functions in a VBScript placed in the HEAD section. This helps to ensure that all procedures have been initialized before being called upon by VBScripts or event handlers located in the HTML page's BODY section.

Reusable Code

Functions and subroutines help make for smaller scripts by allowing the creation of reusable modules of code that can be called upon as many times as necessary from any location within a script. Therefore, functions and subroutines should be used in any situation where a particular task needs to performed more than once within a script.

Procedures also make script maintenance easier because you only have to modify the code located in one procedure instead of making the same change over and over again to code that would otherwise be duplicated throughout a script.

Subroutines vs. Functions

Subroutines and functions perform nearly identical roles within VBScripts. Both provide a means for grouping and executing collections of related statements. Both provide a means of limiting variable scope, which is discussed later in this chapter. They even share a similar syntax. Where they differ is in their ability to return data back to the statement that calls them. Functions provide this capability, whereas subroutines cannot return a result back to their calling statement.

Subroutines

Subroutines are used to execute a collection of statements without returning a result to a calling statement. Once executed, a subroutine returns processing control back to the statement that follows its calling statement.

Subroutines are created using the VBScript `Sub` statement. The `Sub` statement defines the name of the subroutine and any arguments that it expects to receive. The syntax for the `Sub` statement is shown below.

```
[Public ¦ Private] Sub name [(arglist)]
  statements
End Sub
```

`Public` and `Private` are optional keywords. The `Public` keyword specifies that the subroutine can be called upon by other procedures located within the script. The `Private` keyword specifies that the subroutine cannot be called upon by other procedures within the script. `Name` is the name assigned to the subroutine and must be unique within the script. `Arglist` is a list of comma delineated arguments that can be passed to the subroutine when it is called.

To call a subroutine, you type its name in the following format:

```
SubroutineName()
```

The closing parentheses characters `()` are required. You can call a subroutine and pass it arguments by specifying the arguments, separated by commas, within the parentheses, as demonstrated below.

```
SubroutineName(arg1, arg2, arg3, ... argn)
```

For example, the following VBScript statement defines a subroutine called `AboutRoutine()`.

```
Sub AboutRoutine()
  MsgBox "UserAcctMgr.vbs" & vbCrLf & vbCrLf & _
         "Copyright © Jerry Ford 2003" & vbCrLf & vbCrLf & _
         "For more information about UserAcctMgr.vbs please contact " & _
         "jlf04@yahoo.com", ,"About Sample Script"
End Sub
```

This subroutine might be included as part of a larger script to provide information about the script. When called, `AboutRoutine()` uses the `MsgBox()` function to display information about the script. This subroutine has not been designed to accept any arguments as input and can be called from anywhere in the script using the following statement.

```
AboutRoutine()
```

When executed, this subroutine displays the pop-up dialog box shown in Figure 4.1.

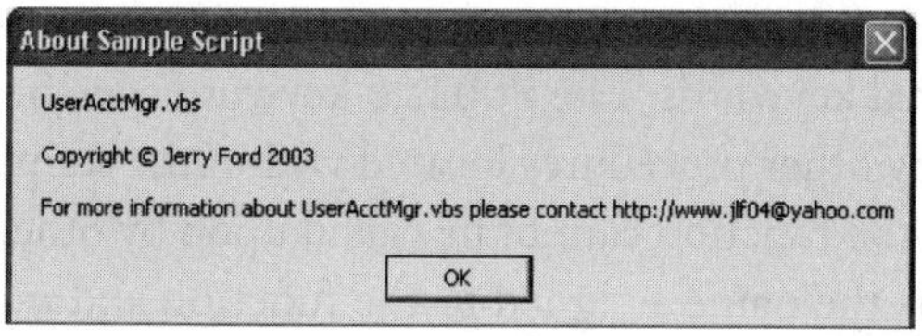

FIGURE 4.1 *Using a subroutine to display information about a script*

The following example demonstrates how to define a subroutine that accepts and processes one argument when called upon to execute.

```
Sub DisplayMsg(strMsgText)
  MsgBox strMsgText, , "VBScript Subroutine Demo"
End Sub
```

This subroutine could be added to any VBScript to provide a generic message display procedure. It accepts a single argument, which in the case of this example would be a text string passed to it by its calling statement. For example, the following statement could be used to execute the `DisplayMsg()` subroutine, which results in displaying the pop-up dialog box shown in Figure 4.2.

```
DisplayMsg("This message will be displayed by a message display subroutine.")
```

FIGURE 4.2 *Viewing a message displayed using a generic message display subroutine*

Functions

Functions are similar to subroutines, except that they also provide the ability to return a result to their calling statements. The syntax for functions is outlined below.

```
[Public ¦ Private] Function name [(arglist)]
  statements
End Function
```

`Public` and `Private` are optional keywords. The `Public` keyword specifies that the function can be called upon by other procedures located within the script. The `Private` keyword specifies that the function cannot be called upon by other procedures within the script. `Name` is the name assigned to the function and must be unique within the script. `Arglist` is a list of comma delimitated arguments that can be passed to the function when it is called.

For example, the following function represents a rewrite of a previous subroutine that displays information about a script in a pop-up dialog box.

```
Function AboutRoutine()
  MsgBox "UserAcctMgr.vbs" & vbCrLf & vbCrLf & _
         "Copyright © Jerry Ford 2003" & vbCrLf & vbCrLf & _
         "For more information about UserAcctMgr.vbs please contact " & _
         "jlf04@yahoo.com", ,"About Sample Script"
End Function
```

This function can be called using the following statement from anywhere within the script that defines it.

```
AboutRoutine()
```

When used in this manner, there is no advantage to using a function over a subroutine. The advantage of using a function in place of a subroutine is the function's ability to return a result to its calling statement. In order to return a result back to its calling statement, a function must define a variable with the same exact name as the function and then assign the result that is to be returned to that variable. When the function stops executing, the value is then returned to the calling statement. For example, the following function might be used to collect the name of a file from the user.

```
Function GetFileName()
  GetFileName = InputBox("Please type the name of the file you wish to open.")
End Function
```

The name of the function is `GetFileName()`. It uses the VBScript `InputBox()` function to collect the name of a file from the user and assigns the file name typed by user to a variable named `GetFileName`. Note that the name of the variable is exactly the same as the name of the function (less the parentheses). To execute this procedure, the calling statement can reference it, as shown below.

```
strFileName = GetFileName()
```

In this example, the name of the file that is returned by the function is assigned to a variable name `strFileName`. Another way to call the function would be to include a reference to it within a VBScript statement, as shown below.

```
MsgBox "Click on OK to delete " & GetFileName()
```

In this example, the `MsgBox()` function includes a reference to the `GetFileName()` function and substitutes the results returned by that function into the message that it has been set up to display.

Functions can also accept arguments passed to them at run time, as demonstrated below.

```
Function DisplayMsg(strMsgText)
  MsgBox strMsgText, , "VBScript Subroutine Demo"
End Function
```

Controlling Variable Scope

Procedures provide VBScript with the ability to localize or isolate variables. Any variable defined outside of a procedure is global in scope, meaning that it can be referenced from any location within the script. A variable with a local scope, on the other hand, is one that is defined within a procedure and can be accessed only from within that procedure. Local variables exist only as long as the procedure that defined them is executing.

By localizing variable values, you eliminate the possibility of accidentally modifying a variable outside of the procedure where it was created. As a programming technique, it is generally preferable to localize variables as much as possible. The following example demonstrates the differences between local and global variables.

```
'*************************************************************************
'Script Name: Script 4.1.vbs
'Author: Jerry Ford
'Created: 01/04/2003
'Description: This script demonstrates global and local variable scopes
'*************************************************************************

'Initialization Section
Option Explicit
Dim X, Y

'Main Processing Section
X = 10
GetNewNumber()
MsgBox "X =  " & X & "  Y =  " & Y

'Procedure Section
Function GetNewNumber()
  Dim Y
  Y = 20
End Function
```

In this script, two variables are defined, X and Y. The X variable and its value are both defined in the script's Main Processing Section and are global in scope. Next, the script executes the `GetNewNumber()` function, which defines the Y variable and sets its value. Once the `GetNewNumber()` function is finished, processing control returns to the Main Processing Section, which then uses the VBScript `MsgBox()` function to try and display the values assigned to `X` and `Y`. However, only the value of `X` can be displayed because the `Y` variable no longer exists.

Figure 4.3 shows the output produced when this script is executed by the WSH.

FIGURE 4.3 A demonstration of variable scope within and outside of VBScript procedures

Browser Event Handling

Within the context of client-side Web page development, VBScript procedures have a special role in building event handlers that respond to browser events. This adds interactivity to Web pages and allows front-end processing to be performed on the client computer. An *event* is an occurrence of an action within a browser. For example, a mouse click on an image, button, or link represents a click event. Other examples of events include double-clicking on Web page objects, typing text into form elements, clicking on form buttons, and moving the pointer over and off of objects. Browser events also occur when Web pages load or unload.

To react to an event, you must add event handlers to your scripts. An *event handler* is a trap that recognizes when an event occurs and executes one or more VBScript statements. For example, if a visitor clicks on a form's submit button, the click event associated with that button can be used to trigger the execution of an event handler that performs form validation.

By defining functions and subroutines and storing them in the head section of an HTML page, you can create a library of event handlers that can be associated with any object on a Web page.

Examining Events and Event Handlers

Table 4.1 provides a list of browser events for which you can define event handlers. Table 4.1 also provides the name of the event handler associated with each event and a description of the event and event handler. As you can see, event handlers are named by adding *on* to the beginning of the event name with which it is associated.

Table 4.1 Browser Events and Event Handlers

Property	Event Handler	Description
Abort	onAbort	Executes when the visitor aborts an image while it is loading
Blur	onBlur	Executes when the currently selected object loses focus
Change	onChange	Executes when the visitor changes an object
Click	onClick	Executes when the visitor clicks an object
DblClick	onDblClick	Executes when the visitor double-clicks an object
DragDrop	onDragDrop	Executes when the visitor drags and drops an object onto a frame or window
Error	onError	Executes when an error occurs on the HTML page
Focus	onFocus	Executes when a visitor selects an object
KeyDown	onKeyDown	Executes when a visitor presses down on a key
KeyPress	onKeyPress	Executes when a visitor presses and releases a key
KeyUp	onKeyUp	Executes when a visitor releases a key
Load	onLoad	Executes when an HTML page or image finishes loading
MouseDown	onMouseDown	Executes when a visitor presses a mouse button
MouseMove	onMouseMove	Executes when a visitor moves the pointer
MouseOut	onMouseOut	Executes when a visitor moves the pointer off of an object
MouseOver	onMouseOver	Executes when a visitor moves the pointer over an object
MouseUp	onMouseUp	Executes when a visitor releases a mouse button
MouseWheel	onMouseWheel	Executes when a mouse wheel is rotated

Table 4.1 Browser Events and Event Handlers (continued)

Property	Event Handler	Description
Move	onMove	Executes when the visitor moves a frame or window
Reset	onReset	Executes when a visitor clicks on a reset button
Resize	onResize	Executes when the visitor resizes a frame or window
Select	onSelect	Executes when a visitor selects the contents of a form select menu
Submit	onSubmit	Executes when a visitor clicks on a submit button
Unload	onUnload	Executes when a visitor closes the browser window or frame or loads a different URL

Setting Up Event Handlers

Events are associated with specific objects. Likewise, event handlers are associated with specific events and objects. When an event occurs, its associated event handler, if one has been written, is automatically executed. There are three different ways in which to set up the execution of an event handler. The first option is to embed the event handler inside an HTML tag, as demonstrated below.

```
<BODY onLoad="window.alert('Greetings')">
```

In the case of this example, the `onLoad` event is automatically triggered when the HTML page is loaded by the browser, displaying a pop-up message. While convenient for performing tasks that require minimal coding, this option is limited. Another option provided by VBScript is to set up event handlers, as demonstrated below.

```
<SCRIPT FOR="SubmitButton" EVENT="onClick" LANGUAGE="VBScript">
  window.alert "Thank you for shopping with us today."
</SCRIPT>
```

The third and most commonly used option is to define event handlers that call procedures stored within VBScripts located within the HTML page's HEAD section, as demonstrated below.

```
Sub SubmitButton_onMouseOver
  window.status = "Click here to submit your request."
End Sub
```

When used in conjunction with event handlers, procedure names are created by combining the name of an object button and the name of the appropriate event handler. For example, the previous subroutine is automatically triggered whenever the pointer is moved over a form button named `SubmitButton` on the HTML page. When executed, it displays a text message in the browser's status bar located at the bottom of the browser.

To further demonstrate the use of VBScript procedures as constructs for storing statements that are called by event handlers, look at two more examples. In the first example shown below, an HTML page has been set up that contains a VBScript in its HEAD section. This VBScript defines a single function called `ShowGreetingMsg()`. This function will execute when called by the `onLoad` event handler specified in the `<BODY>` tag example, as highlighted below.

```
<HTML>

  <HEAD>
    <TITLE>Script 4.2 - onLoad event handler example</TITLE>

    <SCRIPT LANGUAGE="VBScript">
    <!-- Start hiding VBScript statements
      Function ShowGreetingMsg()
        MsgBox("Greetings and thanks for visiting us today.")
      End Function
    ' End hiding VBScript statements -->
    </SCRIPT>

  </HEAD>
  <BODY onLoad=ShowGreetingMsg()>
    onLoad event handler example
  </BODY>

</HTML>
```

Figure 4.4 shows the output produced when this HTML page is loaded by Internet Explorer.

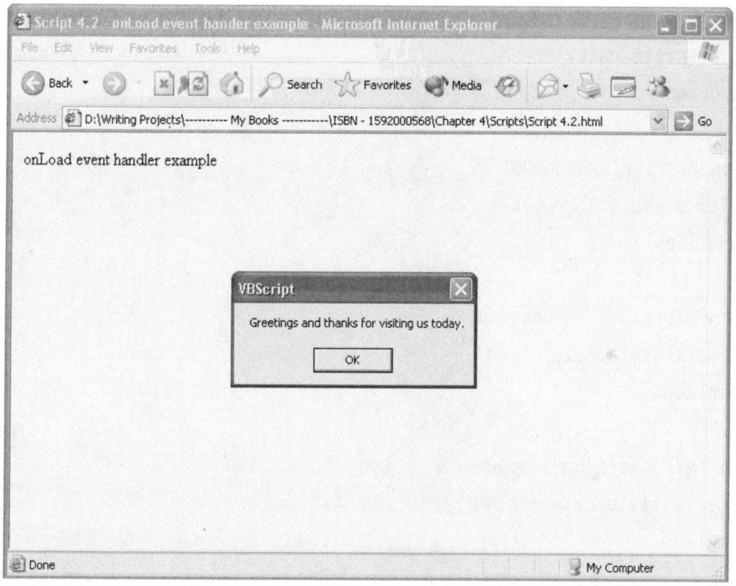

FIGURE 4.4 *A pop-up dialog box displayed by a function that has been called by a VBScript event handler*

Another popular use of event handlers is in the creation of animated rollover effects, which change the appearance of a link, image, or object in some manner whenever the pointer is moved over or off of the object. Rollovers can be created using the `onMouseOver` and `onMouseOut` events, which are listed below.

- **`onMouseOver`**. Triggered whenever the pointer is moved over an object
- **`onMouseOut`**. Triggered whenever the pointer is moved off of an object

For example, the following script demonstrates how to set up an HTML page with two rollover links. One is for the Premier Press Web site and the other is for Microsoft's Web site.

```
<HTML>
  <HEAD>
    <TITLE>Script 4.3 - A demo of how to creak a link rollover</TITLE>

    <SCRIPT LANGUAGE="VBScript">
    <!-- Start hiding VBScript statements
```

```
      Function Premier_onMouseOver
        Premier.style.color="red"
      End Function

      Function Premier_onMouseOut
        Premier.style.color="blue"
      End Function

      Function Microsoft_onMouseOver
        Microsoft.style.color="red"
      End Function

      Function Microsoft_onMouseOut
        Microsoft.style.color="blue"
      End Function

    ' End hiding VBScript statements -->
    </SCRIPT>
  </HEAD>

  <BODY>
    <A HREF="http://www.premierpressbooks.com" NAME="Premier"> Premier</A><P>
<A HREF="http://www.microsoft.com" NAME="Microsoft"> Microsoft</A><P>
   </BODY>
</HTML>
```

In order to set up a rollover for each link, two functions must be set up as event handlers for each link. The first function defines the statements to be executed for the `onMouseOut` event handler and the second function defines the statements to be executed for the `onMouseOver` event handler. Notice that unlike the previous example in which the `<BODY>` tag explicitly called the function specified by the `onLoad` event handler, the functions in this example are automatically associated with links because of the manner in which their names were formulated.

When executed, these functions modify the color of the text used to display each link, depending on which event handler is being executed. Figure 4.5 shows the output produced when this HTML page is loaded by Internet Explorer. However, it is difficult to see how the rollover links work from an examination of Figure 4.5. To get a better understanding, create and run this script yourself.

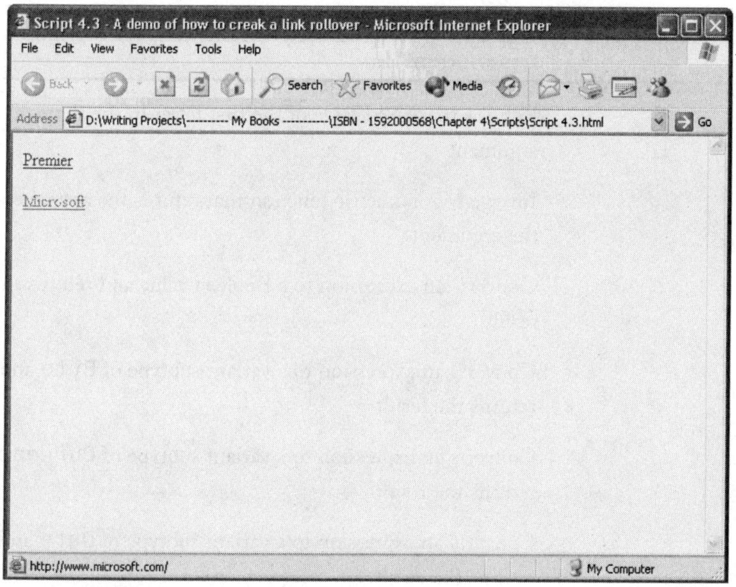

FIGURE 4.5 *Creating rollovers using event handlers*

Built-in Functions

In this chapter, you learned how to create your own custom functions. Using functions, you can create modular scripts and group related VBScript statements together in some logical manner. VBScript also provides a large collection of ready-to-use built-in functions that you can reference from your VBScripts. Using built-in VBScripts saves you the time and trouble required to reinvent a function to perform a task for which Microsoft has already provided a solution. This speeds up script development time while making for smaller scripts that are easier to manage. Table 4.2 provides a list of VBScript's built-in functions.

Table 4.2 VBScript Functions

Function	Description
`Abs`	Returns a number's absolute value
`Array`	Returns an array based on the supplied argument list

continues

Table 4.2 VBScript Functions (*continued*)

Function	Description
`Asc`	Returns the ANSI code of the first letter in the supplied argument
`Atn`	Inverse trigonometric function that returns the arctangent of the argument
`CBool`	Converts an expression to a Boolean value and returns the result
`CByte`	Converts an expression to a variant subtype of `Byte` and returns the result
`CCur`	Converts an expression to a variant subtype of `Currency` and returns the result
`Cdate`	Converts an expression to a variant subtype of `Date` and returns the result
`CDbl`	Converts an expression to a variant subtype of `Double` and returns the result
`Chr`	Returns a character based on the supplied ANSI code
`Cint`	Converts an expression to a variant subtype of `Integer` and returns the result
`CLng`	Converts an expression to a variant subtype of `Long` and returns the result
`Cos`	Trigonometric function that returns the cosine of the argument
`CreateObject`	Creates an automation object and returns a reference to it
`CSng`	Converts an expression to a variant subtype of `Single` and returns the result
`Date`	Returns the current date
`DateAdd`	Adds an additional time interval to the current date and returns the result
`DateDiff`	Compares two dates and returns the number of intervals between them
`DatePart`	Returns a portion of the specified date
`DateSerial`	Returns a variant (subtype `Date`) based on the supplied year, month, and day

Table 4.2 VBScript Functions (*continued*)

Function	Description
DateValue	Converts a string expression into a variant of type Date and returns the result
Day	Converts an expression representing a date into a number between 1 and 31 and returns the result
Eval	Returns the results of an evaluated expression
Exp	Returns the value of an argument raised to a power
Filter	Returns an array based on a filtered set of elements using supplied filter criteria
FormatCurrency	Returns an expression that has been formatted as a currency value
FormatDateTime	Returns an expression that has been formatted as a date or time value
FormatNumber	Returns an expression that has been formatted as a numeric value
FormatPercent	Returns an expression that has been formatted as a percentage (including the accompanying %)
GetLocale	Returns the locale ID
GetObject	Returns a reference for an automation object
GetRef	Returns a reference for a procedure
Hex	Returns a hexadecimal string that represents a number
Hour	Returns a whole number representing an hour in a day (0 to 23)
InputBox	Returns user input from a dialog box
InStr	Returns the starting location of the first occurrence of a substring within a string
InStrRev	Returns the ending location of the first occurrence of a substring within a string
Int	Returns the integer portion from the supplied number
IsArray	Returns a value of True or False depending on whether a variable is an array

continues

Table 4.2 VBScript Functions (*continued*)

Function	Description
`IsDate`	Returns a value of `True` or `False` depending on whether an expression is properly formatted for a data conversion
`IsEmpty`	Returns a value of `True` or `False` depending on whether a variable is initialized
`IsNull`	Returns a value of `True` or `False` depending on whether an expression is set to `Null`
`IsNumeric`	Returns a value of `True` or `False` depending on whether an expression evaluates to a number
`IsObject`	Returns a value of `True` or `False` depending on whether an expression has a valid reference for an automation object
`Join`	Returns a string that has been created by concatenating the contents of an array
`Lbound`	Returns the smallest possible subscript for the specified array dimension
`Lcase`	Returns a lowercase string
`Left`	Returns characters from the left side of a string
`Len`	Returns a number or string's character length
`LoadPicture`	Returns a picture object
`Log`	Returns the natural log of the specified argument
`LTrim`	Trims any leading blank spaces from a string and returns the result
`Mid`	Returns a number of characters from a string based on the supplied start and length arguments
`Minute`	Returns a number representing a minute within an hour in the range of 0 to 59
`Month`	Returns a number representing a month within a year in the range of 1 to 12
`MonthName`	Returns a string containing the name of the specified month
`MsgBox`	Returns a value specifying the button that users click on in a dialog box

Table 4.2 VBScript Functions (*continued*)

Function	Description
`Now`	Returns the current date and time
`Oct`	Returns a string containing an octal number representation
`Replace`	Returns a string after replacing occurrences of one substring with another substring
`RGB`	Returns a number that represents an RGB color
`Right`	Returns characters from the right side of a string
`Rnd`	Returns a randomly generated number
`Round`	Returns a number after rounding it by a specified number of decimal positions
`RTrim`	Trims any trailing blank spaces from a string and returns the result
`ScriptEngine`	Returns a string identifying the current scripting language
`ScriptEngineBuildVersion`	Returns the scripting engine's build number
`ScriptEngineMajorVersion`	Returns the scripting engine's major version number
`ScriptEngineMinorVersion`	Returns the scripting engine's minor version number
`Second`	Returns a number representing a second within a minute in the range of 0 to 59
`Sgn`	Returns the sign of the specified argument
`Sin`	Trigonometric function that returns the sine of the argument
`Space`	Returns a string consisting of a number of blank spaces
`Split`	Organizes a string into an array
`Sqr`	Returns a number's square root
`StrComp`	Returns a value that specifies the results of a string comparison
`String`	Returns a character string made up of a repeated sequence of characters

continues

Table 4.2 VBScript Functions (*continued*)

Function	Description
`Tan`	Trigonometric function that returns the tangent of the argument
`Time`	Returns a variant of subtype `Date` that has been set equal to the system's current time
`Timer`	Returns a value representing the number of seconds that have passed since midnight
`TimeSerial`	Returns a variant of subtype `Date` that has been set equal to containing the specified hour, minute, and second
`TimeValue`	Returns a variant of subtype `Date` that has been set using the specified time
`Trims`	Returns a string after removing any leading or trailing spaces
`TypeName`	Returns a string that specified the variant subtype information regarding the specified variable
`Ubound`	Returns the largest subscript for the specified array dimension
`Ucase`	Returns an uppercase string
`VarType`	Returns a string that specified the variant subtype information regarding the specified variable
`Weekday`	Returns a whole number in the form of 1 to 7, which represents a given day in a week
`WeekdayName`	Returns a string identifying a particular day in the week
`Year`	Returns a number specifying the year

As a quick example of the benefit of using a built-in VBScript function to save time and simplify your VBScripts, look at the following custom function, which consists of five VBScript statements.

```
Function SqrRootSolver()
  intUserInput = InputBox ("Type a number", "Custom Square Root Function")
  X = 1
  For Counter = 1 To 15
    X = X - ((X^2 - intUserInput) / (2 * X))
  Next
```

```
    MsgBox "The square root of " & intUserInput & " is " & X
End Function
```

The five statements contained in the function ask the user to type a number and then use a `For...Next` loop to determine the square root of that number using some fairly sophisticated math. Figures 4.6 and 4.7 demonstrate the operation of this function.

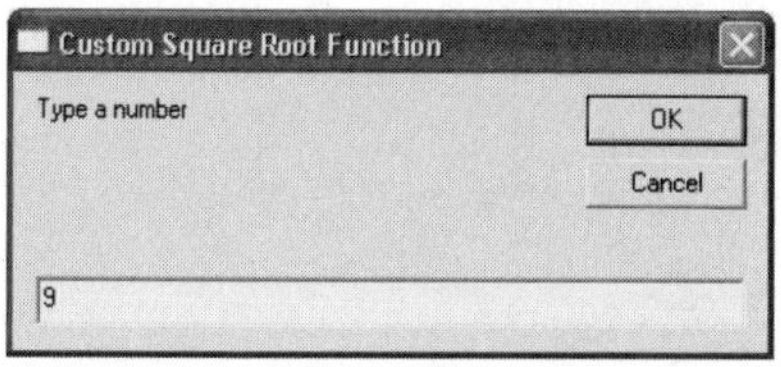

FIGURE 4.6 *Creating a custom function that determines the square root on an input number*

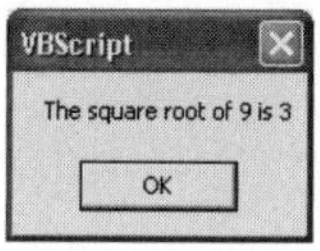

FIGURE 4.7 *Displaying the results of the square root calculation*

Using VBScript's built-in `Sqr()` function, you can perform the same task with just two lines of code, as shown below.

```
UserInput = InputBox ("Type a number", "Square Root Calculator")
MsgBox "The square root of " & UserInput & " is " & Sqr(UserInput)
```

Not only does using the built-in VBScript `Sqr()` function reduce the number of lines of code, but it also greatly reduces the complexity of the script, thus reducing the amount of time that it takes to develop it.

Summary

In this chapter, you learned how to enhance your VBScripts by organizing them into subroutines and functions. This included developing an understanding of the differences between these two types of procedures and how to leverage the power and convenience provided by VBScript's built-in collection of functions. In addition to making scripts easier to read and maintain, procedures provide a mechanism for limiting variable scope. You also learned how to call VBScript procedures using event handlers in order to develop VBScripts that can react dynamically to both user and browser activity.

Chapter 5

Arrays

Up to this point, all discussion has centered on the use of variables as the primary means of storing information in memory during script execution. Variables are limited in their ability to effectively handle large amounts of data. Scripts are generally designed to process data that is related in some manner. VBScript provides the array construct as a means of more efficiently managing large amounts of related data. In this chapter, you will learn how to work with single dimensional and multidimensional arrays. In addition, you will learn various techniques for resizing arrays and how to process and erase their contents.

Storing Related Data in Arrays

Typically, scripts process data that is related in some fashion. When the amount of data to be processed is relatively small, it can be stored in individual variables. However, as the amount of data processed by scripts grows, it becomes increasingly difficult to rely on variables. For example, a script may need to process a collection of user names. Defining 100 unique variable names would be an arduous process. Instead, VBScript provides arrays as a construct for storing large quantities of related data.

An *array* is an indexed list of related data. Arrays provide the ability to store related pieces of information in a manner that is easy to manage. Most arrays are made up of a single dimension and can be thought of as a single column table. VBScript arrays are zero-based, meaning that their first element is always assigned an index number of 0. The second element stored in the array is assigned an index number of 1, and so on. By specifying the name of an array and an index number, you can reference any element stored within the array.

However, VBScript arrays are not limited to a single dimension. For example, a two-dimensional VBScript array can be thought of as a table consisting of multiple columns and rows, as depicted in Figure 5.1.

As additional dimensions are added, arrays become more complex. For example, a three-dimensional array can be thought of as a cube. Anything beyond three dimensions is difficult for most people to conceptualize and is equally difficult to

	Cust_No	Cust_Name	Cust_Phone
Customer1	0,0	1,0	2,0
Customer2	0.1	1,1	2,1
Customer3	0,2	1,2	2,2

FIGURE 5.1 *Examining the structure of a two-dimensional array*

represent graphically. Fortunately, even though VBScript can support arrays with up to 60 dimensions, most situations only call for one or two dimensional arrays.

Each *element* in an array can hold one value. For single-dimension arrays, an element is a row in the table or column. For two-dimensional arrays, an element is the intersection of a row and a column.

Working with Single-Dimension Arrays

A single-dimension array is used to store related collections of data, such as the names of a collection of files, users, or customers. VBScript arrays are zero-based. Therefore, the first element stored in a single-dimension array is assigned an index position of 0. The actual length of an array is equal to the number of elements in the array minus 1.

Defining Single-Dimension Arrays

VBScript supports the establishment of both static and dynamic arrays. A *static* array is one whose length is defined in advance and cannot be changed. A *dynamic* array, on the other hand, can be resized as many times as necessary. You may define a static array using the `Dim` keyword. The syntax for the `Dim` statement when used to define arrays is outlined below.

```
Dim ArrayName(dimensions)
```

ArrayName is the name assigned to the array, and dimensions is a comma-separated list that specifies the number of dimensions in the array as well as their length.

```
Dim astrCustomerList(4)
```

The previous statement defines an array called astrCustomerList that can store up to five elements (that is, elements 0 through 4).

TIP

To make arrays stand out from other variables, develop a unique naming convention for them. In this book, the lowercase letter *a* is appended to the beginning of array names, followed by a three-character Hungarian styled description of the type of data stored in the array and one or more descriptive words that identify the array's contents. In the case of the previous example, the astrCustomerList array contains string data representing the customer names.

Populating a Single-Dimension Array

Once an array has been defined, you can begin storing elements in it. For example, the following statements create an array called astrCustomerList and assign data to each of its five elements.

```
Dim astrCustomerList(4)
astrCustomerList(0) = "XYZ Corp."
astrCustomerList(1) = "ABC Co."
astrCustomerList(2) = "Acme Inc."
astrCustomerList(3) = "A&B Corp"
astrCustomerList(4) = "ZZZ Enterprises"
```

If you want the user to provide data for the array, you might collect it as demonstrated below.

```
Dim astrCustomerList(4)

For i = 0 to 4
  astrCustomerList(i) = InputBox("Please enter a customer name.")
Next
```

A loop has been set up to iterate five times (from 0 to 4). It uses the VBScript `InputBox()` function to prompt the user to type the name of a customer during each iteration of the loop, as demonstrated in Figure 5.2. It then stores the values typed by the user in the array by associating the value of `i` with an index number in the array.

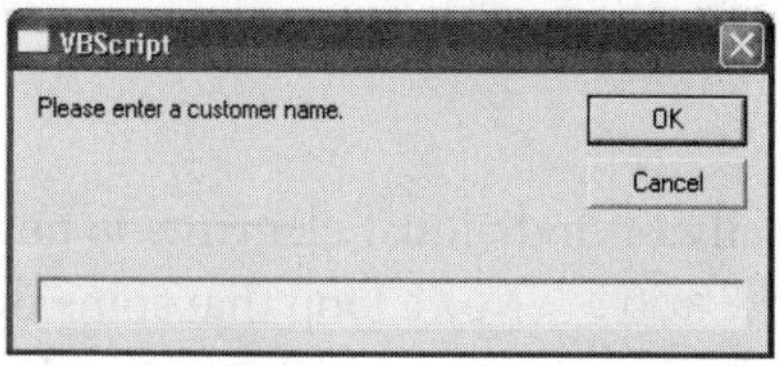

FIGURE 5.2 *Populating an array with user input*

Processing a Single-Dimension Array

There are a couple of different techniques that you can use to access the contents of an array. This includes accessing specific elements by referencing their index number and creating loops that iterate through all of the elements stored within an array. Both of these techniques are reviewed in the sections that follow.

Direct Access

Once an array has been populated with data, you can process it. One way to access the array contents is to specify the index number of a specific array element, as demonstrated below.

```
Dim astrCustomerList(4)

astrCustomerList(0) = "XYZ Corp."
astrCustomerList(1) = "ABC Co."
astrCustomerList(2) = "Acme Inc."
astrCustomerList(3) = "A&B Corp"
astrCustomerList(4) = "ZZZ Enterprises"

MsgBox "The third customer is " & astrCustomerList(2)
```

Figure 5.3 shows the output displayed by this script.

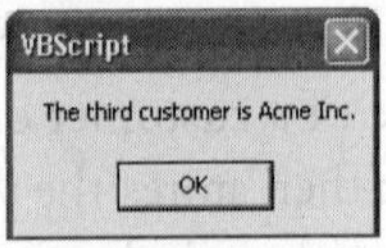

FIGURE 5.3 *Accessing a specific element stored in an array*

For Each...Next

Processing the contents of an array by specifying individual elements is not usually practical. Instead, you can create a `For Each...Next` loop that spins though the array, allowing you to programmatically process each element stored in the array. The syntax of the `For Each...Next` loop is outlined below.

```
For Each element In group
  Statements . . .
Next [element]
```

`Element` is a variable used to control the loop as it iterates through the array. `Group` specifies the name of the array to be processed. `Statements` are the statements that will be used to process the contents of the array.

The `For Each...Next` loop iterates until every element stored within the array is processed as demonstrated in the following example.

```
<HTML>
  <HEAD>
    <TITLE>Script 5.1 Using the For…Each…Next loop to process an
      array</TITLE>
</HEAD>

  <BODY>

    <SCRIPT language="VBScript">
      Option Explicit

      Dim i
      Dim astrCustomerList(4)

      astrCustomerList(0) = "XYZ Corp."
```

```
      astrCustomerList(1) = "ABC Co."
      astrCustomerList(2) = "Acme Inc."
      astrCustomerList(3) = "A&B Corp"
      astrCustomerList(4) = "ZZZ Enterprises"

      Document.Write "<B>" & "Customer Contacts:" & "</B> " & "<BR>"

      For Each i In astrCustomerList
        Document.Write  i & "<BR>"
      Next

    </SCRIPT>

  </BODY>
</HTML>
```

As you can see, a VBScript has been embedded into the BODY section of an HTML page. This script begins by defining an array called `astrCustomerList` that can store up to five elements. The next five statements store values in each element of the array. Next, a `Document.Write` statement is used to display a column heading on the Web page. Finally, a `For Each...Next` loop is used to iterate through the array and display its contents, which are represented by the variable `i`. Figure 5.4 shows the output created when this HTML page is loaded.

NOTE

`Document` is a browser object that represents the currently loaded HTML page. The `Document` object has a number of methods and properties associated with it, including the `Write()` method, which provides the ability to display text directly on HTML pages. For more information on the `Document` object, refer to Chapter 8, "VBScript and Internet Explorer."

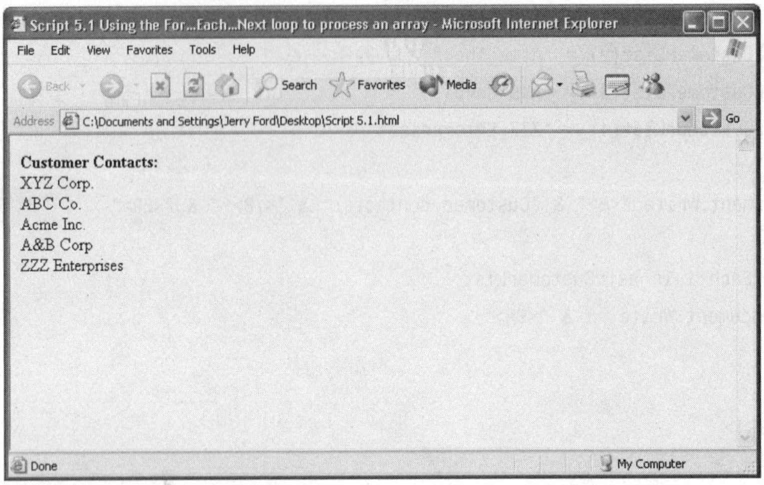

FIGURE 5.4 *Using a* `For Each...Next` *loop to process all the elements stored in an array*

> **NOTE**
>
> More information about how to work with the `For Each...Next` loop is available in Chapter 3, "Conditional Logic and Iterative Structures."

Using the UBound Function

VBScript provides two functions that allow you to programmatically determine the upper and lower bounds of an array. These are the `UBound()` and `LBound()` functions. The `LBound()` function reruns the value of an array's lower bound (that is, its lowest element). However, as VBScript loops are always zero-based, this function is of little value.

> **NOTE**
>
> VBScript is part of the Visual Basic family of programming languages. The other languages in this family are Visual Basic and VBA. VBScript represents a subset of these other languages. In Visual Basic and VBA, programmers have the ability to assign an array's lower bound, whereas in VBScript it is always set to zero. Therefore, while useful in Visual Basic and VBA programs, the `LBound()` function is redundant in VBScript.

The `UBound()` function, on the other hand, has merit. It is used to retrieve the value of an array's upper bound (its highest element). The syntax of the `UBound()` function, when used to process a single-dimension array, is outlined below.

```
UBound(ArrayName)
```

`ArrayName` is the name of the array. The `UBound()` function is typically used as shown below.

```
x = UBound(ArrayName)
```

The value assigned to `x` is equal to one less than the actual number of elements in the array. Therefore, to determine the number of elements stored in the array, add 1 to the value returned by `UBound()`, as shown below.

```
x = UBound(ArrayName) + 1
```

For example, the following VBScript uses the `UBound()` function to terminate the execution of a `For...Next` loop when processing an array.

```
'*************************************************************************
'Script Name: Script 5.2.vbs
'Author: Jerry Ford
'Created: 01/17/2003
'Description: Using UBound() to determine an array's upper boundary
'*************************************************************************


'Initialization Section


Option Explicit


Dim intArrayUpperBound, i, strDisplayString


Dim astrCustomerList(4)
astrCustomerList(0) = "XYZ Corp."
astrCustomerList(1) = "ABC Co."
astrCustomerList(2) = "Acme Inc."
astrCustomerList(3) = "A&B Corp"
astrCustomerList(4) = "ZZZ Enterprises"


'Main Processing Section
```

```
intArrayUpperBound = UBound(astrCustomerList)
For i = 0 to intArrayUpperBound
  strDisplayString = strDisplayString & astrCustomerList(i) & " " & vbCrLf
Next

MsgBox "Contacts:" & vbCrLf & vbCrLf & strDisplayString, , "Customer Contacts"
```

Figure 5.5 shows the output displayed by this script.

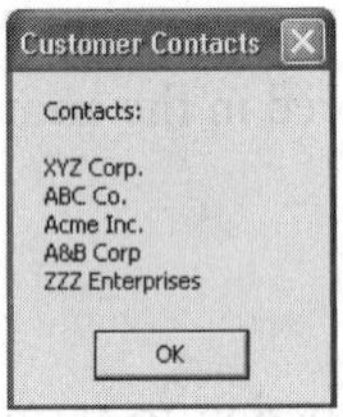

FIGURE 5.5 *Using the* `UBound()` *function to determine an array's upper boundary*

You can use the `UBound()` function to prevent a VBScript from attempting to access elements that do not exist, thus prevent errors from occurring. For example, the following statements define an array and populate it with five elements. The last statement attempts to access an element that does not exist in the array, resulting in the error message shown in Figure 5.6.

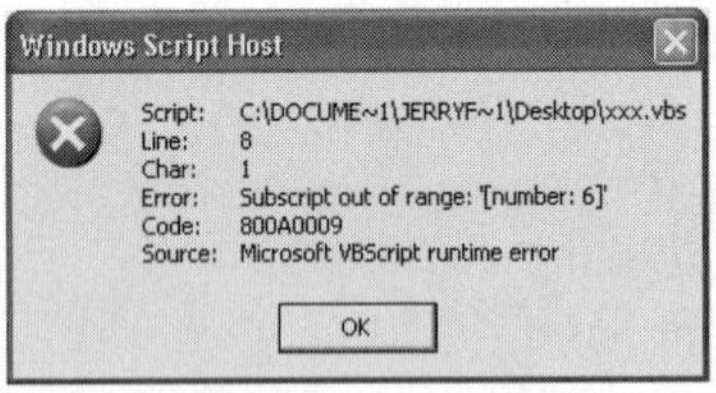

FIGURE 5.6 *An error occurs when VBScript attempts to access an element that is beyond an array's upper boundary*

```
Dim astrCustomerList(4)
astrCustomerList(0) = "ABC Corp"
astrCustomerList(1) = "XYZ Inc"
astrCustomerList(2) = "Acme Co."
```

```
astrCustomerList(3) = "L&F Inc"
astrCustomerList(4) = "IV World"

X = astrCustomerList(6)
```

Working with Multidimensional Arrays

Multidimensional arrays provide a powerful tool for storing and manipulating large amounts of data. Multidimensional arrays provide the ability to store information when the data that is collected consists of different types of related data. For example, a VBScript may need to store numerous pieces of information about a customer, including the customer's name, customer number, and phone number as demonstrated in Table 5.1.

Table 5.1 Organizing Related Data into a Two-Dimensional Table

Customer_ Name	Customer_No	Customer_Phone
XYZ Corp.	12345	800-333-3333
ABC Co.	98765	877-444-4444
Acme Inc.	11122	800-555-5555
A&B Corp.	22233	888-888-9999
ZZZ Enterprises	33344	877-444-1111

Defining Multidimensional Arrays

The `Dim` statement can be used to define a multidimensional array. When used to define arrays in this manner, the `Dim` statement has the following syntax:

```
Dim ArrayName(dimensions)
```

TIP

Another way to think of a two-dimensional array is as a one-dimensional array that consists of a collection of one-dimensional arrays.

ArrayName is the name of the array being defined and dimensions is a comma-separated list of subscripts, each of which defines a dimension of the array. For example, the following statement defines a two-dimensional array.

```
Dim astrCustomerList(4,2)
```

The astrCustomerList array, as defined above, will be able to store five rows' and three columns' worth of information, allowing it to store all the information listed in Table 5.1.

Populating a Multidimensional Array

Once a multidimensional array is defined, it can be populated. In order to populate an element in the array, you must specify the element's index number. In the case of a two-dimensional array, the index number will be specified as (X,Y), which represents a point of intersection in the array between each dimension.

The following script demonstrates how to assign the data listed in Table 5.1 to the astrCustomerList array.

```
Const cCustomerName = 0
Const cCustomerNo = 1
Const cCustomerPhone = 2

Dim astrCustomerList(2,4)

astrCustomerList(cCustomerName,0) = " XYZ Corp."
astrCustomerList(cCustomerNo,0) = 12345
astrCustomerList(cCustomerPhone,0) = "800-333-3333"
astrCustomerList(cCustomerName,1) = " ABC Co "
astrCustomerList(cCustomerNo,1) = 98765
astrCustomerList(cCustomerPhone,1) = "877-444-4444"
astrCustomerList(cCustomerName,2) = " Acme Inc."
astrCustomerList(cCustomerNo,2) = 11122
astrCustomerList(cCustomerPhone,2) =  "800-555-5555"
astrCustomerList(cCustomerName,3) = " A&B Corp."
astrCustomerList(cCustomerNo,3) = 22233
astrCustomerList(cCustomerPhone,3) = "888-888-9999"
astrCustomerList(cCustomerName,4) = " ZZZ Enterprises "
astrCustomerList(cCustomerNo,4) = 33344
astrCustomerList(cCustomerPhone,4) = "877-444-1111"
```

> **TIP**
>
> Notice the use of the constants in the first three statements in the previous example. By assigning constants to represent the value of each of the three columns in the array, the code becomes self-documenting, making it easier to read and support.

Processing Multidimensional Arrays

Once a multidimensional array has been defined and populated with data, it can be processed. Like static arrays, you can specify the location of individual elements in order to access their values. In the case of a two-dimensional array, this means specifying both the row and column coordinates, as demonstrated below.

```
WScript.Echo astrCustomerList(cCustomerName,2)
WScript.Echo astrCustomerList(cCustomerPhone,2)
```

However, to process multidimensional arrays with large amounts of data, you will need to establish a loop, as demonstrated in the following example.

```
'*************************************************************************
'Script Name: Script 5.3.vbs
'Author: Jerry Ford
'Created: 01/17/2003
'Description: A multidimensional array example
'*************************************************************************


'Initialization Section


Option Explicit


Const cCustomerName = 0
Const cCustomerNo = 1
Const cCustomerPhone = 2


Dim intArrayUpperBound, i, strDisplayString


Dim astrCustomerList(2,4)
```

```
'Main Processing Section

LoadArray()

intArrayUpperBound = UBound(astrCustomerList,2)
For i = 0 to intArrayUpperBound
  strDisplayString = strDisplayString & _
    astrCustomerList(cCustomerName, i) & _
    vbTab & astrCustomerList(cCustomerPhone, i) & " " & vbCrLf
Next
MsgBox strDisplayString, , "Multidimensional Array Example"

'Procedure Section

Function LoadArray()
  astrCustomerList(cCustomerName,0) = "XYZ Corp."
  astrCustomerList(cCustomerNo,0) = 12345
  astrCustomerList(cCustomerPhone,0) = "800-333-3333"
  astrCustomerList(cCustomerName,1) = "ABC Co.    "
  astrCustomerList(cCustomerNo,1) = 98765
  astrCustomerList(cCustomerPhone,1) = "877-444-4444"
  astrCustomerList(cCustomerName,2) = "Acme Inc."
  astrCustomerList(cCustomerNo,2) = 11122
  astrCustomerList(cCustomerPhone,2) =  "800-555-5555"
  astrCustomerList(cCustomerName,3) = "A&B Corp."
  astrCustomerList(cCustomerNo,3) = 22233
  astrCustomerList(cCustomerPhone,3) = "888-888-9999"
  astrCustomerList(cCustomerName,4) = "ZZZ Enterprises"
  astrCustomerList(cCustomerNo,4) = 33344
  astrCustomerList(cCustomerPhone,4) = "877-444-1111"
End Function
```

The script begins by defining constants to represent each column in a two-dimensional array. Next, the variables to be used by the script are defined, followed by the definition of a two-dimensional array. Then the `LoadArray()` function is executed. This function assigns values to each element of the array. Finally, a loop is set up to process the contents of the array. The `Ubound()` function is used to determine upper boundary of the array's second dimension (the length of the column dimension). A `For` loop is then set up to process all elements of the array beginning with the first element (0) and going through the last element (intArrayUpperBound). As the loop iterates, a display string is assembled. This string consists of the values stored in the first (astrCustomerList(cCustomerName, i)) and third (astrCustomerList(cCustomerPhone, i)) columns of the array. The last statement in the script displays the fully assembled string using the VBScript MsgBox() function. Figure 5.7 shows the output produced by this script.

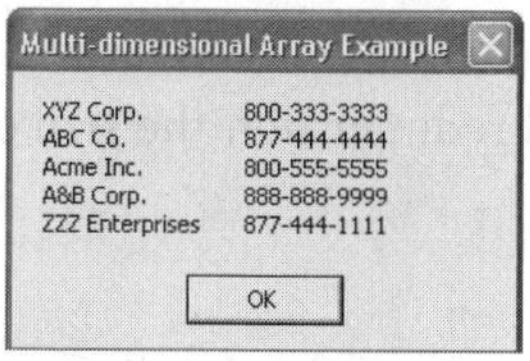

FIGURE 5.7 *Processing data stored in a multidimensional array*

NOTE

The syntax of the UBound() function when used to work with multidimensional arrays is shown below:

```
LBound(ArrayName, dimension)
```

ArrayName specifies the array to be tested. The Dimension parameter is optional. When used, the dimension parameter specifies the array dimension whose upper bound should be returned. Specify 1 for the first dimension, 2 for the second dimension, and so on.

Creating Dynamic Arrays

In all of the preceding examples, the number of elements that were to be stored in each array were known at design time. However, in the real world, it is common not to know the number of elements that will need to be stored in advance. For example, if a script is set up to collect information about customers using the VBScript InputBox() function, there is often no way of knowing in advance how many different customers the user will enter data for. VBScript provides a solution to this dilemma in the form of dynamic arrays. A dynamic array is an array that can be resized during the execution of the script, meaning that its size can be increased or decreased.

Defining Dynamic Arrays

One way to define a dynamic array is to use the `Dim` statement to define it without specifying its size, as demonstrated below.

```
Dim astrCustomerList()
```

This allows you to come back later in your script and redimension the size of the array using the `ReDim` statement, as follows.

```
ReDim astrCustomerList(4)
```

In this example, the `astrCustomerList` array has been redimensioned so that it can store five elements. Another option when working with dynamic arrays is to define them initially with the `ReDim` statement instead of the `Dim` statement. This option allows you to assign an initial size to the array. There is no limit to the number of times that a dynamic array can be resized.

Resizing Single-Dimension Dynamic Arrays

By default, all the data stored in a dynamic array is lost when it is resized. However, you can prevent this behavior by adding the `Preserve` keyword to the `ReDim` statement, as demonstrated below.

```
ReDim Preserve astrCustomerList(49)
```

In the case of this example, the array `astrCustomerList` is resized to allow it to store 50 elements without causing it to lose any data that it contained before it was increased in size.

NOTE

If you resize a dynamic array by making it smaller, all of the data stored in the elements of the array that were removed are lost, even if you use the `Preserve` keyword when redimensioning the array. For example, if you define a single-dimension dynamic array, assign 10 elements to it, and then later resize it so that it can only store 5 elements, then the last 5 elements in the array will be lost.

The following example provides a simple demonstration of how to redimension a dynamic array.

```
'*************************************************************************
'Script Name: Script 5.4.vbs
'Author: Jerry Ford
'Created: 01/17/2003
'Description: A demonstration of how to resize an array
'*************************************************************************

'Initialization Section

Option Explicit

Dim strMessage, astrCustomerList, i
strMessage = "Dynamic Array Demonstration" & vbCrLf & vbCrLf


'Main Processing Section

DimTheArray()
ReDimTheArray()
DisplayResults()


'Procedure Section

Function DimTheArray()
  ReDim astrCustomerList(2)
  astrCustomerList(0) = "XYZ Corp."
  astrCustomerList(1) = "ABC Co."
  astrCustomerList(2) = "Acme Inc."
End Function

Function ReDimTheArray()
  ReDim Preserve astrCustomerList(4)
  astrCustomerList(3) = "A&B Corp"
  astrCustomerList(4) = "ZZZ Enterprises"
```

```
End Function

Function DisplayResults()
  For Each i In astrCustomerList
    strMessage = strMessage & i & vbCrLf
  Next
  MsgBox strMessage, , "Resizing an Array" & Space(25)
End Function
```

Three statements in the script's Main Processing Section control the overall execution of the script by calling upon three functions located in the Procedure Section. The `DimTheArray()` function defines a single-dimension dynamic array with an initial size of three elements. It then assigns values to each of these elements.

Next, the `ReDimTheArray()` function executes. This function redimensions the size of the array to allow it to store up to five elements. The `Preserve` keyword is included in order to ensure that no data currently stored in the array is lost. The function then assigns values to the two new array elements.

The final function that is executed is `DisplayResults()`. It uses a `For Each...Next` loop to process the contents of the newly expanded array so that it can display its contents. Figure 5.8 shows the output displayed by this script.

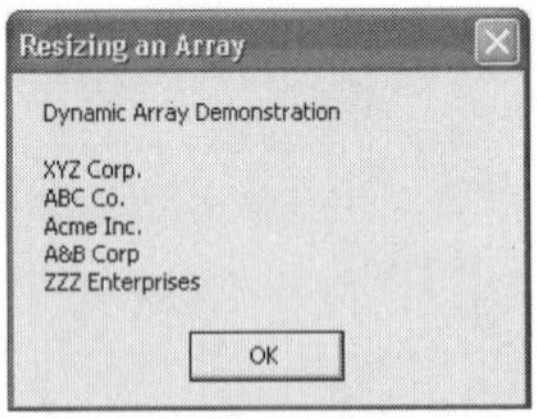

FIGURE 5.8 *A demonstration of how to resize a dynamic array*

The previous example demonstrated how to resize a dynamic array based on the assumption that you know in advance what size the array will need to be expanded to. However, in many cases you will not know in advance how big the dynamic array should be. This following example demonstrates how to write a script that dynamically resizes an array each time a new element is added. This allows the script to increase the size of the array as necessary to accommodate whatever amount of data is required.

```
'*************************************************************************
'Script Name: Script 5.5.vbs
'Author: Jerry Ford
'Created: 01/17/2003
'Description: Resizing a dynamic array based on user input
'*************************************************************************

'Initialization Section

Option Explicit

Dim strUserInput, strMessage

ReDim astrCustomerList(0)


'Main Processing Section

CollectInputData()
ProcessInputData()

'Procedure Section

Function CollectInputData()

  Dim i
  i = 0

  Do While UCase(strUserInput) <> "QUIT"

    strUserInput = InputBox("Type a customer name")

    If UCase(strUserInput) <> "QUIT" Then
      astrCustomerList(i) = strUserInput
    Else
      Exit Do
    End If
```

```
        i = i + 1

        ReDim Preserve astrCustomerList(i)

Loop

End Function

Function ProcessInputData()

  Dim i
  i = 0

  For Each i In astrCustomerList
    strMessage = strMessage & i & vbCrLf
  Next

  MsgBox strMessage

End Function
```

The script begins by defining its variables and defining an array called `astrCustomerList` with an initial size of `0`. This allows the array to store a single element. The controlling logic of the script is located in the Main Processing Section, and it consists of two function calls. The first function called is `CollectInputData()`. This function uses a `Do...While` loop to control data collection. The VBScript `InputBox()` function is used to collect text input from the user. Data collection occurs until the user types the word `quit`. The `Ucase()` function is used to test each piece of data typed by the user to search for the word **Quit**. Each time a new entry is typed, the script assigns it as the last element in the array and then resizes the array to accommodate a new element.

TIP

The `Ucase()` function can be used to convert text to all uppercase. This allows you to perform an all uppercase text comparison without being concerned about the case that the user uses. For example, in the previous script the user could type **QUIT**, **quit**, or **QuIt** to terminate the data entry process.

The last function called in the script uses a `For Each...Next` loop to process each element stored in the array, to build a display string, and to display its results.

Resizing Multidimensional Dynamic Arrays

When preserving data stored in a multidimensional array, only the last dimension that is defined can be resized. For example, in the two-dimensional array presented earlier in this chapter, an array was set up to store the customer names, customer numbers, and customer phone numbers. Because the second dimension of the array was used to store customer phone numbers, it is the only dimension that can be resized. Fortunately, this works out well in this case, because it is unlikely that customers will change their names. It is also unlikely that the number assigned to the customer will change. However, the customer's phone number may change from time to time.

As another example, consider the following two-dimensional array.

```
ReDim astrCustomerList(2,2)
```

The array defined by this statement can be viewed as a table made up of three columns and three rows. However, since only the last dimension of a multidimensional array can be resized, only the elements stored in the second dimension of the array can be resized. To resize the array to contain additional data, you could increase the size of its second dimension as demonstrated below.

```
ReDim astrCustomerList(2,9)
```

This statement allows to you expand the size of the second dimension to store 10 elements.

Keep the following points in mind when resizing multidimensional arrays.

- You can redimension a multidimensional array by changing both the number of dimensions and the size of each dimension, but doing so will result in the loss of its data.
- To prevent the loss of data when resizing a multidimensional array, you may add the `Preserve` keyword to the `ReDim` statement, but in doing so, you limit the ability to modify the array to resizing only the length of the last dimension.

Erasing Arrays

VBScript provides the ability to erase the contents of an array using the `Erase` statement. The syntax of this statement is outlined below.

```
Erase arrayname
```

The `Erase` statement erases the contents of a static array but does not reduce the size of the array. When used to erase a dynamic array, the `Erase` statement erases the contents of the array and deallocates all storage used by the array, thus freeing up memory.

For example, the following statement erases the contents of an array called `astrCustomerList`.

```
Erase astrCustomerList
```

Using VBScript Functions to Work with Arrays

VBScript supplies two functions that are useful when working with arrays. These functions are briefly defined below.

- **`Array()`.** Retrieves a variant that contains an array
- **`IsArray()`.** Provides the ability to determine whether a variable is an array

Using the VBScript Array() Function

The `Array()` function provides a tool for quickly defining arrays. Its syntax is outlined below.

```
Array(arglist)
```

`Arglist` is a comma-separated list of elements to be stored in the array. If `arglist` is omitted, then a zero length array is set up. Otherwise the initial size of the array is determined by the number of elements supplied in the `arglist`. For example, the following statement defines an array that contains five elements.

```
astrCustomerList = Array("ABC Corp", "XYZ Inc", "Acme Co.", "L&F Inc", "IV World")
```

The `Array()` function allows you to reduce the number of statements required to create small arrays. For example, the above array could have just as easily been defined as shown below.

```
ReDim astrCustomerList(4)
astrCustomerList(0) = "XYZ Corp."
astrCustomerList(1) = "ABC Co."
astrCustomerList(2) = "Acme Inc."
astrCustomerList(3) = "A&B Corp"
astrCustomerList(4) = "ZZZ Enterprises"
```

Using the IsArray() Function

The VBScript `IsArray()` function is used to test whether the specified variable is an array. It returns a value of `True` if the tested variable is an array. Otherwise it returns a value of `False`.

Except for arrays, VBScript variables are scalar, meaning that they only contain one value. If a VBScript attempts to use an array-related function such as `UBound()` or `LBound()` against a scalar variable, an error occurs, terminating script execution. An error will also occur if the script attempts to treat a scalar variable like an array by specifying an index number when referencing it. One way to guard against accidentally attempting to treat a scalar variable as if it were an array is to first test it using the `IsArray()` function.

The syntax of the `IsArray()` function is outlined below.

```
IsArray(variablename)
```

For example, the following statements define an array and then demonstrate how to use the `IsArray()` function.

```
ReDim astrCustomerList(4)
X = IsArray(astrCustomerList)
If x = "True" then
  MsgBox "This variable is an array."
Else
  MsgBox "This is a scalar variable."
End If
```

Summary

In this chapter, you learned how to work with single-dimension and multidimensional arrays. You also learned how to work with static and dynamic arrays. In addition, you learned different techniques for processing array contents, including how to access data stored in specific array cells and how to create loops that iteratively process the contents of an entire array. Other topics covered in this chapter included how to resize arrays as well as how to both preserve and erase their contents.

Chapter 6

Data Collection, Notification, and Error Reporting

In this chapter, you will learn how the VBScript `InputBox()` and `MsgBox()` functions display pop-up dialog boxes that can be used to collect user input and to display output. You will also learn how to control the presentation of text within these pop-up dialog boxes, as well as how to interrogate the input specified by the user. In addition, this chapter will present information on error handling, including how to generate more user-friendly error messages.

Interacting with Users

Depending on the programming environment for which you are developing your VBScripts, you have a number of different options for displaying output and interacting with users. For example, within HTML pages you can display output using methods provided by the `Window` and `Document` objects. These methods are described in Table 6.1.

> **NOTE**
>
> The `Window` and `Document` objects are browser objects. The `Window` object represents the currently opened browser window or frame. The `Document` object represents the currently loaded HTML page. More information about these objects is available in Chapter 8, "VBScript and Internet Explorer."

Table 6.1 VBScript String Constants

Object	Method	Description
`Document`	`Write`	Displays text directly on HTML pages
`Window`	`Alert`	Displays text in a pop-up dialog box that displays an `OK` button
	`Prompt`	Displays text in a pop-up dialog box that displays a text entry field and the `OK` and `Cancel` buttons
	`Confirm`	Displays a text message in a pop-up dialog box and requires the user to provide confirmation by clicking on either the `OK` or the `Cancel` button
	`Status`	Displays text messages in the browser status bar

When developing scripts for the WSH, programmers have the option of displaying output using methods provided by the `WScript` and `WshShell` objects. These methods are specified below.

- **`Echo()`**. A method belonging to the `WScript` object that displays text messages in either the Windows console or in a pop-up dialog box
- **`Popup()`**. A method belonging to the `WshShell` object that displays text messages in pop-up dialog boxes with control over icon and button selection and the ability to determine the button clicked by the user

NOTE

The `WScript` and `WshShell` objects are WSH objects. The `WScript` object is the topmost or parent object for other WSH objects. The `WshShell` object provides access to methods and properties that can be used to access the Windows file system, registry, and other Windows resources. More information about these objects is available in Chapter 9, "VBScript and the WSH."

In addition to the environment-specific output options provided by Internet Explorer and the WSH, VBScript provides a pair of functions that are always available for displaying output and collecting user input. These two functions are described below.

- **`InputBox()`**. Displays a pop-up dialog box that collects text input from the user using a text entry field
- **`MsgBox()`**. Displays a pop-up dialog box that contains a text message, one or more buttons, and an optional icon

The features and capabilities of the `InputBox()` and `MsgBox()` functions will be further explored throughout the rest of this chapter.

The InputBox() Function

The VBScript `InputBox()` function provides the ability to prompt the user to type data input during script execution. This allows you to develop scripts that can interact directly with the user. The `InputBox()` function displays a pop-up dialog box that has the following capabilities:

- A text field used to collect user input
- The ability to display a text message up to 1,024 characters long
- OK and Cancel buttons that allow the user to control the pop-up dialog box

Defining the InputBox() Function

The syntax of the `InputBox()` function is outlined below.

```
Response = InputBox(Prompt[, Titlebarmsg][, Default][, Xpos]
  [, Ypos][, Hhelpfile, Context])
```

`Response` is a variant with a string subtype that stores the text supplied by the user. `Prompt` is a text message up to 1,024 characters long that provides instructions and directions for the user. `Titlebarmsg` is optional. When supplied, it displays its text in the pop-up dialog box's title bar. If omitted, the word "VBScript" will be displayed in the title bar. `Default` is optional. When used, it supplies a default answer that is automatically displayed in the pop-up dialog box's text field. `Xpos` and `Ypos` are optional measurements specified as twips. When used, `Xpos` specifies the distance from the left side of the display to the left side of the pop-up dialog box. `Ypos` specifies the distance from the top of the pop-up dialog box to the top of the display. `Helpfile` and `Context` are optional. They specify the location of an external file where context-sensitive help is available.

NOTE

Twip is a measurement of space and represents 1/20 of a point or 1/1440 of an inch.

The following statement demonstrates how to use the `InputBox()` function.

```
strUserName = InputBox("Please enter your name")
MsgBox ("Greetings " & strUserName)
```

The first statement in this example displays the pop-up dialog box shown in Figure 6.1. As you can see, it displays a message and waits for the user to either type in a name and click on the OK button or abort the operation by clicking on the Cancel button.

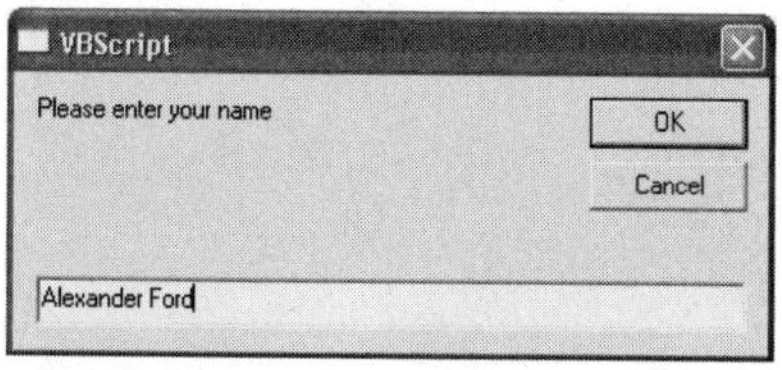

FIGURE 6.1 *Using the* `InputBox()` *function to collect data input from the user*

The `InputBox()` function returns the text typed by the user when the OK button is clicked. However, if the user clicks on OK without entering any text, or if the user clicks on the `Cancel` button, a zero-length string is returned (that is, `""`). In the previous example, the data typed by the user is saved as a variant with a string subtype in a variable called `strUserName`. Figure 6.2 shows the pop-up dialog box displayed by the second statement shown above.

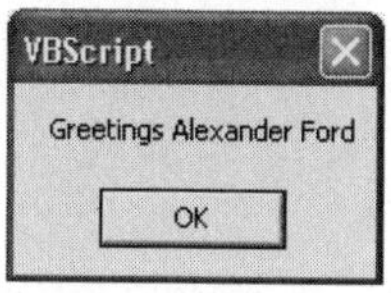

FIGURE 6.2 *Greeting a user by name*

`InputBox()` function parameters are position sensitive. If you do not use a specific parameter, you must substitute a comma in order to continue to add other parameters that follow the omitted parameter. For example, the following statements display the pop-up dialog box shown in Figure 6.3. This example will display a message and a default answer without specifying any message text for display in the pop-up dialog box's title bar.

```
strFileName = InputBox("Please specify a temporary file name.", ,"C:\Temp")
```

NOTE

If you omit the `titlebarmsg` parameter when using the `InputBox()` function, VBScript will display the word "VBScript" in the pop-up dialog box's title bar.

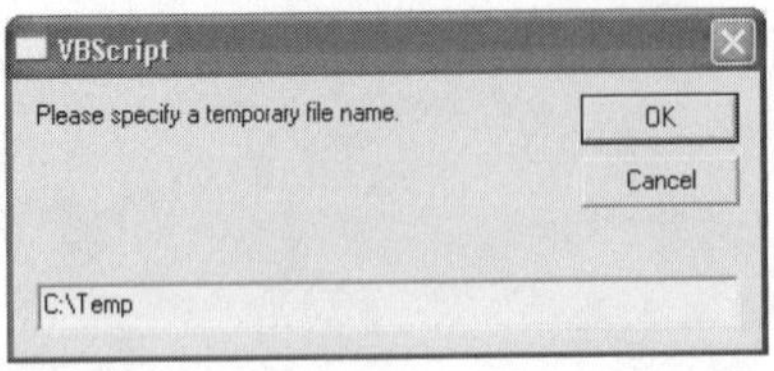

FIGURE 6.3 *Using the* `InputBox()` *function to display a pop-up dialog box with a default answer*

Input Validation

Users can be completely unpredictable. It is therefore essential that you interrogate and validate all data returned by the `InputBox()` function to ensure that it complies with the requirements of your VBScripts. For example, you may write a script in which you intend to collect the user's name. However, instead of typing a name, the user might perform one of the following actions:

- Click on the Cancel button
- Press the Escape key
- Click on OK without typing any text

Each of these actions results in a zero-length string. The following statements demonstrate how to check for the presence of data when using the `InputBox()` function.

```
strUserName = InputBox("Please enter your name.", "User Questionnaire")

If strUserName = "" Then
  MsgBox "You did not provide any information!"
Else
  MsgBox "Greetings " & strUserName
End If
```

The second statement checks to see whether the data returned by the `InputBox()` function and stored as `strUserName` is equal to `""`.

The following example shows another way to see whether the user has provided any data to the `InputBox()` function.

```
strChoice = InputBox("What do you prefer: Games, Utilities or Other?")
If Len(strChoice) = 0 Then
```

```
  MsgBox "You did not enter any data."
End If
```

In this example, the VBScript `Len()` function is used to see whether the value stored in `strChoice` is zero-length. Sometimes it may be appropriate to supply a default answer in the event that the user fails to provide any data, as demonstrated below.

```
strChoice = InputBox("What do you prefer: Games, Utilities or Other?")
If Len(strChoice) = 0 Then
  strChoice = "Other"
End If
```

In this example, the value of `strChoice` is automatically set equal to `Other` in the event that the user fails to type any data. There will be times in which supplying a default answer will not suffice. In these circumstances, you can wrap the `InputBox()` function inside a loop that iterates until the user provides a proper response. For example, the following statements use a `Do...While` loop to force the user to type **quit** when prompted by the `InputBox()` function in order to exit the loop.

```
Do While UCase(strChoice) <> "QUIT"

  strChoice = InputBox("What do you want to do?")

  If UCase(strChoice) <> "QUIT" Then
    MsgBox "Invalid option. Please specify your selection again."
  Else
    Exit Do
  End If

Loop
```

In this example, the `UCase()` function is used to convert all user responses to uppercase. The user's response is then checked to see if the correct input has been supplied.

VBScript provides you with tools for controlling the format of the prompt message displayed by the `InputBox()` function. You can use any of the VBScript constants listed in Table 6.2 to format the text output.

Table 6.2 VBScript String Constants

Function	Description
VbCr	Performs a carriage return operation
vbCrLf	Performs a carriage return and a line feed operation
vbLf	Performs a line feed operation
VbTab	Performs a horizontal tab operation

The following example demonstrates how to display a menu of options using the `InputBox()` function and then to select the appropriate action based on the user's selection.

```
intAnswer = InputBox("Please enter the number of one of the " & _
  "following options:" & vbCrLf & _
  vbCrLf & vbTab & "—— Choices ——" & vbCrLf & vbCrLf & _
  "1. View copyright information." & vbCrLf & _
  "2. View information about the script." & vbCrLf & _
  "3. View help information." & vbCrLf, "Menu List")
If IsNumeric(intAnswer) Then
  Select Case intAnswer
    Case 1
      MsgBox "Copyright 2003, Jerry Lee Ford, Jr."
    Case 2
      MsgBox "This script demonstrates how to format text in " & _
        "InputBox() dialogs"
    Case 3
      MsgBox "For additional assistance visit " & _
        "msdn.microsoft.com/scripting"
    Case Else
      MsgBox "Invalid selection."
  End Select
Else
  MsgBox "The only valid options are 1, 2 or 3."
End If
```

Data Coercion

VBScript only supports the variant data type. However, it supports multiple variant subtypes. VBScript does its best to determine the type of data stored in a variable in order to associate it with the correct data subtype. Sometimes VBScript will not identify the data subtype in the manner in which you desire. To remedy this situation, VBScript provides two ways of changing data subtypes, implicit coercion and explicit coercion.

Implicit Coercion

The `InputBox()` function only returns string data regardless of what the user enters into its text field. However, VBScript provides ways around this. In most cases, VBScript is able to automatically convert data stored in variables as required by the situation. For example, if a user enters the number 66 as input into the text field of an `InputBox()` pop-up dialog box, VBScript will treat it as a string equivalent to `"66"`. If a mathematical operation is performed that uses the variable, VBScript will automatically convert its subtype to numeric. This is known as *implicit coercion.*

Using implicit coercion, the following VBScript is able to automatically convert any number entered by the user from a string to a numeric value.

```
dblAnswer = InputBox("Enter the number", "Implicit Coercion Example")
MsgBox TypeName(dblAnswer)
dblAnswer = 100 + dblAnswer
MsgBox TypeName(dblAnswer)
```

NOTE

The VBScript `TypeName()` function used in the previous example returns a string that displays the subtype of the specified variable. The `TypeName()` function can return any of the following strings.

- Byte
- Integer
- Long
- Single
- Double

continues

NOTE (*continued*)

- Currency
- Decimal
- Date
- String
- Boolean
- Empty
- Null
- Object
- Unknown
- Error

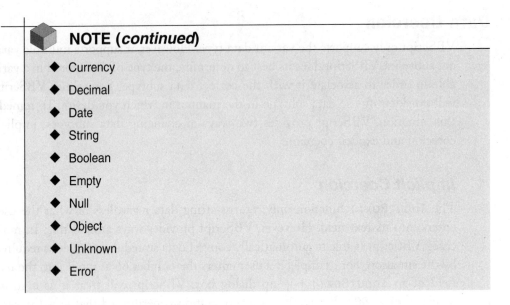

When executed, the second statement in this example displays the output shown in Figure 6.4, proving that the `InputBox()` function always returns a string value.

FIGURE 6.4 *The `InputBox()` function always returns a string value*

The third line in the script performs a mathematical operation, adding 100 to the number entered by the user. Using implicit coercion, VBScript automatically converts the value of the variable to a variant with a subtype of double. The output displayed by the last line in the script, shown in Figure 6.5, proves that the variable has been converted.

FIGURE 6.5 *VBScript automatically attempts to convert a variable from one subtype to another as required by the situation*

Explicit Coercion

While VBScript does its best to automatically adjust the subtype of a variable as each situation requires, there may be occasions when it fails to make the adjustment as you might expect. When this happens, you can attempt to use *explicit coercion* to force subtype conversion. VBScript provides a large number of conversion functions, as listed in Table 6.3.

Table 6.3 VBScript Conversion Functions

Function	Description
`Asc`	Returns the ANSI character code of the first letter in a string
`CBool`	Converts to a variable to a `Boolean` subtype
`CByte`	Converts to a variable to a `Byte` subtype
`CCur`	Converts to a variable to a `Currency` subtype
`CDate`	Converts to a variable to a `Date` subtype
`CDbl`	Converts to a variable to a `Double` subtype
`Chr`	Returns the specified ANSI character code character
`CInt`	Converts to a variable to an `Integer` subtype
`CLng`	Converts to a variable to a `Long` subtype
`CSng`	Converts to a variable to a `Single` subtype
`CStr`	Converts to a variable to a `String` subtype
`Hex`	Returns a string representing a number's hexadecimal value
`Oct`	Returns a string representing a number's octal value

The following example demonstrates the application of the `CInt()` conversion function.

```
intUserNumber = InputBox("Type a number between 0 and 9", _
  "Type Your Answer")

If IsNumeric(intUserNumber) = "True" Then
  intUserNumber = CInt(intUserNumber)
  If Len(intUserNumber) = 1 Then
    MsgBox "You entered " & intUserNumber
  Else
```

```
      MsgBox "Invalid selection!"
    End If
  Else
    MsgBox "Invalid non-number"
  End If
```

The `InputBox()` function is used to prompt the user to type a value between 0 and 9. To make sure that the user types a number and not a letter or special character, the `IsNumeric()` function is used. If a number is typed, then the value returned by this function will be equal to `True`. In this case the `CInt()` function is used to explicitly coerce the input value to an Integer value. While not strictly required in this example, the use of the `CInt()` function makes the programmer's intentions clearer.

NOTE

The `IsNumeric()` function returns a Boolean value specifying whether or not the tested value is a number.

Type Mismatch

If VBScript attempts to perform an operation on a variable that is not supported by its subtype, an error occurs. VBScript cannot perform arithmetic comparison of non-numeric data. For example, the following script prompts the user to type a numeric value between 1 and 9.

```
intAnswer = InputBox("Enter the number between 1 and 9", "Menu List")

If intAnswer > 0 Then
  If intAnswer < 10 Then
    MsgBox "You entered " & intAnswer
  End if
End If
```

If the user types a number between 1 and 9, a message is displayed. If the user types a number outside of this range, nothing happens. However, if the user types a letter or special character instead of a numeric value, a Type Mismatch error occurs, as demonstrated in Figure 6.6.

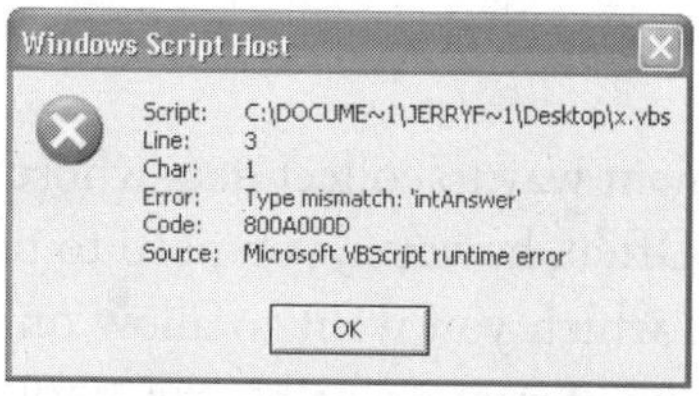

FIGURE 6.6 *A Type Mismatch error occurs when VBScript attempts to perform a operation on a variant that is not supported by its subtype*

To avoid the occurrence of Type Mismatch errors, you need to perform input validation. This typically involves testing variables to determine their subtype assignment using the `TypeName()` function or any of the subtype testing functions listed in Table 6.4.

Table 6.4 VBScript Functions That Test Variant Subtype

Function	Description
`IsArray`	Returns a value of `True` or `False` based on whether the specified variable is an array
`IsDate`	Returns a value of `True` or `False` based on whether the specified variable is a date
`IsEmpty`	Returns a value of `True` or `False` based on whether the specified variable has been initialized
`IsFinite`	Returns a value of `True` or `False` based on whether the specified number is finite
`IsNaN`	Returns a value of `True` or `False` based on whether the specified variable has the `NaN` (*not a number*) value
`IsNull`	Returns a value of `True` or `False` based on whether the specified variable contains any data
`IsNumeric`	Returns a value of `True` or `False` based on whether the specified variable is numeric

The MsgBox() Function

The `InputBox()` function provides a convenient way to collect data whose value cannot be determined in advance from users. Often, however, you need to present the user with a limited range of choices from which you want to allow only one selection. You can accomplish this type of user interaction using the `MsgBox()` function. Like the `InputBox()` function, you can use VBScript string constants to control the presentation of the text displayed by the `MsgBox()` function. In addition, you have control over what types of buttons and icons are displayed.

Defining the MsgBox() Function

The syntax of the `MsgBox()` function is outlined below.

```
MsgBox(Prompt[, Buttons][, TitleBarMsg][, Helpfile, Context])
```

`Prompt` is a text message up to 1,024 characters long that provides instructions and directions to the user. `Buttons` is a value specifying which buttons and icons should appear in the pop-up dialog box. `Titlebarmsg` is optional. When supplied, it displays its text in the pop-up dialog box's title bar. If omitted, the word "VBScript" will be displayed in the title bar. `Helpfile` and `Context` are optional. They specify the location of external files where context-sensitive help is available.

The `MsgBox()` function provides the ability to customize four pop-up dialog box features. These features are outlined below.

- ◆ The combination of buttons to be displayed
- ◆ The icon to be displayed
- ◆ The default button
- ◆ The modality of the pop-up dialog box

Each of these options is described in the tables that follow. You have the chance to specify one option from each table when using the `MsgBox()` function to display a pop-up dialog box. Table 6.5 lists the different buttons that can be displayed by the `MsgBox()` function.

Table 6.5 VBScript MsgBox() Function Buttons

Constant	Value	Description
vbOKOnly	0	Displays the OK button
vbOKCancel	1	Displays the OK and Cancel buttons
vbAbortRetryIgnore	2	Displays the Abort, Retry, and Ignore buttons
vbYesNoCancel	3	Displays the Yes, No, and Cancel buttons
vbYesNo	4	Displays the Yes and No buttons
vbRetryCancel	5	Displays the Retry and Cancel buttons

The following example demonstrates how to create a pop-up dialog box that displays an OK button.

```
MsgBox "Click on OK to continue."
```

Since the `vbOKOnly` constant represents the default selection for the `MsgBox()` function, it does not have to be specified. However, you can specify it as shown below and achieve the same results as shown in Figure 6.7.

```
MsgBox "Click on OK to continue.", vbOKOnly
```

Alternatively, you can substitute the numeric value of the `vbOKOnly` constant as shown below.

```
MsgBox "Click on OK to continue.", 0
```

Table 6.6 lists the different icons that can be displayed by the `MsgBox()` function.

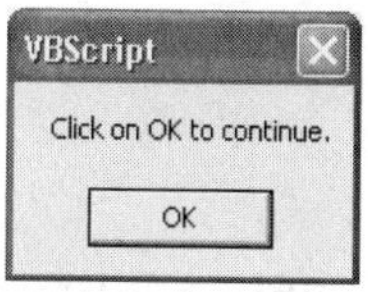

FIGURE 6.7 *Using the* `MsgBox()` *function to display a pop-up dialog box with an* OK *button*

Table 6.6 VBScript MsgBox() Function Icons

Constant	Value	Description
vbCritical	16	Displays the critical icon
vbQuestion	32	Displays the question mark icon
vbExclamation	48	Displays the exclamation mark icon
vbInformation	64	Displays the information icon

The following example demonstrates how to create a pop-up dialog box that displays `OK` and `Cancel` buttons as well as the question mark icon.

```
MsgBox "Click on OK to try again.", vbOKCancel + vbQuestion
```

Alternatively, you could rewrite this statement as shown below.

```
MsgBox "Click on OK to try again.", 1 + 32
```

You could also rewrite it as follows.

```
MsgBox "Click on OK to try again.", 33
```

The format of the first example is the clearest and easiest to read. Regardless of which of the above formats you use, the output shown in Figure 6.8 will always be the same.

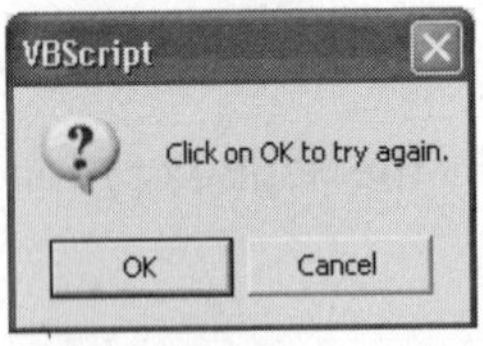

FIGURE 6.8 *Using the* `MsgBox()` *function to prompt the user for instructions*

Table 6.7 provides a list of constants that you can use to specify a pop-up dialog box's default button.

Table 6.7 VBScript MsgBox Button Default Constants

Constant	Value	Description
`vbDefaultButton1`	0	Makes the first button the default
`vbDefaultButton2`	256	Makes the second button the default
`vbDefaultButton3`	512	Makes the third button the default
`vbDefaultButton4`	768	Makes the fourth button the default

The following example demonstrates how to create a pop-up dialog box that displays `Yes`, `No`, and `Cancel` buttons. In addition, the `Cancel` button has been set up as the default button.

```
MsgBox "Please select an option.", vbYesNoCancel + vbDefaultButton3
```

Figure 6.9 shows how the pop-up dialog box appears when this statement is executed.

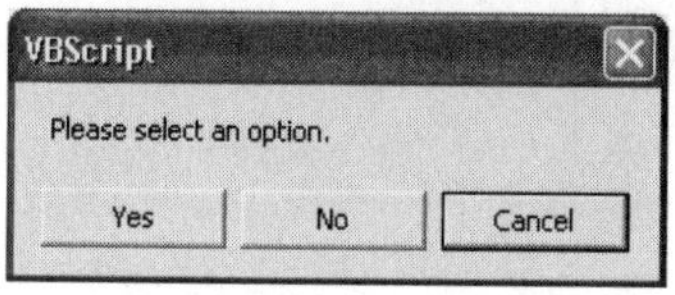

FIGURE 6.9 *Using the* `MsgBox()` *function to present the user with multiple options*

Table 6.8 provides a list of constants that you can use to specify the modality of a pop-up dialog box produced by the `MsgBox()` function.

Table 6.8 VBScript MsgBox Modal Setting Constants

Constant	Value	Description
`vbApplicationModal`	0	User must respond before the script can continue.
`vbSystemModal`	4096	User must respond before the script can continue. Also, the pop-up dialog box remains displayed on top of other active applications.

The following example demonstrates how to create a pop-up dialog box that displays `Retry` and `Cancel` buttons as well as the exclamation mark icon. In addition, the Cancel button has been set up as the default button and the pop-up dialog box has been set as the application model.

```
MsgBox "Click on Retry to try again.", vbRetryCancel + vbExclamation  +
vbDefaultButton2 +
vbApplicationModal
```

Figure 6.10 shows how the pop-up dialog box appears when this statement is executed.

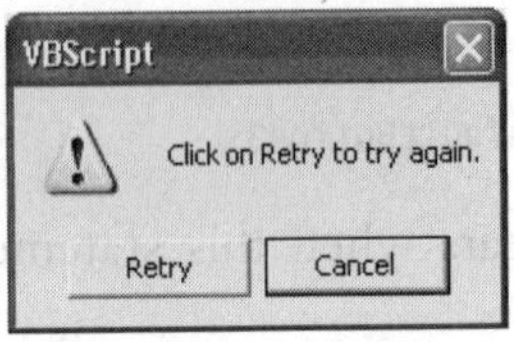

FIGURE 6.10 *Using the* `MsgBox()` *function to create an application modal pop-up dialog box*

Interrogating Results

In order to determine which button the user clicked on, you need to use the `MsgBox()` function, as demonstrated below.

```
intChoice = MsgBox("Would you like to continue?", vbYesNo, _
  "Confirmation dialog")
```

Here the numeric value of the button that the user clicks on is returned by the `MsgBox()` function and is stored in a variable called `intChoice`. Table 6.9 outlines the possible values that the `MsgBox()` function can return. In the case of the previous example, a value of 6 is returned if the user clicks on the Yes button and a value of 7 is returned if the user clicks on the No button.

Table 6.9 VBScript MsgBox() Function Return Values

Constant	Value	Description
vbOK	1	User clicked on OK
vbCancel	2	User clicked on Cancel
vbAbort	3	User clicked on Abort
vbRetry	4	User clicked on Retry
vbIgnore	5	User clicked on Ignore
vbYes	6	User clicked on Yes
vbNo	7	User clicked on No

Handling VBScript Errors

Errors can occur in VBScripts for a variety of reasons, including syntax errors, invalid user input, and unavailable system resources. VBScripts automatically terminate their execution and display an error message when an error occurs. With proper planning and testing most, but not all, errors can be eliminated. Unfortunately, VBScript errors tend to be fairly cryptic and only serve to confuse most users.

In Chapter 2, "Errors, Constants, and Variables," you learned about VBScript syntax errors. Another category of errors that can occur within VBScripts is run-time errors. Run-time errors occur when a VBScript statement attempts to perform an invalid action, such as trying to access a crashed hard disk drive. Run-time errors can be difficult to track down because, unlike syntax errors, they are not automatically detected during script interpretation. Instead they only occur if the portion of code that contains them executes. Unless every part of a VBScript is tested, it is possible that run-time errors may not be caught. In many cases, you can add programming logic to your VBScripts that anticipates and recovers from run-time errors. However, there will be occasions, such as when a disk drive crashes or the network goes down, that are beyond your ability to control or anticipate. In these circumstances, the best you can usually do is to present the user with a custom error message that clearly explains why the script has ended without accomplishing its task.

Deciding Not to Take Action

Many VBScripts consist of only a handful of statements and are written within minutes in order to quickly automate the execution of a particular common task. Under these circumstances, it is often best to omit any error handling logic and to allow errors to simply occur, since the time required to anticipate them and write code that attempts to deal with them would be prohibitive. This is usually acceptable when programmers develop small utility scripts that only they will use. In the event that the scripts will be shared with other users, instructions can be provided that ask the user to report any problems that they may experience with the scripts.

Telling VBScript to Ignore Errors

Another option for dealing with run-time errors is to tell VBScript to ignore them and to continue processing. This can be an effective technique in many cases. The following example prompts the user to type in three numbers, which are then added together.

```
intNoOne = CInt(InputBox("Enter the first number"))

intNoTwo = CInt(InputBox("Enter the second number"))

intNoThree = CInt(InputBox("Enter the final number"))


intTotal = intNoOne + intNoTwo
intTotal = intTotal + intNoThree

MsgBox intTotal
```

Everything works correctly if the user types in three numbers as requested. But often users do not behave as expected. If, for example, the user types the number 3 followed by the number 3 and then the word three, a run-time error would occur. However, if you modify the script by adding the following statement as its first line, VBScript will ignore the error and display a value of 6 (that is, the value of `intTotal` prior to the statement where the error occurred).

```
On Error Resume Next
```

While sometimes effective, this approach should be used with caution. There are few situations in which ignoring an error in one part of a script does not result in another error later in the script's execution. In addition, there will be some errors that the statement will be unable to ignore and prevent from terminating script execution.

When added to the beginning of a script, the `On Error Resume Next` statement is in effect for the entire script. If you wish, you can later disable the effects of this statement; you may do so by adding the following statement to your VBScript:

```
On Error GoTo 0
```

NOTE

Just like variables, you can localize the effects of the `On Error Resume Next` statement to procedures. This provides you with the ability to limit the effects of this statement to portions of the script where it may be useful without affecting the behavior of the entire script.

Developing Error-Handling Routines

Another option for dealing with run-time errors is to try to develop error-handling routines that deal with them. In order to be able to effectively implement error handlers, you need to be able to anticipate the locations within your scripts where errors are likely to occur and to be able to devise the appropriate logic to deal with the situation. Examples of possible error recovery actions include:

- Requesting that the user report the error
- Giving the user instructions on what to do next
- Providing more descriptive error messages
- Attempting to automatically perform a corrective action
- Giving the user another try if data entry is involved
- Apologizing to the user for the error

In order to create error handling routines, you need to know how to work with the VBScript `Err` object. This VBScript object provides access to error messages as well as to the methods that can be used to deal with them. The `Err` object has three properties that provide the following information about an error event:

- **`Number`**. The error number of the last error event
- **`Description`**. The description of the last error event

◆ **Source**. The source object that caused the error

Each of these properties can be modified, allowing you to reword them and make them more understandable before allowing them to be displayed to the user. The following example demonstrates how to create a custom error-handling routine.

```
On Error Resume Next

BogusProcedure()

If Err > 0 then
  Err.Number = 9000
  Err.Description = "This script has attempted to execute a " _
    "procedure that  has not been defined by the programmer."
  MsgBox "Error: " & Err.Number & " - " & Err.description
End if
```

The first step in setting up an error handler is to add the `On Error Resume Next` statement to the beginning of the script or procedure. Then you must add a statement that checks for an error immediately after a statement where you think an error might occur. You can check for a specific error or for any error by determining whether the error number assigned to the error `Err.Number` is greater than 0. You can check for errors at any point in your VBScript where you think they may occur and take different actions based upon each situation. In the case of the previous example, the error handler provides the user with a more descriptive error message.

Figure 6.11 shows the output displayed by the previous example.

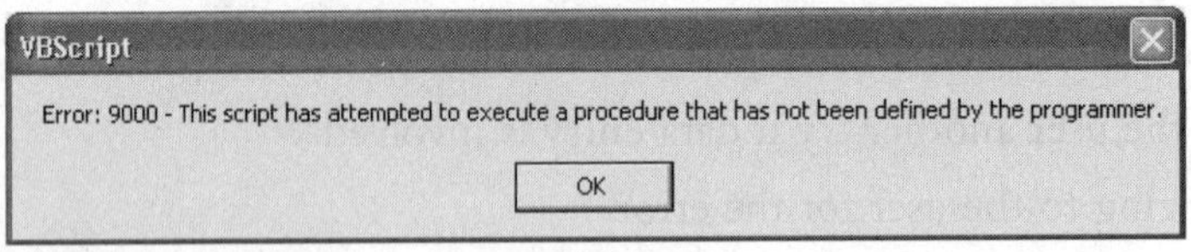

FIGURE 6.11 *VBScript provides the ability to recognize and react to error events*

Table 6.10 provides a list of VBScript run-time errors.

Table 6.10 VBScript Run-Time Errors

Hexadecimal	Decimal	Description
800A0005	5	Invalid procedure call or argument
800A0006	6	Overflow
800A0007	7	Out of memory
800A0009	9	Subscript out of range
800A000A	10	This array is fixed or temporarily locked
800A000B	11	Division by zero
800A000D	13	Type mismatch
800A000E	14	Out of string space
800A0011	17	Can't perform requested operation
800A001C	28	Out of stack space
800A0023	35	Sub or function not defined
800A0030	48	Error in loading DLL
800A0033	51	Internal error
800A005B	91	Object variable not set
800A005C	92	For loop not initialized
800A005E	94	Invalid use of Null
800A01A8	424	Object required
800A01AD	429	ActiveX component can't create object
800A01AE	430	Class doesn't support automation
800A01B0	432	File name or class name not found during automation operation
800A01B6	438	Object doesn't support this property or method
800A01BD	445	Object doesn't support this action
800A01BF	447	Object doesn't support current locale setting
800A01C0	448	Named argument not found
800A01C1	449	Argument not optional

continues

Table 6.10 VBScript Run-Time Errors (*continued*)

Hexadecimal	Decimal	Description
800A01C2	450	Wrong number of arguments or invalid property assignment
800A01C3	451	Object not a collection
800A01CA	458	Variable uses an automation type not supported in VBScript
800A01CE	462	The remote server machine does not exist or is unavailable
800A01E1	481	Invalid picture
800A01F4	500	Variable is undefined
800A01F6	502	Object not safe for scripting
800A01F7	503	Object not safe for initializing
800A01F8	504	Object not safe for creating
800A01F9	505	Invalid or unqualified reference
800A01FA	506	Class not defined
800A01FB	507	An exception occurred
800A1390	5008	Illegal assignment
800A1399	5017	Syntax error in regular expression
800A139A	5018	Unexpected quantifier
800A139B	5019	Expected] in regular expression
800A139C	5020	Expected) in regular expression
800A139D	5021	Invalid range in character set

Clearing Out Errors

The `Err` object provides two methods that you will find useful. The first method is the `Clear()` method. If an error occurs within a script and is handled, allowing the script to continue, and later a new error occurs, the information about the new error will overwrite the information stored by the `Err` object about the previous error. However, if your script later checks for an error and a new error has not occurred, the information about the old error will be reported again. To prevent this behavior, use the `Clear()` method to delete the information for a previously handled error. To use the `Clear()` method, place it at the end of your error-handling routine, as demonstrated below.

```
If Err > 0 then
  Err.Number = 9000
  Err.Description = "This script has attempted to execute a procedure " _
    "that has not been defined by the programmer."
  MsgBox "Error: " & Err.Number & " - " & Err.description
  Err.Clear
End if
```

> **NOTE**
>
> VBScript will automatically execute the `Clear()` method when the `On Error Resume Next` statement executes. It also executes the `Clear()` method when the `Exit Sub` and `Exit Function` statements execute.

Raising Errors

The `Err` object's `Raise()` method provides the ability to simulate errors when testing your error handlers. To use this method, place it in your code just before your error handler, as demonstrated below.

```
Err.Raise(92)
```

This statement simulates a "For loop not initialized" error. Without the `Raise()` method, the only way to test your error-handling routines would be to deliberately introduce an error situation into your code or to simulate environmental problems such as disk drive and network outages.

Summary

This chapter described the ins and outs of working with the VBScript `InputBox()` function. This included how to format text displayed within pop-up dialog boxes, as well as how to interrogate and validate the data that the `InputBox()` function collects. You also learned about VBScript implicit variable coercion and how to manually perform explicit variable coercion. The chapter covered how to work with the `MsgBox()` function, including a review of how to specify buttons, icons, the default button, and modality. In addition, you learned how to determine which button the user selected. This chapter also showed you how to trap and reformat error messages to make them more descriptive and understandable to the user.

Chapter 7

VBScript Objects

In this chapter, you will examine how VBScript interacts with its environment by working with objects. This will include an examination of VBScript's built-in and run-time objects as well as a complete listing of the objects' associated properties and methods. In addition, you'll get a brief overview of the importance of browser- and WSH-specific objects. You will also learn how to create your own custom objects replete with their own sets of properties and methods.

VBScript Object-Based Programming

In order to get any real work done, VBScript depends upon the use of objects. An *object* provides access to system resources and data manipulation structures by way of methods and properties. *Methods* are functions built into objects that, when executed, interact with or manipulate the resources represented by the objects. *Properties* are qualities of the resources represented by objects that describe the resource in some manner. Some properties are read-only, allowing VBScript to collect information about the resource. Other properties can be modified, thus providing the ability to directly change some quality of a resource represented by an object.

By itself, VBScript has only limited capabilities. It cannot access HTML page elements, the Windows file system, or other system resources. VBScript supplies only a small collection of built-in objects. These objects provide VBScript with the ability to react to errors and to parse and extract data from strings. VBScript's built-in objects are listed in Table 7.1.

NOTE

VBScript's built-in collection of objects is provided by the VBScript interpreter. These objects are available to all VBScripts regardless of the environment in which they are executed.

Table 7.1 VBScript Built-in Objects

Object	Description
`Class`	Provides the ability to create custom objects Properties: This object does not support any properties Methods: This object does not support any methods Events: `Initialize`, `Terminate`
`Err`	Provides details about run-time errors Properties: `Description`, `HelpContext`, `HelpFile`, `Number`, `Source` Methods: `Clear`, `Raise` Events: This object does not support any events
`Match`	Accesses read-only properties of a regular expression match Properties: `FirstIndex`, `Length`, `Value` Methods: This object does not support any methods Events: This object does not support any events
`Matches Collection`	A collection of regular expression `Match` objects Properties: This object does not support any properties Methods: This object does not support any methods Events: This object does not support any events
`RegExp`	Supports regular expressions Properties: `Global`, `IgnoreCase`, `Pattern` Methods: `Execute`, `Replace`, `Test` Events: This object does not support any events
`SubMatches Collection`	Accesses read-only values of regular expression submatch strings Properties: This object does not support any properties Methods: This object does not support any methods Events: This object does not support any events

Properties Belonging to VBScript's Built-in Objects

As Table 7.1 indicates, VBScript's built-in collection of objects provides access to a number of different properties. Table 7.2 lists each of these properties and describes their purpose.

Table 7.2 VBScript Object Properties

Property	Description
`Description`	Retrieves an error message
`FirstIndex`	Returns the first position of a specified substring in a string
`Global`	Changes or retrieves a `Boolean` value
`HelpContext`	Retrieves the context ID of a Help file topic
`HelpFile`	Returns the path to a Help file
`IgnoreCase`	Retrieves a `Boolean` value that indicates whether a pattern search is case-sensitive
`Length`	Returns the length of a search string match
`Number`	Returns the error number for the specified error
`Pattern`	Retrieves the regular expression pattern in a search operation
`Source`	Retrieves the name of the object that generates an error
`Value`	Returns the value of a search string match

Methods Belonging to VBScript's Built-in Objects

VBScript's built-in `Err` and `RegExp` objects provide access to a small number of methods. Table 7.3 lists each of these methods and describes their purpose.

Table 7.3 VBScript Object Methods

Object	Method	Description
`Err`	`Clear`	Clears an `Err` object's property settings
`Err`	`Raise`	Used to simulate a run-time error
`RegExp`	`Execute`	Performs a regular expression search against a string
`RegExp`	`Replace`	Replaces text in a regular expression search
`RegExp`	`Test`	Performs a regular expression search against a string

Working with VBScript's Built-in Objects

As Table 7.1 shows, VBScript provides a number of built-in objects. These objects provide the ability to perform all of the following actions:

- Work with VBScript run-time errors
- Define custom objects and assign to them properties and methods
- Perform character and pattern matching using regular expressions

The next several sections cover some of these objects and their capabilities.

The Err Object

You already learned how to work with the built-in `Err` object back in Chapter 6, "Data Collection, Notification, and Error Reporting." This object provides access to run-time error information by providing access to the following properties:

- **`Description`**. A string describing the error condition
- **`Error Number`**. The VBScript error number associated with the error
- **`Source`**. The name of the resource that reported the error
- **`HelpContext`**. Sets a context ID for a topic in the specified Help file
- **`HelpFile`**. The name and location of an external file containing help information

In addition, this object provides two methods for working with errors:

- **`Clear()`**. Deletes information stored by the `Err` object regarding the current error
- **`Raise()`**. Provides the ability to generate and test run-time errors

The Class Object

VBScript provides support for a number of different data subtypes, including strings and dates. VBScript also supports the more complex array data structure. VBScript provides the `Class` object as a means of creating a customized complex data structure, or custom objects. By creating your own custom objects, you can encapsulate data functions to create new objects, which your VBScripts can then access like any other objects. Creating custom objects provides your scripts with a tool that helps ensure data consistency, because it allows you to define procedures for validating and enforcing object properties and for controlling object manipulation.

Class Object Syntax

Custom objects are created using the `Class...End Class` statement. The `Class` object therefore provides a template for defining other objects and their structures. Once defined, these objects can be instantiated just like another object. The syntax for this statement is outlined below.

```
Class ClassName
   Statements
End Class
```

`ClassName` represents the name to be assigned to the new object. `Statements` represent the variables, properties, and methods defined within the object. Methods are established by defining the `Sub` or `Function` procedures. Properties are defined by using any of the following statements to manipulate variables defined within the `Class...End Class` statement:

- **`Property Get`**. Provides the ability to retrieve the value assigned to a private variable
- **`Property Let`**. Provides the ability to change the value assigned to a private variable
- **`Property Set`**. Provides the ability to change the value of an object variable

Creating Variables, Properties, and Methods

Variables, properties, and methods can be defined as public (accessible throughout the script) or private (available only within the `Class`) using the `Public` and `Private` keywords. Unless specified, `Public` is always assumed.

NOTE

Although you can allow variables defined within the `Class...End Class` statement to have a public scope, this is not recommended. This prevents you from being able to validate the value assigned to the variable from within the object. Instead, it is recommended that you make all variables private and expose them using the `Property Get` and `Property Let` statements. This way, you can build data-validation logic into your object and ensure data integrity.

The following example demonstrates how to use the `Class` object to create a custom object called `Customer`.

```
Class Customer

  Private strCustName

  Public Property Get CustomerName
    CustomerName = strCustName
  End Property

  Public Property Let CustomerName (strNameAssignment)
    StrCustName = strnameAssignment
  End property

  Function DisplayName
    MsgBox(strCustName)
  End Function
End Class
```

The first statement defines a private variable named `strCustName`. The next three statements use that variable to create a property and make it readable. The three statements that follow make the property writable. Finally, the last three statements within the `Class...End Class` statement define a function that will serve as an object method.

Now that a new object has been defined, you can instantiate it, as shown below.

```
Dim objCustName
Set objCustName = New Customer
```

You can then store a customer's name to the object.

```
objCustName.CustomerName = "ABC Inc."
```

You can then execute the object's `DisplayGreeting()` method.

```
objCustName.DisplayName()
```

NOTE

Data stored in objects is destroyed as soon as the script ends. This has a somewhat limiting effect on its value. However, there are a number of ways to store and retrieve object data. For example, when working with the WSH, you could write object data to a file or store it in a system variable. Similarly, when using VBScript in Web page development, you could store nonsensitive object data locally on client computers using cookies.

Setting Up Initialization and Termination Procedures

Objects created by the `Class...End Class` statement support the following events:

- **`Class_Initialize`**. If present, this method executes whenever an instance of the object is created, providing an opportunity to perform initialization tasks such as defining initial variable values.
- **`Class_Terminate`**. If present, this method executes whenever an instance of the object is destroyed, providing an opportunity to perform any required cleanup tasks.

The following statements demonstrate how to trigger statement execution based on the occurrence of the `Class_Initialize` and `Class_Terminate` events.

```
Private Sub Class_Initialize
  MsgBox("The Class_Initialize Subroutine is executing!")
End Sub

Private Sub Class_Terminate
  MsgBox("The Class_Terminate Subroutine is executing!")
End Sub
```

Once added inside a `Class...End Class` statement, these events will automatically execute whenever a new instance of the associated object is created or destroyed.

NOTE

You can create a new instance of a custom object using the `Set` statement and the `New` keywords, as demonstrated below.

```
Set objCustName = New Customer
```

Similarly, you can destroy a custom object using the `Set` statement.

```
Set objCustName = Nothing
```

`Nothing` is a VBScript keyword that disassociates an object variable from an object. As long as no other object variables refer to the object in question, the memory used to store its data is released.

The RegExp Object and Other Related Objects

Except for the `Err` object and the `Class` object, all the rest of VBScript's built-in objects are designed to work with regular expressions. A *regular expression* is a pattern of text made up of characters and metacharacters. Regular expressions provide the ability to identify patterns and perform complex search and replace operations.

The `RegExp` object allows you to work with regular expressions in VBScript. To add a `RegExp` object to your VBScripts, you must first define a variable to represent it and then use the `New` keyword to instantiate it, as demonstrated below.

```
Dim regExpObj
Set regExpObj = New RexExp
```

The `RegExp` object has three properties:

- **`Pattern`**. Specifies the regular expression pattern to be matched
- **`IgnoreCase`**. A Boolean value that determines whether a case-sensitive search is performed
- **`Global`**. A Boolean value that determines whether all occurrences of a pattern match should be replaced

In addition, the `RegExp` object provides a number of methods, one of which is the `Replace()` method. This method replaces the matching text patterns in a search string. Its syntax is shown in the following statement.

```
RegExp.Replace(String1, String2)
```

String1 is the string in which the replacements are to occur and String2 is the replacement string.

For example, the following statements demonstrate how to use the RegExp object to search a string variable called strQuote and replace an occurrence of the word child.

```
Dim regExpObj, strQuote
Set regExpObj = New RegExp
regExpObj.Pattern = "boy"
strQuote = "Once upon a time there was a little boy."
MsgBox RegExpObj.Replace(strQuote, "child")
```

The first two statements in this example define and create an instance of the RegExp object named regExpObj. The next line uses the RegExp project's Pattern property to set a search pattern. The statement that follows sets up the string to be searched. Finally, the last statement in the example replaces the first occurrence of the characters boy with the characters child (the value assigned to the RegExp Pattern property).

The previous example replaces only the first occurrence of the specified pattern match. However, you can modify the search pattern as shown below to search for and replace all pattern matches in the search string.

```
Dim regExpObj, strQuote
Set regExpObj = New RegExp
regExpObj.Pattern = "boy"
regExpObj.Global = True
strQuote = "Once upon a time there was a little boy."
MsgBox RegExpObj.Replace(strQuote, "child")
```

As you can see, a new statement has been added to the example, which uses the Global property of the RegExp property to replace all matching instances in the search string. VBScript also supplies a number of metacharacters that you can use when working with the RegExp object's Pattern property. For example, the following statements perform a pattern replacement using a range of values:

```
Dim regExpObj, strQuote
Set regExpObj = New RegExp
regExpObj.Pattern = "[\d]"
```

```
regExpObj.Global = True
strQuote = "Your customer number is 8."
MsgBox RegExpObj.Replace(strQuote, "1008")
```

The `\d` metacharacter specifies that any single digit should be used as the replacement string. In the case of this example, the number 8 is replaced with the number 1008. Table 7.4 lists the metacharacters supported by VBScript regular expressions.

Table 7.4 VBScript Object Methods

Character	Description
\	Sets the next character as a special character, a back reference, a literal, or an octal escape
^	Matches the beginning of the input string
$	Matches the end of the input string
*	Matches the preceding expression (zero or more times)
+	Matches the preceding expression (one or more times)
?	Matches the preceding expression (zero or one time)
{*n*}	Matches exactly *n* times
{*n*,}	Matches a minimum of *n* times
{*n*,*m*}	Matches a minimum of *n* times and a maximum of *m* times
.	Matches any individual character except the newline character
(*pattern*)	Matches a pattern and allows the matched substring to be retrieved from the `Matches` collection.
x|*y*	Matches *x* or *y*
[*xyz*]	Matches any of the specified characters
[^*xyz*]	Matches any character except those specified
[*a-z*]	Matches any character specified in the range
[^*a-z*]	Matches any character except for those specified in the range
\b	Matches on a word boundary
\B	Matches on a non-word boundary
\c*x*	Matches the control character specified as *x*

continues

Table 7.4 VBScript Object Methods (*continued*)

Character	Description
\d	Matches a single digit number
\D	Matches any single non-numeric character
\f	Matches the form-feed character
\n	Matches the newline character
\r	Matches the carriage return character
\s	Matches any white space character (for example, space, tab, form-feed)
\S	Matches any non-white-space character
\t	Matches the tab character
\v	Matches the vertical tab character
\w	Matches any word character
\W	Matches any non-word character
\x*n*	Matches *n*, where *n* is a two-digit hexadecimal escape value
num	Matches *num*, where *num* is a positive integer in a backward reference to captured matches
\n	Specifies an octal escape value or a back reference
nml	Matches octal escape value *nml* where *n* is an octal digit in the range of 0–3 and *m* and *l* are octal digits in the range of 0–7
\u*n*	Matches *n*, where *n* is a four-digit hexadecimal Unicode character

The `RegExp` object provides two additional methods, as outlined below.

- **`Test()`**. Searches a regular expression and returns a Boolean value indicating whether a matching pattern was found
- **`Execute()`**. Creates a Matches collection from a search of a regular expression

The Test() Method

The `Test()` method allows you to check whether a string contains a pattern match. It has the following syntax:

```
RegExp.Test(string)
```

For example, the following statements demonstrate how to use the `Text()` method to report on the presence or absence of a pattern match:

```
Dim regExpObj, strQuote
Set regExpObj = New RegExp
regExpObj.Pattern = "boy"
strQuote = "Once upon a time there was a little boy."
If regExpObj.Test(strQuote) = True Then
  MsgBox "Match Found"
Else
  MsgBox "No Match Found"
End If
```

The Execute() Method

The `RegExp` object's `Execute()` method creates a `Matches` collection from a search of a regular expression and has the following syntax:

```
RegExp.Execute(string)
```

The resulting `Matches` collection is read-only, as are the individual `Match` objects that make up the collection. Once created, you can loop through each object in the `Matches` collection and process it, as demonstrated in the following example.

```
'*************************************************************************
'Script Name: Script 7.1.vbs
'Author: Jerry Ford
'Created: 02/05/2003
'Description: Performing Regular Expression pattern replacements
'*************************************************************************

'Initialization Section

Option Explicit

Dim regExpObj, strQuote, colMatchStmts, strDisplayText, intCount, Match
Set regExpObj = New RegExp

regExpObj.Pattern = "File"  'Specify the string to search for
```

```
regExpObj.Global = True  'Perform a global pattern match

'Specify the string to be searched
strQuote = "Filename filename logFile logfile File file"


'Main Processing Section

CreateMatchesCollection()
ProcessMatchesConnection()
DisplayResults()


'Procedure Section

Sub CreateMatchesCollection()
  'Use the RegExp object's Execute() method to create a matches collection
  Set colMatchStmts = regExpObj.Execute(strQuote)
End Sub

Sub ProcessMatchesConnection()
  'Set up a counter to count the number of matches found
  intCount = 0
  'Loop through the Matches collection
  For Each Match in colMatchStmts
    'Build a string that displays the location where each match was found
    strDisplayText = strDisplayText & "A match occurred at position " & _
      Match.FirstIndex & vbCrLf
    intCount = intCount + 1
  Next
End Sub

Sub DisplayResults()
  'Display the results
  MsgBox "Total number of matches = " & intCount & vbCrLf & vbCrLf & "" & _
    strDisplayText
End Sub
```

In this example, a `Matches` collection consisting of three `Match` objects is created using the `RegExp` object's `Execute()` method. Each of these match objects has its own set of associated properties, including the `FirstIndex` property, which specifies the location in the search string where a match is found. A `For Each...Next` loop is then used to assemble a display string that shows the location of each pattern match, as shown in Figure 7.1.

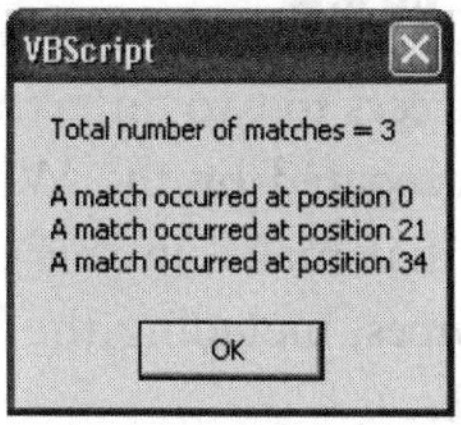

FIGURE 7.1 *Processing the contents of a* `Matches` *collection created by the* `RegExp` *object's* `Execute()` *method*

Other Collections of Objects Available to VBScript

VBScript's limited built-in collection of objects makes it a safe scripting language, meaning that it has no inherent ability to affect the environment in which it operates. In order to operate in and control the environment in which it executes, VBScript depends on external collections of objects.

Browser-Based Objects

VBScripts that are executed within HTML pages and loaded into Internet Explorer have access to two different collections of objects. The first collection of objects is referred to as the DHTML (*Dynamic HTML*) object model. This is an older object model originally developed for Internet Explorer versions 3 and 4. The DHTML object model is also supported by Internet Explorer 5 and 6 for the purposes of backward compatibility. The second collection of objects is known as the DOM (*Document Object Model*). This object model provides VBScript with the ability to access and control objects on an HTML page, such as links, images, frames, forms, and form elements.

NOTE

For more information on the object models provided by Internet Explorer, refer to Chapter 8, "VBScript and Internet Explorer."

Objects Available When Executed in the WSH

When VBScripts are executed by the WSH, they have access to two different sets of objects. One set of objects available to VBScripts executed by the WSH is referred to as the WSH *core object model*. The objects that make up this object model provide access to a collection of Windows resources, including the Windows desktop, file system, registry, and network resources.

NOTE

For more information on the WSH object model, refer to Chapter 9, "VBScript and the WSH."

The second set of objects is referred to as VBScript *run-time objects*. These objects are provided by an external DLL (*Dynamic Link Library*) named `scrrun.dll`. They provide VBScript with the ability to access the Windows file system. In addition, the VBScript run-time objects include an object known as a `Dictionary` object. The `Dictionary` object allows you to store data in an associative array and to retrieve the data stored in that array using keys instead of an index position as is the case with regular VBScript arrays. VBScript's run-time objects are listed in Table 7.5.

Table 7.5 VBScript Run-Time Objects

Object Name	Description
`Dictionary`	Stores data key, item pairs Properties: `Count`, `Item`, `Key` Methods: `Add`, `Exists`, `Items`, `Keys`, `Remove`, `RemoveAll`
`Drive`	Provides script with access to disk properties

Table 7.5 VBScript Run-Time Objects (*continued*)

Object Name	Description
	Properties: AvailableSpace, DriveLetter, DriveType, FileSystem, FreeSpace, IsReady, Path, RootFolder, SerialNumber, ShareName, TotalSize, VolumeName
	Methods: This object does not support any methods
Drives Collection	Provides script with access to information regarding a drive's location
	Properties: Count, Item
	Methods: This object does not support any methods
File	Provides script with access to file properties
	Properties: Attributes, DateCreated, DateLastAccessed, DateLastModified, Drive, Name, ParentFolder, Path, ShortName, ShortPath, Size, Type
	Methods: Copy, Delete, Move, OpenAsTextStream
Files Collection	Provides scripts with access to files stored in a specified folder
	Properties: Count, Item
	Methods: This object does not support any methods
FileSystemObject	Provides scripts with access to the file system
	Properties: Drives
	Methods: BuildPath, CopyFile, CopyFolder, CreateFolder, CreateTextFile, DeleteFile, DeleteFolder, DriveExists, FileExists, FolderExists, GetAbsolutePathName, GetBaseName, GetDrive, GetDriveName, GetExtensionName, GetFile, GetFileName, GetFolder, GetParentFolderName, GetSpecialFolder, GetTempName, MoveFile, MoveFolder, OpenTextFile
Folder	Provides scripts with access to folder properties
	Properties: Attributes, DateCreated, DateLastAccessed, DateLastModified, Drive, Files, IsRootFolder, Name, ParentFolder, Path, ShortName, ShortPath, Size, SubFolders, Type
	Methods: Copy, Delete, Move, OpenAsTextStream

continues

Table 7.5 VBScript Run-Time Objects (*continued*)

Object Name	Description
Folders Collection	Provides scripts with access to folders located within another folder Properties: Count, Item Methods: Add

Properties Belonging to VBScript Run-Time Objects

VBScript run-time objects provided by the WSH offer an extensive collection of properties. These properties provide information about the Windows file system and Windows files and folders. Table 7.6 contains a complete list of run-time properties.

Table 7.6 VBScript Run-Time Properties

Property Name	Description
AtEndOfLine	Returns a value of either True or False based on whether the file pointer has reached the TextStream file's end-of-line marker
AtEndOfStream	Returns a value of either True or False based on whether the end of a TextStream file has been reached
Attributes	Modifies or retrieves file and folder attributes
AvailableSpace	Retrieves the amount of free space available on the specified drive
Column	Retrieves the current column position in a TextStream file
CompareMode	Sets or returns the comparison mode used to compare a Dictionary object's string keys
Count	Returns a value representing the number of items in a collection or Dictionary object
DateCreated	Retrieves a file or folder's creation date and time
DateLastAccessed	Retrieves the date and time that a file or folder was last accessed
DateLastModified	Retrieves the date and time that a file or folder was last modified
Drive	Retrieves the drive letter where a file or folder is stored
DriveLetter	Retrieves the specified drive's drive letter
Drives	Establishes a Drives collection representing all the drives found on the computer

Table 7.6 VBScript Run-Time Properties (*continued*)

Property Name	Description
`DriveType`	Returns a value identifying a drive's type
`Files`	Establishes a `Files` collection to represent all of the `File` objects located within a specified folder
`FileSystem`	Retrieves the name of the file system used on the specified drive
`FreeSpace`	Retrieves the amount of free space available on the specified drive
`IsReady`	Returns a value of either `True` or `False` based on the availability of the specified drive
`IsRootFolder`	Returns a value of either `True` or `False` based on whether the specified folder is the root folder
`Item`	Retrieves or sets an item based on the specified `Dictionary` object key
`Key`	Sets a `Dictionary` object key
`Line`	Retrieves the current line number in the `TextStream` file
`Name`	Gets or modifies a file or folder's name
`ParentFolder`	Returns a reference the specified file or folder's parent folder object
`Path`	Retrieves the path associated with the specified file, folder, or drive
`RootFolder`	Retrieves the `Folder` object associated with the root folder on the specified drive
`SerialNumber`	Retrieves the specified disk volume's serial number
`ShareName`	Retrieves the specified network drive's share name
`ShortName`	Retrieves the specified file or folder's 8.3 character short name
`ShortPath`	Retrieves a file or folder's short path name associated with a file or folder's 8.3 character name
`Size`	Returns the number of bytes that make up a file or folder
`SubFolders`	Establishes a `Folders` collection made up of the folders located within a specified folder
`TotalSize`	Retrieves a value representing the total number of bytes available on a drive
`Type`	Retrieves information about the specified file's or folder's type
`VolumeName`	Gets or modifies a drive's volume name

Methods Belonging to VBScript Run-Time Objects

VBScript's run-time methods provide the ability to access the Windows file system; to create, modify, and delete files and folders; and to create and process text files. Table 7.7 contains a complete list of the methods provided by VBScript's run-time objects.

Table 7.7 VBScript Run-Time Methods

Method Name	Description
`Add (Dictionary)`	Adds a key and item pair to a `Dictionary` object
`Add (Folders)`	Adds a `Folder` to a collection
`BuildPath`	Appends a name to the path
`Close`	Closes an open `TextStream` file
`Copy`	Copies a file or folder
`CopyFile`	Copies one or more files
`CopyFolder`	Recursively copies a folder
`CreateFolder`	Creates a new folder
`CreateTextFile`	Creates a file and a `TextStream` object so that it can be read from and written to
`Delete`	Deletes a file or folder
`DeleteFile`	Deletes a file
`DeleteFolder`	Deletes a folder's contents
`DriveExists`	Returns a value of `True` or `False` based on whether a drive exists
`Exists`	Returns a value of `True` or `False` based on whether a key exists in a `Dictionary` object
`FileExists`	Returns a value of `True` or `False` based on whether the specified file can be found
`FolderExists`	Returns a value of `True` or `False` based on whether the specified folder can be found
`GetAbsolutePathName`	Retrieves a complete path name
`GetBaseName`	Retrieves a file name without its file extension
`GetDrive`	Returns the `Drive` object associated with the drive in the specified path

Table 7.7 VBScript Run-Time Methods (*continued*)

Method Name	Description
GetDriveName	Returns the name of a drive
GetExtensionName	Returns a file's extension
GetFile	Returns a File object
GetFileName	Returns the last file name or folder of the specified path
GetFileVersion	Returns a file's version number
GetFolder	Returns the Folder object associated with the folder in the specified path
GetParentFolderName	Returns the name of the parent folder
GetSpecialFolder	Returns a special folder's name
GetTempName	Returns the name of a temporary file or folder
Items	Returns an array where items in a Dictionary object are stored
Keys	Returns an array containing the keys in a Dictionary object
Move	Moves a file or folder
MoveFile	Moves one or more files
MoveFolder	Moves one or more folders
OpenAsTextStream	Opens a file and retrieves a TextStream object in order to provide a reference to the file
OpenTextFile	Opens a file and retrieves a TextStream object in order to provide a reference to the file
Read	Returns a string containing a specified number of characters from a TextStream file
ReadAll	Reads the entire TextStream file and its contents
ReadLine	Reads an entire line from the TextStream file
Remove	Deletes a Dictionary object's key, item pair
RemoveAll	Deletes all Dictionary objects' key, item pairs
Skip	Skips a specified number of character positions when processing a TextStream file

(continues)

Table 7.7 VBScript Run-Time Methods (*continued*)

Method Name	Description
SkipLine	Skips an entire line when processing a TextStream file
Write	Places a specified string in the TextStream file
WriteBlankLines	Writes a specified number of newline characters to the TextStream file
WriteLine	Writes the specified string to the TextStream file

The Run-Time Dictionary Object

All of the VBScript run-time objects, except for the Dictionary object, are designed to work with files and the Windows file system. Use of these objects is covered extensively in Parts III, IV, and V of this book. This section provides a review of the Dictionary object.

The Dictionary object and the FileSystemObject object are the two top-level VBScript run-time objects. The Dictionary object provides the ability to set up an associative array based on key and item pairs. In other words, unlike traditional VBScript arrays, which store and retrieve data based on its indexed position within the array, items stored in a Dictionary object are stored and retrieved using a key. This key can be a number, a string, or any of the data subtypes supported by VBScript. The Dictionary object does not even support the use of index numbers because it does not store items based on order. The Dictionary object has all the benefits of an array while providing greater flexibility in storing and retrieving data. In addition, the Dictionary object provides a number of properties and methods that enhance your ability to control data stored in a Dictionary object.

The Dictionary object supports three properties:

- **Count**. Retrieves the number of items stored in a Dictionary object
- **Item**. Retrieves or adds an item with a specified key in a Dictionary object
- **Key**. Adds a key in a Dictionary object

In addition, the Dictionary object provides access to the following methods:

- **Add**. Adds a key and item pair to a Dictionary object

- **Exists**. Returns a Boolean value of `True` if a specified key exists in the `Dictionary` object and `False` if it does not
- **Items**. Returns an array containing all the items in a `Dictionary` object
- **Keys**. Returns an array containing all existing keys in a `Dictionary` object
- **Remove**. Removes a key, item pair from a `Dictionary` object
- **RemoveAll**. Removes all key, item pairs from a `Dictionary` object

To better demonstrate the implementation of the `Dictionary` object, consider the following example. To add an instance of the `Dictionary` object to a VBScript, you must first define a variable by which it can be referenced and then create an instance of the object.

```
Dim dicObject
Set dicObject = CreateObject("Scripting.Dictionary")
```

Once instantiated, you may then store items in the object along with their associated keys, as demonstrated below.

```
dicObject.Add "Aug2003Rpt", "AugReports.txt"
dicObject.Add "Sep2003Rpt", "SepReports.txt"
dicObject.Item("Oct2003Rpt") = "OctReports.txt"
```

The first two statements add data to the `Dictionary` object using the `Add()` method. The first argument specified is the key that is to be associated with the data, which follows as the second argument. The last statement adds a third piece of data by using the `Item()` property, thus demonstrating that if you reference a key/item pair that does not exist, VBScript will automatically add it for you.

Once you have populated your `Dictionary` object with data, you can come back and work with its data. For example, the following statements use the `Exists()` method to determine whether a key/item pair exists. If it does, then the `Item()` method retrieves and displays a data element by supplying its associated key.

```
If dicObject.Exists("Sep2003Rpt") = True Then
  MsgBox "The value stored in Sep2003Rpt is " & dicObject.Item("Sep2003Rpt")
End If
```

Removing key/item pairs from a `Dictionary` object is just as easy as adding them. For example, the following statement shows how to use the `Remove()` method to delete a data element using its associated key:

```
DicObject.Remove "Sep2003Rpt"
```

Alternatively, if you prefer to delete all the data stored in a `Dictionary` object, you may do so using the `RemoveAll()` method, as shown below.

```
DicObject.RemoveAll
```

Summary

In this chapter, you were presented with a complete listing of VBScript's built-in and run-time objects. In addition to reviewing these objects and their associated properties and methods, you learned how to create your own custom objects. You also learned how to create an associative array using the `Dictionary` object when developing VBScripts that run with the WSH. Other object models were also discussed, including those provided by Internet Explorer and the WSH.

Chapter 8

VBScript and Internet Explorer

In the previous chapters, you learned the basics of VBScript programming and were introduced to VBScript's built-in and run-time objects. This chapter focuses on the specifics of the two object models provided to VBScript when executing within Internet Explorer. As you'll see, these objects provide you with the ability to develop scripts that can interact with browser objects using browser object methods and properties. This allows you to open and close browser windows, display pop-up messages, validate form input, create visual effects, and control numerous other aspects of the users' experience when they are visiting your Web pages. This chapter will also discuss browser-based events and how to develop code that can react to them in order to make your Web pages more interactive.

Internet Explorer Objects

Browser-based objects represent specific features or components of a Web page or browser. They are programming constructs that supply properties and methods, which VBScript can use to interact with and control features and components. These objects are made available to VBScript by Internet Explorer, which exposes the objects based on the content of each Web page that it loads.

Beginning with Internet Explorer version 3, each new version of the browser has introduced support for additional browser objects. Many of the objects found in the current version of Internet Explorer, version 6.X, are not found in earlier versions. This makes for a challenging programming environment, because you cannot control which version of Internet Explorer your visitors will use to view your Web pages. For example, if you develop a Web page that contains a VBScript that takes advantage of objects available in Internet Explorer version 6, and a visitor attempts to view your Web page using Internet Explorer version 4, your scripts will fail and the results will be less than satisfactory.

Of course, you can always develop your scripts based on the lowest common denominator (the lowest version of Internet Explorer that you intend on supporting), but this means forfeiting many of the features made available in Internet Explorer version 6. Such is the way of the Internet. Fortunately, if you are developing your Web pages to run on a corporate intranet, you'll typically find that all users are running the same version of Internet Explorer. This allows you to develop VBScripts based on the features and functionality supported by that particular browser version. Alternatively, you could develop different versions of your Web pages, add code to test the browser type of each visitor, and redirect the browser to the appropriate set of Web pages.

NOTE

As of the writing of this book, Microsoft has released four different major versions of Internet Explorer that support VBScript (versions 3.X, 4.X, 5.X, and 6.X). All scripts that you see in this book were developed and tested using Internet Explorer 6.0.

Internet Explorer organizes Web pages into a logical tree-like structure, with parent, child, and sibling relationships between the objects found on the Web page. To demonstrate how Internet Explorer applies this structure to a typical Web page, consider the following example.

```
<HTML>

  <HEAD>
    <TITLE>Script 8.1 - HTML Page Object Organization Example</TITLE>
  </HEAD>

  <BODY>
    <P>Welcome to the home page of</P>
    <P>ABC Enterprises Inc.</P>
  </BODY>

</HTML>
```

Figure 8.1 shows how this Web page is logically represented by Internet Explorer. The `document` object is always at the top of the hierarchy. The `document` object's child is the `<HTML>` element. The `<HTML>` element has two children, the `<HEAD>` and `<BODY>` elements. The `<HEAD>` element has one child of its own, and the `<BODY>` element has two children.

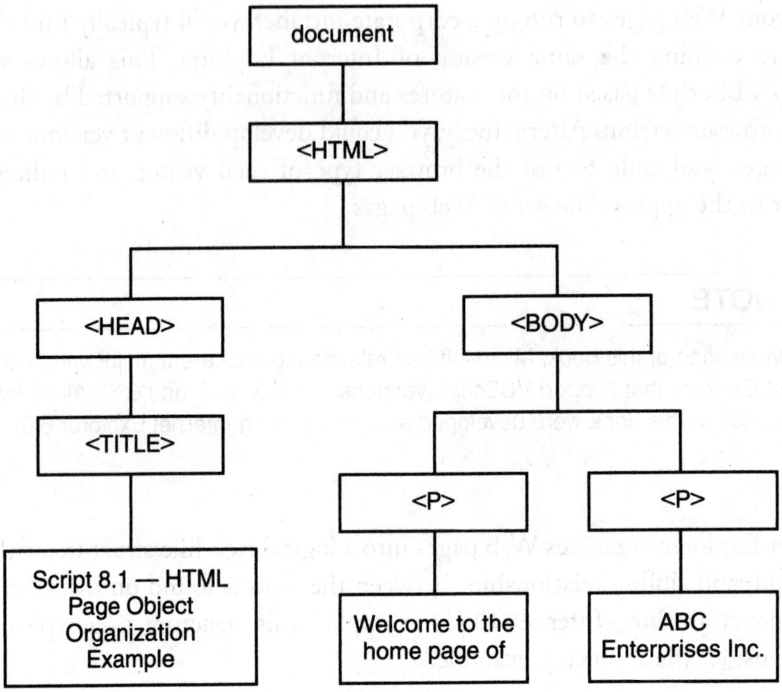

FIGURE 8.1 *Examining the manner in which Internet Explorer logically represents the contents of a Web page*

Internet Explorer versions 3 and 4 support a collection of objects called the DHTML object model. Starting with Internet Explorer version 5, the browser began supporting a second object model, the DOM. Internet Explorer versions 5 and 6 support the DOM as their primary object model while providing support for the DHTML object model for purposes of backward compatibility. The DHTML object model provides VBScript with access to most of the elements found on Web pages, whereas the DOM provides access to every element.

NOTE

The DOM was developed by a group called the World Wide Web Consortium and has been incorporated into all major Internet browsers. To learn more about the DOM, check out **www.w3c.org/DOM**.

Examining the DHTML Object Model

The DHTML object model organizes the elements found on Web pages into a logical hierarchy. The `window` object resides at the top of the DHTML object model. Every Web page has one `window` object, except for pages that contain frames, in which case there is a `window` object for each frame that has been defined in addition to a single parent `window` object. The `window` object provides access to a number of child objects, as depicted in Figure 8.2.

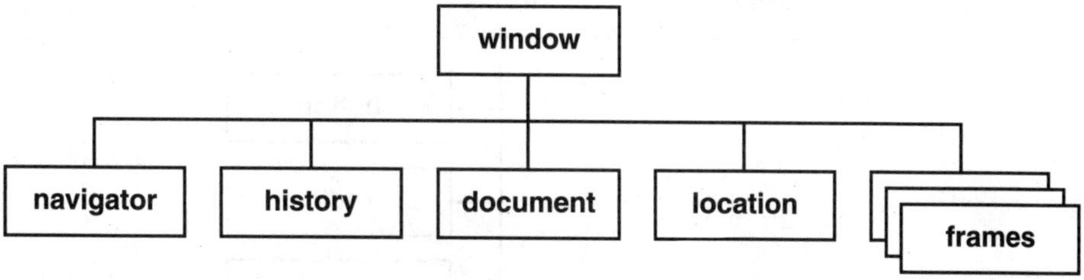

FIGURE 8.2 *The* `window` *object provides access to other objects that allow VBScript to interact with and control the elements found on HTML pages*

The `window` object provides properties and methods that you can use to open and close windows, display text on the browser's status bar or in pop-up dialog boxes, and load URLs into Web pages. The following list outlines the capabilities provided by its child objects.

- **`navigator` object.** Provides access to information about the browser being used to view an HTML page
- **`history` object.** Provides access to the `document` object's history list (that is, the Web pages visited since the browser window was opened)
- **`document` object.** Provides access to elements residing on the current HTML page
- **`location` object.** Provides information about the currently loaded HTML page and the ability to load a new URL
- **`frames` collection.** Provides access to an indexed list representing each of the frames defined on the HTML page

Of all the `window` object's children, you'll find that the `document` object is the one that you work with the most. As depicted in Figure 8.3, the `document` object provides access to a number of other objects that represent specific types of HTML page elements.

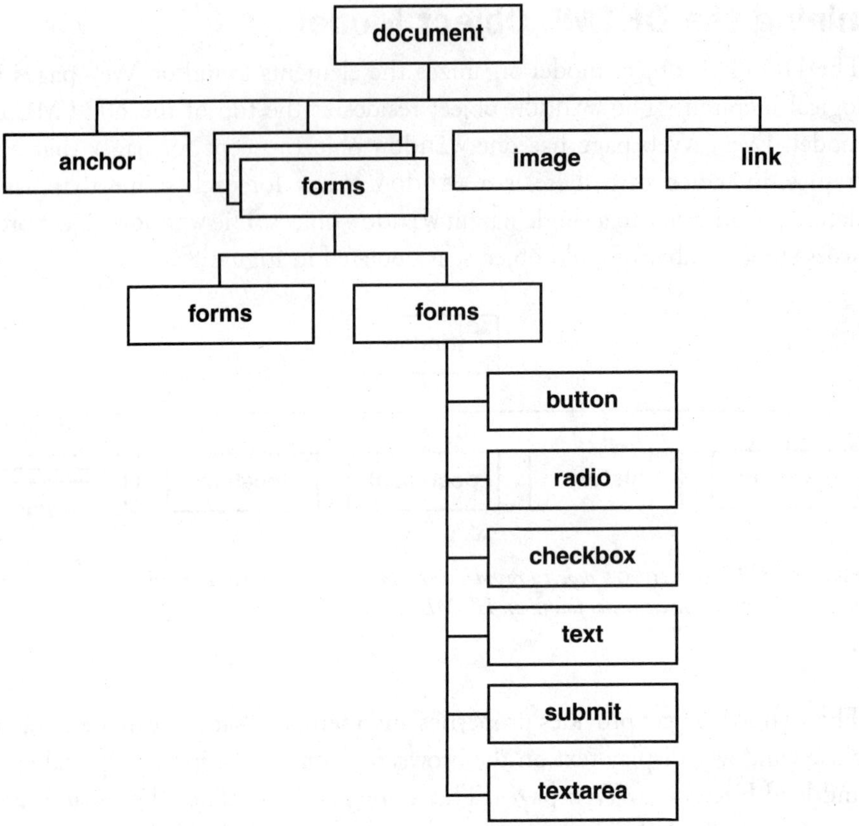

FIGURE 8.3 *The* `document` *object provides access to a number of other objects that allow VBScript to interact with specific HTML page elements*

To reference any element on an HTML page using the DHTML object model, you must reference the objects that provide access to it according to its location in the logical hierarchy provided by the DHTML object model. For example, look at the following HTML statements.

```
<FORM NAME="ApplicationForm">
  Last Name:
  <INPUT NAME="FirstName" TYPE="text" SIZE="10" MAXLENGTH="25">
</FORM>
```

These statements define an HTML form called `ApplicationForm` that contains a text field called `FirstName`. Although you have the option of developing HTML pages that do not assign names to HTML elements, names must be assigned in order for VBScript to be able to reference the page's elements using the DHTML object model. For example, the following VBScript statements could be added to a VBScript inserted in the HTML page to determine whether or not the visitor entered any text into the form's text field.

```
If Len(document.ApplicationForm.FirstName.value) < 1 Then
  MsgBox "Last name is a required field"
End If
```

As you can see, to determine whether anything was typed into the text field, you must specify its location, beginning with the top element of the HTML page (`document`), followed by the name of the form that contains it (`ApplicationForm`), the name of the text field (`FirstName`), and finally the `value` property.

Examining the DOM

The DOM provides complete control over all elements found on an HTML page and makes them more accessible than the DHTML object model does. In addition to being able to access any element on an HTML page by specifying its location within the HTML page's logical hierarchy, the DOM allows you to navigate up, down, and sideways within the hierarchy without having to reference elements by name. The DOM provides this capability by using the properties outlined in Table 8.1.

Table 8.1 DOM Properties

Property	Description
`firstChild`	The object's first child node
`lastChild`	The object's last child node
`childNodes`	A collection/array of all an object's child objects
`parentNode`	The object's parent object
`nextSibling`	The child node that follows next in the DOM tree
`prevSibling`	The child node that precedes the current child
`nodeName`	The name of the HTML tag
`nodeType`	Specifies a value representing the type of HTML element (tag, attribute, or text)

continues

Table 8.1 DOM Properties (*continued*)

Property	Description
`nodeValue`	The value assigned to a text node
`data`	The value of the specified text node
`specified`	Specifies whether an attribute has been set
`attributes`	A collection/array of all an object's attributes

To demonstrate how this works, consider the following HTML page:

```
<HTML>
  <HEAD>
    <TITLE>Script 8.2 - A DOM Navigation Example</TITLE>
  </HEAD>

  <BODY ID="BodyTag">
    <P ID="TopParagraph" Name="FirstTag">Welcome to the home page of</P>
    <P ID="BottomParagraph">ABC Enterprises Inc.</P>
  </BODY>
</HTML>
```

Figure 8.4 depicts how this page is viewed by the DOM. As you can see, the `document` object is the parent object, and it has just one child, the `<HTML>` tag, which is also referred to as the `documentElement`.

The following statement demonstrates how to use the DOM to navigate the elements located on the HTML page.

```
window.alert("The ID for the first element is: " & _
   document.documentElement.firstChild.tagName)
```

This VBScript statement references the `<HEAD>` tag on the HTML page by specifying its relationship to the `document` object. The next statement displays the name of the `<BODY>` tag by again referencing the `<BODY>` tag's relationship to the `document` object.

```
window.alert("The ID for the second element is: " & _
  document.documentElement.firstChild.nextSibling.tagName)
```

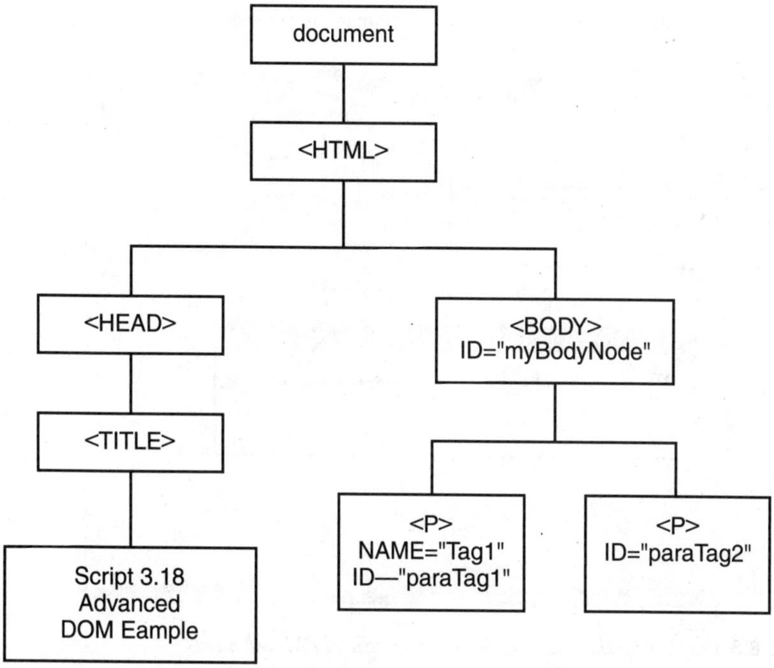

FIGURE 8.4 *Examining an HTML page from the point of view of the DOM*

The next VBScript statement shows how to display the value of the first child of the `<P>` tag whose ID is `BottomParagraph`. This VBScript uses the DOM `getElementById()` method to perform this operation, as shown below.

```
window.alert("The Value associated with the BottomParagraph tag "& _
  element is: " & _
  document.getElementById("BottomParagraph").firstChild.nodeValue)
```

Using the DOM, you may also change the value assigned to HTML elements, as demonstrated by the following VBScript statement.

```
document.getElementById("BottomParagraph").firstChild.nodeValue="ABC Inc."
```

The value associated with the Bottom Paragraph element

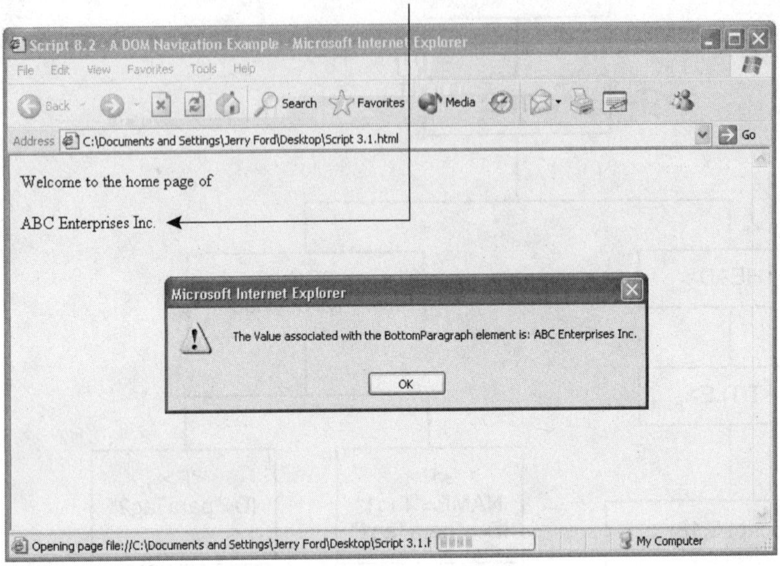

FIGURE 8.5 *Displaying the values assigned to specific HTML elements*

This statement begins by using the `document` object's `getElementById()` method to reference the second `<P>` tag (that is, `BottomParagraph`). It then references the `nodeValue` property of the `firstChild` object of the `<P>` tag. The end result is that the contents of the HTML page are dynamically altered, as shown in Figure 8.6.

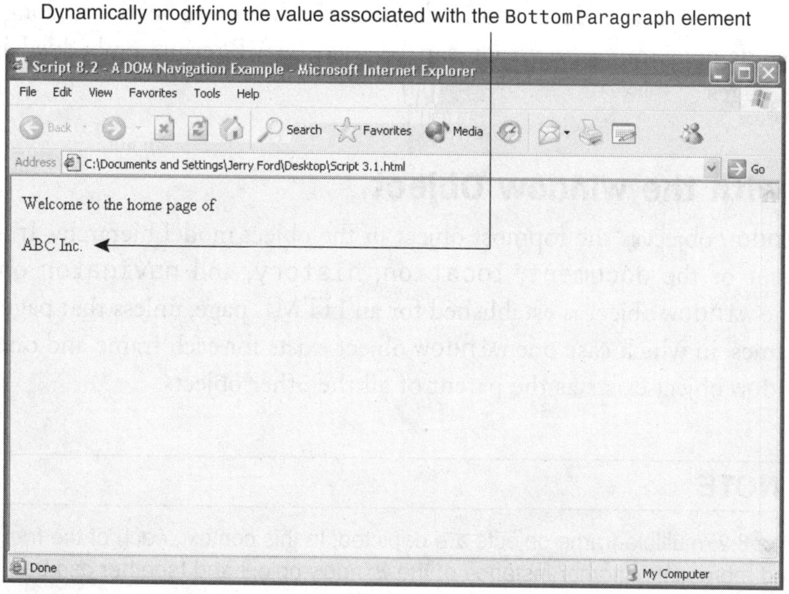

FIGURE 8.6 *Dynamically altering the content of an HTML page*

Obviously, the DOM provides a powerful tool for navigating HTML pages and accessing and manipulating their content. The DOM is too complex to fully cover all its objects, properties, and methods in this book. However, you can visit **www.w3c.org/DOM** to learn more.

High-Level Browser Objects

A number of high-level browser objects merit specific attention. These objects are listed below.

- `window`
- `document`
- `location`
- `history`
- `navigator`

Each of these objects is described in detail in the following sections, along with examples demonstrating how they can be used by VBScripts embedded inside HTML pages.

Working with the window Object

The `window` object is the topmost object in the object model hierarchy. It is also the parent of the `document`, `location`, `history`, and `navigator` objects. Only one `window` object is established for an HTML page, unless that page contains frames, in which case one `window` object exists for each frame and one parent `window` object exists as the parent of all the other objects.

NOTE

In Figure 8.2, multiple-frame objects are depicted. In this context, each of the frames depicted represents another instance of the `window` object and together can be referred to as a *collection*.

In addition to its child objects and collections, the `window` object provides access to a collection of properties and methods, which are demonstrated in this chapter as well as in Part V of this book. For example, the following HTML page contains a VBScript that demonstrates how to use a number of the `window` object's methods.

```
<HTML>

  <HEAD>
    <TITLE>Script 8.3 - Working with window object's methods</TITLE>
  </HEAD>

  <BODY onLoad="window.status = 'Welcome to the ABC Inc. Home page'">
    <H3>ABC Inc. Home Page!<H3>

    <SCRIPT LANGUAGE="VBScript">
    <!— Start hiding VBScript statements

      Option Explicit
```

```
        Dim blnValue, strUserName

        blnValue = window.confirm("This web site is the exclusive " & _
          "property of ABC Inc. All material listed here is " & _
          "strictly confidential. Click on OK to confirm your " & _
          "acceptance of these terms and access this site.")

        If blnValue = "True" Then
          strUserName = window.prompt("Please type your name.", "")
          window.alert("Welcome " & strUserName)
        Else
          window.open "http://www.yahoo.com", "Window1", "toolbar=no", _
            "menubar=No", "scroolbar=no"
          window.close()
        End If

      'End hiding VBScript statements —>
      </SCRIPT>

    </BODY>

</HTML>
```

The basic premise behind this example is to give visitors a URL to an intermediate Web page, where they are prompted to acknowledge the company's privacy statement before being redirected to the company's real Web site. For starters, the `window` object's `status` property is used to display a text message in the browser's status bar. Then its `confirm()` method is used to prompt the visitor to acknowledge the company's privacy rights before accessing the Web site. Next the document object's `prompt` method is used to collect the visitor's name, which is then used by the `alert()` method to greet the visitor by name. Finally, a new browser window is opened using the window object's `open()` method, and the visitor is redirected to the company's actual Web site (**www.yahoo.com** was used in this example to have someplace for the browser to go). This new window is configured to open without a scroll bar, menu bar, or toolbar. This example ends with the `close()` method to close the original browser window. Figure 8.7 shows how the second browser window looks when displaying the Web site to which the visitor is redirected.

FIGURE 8.7 *Using properties and methods belonging to the* `document` *object to control browser activity*

Working with the document Object

The `document` object is the most commonly used object. The properties and methods of the `document` object provide access to elements located on the currently loaded HTML page. The following example demonstrates how to use these `document` object properties and methods:

- **`bgColor`.** Retrieves or sets the background color of the currently loaded HTML page
- **`fgColor`.** Retrieves or sets the foreground color of the currently loaded HTML page
- **`write()`.** Displays or writes text strings on the currently loaded HTML page

```
<HTML>

  <HEAD>
    <TITLE>Script 8.4- Working with the document object</TITLE>
  </HEAD>
```

```
  <BODY>

    <SCRIPT LANGUAGE="VBScript">
    <!-- Start hiding VBScript statements

      Option Explicit

      document.bgColor="black"
      document.fgColor="yellow"

      document.write("<B>Using the write method() to display </B> <P>")
      document.write("<B>document object properties! </B> <P>")

      document.write("Document Title: " & document.title & "<P>")
      document.write("Last Modified on: " & document.lastModified & "<P>")

    ' End hiding VBScript statements -->
    </SCRIPT>

  </BODY>

</HTML>
```

As you can see, the script begins by changing the HTML page's background and foreground colors to black and yellow. Then the `document` object's `write()` method is used to display a number of lines of output on the HTML page. Figure 8.8 shows the HTML page generated by the example.

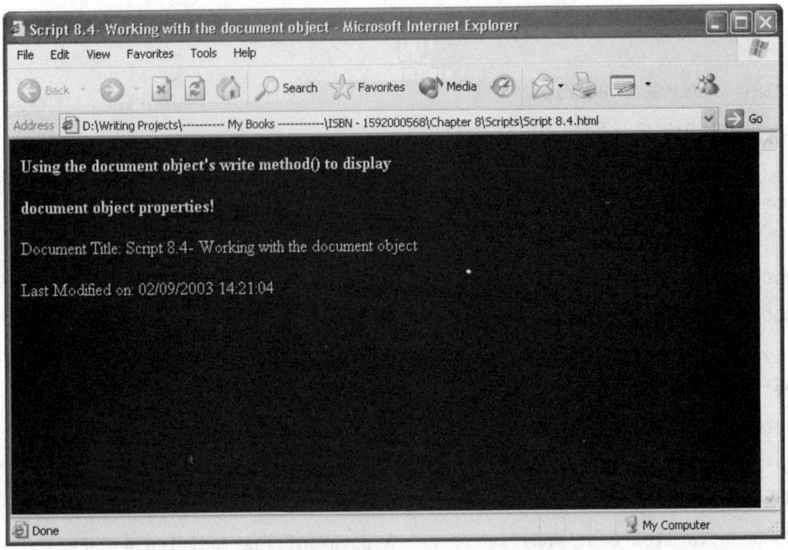

FIGURE 8.8 *Using properties and methods belonging to the* `document` *object to control the content and appearance of an HTML page*

> **NOTE**
>
> The `document` object provides access to numerous other properties that you will see used in Part V of this book. One particularly useful property is the `cookie` property, which provides you with the ability to store small amounts of data on each visitor's computer. For example, using a cookie, you could store and later retrieve a visitor's name and use it to create a personal greeting message the next time a user returns to your Web site.

Working with the location Object

The `location` object provides the ability to refresh the currently displayed HTML page or to load a different URL using its `replace()` and `reload()` methods. In addition, the `location` object's `href` property can be used to set or retrieve the name of the currently loaded URL. For example, you can add the following statement to a VBScript embedded inside a HTML page to load Microsoft's main URL:

```
location.href="http://www.microsoft.com"
```

As a working example, the following VBScript shows how to use the location object's `href` property to load a URL selected by the user by way of an HTML drop-down selection form element.

```
<HTML>

  <HEAD>
    <TITLE>Script 8.5 - Using the navigator object to load web pages</TITLE>
  </HEAD>

  <BODY>

    <SCRIPT LANGUAGE="VBScript">
    <!-- Start hiding VBScript statements

        Option Explicit

        Function OpenButton_onClick()
          location.href=document.OnLineSitesForm.SupportList.value
        End Function

    ' End hiding VBScript statements -->
    </SCRIPT>

    <H2>On-Line Support Sites</H2>

      <FORM NAME="OnLineSitesForm">
        <SELECT NAME="SupportList" size=1>
        <OPTION VALUE="http://www.microsoft.com"> Microsoft
        <OPTION VALUE="http://www.compaq.com"> Compaq
        <OPTION VALUE="http://www.dell.com"> Dell
        <OPTION VALUE="http://www.ibm.com"> IBM
        <OPTION VALUE="http://www.gateway.com"> Gateway
        </SELECT>
        <INPUT NAME="OpenButton" TYPE="button" VALUE="Open Vendor Site">
      </FORM>
  </BODY>

</HTML>
```

The HTML page and VBScript work by triggering the `click` event for the `OpenButton` form element when the visitor selects one of the entries in the form's drop-down list. This in turn executes the `OpenButton_onClick` function. This function uses the `location` object's `href` property to load the URL associated with the visitor's selection, as shown below.

```
window.location=document.myForm.myList.value
```

Figure 8.9 shows the HTML page that allows the visitor to make a new URL selection. After selecting a vendor name from the drop-down list, the URL associated with that selection is loaded, replacing the currently loaded URL.

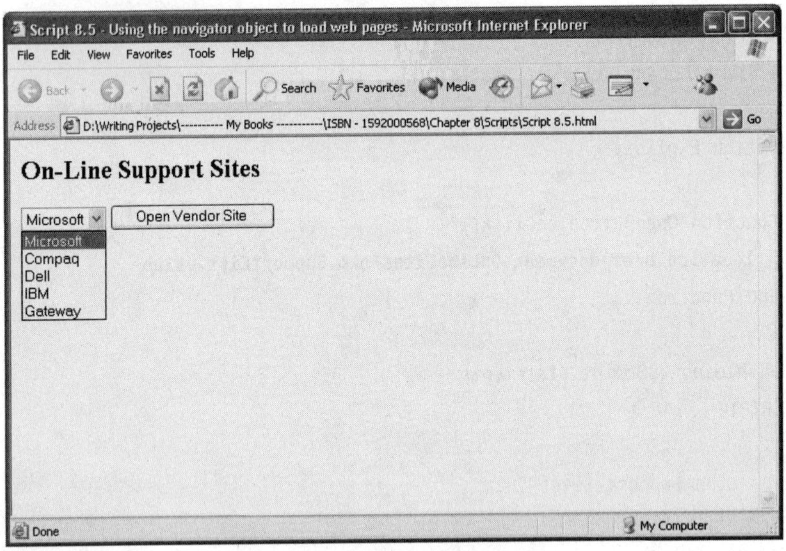

FIGURE 8.9 *Using the* `location` *object's* `href` *property to develop a custom navigation control*

Working with the history Object

The `history` object provides another way to control browser navigation. By using this object's `back()` and `forward()` methods, you can programmatically navigate through the list of URLs stored in the browser's history (the list of URLs that have been recently opened by this browser). In addition, you can use the `history` object's `go()` method to load any URL in the list. For example, the following statement instructs Internet Explorer to load the previously viewed URL:

```
history.back()
```

Likewise, to go forward one position in the history list, you could use the following statement:

```
history.forward()
```

To refresh the currently loaded URL, use the following statement:

```
history.go(0)
```

To jump backward or forward a number of positions in the history list, pass the `go()` method a positive or negative number.

Working with the navigator Object

The `navigator` object has properties that you can use to collect information about the operating system the visitor is using and the version of Internet Explorer that has been used to load the HTML page. Using these properties, you can develop a script that can adjust its presentation based on the version of Internet Explorer being used. Alternatively, you might use this information so you can redirect visitors to HTML pages specifically designed to support their version of Internet Explorer.

The `navigator` object provides access to the following collection of properties:

- **`appCodeName`.** Returns the code name assigned to the version of the browser that has loaded the HTML page
- **`appName`.** Returns the name of the browser that has loaded the HTML page
- **`appVersion`.** Returns version information about the browser that has loaded the HTML page

The following example demonstrates one way to use the `appName` and `appVersion` properties. The VBScript in this example interrogates the visitor's browser and either redirects the browser to another URL or displays a message stating that a specific version of Internet Explorer is required. This technique might be useful when a company wishes to standardize the features provided by a specific version of Internet Explorer. It displays a message informing its visitors that Internet Explorer version 5 or higher is required to access the company's Web site. This example also works for non-Internet Explorer browsers, displaying the same message.

```
<HTML>

  <HEAD>
    <TITLE>Script 8.6 - Detecting browser type and version</TITLE>
  </HEAD>

  <BODY>

    <SCRIPT LANGUAGE="VBScript">
    <!-- Start hiding VBScript statements

      Option Explicit

      Dim strBrowserName, strBrowserVersion, strFindString
      Dim intVersionNumber

      strBrowserName=navigator.appName

      If strBrowserName = "Microsoft Internet Explorer" Then

        strBrowserVersion = navigator.appVersion

        strFindString = Instr(1, strBrowserVersion, "MSIE")
        strFindString = strFindString + 5
        intVersionNumber = Mid(strBrowserVersion, strFindString, 1)

        If intVersionNumber < 5 then
          'document.write("This web sites requires IE ver. 5 or higher")
        Else
          window.location="http://www.yahoo.com"
        End If
      End If

    ' End hiding VBScript statements -->
    </SCRIPT>

    To access this web site use Internet Explorer 5 or above.
```

```
</BODY>

</HTML>
```

This example begins by setting a variable called `strBrowserName` equal to `navigator.appName`. It then checks to see if the value assigned to this variable is equal to `Microsoft Internet Explorer`. If it is, then the value of `navigator.version` is assigned to a variable named `strBrowserVersion`. The following three statements then parse out the browser's version number.

```
strFindString = Instr(1, strBrowserVersion, "MSIE")
strFindString = strFindString + 5
intVersionNumber = Mid(strBrowserVersion, strFindString, 1)
```

For example, the value assigned to `strBrowserName` will be set equal to the following if Internet Explorer version 6.X has been used to load the HTML page.

```
4.0 (compatible; MSIE 6.0; Windows NT 5.1; Q312461)
```

The first statement uses the VBScript `Instr()` function to set a value indicating the starting position of the letters MSIE in `strFindString`. The second statement then adds 5 to this number. The third statement then uses the VBScript `Mid()` function to strip off the browser's major version number (that is, 6).

If the browser's version number is less than 5 (for example, Internet Explorer version 4.X) then a message is displayed on the Web page informing the visitor that Internet Explorer version 5.X or above is required to access the Web site. If the version number is 5 or greater, then the `location` object's `href` property is used to load the specified URL.

NOTE

If a visitor is using Netscape Communicator or any other non-Internet Explorer compatible browser, then the browser automatically ignores the embedded VBScript and instead displays the following message located at the bottom of the HTML page:

```
Sorry. To access this web site use Internet Explorer version 5 or above.
```

Handling Browser Events

In order to truly interact with the visitors to your Web site, you need to develop VBScripts that react to visitors as they navigate through and interact with your Web site. Anytime something happens to your HTML pages, an event occurs. For example, when an HTML page is loaded into the browser, the `load` event occurs, and when it is unloaded, the `unload` event occurs. Events also occur when visitors move the pointer on to and off of links, buttons, and images or when visitors interact with various elements on HTML forms.

You can use VBScript to create event handlers to react to events as they occur. An *event handler* is a trigger that fires when an event occurs. For example, you could create an event handler that displays a welcome message in a pop-up dialog box when visitors first load your HTML pages or to thank the user for visiting just before the browser unloads your HTML page. In addition, you can use an event handler to create graphic effects by changing the colors of text as visitors move the pointer over links. You might also use event handlers to validate the fields on an HTML form as the user interacts with them.

Event handlers are associated with specific objects. In other words, if you have an HTML page that defines four links, then you can create separate event handlers that manage user interactivity for each individual link.

Table 8.2 provides a list of browser events and their associated event handlers. As you can see, the name of an event handler is determined by appending the word `on` to the beginning of the event name that it is associated with.

Table 8.2 Document Object Model Events and Event Handlers

Property	Event	Description
`Abort`	`onAbort`	Executes when the visitor aborts an image while it is loading
`Blur`	`onBlur`	Executes when the currently selected object loses focus
`Change`	`onChange`	Executes when the visitor changes an object
`Click`	`onClick`	Executes when the visitor clicks an object
`DblClick`	`onDblClick`	Executes when the visitor double-clicks an object
`DragDrop`	`onDragDrop`	Executes when the visitor drags and drops an object onto a frame or window

Table 8.2 Document Object Model Events and Event Handlers (*continued*)

Property	Event	Description
`Error`	`onError`	Executes when an error occurs on the HTML page
`Focus`	`onFocus`	Executes when a visitor selects an object
`KeyDown`	`onKeyDown`	Executes when a visitor presses down on a key
`KeyPress`	`onKeyPress`	Executes when a visitor presses and releases a key
`KeyUp`	`onKeyUp`	Executes when a visitor releases a key
`Load`	`onLoad`	Executes when an HTML page or image finishes loading
`MouseDown`	`onMouseDown`	Executes when a visitor presses a mouse button
`MouseMove`	`onMouseMove`	Executes when a visitor moves the pointer
`MouseOut`	`onMouseOut`	Executes when a visitor moves the pointer off of an object
`MouseOver`	`onMouseOver`	Executes when a visitor moves the pointer over an object
`MouseUp`	`onMouseUp`	Executes when a visitor releases a mouse button
`MouseWheel`	`onMouseWheel`	Executes when a mouse wheel is rotated
`Move`	`onMove`	Executes when the visitor moves a frame or window
`Reset`	`onReset`	Executes when a visitor clicks on a reset button
`Resize`	`onResize`	Executes when the visitor resizes a frame or window
`Select`	`onSelect`	Executes when a visitor selects the contents of a form text field
`Submit`	`onSubmit`	Executes when a visitor clicks on a submit button
`Unload`	`onUnload`	Executes when a visitor closes the browser window or frame or loads a different URL

There are a number of different ways to set up event handlers within your HTML pages. For example, you can embed them directly into HTML tags, as demonstrated below.

```
<BODY onLoad="window.status = 'Welcome to ABC Enterprises Inc.'s Home Page!'">
```

This statement displays a welcome message in the browser's status bar when the HTML page is initially loaded. A second way to set up event handlers is to set them up as procedures. In order to do this, you must name your procedures after the events for which you intend them to react. You do this by providing the name of an HTML page element followed by the underscore character and then the name of the event handler for which the procedure is designed to accommodate. For example, to create an event handler that reacts anytime the user moves the pointer over a link named `strCorpLogo`, you would need to name your procedure as demonstrated below.

```
Sub strCorpLogo_onMouseOver
  window.status = "ABC Enterprises, Inc - Where your problems " & _
    "become our problems!"
End Sub
```

Yet another way to set up event handlers is to embed them within the HTML `<SCRIPT>` tag, as demonstrated below.

```
<SCRIPT FOR=" strCorpLogo" EVENT=" onMouseOver" LANGUAGE="VBScript">
  window.status = "ABC Enterprises, Inc - Where your problems " & _
    "become our problems!"
</SCRIPT>
```

As Table 8.2 shows, there are a number of types of events and event handlers. The next few sections demonstrate how to write VBScripts that interact with various browser events.

Window and Frame Events

You can set up event handlers that respond to many types of window and frame events. These event handlers include:

- `onLoad`
- `onResize`
- `onUnload`
- `onMove`

To respond to the `load`, `resize`, `unload`, and `move` events, you must place these event handlers inside the HTML page's opening `<BODY>` tag. For example, the following HTML page demonstrates how to make use of the `onLoad()` and `onUnload()` event handlers.

```
<HTML>
```

```
  <HEAD>
    <TITLE>Script 8.7 - Using the onLoad & onUnload event handlers</TITLE>

    <SCRIPT LANGUAGE="VBScript">
    <!— Start hiding VBScript statements

      Function Greeting()
        MsgBox("Greetings and welcome to our web site!")
      End Function

      Function Goodbye()
        MsgBox("Thank you for visiting and please return soon!")
      End Function

    ' End hiding VBScript statements —>
    </SCRIPT>

  </HEAD>

  <BODY onLoad=Greeting()
    onUnload=Goodbye()>
    <H4>ABC Enterprises Inc. Home Page</H4>
  </BODY>

</HTML>
```

As you can see, the <BODY> tag has been modified by adding the following statements:

- `onLoad=Greeting()`
- `onUnload=Goodbye()`

These two statements execute two VBScript procedures located in the HEAD section of the HTML page. The first statement executes when the HTML page is initially loaded by the browser or when the visitor refreshes the page. The second statement executes when the visitor loads a different URL or closes the browser. In either case, a pop-up message is displayed that either greets the visitor or says goodbye. Figure 8.10 shows the pop-up dialog box when the script's `Goodbye()` function executes (that is, when the `Unload` event is triggered).

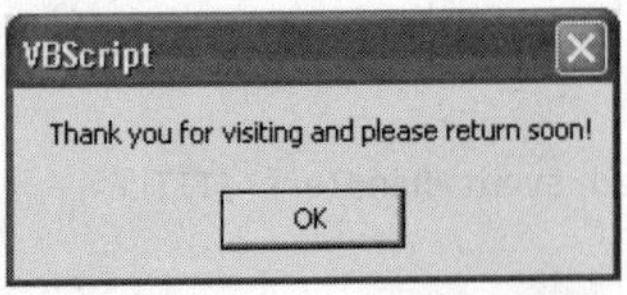

FIGURE 8.10 *Using the* `onLoad` *and* `onUnload` *event handlers to trigger the display of text messages*

Mouse and Keyboard Events

As a final example of how to set up event handlers, the following VBScript uses the `onMouseOver` and `onMouseOut` event handlers to create a graphical menu rollover effect for several HTML links. In order to set up rollover effects for the links, the NAME attribute must be added to each link defined on the HTML page. Then a pair of procedures must be defined for each link, one for the `onMouseOver` event handler and the other for the `onMouseOut` event handler. Each procedure must then modify the color property assigned to the link's text.

```
<HTML>
  <HEAD>
    <TITLE>Script 8.8 - Use Mouse events to create rollovers</TITLE>

    <SCRIPT LANGUAGE="VBScript">
    <!— Start hiding VBScript statements

      Function gateway_onMouseOver
        gateway.style.color="red"
      End Function
      Function gateway_onMouseOut
        gateway.style.color="blue"
      End Function

      Function compaq_onMouseOver
        compaq.style.color="red"
      End Function
      Function compaq_onMouseOut
        compaq.style.color="blue"
      End Function
```

```
    Function dell_onMouseOver
      dell.style.color="red"
    End Function
    Function dell_onMouseOut
      dell.style.color="blue"
    End Function

  ' End hiding VBScript statements —>
  </SCRIPT>
</HEAD>

<BODY>
  <B>Select A Vendor Site:</B><P>
  <A HREF="http://www.gateway.com" NAME="gateway"> Gateway</A><P>
  <A HREF="http://www.compaq.com" NAME="compaq"> Compaq</A><P>
  <A HREF="http://www.dell.com" NAME="dell"> Dell</A><P>
 </BODY>
</HTML>
```

Figure 8.11 shows how the Web page appears when loaded by Internet Explorer. Unfortunately, this figure cannot do the example justice. In order to examine this figure in greater detail, download it from **www.premierpressbooks.com/download.asp**. As you'll see when you run it, the color changes from red to blue as you pass the pointer on to and off of each link.

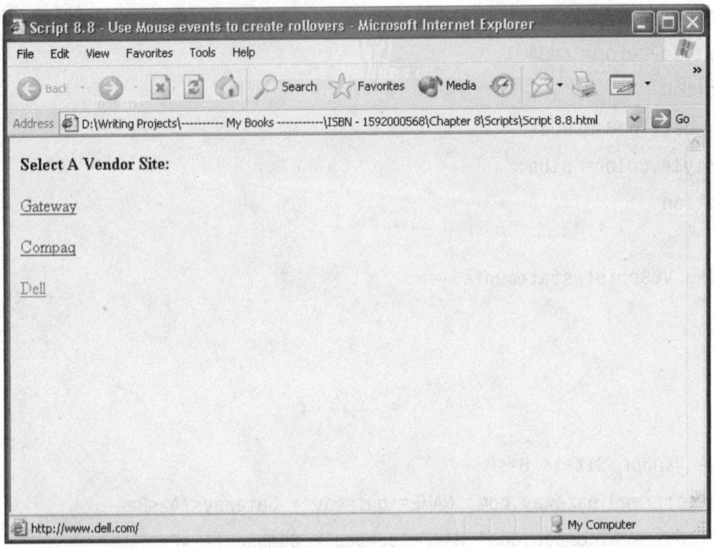

FIGURE 8.11 *Using the* `onMouseOver` *and* `onMouseOut` *event handlers to create graphical rollover effects*

Summary

In this chapter, you learned about the DOM and DHTML object models. You also learned how to develop scripts that interact with the objects provided by these object models in order to enhance your control over your HTML pages. In addition, you learned about browser events and how to set up event handlers in order to develop procedures that allow you to create interactive HTML pages.

Chapter 9

VBScript and the WSH

In this chapter, you will learn about the objects, properties, and methods provided by the WSH. Later, you will learn how to use these objects to access and manipulate a host of Windows resources. This chapter will also demonstrate how to create scripts that can receive and process arguments passed at run time. Finally, you'll learn how to create a new kind of script file using XML (*Extensive Markup Language*) that will allow you to combine two or more separate scripts, written in different scripting languages, together into one new Windows Script File.

The WSH Object Model

At the heart of the WSH is its core object model. The objects that make up this model provide direct access to the Windows resources that they represent. In total, the WSH core object model is made up of 14 objects. These objects and their relationship to one another are depicted in Figure 9.1.

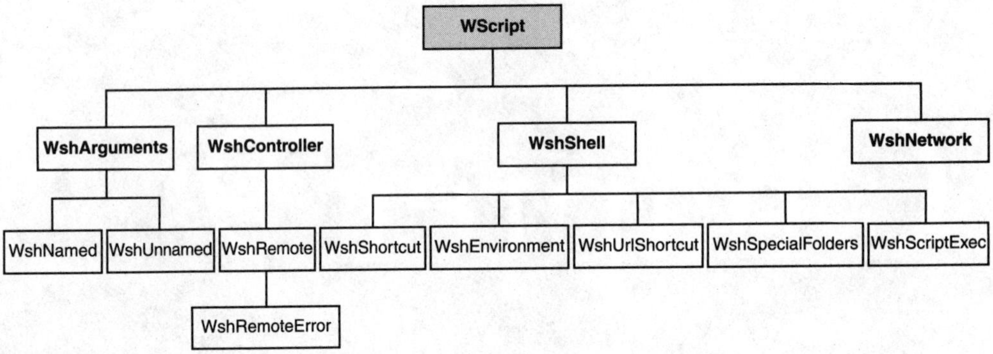

FIGURE 9.1 *The WSH core object model is made up of 14 individual objects*

The `WScript` object resides at the top or root of the object model. The `WScript` object is implicitly instantiated by the WSH at the start of script execution, meaning that scripts can automatically access any of its properties or methods. All of the other objects in the WSH core object model must first be instantiated in order to use their properties and methods.

Public Objects

The `WScript` object is automatically exposed at the start of script execution. The `WScript` object is also referred to as a public object. The WSH core object model has three other public objects, which are the `WshController`, `WshShell`, and `WshNetwork` objects. In order to instantiate any of these three objects, you must use the `WScript` object's `CreateObject()` method. The remaining WSH core objects are instantiated by using one of the properties or methods of these four public objects.

> **NOTE**
>
> The `WScript` object's `CreateObject()` method provides the means of instantiating other objects in the WSH core object model.

Table 9.1 provides a list of the other 10 objects that make up the WSH core object model and a list of object properties or methods that are required to instantiate them.

Table 9.1 Working with Lower-Level WSH Objects

Object	Method of Instantiation
WshArguments	WScript.Arguments
WshNamed	WScript.Arguments.Named
WshUnnamed	WScript.Arguments.Unnamed
WshRemote	WshController.CreateScript()
WshRemoteError	WshRemote.Error
WshShortcut	WshShell.CreateShortcut()
WshUrlShortcut	WshShell.CreateShortcut()
WshEnvironment	WshShell.Environment
WshSpecialFolders	WshShell.SpecialFolders
WshScriptExec	WshShell.Exec()

WSH Object Properties and Methods

Each object in the WSH core object model has its own unique set of properties and methods. Table 9.2 provides a brief description of the WSH core objects. In addition, it provides a list of properties and methods associated with each object.

Table 9.2 WSH Core Objects

Object	Description
`WScript`	This is the WSH root object. It provides access to a number of useful properties and methods. It also provides access to the rest of the objects in the WSH core object model. Properties: `Arguments`, `FullName`, `Interactive`, `Name`, `Path`, `ScriptFullName`, `ScriptName`, `StdErr`, `StdIn`, `StdOut`, and `Version` Methods: `ConnectObject()`, `CreateObject()`, `DisconnectObject()`, `Echo()`, `GetObject()`, `Quit()`, and `Sleep()`
`WshArguments`	This object allows you to access command-line arguments passed to the script at execution time. Properties: `Count`, `Item`, and `Length`; `Named` and `Unnamed` Methods: `Count()` and `ShowUsage()`
`WshNamed`	This object provides access to a set of named command-line arguments. Properties: `Item` and `Length` Methods: `Count()` and `Exists()`
`WshUnnamed`	This object provides access to a set of unnamed command-line arguments. Properties: `Item` and `Length` Methods: `Count()`
`WshController`	This object provides the ability to create a remote script process. Properties: This object does not support any properties. Methods: `CreateScript`
`WshRemote`	This object provides the ability to administrate remote computer systems using scripts over a network. Properties: `Status` and `Error` Methods: `Execute()` and `Terminate()`

Table 9.2 WSH Core Objects (*continued*)

Object	Description
`WshRemoteError`	This object provides access to information on errors produced by remote scripts. Properties: `Description`, `Line`, `Character`, `SourceText`, `Source`, and `Number` Methods: This object does not support any methods.
`WshNetwork`	This object provides access to a number of different network resources such as network printers and drives. Properties: `ComputerName`, `UserDomain`, and `UserName` Methods: `AddWindowsPrinterConnection()`, `AddPrinterConnection()`, `EnumNetworkDrives()`, `EnumPrinterConnection()`, `MapNetworkDrive()`, `RemoveNetworkDrive()`, `RemovePrinterConnection()`, and `SetDefaultPrinter()`
`WshShell`	This object provides access to the Windows registry, event log, environmental variables, shortcuts, and applications. Properties: `CurrentDirectory`, `Environment`, and `SpecialFolders` Methods: `AppActivate()`, `CreateShortcut()`, `ExpandEnvironmentStrings()`, `LogEvent()`, `Popup()`, `RegDelete()`, `RegRead()`, `RegWrite()`, `Run()`, `SendKeys()`, and `Exec()`
`WshShortcut`	This object provides scripts with methods and properties for creating and manipulating Windows shortcuts. Properties: `Arguments`, `Description`, `FullName`, `Hotkey`, `IconLocation`, `TargetPath`, `WindowStyle`, and `WorkingDirectory` Method: `Save()`
`WshUrlShortcut`	This object provides scripts with methods and properties for creating and manipulating URL shortcuts. Properties: `FullName` and `TargetPath` Methods: `Save()`

continues

Table 9.2 WSH Core Objects (*continued*)

Object	Description
`WshEnvironment`	This object provides access to Windows environmental variables. Properties: `Item` and `Length` Methods: `Remove()` and `Count()`
`WshSpecialFolders`	This object provides access to special Windows folders that allow scripts to configure the Start menu, desktop, Quick Launch toolbar, and other special Windows folders. Properties: `Item` Methods: `Count()`
`WshScriptExec`	This object provides access to error information from scripts run using the Exec method. Properties: `Status`, `StdOut`, `StdIn`, and `StdErr` Methods: `Terminate()`

There are too many WSH objects to cover them all in a single chapter. Therefore, this chapter will be limited to providing you with a WSH object reference, while offering a few examples of how to work with some of the WSH objects. The remaining chapters of this book will give you the opportunity to work with many of the properties and methods belonging to the objects shown in Table 9.2.

Core Object Properties

Object properties store information about the resources that they represent. By referencing object properties, VBScript can collect information about the environment in which they execute. Further, by modifying object properties, VBScripts can make direct changes to this environment and the Windows resources that reside within it.

The WSH core objects provide access to dozens of different properties. Table 9.3 lists each of these properties.

NOTE

In some cases, the same property may be shared by more than one object. Use Table 9.2 to determine which properties are associated with which objects.

Table 9.3 WSH Object Properties

Property	Description
`Arguments`	Sets a pointer reference to the `WshArguments` collection
`AtEndOfLine`	Returns either `True` or `False` depending on whether the end-of-line maker has been reached in the stream
`AtEndOfStream`	Returns either `True` or `False` depending on whether the end of the input stream has been reached
`Character`	Identifies the specific character in a line of code where an error occurs
`Column`	Returns the current column position in the input stream
`ComputerName`	Retrieves a computer's name
`CurrentDirectory`	Sets or retrieves a script's current working directory
`Description`	Retrieves the description for a specified shortcut
`Environment`	Sets a pointer reference to the `WshEnvironment`
`Error`	Provides the ability to expose a `WshRemoteError` object
`ExitCode`	Returns the exit code from a script started using `Exec()`
`FullName`	Retrieves a shortcut or executable program's path
`HotKey`	Retrieves the hotkey associated with the specified shortcut
`IconLocation`	Retrieves an icon's location
`Interactive`	Provides the ability to programmatically set script mode
`Item`	Retrieves the specified item from a collection or provides access to items stored in the `WshNamed` object
`Length`	Retrieves a count of enumerated items
`Line`	Returns the line number for the current line in the input stream or identifies the line number within a script where an error occurred
`Name`	Returns a string representing the name of the `WScript` object
`Number`	Provides access to an error number
`Path`	Returns the location of the folder where the `CScript` or `WScript` execution hosts reside
`ProcessID`	Retrieves the PID (*process ID*) for a process started using the `WshScriptExec` object
`ScriptFullName`	Returns an executing script's path

continues

Table 9.3 WSH Object Properties (*continued*)

Property	Description
ScriptName	Returns the name of the executing script
Source	Retrieves the identity of the object that caused a script error
SourceText	Retrieves the source code that created the error
SpecialFolders	Provides access to the Windows Start menu and desktop folders
Status	Provides status information about a remotely executing script or a script started with Exec()
StdErr	Enables a script to write to the error output stream or provides access to read-only error output from an Exec object
StdIn	Enables read access to the input stream or provides access to the write-only input scream for the Exec object
StdOut	Enables write access to the output stream or provides access to the write-only output stream of the Exec object
TargetPath	Retrieves a shortcut's path to its associated object
UserDomain	Retrieves the domain name
UserName	Retrieves the currently logged on user's name
Version	Retrieves the WSH version number
WindowStyle	Retrieves a shortcut's window style
WorkingDirectory	Returns the working directory associated with the specified shortcut

Using WSH Object Properties

As an example of how to work with WSH object properties, review the following VBScript. In this script, the properties belonging to the WshNetwork object are referenced in order to collect network information.

```
'*************************************************************************
'Script Name: Script 9.1.vbs
'Author: Jerry Ford
'Created: 02/12/03
'Description: This script demonstrates how to use properties belonging to
'the WshNetwork object in order to obtain network information
'*************************************************************************
```

```
'Initialization Section

Option Explicit

Dim WshNtwk, strDisplayText

'Instantiate the WshNetwork object
Set WshNtwk = WScript.CreateObject("WScript.Network")


'Main Processing Section

'Call the procedure that collects and displays network information
DisplayNetInfo()

'Terminate script execution
WScript.Quit()



'Procedure Section

'This subroutine Display network information
Sub DisplayNetInfo()

  strDisplayText = "This computer is " & WshNtwk.ComputerName & ". " & _
    "It is connected to the following domain:" & vbCrLf & vbCrLf & _
    WshNtwk.UserDomain & vbCrLf & vbCrLf & vbCrLf

  MsgBox strDisplayText, , "Network Information"

End Sub
```

This script begins by defining two variables, `WshNtwk` and `strDisplayText`. `WshNtwk` is then used to instantiate the `WshNetwork` object, as shown below.

```
Dim WshNtwk, strDisplayText
Set WshNtwk = WScript.CreateObject("WScript.Network")
```

As you can see, both the `Set` statement and the `WScript` object's `Create-Object()` method are required to set up an instance of the `WshNetwork` object. Once instantiated, you can reference any of the object's properties and methods. Next, the script executes a procedure called `DisplayNetInfo()`. This subroutine contains two statements. The first statement creates a display string using the `strDisplayText` variable and the following `WshNetwork` properties:

- **`ComputerName`**. Retrieves the network name assigned to the computer where the script executes
- **`UserDomain`**. Retrieves the domain name of the Windows domain to which the computer belongs, or if the computer is a member of a workgroup-based network, retrieves the name of the workgroup to which the computer has been assigned

The second statement in the `DisplayNetInfo()` subroutine displays the display string as demonstrated in Figure 9.2. Finally, control returns to the Main Processing Section, where the `WScript` object's `Quit()` method is used to terminate the script's execution.

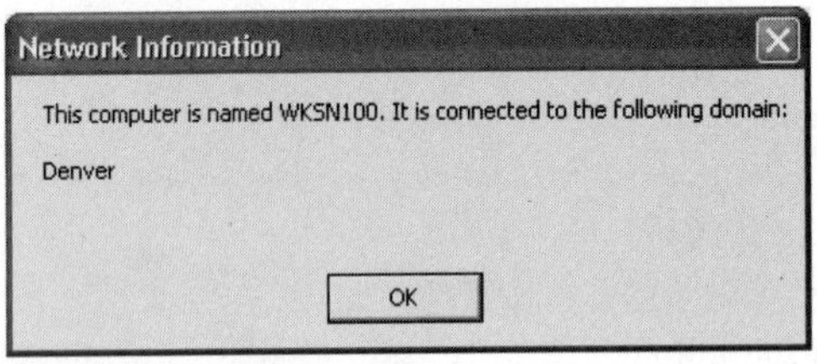

FIGURE 9.2 *Displaying network information collected from properties belonging to the* `WshNetwork` *object*

Core Object Methods

WSH object methods provide the ability to interact with and manipulate the resources that they represent. These resources include desktop shortcuts, the Windows file systems, printers, and the Windows registry. Table 9.4 provides a list of WSH core object methods.

Table 9.4 WSH Object Methods

Method	Description
AddPrinterConnection()	Creates printer mappings
AddWindowsPrinterConnection()	Creates a new printer connection
AppActivate()	Activates the targeted application Window
Close()	Terminates or ends an open data stream
ConnectObject()	Establishes a connection to an object
Count	Retrieves the number of switches found in the WshNamed and WshUnnamed objects
CreateObject()	Creates a new instance of an object
CreateScript()	Instantiates a WshRemote object representing a script that is running remotely
CreateShortcut()	Creates a Windows shortcut
DisconnectObject()	Terminates a connection with an object
Echo()	Displays a text message
EnumNetworkDrives()	Enables access to network drives
EnumPrinterConnections()	Enables access to network printers
Exec()	Executes an application in a child command shell and provides access to the environment variables
Execute()	Initiates the execution of a remote script object
Exists()	Determines a specified key exists within the WshNamed object
ExpandEnvironmentStrings()	Retrieves a string representing the contents of the Process environmental variable
GetObject()	Retrieves an Automation object
GetResource()	Retrieves a resource's value as specified by the <resource> tag
LogEvent()	Writes a message in the Windows event log
MapNetworkDrive()	Creates a network drive mapping
Popup()	Displays a text message in a pop-up dialog box
Quit()	Terminates or ends a script

continues

Table 9.4 WSH Object Methods (*continued*)

Method	Description
`Read()`	Retrieves a string of characters from the input stream
`ReadAll()`	Retrieves the `s` string that is made up of the characters in the input stream
`ReadLine()`	Retrieves a string containing an entire line of data from the input stream
`RegDelete()`	Deletes a registry key or value
`RegRead()`	Retrieves a registry key or value
`RegWrite()`	Creates a registry key or value
`Remove()`	Deletes the specified environmental variable
`RemoveNetworkDrive()`	Deletes the connection to the specified network drive
`RemovePrinterConnection()`	Deletes the connection to the specified network printer
`Run()`	Starts a new process
`Save()`	Saves a shortcut
`SendKeys()`	Emulates keystrokes and sends typed data to a specified Window
`SetDefaultPrinter()`	Establishes a default Windows printer
`ShowUsage()`	Retrieves information regarding the way that a script is supposed to be executed
`Skip()`	Skips `x` number of characters when reading from the input stream
`SkipLine()`	Skips an entire line when reading from the input stream
`Sleep()`	Pauses script execution for *x* number of seconds
`Terminate()`	Stops a process started by `Exec()`
`Write()`	Places a string in the output stream
`WriteBlankLines()`	Places a blank in the output stream
`WriteLine()`	Places a string in the output stream

Using WSH Object Methods

As an example of how to work with WSH object methods, examine the following VBScript. In this VBScript, methods belonging to the `WshShell` object are used to set up a mapped drive connection to a network folder.

```
'*************************************************************************
'Script Name: Script 9.2.vbs
'Author: Jerry Ford
'Created: 02/12/03
'Description: This script demonstrates how to use methods belonging to
'the WshNetwork object in order to map a network drive
'*************************************************************************


'Initialization Section

Option Explicit

Dim WshNtwk, strDriveLetter, strDrivePath

strDriveLetter = "z:"
strDrivePath = "\\FamilyPC\D"

'Instantiate the WshNetwork object
Set WshNtwk = WScript.CreateObject("WScript.Network")


'Main Processing Section

'Call the procedure that maps network drives
MapDrive strDriveLetter, strDrivePath

'Terminate script execution
WScript.Quit()


'Procedure Section
```

```
'This subroutine creates a network drive mapping

Sub MapDrive(strLetter, strPath)

  'Create a mapping to the specified network drive
  WshNtwk.MapNetworkDrive strLetter, strPath

End Sub
```

The script's Initialization Section contains statements that perform the following tasks:

- Define variables to represent the `WshNetwork` object, a drive letter, and the address of a network folder
- Assign a drive letter and the address of the network folder
- Instantiate the `WshNetwork` object

Next, the Main Processing Section executes the `MapDrive()` procedure, passing the drive letter and the address of the network folder, as shown below.

```
MapDrive strDriveLetter, strDrivePath
```

The `MapDrive()` subroutine receives the arguments passed to it and assigns them to two new variables. It then uses the `WshNetwork` object's `MapNetwork-Drive()` method to establish the drive mapping. Finally, control returns to the Main Processing Section, where the `WScript` object's `Quit()` method is used to terminate the script's execution. Figure 9.3 shows how the mapped network drive appears in the My Computer dialog box.

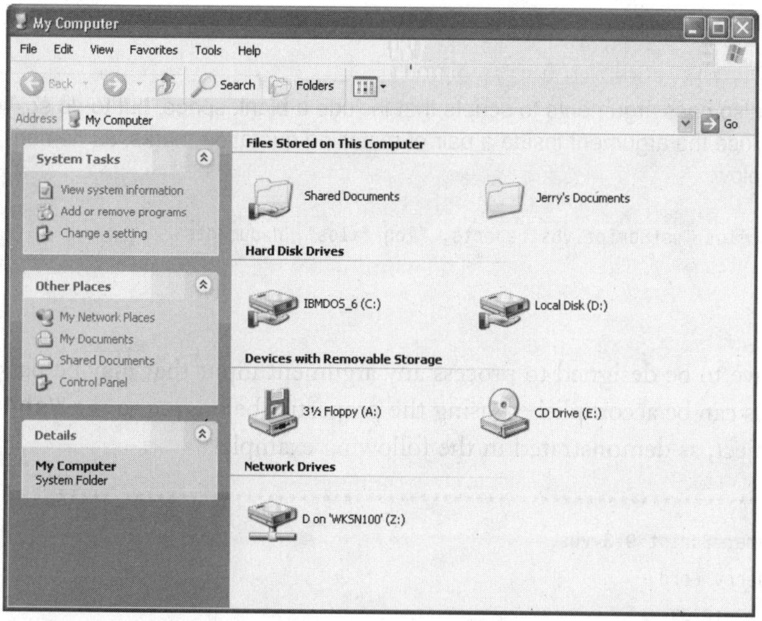

FIGURE 9.3 *Mapping a network drive using the* `WshNetwork` *object's* `MapNetworkDrive()` *method*

Passing Arguments to Scripts

In all the scripts that you have seen thus far, data has been either hard coded into the scripts as constants, variables, and arrays or collected interactively from the user via pop-up dialog boxes. Scripts also frequently receive data to process by having that data passed to them as arguments at run time. For example, you might set up one script to call another script and use the output produced by the first script as input for the second script.

Alternatively, you might pass arguments to a script from the Windows command prompt. For example, the following command would execute a script name `TestScript.vbs` and pass it three arguments:

```
WScript TestScript.vbs log txt doc
```

What happens next depends on the script. For example, a script receiving `log`, `txt`, and `doc` as input might use these arguments to build a list of files that should be processed in some manner.

NOTE

You can also pass arguments to scripts that include a blank space, but to do so, you must enclose the argument inside a pair of matching quotation marks, as demonstrated below.

```
CScript TestScript.vbs reports, "log files", documents
```

Scripts have to be designed to process any argument input that may be passed to them. This can be accomplished using the properties belonging to the `WshArguments` object, as demonstrated in the following example.

```
'*************************************************************************
'Script Name: Script 9.3.vbs
'Author: Jerry Ford
'Created: 02/12/03
'Description: This script demonstrates how to process arguments passed to
'a VBScript
'*************************************************************************

'Initialization Section

Option Explicit

Dim WshArgs
Set WshArgs = WScript.Arguments


'Main Processing Section

If WshArgs.Count < 1 Then
  MsgBox "Error: No arguments were passed to this script."
  WScript.Quit()
Else
  ProcessArguments()
End If
```

```
WScript.Quit()


'Procedure Section

Sub ProcessArguments()

  Dim i, strDisplayString

  strDisplayString = "Total number of arguments passed to this " & _
    script: " & vbTab & WshArgs.Count & vbCrLf & vbCrLf

  For i = 0 to (WshArgs.Count - 1)
    strDisplayString = strDisplayString & WshArgs.Item(i) & vbCrLf
  Next

  MsgBox strDisplayString

End Sub
```

The first thing that this VBScript does is to define a variable and use it to instantiate an instance of the `WshArguments` object, as shown below.

```
Dim WshArgs
Set WshArgs = WScript.Arguments
```

In the script's Main Processing Section, the script then uses the `WshArguments` object's `Count` property to ensure that at least one argument was passed to the script, in which case the `ProcessArguments()` function is called. Otherwise an error message is displayed and the `WScript` object's `Quit()` method is executed, terminating the script's execution.

The `ProcessArguments()` function starts by adding a heading to a display string, as shown below.

```
strDisplayString = "Total number of arguments passed to this script: " & _
   vbTab & WshArgs.Count & vbCrLf & vbCrLf
```

Next it uses a `For...Next` loop to iterate through the list of arguments passed to the script. The `WshArguments` object stores arguments in an indexed list beginning at zero. The loop begins at zero and spins until `WshArgs.Count - 1` (for example, if five arguments are passed, the index will begin at position 0 and end at position 4). The contents of the display string are modified upon each iteration of the loop by adding the value of each argument to the string based on its index number as specified by the variable `i` (for example, `WshArgs.Item(i)`).

Figure 9.4 demonstrates the output produced by this script if it is passed an argument list of `SalesReport.doc`, `MarketReport.doc`, `Forecast.xls`, `MonthlyStats.xls`, and `LogReports.log`.

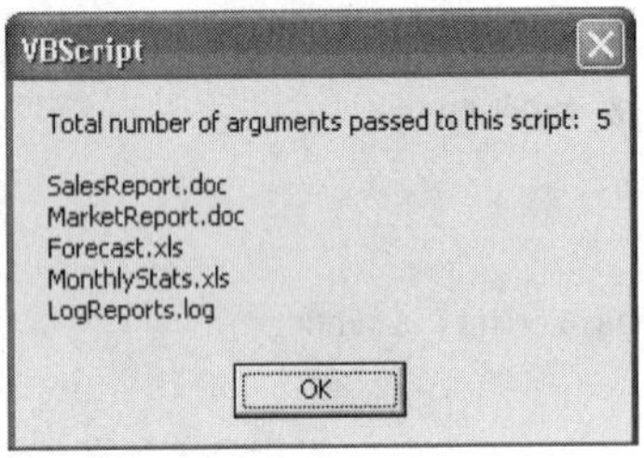

FIGURE 9.4 *Processing arguments passed to a VBScript at run time*

Using XML to Create Windows Script Files

The WSH provides programmers with a robust scripting environment that includes access to a common set of objects. These objects provide access to the Windows resources that they represent by means of the properties and methods. One of the strengths of the WSH is that it provides this same level of access regardless of the scripting language being used by the programmer.

Microsoft ships the WSH with VBScript and JScript, but third-party WSH-compatible scripting languages have been made available that include Perl, Python, and Rexx. The WSH does not stop there. In addition to allowing you to use the scripting language of your choice, it provides you with the ability to combine two or more scripts, including scripts written using different languages, into a single script known as a *Windows Script File*. Windows Script Files are plain text files that are saved with an .wsf file extension.

The WSH uses a subset of XML to create Windows Script Files. XML is a markup language that is syntactically similar to HTML. XML tags are used in

Windows Script Files to identify or mark the components that make up the file. For example, every script contained in a Windows Script File is enclosed within a pair of `<script> </script>` tags. The WSH currently provides support for version XML 1.0.

XML is a case-sensitive markup language. It has a strict set of rules that must be followed when formatting tags. Unlike the HTML markup languages, you cannot get away with excluding required closing tags. The remainder of this chapter is dedicated to demonstrating a number of commonly used XML tags, as outlined in Table 9.5.

Table 9.5 XML Tags Commonly Used in Windows Script Files

Tag	Description
<?XML ?>	This tag specifies the Windows Script File's XML level.
<?job ?>	This tag is used to enable or disable error handling and debugging for a specified job.
<comment> </comment>	This tag provides the ability to embed comments within Windows Script Files.
<script> </script>	This tag identifies the beginning and ending of a script within a Windows Script File.
<job> </job>	This tag identifies the beginning and ending of a job inside a Windows Script File.
<package> </package>	This tag allows multiple jobs to be defined within a single Windows Script File.
<resource> </resource >	This tag defines static data (constants) that can be referenced by a script within a Windows Script File.

TIP

XML version 1.0 allows the use of both uppercase and lowercase spelling in tags. However, the use of uppercase spelling is generally considered to be bad form. You should, therefore, use all lowercase spelling. This will also save you a lot of recoding work in the event that a future release of XML incorporates an all-lowercase requirement.

The <?XML ?> Tag

The `<?XML ?>` tag is an optional tag that specifies the XML version that a Windows Script File requires in order to execute. If used, the `<?XML ?>` tag must be the first statement in the Windows Script File. Its syntax is shown below.

```
<?XML version="X.X" standalone="dtdflag" ?>
```

`version` specifies the required XML version. As of the writing of this book, the current version of XML is version 1.0. `standalone` specifies a Boolean value indicating whether or not the script includes a reference to an external DTD (*Document Type Definition*). The DTD is currently an unsupported WSH feature. However, if you wish, you may include it. If you choose to do so, then you must specify its value as `Yes`. The `<?XML ?>` tag does not have a closing tag.

The purpose of the `<?XML ?>` tag is to allow the programmer to enforce a stricter interpretation of XML statements within Windows Script Files. For example, this tag strictly enforces case sensitivity. In addition, it requires all attribute values to be enclosed within single or double quotes.

The following example demonstrates the use of the `<?XML ?>` tag within a Windows Script File.

```
<?XML version="1.0" standalone="yes" ?>
<job>
  <script language="VBScript">
    MsgBox "Error handling and debugging are now enabled."
  </script>
</job>
```

The <?job ?> Tag

The `<?job ?>` tag is an optional tag that allows you to enable or disable error reporting and debugging. The `<?job ?>` tag does not have a closing tag. Its syntax is shown below.

```
<?job error="errorflag" debug="debugflag" ?>
```

`errorflag` is a Boolean value. When set equal to `True`, error reporting is enabled. If omitted, Windows Script Files automatically disable error reporting. `debugflag` is also a Boolean value that controls whether or not the occurrence of an error will start the Windows Script Debugger.

NOTE

The Microsoft Windows Script Debugger is a utility provided by Microsoft that helps programmers in debugging script errors. Visit **http://msdn.microsoft.com/scripting** to learn more about this utility.

The following example demonstrates how to enable both error reporting and script debugging within a Windows Script File.

```
<job>
  <?job error="true" debug="true"?>
  <script language="VBScript">
    MsgBox "Error handling and debugging are now enabled."
  </script>
</job>
```

The <comment> and </comment> Tags

The `<comment>` and `</comment>` tags provide the ability to place comments within Windows Script Files. The `<comment>` and `</comment>` tags can also be used to spread comments out over multiple lines. The syntax for the `<comment>` and `</comment>` tags is shown below.

```
<comment> comment text  </comment>
```

The following example demonstrates the use of the `<comment>` and `</comment>` tags.

```
<job>
  <comment>Place your comment here</comment>
  <script language="VBScript">
    MsgBox "Error handling and debugging are now enabled."
  </script>
</job>
```

The <script> and </script> Tags

Windows Script Files contain one or more script files written in various WSH-supported scripting languages. The <script> and </script> tags are used to identify the beginning and the ending of individual scripts within a Windows Script File. Their syntax is shown below.

```
<script language="scriptlanguage" [src="externalscript"]>
  ...
</script>
```

`language` is used to specify the scripting language used to develop the script. `src` is optional and can be used to specify the location of an external script.

The following example demonstrates the use of the `<script>` and `</script>` tags to embed a VBScript inside a Windows Script File.

```
<job>
  <script language="VBScript">
    MsgBox "Windows Script Host - Script number 2 executing"
  </script>
</job>
```

The next example demonstrates how to set up a reference to an external VBScript that is located in the same folder as the Windows Script File.

```
<job>
  <script language="VBScript" src="ScriptName.vbs" />
</job>
```

The <job> and </job> Tags

Windows Script Files can contain one or more jobs, each of which may contain any number of scripts. Each job is identified using the `<job>` and `</job>` tags. At a minimum, every Windows Script File must contain at least one job. The syntax for these tags is shown below.

```
<job [id=jobid]>
  . . .
</job>
```

`id` is used to uniquely identify jobs in a Windows Script File that contains more than one job. This parameter can be omitted in Windows Script Files that consist of just one job. By assigning job IDs to each job within a Windows Script File, you provide the ability to specify which job you wish to run when you execute the Windows Script File. The following example shows a Windows Script File that is made up of a single job.

```
<job>

  <script language="VBScript">
    MsgBox "The first VBScript is now executing."
  </script>

  <script language="VBScript" src="SecondVBScript.vbs" />

  <script language="JScript">
    WScript.Echo("The first JScript is now executing.");
  </script>

</job>
```

As you can see, this job executes three scripts, two written in VBScript and one written using JScript. The second VBScript defined within the job represents an external script.

The <package> and </package> Tags

In order to place more than one job within a Windows Script File, you must first specify `<package>` and `</package>` tags and then embed the jobs within these tags. The syntax for the `<package>` and `</package>` tags is shown below.

```
<package>
   . . .
</package>
```

The following example demonstrates how to use the `<package>` and `</package>` tags to add three jobs to a Windows Script File.

```
<package>

  <job id="Job_A">
    <script language="VBScript">
      MsgBox "Job_A is now executing."
    </script>
  </job>

  <job id="Job_B">
```

```
    <script language="VBScript">
      MsgBox "Job_B is now executing."
    </script>
  </job>

  <job id="Job_C">
    <script language="JScript">
      WScript.Echo("Job_C is now executing.");
    </script>
  </job>

</package>
```

The first job is named Job_A. It contains a single VBScript. The second and third jobs are named Job_B and Job_C, respectively.

The <resource> and </resource> Tags

The XML <resource> and </resource> tags allow you to define constants that can be accessed by any scripts defined within the same job in a Windows Script File. Using these tags, you can define one or more constants that individual scripts within the Windows Script Files may need to use. This saves you the trouble of having to redefine constants over and over again for every script in the Windows Script File. This also helps to make your scripts easier to support. It allows you to store and manage constants by limiting the number of locations where constants are defined (for example, once per job).

When specified, the <resource> and </resource> tags must be placed within the <job> and </job> tags. The syntax for these tags is shown below.

```
<resource id="resourceid">
   . . .
</resource>
```

id is used to specify the name of a constant. The value assigned to the constant is specified by typing it between the opening and closing tags, as shown in the following example.

```
<job>

  <resource id="cTitleBarMsg">Windows Script File Demo</resource>
```

```
  <script language="VBScript">
    MsgBox "Script Execution beginning.", , getResource("cTitleBarMsg")
  </script>

</job>
```

In this example, the value of the constant cTitleBarMsg is displayed by a Msg-Box() function using the WSH getResource() method. This built-in WSH method is designed to retrieve the value of constants defined within <resource> and </resource> tags.

Running Your Windows Script Files

You can run any Windows Script File by double-clicking on its icon. If the Windows Script File contains one job, that job and all the scripts that it is made of will execute. However, if the Windows Script File consists of more than one job, the first job that is defined will execute. In order to run other jobs that reside within the Windows Script File, you must execute the Windows Script File from the Windows command prompt and tell it which job you wish to execute by specifying the job's ID.

For example, the following statement could be used to run the first job defined in a Windows Script File called SampleScript.wsh using the WScript execution host.

```
WScript SampleScript.wsf
```

Since the first job defined in the script is to be executed, there is no need to specify its assigned job ID. If the Windows Script File contained a second job that was assigned a job ID of Job_B, then you could run it using the following command:

```
WScript SampleScript.wsf //job:Job_B
```

Summary

In this chapter, you learned about the objects that comprise the WSH object model. In addition, you were presented with a complete listing of the properties and methods associated with these objects and examples that demonstrated how to incorporate the use of WSH objects into your VBScripts. You also learned how to create and execute scripts that can accept and process arguments passed at run time. Finally, you learned how to develop Windows Script Files using XML. This included a review of commonly used XML tags.

PART II

Professional Project 1

Project 1

Desktop Administration Using VBScript and the WSH

Project 1 Overview

In this project, a small company named ABC, Inc. wishes to begin automating administration of its desktop computers. In pursuit of this goal, ABC, Inc.'s managers have created a desktop management project and have assigned a programmer to begin work on developing a collection of VBScripts that will perform the following tasks:

- Automate desktop customization
- Configure the Start menu
- Configure the Quick Launch toolbar
- Establish a remote network drive connection
- Establish a connection to a network printer
- Automate the creation of a new user account

As you go through the development of this project, you will learn how to develop VBScripts that can interact with the operating system and its environment in many ways, including:

- Directly accessing Windows desktop and network resources
- Automating the establishment of network connections using a VBScript logon script
- Directly accessing the contents of Windows folders
- Configuring systems by manipulating registry keys and values
- Directly executing Windows commands from within VBScripts
- Automating the execution of the Windows utilities

Chapter 10

Project Case Study: Desktop Customization and Deployment

In Part I of this book, you learned the basics of VBScript programming, including how to create and execute VBScripts in both the WSH and Internet Explorer execution environments. You also learned about the WSH core object model and the properties and methods associated with its objects. In this chapter, you'll begin work on a collection of desktop management scripts that will allow you to expand your working knowledge of many of the WSH objects.

Project Overview

In this project, you will examine and duplicate a desktop management project recently undertaken by a fictional company named ABC, Inc. ABC, Inc. does radio and newspaper marketing, advertising, and consulting in the central Virginia area. ABC, Inc. is a small company with 50 employees. With only a few exceptions, each of these employees is considered computer savvy.

Currently, each employee in the company has an assigned computer to work from. All the computers are connected to a small Windows domain-based network. The company has a collection of six Windows NT and 2000 servers from which they support a corporate Web site, file and print services, and a customer and projects database. To manage these servers and the Windows network, the company has two IT employees, Rick and Sue. For the most part, things run smoothly on these servers, and the company is very pleased with the way that Rick and Sue maintain things.

However, when it comes to desktop support, things are not going quite so well. Because it has a technically savvy workforce, the company has invested a minimal amount of time and effort on desktop support. Carl, the office manager, and his assistant, Becky, are in charge of corporate desktops. For the most part, their duties have been limited to purchasing and receiving new computers, which they then set up for individual users. After initial setup and configuration, users are left to work out desktop computer problems on their own. Therefore, desktop support at ABC, Inc. can be classified as being loosely supported.

Occasionally, users call Carl or Becky for help with a hardware or software problem that they cannot resolve. This often leads to a visit by Carl or Becky to determine whether something is broken and needs to be replaced of if there is a software or configuration problem that they could solve. Many times Carl and Becky call upon Rick and Sue, who are regarded as the company's computer gurus, for help.

Desktop support is only a part-time task for Carl and Becky, and they paid as little attention to it as possible. Because of this lack of attention, things have become a little messy over the last few years. For one thing, management requires that Carl and Becky shop for the best possible prices each time a new computer is purchased. As a result, the company purchased computers from numerous manufacturers over the years, including IBM, Compaq, Dell, and Gateway. In addition, Carl and Becky now find themselves supporting a number of different Microsoft operating systems, including Windows 98, Workstation NT 4.0, Windows 2000 Professional, and Windows XP Professional.

To make matters worse, users are beginning to find that their computers do not have adequate hardware resources (such as processor, memory, and drive space) to support new applications. As a result, Carl and Becky have noticed a large increase in the amount of time that they have had to dedicate to desktop support in the last six months. After numerous meetings and discussions with the top management, Carl and Becky have finally received authorization to hire a full-time staff member to assume responsibility for managing all corporate desktops. This person is Tom.

Tom started last month and went right to work taking care of existing user problems. It did not take Tom long to come to a number of conclusions, which he quickly documented and passed on to Carl and Becky. Tom also provided them with a formal report in which he identified a number of issues that he felt the company needed to address right away. A brief synopsis of these issues is outlined below.

- All but five computers running Windows 2000 Professional are in need of significant memory, disk drive, or processor upgrades.
- There are too many different models of computers from too many different computer manufacturers to effectively support every computer. Tom recommends replacing all existing computers with new computers over the next year. In addition, he strongly suggests that the company make a single manufacturer's line of computers standard to simplify future upgrades and problem troubleshooting and to gain leverage in negotiating a better deal on the purchase of new computers.
- Tom recommends adopting Windows XP Professional as the standard desktop operating system for all computers. Windows XP provides support for the widest possible range of hardware and business software and

is equipped with numerous software tools and utilities that assist in computer administration. This will help to simplify many support and maintenance issues.

- Tom also referred to a rumor going around the office that the company was about to expand and would be adding another 20 employees by the end of the year. Tom said that further growth in the number of desktops being supported necessitates a move toward standardization.

Management was receptive to Tom's recommendations and decided to implement them. New computers would be purchased in batches of 10, with a complete overhaul of the company's desktop environment in just five months. Dell would be selected as the company's desktop computer vendor. Arrangements were made to purchase 50 new computers, each equipped with 2GHz processors, 256MB of memory, 20GB hard drives, 17-inch monitors, and a preinstalled network adapter. All computers will come with Windows XP Professional and Microsoft Office preinstalled.

With the first batch of computers scheduled to arrive in just three weeks, Tom knows that he will be under a lot of pressure to configure them and get them deployed as quickly as possible. Previously, Carl and Becky took an average of five business days to customize and deploy a newly purchased computer. Given the number of computers that Tom will have to deal with in the coming months, he knows that management would not be pleased with this kind of turnaround. He decides that he wants to set a goal of rolling out 10 computers within four days of their receipt. This will not only impress upper management, but will also provide Tom with more time to assist in training users and help them troubleshoot problems. In addition, it will give Tom more time to work with Rick and Sue to begin training as backup server administrators.

Analyzing the Existing Process

Tom plans to develop a collection of WSH VBScripts to speed up the desktop configuration process, which he refers to collectively as his Desktop Deployment Toolkit. Once developed, these scripts will allow Tom to configure new desktops quickly. These scripts will eliminate problems and issues that result from human error (such as mistyping configuration settings, incorrectly performing procedures, and so on).

To begin, Tom sat down and documented the current desktop setup and configuration process and looked for ways to improve it and speed it up. By the time he was done, Tom broke down the process of setting up and configuring new computers into the following steps.

1. When new computers arrive, they are unpacked, assembled, and placed on a staging table, which can hold up to two computers at a time.
2. The computers are then physically connected to the network using a pair of network connections especially set up for this purpose.
3. Each computer is initially logged on to using the Administrator account.
4. Each computer comes with its operating system and Microsoft Office preinstalled. Each application is tested to verify that it works correctly. Then key hardware, such as the CD-ROM drive and floppy disk drives, is tested to make sure that it is operable.
5. Each computer is configured with a computer name provided by Rick and Sue and added to the corporate domain. It is then rebooted.
6. Next a local administrator account is set up using the User Accounts folder, as shown in Figure 10.1. This account and its password are recorded on paper and stored in a safe to keep them secure. The reason for creating this account is to provide a backdoor entry into the computer in case the user and the network administrators (Rick and Sue) lose their access to the computer.

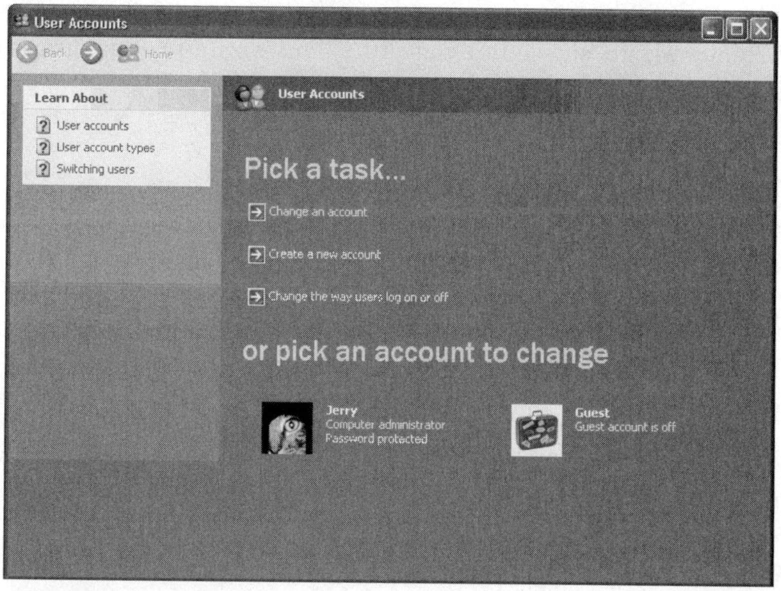

FIGURE 10.1 *Creating a local administrator account to be used in case of emergencies*

7. A monthly execution schedule is set up for two disk maintenance utilities from the Scheduled Tasks folder, as shown in Figure 10.2.

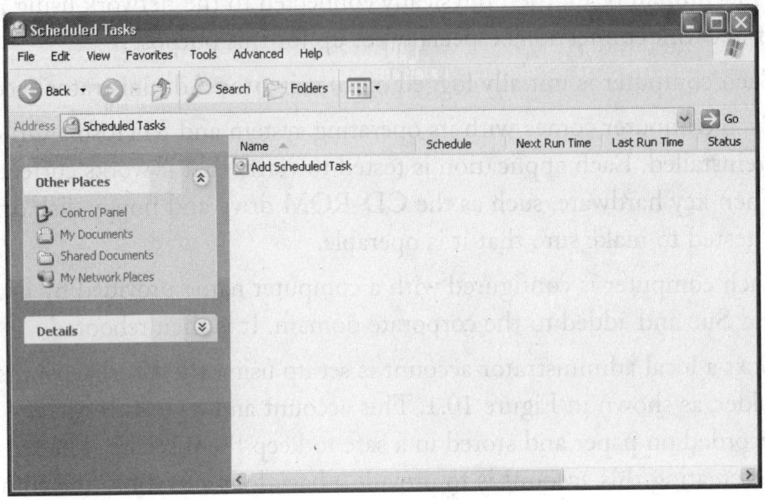

FIGURE 10.2 *The Scheduled Tasks folder is to set up and manage scheduled tasks*

The first of these disk management tasks to be scheduled is the Disk Cleanup wizard, shown in Figure 10.3. This wizard frees up disk space by deleting noncritical files, including:

- Downloaded program files
- Temporary Internet files
- Offline Web pages
- The Recycle Bin
- Setup log files
- Temporary files
- Catalog files for the Content Indexer

The second disk management task to be set up is the Disk Defragmenter utility, shown in Figure 10.4. This utility is used to keep the C: drive on each user's computer defragmented.

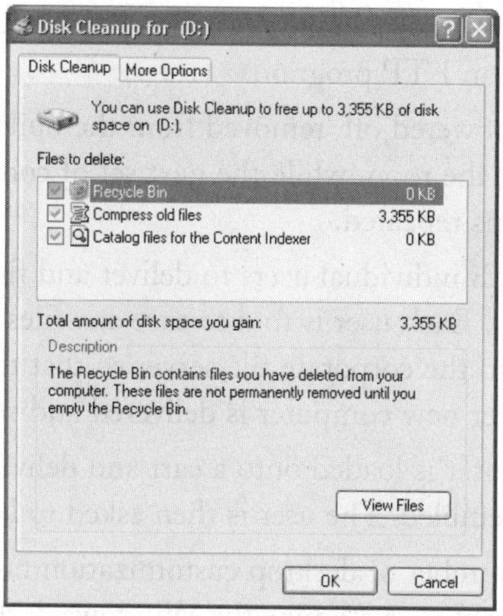

FIGURE 10.3 *Using the Disk Cleanup wizard to remove unnecessary files from the computer*

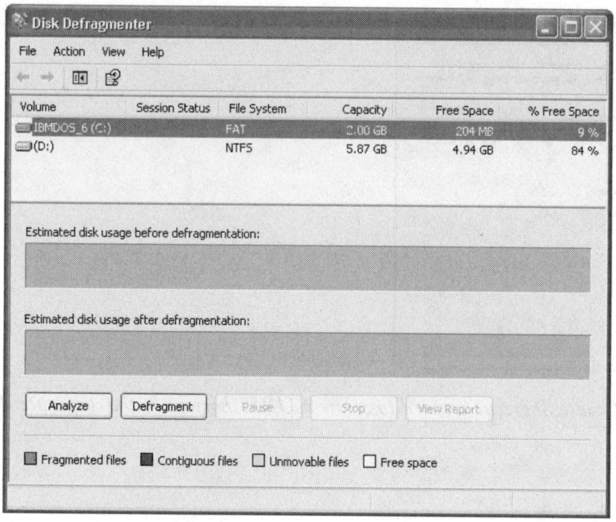

FIGURE 10.4 *Setting up the Disk Defragmenter to run on a monthly basis*

8. An Images folder is created on the root of the computer's D: drive, and a .bmp file that contains a copy of a desktop background file with the corporate logo is copied into that folder.

9. Next, several applications are installed, including WinZip, Adobe Acrobat Reader, Paint Shop Pro, and an FTP program.
10. At this point, each computer is powered off, removed from the build table, and stored in the corner of the room while the next set of computers is set up and the previous steps repeated.
11. Appointments are then made with individual users to deliver and finish the setup of their new computers. Each user is told to save any files stored on her current computer to the corporate file server so that the user can move them back after her new computer is delivered and set up.
12. At the appropriate time, a computer is loaded onto a cart and delivered to the user's desk, where it is assembled. The user is then asked to log in.
13. The user is asked to perform a number of desktop customization tasks. The Create Shortcut wizard is used to customize the Windows desktop by setting up a shortcut to the corporate Web site, as demonstrated in Figure 10.5.

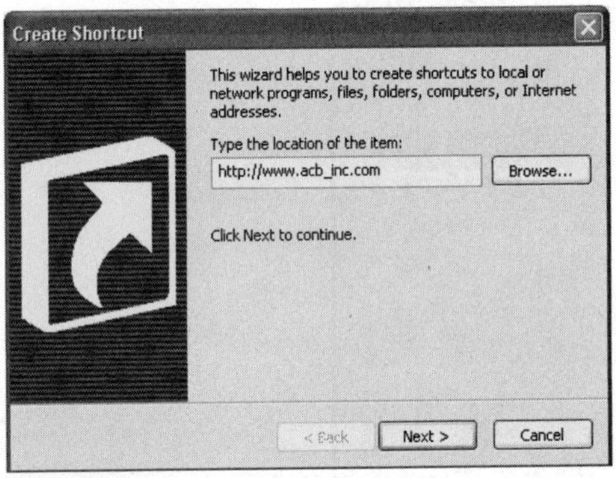

FIGURE 10.5 *Using the Create Shortcut wizard to create a URL shortcut to the corporate Web site*

NOTE

A number of desktop customization tasks are not performed until the computer is delivered to the user because these changes are saved in the user's profile and then are stored in the HKEY_CURRENT_USER root key of the Windows registry. In order to make these changes the user's profile must be loaded into memory (that is, the user needs to be logged on).

14. Using the Windows Display Properties dialog box shown in Figure 10.6, a Windows screen saver is configured that kicks in after 15 minutes of inactivity. Password protection is also configured.

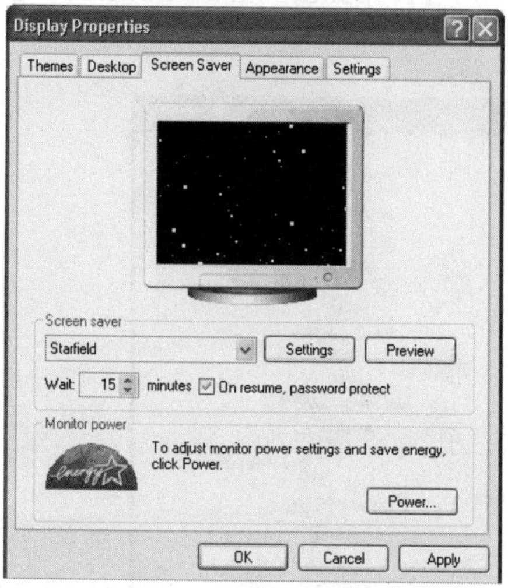

FIGURE 10.6 *Configuring the Starfield screen saver to start running after 15 minutes of inactivity*

15. The Windows desktop background is then configured to display the corporate desktop logo file located in the computer's D:\Images folder, as shown in Figure 10.7.

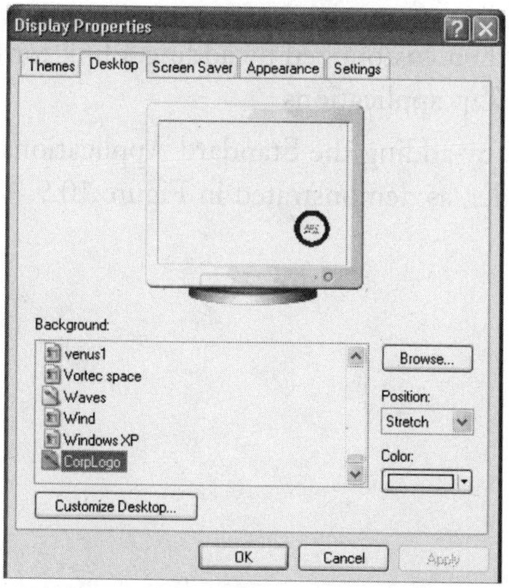

FIGURE 10.7 *Configuring the desktop to display the corporate logo*

16. Several Start menu and taskbar settings are configured. These settings include the creation of a Standard Applications folder, which is then populated with shortcuts to Microsoft Word, Adobe Acrobat Reader, Paint Shop Pro, WinZip, and an FTP application, as shown in Figure 10.8.

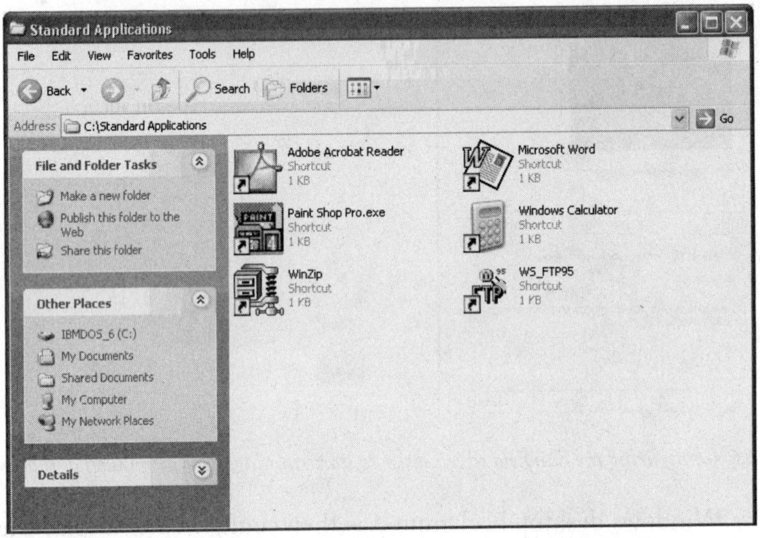

FIGURE 10.8 *Creating a Standard Applications folder that contains shortcuts to applications used by everyone in the company*

17. The Quick Launch toolbar is then customized by adding a link for the Windows Calculator and WinZip applications.
18. The Start menu is customized by adding the Standard Applications folder to the All Programs folder, as demonstrated in Figure 10.9.

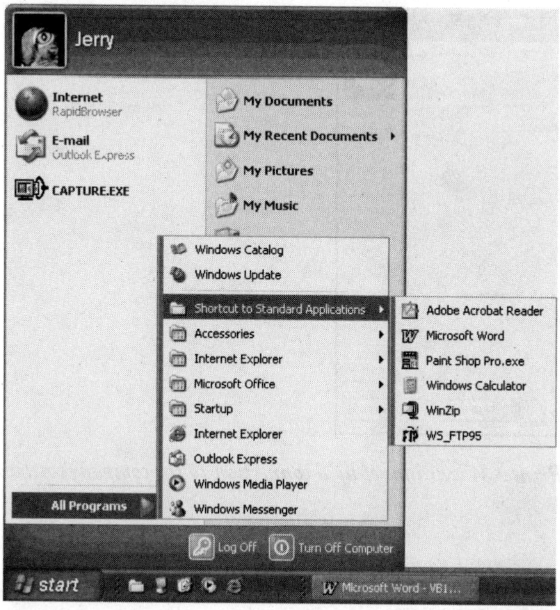

FIGURE 10.9 *Adding a shortcut to the Standard Applications folder on the Start menu*

19. The final tasks that are performed are the setup connections to the corporate file server and to a shared network printer. To set the network printer connection, the Add Printer Wizard is used, as shown in Figure 10.10. The Map Network Drive wizard is then used to create the drive mapping, as shown in Figure 10.11.

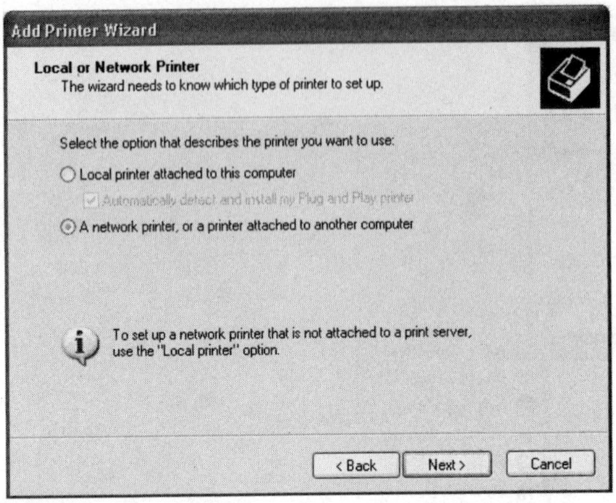

FIGURE 10.10 *Using the Add Printer Wizard to set up a connection to the company's network printer*

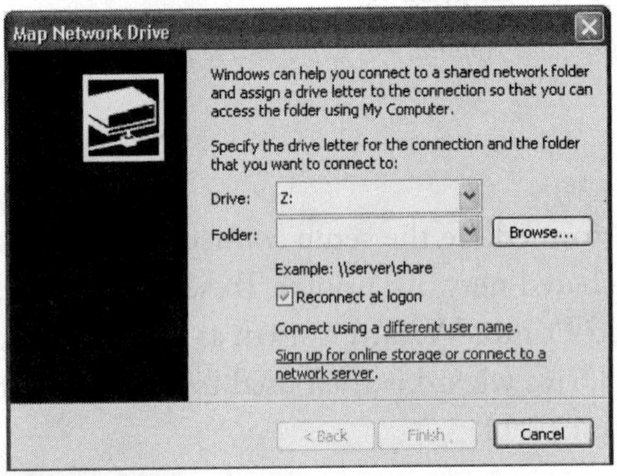

FIGURE 10.11 *Using the Map Network Drive wizard to map a drive connection to the company's shared network drive*

20. Finally, the user's old computer is packed up and taken away.

Determining Which Tasks Can Be Automated

After studying the rollout process for a while, Tom determines that he can significantly speed things up by automating key parts of the process using VBScript and the WSH. Tom produces a list of tasks that he considers to be candidates for automation and that he thinks he'll be able to write within the next three weeks.

He then organizes these tasks into logical groups, thinking that he will focus on automating one group of related tasks at a time. Table 10.1 shows the list that Tom put together.

Table 10.1 Desktop Management Task List

Type of Task	Description
Desktop customization	Customize the Windows desktop by adding a shortcut to the corporate Web site.
	Set up each user's screen saver to kick in after 15 minutes and to display the Starfield screen saver with password protection enabled.
	Set the Windows background to display the corporate logo.
Start menu and taskbar	Create a Standard Applications folder and populate it with shortcuts to Microsoft Word, Adobe Acrobat Reader, Paint Shop Pro, WinZip, and an FTP application.
	Customize the Quick Launch toolbar by adding a link to the Windows Calculator and WinZip applications.
	Customize the Start menu by adding the Standard Applications folder to the Start menu's All Programs folder.
Task scheduling	Schedule the execution of the Disk Cleanup wizard once a month.
	Schedule the execution of the Disk Defragmenter utility once a month.
Network connections	Set up a network printer connection to the corporate network printer pool.
	Set up a mapped drive to the corporate file server.
Account management	Add a local administrative maintenance user account to each computer.

Performing a High-Level Design

As a preliminary task, Tom decides to start by researching the WSH objects and Windows utilities and commands that he'll need to work with to automate each task. As a design strategy, Tom decides that he wants to break down tasks into small scripts and that scripts should be limited to performing no more than one or two tasks. This will help to facilitate rapid script development and testing, which is important to Tom because he only has a few weeks until the first batch of computers are scheduled to arrive.

Desktop Customization

Tom has broken down the desktop customization tasks into two separate tasks, as shown below.

- Adding a URL shortcut to the desktop
- Configuring the screen saver and Windows desktop wallpaper background

Tom has determined that to create a URL shortcut to the corporate Web site, he will need to make use of the WSH `WshUrlShortcut` object, which provides the ability to specify a URL via its `TargetPath` property. In addition, he'll need to use the `WshShell` object's `SpecialFolders` property in order to establish a reference to the Windows desktop.

In order to programmatically configure the Windows screen saver and desktop background, Tom has learned that he needs to make changes to the Windows registry. To do this, he will need to use the WSH `WshShell` object's `RegWrite()` method in order to modify screen saver and desktop wallpaper values stored in the `HKCU\Control Panel\Desktop` key.

In order for changes made to the desktop wallpaper to take effect, Tom will need to have the user log off and back on again. Tom has discovered that Windows XP provides the `logoff.exe` command line utility, which he will be able to use within a script to automatically log off the user.

Start Menu and Taskbar

Tom has broken down the Start menu and taskbar tasks into three separate tasks:

- Create a Standard Applications folder and populate it with application shortcuts
- Customize the Quick Launch toolbar
- Customize the Start menu

Tom has discovered that in order to create a folder, he'll need to learn to work with the VBScript run-time `FileSystemObject`. To create a desktop shortcut, Tom needs to begin by establishing an instance of the `WshShell` object. Then he needs to access the Windows Desktop special folder using the `WScript` object's `SpecialFolders` property. In addition, Tom needs to use the `WshShell` object's `CreateShortCut()` to finish creating the shortcut.

To configure the Quick Launch toolbar, Tom has discovered that he needs to configure and add a shortcut to it. In order to do this, he'll need to learn to work with another special folder called `AppData`. In addition, he'll need to learn how to work with special folders that represent the Start menu and the All Programs menu in order to configure the Start menu.

Task Scheduling

Tom has identified two disk management tasks that he needs to set up to run every 30 days. These utilities are listed below.

- The Disk Cleanup wizard
- The Disk Defragmenter utility

In order to programmatically interact with the Windows scheduler service, Tom plans to use the Windows `At` command. He has discovered that in order to execute this command from within a WSH VBScript, he'll need to learn how to use the `WshShell` object's `Run()` method.

Tom has also learned that he can use the `defrag.exe` command line utility to defrag hard disk drives. He can pass this utility arguments that will allow it to run silently in the background. In addition, he can use the `cleanmgr` command line utility to run the Disk Cleanup utility as a background task.

Network Connections

Tom needs to set up two network connections as part of the computer setup and configuration process. The network resources for which the connections are to be made are outlined below.

- **`\\PrinterServer\LazerPtr`.** A high-speed laser printer located in the photocopier room
- **`\\FileServer\D-drive`.** A high-capacity hard disk drive available to all employees

In order to set up these two network connections, Tom needs to learn how to work with the WSH `WshNetwork` object. Specifically, he'll need to use the following `WshNetwork` object methods:

- **`MapNetworkDrive`.** Maps a connection to the specified network drive
- **`AddPrinterConnection`.** Establishes a connection to the specified network printer

Account Management

Tom plans to use the Windows `net user` command to create a local user account. In order to do so, he'll need to use the `WshShell` object's `Run()` method to be able to execute the commands. Once the new account has been added to the local computer, he'll need to use the `WshShell` object `Run()` method again to add the new account to the administrator's group. To complete this task, he plans to execute the Windows `net localgroup` command.

The Implementation Plan

Now that Tom has an idea of the VBScripts that he wants to develop and the commands, objects, methods, and properties that he'll need to use in order to write them, he decides to develop a brief implementation plan. In this plan, he decides to develop 10 separate VBScripts, one for each task number in the plan.

Tom then presents this plan to Carl, the office manager, for approval so that he can begin writing the scripts as quickly as possible. Table 10.2 shows the implementation plan that Tom developed.

Table 10.2 Desktop Configuration and Management Script Development Schedule

Task No.	Task Type	Description
0100	Desktop	Configure a shortcut to the corporate Web site.
0110	Desktop	Set up a password-protected screen saver with a 15-minute delay and configure the Windows background to display the corporate logo.
0200	Start menu and taskbar	Create a Standard Applications folder and populate the Standard Applications folder with application shortcuts.

Table 10.2 Desktop Configuration and Management Script Development Schedule (*continued*)

Task No.	Task Type	Description
0220	Start menu and taskbar	Add application shortcuts to the Quick Launch toolbar.
0230	Start menu and taskbar	Add application shortcuts to the All Programs menu located on the Start menu.
0300	Scheduling	Schedule the execution of the `defrag.exe` utility.
0310	Scheduling	Schedule the execution of the `cleanmgr` utility.
0400	Network	Automate the setup of the network printer connection.
0410	Network	Automate the setup of a mapped drive to the corporate file server.
0500	Account Admin	Create a local administrative maintenance user account.

Upon reviewing Tom's plan, Carl happily approved it. However, Carl wanted to know how Tom planned on incorporating these scripts into the rollout process. Tom explained that although the steps that make up the overall process would remain unchanged, he would now be able to execute them more quickly while eliminating errors that often occurred in the past.

Tom told Carl that he plans on copying all the scripts onto a floppy disk, which he will insert into each computer when it is first placed on the build table. He will then run each script representing a build-table task from the floppy disk. Then he will take a copy of the floppy disk with him when he delivers each computer. After getting the user to log in, Tom will insert the floppy disk and run the remaining scripts. Not only will this process reduce the disruption imposed on each user, but it will also make it possible for Tom to deploy all the computers, once removed from the build table, in a single day.

Summary

In this chapter, you were introduced to ABC, Inc. You reviewed the challenges that the company faces regarding the support and deployment of desktop computers. In addition, you observed as Tom, the company's new desktop support analyst, devised a plan for streamlining the desktop deployment process by developing VBScripts that automated a number of manual tasks. In the next five chapters, you will get the opportunity to follow along as Tom implements his plan by developing these scripts.

Chapter 11

Customizing the Desktop

In this chapter, you will learn how to develop two VBScripts that customize the Windows desktop in a number of ways. The first script will demonstrate how to create a shortcut to an Internet URL as well as how to work with Windows special folders. The second script will demonstrate how to programmatically manipulate the contents of the Windows registry in order to configure both the Windows desktop wallpaper and the Windows screen saver.

Adding a URL Desktop Shortcut to the Corporate Web Site

The first script that needs to be completed is the one that creates a shortcut on the Windows desktop to the company's Web site. This is the easier of the two scripts to write, and it will give Tom, the new desktop support employee from Chapter 10, a chance to get his feet wet before trying to learn how to programmatically interact with the Windows registry.

There are a number of different pieces of information that you must take into account when developing this first script. First of all, you need to learn how to work with the `WshUrlShortcut` object. In order to add a shortcut to the Windows desktop, you also need to learn about a Windows management feature known as special folders. Special folders are used to represent and administer a number of Windows features, including the Start menu, the Quick Launch toolbar, and the desktop.

Working with Special Folders

Windows special folders represent a number of important system resources. By manipulating the contents of these folders, you are able to directly modify numerous Windows resources, including:

- Desktop
- Favorites
- Fonts
- MyDocuments

- NetHood
- PrintHood
- Programs
- Recent
- SendTo
- StartMenu
- Startup
- Templates

To examine these special folders, right-click on the Windows XP Start button and click on Explore. This will open an Explorer folder. By default, the Document and Settings folder will be expanded, as will a folder representing a number of your personal user profile settings. To view the contents of your Windows desktop, select the Desktop folder, as demonstrated in Figure 11.1.

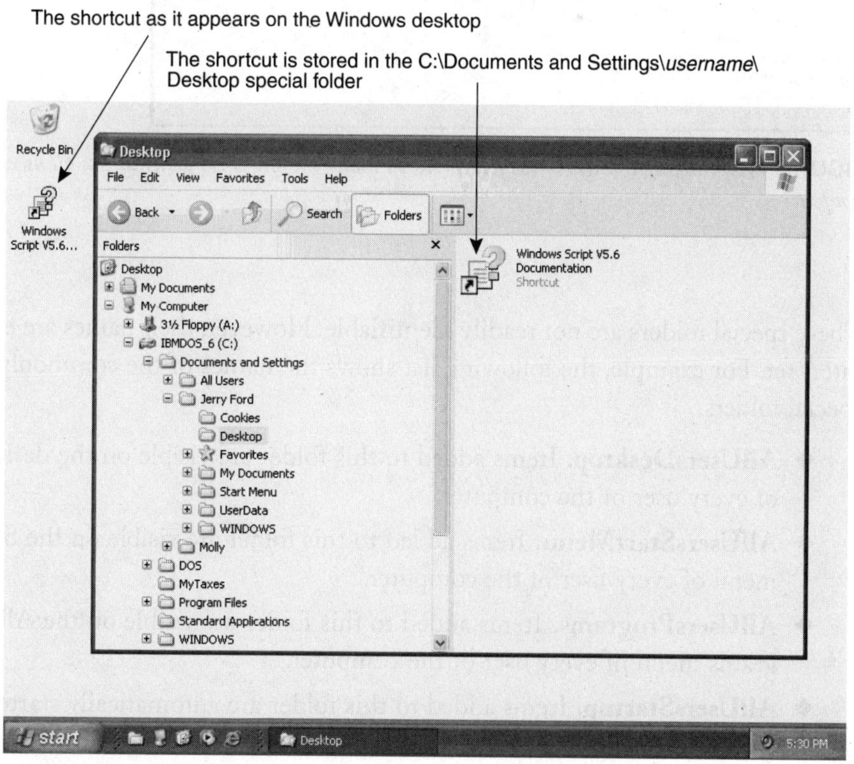

FIGURE 11.1 *Examining the contents of the Desktop special folder*

One way to configure the contents of your Windows desktop is to drag and drop Windows shortcuts to and from this folder.

In addition to the special folders associated with your specific profile, Windows provides a second group of special folders that apply to all users of the computer. To view these folders, expand the All Users folder, as shown in Figure 11.2.

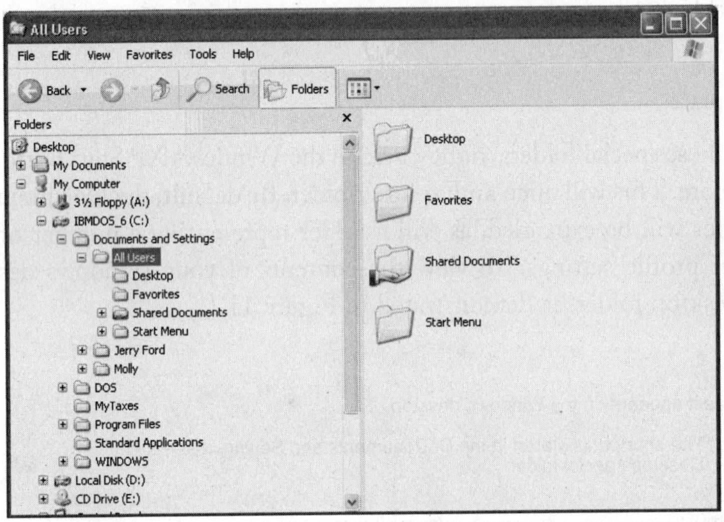

FIGURE 11.2 *Making changes to the folders stored under the All Users folder affects all users of the computer*

These special folders are not readily identifiable. However, their names are easy to interpret. For example, the following list shows the names of the commonly used special folders.

- **AllUsersDesktop.** Items added to this folder are visible on the desktop of every user of the computer.
- **AllUsersStartMenu.** Items added to this folder are visible on the Start menu of every user of the computer.
- **AllUsersPrograms.** Items added to this folder are visible on the All Programs menu of every user of the computer.
- **AllUsersStartup.** Items added to this folder are automatically started each time a user logs on to the computer.

As you can see, the names of these special folders are generated by appending *AllUsers* to the folder names (less any spaces).

Working with the WshUrlShortcut Object

In order to create a shortcut for a URL, you must use the methods and properties belonging to the `WshUrlShortcut` object. This object is a child object of the `WshShell` object. In order to work with the `WshUrlShortcut` object, you must first instantiate the `WshShell` object, as shown below.

```
Set WshShl = WScript.CreateObject("WScript.Shell")
```

In order to place a shortcut on the Windows desktop, you must set up a reference to it using the `WshShell` object's `SpecialFolders` property. The syntax for doing so is outlined below.

```
WshShl.SpecialFolders(SpecialFolderName)
```

`SpecialFolderName` specifies the name of a special folder, which in the case of the Windows desktop is the `Desktop` special folder. A reference to the `Desktop` special folder is set up as follows:

```
DesktopFolder = WshShl.SpecialFolders("Desktop")
```

NOTE

The `WshShell` object's `SpecialFolders` property will return an empty string if the specified folder does not exist.

Once the `WshShell` object is established and the reference to the special folder is set, you can use the `WshShell` object's `CreateShortcut` method to instantiate a `WshUrlShortcut` object. The syntax for doing so is outlined below.

```
WshShell.CreateShortcut(ShortcutPathname)
```

When creating a URL shortcut in a special folder such as the `Desktop` special folder, the value assigned to the `ShortcutPathname` parameter consists of two different pieces of information. The first piece is the name of the special folder reference. The second piece of information is a descriptive string that ends with .url.

These two pieces of information are then concatenated to the special folder name, as shown below.

```
Set UrlShortcut = WshShl.CreateShortcut(DesktopFolder + "\\Premier Press
Publishing.url")
```

The next step to perform when setting up a URL shortcut on the Windows desktop is the specification of the URL address that the shortcut is to represent. Setting the `WshUrlShortcut` object's `TargetPath` property does this.

```
UrlShortcut.TargetPath = "www.premierpressbooks.com"
```

The only remaining step is to use the `WshUrlShortcut` object's `Save()` method to save the object to disk, as shown below.

```
UrlShortcut.Save
```

When fully assembled, the previous statements create a desktop shortcut to the Premier Press Web site, as shown below.

```
Set WshShl = WScript.CreateObject("WScript.Shell")
DesktopFolder = WshShl.SpecialFolders("Desktop")
Set UrlShortcut = WshShl.CreateShortcut(DesktopFolder + "\\Premier Press
Publishing.url")
UrlShortcut.TargetPath = "www.premierpressbooks.com"
UrlShortcut.Save
```

Developing the Desktop URL VBScript

By duplicating the logic of the previous example, you can easily create a VBScript that places a URL shortcut on the Windows desktop, as shown in the following example.

```
'*************************************************************************
'Script Name: Script 11.1.vbs
'Author: Jerry Ford
'Created: 02/17/03
'Description: This script creates a URL to the corporate web site on the
'Windows desktop
'*************************************************************************
```

```
'Initialization Section

Option Explicit

Dim WshShl, DesktopFolder, UrlShortcut

Set WshShl = WScript.CreateObject("WScript.Shell")


'Main Processing Section

CreateUrlShortcut()

WScript.Quit()


'Procedure Section

'Create the desktop URL Shortcut
Sub CreateUrlShortcut()

  DesktopFolder = WshShl.SpecialFolders("Desktop")

  Set UrlShortcut = WshShl.CreateShortcut(DesktopFolder + "\\ABC Inc " & _
    "Home Page.url")
UrlShortcut.TargetPath = "www.abc_inc.com"
  UrlShortcut.Save

End Sub
```

The script begins with the `Option Explicit` statement and then defines the variables that it will need to work with. Next the `WshShell` object is instantiated. The Main Processing Section consists of two statements. The first statement calls a subroutine called `CreateUrlShortcut()`, which creates the desktop URL shortcut. The second statement uses the `WScript` object's `Quit()` method to terminate the script's execution.

The key part of the script is contained in the `CreateUrlShortcut()` subroutine. It begins by setting up a reference to the `Desktop` special folder. Next the shortcut is created. Then its URL address is assigned, and finally it is saved to disk. Once run, this script creates the desktop URL shortcut shown in Figure 11.3.

FIGURE 11.3 *An example of a desktop URL shortcut created by a VBScript*

> **NOTE**
>
> The coverage of desktop shortcuts in this chapter is very limited. For a detailed review of shortcuts, including their attributes and construction, refer to Chapter 12, "Customizing the Start Menu and Taskbar."

Understanding the Windows Registry

Now that you have written a VBScript to configure a desktop URL shortcut, it is time to begin working on a script that will automate the configuration of the Windows background wallpaper and the screen saver. This script must satisfy a number of requirements, including:

- Creating a D:\Images folder if it does not already exist
- Copying the CorpLogo.bmp desktop background file from floppy disk to the D:\Images folder
- Configuring CorpLogo.bmp as the Windows desktop wallpaper
- Setting the Windows desktop background to white so that text displayed on the desktop will not have a background color
- Disabling the Wallpaper Tile setting
- Enabling the screen saver
- Enabling password protection
- Setting up a 15-minute delay before the screen saver begins executing

- Enabling the Starfield screen saver
- Logging the user off in order for changes to take effect

Working with the Registry

The Windows registry is a built-in database that provides a central repository for storing configuration information about:

- User configuration settings and profile information
- Windows operating system settings
- Software configuration settings
- Hardware settings
- Configuration information for Windows services
- Configuration information for software device drivers

The registry contains configuration information about virtually every aspect of a Windows computer. By modifying the contents of the Windows registry, you can configure the operation of many Windows features, including desktop settings, the desktop wallpaper, and the screen saver.

Users and administrators work with the registry every day, often without even realizing it. For example, the utilities or applets located on the Windows Control Panel provide graphical interfaces for making modifications to the registry. The Control Panel applets simplify the process of making changes to the registry by providing intuitive interfaces. An alternative way to work with the Windows registry is to use the `Regedit` registry editor.

TIP

On Windows NT, 2000, and XP you may also use the `Regedt32` registry editor.

Figure 11.4 provides a high-level view of the Windows XP registry, which is made up of five root keys.

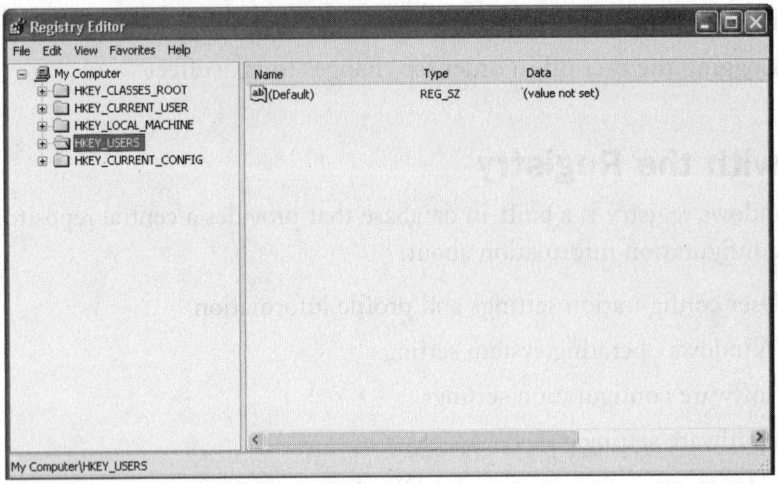

FIGURE 11.4 *Using the* `Regedit` *registry editor to examine the contents of the Windows registry*

> **NOTE**
>
> Making a mistake when modifying the contents of the Windows registry can have a potentially devastating impact on the computer. In certain circumstances, it can even prevent the computer from starting. Unless you are absolutely certain of the effects of a change that you are making to the registry, do not make the change. In addition, take advantage of Control Panel applets and other utilities whenever possible to avoid making manual registry changes with `Regedit`. Finally, make sure that you back up the registry on a regular basis so that you can recover from any changes that result in a problem.

Understanding How the Registry Is Organized

The Windows registry is logically organized in a treelike structure with five root or parent keys, as shown in Table 11.1.

Table 11.1 Windows Registry Root Keys

Key	Abbreviation	Description
HKEY_CLASSES_ROOT	HKCR	Stores information about Windows file associations
HKEY_CURRENT_USER	HKCU	Stores information about the currently logged on user

Table 11.1 Windows Registry Root Keys (*continued*)

Key	Abbreviation	Description
HKEY_LOCAL_MACHINE	HKLM	Stores global computer settings
HKEY_USERS	N/A	Stores information about all users of the computer
HKEY_CURRENT_CONFIG	N/A	Stores information regarding the computer's current configuration

NOTE

There is a sixth root key on Windows 98 and Me called `HKEY_DYN_DATA`. This key references Plug and Play related information.

Physically, the Windows registry is made up of a number of different files. On a computer running Windows 2000 or XP, these files are located in %systemroot%\system32\config and include all of the following:

- `DEFAULT`
- `SAM`
- `SECURITY`
- `SOFTWARE`
- `SYSTEM`
- `Userdiff`

In addition to these files, information is stored in individual user profiles. These user profiles are located in the Documents and Settings folder and are organized by username.

NOTE

On computers running Windows 98 and Me, the contents of the Windows registry are stored in two files called `user.dat` and `system.dat`. `User.dat` stores user-profile-related information and `system.dat` stores system-related information.

Of the five registry keys, the only ones that you will probably need to work with are the first three keys listed in Table 11.1. As a convenience, each of these root keys has an associated abbreviation that you can use within your VBScripts when working with any of these keys. The remaining two keys do not have an abbreviation. To work with these two keys, you will have to reference them using their full names (`HKEY_CURRENT_CONFIG` or `HKEY_USERS`).

Keys, Values, and Data

Within the Windows registry data is stored a complex hierarchy made up of keys and values. A *key* can be thought of as a container that holds other keys or values. The five root keys are analogous to disk drives, while the various levels of subkeys that reside underneath them can be thought of as functioning like folders. Actual data within the registry is stored within values. A *value* is therefore very much like a file, which in turn stores data.

Data is stored in the registry using the following format:

```
Key : key_type : value
```

`Key` represents the name of a registry key. For example, the following statement references a key named `Desktop`, which is a subkey of the `Control Panel` key, which itself is a subkey of the `HKEY_CURRENT_USERS` root key.

```
HKCU\
     Control Panel\
          \Desktop\
```

You specify a key versus a value by adding a closing \ character to the end of a key name, as demonstrated above. Values, on the other hand, are specified without a closing \, as demonstrated below.

```
HKCU\
     Control Panel\
          \Desktop
               \Wallpaper
```

In this example, the `Wallpaper` value, which is located within the `Desktop` key, is specified.

`Key_type` specifies the type of data being stored. The Windows registry supports the storage of a number of different types of data, as listed in Table 11.2. `Value` is used to specify the actual data to be stored.

Table 11.2 Windows Registry Data Types

Type	Description
`REG_BINARY`	Stores a binary value
`REG_DWORD`	Stores a hexadecimal DWORD value
`REG_EXPAND_SZ`	Stores an expandable string
`REG_MULTI_SZ`	Stores multiple strings
`REG_SZ`	Stores a string

There are two types of registry values, `named` and `unnamed`. Most registry values are `named`. A `named` value is one that is assigned a name by which the data stored within the value can be referenced. An `unnamed` value is one without a name. Every registry key has one `unnamed` value that represents its default value (that is, the value that is changed if a named value is not specified). `Unnamed` values are represented within the Windows registry with a label of `Default`, as shown in Figure 11.5.

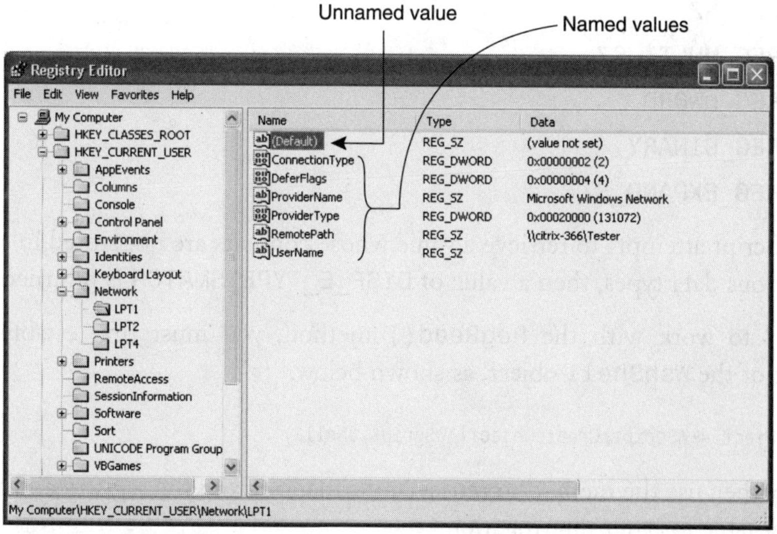

FIGURE 11.5 *`Unnamed` values are represented with a label of `Default` when viewed using the `Regedit` utility*

Writing VBScripts That Programmatically Interact with the Windows Registry

In order to programmatically interact with the Windows registry using VBScript and the WSH, you must first instantiate the `WshShell` object. The `WshShell` object provides three methods that you can use to read, write, add, delete, and modify registry keys and values. These methods are described below.

- **`RegRead()`**. Retrieves a key or value from the registry
- **`RegWrite()`**. Creates or modifies a registry key or value
- **`RegDelete()`**. Deletes a key or value from the registry

Reading Registry Keys and Values

The `WshShell` object's `RegRead()` method provides the ability to examine the contents of registry keys and values. The `RegRead()` method has the following syntax:

```
X = WshShell.RegRead(KeyOrValue)
```

`KeyOrValue` specifies the name of a registry key or value to be retrieved. The `RegRead()` method can only retrieve the following types of data from the registry:

- `REG_SZ`
- `REG_MULTI-SZ`
- `REG_DWORD`
- `REG_BINARY`
- `REG_EXPAND_SZ`

If a VBScript attempts to retrieve a value whose contents are not stored in one of the previous data types, then a value of `DISP_E_TYPEISMATCH` is returned.

In order to work with the `RegRead()` method, you must first establish an instance of the `WshShell` object, as shown below.

```
Set wshObject = WScript.CreateObject("WScript.Shell")
```

You may then use the method to retrieve information from the registry and assign it to a variable for later interrogation.

```
results = wshObject.RegRead("HKCU\TestKey\FileName")
```

In this example, the data assigned to a value named `FileName` (stored in a key named `HKCU\TestKey`) is retrieved.

Adding or Changing Registry Keys and Values

The `WshShell` object's `RegWrite()` method provides the ability to create new registry keys or values. It also provides the ability to modify them if they already exist. The syntax required to work with this method is shown below.

```
WshShell.RegWrite(KeyOrValue, Data, DataType)
```

`KeyOrValue` represents the registry key or value being created or modified. `Data` specifies the data that is being written to the registry, and `DataType` identifies the data's type.

All registry values are typed. The `RegWrite()` method provides VBScript with the ability to write the following types of data to the Windows registry:

- `REG_SZ`
- `REG_DWORD`
- `REG_BINARY`
- `REG_EXPAND_SZ`

By default, all data is stored as a string (for example, `REG_SZ`). VBScript is a loosely typed scripting language that supports only the variant data type. Therefore, when writing nonstring data, it is important that your VBScripts specify the `DataType` parameters to ensure that the data is stored using the proper type.

To write to the registry, you must first instantiate the `WshShell` object. You may then add or modify registry keys or values as demonstrated below.

```
Set WshShell = WScript.CreateObject("WScript.Shell")
WshShell.RegWrite "HKCU\TestKey\FileName", "Error.log", "REG_SZ"
```

In this example, a new value is created, as demonstrated in Figure 11.6. It is stored in a key called `Error.Log`, which is located under `HKCU\TestKey\`. If the `TestKey` key does not exist, the `RegWrite()` method will automatically create it. The data being stored is the name of a file (`Error.log`). This data is stored as a string.

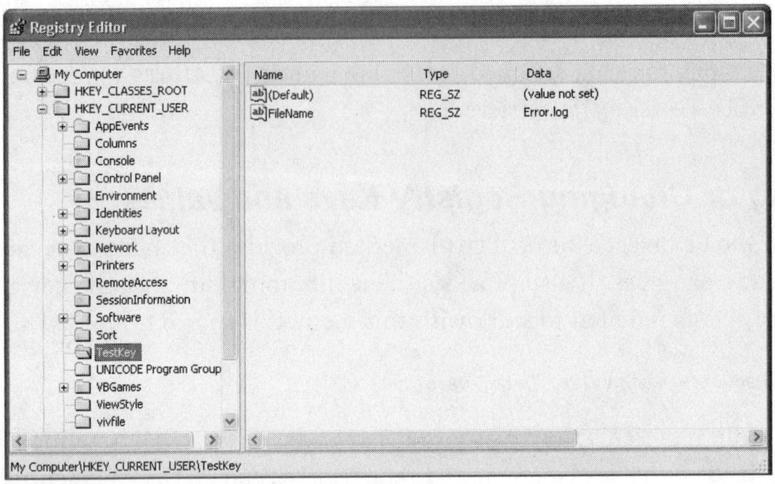

FIGURE 11.6 *Using the* `Regedit` *utility to view the new value*

To later modify this value, all that you have to do is assign it a new string, as demonstrated below.

```
Set WshShell = WScript.CreateObject("WScript.Shell")
WshShell.RegWrite "HKCU\TestKey\FileName", "Error.txt", "REG_SZ"
```

In this example, the file extension of the `Error` file was changed from .log to .txt.

NOTE

A registry key can be used to store an unlimited number of subkeys or values. For example, the following statement could be used to create a second value and store it under `HKCU\TestKey\FileName`:

```
WshShell.RegWrite "HKCU\TestKey\FileStatus", "Active", "REG_SZ"
```

Deleting Registry Keys and Values

The `WshShell` object's `RegDelete()` method provides VBScript with the ability to delete registry keys and values. Use the following syntax when working with this method:

```
WshShell.RegDelete KeyOrValue
```

`KeyOrValue` identifies the name of a key or variable to be deleted.

> **NOTE**
>
> Windows 2000 and XP will not allow you to delete a registry key if it contains other subkeys. You must delete all child keys before deleting a parent key. Things work differently on Windows 98 and Me, where the `RegDelete()` method will allow a parent key that contains child keys to be deleted.

To work with the `RegDelete()` method, you must first instantiate the `WshShell` object. You can then delete a key or value, as demonstrated below.

```
Set wshObject = WScript.CreateObject("WScript.Shell")
wshObject.RegDelete "HKCU\TestKey\FileName"
```

In this example, a value named `FileName` is deleted from `HKCU\TestKey`. In a similar fashion, the `HKCU\TestKey` key can be deleted, as shown below.

```
Set wshObject = WScript.CreateObject("WScript.Shell")
wshObject.RegDelete "HKCU\ TestKey \"
```

Customizing Desktop Wallpaper and Screen Saver Settings

The VBScript that is to modify desktop wallpaper and screen saver settings has a number of tasks that it must perform. These tasks include creating a folder to store the CorpLogo.bmp wallpaper file, modifying Windows desktop wallpaper and screen saver values located in the `HKCU\Control Panel\Desktop` key, and logging off the user once the changes have been made.

The Initialization Section

As with all the VBScripts developed in this book, this VBScript is divided into three sections. The Initialization Section is responsible for defining variables used by the script. It also instantiates both the `WshShell` object and the `FileSystemObject` object, as shown below.

```
Option Explicit

Dim WshShl, ChangeSettings, shellApp, FsoObject
Set WshShl = WScript.CreateObject("WScript.Shell")
Set FsoObject = CreateObject("Scripting.FileSystemObject")
```

The `WshShell` object must be established in order for the script to make use of its `RegWrite()` method. The `FileSystemObject` object is needed in order to have access to methods that will allow the script to create the Images folder on the computer's D: drive and to store a copy of the CorpLogo.bmp wallpaper file in that folder.

The Main Processing Section

The Main Processing Section controls the overall execution of the script, deciding when and if the registry is to be modified. This is accomplished by calling the `GetConfirmation()` function, which returns a value of `6` if permission to run the script has been given. If this is the case, then a series of subroutine calls is made to procedures that copy the CorpLogo.bmp file to the computer's disk drive, modify both the background wallpaper and screen saver settings, and then initiate the logoff process.

```
ChangeSettings = GetConfirmation()

If ChangeSettings = 6 Then
  CopyCorpLogo()
  SetBackground()
  SetScreenSaver()
  ForceLogoff()
End If

WScript.Quit()
```

Once each of these subroutines has executed, control returns to the Main Processing Section, and the `WScript` object's `Quit()` method is called in order to terminate the script's execution.

TIP

The use of the `WScript` object's `Quit()` method is not required in this instance because as it is written, the script would stop executing at this point anyway. However, by adding this method to the end of the Main Processing Section, you make the script easier to read and prevent any code that may have been accidentally placed outside of a procedure in the Procedure Section from inadvertently executing.

The CopyCorpLogo() Subroutine

The `CopyCorpLogo()` subroutine uses several methods belonging to the `FileSystemObject` object to interrogate and manipulate the Windows file system. For starters, the subroutine uses the `FolderExists()` method to determine whether or not the D:\Images folder already exists. If it does not exist, then the `CreateFolder()` method is used to create it. Since Tom is working with all new computers, the folder shouldn't already exist. However, adding this check provides a foundation for expanding the script should Tom ever need to reconfigure computers that have already been deployed. The last thing that the script does is copy the CorpLogo.bmp file to the D:\Images folder.

```
Sub CopyCorpLogo()
  If (FsoObject.FolderExists("D:\Images") = false) Then
    FsoObject.CreateFolder "D:\Images\"
  End If
  FsoObject.CopyFile "a:\CorpLogo.bmp", "D:\Images\"
End Sub
```

The GetConfirmation() Function

The `GetConfirmation()` function displays a message in a pop-up dialog box using the built-in VBScript `MsgBox()` function. This procedure is written as a function instead of as a subroutine because it needs to be able to return a result back to its calling statement. A value of `6` is returned if the Yes button is clicked and a value of `7` is returned if the No button is clicked.

```
Function GetConfirmation()
  GetConfirmation = MsgBox("This script will perform the following " & _
```

```
        "tasks:" & _ vbCrLf & vbCrLf & "1. Configure the display of the " & _
        "Corporate Logo the Windows desktop" & vbCrLf & _
        "2. Configure a password protected screen saver" & vbCrLf & _
        "3. Initiate a restart of the of the computer so that " & _
        "changes may take effect" & vbCrLf & vbCrLf & _
        "Do you wish to continue?", 36)
End Function
```

The SetBackground() Subroutine

The `SetBackground()` subroutine uses the `WshShell` object's `RegWrite()` method to modify three registry values located in the `HKCU\Control Panel\Desktop` subkey. The first value that is modified is `Wallpaper`, which is set to `D:\Images\CorpLogo.bmp`. The second value to be modified is `TileWallpaper`, which is set to 0. Finally, the `Background` value is set to `255 255 255` (white).

```
Sub SetBackground()
  'Set CorpLogo.bmp as the desktop wallpaper
  WshShl.RegWrite "HKCU\Control Panel\Desktop\Wallpaper", _
    "D:\Images\CorpLogo.bmp"

  'Make sure that the Tile option is disabled
  WshShl.RegWrite "HKCU\Control Panel\Desktop\TileWallpaper", "0"


  'Configure the background color to be white
  WshShl.RegWrite "HKCU\Control Panel\Colors\Background", "255 255 255"
End Sub
```

The registry modifications performed by this subroutine are equivalent to opening the Desktop Properties dialog box (by right-clicking on the Windows desktop and selecting Properties from the menu that appears) and then modifying the settings on the Desktop Saver property sheet, as shown in Figure 11.7.

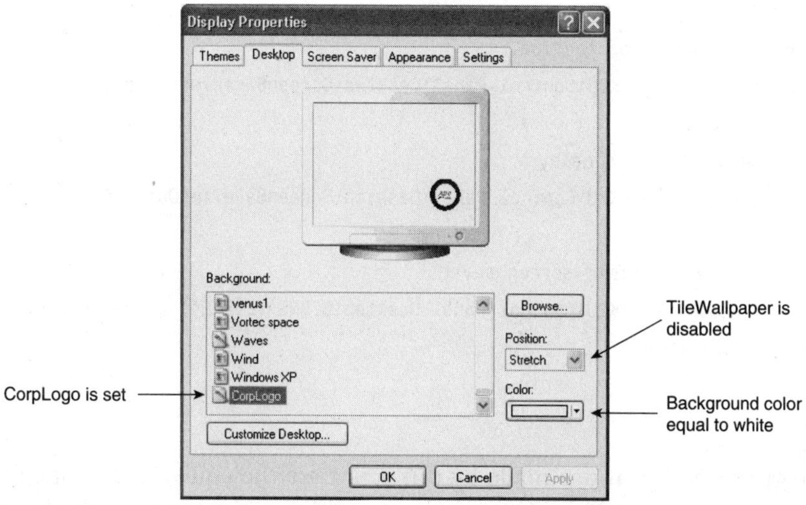

FIGURE 11.7 *Examining the changes made to the desktop wallpaper settings*

The SetScreenSaver() Subroutine

The `SetScreenSaver()` subroutine modifies four screen-saver-related registry values located in the `HKCU\Control Panel\Desktop` subkey. The first value that is changed is `ScreenSaveActive`, which is set to 1. This enables the Windows screen saver. Next the `ScreenSaverIsSecure` value is set to 1. This enables Windows screen saver password protection. The `ScreenSaveTimeOut` value is then set to 900. This configures a 15-minute delay before the screen saver will kick in. Finally, the `SCRNSAVE.EXE` value is set to `("%SystemRoot%") & "System32\ssstars.scr"`. This sets up the Starfield Simulation screen saver.

NOTE

Windows XP screen savers are stored in C:\Windows\System32 and have a .scr file extension. Their file names are rather cryptic, making it difficult to identify them by name. However, you can double-click on them to open and view them.

```
Sub SetScreenSaver()
    'Enable the screen saver
    WshShl.RegWrite "HKCU\Control Panel\Desktop\ScreenSaveActive", 1
```

```
    'Enable password protection
    WshShl.RegWrite "HKCU\Control Panel\Desktop\ScreenSaverIsSecure", 1

    'Set up a 15 minute delay
    WshShl.RegWrite "HKCU\Control Panel\Desktop\ScreenSaveTimeOut", 900

    'Enable the Starfield screen saver
    WshShl.RegWrite "HKCU\Control Panel\Desktop\SCRNSAVE.EXE", ("%SystemRoot%") &
"System32\ssstars.scr"

End Sub
```

The registry modifications made by this script are the equivalent of opening the Desktop properties dialog box and then modifying the settings on the Screen Saver property sheet, as shown in Figure 11.8.

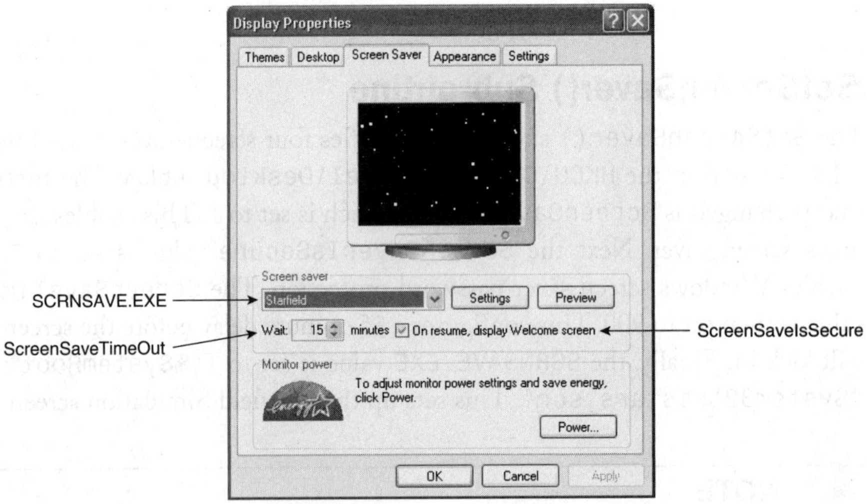

FIGURE 11.8 *Examining the changes made to the desktop screen saver settings*

The ForceLogoff() Subroutine

Desktop wallpaper and screen saver configuration settings are associated with individual users and are stored in each user's profile (for example, HKCU). In order to make changes to HKCU, the user must be logged on to the computer.

Once the script has changed the settings that affect the desktop wallpaper and screen saver, the user must log off for the changes to take effect.

Windows XP comes equipped with a command line utility called `logoff.exe` that can be called by the script in order to automatically log the user off. The `WshShell` object has a method called `Run()` that VBScript can use to execute any Windows command or command line utility. The `ForceLogoff()` subroutine, shown below, takes advantage of both the `Run()` method and `logoff.exe`. When the user logs back in, the changes will be in effect.

```
Sub ForceLogoff()
  WshShl.Run("%SystemRoot%") & "\System32\logoff.exe"
End Sub
```

The Fully Assembled Script

The entire VBScript is assembled below. When run, the VBScript will make the required Windows registry changes and then log the user off.

```
'*************************************************************************
'Script Name: Script 11.2.vbs
'Author: Jerry Ford
'Created: 02/16/03
'Description: This script configures the Windows desktop background and
'screen saver. Then it initiates a system restart.
'*************************************************************************


'Initialization Section

Option Explicit

Dim WshShl, ChangeSettings, shellApp, FsoObject
Set WshShl = WScript.CreateObject("WScript.Shell")
Set FsoObject = CreateObject("Scripting.FileSystemObject")


'Main Processing Section
```

```
'Verify that the user intends to change his or her screen saver settings
ChangeSettings = GetConfirmation()

If ChangeSettings = 6 Then
  CopyCorpLogo()
  SetBackground()
  SetScreenSaver()
  ForceLogoff()
End If

WScript.Quit()



'Procedure Section

'This subroutine copies the CorpLogo.bmp file to D:\Images
Sub CopyCorpLogo()
  If (FsoObject.FolderExists("D:\Images") = false) Then
    FsoObject.CreateFolder "D:\Images\"
  End If
  FsoObject.CopyFile "a:\CorpLogo.bmp", "D:\Images\"
End Sub

'This subroutine prompts for permission to proceed
Function GetConfirmation()
  GetConfirmation = MsgBox("This script will perform the following " & _
    "tasks:" & vbCrLf & vbCrLf & "1. Configure the display of " & _
    "the Corporate Logo the Windows desktop" & vbCrLf & _
    "2. Configure a password protected screen saver" & vbCrLf & _
    "3. Initiate a restart of the computer so that changes " & _
    "may take effect" & vbCrLf & vbCrLf & _
"Do you wish to continue?", 36)
End Function

'This subroutine configures the desktop background
Sub SetBackground()
  'Set CorpLogo.bmp as the desktop wallpaper
  WshShl.RegWrite "HKCU\Control Panel\Desktop\Wallpaper", _
```

```
      "D:\Images\CorpLogo.bmp"

   'Make sure that the Tile option is disabled
   WshShl.RegWrite "HKCU\Control Panel\Desktop\TileWallpaper", "0"


   'Configure the background color to be white
   WshShl.RegWrite "HKCU\Control Panel\Colors\Background", "255 255 255"
End Sub

'This subroutine configures the screen saver
Sub SetScreenSaver()
    'Enable the screen saver
    WshShl.RegWrite "HKCU\Control Panel\Desktop\ScreenSaveActive", 1

    'Enable password protection
    WshShl.RegWrite "HKCU\Control Panel\Desktop\ScreenSaverIsSecure", 1

    'Set up a 15 minute delay
    WshShl.RegWrite "HKCU\Control Panel\Desktop\ScreenSaveTimeOut", 900

    'Enable the Starfield screen saver
    WshShl.RegWrite "HKCU\Control Panel\Desktop\SCRNSAVE.EXE", _
      ("%SystemRoot%") & "System32\ssstars.scr"

End Sub

'This subroutine initiates a system shutdown
Sub ForceLogoff()
  WshShl.Run("%SystemRoot%") & "\System32\logoff.exe"
End Sub
```

Summary

In this chapter, you learned how to programmatically interact with the Windows registry in order to configure desktop wallpaper and screen saver related settings. By using the techniques presented in this chapter, you will be able to write

VBScripts that can configure just about any aspect of a computer running a Windows operating system.

You also learned how to create a desktop URL shortcut and how to work with special folders. In the next chapter, you will get the opportunity to expand upon your knowledge of shortcuts and to use them to configure both the Start menu and the Quick Launch toolbar.

Chapter 12

Customizing the Start Menu and Quick Launch Toolbar

One of Tom's desktop scripting projects at ABC, Inc. is to standardize the look and feel of the Windows desktop on all new computers that he deploys. One of the ways that he plans to accomplish this is by creating a folder called the Standard Applications folder and adding a number of shortcuts to it. These shortcuts will include:

- WinZip
- Adobe Acrobat Reader
- Paint Shop Pro
- An FTP program
- Microsoft Word

This chapter will explain in detail how Windows shortcuts work and how to use the methods and properties belonging to the WSH `WshShortcut` object in order to accomplish this task.

In addition, this chapter will show you how to add menus to the Start menu and how to add menu items to existing menus. Specifically, you will see how to create a submenu under the All Programs menu by adding the Standard Applications folder. The shortcuts in this folder will then function as menu items.

You will also learn how to use shortcuts to manage the configuration of the Quick Launch toolbar. This will include adding shortcuts to the Windows Calculator and WinZip applications. The chapter will conclude by demonstrating how to create two of the scripts required to automate the configuration of computers at ABC, Inc.

Shortcut Construction

Shortcuts provide a tool for organizing access to applications, files, drives, printers and many other Windows resources. Placing shortcuts on the Windows desktop provides quick access to resources that are constantly accessed. However, placing too many shortcuts on the Windows desktop will clutter things up and can be distracting. To prevent this, shortcuts can be added to other convenient locations, such as the Start menu and the Quick Launch toolbar.

NOTE

By default, the Quick Launch toolbar resides just to the right of the Start menu. It provides single-click access to any shortcut that is added to it.

A shortcut represents a link to another Windows resource. By consistently creating and placing shortcuts in the same place on each new Windows XP computer, Tom hopes to begin introducing the idea of desktop standardization to the employees of ABC, Inc.

Figure 12.1 shows a shortcut for the Windows Notepad application.

FIGURE 12.1 *A shortcut to the Notepad application*

You can tell a shortcut apart from the resource that it represents by the presence of a small curved black arrow in the lower left-hand corner of the shortcut's icon. Shortcuts have a number of properties that control their operation. For example, the `Target` property specifies the location and name of the resource that the shortcut represents. To view all the properties associated with a shortcut, right-click on the shortcut and select Properties from the menu that appears. This will open the Properties dialog box for the shortcut and display its Shortcut property sheet. For example, Figure 12.2 shows the properties associated with a shortcut to the Notepad application.

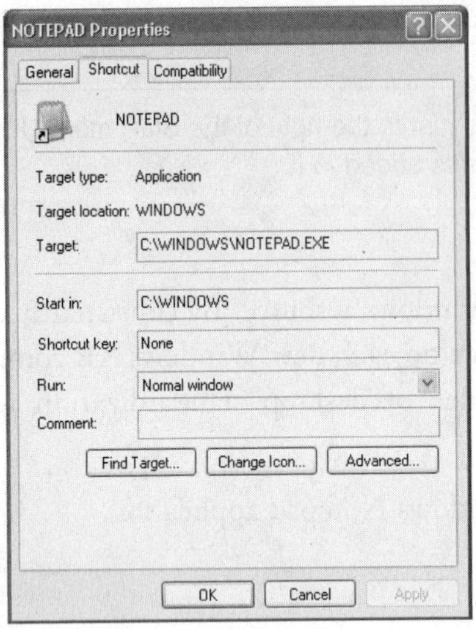

FIGURE 12.2 *Examining the properties of a shortcut to the Notepad application*

Table 12.1 lists and describes all of the properties associated with shortcuts.

Table 12.1 Shortcut Properties

Property	Description
`Target`	Specifies the complete path and file name of the Windows object
`Start in`	Specifies the application's default working directory
`Shortcut key`	Specifies a keyboard keystroke sequence that can be used to open the shortcut
`Run`	Specifies whether the application will be opened in a normal window or in one that is maximized or minimized
`Comment`	Specifies an optional shortcut description
`Icon filename`	Identifies the icon used to represent the shortcut

Working with the WshShortcut Object

To create and manage shortcuts, you will need to learn how to work with the `WshShortcut` object. In addition, you will need to establish a reference to the location where you want to save each shortcut. In order to work with the `WshShortcut` object, you must first instantiate its parent object, the `WshShell`, as shown below.

```
Set WshShl = WScript.CreateObject("WScript.Shell")
```

Before you can proceed with the instantiation of the `WshShortcut` object, you must set up a reference to the location where the shortcut will be saved. For example, to set up a reference to the Windows desktop, you must use the Windows Desktop special folder.

```
DesktopFolder = WshShl.SpecialFolders("Desktop")
```

You can now define the shortcut by using the `WshShell` object's `CreateShortcut()` method to set up an instance of the `WshShortcut` object, as demonstrated below.

```
Set NotepadShortcut = WshShl.CreateShortcut(DesktopFolder & "\\Notepad.lnk")
```

As you can see, the shortcut is defined by concatenating its destination folder to its name (`\\Notepad.lnk`).

NOTE

In the previous chapter, you learned how to work with the `WshUrlShortcut` object. A URL shortcut is created in the same way as a standard shortcut, the only difference being that you specify .url instead of .lnk at the end of the shortcut definition. Specifying .url results in the instantiation of the `WshUrlShortcut` object, and specifying .lnk results in the specification of the `WshShortcut` object.

The next step involved in setting up the shortcut is to specify the Windows resource that the shortcut is to represent. This is done using the `WshShortcut` object's `TargetPath` property, as demonstrated below.

```
NotepadShortcut.TargetPath = "%windir%\Notepad.exe"
```

The final step in the creation of the shortcut is to save the shortcut. This is done using the `WshShortcut` object's `Save()` method:

```
NotepadShortcut.Save()
```

> **NOTE**
>
> The Notepad application resides by default in the `C:\Windows` folder on computers running Windows 98, Me, and XP. However, on Windows 2000 it resides by default in `C:\Winnt`. In addition, it is possible to modify the location of the folder where Windows system files are stored during the installation of the operating system, in which case the Notepad application could reside in an entirely different folder. One way to avoid any confusion and to facilitate the development of a single script that will work on any of these Microsoft operating systems is to take advantage of the `%windir%` environment variable. This variable is automatically created by the operating system. It specifies the location of the Windows system folder, wherever it may reside.

A Desktop Shortcut Example

By using the above statements as a template, it's easy to assemble a VBScript that creates a shortcut to the Notepad application.

```
'*************************************************************************
'Script Name: Script 12.1.vbs
'Author: Jerry Ford
'Created: 02/22/03
'Description: This script creates a desktop for the Windows Notepad
'application
'*************************************************************************


'Initialization Section

Option Explicit

Dim WshShl, DesktopFolder, NotepadShortcut

Set WshShl = WScript.CreateObject("WScript.Shell")


'Main Processing Section
```

```
CreateShortcut()

WScript.Quit()


'Procedure Section

'Create the desktop Shortcut
Sub CreateShortcut()
  DesktopFolder = WshShl.SpecialFolders("Desktop")
  Set NotepadShortcut = WshShl.CreateShortcut(DesktopFolder & _
    "\\Notepad.lnk")
  NotepadShortcut.TargetPath = "%windir%\Notepad.exe"
  NotepadShortcut.Save()
End Sub
```

NOTE

You can also use VBScript to delete Shortcuts. To do so, you need to use the `WshShortcut` object's `Delete()` method as demonstrated below.

```
Set WshShl = WScript.CreateObject("WScript.Shell")
DesktopFolder = WshShl.SpecialFolders("Desktop")
Set FsoObject = CreateObject("Scripting.FileSystemObject")
Set NotepadShortcut = FsoObject.GetFile(DesktopFolder & "\\notepad.lnk")
NotepadShortcut.Delete
```

Modifying Shortcut Properties

The shortcut defined by the previous VBScript was defined using a single `WshShortcut` object property, the `TargetPath` property. As a result, the rest of the shortcut properties either were left undefined or were set using defaults, as shown in Figure 12.3.

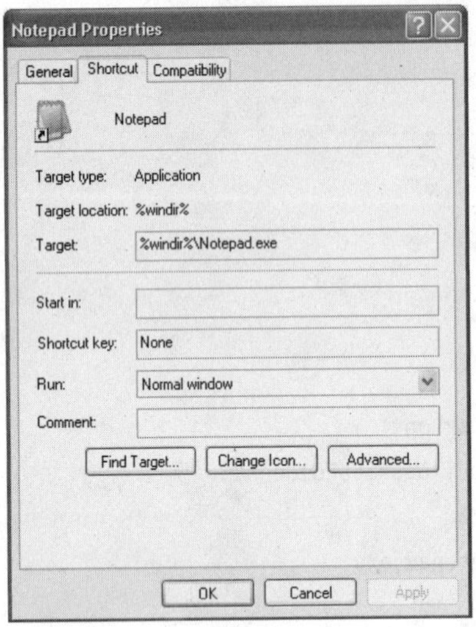

FIGURE 12.3 *Examining the properties assigned to the shortcut for the Notepad application*

As Table 12.2 shows, the `WshShortcut` object provides access to all the properties associated with shortcuts.

Table 12.2 WshShortcut Properties

Property	Description
`Arguments`	Specifies arguments to be passed to the application
`Description`	Specifies a comment
`Hotkey`	Specifies a keystroke sequence that can be used to open the shortcut
`IconLocation`	Specifies the icon to be displayed
`TargetPath`	Specifies the complete path and file name of the object represented by the shortcut
`WindowStyle`	Specifies the window style to be used when the application is started from the shortcut (normal, minimized, or maximized)
`WorkingDirectory`	Specifies the application's default working directory as well as the default location where any output will be saved

Most of these properties are strings that specify a particular piece of information. However, three of these properties require further explanation.

The `WshShortcut` object's `Hotkey` must include a minimum of one modifier key and one key designator. A modifier key can be any of the following:

- **CTRL**. The Ctrl key
- **ALT**. The Alt key
- **SHIFT**. The Shift key
- **EXT**. The Windows logo key

A key designator can be any of the following:

- Letters A–Z
- Numbers 0–9
- F1–F12
- Backspace
- Delete
- Esc
- End
- Spacebar
- Clear
- Tab
- Home
- Enter

The `WshShortcut` object's `IconLocation` is used to specify the index position of an icon to be used to represent a shortcut. Many times a Windows object, such as an application's executable file, contains an indexed list of icons, which can be used to represent the application. For example, Figure 12.4 shows the icons available for the Windows WordPad application. These icons can be viewed by right-clicking on the WordPad application executable's icon, selecting Properties, and then clicking on the Change Icon button on the Shortcut Properties sheet.

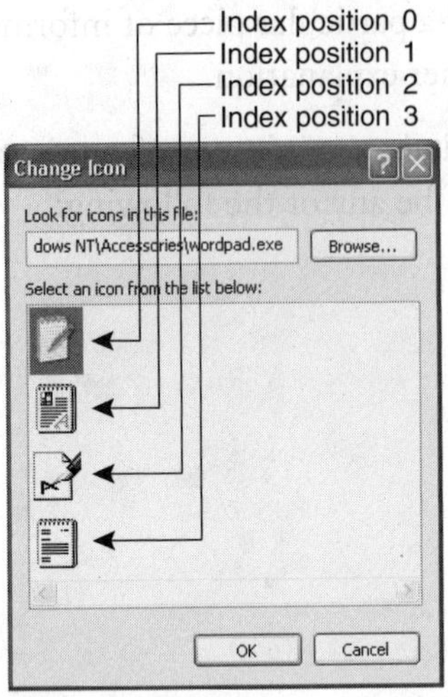

FIGURE 12.4 *Many Windows applications provide an optional indexed list of icons that can be selected*

The `WshShortcut` object's `WindowStyle` is used to specify the type of window that the shortcut should use. Table 12.3 lists the three Windows style types that are supported by the `WshShortcut` object.

Table 12.3 Shortcut Properties

WindowStyle	Description
1	Displays a window by restoring it to its location and size
2	Displays a maximized window
7	Minimizes the window

By setting additional shortcut properties, you can further refine the definition of your shortcuts. For example, the following VBScript is a modified version of the previous example. In addition to creating the Notepad shortcut, this new script sets or modifies a number of additional properties. For example, the value of the `Arguments` property is set to `"D:\DskTpError.log"`. This property specifies a file that is to be opened by the Notepad application whenever the shortcut is used to open it. In addition, the `Description` property is set equal to Desktop Error Log. As a result, this comment will be displayed any time the user moves the pointer over the shortcut. Finally, the `Hotkey` property is set equal to Ctrl+Alt+D. This allows the shortcut to be opened by pressing the Ctrl, Alt, and D keys at the same time.

```
'*************************************************************************
'Script Name: Script 12.2.vbs
'Author: Jerry Ford
'Created: 02/22/03
'Description: This script creates a desktop for the Windows Notepad
'application
'*************************************************************************


'Initialization Section

Option Explicit

Dim WshShl, DesktopFolder, NotepadShortcut

Set WshShl = WScript.CreateObject("WScript.Shell")


'Main Processing Section

CreateShortcut()

WScript.Quit()


'Procedure Section

'Create the desktop Shortcut
Sub CreateShortcut()
  DesktopFolder = WshShl.SpecialFolders("Desktop")
  Set NotepadShortcut = WshShl.CreateShortcut(DesktopFolder & "\\Notepad.lnk")
  NotepadShortcut.TargetPath = "%windir%\Notepad.exe"
  NotepadShortcut.Description = "Desktop Error Log"
  NotepadShortcut.Arguments = "D:\DskTpError.log"
```

```
    NotepadShortcut.Hotkey = "CTRL+Alt+D"
    NotepadShortcut.Save()
End Sub
```

Figure 12.5 shows how the properties are set for the shortcut created by the previous script.

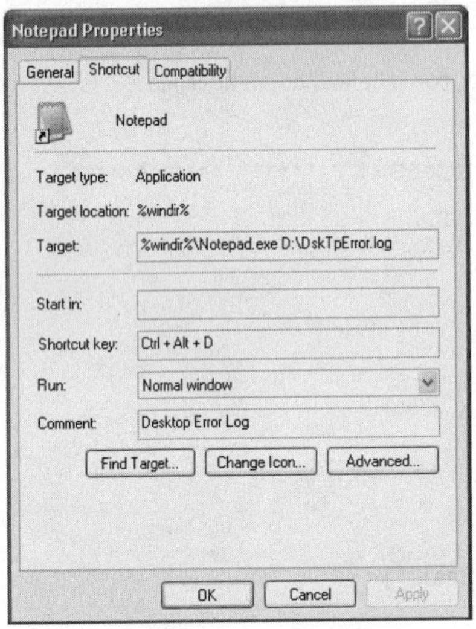

FIGURE 12.5 *Validating property settings for the new shortcut*

Creating a Standard Applications Folder

One of Tom's scripting projects is the development of a Standard Applications folder. Tom plans to create this folder and then populate it with a number of application shortcuts in order to provide quick access to a collection of applications used by everyone in the company.

The first step in writing the script that will perform this task is to create the Standard Applications folder. This can be accomplished using properties and methods associated with the VBScript run-time `FileSystemObject` object.

Scripting Folder Creation

The first step in working with the `FileSystemObject` is to instantiate it, as demonstrated below.

```
Set FsoObject = CreateObject("Scripting.FileSystemObject")
```

Once this is done, you can access all of its properties and methods. You can then use the `FileSystemObject` object's `CreateFolder()` method to create the Standard Applications folder. However, before doing so, it is always a good idea to first verify that the folder does not already exist. You can do this using the `FileSystemObject` object's `FolderExists()` method. The following VBScript statements demonstrate how to test for the existence of the Standard Applications folder and how to create it if it does not already exist.

```
Set FsoObject = CreateObject("Scripting.FileSystemObject")
If (fsoObject.FolderExists("D:\Standard Applications") = false) Then
  Set StndAppsFolder = fsoObject.CreateFolder("D:\Standard Applications")
End If
```

Saving a Shortcut to a Windows Folder

Once the Standard Applications folder is created, you may add shortcuts to it. The following VBScript statements can be added to the end of the previous example to add a shortcut for the Notepad application to the Standard Applications folder.

```
Set WshShl = WScript.CreateObject("WScript.Shell")
Set NotepadShortcut = WshShl.CreateShortcut(StndAppsFolder & "\\Notepad.lnk")
NotepadShortcut.TargetPath = "%windir%\notepad.exe"
NotepadShortcut.Save()
```

Creating and Populating the Standard Applications Folder

The chapter has now covered all of the building blocks required to create the VBScript that creates and populates the Standard Applications folder for ABC, Inc., which is shown below.

```
'*************************************************************************
'Script Name: Script 12.3.vbs
'Author: Jerry Ford
```

```
'Created: 02/22/03
'Description: This script creates a Standard applications folder and
'populates it with a collection of application shortcuts
'*************************************************************************


'Initialization Section

Option Explicit

Dim FsoObject, WshShl, StndAppsFolder, ModelShortcut

Set FsoObject = CreateObject("Scripting.FileSystemObject")

Set WshShl = WScript.CreateObject("WScript.Shell")


'Main Processing Section

CreateStndAppsFolder()
PopulateWinZipShortcut()
PopulatePaintShopProShortcut()
PopulateAdobeAcrobatReaderShortcut()
PopulateWS_FTPShortcut()
PopulateMSWordShortcut()
WScript.Quit()


'Procedure Section

'Look for and if necessary create the Standard Applications folder
Sub CreateStndAppsFolder()
  If (fsoObject.FolderExists("C:\Standard Applications") = false) Then
    Set StndAppsFolder = fsoObject.CreateFolder("C:\Standard Applications")
  Else
    fsoObject.DeleteFolder("C:\Standard Applications")
    Set StndAppsFolder = fsoObject.CreateFolder("C:\Standard Applications")
  End If
```

```
End Sub

'Create and add a WinZip shortcut
Sub PopulateWinZipShortcut()
  Set ModelShortcut = WshShl.CreateShortcut(StndAppsFolder & _
    "\\WinZip.lnk")
  ModelShortcut.TargetPath = "C:\Program Files\WinZip\WinZip32.exe"
  ModelShortcut.Save()
End Sub

'Create and add a Paint Shop Pro shortcut
Sub PopulatePaintShopProShortcut()
  Set ModelShortcut = WshShl.CreateShortcut(StndAppsFolder & _
    "\\Paint Shop Pro.lnk")
  ModelShortcut.TargetPath = "C:\Program Files\Paint Shop Pro\PSP.exe"
  ModelShortcut.Save()
End Sub

'Create and add a Adobe Acrobat Reader shortcut
Sub PopulateAdobeAcrobatReaderShortcut()
  Set ModelShortcut = WshShl.CreateShortcut(StndAppsFolder & _
    "\\Adobe Acrobat Reader.lnk")
  ModelShortcut.TargetPath = _
    "C:\Program Files\Adobe\Acrobat 5.0\Reader\AcroRd32.exe"
  ModelShortcut.Save()
End Sub

'Create and add a WS_FTP LE shortcut
Sub PopulateWS_FTPShortcut()
  Set ModelShortcut = WshShl.CreateShortcut(StndAppsFolder & _
    "\\WS_FTP LE.lnk")
  ModelShortcut.TargetPath = "C:\Program Files\WS_FTP\WS_FTP95.exe"
  ModelShortcut.Save()
End Sub

'Create and add a MS Word shortcut
Sub PopulateMSWordShortcut()
  Set ModelShortcut = WshShl.CreateShortcut(StndAppsFolder & _
```

```
    "\\Microsoft Word.lnk")
  ModelShortcut.TargetPath = _
    "C:\Program Files\Microsoft Office\Office\Winword.exe"
  ModelShortcut.Save()
End Sub
```

The script's `Initialization Section` defines the variables and objects that it will use. The `Main Processing Section` executes a series of procedure calls before finally terminating the script execution using the `WScript` object's `Quit()` method.

The first procedure executed in the `Main Processing Section` is the `CreateStndAppsFolder()` subroutine. It uses the `FileSystemObject` object's `FolderExists()` method to determine whether or not the Standard Applications folder already exists. If it does not, then it is created using the `CreateFolder()` method. If the folder does already exist, then it is deleted using the `DeleteFolder()` method and then recreated, effectively replacing the contents of the folder. The rest of the VBScript's procedures create and add various application shortcuts to the Standard Applications folder.

Configuring the Start Menu and Quick Launch Toolbar

The Start menu is organized as a series of folders with the Start menu as the top of the menu hierarchy. Underneath it is the All Programs menu, which by default contains the Programs folder and shortcuts to several Windows applications, as shown in Figure 12.6.

Each folder located under the Programs folder serves as a menu when viewed from the Start menu, and each shortcut stored on one of these folders serves a menu option. By adding a shortcut to the Standard Applications folder from the Programs menu, you can present users with easy access to their most commonly used applications.

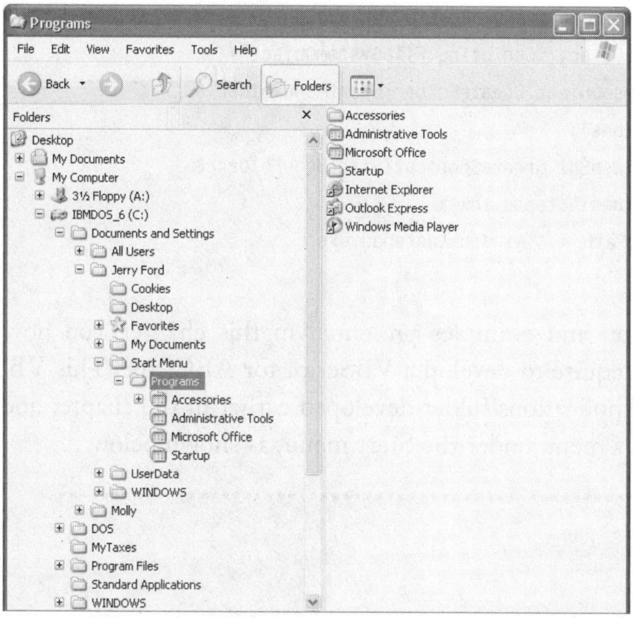

FIGURE 12.6 *Examining the folders and shortcuts stored in the Programs special folder*

Adding a Link to the Programs Folder

In order to programmatically add menus and menu items to the Start menu's All Programs menu, you first need to know how to access it. The following VBScript statements demonstrate how to add a menu entry for the Notepad application on the All Programs menu located on the Start menu.

```
Set WshShl = WScript.CreateObject("WScript.Shell")
StartMenuFolder = WshShl.SpecialFolders("StartMenu")
Set NotepadShortcut = WshShl.CreateShortcut(StartMenuFolder & _
  "\\notepad.lnk")
NotepadShortcut.TargetPath = "%windir%\notepad.exe"
NotepadShortcut.Save
```

In similar fashion, the following VBScript statements demonstrate how to create a Standard Applications folder, add it to the All Programs menu as a submenu, and then add a Notepad shortcut to it.

```
Set WshShl = WScript.CreateObject("WScript.Shell")
```

```
StartMenuFolder = WshShl.SpecialFolders("StartMenu")
Set FsoObject = CreateObject("Scripting.FileSystemObject")
Set StndAppsFolder = fsoObject.CreateFolder(StartMenuFolder & _
  "\Standard Applications")
Set NotepadShortcut = WshShl.CreateShortcut(StartMenuFolder & _
  "\Standard Applications\Notepad.lnk")
NotepadShortcut.TargetPath = "%windir%\notepad.exe"
NotepadShortcut.Save
```

Using the information and examples presented in this chapter, you now have everything that you require to develop a VBScript for ABC, Inc. This VBScript takes the Standard Applications folder developed earlier in the chapter and adds it to the All Programs menu under the Start menu, as shown below.

```
'*************************************************************************
'Script Name: Script 12.4.vbs
'Author: Jerry Ford
'Created: 02/23/03
'Description: This script adds a shortcut to the Standard applications
'folder on the Windows XP All Programs menu
'*************************************************************************


'Initialization Section

Option Explicit

Dim FsoObject, WshShl, StartMenuFolder, StndAppsFolder, StdAppsShortcut

Set FsoObject = CreateObject("Scripting.FileSystemObject")

Set WshShl = WScript.CreateObject("WScript.Shell")


'Main Processing Section

ModifyAllProgramsMenu()

WScript.Quit()
```

```
'Procedure Section

'Add the Standard Applications folders to the All Programs menu
Sub ModifyAllProgramsMenu()
  If (FsoObject.FolderExists("C:\Standard Applications") = false) Then
    MsgBox "Unable to modify All Programs menu - Standard " & _
      "Applications folder not found"
  Else
    StartMenuFolder = WshShl.SpecialFolders("StartMenu")
    Set StdAppsShortcut = WshShl.CreateShortcut(StartMenuFolder & _
      "\\Standard Applications.lnk")
    StdAppsShortcut.TargetPath = "C:\Standard Applications"
    StdAppsShortcut.Save
  End If
End Sub
```

The core logic in this script resides in the `ModifyAllProgramsMenu()` subroutine. It uses the `FileSystemObject` object's `FolderExists()` method to verify that the Standard Applications folder exists. If it does not exist, an error message is displayed. Otherwise a shortcut for the folder is added to the Start menu folder, making it appear under the All Programs menu.

Figure 12.7 demonstrates how the Standard Applications folder will appear once added to the Programs folder belonging to the Start menu.

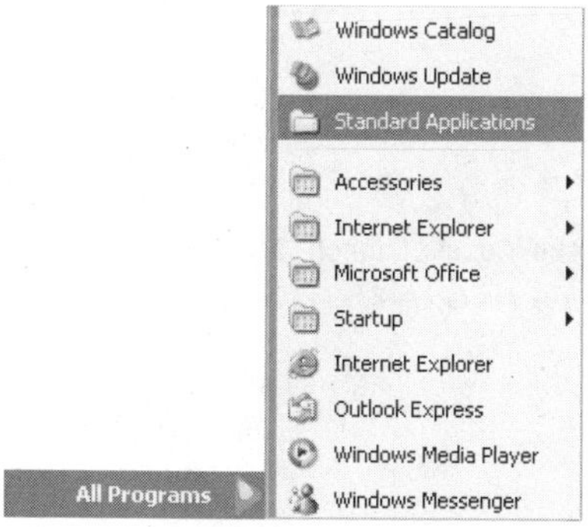

FIGURE 12.7 *Using the Standard Applications folder to add a new menu under the All Programs menu*

Adding Shortcuts to the Quick Launch Toolbar

Another way to provide users with quick access to applications is to add shortcuts to them on the Quick Launch toolbar. The Quick Launch toolbar resides on the Windows taskbar. It provides single-click access to any application that is added to it. By default, Windows XP enables the Quick Launch toolbar and places several icons on it. These icons include those representing Internet Explorer, Outlook Express, and the Windows desktop.

In order to programmatically administer the Quick Launch toolbar, you need to work with the `AppData` special folder. The process of adding shortcuts to the Quick Launch toolbar is a little different than the process of adding them to the Start menu. To add a shortcut to the Quick Launch toolbar, you must specify a reference to the Quick Launch toolbar, which is located within the `AppData` special folder. The following VBScript statements demonstrate how to add a shortcut for the Notepad application to the Quick Launch toolbar.

```
Set WshShl = WScript.CreateObject("WScript.Shell")
QuickLaunchToolbar = WshShl.SpecialFolders("AppData")
ApplicationPath = _
  QuickLaunchToolbar + "\Microsoft\Internet Explorer\Quick Launch"
Set QuickLaunchShortcut = _
  WshShl.CreateShortcut(ApplicationPath + "\\notepad.lnk")
QuickLaunchShortcut.TargetPath = "%windir%\notepad.exe "
QuickLaunchShortcut.Save
```

By expanding on the previous example, you can create the VBScript needed to populate the Quick Launch toolbar for the new computers at ABC, Inc.

```
'*************************************************************************
'Script Name: Script 12.5.vbs
'Author: Jerry Ford
'Created: 02/23/03
'Description: This script adds shortcuts to the Quick Launch Toolbar
'*************************************************************************


'Initialization Section

Option Explicit
```

```
Dim WshShl, QuickLaunchToolbar, ApplicationPath, QuickLaunchShortcut

Set WshShl = WScript.CreateObject("WScript.Shell")


'Main Processing Section

ModifyQuickLaunchToolbar()

WScript.Quit()


'Procedure Section

'Add application shortcuts to the Quick Launch Toolbar
Sub ModifyQuickLaunchToolbar()

  QuickLaunchToolbar = WshShl.SpecialFolders("AppData")
  ApplicationPath = _
    QuickLaunchToolbar + "\Microsoft\Internet Explorer\Quick Launch"

  Set QuickLaunchShortcut = _
    WshShl.CreateShortcut(ApplicationPath + "\\WinZip.lnk")
  QuickLaunchShortcut.TargetPath = "d:\Program Files\WinZip\Winzip32.exe "
  QuickLaunchShortcut.Save


  Set QuickLaunchShortcut = _
    WshShl.CreateShortcut(ApplicationPath + "\\Calculator.lnk")
  QuickLaunchShortcut.TargetPath = "%SystemRoot%\System32\calc.exe"
  QuickLaunchShortcut.Save

End Sub
```

Figure 12.8 shows how the Quick Launch toolbar looks after the two shortcuts have been added to it.

FIGURE 12.8 *Adding shortcuts to the Windows Quick Launch toolbar*

Summary

This chapter showed you how to use the `WshShortcut` object and the VBScript run-time `FileSystemObject` to modify menus and menu options on the Start menu. You learned how to configure a variety of shortcut properties. This chapter also showed you how to manage the configuration of the Quick Launch toolbar. Tom will be able to use the information presented in this chapter to write VBScripts that he'll use to customize the new Windows XP computers being deployed at ABC, Inc.

Chapter 13

Scheduling Disk Maintenance

This chapter addresses Tom's requirements for developing scripts that perform the scheduled execution of two different disk maintenance tasks, disk cleanup and disk defrag. In this chapter, you will learn how to develop scripts that perform these two tasks. You will also learn how to write a setup script that sets up the execution schedule for both disk maintenance scripts.

Working with the Windows Command Prompt

The WSH provides the ability to execute any Windows command or command line utility using the `WshShell` object's `Run()` method. This method runs the specified command or command-line utility as a new process. The `Run()` method has the following syntax:

```
WshShell.Run(Command, [WindowStyle], [WaitState])
```

`Command` identifies the command or command-line utility to be executed and may also include any arguments that need to be passed to the command or command-line utility. `WindowStyle` is an optional parameter that specifies the appearance of the window used to process the command or command-line utility. The value of `WindowStyle` is specified as an integer. Table 13.1 provides a list of the Windows style options supported by the `Run()` method. `WaitState` is an optional Boolean parameter that specifies whether the script will wait on the command or command-line utility to finish executing before continuing to run. Setting `WaitState` to `True` pauses script execution. The default is `False`.

Table 13.1 Run() Method Windows Style Options

Windows Style	Description
0	Hides and deactivates the window
1	Activates and displays a window, restoring it to its original position and size

Table 13.1 Run() Method Windows Style Options (*continued*)

Windows Style	Description
2	Activates the window and minimizes it
3	Activates the window and maximizes it
4	Displays a window using its previous position and size without affecting the currently active window
5	Activates the window, displaying it using its current position and size
6	Minimizes the window and deactivates its focus
7	Displays a minimized window without affecting the currently active window
8	Displays the window using its current position and size without affecting the currently active window
9	Activates and displays the window restoring it to its original position and size
10	Uses the display status of the calling program to display the window

The following example demonstrates how to start the Windows Notepad application from within a VBScript using the `Run()` method.

```
Set WshShl = WScript.CreateObject("WScript.Shell")
WshShl.Run "%windir%\notepad"
```

The next example demonstrates how to start Notepad and pass it the name of a file to open.

```
Set WshShl = WScript.CreateObject("WScript.Shell")
WshShl.Run "%windir%\notepad c:\docs\Activity.doc"
```

This final example demonstrates how to start the Notepad application and have it display a copy of the script that opened it. In order to accomplish this trick, the script uses the `WScript` object's `ScriptFullName` property, which identifies the name of the currently executing script.

```
Set WshShl = WScript.CreateObject("WScript.Shell")
WshShl.Run "%windir%\notepad " & WScript.ScriptFullName
```

Disk Management Utilities and Command-Line Utilities

In recent years, the capacity of hard disk drives has increased greatly. At the same time, the cost of hard drives has been decreasing. As quickly as disk capacity has grown, so have the storage requirements for new applications. As a result, careful disk drive management is an important consideration for many desktop administrators who are wary of continued complaints from the users that they support.

The policy at ABC, Inc. has been to ask all employees to run two Windows disk management utilities at the beginning of each month in order to help manage disk storage on their desktop computers. These utilities are Disk Cleanup and Disk Defragmenter. The Disk Cleanup utility frees up disk space by removing unnecessary files. The Disk Defragmenter reorganizes files that have been stored in fragments on disk drives.

Fortunately, like many Windows utilities, the Disk Cleanup and Disk Defragmenter utilities provide a command-line interface which exposes their functionality and makes it available to the Windows command line. Using the `WshShell` object's `Run()` method, you can execute either of these two utilities from within a VBScript.

Examining the Manual Disk Cleanup Process

Windows applications usually create temporary files while executing. Usually applications clean up these files when they close. However, events such as a system crash or a hung program often leave these files behind, unnecessarily using up disk space.

A computer's performance is directly related to the amount of free space available on its hard disk drives. As drives begin to fill up, a noticeable slowdown in performance will occur. Often the removal of unnecessary files will free up enough disk space to improve performance and prolong the storage capacity of the disk drive.

One way to reclaim lost space is to manually search for and delete unnecessary files. This not only is time consuming, but also opens up the possibility that a critical system or application file may accidentally get deleted in the process. Fortunately, Windows XP provides the Disk Cleanup utility. This utility provides users with a tool for manually tracking down and deleting many types of unnecessary files from their computer. The disk Cleanup utility can be used to delete any of the following types of files:

- Downloaded program files
- Temporary Internet files
- Files found in the Recycle Bin
- Temporary files
- WebClient/Publisher temporary files
- Catalog files for the Content Indexer

The employees at ABC, Inc. have been instructed to run the Disk Cleanup utility at the beginning of every month. Unfortunately, when Disk Cleanup is running, working on the computer is a painful process. Most users have fallen into the habit of either not running it as requested or using it as an opportunity to take extended coffee breaks.

In order to understand how Disk Cleanup works, it is helpful to run it at least once. The following procedure outlines the basic steps involved in performing this process.

1. Click on Start/All Programs/Accessories/System tools and then select Disk Cleanup. If more than one hard disk drive is installed, the Select Drive dialog box will appear, as shown in Figure 13.1.

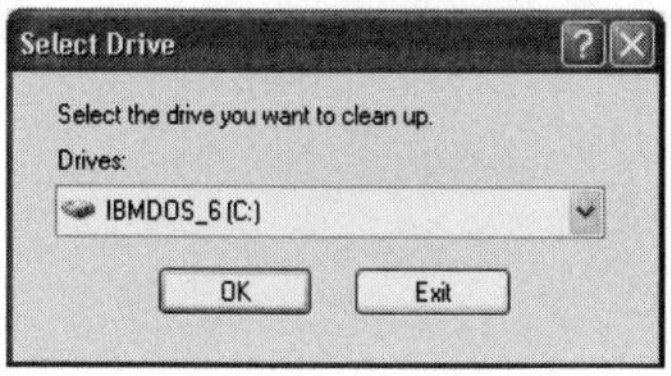

FIGURE 13.1 *Specifying the disk drive to be cleaned up by the Disk Cleanup utility*

2. Select a disk drive and click on OK. The dialog box shown in Figure 13.2 appears. The options that are displayed will vary depending on the drive that is selected.
3. Select the types of file to be deleted and click on OK.
4. Click on Yes when prompted for confirmation.

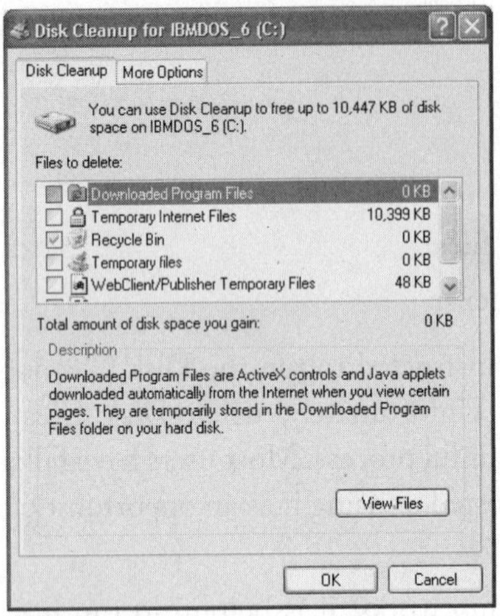

FIGURE 13.2 *Specifying the files to be removed by the Disk Cleanup utility*

> **NOTE**
>
> The Disk Cleanup utility can also be run from the Windows command prompt by invoking its executable. To initiate its execution in this manner, click on Start/Run and then type `cleanmgr` and click on OK.

Configuring Disk Cleanup

After doing some research on the Internet, Tom has learned that the Disk Cleanup utility provides a command-line interface. Therefore, its execution can be initiated by a VBScript. Once scripted, Tom plans to set up an automated execution schedule for the script. This way it can be scheduled to run after hours, when the users are not using their computers.

Before the execution of the Disk Cleanup utility can be automated, it has to be configured. Unfortunately, this is a manual process. But the good news is that it only has to be done once. The following procedure outlines the steps involved in configuring the Disk Cleanup utility.

1. Click on Start and then Run. The Run dialog box appears.
2. Type cleanmgr /sageset:1 as shown in Figure 13.3 and then click on OK.

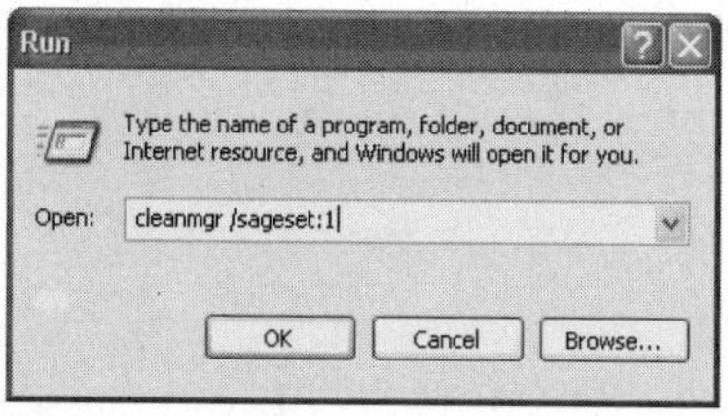

FIGURE 13.3 *Configuring the command-line execution of the Disk Cleanup utility*

3. The Disk Cleanup dialog box appears. Select the options that specify the types of files to be removed and then click on OK.

NOTE

You can create additional `sageset` profiles by specifying a different number. The Disk Cleanup utility will support up to 65,536 difference profiles. By creating two or more difference profiles, you can break up the cleanup process into small chunks and vary the scheduled execution of each profile.

Creating the Cleanup Script

Once the Disk Cleanup utility has been configured to support command-line execution, its execution can be scripted, as demonstrated by the following example.

```
'*************************************************************************
'Script Name: Script 13.3.vbs
'Author: Jerry Ford
'Created: 02/24/03
'Description: This script schedules the execution of the Cleanup utility
'at 20:00 on the first day of each month. This utility removes unnecessary
'files from the local disk drive.
'*************************************************************************


'Initialization Section

Option Explicit
```

```
Dim WshShl, FsoObject, LogFile

Set WshShl = WScript.CreateObject("WScript.Shell")

Set FsoObject = WScript.CreateObject("Scripting.FileSystemObject")


'Main Processing Section

CheckForCleanupLog()

PerformCleanup()

WScript.Quit()


'Procedure Section

'This procedure ensures that a cleanup.log file exists
Sub CheckForCleanupLog()
  If (FsoObject.FileExists("D:\cleanup.log")) Then
    Set LogFile = FsoObject.OpenTextFile("D:\cleanup.log", 8)
    LogFile.WriteLine "Cleanup process Started on " & Date & " at " & Time
  Else
    Set LogFile = FsoObject.OpenTextfile("D:\cleanup.log", 2, "True")
    LogFile.WriteLine "Cleanup process Started on " & Date & " at " & Time
  End If
End Sub

'This procedure executes the cleanup utility
Sub PerformCleanup()
  WshShl.Run "C:\WINDOWS\SYSTEM32\cleanmgr /sagerun:1"
End Sub
```

The `Main Processing Section` executes a subroutine called `CheckForCleanupLog()`, which begins by writing a message to a file named `cleanup.log` on the computer's D:\ drive. This log is used to keep a record of the script's execution, making it easy to later check and see the last time that the script ran. If `cleanup.log` does not exist, which will be the case the first time the script is run, it is created by the statement shown below.

```
Set LogFile = FsoObject.OpenTextFile("D:\cleanup.log", 8)
```

This statement uses the `FileSystemObject` object's `OpenTextFile()` method to open the specified file so that it can be written to. The method is passed two parameters. The first parameter is the name and location of the file, and the second parameter is an integer that specifies how the file is to be opened. The following options are available.

- **ForReading**. As specified by a value of 1
- **ForWriting**. As specified by a value of 2
- **ForAppending**. As specified by a value of 8

Once the file is opened, the subroutine executes the following statement:

```
LogFile.WriteLine "Cleanup process Started on " & Date & " at " & Time
```

This statement uses the `FileSystemObject` object's `WriteLine()` method to write an entire line of text to the file and then performs a line feed and carriage return.

Once a record of its execution has been recorded, the script processes the `PerformCleanup()` subroutine. This subroutine runs the Disk Cleanup utility as shown below. Note that this time the `sagerun` parameter is passed to the `cleanmgr` command-line utility and that the number of the previously configured profiles is provided.

```
WshShl.Run "C:\WINDOWS\SYSTEM32\cleanmgr /sagerun:1"
```

Now that the script has been written, Tom can set up its scheduled execution, as described later in this chapter.

Examining the Manual Disk Defrag Process

Over time, all disk drives fill up. As free space becomes scarce, Windows is forced to begin breaking files up into smaller pieces that are then stored in different locations on the disk drive, wherever space permits. Because the files are not stored in contiguous disk space, it takes longer to read and write to them, thus slowing the computer's overall performance.

In order to limit the amount of fragmentation and keep computers running efficiently, Tom plans on developing a VBScript to automate the execution of the defrag process. Up to this point in time, employees at ABC, Inc. have been responsible for defragging their own hard disk drives using Windows XP's Disk Defragmenter utility. The Disk Defragmenter provides a command-line interface in the form of an executable called `defrag.exe`, thus providing the ability to execute it from the Windows command prompt.

Running the Disk Defragmenter Utility

In order to understand how the Disk Defragmenter utility works, it is helpful to manually run it at least once. The following procedure outlines the basic steps involved in performing this process.

1. Click on Start/All Programs/Accessories/System Tools and then select Disk Defragmenter. The Disk Defragmenter console opens.
2. Select a hard disk drive and click on Analyze to view the fragmentation status of the disk drive, as demonstrated in Figure 13.4.

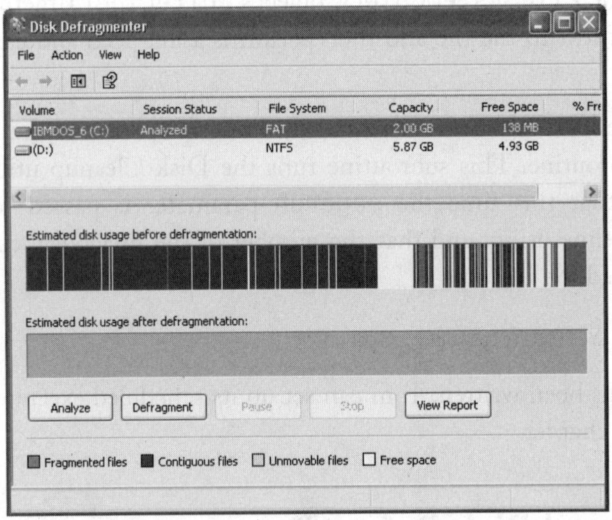

FIGURE 13.4 *Analyzing the fragmentation status of the computer's hard disk drive*

3. Click on Defragment to initiate the defrag process.

4. A pop-up dialog box will appear announcing when the defrag process has completed. Click on Close.

Running Defrag.exe

Using the `defrag.exe` command, you can defrag hard disk drives from the Windows command prompt. The `defrag.exe` command has the following syntax:

```
defrag <volume:> [/a] [/f] [/v]
```

`Volume` specifies the disk drive to be defragged. All remaining parameters are optional. The `/a` parameter displays an analysis of the specified drive's current fragmentation status. By default, `defrag.exe` requires 15 percent of free space on the disk drive in order to execute. The `/f` parameter provides the ability to force the execution of `defrage.exe` when less than 15 percent of free space is available. The `/v` parameter provides for verbose output.

NOTE

Schedule the Disk Cleanup utility to run before `defrag.exe` to ensure that as much free space as possible is available.

The following procedure demonstrates how to run `defrag.exe` from the Windows command prompt.

1. Click on Start/All Programs/Accessories and then Command Prompt. A Windows console opens and displays the Windows command prompt.
2. Type `defrag` *`volume:`* `/a` and press Enter to view an analysis of the specified disk drive.
3. Type `defrag` *`volume:`* `/f` and press Enter to defrag the specified disk drive.

Creating the Defrag Script

The following example demonstrates how to script the execution of the Disk Defragmenter utility.

```
'*************************************************************************
'Script Name: Script 13.2.vbs
'Author: Jerry Ford
'Created: 02/24/03
'Description: This script schedules the execution of the Windows defrag.exe
'at 22:00 on the first day of each month. This utility defrags disk drives.
'*************************************************************************


'Initialization Section

Option Explicit

Dim WshShl, FsoObject, LogFile

Set WshShl = WScript.CreateObject("WScript.Shell")

Set FsoObject = WScript.CreateObject("Scripting.FileSystemObject")


'Main Processing Section

CheckForDefragLog()

PerformDefrag()

WScript.Quit()


'Procedure Section

'This procedure ensures that a defrag.log file exists
Sub CheckForDefragLog()
  If (FsoObject.FileExists("D:\defrag.log")) Then
    Set LogFile = FsoObject.OpenTextFile("D:\defrag.log", 8)
    LogFile.WriteLine "Defrag.exe Started on " & Date & " at " & Time
  Else
    Set LogFile = FsoObject.OpenTextfile("D:\defrag.log", 2, "True")
```

```
    LogFile.WriteLine "Defrag.exe Started on " & Date & " at " & Time
  End If
End Sub

'This procedure executes the defrage.exe command line utility
Sub PerformDefrag()
  WshShl.Run "c:\Windows\System32\defrag C: /f"
End Sub
```

The `Main Processing Section` starts things off by executing a subroutine called `CheckForDefragLog()`. This subroutine works exactly as the similarly named subroutine in the previous cleanup script by creating a log file if it does not already exist and writing a message that records the execution of the script.

Next the `PerformDefrag()` subroutine is executed. This subroutine executes the following statement:

```
WshShl.Run "c:\Windows\System32\defrag C: /f"
```

As you can see, the `WshShell` object's `Run()` method is used to run the `defrag.exe` command, which is passed the `/f` parameter to ensure its execution in the event that the hard disk drive is beginning to run low on space.

Scheduling Script Execution

Windows XP provides a background service called the Task Scheduler as a tool for setting up the scheduled execution of applications, utilities, commands, and scripts. By leveraging the capabilities of this service, you can schedule the execution of scripts at times that are more appropriate and convenient.

Windows XP provides two ways of interacting with the Task Scheduler, as outlined below.

- **`at` command.** A command-line interface that can be used to create and manage scheduled tasks from the Windows command prompt.
- **Scheduled Tasks folder.** A special folder that can be used to view, delete, and configure scheduled tasks. This folder also provides access to the Scheduled Task Wizard, which walks you through the process of manually setting up new scheduled tasks.

NOTE

When you manually run a VBScript, it executes using the security privileges and permissions assigned to your user account. This allows VBScripts to perform any task that you are authorized to complete. However, scripts executed by the Task Scheduler service are run using a different set of security privileges and permissions. By default, the Task Scheduler service is configured to run using the Local System account. This account has limited security access and may not be able to run all of your VBScripts. One way around this dilemma is to associate a user account with a specific script when scheduling it, thus allowing the script to run using that account's security privileges and permissions.

TIP

Another problem faced by scripts run by the Task Scheduler service is that they do not have access to the same execution environment that is available when run by you. For example, if you wrote a script that depends on the existence of a mapped network drive that you set up, the script will fail when run by the Task Scheduler service. Resources such as mapped network connections are associated with individual profiles, which are available to scripts only when run by a logged-on user. One way to work around this type of situation is to provide the script with the ability to set up its own temporary network drive connections, as provided by the `WshNetwork` object's `MapNetworkDrive()` method.

In order to understand how to schedule the execution of your VBScripts using the Scheduled Task Wizard or the `at` command, it is helpful to manually go through the process of using each tool. The next two sections briefly outline the steps involved in manually scheduling the execution of a VBScript using both of these options.

Working with the Scheduled Task Wizard

One of the resources found on the Scheduled Tasks folder is a link to the Scheduled Task Wizard. This wizard guides you through the process of creating new scheduled tasks, as demonstrated by the following procedure.

1. Click on Start/All Programs/Accessories/System Tools and then Scheduled Tasks. The Scheduled Tasks folder opens.

2. Double-click on the Add Scheduled Task icon. The Scheduled Task Wizard appears.
3. Click on Next.
4. A list of Windows XP applications is displayed. Click on Browse, locate your script, and click on Open.
5. Type a descriptive name for the scheduled task, select a time frame for its execution, as shown in Figure 13.5, and click on Next.

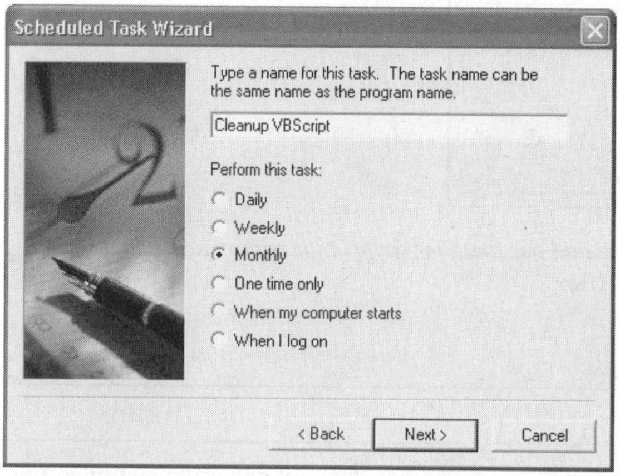

FIGURE 13.5 *Specify an execution schedule for your script*

6. Specify additional execution time frame options, as demonstrated in Figure 13.6, and click on Next. The specific time frame options shown will vary depending on the type of time frame previously selected.

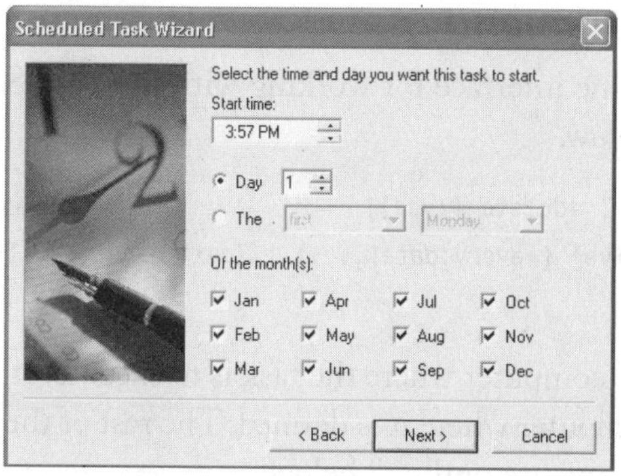

FIGURE 13.6 *Fine-tuning a script's execution schedule*

7. Next, you are prompted to specify an optional user name and password under which the scheduled task can be run, as shown in Figure 13.7. Click on Next.

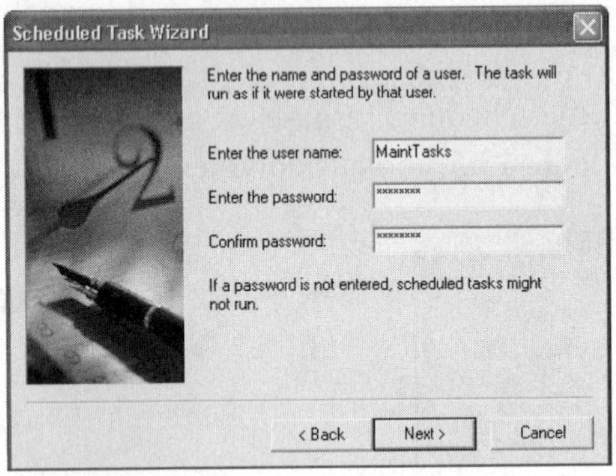

FIGURE 13.7 *Specify a user name and password for scripts that require additional security privileges and permissions in order to execute*

NOTE

You may want to consider creating a special user account with administrative privileges and a nonexpiring password to support the execution of scripts that require greater security access than that provided by the Local System account.

8. Click on Finish. The task that you just created will now be visible on the Scheduled Tasks folder.

Using the Windows at Command

The `at` command is a command-line interface for working with the Task Scheduler service. Its syntax is shown below.

```
at [\\ComputerName] [[id] [/delete] ¦ /delete [/yes]]
at [\\ComputerName] time [/interactive] [/every:date[,...] ¦ /next:date[,...]] command
```

`ComputerName` is the name of the computer where the task is to execute. If omitted, the task will execute on the computer where it is defined. The rest of the parameters supported by the `at` command are outlined below.

- **id.** Specifies the ID number assigned to an existing scheduled task
- **/delete.** Terminates the specified scheduled task
- **/yes.** Requires a confirmation before performing the specified action
- ***Time.*** Specifies the task's execution time using a 24-hour clock (hh:mm)
- **/interactive**. Allows interaction with the logged-on user
- **/every:*date*[,...].** Specifies the tasks execution schedule based on specified days of the week or month; valid dates include M, T, W, Th, F, S, Su or 1–31 and are separated by commas
- **/next:*date*[,...].** Sets the task to execute on the next occurrence of the specified date
- ***Command.*** Identifies the task, application, or script to be scheduled

You work with the `at` command from the Windows command prompt. To view all currently scheduled tasks, type the `at` command and press the Enter key, as demonstrated below.

```
C:\>at
Status ID   Day                     Time          Command Line
-------------------------------------------------------------------------------
        1   Each 1                   8:00 PM      c:\Cleanup.vbs
        2   Each 1                  10:00 PM      c:\Defrag.vbs
```

As you can see, there are currently two scheduled tasks. The first task has been assigned an ID of 1 and the second task has an ID of 2. Both tasks are scheduled to run on the first day of each month, the first at 8 P.M. and the second at 10 P.M.

The following command demonstrates how to set up a third scheduled task that executes every Monday, Wednesday, and Friday at 11 P.M.

```
at 23:00 /every:M,W,F cmd /c "Script 13.1.vbs"
```

If you reissued the `at` command, you would see that the Task Scheduler is now managing three tasks, as shown below.

```
C:\>at
Status ID   Day                     Time          Command Line
-------------------------------------------------------------------------------
        1   Each 1                   8:00 PM      c:\Cleanup.vbs
        2   Each 1                  10:00 PM      c:\Defrag.vbs
        3   Each M W F              11:00 PM      cmd /c "Script 13.1.vbs"
```

The following statement demonstrates how to schedule the execution of a task on a different network computer.

```
\\Desktop10 23:00 /every:M,W,F cmd /c "Script 13.1.vbs"
```

The `at` command also provides the ability to delete scheduled tasks by specifying the task's ID assignment, as demonstrated below.

```
at 3 /delete
```

Creating a Scheduler Script

Once you understand the basic elements of task scheduling, you can develop VBScripts that can interact with and manage the task execution. To accomplish this, you will need to use the `WshShell` object's `Run()` method and the Windows `at` command.

The following example shows the script that Tom developed to schedule the execution of the cleanup and defrag VBScripts.

```
'*************************************************************************
'Script Name: Script 13.1.vbs
'Author: Jerry Ford
'Created: 02/24/03
'Description: This script schedules the execution of the Windows
'Cleanup.exe utility.
'*************************************************************************


'Initialization Section

Option Explicit

Dim WshShl

'Instantiate the WshShell object
Set WshShl = WScript.CreateObject("WScript.Shell")
```

```
'Main Processing Section

ScheduleScripts()

WScript.Quit()


'Procedure Section

'This procedure schedules the execution of other VBScripts
Sub ScheduleScripts()
  'Use the WshShell object's Run() method to run the at command
  WshShl.Run "at 20:00 /every:1 c:\Cleanup.vbs"
  WshShl.Run "at 22:00 /every:1 c:\Defrag.vbs"
End Sub
```

As you can see, the `ScheduleScripts()` subroutine is responsible for scheduling the execution of both scripts.

Configuring the Task Scheduler Service

At this point, Tom has written three VBScripts. One is to automate the execution of the Disk Cleanup utility. Another is to run the `defrag.exe`, and a third script is to schedule the first two scripts. In addition, Tom knows that in order to run the Disk Cleanup script, he must first configure a `sageset` profile for it on each computer.

One last pair of tasks still remains. The default Local System account used by the Task Scheduler service lacks sufficient access privileges and permissions to run either the Disk Cleanup or Disk Defragmenter scripts. In order to run the Disk Defragmenter VBScript, Tom will have to configure the task that runs the script to use a user account with sufficient security privileges and permissions. This account will be named `MaintTasks`. Its creation will be automated in Chapter 15, "Creating Administrator Accounts."

The Disk Cleanup script has a slightly different requirement. Although it does not require administrative privileges in order to run, it must be associated with a specific user account in order to perform certain tasks, such as emptying the user's Recycle Bin.

The following procedure outlines the steps required to associate a user account with an existing scheduled task.

1. Click on Start/All Programs/Accessories/System Tools and then Scheduled Tasks. The Scheduled Tasks folder appears.
2. Double-click on the schedule to open its properties dialog box.
3. Type the name of the account to be associated with the tasks in the Run as field, as shown in Figure 13.8.

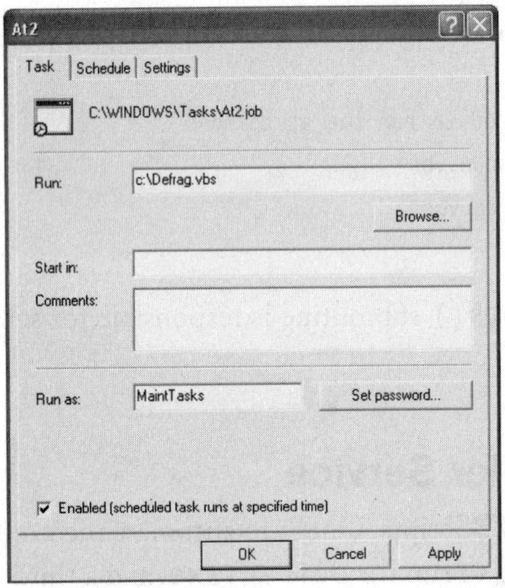

FIGURE 13.8 *Type the name of a user account with sufficient privileges to run the script*

4. Click on Set password, specify the password associated with the user account, and then click on OK.
5. Click on OK to close the Scheduled Task Properties dialog box.

NOTE

Tom will be able to configure and set up both the Disk Defragmenter and Disk Cleanup tasks while setting up the computers in the build area. However, he will have to wait until he delivers the desktops to the users in order to finish configuring the Disk Cleanup task, because he needs the users to log in and type their passwords. Also, unless the users have an account whose password never expires, the users will have to repeat this process whenever they change their passwords. Otherwise, the scheduled tasks will fail the next time the users change their passwords.

Summary

In this chapter, you learned more about the `WshShell` object's `Run()` method. You learned how to use it to create scripts that interact with the Disk Cleanup and Disk Defragmenter utilities, as well as the Task Scheduler service. You also learned how to configure individual scheduled tasks so that they could run using the security privileges and permissions of user accounts other than the Local System account.

Chapter 14

Mapping Network Printers and Disks

It is now time for Tom to begin working on automating the setup of desktop connections to the corporate print server and file server. This requires Tom to learn how to work with the properties and methods associated with the `WshNetwork` object. In addition, Tom will have to determine the best means for deploying and executing his VBScript.

A Change of Plans

Tom's original plan was to develop two separate scripts and to execute them using local Group Policy on each computer as part of the user login process. When implemented locally, Group Policy is administered using *`GPEDIT.MSC`*. `GPEDIT.MSC` is a preconfigured MMC (*Microsoft Management Console*) that contains the Group Policy snap-in.

To implement these scripts in this manner, Tom would open `GPEDIT.MSC` by clicking on Start, Run, typing `GPEDIT.MSC`, and then clicking on OK. This opens the Group Policy folder, as shown in Figure 14.1.

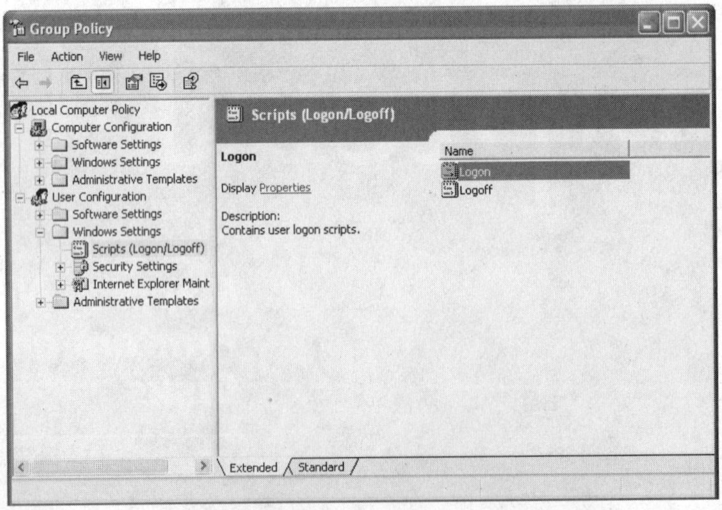

FIGURE 14.1 *Setting Group Policy locally using GPEDIT.MSC*

Script policies are a component of Group Policy. Windows 2000 and XP support the automatic execution of scripts based on four different events, as listed below.

- **Startup**. The script executes using the authority of the Local System account during system startup and before the user is permitted to log in.
- **Logon**. The script executes when the user logs on to the computer using the access rights and permissions assigned to the user.
- **Logoff**. The script executes using the access rights and permissions assigned to the user during the logoff process.
- **Shutdown**. The script executes using the authority of the Local System account as part of the computer's shutdown process.

Group Policy can be configured for both users and computers. Startup and Shutdown scripts apply to computers. Logon and Logoff scripts apply to users. Disk and printer network connections are associated with individual users. By expanding User Configuration\Windows Settings\Script, you can display the Logon and Logoff policies. To add a script to the Logon policy, double-click on Logon. This opens the Logon Properties dialog box, as shown in Figure 14.2. Then click on Add, type the name of the logon script, and click on OK.

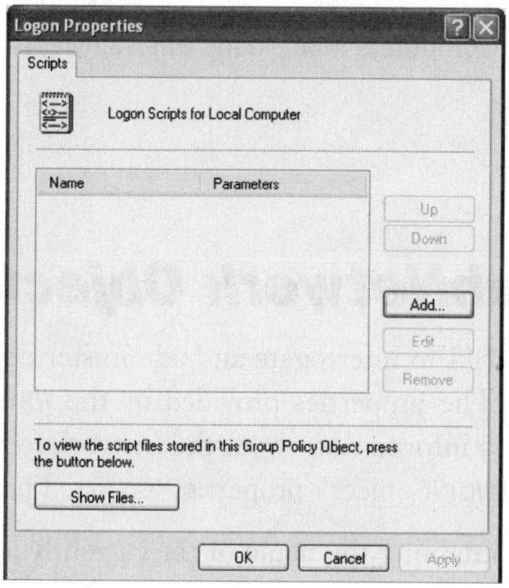

FIGURE 14.2 *Adding a new logon script to Group Policy*

After sharing this plan with Rick and Sue, ABC, Inc.'s two IT analysts, Tom changed his mind. Rick and Sue explained that they could easily take Tom's scripts and use AD (*Active Directory*) Group Policy to implement its execution. This would eliminate the need to configure the scripts to execute on each individual server and allow the scripts to be administered from a single location. In addition, Tom has decided to combine the logic of both scripts into a single script in order to simplify its turnover when he hands it off to Rick and Sue for implementation within AD Group Policy.

NOTE

AD Group Policy provides the ability to implement policy at any of the following levels:

- OU (*organizational unit*)
- Domain
- Site

At the AD level, Group Policy is set from either of two locations:

- **The Active Directory Sites and Services MMC**. Used when setting Group Policy at a site level
- **The Active Directory Users and Computers MMC**. Used when setting Group Policy at the Domain or OU level

Working with the WshNetwork Object

The key to using VBScript and the WSH to interrogate and administer network resources is the `WshNetwork` object. The properties provided by the `WshNetwork` object enable VBScripts to access information about the network to which a computer is connected. The `WshNetwork` object's properties are listed below.

- **`UserName`**. Returns a string containing the name of the currently logged on user
- **`ComputerName`**. Returns a string containing the name assigned to the computer on which the script is executing
- **`UserDomain`**. Returns a string containing the name of the Windows domain to which the user has logged on

The WshNetwork object also provides methods that enable VBScripts to enumerate printers and network drives, establish printer and drive connections, and disconnect existing printer and drive connections. The WshNetwork object's methods are listed below.

- **EnumNetworkDrives()**. Retrieves information about all currently established mapped network drive connections
- **MapNetworkDrive()**. Provides the ability to map connections to network drives using local drive letters
- **RemoveNetworkDrive()**. Disconnects or deletes the specified mapped drive connection
- **EnumPrinterConnections()**. Retrieves information about all currently established printer connections
- **AddPrinterConnection()**. Provides the ability to establish an MS-DOS printer connection
- **AddWindowsPrinterConnection()**. Provides the ability to establish a Windows printer connection
- **RemovePrinterConnection()**. Disconnects or deletes the specified network printer connection
- **SetDefaultPrinter()**. Specifies the printer to which all print jobs are sent by default

Accessing WshNetwork Properties

The properties of the WshNetwork object are read-only, meaning that they cannot be changed by a VBScript. These properties are easily accessible once an instance of the WshNetwork object has been set up. The WshNetwork object is instantiated using the WScript object's CreateObject() method, as shown below.

```
Set WshNet = WScript.CreateObject("WScript.Network")
```

The following example demonstrates how to reference each of the WshNetwork object's properties and to display then in a pop-up dialog box.

```
Set WshNet = WScript.CreateObject("WScript.Network")
MsgBox "UserName:" & vbTab & WshNet.UserName & vbCrLf & _
  "UserDomain:" & vbTab & WshNet.UserDomain & vbCrLf & _
  "ComputerName:" & vbTab & WshNet.ComputerName, ,"Examining WshNetwork Properties"
```

Figure 14.3 demonstrates the output produced by this example when run on a computer named Desktop10.

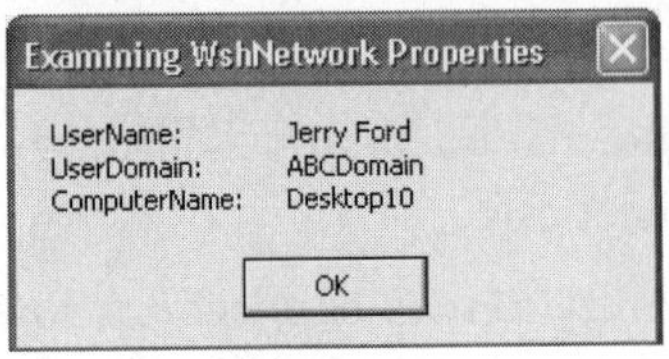

FIGURE 14.3 *Examining WshNetwork properties*

Working with Network Drives

The `WshNetwork` object provides several methods that allow you to enumerate information about currently mapped network drives and to create and disconnect network connections to network drives. Each of these methods is demonstrated in the sections that follow.

Enumerating Network Drives

The `WshNetwork` object's `EnumNetworkDrives` method can be used to retrieve information about all currently established mapped network drive connections. The syntax of the `EnumNetworkDrives` method is shown below.

```
objDriveList = WshNetwork.EnumNetworkDrives
```

`ObjDriveList` is a variable that will store the information returned by the `EnumNetworkDrives` method.

The following example demonstrates how to use the `EnumNetworkDrives` method to display a list of currently mapped network drives in a pop-up dialog box.

```
Set WshNet = WScript.CreateObject("WScript.Network")
Set objMappedDrives = WshNet.EnumNetworkDrives

strDisplayString = "Currently mapped network drives:" & vbCrLf & vbCrLf
```

```
strDisplayString = strDisplayString + "Drive Letter:" & vbTab & "Address" & _
   vbCrLf

For i = 0 to objMappedDrives.Count - 1 Step 2
  strDisplayString = strDisplayString & "Drive " & objMappedDrives.Item(i) & _
  vbTab & vbTab & objMappedDrives.Item(i+1) & vbCrLf
Next

MsgBox strDisplayString
```

The `EnumNetworkDrives` method returns a collection, which the script assigns to `objMappedDrives`. This collection is simply an indexed array that has a zero index. Elements of the array are added in pairs. The first element in each pair stores the drive letter associated with a drive mapping, and the second element stores its network address (in UNC [*Universal Naming Convention*] format). To process all of the contents of the array, a `For...Next` loop is set up. It is assigned a `Step` of `2` in order to facilitate the processing of items, which is done by reference array element in pairs (as `i` and `i + 1`).

Figure 14.4 demonstrates the output produced by the execution of this example.

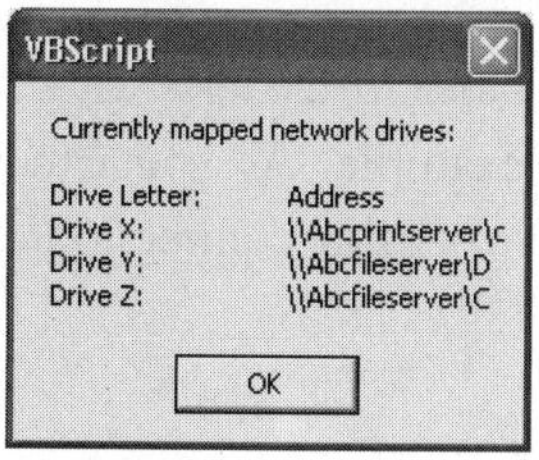

FIGURE 14.4 *Enumerating the list of network drives to which the user is currently mapped*

Mapping a Network Drive

A network drive is a special Windows file sharing service that allows a remote computer to access the contents of a hard disk drive or a directory within a drive via the network. A mapped network drive is a network connection to a network drive. By mapping a connection to a network drive, you make the network drive look and act as if it were a local disk drive. Once connected in this manner, your scripts can read and write to the network drive, assuming that you have the appropriate security access permissions.

The WshNetwork object's MapNetworkDrive method provides the ability to map connections to network drives using local drive letters. The syntax of the MapNetworkDrive method is shown below.

```
WshNetwork.MapNetworkDrive(LocalName, NetworkName, [ChangeProfile],

[UserName], [UserPassword])
```

LocalName specifies the drive letter to be assigned to the drive connection. NetworkName specifies the drive's network name. ChangeProfile is an optional Boolean parameter. When set equal to True, the mapped drive connection is stored in the user's profile. Its default setting is False. UserName is an optional string that specifies a user account name to be used in setting up a mapped drive connection. UserPassword is also optional and is used in conjunction with the UserName parameter to specify the password associated with a specific user account name.

The following example demonstrates how to use this method to set up a connection to a shared drive located on a server called ABCFileSvr.

```
Set WshNet = WScript.CreateObject("WScript.Network")
WshNet.MapNetworkDrive "Z:", "\\ABCFileServer\D"
```

The name of the shared drive is D, and it is assigned a local drive letter of Z:. Figure 14.5 shows the mapped drive created by this example. As you can see, a mapped drive's icon is represented by showing a network cable connection underneath it.

Disconnecting a Network Drive

The WshNetwork object's RemoveNetworkDrive method is used to disconnect or delete a mapped connection to a network drive. The syntax of the RemoveNetworkDrive method is shown below.

```
WshNetwork.RemoveNetworkDrive(Name, [Force], [ChangeProfile])
```

Name identifies the drive letter of the mapped drive to be disconnected. Force is an optional Boolean parameter. When used, Force specifies whether or not the connection is forcefully disconnected (in the event it is currently in use). ChangeProfile is an optional parameter that specifies whether or not the mapped drive should be deleted from the user's profile. The default for this option is False.

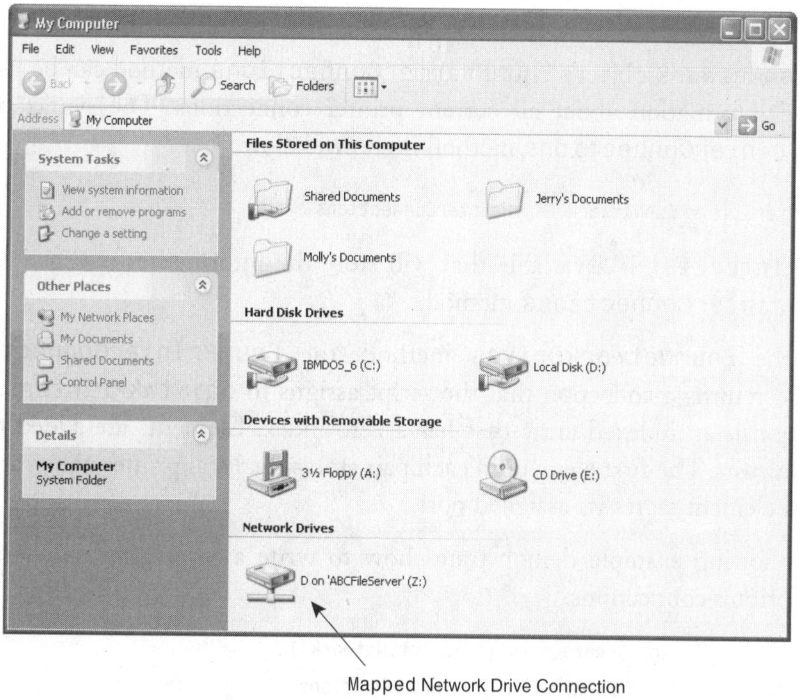

FIGURE 14.5 *Examining the network drive created by the previous example*

The following example demonstrates how to use this method to disconnect the mapped drive set up in the previous example.

```
Set WshNet = WScript.CreateObject("WScript.Network")
WshNet.RemoveNetworkDrive "Z:"
```

Working with Network Printers

The `WshNetwork` object provides several methods that provide the ability to enumerate or discover printers and to create and disconnect printer connections. Each of these methods is demonstrated in the sections that follow.

Enumerating Network Printers

The WshNetwork object's EnumPrinterConnections method can be used to retrieve information about all current printer connections. The syntax of the EnumPrinterConnections method is shown below.

```
objPrinterList = WshNetwork.EnumPrinterConnections
```

ObjPrinterList is a variable that will store the information returned by the EnumPrinterConnections method.

Like the EnumNetworkDrives method, the EnumPrinterConnections method returns a collection that the script assigns to objNtwkPrinters. This collection is an indexed array that has a zero index. Elements are added to the array in pairs. The first element in each pair stores the local printer name, and the second element stores its assigned port.

The following example demonstrates how to write a script that enumerates a user's printer connections.

```
Set WshNet = WScript.CreateObject("WScript.Network")
Set objNtwkPrinters = WshNet.EnumPrinterConnections

strDisplayString = "Currently established network printer connections:" & _
  vbCrLf & vbCrLf

strDisplayString = strDisplayString + "Network printer name" & vbTab & _
  vbTab & "Port:" & vbCrLf

For i = 0 to objNtwkPrinters.Count - 1 Step 2
  strDisplayString = strDisplayString & objNtwkPrinters.Item(i+1) & vbTab & _
  vbTab & objNtwkPrinters.Item(i)  & vbCrLf
Next

MsgBox strDisplayString
```

A For...Next loop is set up to process the contents of the collection. As with the earlier network drive enumeration example, this example uses a Step of 2 to process the contents of the collection (that is, an array) and references each pair of related elements as i and i + 1.

Figure 14.6 demonstrates the output produced by this example.

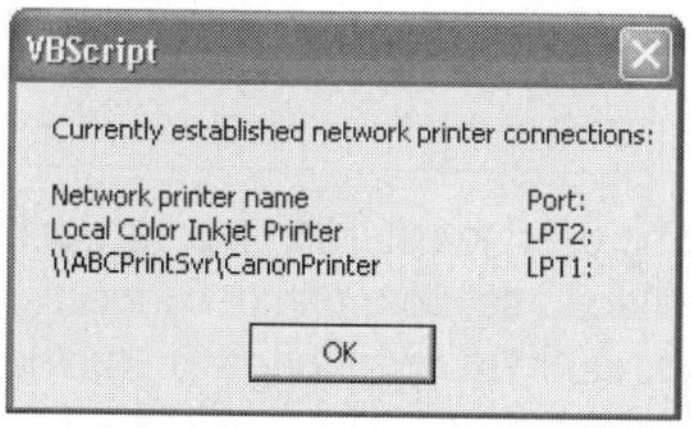

FIGURE 14.6 *Enumerating through the list of printers to which the user is currently connected*

Setting Up a Network Printer Connection

The `WshNetwork` object provides two methods for establishing printer connections. The `AddPrinterConnection` method should be used to set up connections to non-Windows printer connections. The `AddWindowsPrinterConnection` method should be used to set up access to Windows printer connections, which is the case at ABC, Inc.

Using the AddPrinterConnection() Method

The `WshNetwork` object's `AddPrinterConnection` method provides the ability to establish an MS-DOS printer connection. The syntax of the `AddPrinterConnection` method is shown below.

```
WshNetwork.AddPrinterConnection(LocalName, NetworkName [,ChangeProfile] [, UserName]
[,
UserPassword])
```

`LocalName` specifies the name to be assigned to the printer connection. `NetworkName` specifies the printer's network name. `ChangeProfile` is an optional Boolean parameter. When set equal to `True`, the printer connection is stored in the user's profile. Its default setting is `False`. `UserName` is an optional string that specifies a user account name to be used in setting up a network printer connection. `UserPassword` is also optional and is used in conjunction with the `UserName` parameter to specify the password associated with a specific user account name.

TIP

The AddPrinterConnection method should only be used to establish a printer connection with a remote non-Windows-based network printer. To set up a printer connection to a Windows-based network printer, use the AddWindowsPrinterConnection method.

The following example demonstrates how to use the AddPrinterConnection method to set up a network printer connection.

```
Set WshNet = WScript.CreateObject("WScript.Network")
WshNet.AddPrinterConnection "LPT1", "\\ABCPrintServer\LaserPrinter"
```

Using the AddWindowsPrinterConnection() Method

The WshNetwork object's AddWindowsPrinterConnection method provides the ability to establish a Windows printer connection. This method does not require you to specify a specific port to be used in setting up the printer connection. The AddWindowsPrinterConnection method has two different forms of syntax, one of which is applicable to scripts run on Windows 98 and Me, while the second format applies only to Windows 2000 and XP.

The syntax of the AddWindowsPrinterConnection method as applied to scripts running on Windows 98 and Me is shown below.

```
WshNetwork.AddWindowsPrinterConnection(PrinterPath, DriverName [,Port])
```

The syntax of the AddWindowsPrinterConnection method as applied to scripts running on Windows 2000 and XP is shown below.

```
WshNetwork.AddWindowsPrinterConnection(PrinterPath)
```

PrinterPath specifies the path to the printer. DriverName identifies the name of the printer's software driver. Port is an optional parameter that specifies the port to be used in making the printer connection.

NOTE

In order for the AddWindowsPrinterConnection method to work on a computer running Windows 98 or Me, the printer software driver must be preinstalled on the computer, otherwise an error will occur.

The following example demonstrates how to use the `AddWindowsPrinterConnection` method to set up a printer connection on a computer running Windows 98 or Me.

```
Set WshNet = WScript.CreateObject("WScript.Network")
WshNet.AddWindowsPrinterConnection _

  "\\ABCPrintServer\LaserPrinter", "HP DeskJet 710C"
```

The following example demonstrates how to use the `AddWindowsPrinterConnection` method to set up a printer connection on a computer running Windows 2000 or XP.

```
Set WshNet = WScript.CreateObject("WScript.Network")
WshNet.AddWindowsPrinterConnection "\\ABCPrintServer\LaserPrinter"
```

Removing a Network Printer Connection

The `WshNetwork` object's `RemovePrinterConnection` method provides the ability to disconnect an existing network printer connection. The syntax of the `RemovePrinterConnection` method is shown below.

```
WshNetwork.RemovePrinterConnection(PrinterName, [Force], [ChangeProfile])
```

`PrinterName` is a string specifying the name of the printer connection to be deleted. `PrinterName` can be specified using either of the following formats.

- UNC name (\\ComputerName\PrinterName)
- Port (LPT1, LPT2, and so on)

`Force` is an optional Boolean value that specifies whether or not the printer connection should be forcefully removed (in the event that the connection is currently in use). The default value is set to `False`.

`ChangeProfile` is an optional Boolean value that specifies whether the change should be made to the user's profile (for example, saved across login sessions). The default value is set to `False`.

The following example demonstrates how to use the `RemovePrinterConnection` method to disconnect the printer connection set up in the previous example.

```
Set WshNet = WScript.CreateObject("WScript.Network")
WshNet.RemovePrinterConnection "\\ABCPrintServer\LaserPrinter"
```

Establishing a Default Printer

The `WshNetwork` object's `SetDefaultPrinter` method can be used to specify the printer to which all print jobs will be submitted by default. The syntax of the `SetDefaultPrinter` Method is shown below.

```
WshNetwork.SetDefaultPrinter(PrinterName)
```

`PrinterName` is the name of the printer to be made the default printer. Its value is specified using its UNC name.

The following example demonstrates how to modify the previous example in order to make the new network printer the default.

```
Set WshNet = WScript.CreateObject("WScript.Network")
WshNet.AddWindowsPrinterConnection "\\ABCPrintServer\LaserPrinter"
WshNet.SetDefaultPrinter "\\ABCPrintServer\LaserPrinter"
```

Creating a Login Script

As mentioned at the beginning of this chapter, Tom has decided to combine the tasks of setting up the network drive and printer connections into a single script. Once the script is finished, he will hand it off to Rick and Sue for implementation using AD Group Policy. Rick and Sue will then set Tom's VBScript up as a login script, thus ensuring that it will execute as part of each user's login process.

The Initialization Section

This script begins by defining the variables and objects that the script will require to execute. In addition to using `Option Explicit`, the `On Error Resume Next` statement has been added. This allows the script to continue processing in the event that a network resource is temporarily unavailable. The script will be written to create its mapped network drive connection before moving on to create its printer connection. The `On Error Resume Next` statement will allow the script to continue running in the event that the network drive is unavailable. It will also lessen user confusion by preventing the display of error messages during login.

```
Option Explicit
```

```
On Error Resume Next

Dim WshNet, strDriveLetter, strNetworkDrive, strNetworkPrinter, FsoObject
Dim strUserName

Set WshNet = WScript.CreateObject("WScript.Network")

Set FsoObject = CreateObject("Scripting.FileSystemObject")

strDriveLetter = "Z:"
strNetworkDrive = "\\ABCFileSvr\D"
strCopyRoomPrinter = "\\ABCPrintSvr\HPLaserPrinter"
strMgmtPrinter = "\\ABCPrintSvr\CanonColorPrinter"
```

In addition to defining an instance of the `WshNetwork` and `FileSystemObject` objects, the `Initialization Section` assigns values to four variables that specify the drive letter, network drive address, and the network addresses of the company's two network printers. The network printer assigned to the `strCopyRoomPrinter` variable will be set up as the network printer connection on all computers used by nonmanagers, whereas the `strMgmtPrinter` variable will be used to set up a network printer connection on all computers used by company managers.

The Main Processing Section

The VBScript `Main Processing Section` consists of a series of subroutine calls, as shown below.

```
DisplayNetworkData()

MapNetworkDrive strDriveLetter, strNetworkDrive

strUserName = WshNet.UserName

If Left(strUserName, 1) = "A" Then
  SetupPrinterConnection strCopyRoomPrinter
  SetDefaultPrinter strCopyRoomPrinter
  MsgBox "Copy Room Printer connected!"
Else
```

```
  SetupPrinterConnection strMgmtPrinter
  SetDefaultPrinter strMgmtPrinter
  MsgBox "Mgmt Printer connected!"
End If

WScript.Quit()
```

When this script runs, the user will see a command console appear on the desktop. The `DisplayNetworkData()` subroutine displays information about the user's network connection. Next, the `MapNetworkDrive()` subroutine is executed. It is responsible for mapping the connection to the company's file server. The UNC address of the network file server is passed to the subroutine for processing.

Then the `strUserName` variable is assigned the username of the person logging on to the computer. Each user at ABC, Inc. is assigned a username that is created based on the following guidelines:

- The first character of the username is an *M* for managers or *A* for other associates.
- The next three letters of the username are the first letters of the user's first, middle, and last names.
- The last two characters of the username are a number used to differentiate between two users with the same initials.

If the first character of the username is an *A*, then a connection is set up for the printer represented by the `strCopyRoomPrinter` variable. That printer is then set up as the user's default printer. Otherwise a connection is set up to the printer represented by the `strMgmtPrinter` variable and this printer is made the default printer.

Once both the network drive and printer connections have been established, the script executes the `WScript` object's `Quit()` method to cleanly terminate the script's execution.

The DisplayNetworkData() Subroutine

The `DisplayNetworkData()` subroutine displays information about the user's network connection, as shown below. This information displayed inside the Windows console will briefly appear on the user's desktop while the login script executes.

```
Sub DisplayNetworkData()
  WScript.Echo "Now configuring network drive and printer connections for:"
```

```
  WScript.Echo "Computer name: " & WshNet.ComputerName
  WScript.Echo "Domain name:   " & WshNet.UserDomain
  WScript.Echo "User name:     " & WshNet.UserName
End Sub
```

The MapNetworkDrive() Subroutine

The `MapNetworkDrive()` subroutine processes two input arguments, the drive letter to use when setting up the drive mapping and the UNC of the network drive. It begins by determining whether or not the network drive is available. If it is not then a message is displayed to that effect. If it is available, then a check is made to determine whether or not the drive letter to be used in setting up the network drive connection is already in use. If it is, then its connection is deleted. The new network connection is established.

```
Sub MapNetworkDrive(strLetter, strDrive)
  If FsoObject.DriveExists(strDrive) Then
    If FsoObject.DriveExists(strLetter) Then
      WshNet.RemoveNetworkDrive strLetter
    End If
    WScript.Echo "Mapping drive to " & strDrive & " as drive letter " & _
      strLetter
    WshNet.MapNetworkDrive strLetter, strDrive
  Else
    WScript.Echo "Unable to map to network drive " & strDrive & _
      ". Resource not available"
  End If
End Sub
```

The SetupPrinterConnection() Subroutine

The `SetupPrinterConnection()` subroutine displays a message documenting its execution and then uses the UNC of the printer passed to it as an argument to establish the connection to the network printer.

```
Sub SetupPrinterConnection(strPrinter)
  WScript.Echo "Connecting to network printer " & strPrinter
  WshNet.AddWindowsPrinterConnection strPrinter
End Sub
```

The SetDefaultPrinter() Subroutine

The `SetDefaultPrinter()` subroutine displays a message documenting its execution and then uses the UNC of the printer passed to it as an argument to set the network printer up as the user's default printer.

```
Sub SetDefaultPrinter(strPrinter)
  WScript.Echo "Setting connection to network printer " & strPrinter & _
    " as default"
  WshNet.SetDefaultPrinter strPrinter
End Sub
```

The Fully Assembled Script

The entire VBScript is assembled below. It will run as a script policy under the control of Active Directory when the user logs in. It will establish a standardized collection of network connections, thus ensuring that all users have the same base set of network connections. Figure 14.7 shows the Windows console that will briefly appear on the user's desktop when the script executes.

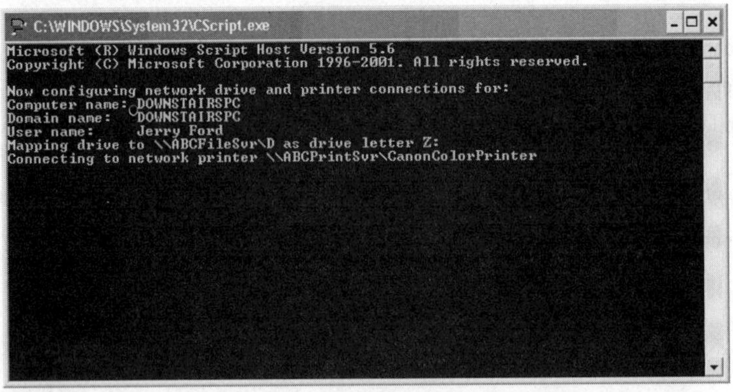

FIGURE 14.7 *The login script displays information about the user's network connection as part of the network connection configuration process*

```
'*************************************************************************
'Script Name: Script 14.1.vbs
'Author: Jerry Ford
'Created: 02/23/03
```

```
'Description: This script will be used as a login script at ABC
'Inc to configure network printer and network drive access
'*************************************************************************


'Initialization Section

Option Explicit

On Error Resume Next

Dim WshNet, strDriveLetter, strNetworkDrive, strNetworkPrinter, FsoObject
Dim strUserName

Set WshNet = WScript.CreateObject("WScript.Network")

Set FsoObject = CreateObject("Scripting.FileSystemObject")

strDriveLetter = "Z:"
strNetworkDrive = "\\ABCFileSvr\D"
strCopyRoomPrinter = "\\ABCPrintSvr\HPLaserPrinter"
strMgmtPrinter = "\\ABCPrintSvr\CanonColorPrinter"

'Main Processing Section

DisplayNetworkData()

MapNetworkDrive strDriveLetter, strNetworkDrive

strUserName = WshNet.UserName

If Left(strUserName, 1) = "A" Then
  SetupPrinterConnection strCopyRoomPrinter
  SetDefaultPrinter strCopyRoomPrinter
Else
  SetupPrinterConnection strMgmtPrinter
  SetDefaultPrinter strMgmtPrinter
End If
```

```
WScript.Quit()


'Procedure Section

'Display network information
Sub DisplayNetworkData()
  WScript.Echo "Now configuring network drive and printer connections for:"
  WScript.Echo "Computer name: " & WshNet.ComputerName
  WScript.Echo "Domain name:   " & WshNet.UserDomain
  WScript.Echo "User name:     " & WshNet.UserName
End Sub

'Map a drive to the Corporate network drive
Sub MapNetworkDrive(strLetter, strDrive)
  If FsoObject.DriveExists(strDrive) Then
    If FsoObject.DriveExists(strLetter) Then
      WshNet.RemoveNetworkDrive strLetter
    End If
    WScript.Echo "Mapping drive to " & strDrive & " as drive letter " & _
      strLetter
    WshNet.MapNetworkDrive strLetter, strDrive
  Else
    WScript.Echo "Unable to map to network drive " & strDrive & _
      ". Resource not available"
  End If
End Sub

'Set up a connection to the corporate network printer
Sub SetupPrinterConnection(strPrinter)
  WScript.Echo "Connecting to network printer " & strPrinter
  WshNet.AddWindowsPrinterConnection strPrinter
End Sub

'Set up the network printer connection as the user's default printer
Sub SetDefaultPrinter(strPrinter)
  WScript.Echo "Setting connection to network printer " & strPrinter & _
```

```
    " as default"
  WshNet.SetDefaultPrinter strPrinter
End Sub
```

Summary

In this chapter, you learned how to work with the WshNetwork object. This included learning how to write a login script that sets up connections to network drives and printers. You also learned how to apply Group Policy locally on a computer running Windows XP Professional. In addition, you were presented with a basic overview of AD Group Policy.

Chapter 15

Creating Administrator Accounts

The final desktop setup task that Tom wants to tackle is the automated creation of two user accounts. One of these accounts will be used as an emergency account that will provide Tom with the ability to locally log on to a user's computer in the event that a problem occurs. The other account will be used to configure scheduled tasks, such as the execution of the defrag script, that require administrative level privileges in order to execute.

Creating a Local Administrator Account

Tom's final scripting assignment is to develop a script that will create the following user accounts:

- **ADMA01**. A local desktop management account that is a member of the local administrators group. Tom will use this account only in the event that he needs to locally log on to the computer to resolve a problem or perform emergency maintenance.
- **ASAT01**. A local scheduling account that is a member of the local administrators group, giving the account sufficient security privileges to run any script set up as a scheduled task.

Tom plans to write down the passwords associated with these two accounts (on a computer-by-computer basis) and to store them in sealed envelopes that he will lock up in the corporate safe, where they can be retrieved in an emergency.

NOTE

In order to administer user accounts, Tom must have administrative privileges within the context of the environment in which he is working. In other words, Tom must be a member of the local administrators group on the computer on which he is creating the new accounts. Likewise, to administer domain user accounts, Tom would have to be a member of the domain administrators group. Since these are new computers that are right out of the box, Tom will use the built-in administrators account to set everything up and run his desktop management configuration scripts.

Options for Manually Creating New User Accounts

Windows XP Professional provides Tom with two different utilities that can be used to create local user accounts. These utilities are listed below.

- The User Accounts folder
- The Local Users and Groups snap-in

The User Accounts folder is found on the Windows XP Control Panel. It provides only limited control over the creation of a new account. It can be used to create, modify, and delete user accounts but has only limited control over account features such as the assignment of group membership. The Local Users and Groups snap-in can be found in the Computer Management console. The Computer Management console is a built-in MMC (*Microsoft management console*) that can be used to perform a number of computer administration tasks, including user account creation and management.

Using the Local User and Groups Snap-In

Ordinarily, Tom would create the desktop management and schedule administrative accounts by hand using the Local Users and Groups snap-in. The following procedure outlines the steps that Tom goes through when manually creating the local ADMA01 desktop management account using this snap-in. This same procedure can also be used to create the local ASAT01 scheduling account.

1. Click on Start, right-click on My Computer, and select Manage. The Computer Management console opens, as shown in Figure 15.1.

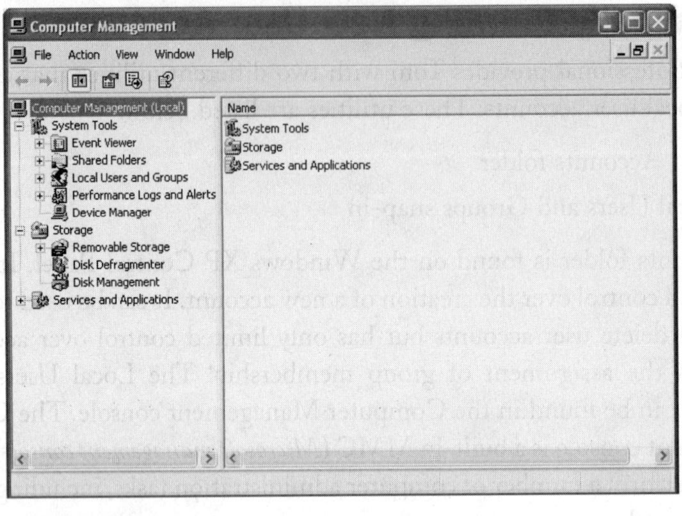

FIGURE 15.1 *Using the Computer Management console to manually administer user accounts*

2. If necessary, expand the System Tools node in the console tree.
3. Expand the Local Users and Groups node.
4. Select the Users node. A list of user accounts defined in the computer's local security database is displayed in the right-hand pane of the Computer Management console, demonstrated in Figure 15.2.

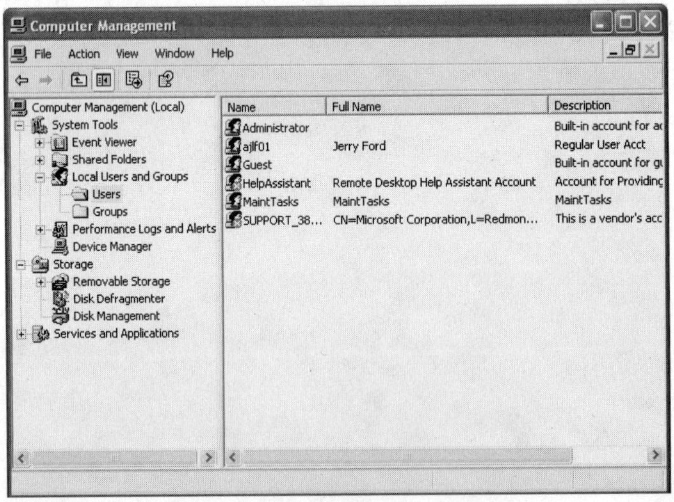

FIGURE 15.2 *Examining currently defined user accounts on the Windows XP computer*

5. Right-click on Users and select New User. The New User dialog box opens, as shown in Figure 15.3.

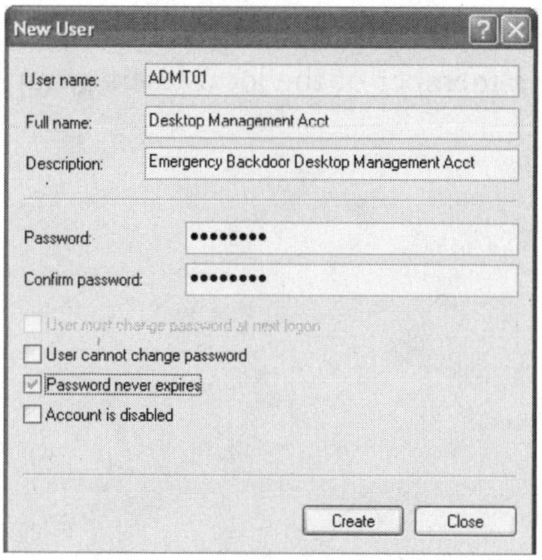

FIGURE 15.3 *Assign a username and password to the new user account*

6. Type ADMT01 in the User name field. Type Desktop Management Acct in the Full name field, Emergency Backdoor Desktop Management Acct in the Description field, and a password in the Password and Confirm password fields.

NOTE

Tom assigns different passwords to each account and never uses the same passwords again on other computers. To ensure that he is creating a strong password, he always makes them 10 characters long, never uses words or phrases, and always includes a combination of numbers, special characters, and uppercase and lowercase letters.

7. Select Password never expires to prevent the account's password from expiring and locking the account until its password is changed.
8. Click on Create and then Close.

9. The new account will appear in the right-hand pane of the Computer Management console. Right-click on it and then select Properties. The account's properties dialog box appears.
10. Select the Member of property sheet, as shown in Figure 15.4. By default the new account is made a member of the local Users group.

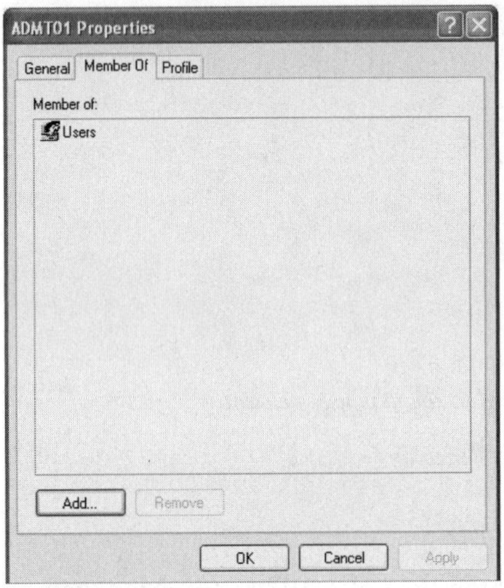

FIGURE 15.4 *Examining the new account's group memberships*

11. Click on Add. The Select Groups dialog box appears.
12. Click on Advanced. The Select Groups dialog box expands to show additional options.
13. Click on Find Now. A list of local group accounts will be displayed, as shown in Figure 15.5. Table 15.1 lists and describes the built-in local groups listed in Figure 15.5.

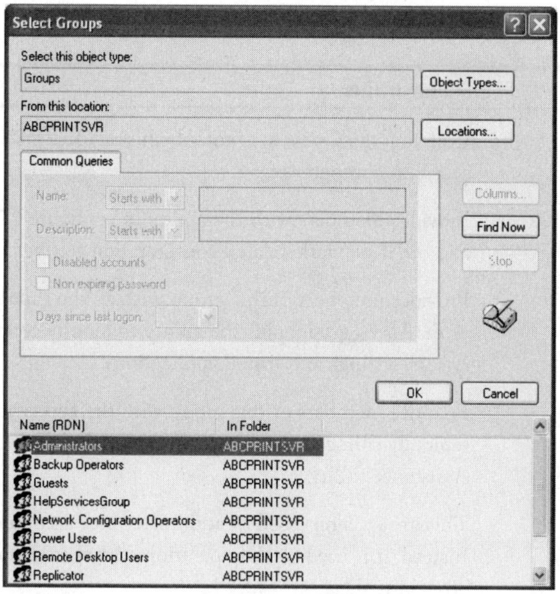

FIGURE 15.5 *Locating local group accounts to which the user account may be added*

14. Select the Administrators group and click on OK twice.
15. The local Administrators group is now displayed as one of the groups to which the account has been added. Click on OK.
16. Close the Computer Management console.

Table 15.1 provides a complete list of Windows XP Professional's built-in collection of local group accounts.

Table 15.1 Windows XP Professional's Built-in Local Group Accounts

Local Group Account	Description
Administrators	Provides its members with control over all computer resources as well as the ability to perform any Windows administration task.
Backup Operators	Provides its members with the ability to back up and restore all files stored on the computer.

(continues)

Table 15.1 Windows XP Professional's Built-in Local Group Accounts (*continued*)

Local Group Account	Description
Guests	Contains the Guest account which provides very limited access to computer resources.
Network Configuration Operators	Provides members with the ability to configure TCP/IP and other network-related configuration settings.
Power Users	Provides members of this group with all the capabilities of the Users group, plus the ability to modify certain system settings and install applications.
Remote Desktop Users	Provides members of this group with the ability to remotely connect to the computer using the Remote Assistance utility.
Replicator	This group is not used to administer user accounts. Instead, it is used by the operation system to support domain replication.
Users	Provides members of this group with the ability to run applications, work with files, submit print jobs, turn off the computer, and perform an assortment of nonadministrative tasks.
HelpServicesGroup	This group is not used to administer user accounts. Instead it is used by the operating system to support the Help and Support Center service.

Net Commands

In researching his options for scripting the creation of local user accounts on computers running Windows XP Professional, Tom determined that he wanted to use either the Windows XP `Net User` command or the Windows XP Resource Kit's `Addusers` command-line utility.

The `Addusers` command-line utility provides the ability to create new accounts and configure account passwords as nonexpiring. Unfortunately, when Tom requested the funds to purchase the Windows XP Resource Kit, he was told that given the capital outlay the company has already committed to upgrading its desktop infrastructure, there were not additional funds available at this time.

Net User

Tom's plan is to use the WshShell object's Run() method to execute the Windows XP Net User command and automate the creation of the two new user accounts. The Net User command can be used in several different ways. The syntax for each of the forms of the Net User command is outlined below.

```
net user [username [password ¦ *] [options]] [/domain]
net user [username {password ¦ *} /add [options] [/domain]
net user [username [/delete] [/domain]
```

When Net User is executed without arguments, it displays a list of user accounts on the local computer. Username specifies the account name to be added, deleted, modified, or viewed. Password is used to assign a password to a new account or change the password of an existing account. The asterisk symbol * prompts for the password. The /domain parameter causes the account to be created on the domain that is currently logged on. The /add parameter defines an add operation and the /delete parameter defines a delete operation. Finally, the options parameter specifies a list of one or more optional subparameters that sets specific account attributes. Table 15.2 defines the list of parameters that are available as options for the Net User command.

Table 15.2 Net User Command Options

Parameter	Description
/active:{no ¦ yes}	Enables or disables the account
/comment:"*text*"	Adds comments to an account
/countrycode:*nnn*	Specifies the Country/Region codes to be used for help and error messages
/expires:{*date* ¦ never}	Specifies the status of account expiration
/fullname:"*name*"	Sets a user's full name rather than a username
/homedir:*path*	Establishes the user's home directory
/passwordchg:{yes ¦ no}	Determines whether the user can change a password
/passwordreq:{yes ¦ no}	Specifies a password requirement
/profilepath:[*path*]	Establishes the user's logon profile

(continues)

Table 15.2 Net User Command Options (*continued*)

Parameter	Description
`/scriptpath:path`	Establishes the path for the user's logon script
`/times:{times ¦ all}`	Defines time frames in which the user is permitted to use the computer, for example: W,8AM-5PM; F,8AM-1PM
`/usercomment:"text"`	Determines whether an administrator can change or add to the user comment
`/workstations: {computername[,...] ¦ *}`	Specifies up to eight workstations where the user is permitted to log on

The following VBScript statements demonstrate how to use the `Net User` command to automate the creation of a user account named `TestAcct` and assign it an initial password of `Wql#5?yi`.

```
Set WshShl = WScript.CreateObject("WScript.Shell")
WshShl.Run "net user TestAcct Wql#5?yi /add", 0
```

Similarly, the same account could have been defined at a Windows domain level by adding the `/domain` parameter, as demonstrated below.

```
Set WshShl = WScript.CreateObject("WScript.Shell")
WshShl.Run "net user TestAcct Wql#5?yi /add /domain", 0
```

Unfortunately, the `Net User` command has one drawback. You cannot use it to create or configure user accounts with passwords that do not expire. This will cause a problem for Tom because these passwords assigned to the ADMA01 and ASAT01 accounts will eventually expire, in effect disabling the accounts until Tom changes their passwords. Although this will not impact the usefulness of the desktop management account, it affects the scheduler account and can cause the defrag script to fail when it executes. To get around this issue, Tom will have to manually modify the user account to set its password to nonexpiring after the script has created it.

Net Localgroup

In addition to the `Net User` command, which provides the ability to create, modify, and delete local and domain user accounts, Tom needs a way to automate the addition of user accounts to the local administrators group. After looking around, he has discovered that he can use another Windows command to perform this task. This command is the `Net Localgroup` command, which provides the ability to add user accounts to local groups on both the local computer and a Windows domain.

NOTE

Group accounts provide a way to easily manage large numbers of user accounts. When an account is made a member of a group account it inherits all the security permissions and rights assigned to that group.

The `Net Localgroup` command can be used in several different ways. The syntax for each of these forms of the `Net Localgroup` command is outlined below.

```
net localgroup [groupname [/comment:"text"]] [/domain]
net localgroup groupname {/add [/comment:"text"] ¦ /delete} [/domain]
net localgroup groupname name [ ...] {/add ¦ /delete} [/domain]
```

When `Net Localgroup` is executed without arguments, it displays the name of the computer and the local groups defined on that computer. `Groupname` specifies the name of the local group to be administered. The `/comment:"`*`text`*`"` parameter adds or modifies a comment to a new or existing group. Specifying `/domain` causes the operation to occur on the domain level instead of the local computer. The *`name`* `[ ...]` parameter is used to list one or more usernames or group names to be added or removed from a local group. The `/add` parameter specifies an add operation and `/delete` specifies a delete operation.

NOTE

Another Windows XP command that can be used to configure group membership is the `Net Group` command. This command provides the ability to add, display, and modify user accounts in global groups located on the local computer or on the domain to which the computer is connected. The various forms of syntax supported by this command are outlined below.

```
net group [groupname [/comment:"text"]] [/domain]
net group groupname {/add [/comment:"text"] ¦ /delete} [/domain]
net group groupname username[ ...] {/add ¦ /delete} [/domain]
```

NOTE (*continued*)

When executed without any parameters, the `Net Group` command displays a list of groups on the server. The `groupname` parameter specifies the group name to be added, expanded, or deleted. The `/comment:"text"` parameter is used to add a comment to a new or existing group. When specified, the `/domain` parameter performs the operation at the domain level instead of on the local computer. The `username[ ...]` parameter is used to specify a list of one or more usernames to be added or removed from the specified group. The `/all` parameter specifies an add operation and the `/delete` parameter specifies a delete operation.

Creating a Login Script

At this point, Tom has reviewed the manual account creation process and has identified the Windows commands that he will need to use when developing the VBScript that will automate account creation. He is now ready to write the script. As with the previous scripts, Tom will develop it in a modular fashion. First he will define the statements that make up the `Initialization Section` and `Main Processing Section` and then he will develop each of the script's functions and subroutines.

The Initialization Section

As with all his other scripts, Tom begins by specifying the `Option Explicit` and the `On Error Resume Next` statements, as shown below.

```
'Initialization Section

Option Explicit

On Error Resume Next
```

The reason for adding the `On Error Resume Next` statement is to prevent the scripts from terminating in the event of an error and to provide the ability to interrogate the return status of each command after it executes. This way, if for some reason the script should run into an error when trying to create the first user account, it can continue to run and try and create the second account.

Next, a constant is defined that will be used to display a title bar message in all pop-up dialog boxes generated by the script. This will provide for a consistent and professional-looking presentation.

```
Const cTitlebarMsg = "Administrative Account Creator"
```

The next four statements, shown below, define a number of variables used by the script. The first variable represents the `WshShell` object and the rest of the defined variables used in the script's `Main Processing Section`.

NOTE

A number of other variables are used by the script. These variables are defined in the functions and subroutines that use them. Moving variable declaration to the procedure level whenever possible helps to tighten variable scope and ensure that variables are not accidentally reused or modified inappropriately in other parts of the script.

```
Dim WshShl
Dim intRunStatus
Dim strDskMgtAcct
Dim strSchedAcct
```

Next, an instance of the `WshShell` object is set up, as shown below, in order to later facilitate the use of the `Net User` and `Net Localgroup` commands using this object's `Run()` method.

```
'Instantiate the WshShell object
Set WshShl = WScript.CreateObject("WScript.Shell")
```

The last two statements in the `Initialization Section` assign values to the `strDskMgtAcct` and `strSchedAcct` variables. These values represent the names of the desktop management and scheduling accounts that are to be created by the script.

```
strDskMgtAcct = "ADMA01"
strSchedAcct = "ASAT01"
```

The Main Processing Section

The Script's `Main Processing` section begins by calling the `CallRunVerification()` function, as shown below.

```
'Get permission to proceed
intRunStatus = CallRunVerification()
```

This function displays a pop-up dialog box asking for permission to continue executing the script. It returns a value of `6` if permission is granted. The value returned by the function is assigned to the `intRunStatus` variable, allowing it to be interrogated, as shown below.

```
If intRunStatus = 6 Then

  'Call the procedure that creates new accounts
  CreateAdminAcct(strDskMgtAcct)
  CreateAdminAcct(strSchedAcct)

End If
```

If a value of `6` is returned by the function, then two new procedure calls are executed. In both instances the same procedure is called. This procedure is named `CreateAdminAcct()`. It is written as a subroutine because it does not need to return any information back to its calling statement. It is designed to accept and process one argument. This argument is the name of the account that it is to create. The first statement that calls this subroutine passes it the `strDskMgtAcct` variable, representing the name of the desktop management account. The second statement that calls this subroutine passes it the `strSchedAcct` variable, which represents the name of the scheduling management account.

The script's `Main Processing Section` ends like all earlier scripts by executing the `WScript` object's `Quit()` method, as shown below.

```
'Terminate script execution
WScript.Quit()
```

The CallRunVerification() Function

The `CallRunVerification()` function is designed to display the pop-up dialog box shown in Figure 15.6 in order to confirm its execution.

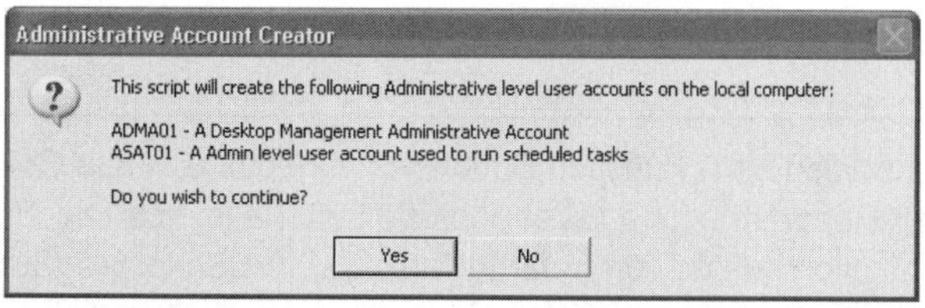

FIGURE 15.6 *Using VBScript's built-in* `MsgBox()` *function to create a confirmation prompt*

The `CallRunVerification()` function, shown below, begins by defining a localized variable called `strMsgText`. It then assigns a text string to this variable. In order to make the text string more readable, the VBScript `vbTab` and `vbCrLf` string formatting constants are used to restructure the string's presentation within the pop-up dialog box. The `MsgBox()` function is then executed and passed three arguments. The first argument is the value assigned to the `strMsgText` variable.

```
Function CallRunVerification()

  Dim strMsgText

  'Display the splash screen and ask the user if he or she wants to play
  strMsgText = "This script will create the following Administrative level" & _
    " user accounts on the local computer:" & vbTab & vbCrLf & vbCrLf & _
    strDskMgtAcct & " - A Desktop Management Administrative Account" & vbCrLf & _
    strSchedAcct & " - A Admin level user account used to run scheduled tasks" & _
    vbCrLf & vbCrLf & "Do you wish to continue?"

  CallRunVerification = MsgBox(strMsgText, 36, cTitlebarMsg)

End Function
```

The second argument passed to the `MsgBox()` function is `36`. This number represents the accumulation of the numeric values assigned to the `vbYesNo` (that is, 4) and `vbQuestion` (that is, 32) constants. The net effect of this argument is to display a pop-up dialog box that displays the Yes and No buttons along with a graphic question mark icon.

NOTE

Refer to Table 6.5, "VBScript MsgBox() Function Buttons," in Chapter 6, "Data Collection, Notification, and Error Reporting," for a list of possible buttons that can be displayed by the `MsgBox()` function. In addition, refer to Table 6.6, "VBScript MsgBox() Function Icons," in Chapter 6 to review the list of icons that can be displayed.

The third and final argument passed to the `MsgBox()` function is `cTitlebarMsg`. This argument represents the constant defined in the script's `Initialization Section` that specifies a standard title bar message to be used in all pop-up dialog boxes displayed by the script.

The CreateAdminAcct() Subroutine

The `CreateAdminAcct()` subroutine, shown below, is responsible for the actual creation of user accounts as well as for their addition to the local administrators group. It accepts and processes one argument, called `strNewAcctName`, that is passed to it as input. This variable will contain the name of the user account that the subroutine is to create. It begins by defining two localized variables. The first variable is `strPasswd` and it will be used to store the password for the account. The second variable is `intCmdResult`. It will be used to store the return code generated by the `Net User` and `Net Localgroup` commands. The `strCmdResult` value is then assigned a initial default value of 0.

The subroutine then calls the `GetValidPassword()` function, which prompts for the specification of a valid password. The value returned by this function call is then assigned to the `strPasswd` variable.

```
Sub CreateAdminAcct(strNewAcctName)

  Dim strPasswd
  Dim intCmdResult

  intCmdResult = 0

  strPasswd = GetValidPasswd()

  'Create the new account
```

```
    intCmdResult = WshShl.Run("net user " & strNewAcctName & " " &_
      strPasswd & " /add", 0)

    'Add the account to the local administrators group
    If intCmdResult = 0 then
      intCmdResult= WshShl.Run("net localgroup Administrators /add " & _
        strNewAcctName, 0)
      If intCmdResult <> 0 then
        MsgBox "Error Code 2: Account creation failed for " & _
          strNewAcctName, , cTitlebarMsg
      Else
        MsgBox "Account creation successful for " & strNewAcctName, , cTitlebarMsg
      End If
    Else
      If intCmdResult <> 0 then
        MsgBox "Error Code 1: Account creation failed for " & _
          strNewAcctName, , cTitlebarMsg
      End If
    End If

End Sub
```

Next, the subroutine executes the `WshShell` object's `Run()` method, passing it the `Net User` command, the `strNewAcctName` variable, the `strPasswd` variable, the `/add` option, and a `0` (which causes the command to run hidden in the background). The result of this command is stored in the `intCmdResult` variable, which is then checked to ensure that an error has not occurred. If the return code generated by the command was not zero (that is, an error occurred), then an error message is displayed. Otherwise the `WshShell` object's `Run()` method is executed again, this time to process the `Net Localgroup` command. The result of this command's execution is then checked. If all goes well, a pop-up dialog box like the one shown in Figure 15.7 will be displayed.

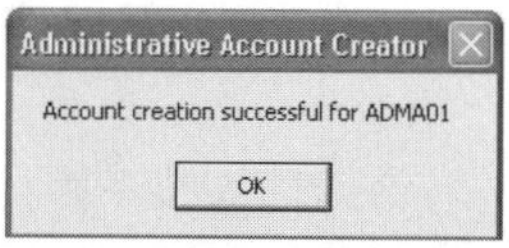

FIGURE 15.7 *A message is displayed for each account that is successfully created*

The GetValidPasswd() Function

The script's final procedure, shown below, is a function named `GetValidPassword()`. Its job is to display the pop-up dialog box shown in Figure 15.8. The script begins by defining two localized variables. The `strPasswd` variable is used to store the password that Tom will type in and the `strValidPassword` variable will be used to store a variable that the function will use to test whether a valid password has been supplied.

```
Function GetValidPasswd()

  Dim strPasswd
  Dim strValidPassword

  strValidPassword = "NO"

  Do Until strValidPassword = "YES"

    'Prompt for a password to assign to the account
    strPasswd = InputBox("Type a password for the " & strDskMgtAcct & _
    " account and click on OK." , cTitleBarMsg)

    If strPasswd = "" Then
      MsgBox "Password Missing: You must enter a valid 8 character " & _
        "Password to continue.", , cTitlebarMsg
    Else
      If Len(strPasswd) < 8 Then
        MsgBox "Incorrect password length. Password must be at least " & _
          "8 characters long", , cTitlebarMsg
      Else
        GetValidPasswd = strPasswd
        strValidPassword = "YES"
      End If
    End If

  Loop

End Function
```

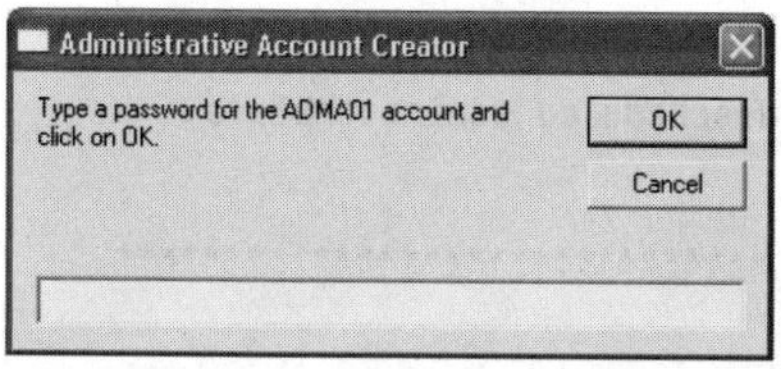

FIGURE 15.8 *Rather than embed passwords into the script, the script is designed to manually collect them*

A `Do...Until` loop is set up, which iterates until a valid password is supplied. It begins by displaying a pop-up dialog box using the built-in VBScript `InputBox()` function. The password that is entered is then interrogated to ensure that it is not blank (that is, either the Cancel button was clicked or the OK button was clicked without a password being typed).

The length of the password is then checked to ensure that it is at least eight characters long. If the value assigned to `strPasswd` is blank or is less than eight characters long, an error message is displayed and a new pop-up dialog box is displayed to once again try and collect a valid password. Once a valid password is entered, its value is assigned to `GetValidPassword` (a variable with the same name as the function) in order to return it to the statement that called in the function the first place. Then, to break out of the `Do...Until` loop, the value of `strValidPassword` is set equal to `YES`.

The Fully Assembled Script

The entire administrative account creation script is assembled below. When executed, it will create both administrative level management accounts. It will then be up to Tom to remember to set the password for the `ASAT01` account to non-expiring in order to prevent the account from getting locked out, which would prevent the execution of the defrag script. Tom will also have to modify the scheduled task that runs the defrag script to run using this account.

```
'*************************************************************************

'Script Name: Script 15.1.vbs

'Author: Jerry Ford

'Created: 03/15/03

'Description: This script creates 2 administrative level user accounts.
```

```
'One provides the Desktop Support Team with a backdoor into the computer.
'The other provides sufficient access to run scheduled administrative
'scripts.
'*************************************************************************


'Initialization Section

Option Explicit

On Error Resume Next

Const cTitlebarMsg = "Administrative Account Creator"

Dim WshShl
Dim intRunStatus
Dim strDskMgtAcct
Dim strSchedAcct

'Instantiate the WshShell object
Set WshShl = WScript.CreateObject("WScript.Shell")

strDskMgtAcct = "ADMA01"
strSchedAcct = "ASAT01"


'Main Processing Section

'Get permission to proceed
intRunStatus = CallRunVerification()

If intRunStatus = 6 Then

  'Call the procedure that creates new accounts
  CreateAdminAcct(strDskMgtAcct)
  CreateAdminAcct(strSchedAcct)

End If
```

```
'Terminate script execution
WScript.Quit()


'Procedure Section

Function CallRunVerification()

  Dim strMsgText

  'Display the splash screen and ask the user if he or she wants to play
  strMsgText = "This script will create the following Administrative level" & _
    " user accounts on the local computer:" & vbTab & vbCrLf & vbCrLf & _
    strDskMgtAcct & " - A Desktop Management Administrative Account" & vbCrLf & _
    strSchedAcct & " - A Admin level user account used to run scheduled tasks" & _
    vbCrLf & vbCrLf & "Do you wish to continue?"

  CallRunVerification = MsgBox(strMsgText, 36, cTitlebarMsg)

End Function

Sub CreateAdminAcct(strNewAcctName)

  Dim strPasswd
  Dim intCmdResult

  intCmdResult = 0

  strPasswd = GetValidPasswd()

  'Create the new account
  intCmdResult = WshShl.Run("net user " & strNewAcctName & " " & _
    strPasswd & " /add", 0)

  'Add the account to the local administrators group
  If intCmdResult = 0 then
    intCmdResult= WshShl.Run("net localgroup Administrators /add " & _
```

```
      strNewAcctName, 0)
    If intCmdResult <> 0 then
      MsgBox "Error Code 2: Account creation failed for " & _
        strNewAcctName, , cTitlebarMsg
    Else
      MsgBox "Account creation successful for " & strNewAcctName, , cTitlebarMsg
    End If
  Else
    If intCmdResult <> 0 then
      MsgBox "Error Code 1: Account creation failed for " & _
        strNewAcctName, , cTitlebarMsg
    End If
  End If

End Sub

'This procedure creates a backdoor account for the desktop management team
Function GetValidPasswd()

  Dim strPasswd
  Dim strValidPassword

  strValidPassword = "NO"

  Do Until strValidPassword = "YES"

    'Prompt for a password to assign to the account
    strPasswd = InputBox("Type a password for the " & strDskMgtAcct & _
    " account and click on OK." , cTitleBarMsg)

    If strPasswd = "" Then
      MsgBox "Password Missing: You must enter a valid 8 character " & _
        "password to continue.", , cTitlebarMsg
    Else
      If Len(strPasswd) < 8 Then
        MsgBox "Incorrect password length. Password must be at " & _
          "least 8 characters long", , cTitlebarMsg
      Else
```

```
            GetValidPasswd = strPasswd
            strValidPassword = "YES"
          End If
        End If

      Loop

    End Function
```

Summary

In this chapter, you reviewed the steps that are required to manually create new user accounts and add them to groups. You also learned how to script the creation of new user accounts, as well as how to add those accounts to groups. Using the techniques presented here, you can begin developing an assortment of account management scripts that can be used to create or modify user accounts on both the local computer and a Windows domain.

PART III

Professional Project 2

Project 2

Analyzing Application Logs

Project 2 Overview

In this project, a programmer at Intuit Mechanical Tools has been assigned to improve the reporting process for an order/inventory system developed in-house. Using VBScript, you will learn how to rapidly develop a collection of scripts that read and process reports created by the order/inventory system in order to create a single consolidated summary report.

In order to develop these scripts, you will learn the basic steps involved in file input processing. This will include verifying whether input files exist before attempting to work with them, opening files, and various techniques for reading files. You will also learn how to create new files, how to write data to these files, and how to close the files when your script has finished working with them.

This project will also show you how to perform file management operations such as moving and deleting files. As you go through the development of this project, you will learn a number of new programming techniques, including:

- How to read and process configuration settings stored in INI files
- How to read and process the contents of formatted log and report files
- How to create new text files
- How to append information to existing text files
- How to programmatically automate the execution of VBScripts
- How to write messages to the Windows application event log

Chapter 16

Project Case Study: Analyzing Application Logs

This chapter marks the beginning of a new project case study in which you will get to observe how Molly Masterson, a new programmer at Intuit Mechanical Tools, uses VBScript to improve the reporting process for an in-house developed order/inventory system. As you work through this chapter and the four chapters that follow, you will get the opportunity to see how to develop VBScripts that perform a number of tasks, including:

- Processing initialization or INI files
- Reading and analyzing formatted report and log files
- Creating and writing to new reports
- Scheduling script execution
- Recording messages to the Windows event log
- Performing report archive management

Project Overview

Intuit Mechanical Tools is a small company that manufactures high-powered computerized mechanical tools and supplies. Its products are commonly used to build large chemical processing facilities. The company uses an in-house developed order/inventory application to track all product sales and returns. The system also tracks current inventory levels and maintains an error log where program and hardware error messages are recorded. The order/inventory system is a distributed application written mostly in C and C++.

Unfortunately, things have been rough for Intuit Mechanical Tools over the last five years. While the number of competing firms has steadily grown, profits have been steadily declining. As a result, many of the application programmers that developed the company's order/inventory system have left the company looking for greener pastures. Today, a limited staff of three programmers remains, including Molly Masterson.

Because of the small size of their group, the programmers at Intuit Mechanical Tools are kept very busy. Recently things have become so bad that they have started to fall behind in their workload. Management has requested that they look for ways to streamline their daily activities in order to free up time for a new application that the company wants to develop for a computerized cooling system.

One of the daily tasks that Molly has been assigned to perform is the manual review and consolidation each morning of four application files generated by the order/inventory application into a report for management to review. Although not particularly complicated, it takes Molly over an hour each day to perform this task. In order to help streamline her workload, she has suggested automating this process.

At first she thought about modifying the in-house application, but decided that it would take too much time, effort, and testing to automate the functionality that she was looking for using C and C++. What she wants is a quick and easy way to develop an add-on process that she can create with a minimum level of work and that will be easy for other members of her team to support. Ultimately, she decided that VBScript is the right tool for the job. Like the other programmers on her team, Molly is already somewhat familiar with Visual Basic. She figures that her learning curve for VBScript will be relatively small. She also knows that as a scripting language, VBScript is well-suited to rapid application development and for filling in holes in applications that do not justify a lot of development time (and hence often go undone).

Analyzing the In-House Application Logs

Unfortunately for Molly, though management approved her new VBScript project, they did not take any work off of her plate in order to provide her with additional time to work on the project. This means that she will have to develop her solution quickly, so as not to backlog her current workload any further.

To begin, Molly decides to take a few moments to document the existing manual process that she goes through every day. By the time she is done, Molly has broken the process of analyzing and consolidating the order/inventory system's reports down into the following steps.

1. The reports generated by the order/inventory application are created by 20:00 each night. Each morning, she goes over to the Windows 2000 server where the application stores its report and log files.
2. She then copies each of the four reports onto a floppy disk and logs off.
3. Next, she renames each of these reports as shown below:

◆ Error.log	ER-MM-DD-YY.txt
◆ DailySales.txt	DS-MM-DD-YY.txt
◆ DailyReturns.txt	DR-MM-DD-YY.txt
◆ DailyProduction.txt	DP-MM.DD.YY.txt

4. After returning to her own desktop, she opens each report and examines its contents.
5. She begins cutting and pasting portions of each report into a new report, which she saves on her computer's hard drive.
6. Finally, she prints a copy of the report, which she places in the inbox of Hank, the company's operations manager.

In addition, Molly keeps a one-month minimum history of log and report files. She does this by logging on the Windows 2000 Server, where the report and log files reside, on the first business day of each new month and deleting all files other than those for the current and previous months.

Examining the Error Log

As the order/inventory application runs each day, it reports any hardware- or software-related errors that are encountered to a log file called Error.log. This file, an example of which is shown in Figure 16.1, is simply a plain text file. All error messages are made up of several pieces of information, as outlined below.

- A time stamp in the form of HH:MM:SS
- A date stamp in the form of MM/DD/YY
- An error code in the range of 1–5, where a 1 indicates a severe error and a 5 indicates an informational error
- Free-form message text that provides a detailed explanation of the error

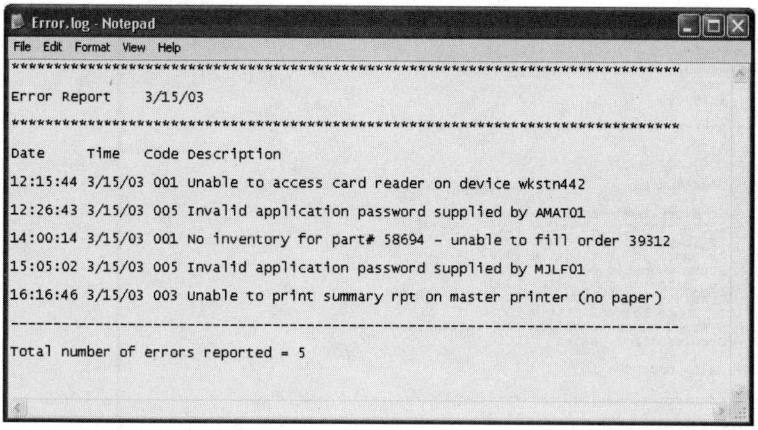


```
*******************************************************************************
Error Report    3/15/03
*******************************************************************************
Date     Time    Code Description
12:15:44 3/15/03 001 Unable to access card reader on device wkstn442
12:26:43 3/15/03 005 Invalid application password supplied by AMAT01
14:00:14 3/15/03 001 No inventory for part# 58694 - unable to fill order 39312
15:05:02 3/15/03 005 Invalid application password supplied by MJLF01
16:16:46 3/15/03 003 Unable to print summary rpt on master printer (no paper)
-------------------------------------------------------------------------------
Total number of errors reported = 5
```

FIGURE 16.1 *Error messages written to Error.log are date- and time-stamped and include an error code and a description*

When Molly reviews this report, she generally looks only for errors that have been assigned a code 1, 2, or 3 severity. She then cuts and pastes these errors as the first entries in the new daily report that she is responsible for creating.

Examining the Daily Sales Report

The first report that Molly usually examines is the Daily Sales report, which is named DailySales.txt. An example of a typical DailySales.txt report is shown in Figure 16.2.

When reviewing this report, Molly copies the information located at the bottom of the report in the Sales summary by part number section to her new report.

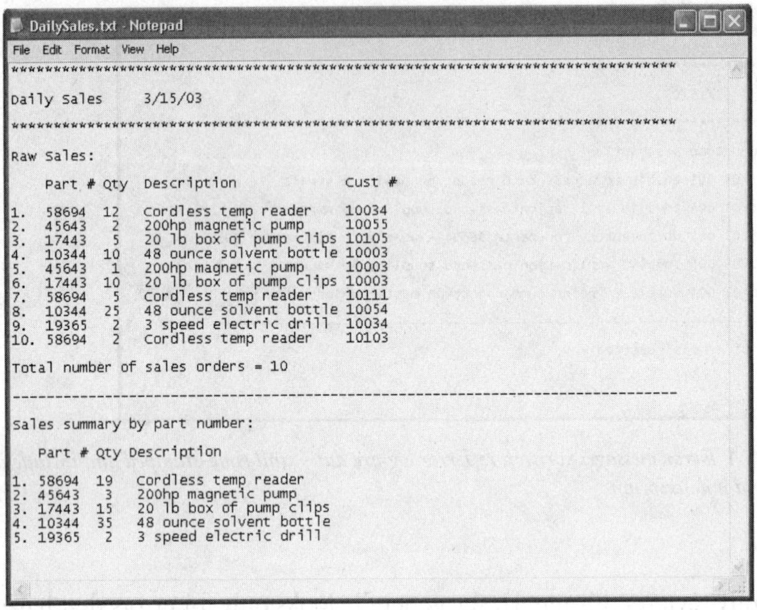

```
DailySales.txt - Notepad
File Edit Format View Help
************************************************************************************

Daily Sales     3/15/03

************************************************************************************

Raw Sales:

    Part # Qty  Description            Cust #

1.   58694  12  Cordless temp reader    10034
2.   45643   2  200hp magnetic pump     10055
3.   17443   5  20 lb box of pump clips 10105
4.   10344  10  48 ounce solvent bottle 10003
5.   45643   1  200hp magnetic pump     10003
6.   17443  10  20 lb box of pump clips 10003
7.   58694   5  Cordless temp reader    10111
8.   10344  25  48 ounce solvent bottle 10054
9.   19365   2  3 speed electric drill  10034
10.  58694   2  Cordless temp reader    10103

Total number of sales orders = 10

--------------------------------------------------------------------------------

Sales summary by part number:

   Part # Qty Description

1. 58694  19   Cordless temp reader
2. 45643   3   200hp magnetic pump
3. 17443  15   20 lb box of pump clips
4. 10344  35   48 ounce solvent bottle
5. 19365   2   3 speed electric drill
```

FIGURE 16.2 *The Daily Sales report consists of detailed and summary information*

Examining the Daily Returns Report

When reviewing the Daily Returns report, an example of which is shown in Figure 16.3, Molly focuses on the summary information provided at the bottom of the report. She copies this information into the summary report that she is creating.

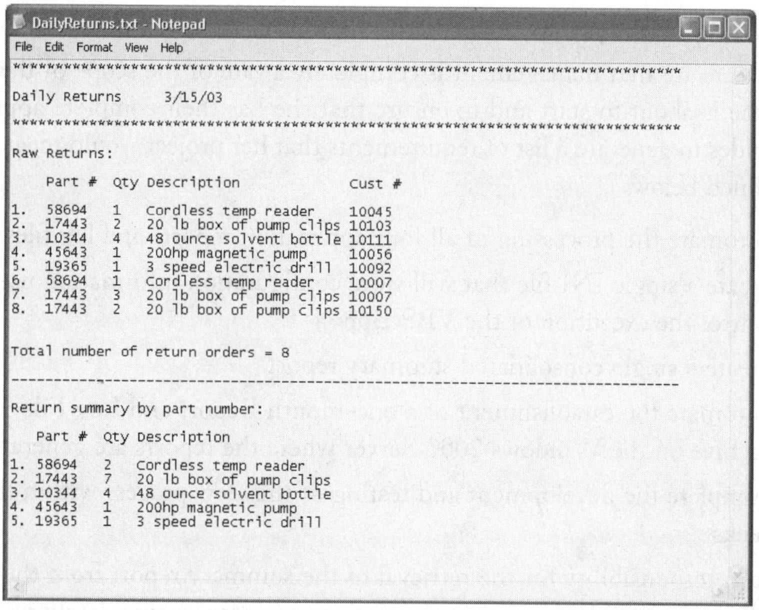

```
DailyReturns.txt - Notepad
File Edit Format View Help
******************************************************************************
Daily Returns     3/15/03
******************************************************************************
Raw Returns:

    Part #  Qty Description             Cust #

1.  58694   1   Cordless temp reader    10045
2.  17443   2   20 lb box of pump clips 10103
3.  10344   4   48 ounce solvent bottle 10111
4.  45643   1   200hp magnetic pump     10056
5.  19365   1   3 speed electric drill  10092
6.  58694   1   Cordless temp reader    10007
7.  17443   3   20 lb box of pump clips 10007
8.  17443   2   20 lb box of pump clips 10150

Total number of return orders = 8
------------------------------------------------------------------------------
Return summary by part number:

   Part #  Qty Description
1. 58694   2   Cordless temp reader
2. 17443   7   20 lb box of pump clips
3. 10344   4   48 ounce solvent bottle
4. 45643   1   200hp magnetic pump
5. 19365   1   3 speed electric drill
```

FIGURE 16.3 *The Daily Returns report provides both line-item details and a summary analysis*

Examining the Daily Production Report

The fourth report that Molly reviews each morning is the Daily Production report, which is called DailyProduction.txt. This report breaks the previous day's production work down into two separate groups, Hardware and Supplies. Molly copies information from both sections into the new summary report.

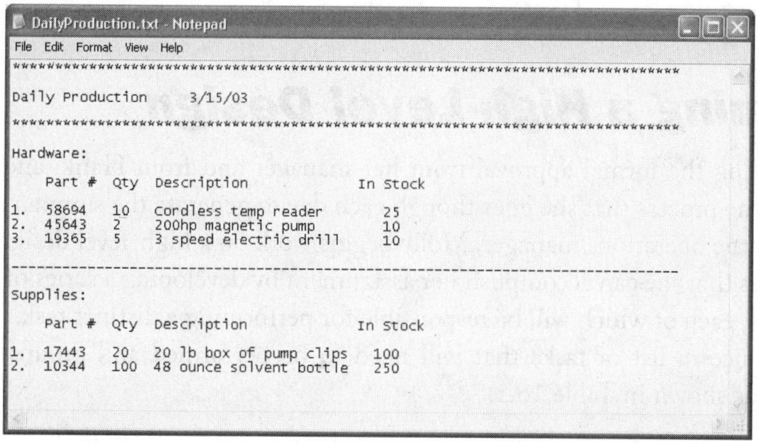

```
DailyProduction.txt - Notepad
File Edit Format View Help
******************************************************************************
Daily Production    3/15/03
******************************************************************************
Hardware:
    Part #  Qty  Description              In Stock

1.  58694   10   Cordless temp reader      25
2.  45643   2    200hp magnetic pump       10
3.  19365   5    3 speed electric drill    10
------------------------------------------------------------------------------
Supplies:
    Part #  Qty  Description              In Stock

1.  17443   20   20 lb box of pump clips   100
2.  10344   100  48 ounce solvent bottle   250
```

FIGURE 16.4 *The Daily Production report breaks information down into multiple categories*

Requirements Analysis

In order to ensure that management is completely aware of the scope of the project that she is about to start and to ensure that she has their complete approval, Molly decides to generate a list of requirements that her project would meet. This list is outlined below.

- Automate the processing of all four application reports and log files
- Create a single INI file that will store configuration information used to control the execution of the VBScripts
- Create a single consolidated summary report
- Automate the establishment of a one-month Report and Log File Archive on the Windows 2000 Server where the reports are generated
- Complete the development and testing of this new process within three weeks
- Turn responsibility for the retrieval of the summary report from the Windows 2000 Server over to operations in order to completely remove the application programmers from the process

After completing this list, she e-mails it to her boss for approval. He then forwards it on to Hank, the operations manager. Although hesitant at first, Hank agrees to assign someone on his staff to the task of retrieving and printing the consolidated summary report. Hank then forwards the e-mail on to the night shift operations supervisor as notification that in a few weeks, this task will need to be added as a step to the nightly checklist that the operations staff perform on the server.

Performing a High-Level Design

After getting the formal approval from her manager and from Hank, and after studying the process that she goes though each day to generate the summary sales report for the operations manager, Molly begins work on a high-level design. She determines that she can accomplish her assignment by developing a series of small VBScripts, each of which will be responsible for performing a distinct task. Molly then produces a list of tasks that will need to be performed and groups them together, as shown in Table 16.1.

Table 16.1 Log Analyzer Ad Report Consolidation Task List

Type of Task	Description
Initialization File	Develop a single INI file that will store configuration information used to control the execution of scripts that process each of the order/inventory system's report and log files.
	Develop a scripted process for reading and processing INI configuration file settings.
Log Analyzers	Develop a VBScript log analyzer to read and process the contents of the Error.log file.
	Develop a VBScript log analyzer to read and process the contents of the DailySales.txt file.
	Develop a VBScript log analyzer to read and process the contents of the DailyReturns.txt file.
	Develop a VBScript log analyzer to read and process the contents of the DailyProduction.txt file.
Script Scheduling	Schedule the execution script that processes the reports and log files.
	Schedule the execution of a monthly VBScript that maintains a month-long archive of report and log files.
Archive Management	Develop a VBScript that, when executed, ensures that a month's worth of log and report files are maintained on the Windows 2000 Server where they are generated.

Developing and Processing the INI Configuration File

Rather than embed script execution settings inside each VBScript that she will be developing, Molly wants to create a single INI file and store as many settings as possible there. This way, some of the changes to the scripts that operations might one day ask of her can be made by modifying the INI file instead of the scripts. This will help make configuration changes easier to perform and eliminate opportunities for accidentally introducing errors in scripts that would otherwise have to be manually edited.

Molly is still in the process of determining the exact format and content of the INI file. For now, she knows that she wants to create a section in the INI file for each of the log analyzer scripts, as demonstrated in Figure 16.5.

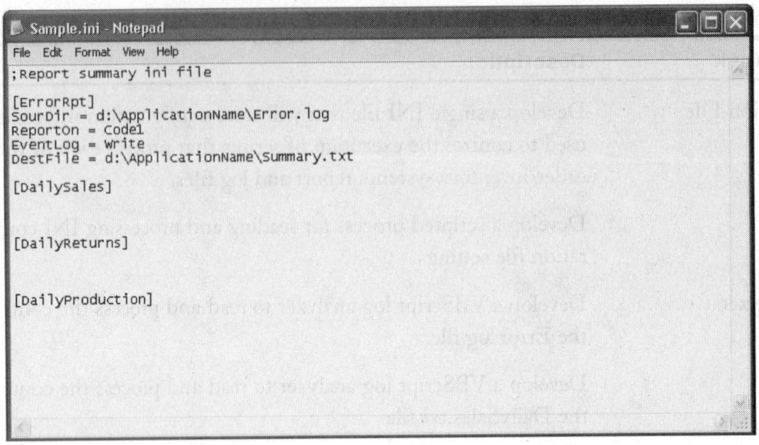

FIGURE 16.5 *A rough outline of how the INI file that Molly is currently developing will look*

As you can see, Molly has started adding settings in the first section in the INI file. These settings and their purpose will be covered in detail in Chapter 17, "Using Configuration Files to Control Script Execution."

In order to develop a VBScript procedure to process the INI file, Molly will have to learn how to work with the VBScript run-time `FileSystemObject`. In particular, she will need to learn how to use a number of its methods, including:

- **`FileExists()`**.Validate whether the INI file exists before trying to open it
- **`OpenTextFile()`**. Work with the contents of the INI file
- **`ReadLine()`**. Read a line at a time from the INI file
- **`Close()`**. Close the INI file when done processing it

Creating Log and Report Analyzers

At first Molly toyed with the idea of creating a single script that could process each of the reports and log files created by the order/inventory application. However, distinct differences in each report would make this a cumbersome development task, so she has decided instead to develop a log analyzer for each file. One benefit of this approach is that she can come back and modify a single log analyzer script without running the risk of making a modification mistake that would disable all of the log analyzers. This approach provides the most flexibility should the report and log files later grow in complexity and require further modification.

For the log analyzer that will process the `Error.log` file, Molly wants to be able to read the report and to be able to pull out errors based on their error codes. She plans to use the INI file to specify the level of alerts that will be reported on. For now, she plans on reporting only on level 1, 2, or 3 error messages.

The report analyzers for the `DailySales.txt` and `DailyReturns.txt` reports will be almost identical. Both will by default only extract summary reporting information as specified by settings stored in the INI file. However, the report analyzers for these two files will also be designed to support the extraction of detailed information should it become necessary.

By default, the report analyzer that will process the `DailyProduction.txt` file will be set up to consolidate and report on the detailed information located in both the Hardware and Supplies sections. However, by modifying a setting located in its section of the INI file, Molly can limit reporting to either the Hardware or the Supplies sections or to disable the reporting of both sections from this file altogether.

In order to develop the log analyzer scripts, Molly will have to learn how to work with the VBScript run-time `FileSystemObject`. In particular, she will need to learn how to use a number of its methods, including:

- **`FileExists()`**.Validate whether a log or report file exists before trying to open it
- **`OpenTextFile()`**. Work with the contents of the log or report file
- **`ReadLine()`**. Read a line at a time from the log file
- **`SkipLines()`**. Skip header lines when reading the log file
- **`Close()`**. Close the log or report file when done processing it
- **`WriteLine()`**. Write a line of output to the summary report file
- **`WriteBlankLines()`**. Write blank lines and format the presentation of data in the summary report file

Molly also plans to provide these scripts with the ability to write messages about their operation to the Windows application event log. To perform this task, she will have to learn to work with the `WshShell` object's `LogEvent()` method.

Figure 16.6 shows an example of the summary report that Molly manually creates each month. As you can see, it consists of statements that she manually copied and pasted from each of the four log and report files.

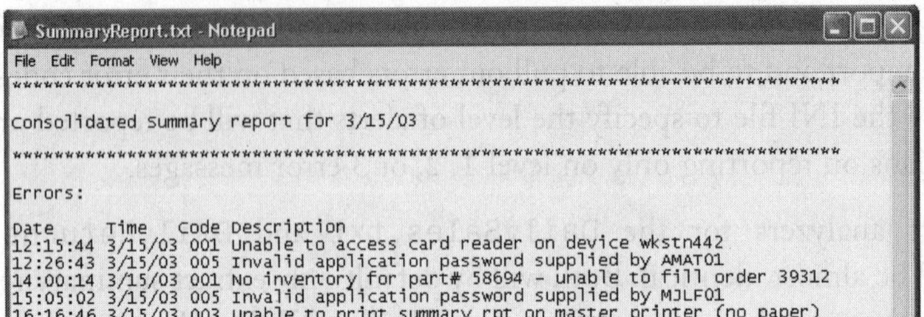


```
****************************************************************************

Consolidated Summary report for 3/15/03

****************************************************************************

Errors:

Date     Time    Code Description
12:15:44 3/15/03 001 Unable to access card reader on device wkstn442
12:26:43 3/15/03 005 Invalid application password supplied by AMAT01
14:00:14 3/15/03 001 No inventory for part# 58694 - unable to fill order 39312
15:05:02 3/15/03 005 Invalid application password supplied by MJLF01
16:16:46 3/15/03 003 Unable to print summary rpt on master printer (no paper)

----------------------------------------------------------------------------

Sales summary:

Part # Qty Description

58694  19   Cordless temp reader
45643   3   200hp magnetic pump
17443  15   20 lb box of pump clips
10344  35   48 ounce solvent bottle
19365   2   3 speed electric drill

----------------------------------------------------------------------------

Return summary:

Part #  Qty Description

58694   2   Cordless temp reader
17443   7   20 lb box of pump clips
10344   4   48 ounce solvent bottle
45643   1   200hp magnetic pump
19365   1   3 speed electric drill

----------------------------------------------------------------------------

Daily Production Summary

Part #  Qty  Description               In Stock

58694   10   Cordless temp reader        25
45643   2    200hp magnetic pump         10
19365   5    3 speed electric drill      10
17443   20   20 lb box of pump clips     100
10344   100  48 ounce solvent bottle     250
```

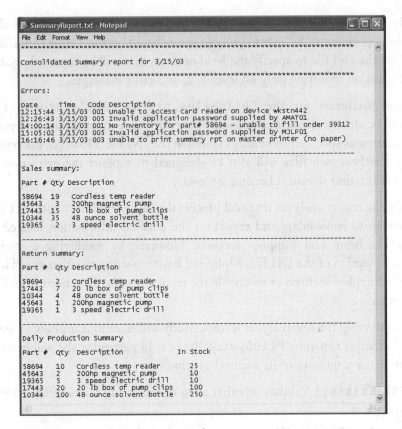

FIGURE 16.6 *A sample of a consolidated summary report*

By automating the creation of this report using VBScript, Molly will eliminate a daily chore that she has been performing. In addition, she will eliminate the occasional errors that are sometimes made when manually creating the report, such as pasting data twice or not at all.

Scheduling the Execution of the Analyzer Scripts

The Windows Task Scheduler service will be used to set up the schedule execution of the first log analyzer file, which will then run and call upon the second analyzer when it is done. By single threading script execution in this manner, Molly ensures that each script will be able to access the summary report file that is to be generated, without having to worry about whether another log analyzer is currently accessing it. The first log analyzer will create a new summary report and the rest of the analyzers will append their data to it when they execute.

In addition to the log analyzers, Molly will create a VBScript that runs once a month under the control of the Task Scheduler service in order to clear out old log, report, and summary files. Since the schedule of these scripts is a one-time task that needs to be performed only on one server, Molly will manually set up their scheduled execution using the Windows 2000 Scheduled Task Wizard.

Creating a Report and Log Archive

Approximately two years ago, Intuit Mechanical Tools underwent a thorough audit of all its manufacturing and related processes. One of the results of this audit was a suggestion that a minimum of a month's worth of order/inventory reports and log files be kept on hand (to supplement the nightly backup and archival of data files on the Windows 2000 Server). Since that time, Molly has been instructed to log on to the Windows 2000 Server on the first business day of each month and to delete all but the previous month's report and log files.

In order to automate the execution of this task, Molly will have to work with the VBScript run-time `FileSystemObject`. In particular she will need to learn how to use a number of its methods, including:

- **`FileExists()`**. Validate whether a log or report file exists before trying to open it
- **`MoveFile()`**. Move one or more files to an archive folder for a minimum one-month retention
- **`DeleteFile()`**. Delete one or more files stored in the archive after their one-month retention period has passed

Molly also plans to provide this script with the ability to write messages about its operation to the Windows application event log. To perform this task, she will need to use the `WshShell` object's `LogEvent()` method.

Summary

In this chapter, you were introduced to Molly Masterson and the challenge presented to her to streamline the reporting process for the order/inventory application at Intuit Mechanical Tools. In preparing to tackle this assignment, Molly has decided that VBScript and the WSH will provide her with the best tools for rapidly developing a new report summary generation and archive management process.

Chapter 17

Using Configuration Files to Control Script Execution

In this chapter you will observe as Molly learns how to use INI files (pronounced "eye 'n eye") and determines what information she will add to her INI file. You will also learn how to work with methods belonging to the VBScript run-time `FileSystemObject` in order to develop a procedure that can process the contents of an INI file. This will include opening the INI file, locating the appropriate section, reading its settings, and then closing the INI file.

Creating a Configuration File to Control Script Execution

One of Molly's design goals for developing the report and log analyzer scripts is to externalize as much of the configuration of the scripts as possible. Molly works with a number of applications that use INI files to store configuration settings and user preferences. From time to time, she has to edit these files, usually by following instructions provided by an application developer or as part of an effort to try and debug a problem with an application or hardware device.

For the most part, she never paid much attention to these files. However, in deciding how best to design her VBScripts, she has decided that she would like to externalize their configuration settings in much the same way that she has seen other applications use them. To this end, she has decided to create a single INI file and to store configuration settings for each of the report and log analyzer scripts that she plans on developing.

Before getting too deep into the script development process, Molly decided to spend a little time on the Internet learning more about INI files and their structure. INI or initialization files are plain ASCII text files with a .ini file extension. They have been used for years to store settings for Windows operating systems and their hardware and software applications.

INI files provide the ability to modify the behavior of an application, utility, or script without modifying its code. INI files make it easier to maintain these types of resources and prevent the possibility of introducing an error when modifying hard-coded configuration settings. In addition, INI files provide inexperienced programmers, worried about accidentally corrupting the registry, with an alternative place to store application settings.

INI files do have some disadvantages. Unlike the Windows registry, which remains a complete mystery to many people, INI files are easy to come across and delete. INI files are stored on the computer's hard drive, which means that disk I/O must occur when processing them, naturally slowing down the applications or scripts that must access them.

How INI Files Are Used

INI files are used to store customization settings and preferences. Because they are just plain ASCII text files, INI files can be created and modified by any text editor. Since the release of Windows 95, Microsoft has strongly encouraged application and hardware developers to begin storing all configuration settings in the registry. Most application developers have gone this direction. However, if you do a search on *.INI on a computer running Windows 2000 or Windows XP, for example, you will still find dozens, if not hundreds, of INI files in use.

Despite Microsoft's continued push to get application and hardware vendors to move all settings to the Windows registry, you'll find many that still use INI files. This is especially true for older hardware and software. To accommodate these older programs and devices, Microsoft has left many of its old INI files in place. This way, older applications that were written before the days of the Windows registry still have a place to store and retrieve application settings. You will find plenty of INI files in the Windows system directory. You'll also find them scattered in folders all over your hard drive.

Microsoft operating systems also make use of INI files. For example, both Windows 2000 and XP store startup information in a file called boot.ini. This INI file is referenced every time the computer starts and is used to present a list of startup options.

Microsoft also uses INI files to store configuration settings for many of its utilities and applications. For example, if you play Solitaire, you'll find that configuration settings for the application are maintained in a file called Win.ini. To demonstrate that point, you can open Win.ini and look at the settings for the Solitaire application. Close Win.ini, open the Solitaire application, and make a configuration change. When you reopen the Win.ini file and examine the settings in the [Solitaire] sections, you will see that they have changed.

NOTE

You can also use applications such as Microsoft Word to modify INI files. However, word processing applications such as Microsoft Word embed a lot of hidden characters inside files, which will wreak havoc on INI files. If you use an application such as Microsoft Word to modify your INI files, be sure that you save them as plain text files.

INI File Structure

An INI file is a file that can be read from or written to by any program, utility, or script. INI files have a very specific structure and are generally processed in a top-down order. INI files are made up of one or more *sections*. Section names are enclosed within a pair of brackets. Sections can be placed in any order within an INI file.

Sections contain zero or more *key=value* pairs, which can also be placed in any order within a section. If a key=value pair is specified more than once within a section, the last instance usually overrides the previous instances.

INI files can also contain comments. Comments are labeled using the semicolon (;) character. You can also add blank lines to an INI file to improve its presentation. However, the blank spaces have no real purpose and are ignored when the INI file is processed.

The following statements demonstrate the format and structure of a small INI file.

```
;Sample INI file

[Section1]
key1=value1
key2=value2
```

As you can see, this INI file example begins with a comment. It has a single section called [Section1]. Two key=value pairs are stored within the section. Additional sections can be added as required. Typically, an INI file is named after the application executable for which it stored settings. For example, the INI file for an application named WordDoc.exe would probably be WordDoc.ini.

TIP

Consider naming your INI files after your VBScript file names. This will make them easier to identify and manage. If you create a VBScript application that consists of a number of separate scripts, all of which share the same INI file, you might want to name an INI file after the main or first VBScript that accesses it. The most important thing is to be consistent and predictable in your naming scheme.

It's typical for an application to have one INI file, although an application certainly can have more than one. Sometimes a collection of related applications may share the same INI file. When this is the case, each application usually has its own section within the INI file. When processing the INI file, these applications search for their specific section and parse through its key=value pairs in order to extract the configuration settings they require.

Designing the Report and Log Analyzer INI File

As the first step in creating an INI file for the report and log analyzer scripts, Molly used the Windows Notepad application to create a blank file named Rpt-Log.ini. She then added a comment and a section heading for each script that will be using the INI file, as demonstrated below.

```
;Report and Log Analyzer INI File

[ErrorRpt]

[DailySales]

[DailyReturns]

[DailyProduction]
```

Next, she began work on the Error Report section. Molly determined that she wanted to externalize the following configuration settings:

- **SourDir**. The path and file name of the Error.log report
- **ReportOn**. The minimum level of error messages to report on
- **EventLog**. A Boolean value indicating whether or not the script should write messages in the local Windows application event log
- **DestFile**. The path and file name of the summary report
- **Debug**. A Boolean value indicating whether or not the script should display intermediate results in the form of pop-up dialog boxes when processing

To begin, Molly modifies the `[ErrorRpt]` section, as shown below.

```
[ErrorRpt]
SourDir=d:\Order_Inventory\Logs\Error.log
ReportOn=3
EventLog=True
DestFile=d:\Order_Inventory\Logs\Summary.txt
Debug=False
```

When the VBScript that processes the Daily Error log analyzer script runs, it will look for the report file in d:\Order_Inventory\Logs\Error.log. It will only report on errors that have been assigned a severity of 3 or higher. The script will write messages to the Windows application event log when it runs. It will write its output to d:\ApplicationName\Summary.txt. Finally, it will not display any debugging information.

Next, she modifies the `[DailySales]` section, as shown below.

```
[DailySales]
SourDir=d:\Order_Inventory\Logs\DailySales.txt
ReportOn=SummaryOnly
EventLog=True
DestFile=d:\Order_Inventory\Logs\Summary.txt
Debug=False
```

The only difference in the settings for this script is the modification of the `SourDir` key and the `ReportOn` key, which has been assigned a value of `SummaryOnly`. This value will be used to limit the data collected by the Daily Sales Report log analyzer script to just the summary information at the bottom of the report.

NOTE

Each of the report and log analyzer scripts will be designed to use default configuration settings in the event that the INI file is deleted or that settings are omitted from the INI file. For example, if the `ReportOn` key was removed from the `[DailySales]` section, then the VBScript would by default process the entire file.

Molly then modifies the `[DailyProduction]` section.

```
[DailyReturns]
SourDir=d:\Order_Inventory\Logs\DailyReturns.txt
ReportOn=SummaryOnly
Eventlog=True
DestFile=d:\Order_Inventory\Logs\Summary.txt
Debug=False
```

As you can see, the only difference between this section and the `[DailySales]` section is the value assigned to the `SourDir` key.

Then Molly modifies the `[DailyReturns]` section, as shown below.

```
[DailyProduction]
SourDir=d:\Order_Inventory\Logs\DailyProduction.txt
Eventlog=True
ReportOn=HardAndSupl
DestFile=d:\Order_Inventory\Logs\Summary.txt
Debug=False
```

Again, the only difference between this and the previous sections are the `SourcDir` key and the `ReportOn` key, which is set to `HardAndSupl` (instructing the script to report on both the report's hardware and supplies information).

When completely assembled, the finished INI file looks like the one shown below.

```
;Report summary ini file

[ErrorRpt]
SourDir=d:\Order_Inventory\Logs\Error.log
ReportOn=3
EventLog=True
```

```
DestFile=d:\Order_Inventory\SummaryRpts\
Debug=False

[DailySales]
SourDir=d:\Order_Inventory\Logs\DailySales.txt
ReportOn=SummaryOnly
EventLog=True
DestFile=d:\Order_Inventory\SummaryRpts\
Debug=False

[DailyReturns]
SourDir=d:\Order_Inventory\Logs\DailyReturns.txt
ReportOn=SummaryOnly
EventLog=True
DestFile=d:\Order_Inventory\SummaryRpts\
Debug=False

[DailyProduction]
SourDir=d:\Order_Inventory\Logs\DailyProduction.txt
EventLog=True
ReportOn=HardAndSupl
DestFile=d:\Order_Inventory\SummaryRpts\
Debug=False
```

Creating an INI File Processing Procedure

Now that Molly has designed the RptLog.ini file, she puts a copy of it in d:\VBScripts\Analyzers on the Windows 2000 Server where the order/inventory system resides. She begins work on developing a procedure that can be used to process the INI file. Later, when she begins working on each of the report and log analyzer scripts, she'll incorporate this procedure into those scripts. In order to access and process the INI file, she will have to learn how to work with the following `FileSystemObject` methods:

- `FileExists()`
- `OpenTextFile()`

- ReadLine()
- Close()

The first step in using methods belonging to the FileSystemObject is to set up an instance of it within your VBScript. This is done using the WScript object's CreateObject() method and by referencing it as Scripting.FileSystemObject, as demonstrated below:

```
Set FsoObject = WScript.CreateObject ("Scripting.FileSystemObject")
```

Once instantiated as shown above, you can reference the FileSystemObject within your scripts as FsoObject.

NOTE

If your VBScripts will be run on a computer that uses the Windows NT, 2000, or XP operating system along with the NTFS file system, then you must take steps to make sure that you have the appropriate set of security permissions required to perform the tasks for which your VBScripts are written.

Verifying Whether the INI File Exists

The first step that you should always take when getting ready to process a file is to verify that the file exists before attempting to open it. This allows you to avoid an error if it does not exist or to create a new file if appropriate to the task at hand. To determine whether a file exists or not, use the FileSystemObject object's FileExists() method. This method has the following syntax.

```
ObjectReference.FileExists(FileName)
```

ObjectReference is the name assigned to the instance of the FileSystemObject defined within the script, and FileName is the name and path of the file whose existence is to be verified. The FileExists() method returns a value of True if the file exists and a value of False if it does not exist.

NOTE

INI files can be accidentally deleted or renamed for an assortment of reasons. One way to deal with this possible situation is to work with your system administrator to tighten up Windows security permissions to prevent nonadministrators from being able to access the contents of the folder where your scripts and INI files reside. Another way of coping with this type of situation is to hard-code a set of default configuration settings whenever possible. This way, the script can still continue to execute and possibly log an error notification event message in the Windows event log to inform you of the situation.

The following VBScript statements demonstrate how to use the `FileExists()` method to determine where a file named Sample.ini resides in the same folders as the VBScript.

```
If (FsoObject.FileExists("Sample.ini ")) Then
  MsgBox "Sample.ini already exists."
Else
  MsgBox "Sample.ini does not exist."
End If
```

NOTE

If the file whose existence is to be verified does not reside in the same folder as the VBScript, you must specify its complete path and file name.

Opening the INI File

Once you have verified that the INI file that stores the VBScript's configuration settings exists, you can open it. To open a file, use the `FileSystemObject` object's `OpenTextFile()` method. This method opens the specified file and returns a TextStream object that can be used to process the contents of the file. The TextStream object represents a file as a contiguous stream of data. The `OpenTextFile()` method has the following syntax.

```
ObjectReference.OpenTextFile(FileName, [OpenMode, [Create, [FormatType]]])
```

ObjectReference is the name assigned to the instance of the FileSystemObject defined within the script, and FileName is the name and path of the file to be opened. OpenMode is an optional parameter that specifies the mode in which the file should be opened and is specified using one of the numeric values shown in Table 17.1.

Table 17.1 OpenTextFile() Constants

Constant	Description	Value
ForReading	Opens or creates a file so that it can be read	1
ForWriting	Opens a new file and writes to it	2
ForAppending	Opens an existing file and appends to the end of it	8

Create is an optional Boolean parameter. When set to True, it specifies that if the specified file does not exist, it should be created. When set to False, a new file is not created if the specified file does not exist. The default is False. FormatType is an optional parameter that specifies the format of the file when a new file is created. The available options for this parameter are listed in Table 17.2.

Table 17.2 OpenTextFile() File Format Type Options

Value	Description
TristateTrue	Opens the file as Unicode
TristateFalse	Opens the file as ASCII
TristateUseDefault	Opens the file using the operating system default file type

NOTE

Be especially careful when specifying whether you wish to read, write, or append to a file. If you open a file in ForWriting mode and the file already exists, its contents are reinitialized, resulting in a loss of all existing data.

The following example demonstrates how to open a file in order to write to it. In this example, the file is created if it does not exist by specifying `ForWriting` as its `OpenMode` setting. However, if the file already exists, it is instead opened using the `ForAppending` mode.

```
Dim FsoObject, strSourceFile, OpenFile
Const cForReading = 1
Const cForWriting = 2
Const cForAppending = 8
Set FsoObject = WScript.CreateObject("Scripting.FileSystemObject")
strSourceFile = "D:\LogFiles\DailyRpt.log"

If (FsoObject.FileExists(strSourceFile)) Then
  Set OpenFile = FsoObject.OpenTextFile(strSourceFile, cForAppending)
Else
  Set OpenFile = FsoObject.OpenTextFile(strSourceFile, cForWriting, "True")
End If
```

NOTE

It is not possible to perform different types of operations on an open file at the same time. In other words if you open a file using the `ForReading` mode, you cannot switch over to `ForWriting` or `ForAppending` modes without first closing and then reopening the file again.

Reading the INI File

Once you know how to open a file and set the appropriate mode, you are ready to read, write, or append to the file. Several steps need to be taken when reading a file, as outlined below.

- Determine whether the file contains any data
- Read the file
- Close the file when done

Each of these tasks will be examined in the sections that follow.

Determining Whether a File Contains Any Data

The first thing to do when opening a file is to determine whether or not it contains any data. Otherwise, there is no point in opening it and attempting to read from it. This can be done using the `AtEndOfStream` property, which will return a Boolean value of `True` if the file contains data and `False` if it does not.

You can also continue to check the value of the `AtEndOfStream` property just before performing any read operation to make sure that you have not reached the end of the file. For example, the following VBScript statements demonstrate how to determine whether a file exists and whether or not it contains any data. If the file is found to contain data, then a loop is set up to process the file, terminating when the value of `AtEndOfStream` becomes equal to `True`.

```
Dim FsoObject, strSourceFile, OpenFile


Const cForReading = 1
Const cForWriting = 2
Const cForAppending = 8


Set FsoObject = WScript.CreateObject("Scripting.FileSystemObject")


strSourceFile = "d:\VBScripts\Analyzers\RptLog.ini"


If (FsoObject.FileExists(strSourceFile)) Then
  Set OpenFile = FsoObject.OpenTextFile(strSourceFile, cForReading)
    Do while False = OpenFile.AtEndOfStream
      ……………..
    Loop
Else
  MsgBox strSourceFile & " does not exist."
End If
```

As you can see, three constants have been defined at the beginning of the example in order to make it easier to read. These three constants represent the different ways that a file can be processed by VBScript. Next an instance of the `FileSystemObject` is instantiated and the location of the INI file to be processed is specified. Then an `If` statement is executed in order to determine whether or not the INI file contains any data. If it does, then the file is opened for reading and a `Do...Until` loop is executed that would then contain other statements required to process the INI file. The loop will iterate until the end of the file is reached.

Reading the Entire INI File

One way to process the contents of a file requires you to use the `FileSystemObject` object's `ReadLine()` method. This method returns a string representing an entire line of output in a file. The syntax of the `ReadLine()` method is shown below.

```
ObjectReference.ReadLine()
```

`ObjectReference` is the name assigned to the instance of the `FileSystemObject` defined within the script.

By modifying the previous example as shown below, you can develop a procedure to process the entire contents of the RptLog.ini that was developed earlier by Molly.

```
Dim FsoObject, strSourceFile, OpenFile

Const cForReading = 1
Const cForWriting = 2
Const cForAppending = 8

Set FsoObject = WScript.CreateObject("Scripting.FileSystemObject")

strSourceFile = "d:\VBScripts\Analyzers\RptLog.ini"

If (FsoObject.FileExists(strSourceFile)) Then
 Set OpenFile = FsoObject.OpenTextFile(strSourceFile, cForReading)
  Do while False = OpenFile.AtEndOfStream
    WScript.Echo(OpenFile.ReadLine())
  Loop
  OpenFile.Close
Else
  MsgBox strSourceFile & " does not exist."
End If
```

The preceding example ensures that the INI file exists and that it has data in it before beginning to read its contents a line at a time. The INI file is read from the beginning to the end of the file using the `FileSystemObject` object's `ReadLine()` method. It ends by executing the `FileSystemObject` object's `Close()` method. This method closes an open TextStream file and has the following syntax:

```
ObjectReference.Close( )
```

`ObjectReference` is the name assigned to the instance of the `FileSystemObject` defined within the script

> **NOTE**
>
> Always use the `FileSystemObject` object's `Close()` method before allowing your VBScripts to terminate their execution. Otherwise, you run the risk of causing an error the next time you try to process the file. The reason is that the file's end-of-file maker may not get created.

If you were to save the previous VBScript statements as a script and run them against Molly's RptLog.ini file, you would see the results shown in Figure 17.1.

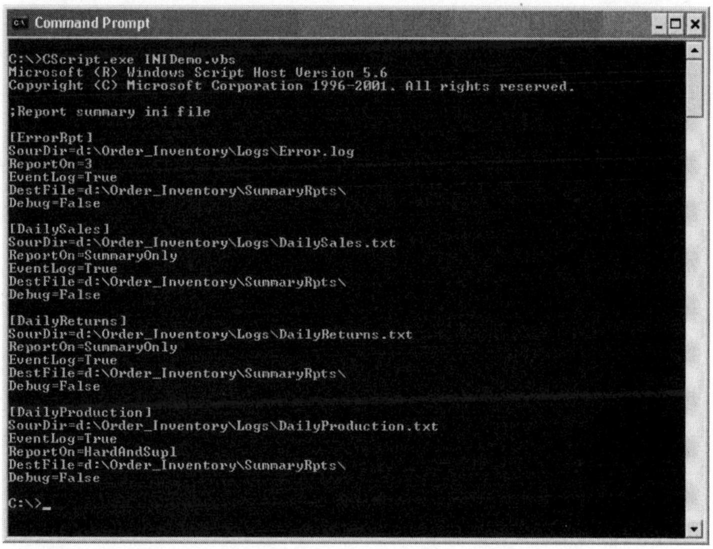
Command Prompt
C:\>CScript.exe INIDemo.vbs
Microsoft (R) Windows Script Host Version 5.6
Copyright (C) Microsoft Corporation 1996-2001. All rights reserved.
;Report summary ini file
[ErrorRpt]
SourDir=d:\Order_Inventory\Logs\Error.log
ReportOn=3
EventLog=True
DestFile=d:\Order_Inventory\SummaryRpts\
Debug=False
[DailySales]
SourDir=d:\Order_Inventory\Logs\DailySales.txt
ReportOn=SummaryOnly
EventLog=True
DestFile=d:\Order_Inventory\SummaryRpts\
Debug=False
[DailyReturns]
SourDir=d:\Order_Inventory\Logs\DailyReturns.txt
ReportOn=SummaryOnly
EventLog=True
DestFile=d:\Order_Inventory\SummaryRpts\
Debug=False
[DailyProduction]
SourDir=d:\Order_Inventory\Logs\DailyProduction.txt
EventLog=True
ReportOn=HardAndSupl
DestFile=d:\Order_Inventory\SummaryRpts\
Debug=False
C:\>_

FIGURE 17.1 *Processing the entire contents of an INI file*

Reading a Section of an INI File

In many cases, it may be appropriate to read and process the entire contents of an INI file at one time. For example, when more than one script shares the same INI file, as is the case in Molly's project, you need a way to selectively process a single section of the INI file at a time. The following VBScript statements demonstrate one way to achieve this goal.

```
Dim FsoObject, strSourceFile, OpenFile, strInputLine, intCounter

Const cForReading = 1
Const cForWriting = 2
Const cForAppending = 8

Set FsoObject = WScript.CreateObject("Scripting.FileSystemObject")

strSourceFile = "d:\VBScripts\Analyzers\RptLog.ini"

If (FsoObject.FileExists(strSourceFile)) Then
 Set OpenFile = FsoObject.OpenTextFile(strSourceFile, cForReading)

    Do Until Mid(strInputLine, 1, 15) = "[DailyReturns]"
      strInputLine = OpenFile.ReadLine
    Loop

    Do Until OpenFile.AtEndOfStream = "True"
      strInputLine = OpenFile.ReadLine
      If Mid(strInputLine, 1, 1) = "[" Then
        Exit do
      End If
        WScript.Echo strInputLine
    Loop

  OpenFile.Close

Else
  MsgBox strSourceFile & " does not exist."
End If
```

A `Do...Until` loop is set up to begin the initial processing of the INI file. In the case of this example, the `Do...Until` loop runs until it finds the `[DailyReturns]` section header. This is done using the VBScript `MID()` function, by passing it the parameters of 1 and 15, which represent the starting and ending character position of the opening and closing brackets in the `[DailyReturns]` section header. When located, the `Do...Until` loop stops executing and a second `Do...Until` loop begins running. This loop executes and processes the key=value pairs stored in the `[DailyReturns]` section using the `ReadLine()` method. This loop runs until either the next section header is found (for example, by looking for the `[` character as the first character in each line that follows) or the end of the file is reached (for example, when the value of `AtEndOfStream` equals `"True"`).

NOTE

The `Mid()` function is used to retrieve or parse out a specified number of characters from a script. Its syntax is shown below.

```
Mid(string, StartPosition[, Length])
```

`String` represents the string from which the characters are to be parsed. `StartPosition` specifies the character position within the string where the parse operation should begin, and `Length` is an optional parameter that specifies the number of characters to be returned. If the `Length` parameter is omitted, then all of the characters from the start position until the end of the string are returned.

If you were to save the previous VBScript statements as a script and run it against Molly's RptLog.ini file, you would see the results shown in Figure 17.2.

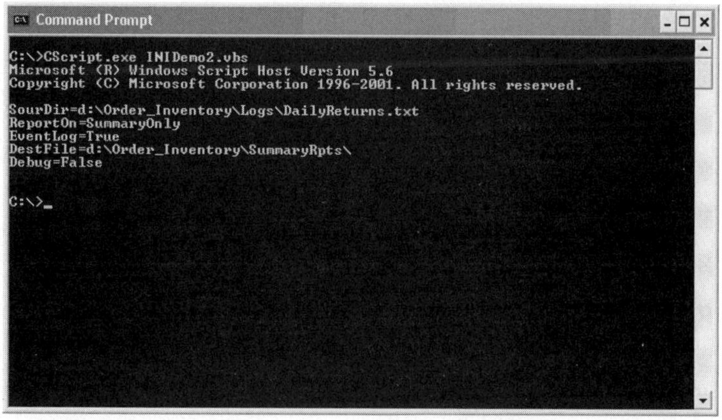
Command Prompt
C:\>CScript.exe INIDemo2.vbs
Microsoft (R) Windows Script Host Version 5.6
Copyright (C) Microsoft Corporation 1996-2001. All rights reserved.
SourDir=d:\Order_Inventory\Logs\DailyReturns.txt
ReportOn=SummaryOnly
EventLog=True
DestFile=d:\Order_Inventory\SummaryRpts\
Debug=False
C:\>_

FIGURE 17.2 *Limiting the processing of an INI file to a single section*

Using the previous example as a template, you can develop a procedure that you can incorporate into the report and log analyzer scripts in order to enable them to retrieve their configuration settings from Molly's INI file.

Summary

In this chapter, you learned how to use INI files as a means of storing configuration settings for your VBScripts. This included a review of their structure and design, as well as an explanation of the steps involved in validating their existence, opening and reading one or all of the sections that make up INI files, and how to close them when done. Using the techniques presented in this chapter, you will be able to incorporate the processing of INI files within your VBScripts and to develop the report and log analyzer scripts required in the next chapter.

Chapter 18

Developing Script Log Analyzers

In this chapter, you will learn how to write a collection of report and log analyzer scripts, each of which is designed to process a uniquely formatted file. In doing so, you will continue to expand your understanding of the techniques involved in reading and processing files. In addition, you will learn the basic techniques involved in creating output files and reports. This chapter will also introduce you to a number of VBScript functions and methods.

Reading Report and Log Files

In the previous chapter, you learned how to apply a number of methods belonging to the `FileSystemObject` in order to read the contents of report and log files. In this chapter, you will continue to expand upon your knowledge of file I/O scripting techniques as you learn how to develop this project's report and log analyzer scripts. You will also learn how to use the `SkipLine()` method. This method allows you to skip lines, such as headers, within input files and to develop more streamlined techniques for processing input files.

The syntax of the `SkipLine()` method is shown below.

```
ObjectReference.SkipLine()
```

`ObjectReference` is the variable representing the instance of the file that is being processed.

NOTE

`SkipLine()` will not permit you to traverse backwards through a file and is only applicable when the input file is opened for reading.

The `SkipLine` method does not accept any arguments and is limited to skipping a single line at a time. However, by wrapping it inside a loop, you can execute the method repeatedly to skip as many lines as necessary, as demonstrated below.

```
Set FsoObject = CreateObject("Scripting.FileSystemObject")
```

```
Set SampleRpt = FsoObject.OpenTextFile("d:\VBScripts\Demo\SampleRpt.txt", 1)
For i = 1 to 3
 SampleRpt.SkipLine()
Next
```

In this example, a file named SampleRpt.txt is opened and the first three lines are skipped. As a result, the next operation performed on the file would occur on the fourth line of the file.

Writing to Files

In order to complete the development of the report and log analyzer scripts you will need to know how to write text output to files in order to generate the summary report. To perform this task, you will need to learn to work with the `FileSystemObject` object's `WriteLine()` method, which has the following syntax:

```
ObjectReference.WriteLine([TextMsg])
```

`ObjectReference` is the variable representing the instance of the `FileSystemObject`. `TextMsg` is an optional parameter that represents a text string to be written as the next line in the file.

NOTE

`WriteLine()` automatically appends a newline character to the end of each text string that it writes to a file. Another way to write text data to a file is with the `Write()` method, which writes a text string to a file without appending a newline character, thus allowing you to create a single line of text in a file using multiple write operations.

The following example demonstrates how to use the `WriteLine()` method to append a text string to the end of a report file.

```
Set FsoObject = CreateObject("Scripting.FileSystemObject")
Set SampleRpt = FsoObject.OpenTextFile("d:\VBScript\s\Demo\SampleRpt.txt", 8)
SampleRpt.WriteLine("--- Account Summary Report ---")
SampleRpt.Close()
```

If you call the `WriteLine()` method without supplying a text string, it will write a blank line. You will need to add blank lines in order to improve the presentation of the text output in the summary report. However, the preferred way to write blank lines is using the `WriteBlankLines()` method, which has the following syntax.

```
ObjectReference.WriteBlankLines(NoOfLines)
```

`ObjectReference` is the variable representing the instance of the `FileSystemObject`. `NoOfLines` represents the number of blank lines to be written.

The following example demonstrates how to use the `WriteBlankLines()` method to append two blank lines to the end of a report file.

```
Set FsoObject = CreateObject("Scripting.FileSystemObject")
Set SampleRpt = FsoObject.OpenTextFile("d:\VBScript\s\Demo\SampleRpt.txt", 8)
SampleRpt.WriteLine("--- Account Summary Report ---")
SampleRpt.WriteBlankLines(2)
SampleRpt.Close()
```

Creating the Error Log Analyzer

The first report and log analyzer script that Molly will tackle is the ErrorAnalyzer.vbs, which will be responsible for performing the following tasks:

- Setting up script configuration setting defaults in case the RptLog.ini file is missing certain key=value pairs or has been removed from the Windows 2000 server
- Reading and processing the INI file
- Creating a new summary report
- Recording a message to the Windows application event log
- Reading and parsing the Error.Log log file looking for level 3 or higher event messages
- Writing the `Errors:` section of the summary report file

ErrorAnalyzer.vbs will need to read the RptLog.ini file, which will reside in D:\VBScripts\Analyzers, and process the key=value pair entries from the `[ErrorRpt]` section, as shown in the following example.

```
[ErrorRpt]
SourDir=d:\Order_Inventory\Logs\Error.log
ReportOn=3
EventLog=True
DestFile=d:\Order_Inventory\SummaryRpts\
Debug=False
```

In addition, ErrorAnalyzer.vbs will have to read and process the Error.log file located in D:\Order_Inventory\Logs on the Windows 2000 Server. A copy of this file is shown below.

```
*******************************************************************************

Error Report  3/15/03

*******************************************************************************

Date           TimeCode Description

12:15:44 3/15/03 001 Unable to access card reader on device wkstn442

12:26:43 3/15/03 005 Invalid application password supplied by AMAT01

14:00:14 3/15/03 001 No inventory for part # 58694 - unable to fill order 39312

15:05:02 3/15/03 005 Invalid application password supplied by MJLF01

16:16:46 3/15/03 003 Unable to print summary rpt on master printer (no paper)

-------------------------------------------------------------------------------

Total number of errors reported = 5
```

The Initialization Section

The script's `Initialization Section`, shown on the following page, begins by defining variables, constants, and objects needed globally by the script. This includes setting up a single dimension array called `astrReportArray` that will be used to hold selected lines of text from the `Error.log` file as it is being read.

Three constants are also defined to make the script easier to read. These constants are called `cForReading`, `cForWriting`, and `cForAppending`. Each represents a different type of file I/O mode. The `FileSystemObject` is also instantiated globally since it will be used by multiple procedures within the script. Lastly, the variable `strSourceFile` is assigned the name and path of the script's INI file.

```
'*************************************************************************
'Script Name: Script 18.3.vbs
'Author: Jerry Ford
'Created: 03/22/03
'Description: This script retrieves configuration settings from an INI file,
'processes a Report file and creates a Summary Report file.
'*************************************************************************


'Initialization Section

Option Explicit

Dim FsoObject, strSourceFile, OpenFile, strInputLine, intCounter
Dim strSourDir, strReportOn, strEventLog, strDestFile, strDebug

ReDim astrReportArray(0)

Const cForReading = 1
Const cForWriting = 2
Const cForAppending = 8

Set FsoObject = WScript.CreateObject("Scripting.FileSystemObject")

strSourceFile = "d:\VBScripts\Analyzers\RptLog.ini"
```

The Main Processing Section

The `Main Processing Section`, shown on the following page, makes six procedure calls and then executes the `WScript` object's `Quit()` method. `SetUpDefault()` calls a subroutine that establishes default configuration settings for the script. `ProcessIniFile()` opens the `RptLog.ini` file, extracts the key=value pairs from the [ErrorRpt] section, and assigns them to local variables, overriding any matching default variable settings. RefineOutputFileName() uses the VBScript Date() and Replace() functions to create a date-stamped file name for the summary report that the script will create and write output to.

Next, an If statement is set up to determine whether or not the script should write an event message to the Windows application event log, by checking the value of the strEventLog variable and calling the WriteToEvenLog() subroutine if appropriate. The ProcessReportFile() subroutine is called next. It reads the Error.log file, parsing out lines of text that contain level 3 or higher error messages and storing them as entries in astrReportArray. Next the RecordSummaryData() subroutine is called. It creates a new summary report and writes the Errors: section, retrieving report data from astrReportArray. Finally, the WScript object's Quit() method is used to terminate the script's execution.

```
'Main Processing Section

SetUpDefaults()

ProcessIniFile()

RefineOutputFileName()

If strEventLog = "True" Then
  WriteToEventLog()
End If

ProcessReportFile()

RecordSummaryData()

'Terminate script execution
WScript.Quit()
```

The SetUpDefaults() Subroutine

The SetUpDefaults() subroutine assigns default values to the following five global variables, each of which represents a default configuration setting for the script.

- **strSourDir**. Specifies the location of the Error.log file.
- **strReportOn**. Specifies the minimum level of message event errors to report on.
- **strEventLog**. Specifies whether or not the script should record a message to the Windows application event log.
- **strDestFile**. Specifies the folder where the summary report is to be saved.
- **strDebug**. Specifies whether or not the script is run in debug mode. When run in debug mode, pop-up dialog boxes display intermediate variable values and identify when various procedures execute in order to track the progress of the script when it executes.

```
'Procedure Section

Sub SetUpDefaults()

  strSourDir = "d:\Order_Inventory\Logs\Error.log"
  strReportOn = 3
  strEventLog = "True"
  strDestFile = "d:\Order_Inventory\SummaryRpts\"
  strDebug = "False"

End Sub
```

The ProcessIniFile() Subroutine

The `ProcessIniFile()` subroutine, shown below, adapts the logic developed from the sample INI processing script in Chapter 17, "Using Configuration Files to Control Script Execution." It processes the RptLog.ini files and extracts the key=value pairs located in the `[ErrorRpt]` section.

```
Sub ProcessIniFile()

  Dim strKeyName, intGetEqualsPosition

  If (FsoObject.FileExists(strSourceFile)) Then
    Set OpenFile = FsoObject.OpenTextFile(strSourceFile, cForReading)
```

```
  Do Until Mid(strInputLine, 1, 10) = "[ErrorRpt]"
    strInputLine = OpenFile.ReadLine
  Loop

  Do Until OpenFile.AtEndOfStream = "True"
    strInputLine = OpenFile.ReadLine

    If Mid(strInputLine, 1, 1) = "[" Then
      Exit do
    End If
    If Len(strInputLine) <> 0 Then
      intGetEqualsPosition = Instr(strInputLine, "=")
      strKeyName = Mid(strInputLine, 1, intGetEqualsPosition - 1)

      Select Case strKeyName
        Case "SourDir"
          strSourDir = Mid(strInputLine, intGetEqualsPosition + 1, _
            Len(strInputLine))
        Case "ReportOn"
          strReportOn = Mid(strInputLine, intGetEqualsPosition + 1, _
            Len(strInputLine))
        Case "EventLog"
          strEventLog = Mid(strInputLine, intGetEqualsPosition + 1, _
            Len(strInputLine))
        Case "DestFile"
          strDestFile = Mid(strInputLine, intGetEqualsPosition + 1, _
            Len(strInputLine))
        Case "Debug"
          strDebug = Mid(strInputLine, intGetEqualsPosition + 1, _
            Len(strInputLine))
      End Select

    End If

  Loop

OpenFile.Close()
```

```
    End If

    If strDebug = "True" Then
      MsgBox "strSourDir = " & strSourDir
      MsgBox "strReportOn = " & strReportOn
      MsgBox "strEventLog = " & strEventLog
      MsgBox "strDestFile = " & strDestFile
      MsgBox "strDebug = " & strDebug
    End If

  End Sub
```

As key=value pairs are parsed out, a `Select Case` statement is set up in order to assign script configuration settings to local variables, thus overriding any matching default settings.

At the end of this subroutine, an `If` statement is set up to check the value assigned to the `strDebug` variable in order to determine whether the script is being run in debug mode. If it is, then the value of each of these variables is displayed in order to show the state of the script's configuration settings.

The RefineOutputFileName() Subroutine

The `RefineOutputFileName()` subroutine, shown on the next page, is responsible for determining the file name under which the summary report is to be saved. In order to facilitate the maintenance of an archive of summary reports, each report is assigned a unique file name that includes a date stamp. This subroutine uses the `Date()` function to retrieve the current date in the format of `mm/dd/yyyy`. It then uses the `Replace()` function to replace each instance of the backslash (/) character with the dash (-) character.

> **NOTE**
>
> Windows does not permit the backslash (/) character to be used in file names. Therefore the dash (-) character is used as a replacement character to separate the month, day, and year components of the date.

```
Sub RefineOutputFileName()

  Dim DataString

  DataString = Replace(Date(), "/", "-")

  strDestFile = strDestFile & DataString & "_SumRpt.txt"

End Sub
```

The ProcessReportFile() Subroutine

The `ProcessReportFile()` subroutine, shown below, opens the Error.log file for reading, establishes a `Do...Loop` that locates the line that begins with the word `Date`, and then sets up a second loop to process the remainder of the file. During each iteration of the second loop, the `Instr()` function is used to determine the location of the `00` characters (each error event number begins with two leading zeros) and then uses the `Mid()` function to determine the error message's event error level. Messages with a level 3 or higher error event level are added to a dynamic array called `astrReportArray`.

If the script is being executed in debug mode, the `MsgBox()` function is used to display each error message that is added to the array. The second `Do...Loop` continues to iterate until all remaining error messages have been examined. Finally the Error.log file is closed.

```
Sub ProcessReportFile()

  Dim FileRef, strRptLine, intGetFirstBlankPosition, OutPutFile

  Dim intArrayCounter, IntErrLevel
  intArrayCounter = 0

  If (FsoObject.FileExists(strSourDir)) Then
    Set FileRef = FsoObject.OpenTextFile(strSourDir, cForReading)
        Do Until Mid(strRptLine, 1, 4) = "Date"
          strRptLine = FileRef.ReadLine()
        Loop
        Do Until FileRef.AtEndOfStream
```

```
            FileRef.SkipLine()
            strRptLine = FileRef.ReadLine()
            If Left(strRptLine, 1) = "-" Then
              Exit Do
            End If
            intGetFirstBlankPosition = Instr(strRptLine, " 00")
            intErrLevel = Mid(strRptLine, intGetFirstBlankPosition + 3, 1)
            If intErrLevel <= 3 Then
              ReDim Preserve astrReportArray(intArrayCounter)
              astrReportArray(intArrayCounter) = strRptLine
            End If

            If strDebug = "True" Then
              MsgBox "Storing '" & strRptLine & "' in the astrReportArray array"
            End If

            intArrayCounter = intArrayCounter + 1
          Loop
        FileRef.Close()

      Else

        astrReportArray(intArrayCounter) = "Error.log file was not available."
      End If

    End Sub
```

The RecordSummaryData() Subroutine

The `RecordSummaryData()` subroutine, shown on the next page, creates a new summary report file and writes its top-level header, followed by the `Errors:` section using the `WriteLine()` and `WriteBlankLines()` functions. A `For...Each` loop is then set up that processes the text strings stored in the `astrReportArray` and writes them to the `Errors:` section of the summary report file. The summary report file is then closed. Finally, if the script is run in debug mode, the `MsgBox()` function is used to display a pop-up message showing that this procedure has executed.

```
Sub RecordSummaryData()

  Dim intArrayCounter, OutPutFile, strMessage

  intArrayCounter = 0

  Set OutPutFile = FsoObject.OpenTextFile(strDestFile, 2, "True")

  If strDebug = "True" Then
    MsgBox "Now writing to the Summary Report"
  End If

  OutPutFile.WriteLine
"*******************************************************************************"
  OutPutFile.WriteBlankLines(1)
  OutPutFile.WriteLine "Consolidated Summary report for " & Date()
  OutPutFile.WriteBlankLines(1)
  OutPutFile.WriteLine
"*******************************************************************************"
  OutPutFile.WriteBlankLines(1)

  OutPutFile.WriteLine "Errors:"
  OutPutFile.WriteBlankLines(1)
  OutPutFile.WriteLine "Date      Time   Code Description"

  For Each intArrayCounter In astrReportArray
    If Len(intArrayCounter) <> 0 Then
      OutPutFile.WriteLine intArrayCounter
    End If
  Next

  OutPutFile.Close()

  If strDebug = "True" Then
    MsgBox "Done writing to the Summary Report"
  End If

End Sub
```

The WriteToEventLog() Subroutine

The `WriteToEventLog()` subroutine, shown below, instantiates the `WshShell` object and uses its `LogEvent()` method to record a message to the Windows application event log. The message is assigned a value of 4, making it an informational message. Finally, if the script is run in debug mode, the `MsgBox()` function is used to display a pop-up message showing that this procedure has executed.

```
Sub WriteToEventLog()

  Dim WshShl

  Set WshShl = WScript.CreateObject("WScript.Shell")

  '4 indicates an information message
  WshShl.LogEvent 4, "The Daily Error Log Analyzer Script is now running."

  If strDebug = "True" Then
    MsgBox "Event log message has been recorded"
  End If

End Sub
```

NOTE

To write error messages to the Windows application event log, you need to know how to work with the `WshShell` object's `LogEvent()` method. While this chapter uses this method to demonstrate how to write event log messages, it is not covered in great detail. For detailed instructions on how to work with the `LogEvent()` method, read Chapter 20, "Maintaining a 30-Day Log Archive."

Creating the Daily Sales Report Analyzer

Like the Error log analyzer script, the Daily Sales report analyzer script reads the RptLog.ini file located in D:\VBScripts\Analyzers. Specifically, it processes the `[DailySales]` section as shown in the following example.

```
[DailySales]
SourDir=d:\Order_Inventory\Logs\DailySales.txt
ReportOn=SummaryOnly
EventLog=True
DestFile=d:\Order_Inventory\SummaryRpts\
Debug=False
```

Once its configuration settings have been read, the script processes the `DailySales.txt` file located in `D:\Order_Inventory\Logs`, as shown below.

```
*******************************************************************************

Daily Sales  3/15/03

*******************************************************************************

Raw Sales:

    Part # Qty  Description                Cust #

1.  58694  12   Cordless temp reader        10034
2.  45643   2   200hp magnetic pump         10055
3.  17443   5   20 lb box of pump clips      10105
4.  10344  10   48 ounce solvent bottle     10003
5.  45643   1   200hp magnetic pump         10003
6.  17443  10   20 lb box of pump clips      10003
7.  58694   5   Cordless temp reader        10111
8.  10344  25   48 ounce solvent bottle    10054
9.  19365   2   3 speed electric drill       10034
10. 58694   2   Cordless temp reader        10103

Total number of sales orders = 10

-------------------------------------------------------------------------------

Sales summary by part number:

   Part # Qty Description
```

```
1. 58694  19   Cordless temp reader
2. 45643   3   200hp magnetic pump
3. 17443  15   20 lb box of pump clips
4. 10344  35   48 ounce solvent bottle
5. 19365   2   3-speed electric drill
```

The Daily Sales report analyzer script, shown below, is structured very similarly to the Error log analyzer script.

```
'*************************************************************************
'Script Name: Script 18.2.vbs
'Author: Jerry Ford
'Created: 03/22/03
'Description: This script retrieves configuration settings from an INI file,
'processes a Report file, and creates a Summary Report file.
'*************************************************************************


'Initialization Section

Option Explicit

Dim FsoObject, strSourceFile, OpenFile, strInputLine, intCounter
Dim strSourDir, strReportOn, strEventLog, strDestFile, strDebug

ReDim astrReportArray(0)

Const cForReading = 1
Const cForWriting = 2
Const cForAppending = 8

Set FsoObject = WScript.CreateObject("Scripting.FileSystemObject")

strSourceFile = "d:\VBScripts\Analyzers\RptLog.ini"


'Main Processing Section

SetUpDefaults()
```

```
ProcessIniFile()

RefineOutputFileName()

If strEventLog = "True" Then
  WriteToEventLog()
End If

ProcessReportFile()

RecordSummaryData()

'Terminate script execution
WScript.Quit()


'Procedure Section

Sub SetUpDefaults()

  strSourDir = "d:\Order_Inventory\Logs\DailySales.txt"
  strReportOn = "All"
  strEventLog = "False"
  strDestFile = "d:\Order_Inventory\SummaryRpts\"
  strDebug = "False"

End Sub

Sub ProcessIniFile()

  Dim strKeyName, intGetEqualsPosition

  If (FsoObject.FileExists(strSourceFile)) Then
    Set OpenFile = FsoObject.OpenTextFile(strSourceFile, cForReading)

      Do Until Mid(strInputLine, 1, 15) = "[DailySales]"
        strInputLine = OpenFile.ReadLine
```

```
        Loop

        Do Until OpenFile.AtEndOfStream = "True"
          strInputLine = OpenFile.ReadLine

          If Mid(strInputLine, 1, 1) = "[" Then
            Exit do
          End If
          If Len(strInputLine) <> 0 Then
            intGetEqualsPosition = Instr(strInputLine, "=")
            strKeyName = Mid(strInputLine, 1, intGetEqualsPosition - 1)

            Select Case strKeyName
              Case "SourDir"
                strSourDir = Mid(strInputLine, intGetEqualsPosition + 1, _
                  Len(strInputLine))
              Case "ReportOn"
                strReportOn = Mid(strInputLine, intGetEqualsPosition + 1, _
                  Len(strInputLine))
              Case "EventLog"
                strEventLog = Mid(strInputLine, intGetEqualsPosition + 1, _
                  Len(strInputLine))
              Case "DestFile"
                strDestFile = Mid(strInputLine, intGetEqualsPosition + 1, _
                 Len(strInputLine))
              Case "Debug"
                strDebug = Mid(strInputLine, intGetEqualsPosition + 1, _
                  Len(strInputLine))
            End Select

          End If

        Loop

      OpenFile.Close()

    End If
```

```
  If strDebug = "True" Then
    MsgBox "strSourDir = " & strSourDir
    MsgBox "strReportOn = " & strReportOn
    MsgBox "strEventLog = " & strEventLog
    MsgBox "strDestFile = " & strDestFile
    MsgBox "strDebug = " & strDebug
  End If

End Sub

Sub RefineOutputFileName()

  Dim DataString

  DataString = Replace(Date(), "/", "-")

  strDestFile = strDestFile & DataString & "_SumRpt.txt"

End Sub

Sub ProcessReportFile()

  Dim FileRef, strRptLine, intGetFirstBlankPosition, OutPutFile

  Dim intArrayCounter
  intArrayCounter = 0

  If (FsoObject.FileExists(strSourDir)) Then
    Set FileRef = FsoObject.OpenTextFile(strSourDir, cForReading)
    Do While False = FileRef.AtEndOfStream

      If strReportOn = "SummaryOnly" Then
        Do Until Mid(strRptLine, 1, 13) = "Sales summary"
          strRptLine = FileRef.ReadLine()
        Loop

        FileRef.SkipLine()
        FileRef.SkipLine()
```

```
          FileRef.SkipLine()

          Do Until FileRef.AtEndOfStream
            strRptLine = FileRef.ReadLine()
            intGetFirstBlankPosition = Instr(strRptLine, " ")
            strRptLine = Mid(strRptLine, intGetFirstBlankPosition + 1)

            ReDim Preserve astrReportArray(intArrayCounter)
            astrReportArray(intArrayCounter) = strRptLine

            If strDebug = "True" Then
              MsgBox "Storing '" & strRptLine & "' in the astrReportArray array"
            End If

            intArrayCounter = intArrayCounter + 1
          Loop
        Else
          Do Until FileRef.AtEndOfStream
            strRptLine = FileRef.ReadLine()
            ReDim Preserve astrReportArray(intArrayCounter)
            astrReportArray(intArrayCounter) = strRptLine

            If strDebug = "True" Then
              MsgBox "Storing " & strRptLine & " in the astrReportArray array"
            End If

            intArrayCounter = intArrayCounter + 1
          Loop
        End If
    Loop
     FileRef.Close()

  Else

     astrReportArray(intArrayCounter) = "DailySales.txt file was not available."
  End If
End Sub
```

```
Sub RecordSummaryData()

  Dim intArrayCounter, OutPutFile, strMessage

  intArrayCounter = 0

  Set OutPutFile = FsoObject.OpenTextFile(strDestFile, 8)

  If strDebug = "True" Then
    MsgBox "Now writing to the Summary Report"
  End If

  OutPutFile.WriteBlankLines(1)
  OutPutFile.WriteLine "--------------------------------------------" & _
    "----------------------------------"
  OutPutFile.WriteBlankLines(1)

  If strReportOn = "SummaryOnly" Then
    OutPutFile.WriteLine "Sales summary:"
    OutPutFile.WriteBlankLines(1)
    OutPutFile.WriteLine "Part #  Qty Description"
    OutPutFile.WriteBlankLines(1)
  End If

  For Each intArrayCounter In astrReportArray
    OutPutFile.WriteLine intArrayCounter
  Next

  OutPutFile.Close()

  If strDebug = "True" Then
    MsgBox "Done writing to the Summary Report"
  End If

End Sub

Sub WriteToEventLog()
```

```
  Dim WshShl

  Set WshShl = WScript.CreateObject("WScript.Shell")

  '4 indicates an information message
  WshShl.LogEvent 4, "The Daily Sales Report Analyzer Script is now running."

  If strDebug = "True" Then
    MsgBox "Event log message has been recorded"
  End If

End Sub
```

One of the areas where the Daily Sales report analyzer script differs from the Error log analyzer scripts is in its default variable settings, which are specified in the `SetUpDefaults()` subroutine. Also, the `ProcessIniFile()` subroutine has been modified to look for the `[DailySales]` header. In addition, the `ProcessReportFile()` subroutine has been modified to look for the `Sales Summary` section of the Daily Sales report and to process all of the entries in that section. One final significant difference between the two analyzers is in the `RecordSummaryData()` subroutine, where the summary report is opened in `ForAppending` mode instead of in `ForWriting` mode.

Creating the Daily Returns Report Analyzer

The Daily Returns report analyzer script is nearly identical to the Daily Sales report analyzer script. Both read the RptLog.ini file located in D:\VBScripts\Analyzers. However, the Daily Returns report analyzer script processes the `[DailyReturns]` section, as shown below.

```
[DailyReturns]
SourDir=d:\Order_Inventory\Logs\DailyReturns.txt
ReportOn=SummaryOnly
EventLog=True
DestFile=d:\Order_Inventory\SummaryRpts\
Debug=False
```

Once its configuration settings have been read, the script processes the DailyReturns.txt file, located in D:\Order_Inventory\Logs as shown below.

```
*******************************************************************************

Daily Returns     3/15/03

*******************************************************************************

Raw Returns:

    Part #  Qty  Description                     Cust #

1.  58694   1    Cordless temp reader            10045
2.  17443   2    20 lb box of pump clips         10103
3.  10344   4    48 ounce solvent bottle         10111
4.  45643   1    200hp magnetic pump             10056
5.  19365   1    3 speed electric drill          10092
6.  58694   1    Cordless temp reader            10007
7.  17443   3    20 lb box of pump clips         10007
8.  17443   2    20 lb box of pump clips         10150


Total number of return orders = 8

-------------------------------------------------------------------------------

Return summary by part number:

   Part #  Qty Description

1. 58694   2   Cordless temp reader
2. 17443   7   20 lb box of pump clips
3. 10344   4   48 ounce solvent bottle
4. 45643   1   200hp magnetic pump
5. 19365   1   3 speed electric drill
```

The Daily Returns report analyzer script, shown on the following page, is structured very similarly to the Daily Sales report analyzer script.

```
'*************************************************************************
'Script Name: Script 18.1.vbs
'Author: Jerry Ford
'Created: 03/22/03
'Description: This script retrieves configuration settings from an INI file,
'processes a Report file, and creates a Summary Report file.
'*************************************************************************


'Initialization Section

Option Explicit

Dim FsoObject, strSourceFile, OpenFile, strInputLine, intCounter
Dim strSourDir, strReportOn, strEventLog, strDestFile, strDebug

ReDim astrReportArray(0)

Const cForReading = 1
Const cForWriting = 2
Const cForAppending = 8

Set FsoObject = WScript.CreateObject("Scripting.FileSystemObject")

strSourceFile = "d:\VBScripts\Analyzers\RptLog.ini"


'Main Processing Section

SetUpDefaults()

ProcessIniFile()

RefineOutputFileName()

If strEventLog = "True" Then
  WriteToEventLog()
End If
```

```
ProcessReportFile()

RecordSummaryData()

'Terminate script execution
WScript.Quit()


'Procedure Section

Sub SetUpDefaults()

  strSourDir = "d:\Order_Inventory\Logs\DailyReturns.txt"
  strReportOn = "All"
  strEventLog = "False"
  strDestFile = "d:\Order_Inventory\SummaryRpts\"
  strDebug = "False"

End Sub

Sub ProcessIniFile()

  Dim strKeyName, intGetEqualsPosition

  If (FsoObject.FileExists(strSourceFile)) Then
    Set OpenFile = FsoObject.OpenTextFile(strSourceFile, cForReading)

      Do Until Mid(strInputLine, 1, 15) = "[DailyReturns]"
        strInputLine = OpenFile.ReadLine
      Loop

      Do Until OpenFile.AtEndOfStream = "True"
        strInputLine = OpenFile.ReadLine

        If Mid(strInputLine, 1, 1) = "[" Then
          Exit do
        End If
```

```
        If Len(strInputLine) <> 0 Then
          intGetEqualsPosition = Instr(strInputLine, "=")
          strKeyName = Mid(strInputLine, 1, intGetEqualsPosition - 1)

          Select Case strKeyName
            Case "SourDir"
              strSourDir = Mid(strInputLine, intGetEqualsPosition + 1, _
                Len(strInputLine))
            Case "ReportOn"
              strReportOn = Mid(strInputLine, intGetEqualsPosition + 1, _
                Len(strInputLine))
            Case "EventLog"
              strEventLog = Mid(strInputLine, intGetEqualsPosition + 1, _
                Len(strInputLine))
            Case "DestFile"
              strDestFile = Mid(strInputLine, intGetEqualsPosition + 1, _
                Len(strInputLine))
            Case "Debug"
              strDebug = Mid(strInputLine, intGetEqualsPosition + 1, _
                Len(strInputLine))
          End Select

        End If

      Loop

    OpenFile.Close()

  End If

  If strDebug = "True" Then
    MsgBox "strSourDir = " & strSourDir
    MsgBox "strReportOn = " & strReportOn
    MsgBox "strEventLog = " & strEventLog
    MsgBox "strDestFile = " & strDestFile
    MsgBox "strDebug = " & strDebug
  End If
```

```
End Sub

Sub RefineOutputFileName()

  Dim DataString

  DataString = Replace(Date(), "/", "-")

  strDestFile = strDestFile & DataString & "_SumRpt.txt"

End Sub

Sub ProcessReportFile()

  Dim FileRef, strRptLine, intGetFirstBlankPosition, OutPutFile

  Dim intArrayCounter
  intArrayCounter = 0

  If (FsoObject.FileExists(strSourDir)) Then
    Set FileRef = FsoObject.OpenTextFile(strSourDir, cForReading)
    Do While False = FileRef.AtEndOfStream

      If strReportOn = "SummaryOnly" Then
        Do Until Mid(strRptLine, 1, 14) = "Return summary"
          strRptLine = FileRef.ReadLine()
        Loop

        FileRef.SkipLine()
        FileRef.SkipLine()
        FileRef.SkipLine()

        Do Until FileRef.AtEndOfStream
          strRptLine = FileRef.ReadLine()
          intGetFirstBlankPosition = Instr(strRptLine, " ")
          strRptLine = Mid(strRptLine, intGetFirstBlankPosition + 1)

          ReDim Preserve astrReportArray(intArrayCounter)
```

```
            astrReportArray(intArrayCounter) = strRptLine

            If strDebug = "True" Then
              MsgBox "Storing '" & strRptLine & "' in the astrReportArray array"
            End If

            intArrayCounter = intArrayCounter + 1
          Loop
        Else
          Do Until FileRef.AtEndOfStream
            strRptLine = FileRef.ReadLine()
            ReDim Preserve astrReportArray(intArrayCounter)
            astrReportArray(intArrayCounter) = strRptLine

            If strDebug = "True" Then
              MsgBox "Storing " & strRptLine & " in the astrReportArray array"
            End If

            intArrayCounter = intArrayCounter + 1
          Loop
        End If
    Loop
      FileRef.Close()

  Else

    astrReportArray(intArrayCounter) = "DailyReturns.txt file was not available."
  End If
End Sub

Sub RecordSummaryData()

  Dim intArrayCounter, OutPutFile, strMessage

  intArrayCounter = 0

  Set OutPutFile = FsoObject.OpenTextFile(strDestFile, 8)
```

```
  If strDebug = "True" Then
    MsgBox "Now writing to the Summary Report"
  End If

  OutPutFile.WriteBlankLines(1)
  OutPutFile.WriteLine "-----------------------------------------" & _
    "---------------------------------"
  OutPutFile.WriteBlankLines(1)

  If strReportOn = "SummaryOnly" Then
    OutPutFile.WriteLine "Return summary:"
    OutPutFile.WriteBlankLines(1)
    OutPutFile.WriteLine "Part #  Qty Description"
    OutPutFile.WriteBlankLines(1)
  End If

  For Each intArrayCounter In astrReportArray
    OutPutFile.WriteLine intArrayCounter
  Next

  OutPutFile.Close()

  If strDebug = "True" Then
    MsgBox "Done writing to the Summary Report"
  End If

End Sub

Sub WriteToEventLog()

  Dim WshShl

  Set WshShl = WScript.CreateObject("WScript.Shell")

  '4 indicates an information message
  WshShl.LogEvent 4, "The Daily Returns Report Analyzer Script is now running."

  If strDebug = "True" Then
```

```
    MsgBox "Event log message has been recorded"
  End If

End Sub
```

The main differences between the Daily Sales and Daily Returns report analyzer scripts are as follows:

- Variable settings in the `SetUpDefaults()` subroutine have been modified.
- The `ProcessIniFile()` subroutine is set up to process the key=pair items located in the `[DailyReturns]` section.

Creating the Daily Production Report Analyzer

The Daily Production report analyzer is very similar to the Daily Sales and Daily Returns report analyzer scripts. All three read the RptLog.ini file located in D:\VBScripts\Analyzers. However, the Daily Production report analyzer processes the `[DailyProduction]` section, as shown below.

```
[DailyProduction]
SourDir=d:\Order_Inventory\Logs\DailyProduction.txt
EventLog=True
ReportOn=HardAndSupl
DestFile=d:\Order_Inventory\SummaryRpts\
Debug=False
```

Once its configuration settings have been read, the script processes the DailyProduction.txt file located in D:\Order_Inventory\Logs as shown below.

```
*******************************************************************************

Daily Production      3/15/03

*******************************************************************************

Hardware:
```

```
    Part #  Qty    Description              In Stock

1.  58694   10     Cordless temp reader       25
2.  45643    2     200hp magnetic pump        10
3.  19365    5     3 speed electric drill      10

--------------------------------------------------------------------------------

Supplies:

    Part #  Qty    Description                  In Stock

1.  17443    20    20 lb box of pump clips       100
2.  10344   100    48 ounce solvent bottle       250
```

The Daily Production report analyzer script, shown below, is structured very similarly to the Daily Sales and Daily Returns report analyzer scripts.

```
'*************************************************************************
'Script Name: Script 18.4.vbs
'Author: Jerry Ford
'Created: 03/22/03
'Description: This script retrieves configuration settings from an INI file,
'processes a Report file, and creates a Summary Report file.
'*************************************************************************


'Initialization Section

Option Explicit

Dim FsoObject, strSourceFile, OpenFile, strInputLine, intCounter
Dim strSourDir, strReportOn, strEventLog, strDestFile, strDebug

ReDim astrReportArray(0)

Const cForReading = 1
Const cForWriting = 2
Const cForAppending = 8
```

```
Set FsoObject = WScript.CreateObject("Scripting.FileSystemObject")

strSourceFile = "d:\VBScripts\Analyzers\RptLog.ini"


'Main Processing Section

SetUpDefaults()

ProcessIniFile()

RefineOutputFileName()

If strEventLog = "True" Then
  WriteToEventLog()
End If

ProcessReportFile()

RecordSummaryData()

'Terminate script execution
WScript.Quit()


'Procedure Section

Sub SetUpDefaults()

  strSourDir = "d:\Order_Inventory\Logs\DailyProduction.txt"
  strReportOn = "HardAndSupl"
  strEventLog = "False"
  strDestFile = "d:\Order_Inventory\SummaryRpts\"
  strDebug = "False"

End Sub
```

```
Sub ProcessIniFile()

  Dim strKeyName, intGetEqualsPosition

  If (FsoObject.FileExists(strSourceFile)) Then
    Set OpenFile = FsoObject.OpenTextFile(strSourceFile, cForReading)

      Do Until Mid(strInputLine, 1, 17) = "[DailyProduction]"
        strInputLine = OpenFile.ReadLine
      Loop

      Do Until OpenFile.AtEndOfStream = "True"
        strInputLine = OpenFile.ReadLine

        If Mid(strInputLine, 1, 1) = "[" Then
          Exit do
        End If
        If Len(strInputLine) <> 0 Then
          intGetEqualsPosition = Instr(strInputLine, "=")
          strKeyName = Mid(strInputLine, 1, intGetEqualsPosition - 1)

          Select Case strKeyName
            Case "SourDir"
              strSourDir = Mid(strInputLine, intGetEqualsPosition + 1, _
                Len(strInputLine))
            Case "ReportOn"
              strReportOn = Mid(strInputLine, intGetEqualsPosition + 1, _
                Len(strInputLine))
            Case "EventLog"
              strEventLog = Mid(strInputLine, intGetEqualsPosition + 1, _
                Len(strInputLine))
            Case "DestFile"
              strDestFile = Mid(strInputLine, intGetEqualsPosition + 1, _
                Len(strInputLine))
            Case "Debug"
              strDebug = Mid(strInputLine, intGetEqualsPosition + 1, _
                Len(strInputLine))
          End Select
```

```
          End If

        Loop

      OpenFile.Close()

    End If

    If strDebug = "True" Then
      MsgBox "strSourDir = " & strSourDir
      MsgBox "strReportOn = " & strReportOn
      MsgBox "strEventLog = " & strEventLog
      MsgBox "strDestFile = " & strDestFile
      MsgBox "strDebug = " & strDebug
    End If

End Sub

Sub RefineOutputFileName()

  Dim DataString

  DataString = Replace(Date(), "/", "-")

  strDestFile = strDestFile & DataString & "_SumRpt.txt"

End Sub

Sub ProcessReportFile()

  Dim FileRef, strRptLine, intGetFirstBlankPosition, OutPutFile

  Dim intArrayCounter
  intArrayCounter = 0

  If (FsoObject.FileExists(strSourDir)) Then
    Set FileRef = FsoObject.OpenTextFile(strSourDir, cForReading)
```

```
'Do While False = FileRef.AtEndOfStream

 If Instr(1, strReportOn, "Hard") Then
   Do Until Mid(strRptLine, 1, 8) = "Hardware"
     strRptLine = FileRef.ReadLine()
   Loop

   FileRef.SkipLine()
   FileRef.SkipLine()
   FileRef.SkipLine()

   Do Until FileRef.AtEndOfStream
     strRptLine = FileRef.ReadLine()
     intGetFirstBlankPosition = Instr(strRptLine, " ")
     strRptLine = Mid(strRptLine, intGetFirstBlankPosition + 2)

     If Left(strRptLine, 1) = "-" Then
       Exit Do
     End If

     ReDim Preserve astrReportArray(intArrayCounter)
     astrReportArray(intArrayCounter) = strRptLine

     If strDebug = "True" Then
       MsgBox "Storing '" & strRptLine & "' in the astrReportArray array"
     End If

     intArrayCounter = intArrayCounter + 1
   Loop
 End If
 If Instr(1, strReportOn, "Supl") Then

   Do Until Mid(strRptLine, 1, 8) = "Supplies"
     strRptLine = FileRef.ReadLine()
   Loop

   FileRef.SkipLine()
   FileRef.SkipLine()
```

```
        FileRef.SkipLine()

        Do Until FileRef.AtEndOfStream
          strRptLine = FileRef.ReadLine()
          intGetFirstBlankPosition = Instr(strRptLine, " ")
          strRptLine = Mid(strRptLine, intGetFirstBlankPosition + 2)

          If Left(strRptLine, 1) = "-" Then
            Exit Do
          End If

          ReDim Preserve astrReportArray(intArrayCounter)
          astrReportArray(intArrayCounter) = strRptLine

          If strDebug = "True" Then
            MsgBox "Storing '" & strRptLine & "' in the astrReportArray array"
          End If

          intArrayCounter = intArrayCounter + 1
        Loop

      End If
    'Loop
     FileRef.Close()

  Else

     astrReportArray(intArrayCounter) = "DailyProducton.txt file was not available."
  End If
End Sub

Sub RecordSummaryData()

  Dim intArrayCounter, OutPutFile, strMessage

  intArrayCounter = 0

  Set OutPutFile = FsoObject.OpenTextFile(strDestFile, 8)
```

```
  If strDebug = "True" Then
    MsgBox "Now writing to the Summary Report"
  End If

  OutPutFile.WriteBlankLines(1)
  OutPutFile.WriteLine "--------------------------------------------" & _
    "----------------------------------"
  OutPutFile.WriteBlankLines(1)

  OutPutFile.WriteLine "Daily Production Summary"
  OutPutFile.WriteBlankLines(1)
  OutPutFile.WriteLine "Part #  Qty  Description              In Stock"
  OutPutFile.WriteBlankLines(1)

  For Each intArrayCounter In astrReportArray

    If Len(intArrayCounter) <> 0 Then
      OutPutFile.WriteLine intArrayCounter
    End If
  Next

  OutPutFile.Close()

  If strDebug = "True" Then
    MsgBox "Done writing to the Summary Report"
  End If

End Sub

Sub WriteToEventLog()

  Dim WshShl

  Set WshShl = WScript.CreateObject("WScript.Shell")

  '4 indicates an information message
  WshShl.LogEvent 4, "The Daily Production Report Analyzer Script is now running."
```

```
    If strDebug = "True" Then
      MsgBox "Event log message has been recorded"
    End If

End Sub
```

The main differences between the Daily Production and the Daily Sales and Daily Returns report analyzer scripts are as follows:

- Variable settings in the `SetUpDefaults()` subroutine have been modified.
- The `ProcessIniFile()` subroutine is set up to process the key=pair items located in the `[DailyProduction]` section.
- The `ProcessReportFile()` subroutine is designed to look for and process the `Hardware` and `Software` sections of the Daily Production report.

Examining the Order/Inventory Summary Report

The four report and log analyzer scripts will ultimately be set up to run on an automated basis. The scripts will be run sequentially, with the Error report processed, first followed by the Daily Sales and Daily Returns reports and finally the Daily Production reports. The following sample summary report shows how a typical summary report will look once all the scripts have been run.

```
********************************************************************************

Consolidated Summary report for 3/23/2003

********************************************************************************

Errors:

Date      Time    Code Description
12:15:44 3/15/03 001 Unable to access card reader on device wkstn442
```

```
14:00:14 3/15/03 001 No inventory for part # 58694 - unable to fill order 39312
16:16:46 3/15/03 003 Unable to print summary rpt on master printer (no paper)

-------------------------------------------------------------------------------

Sales summary:

Part # Qty Description

58694  19   Cordless temp reader
45643   3   200hp magnetic pump
17443  15   20 lb box of pump clips
10344  35   48 ounce solvent bottle
19365   2   3 speed electric drill

-------------------------------------------------------------------------------

Return summary:

Part #  Qty Description

58694   2   Cordless temp reader
17443   7   20 lb box of pump clips
10344   4   48 ounce solvent bottle
45643   1   200hp magnetic pump
19365   1   3 speed electric drill

-------------------------------------------------------------------------------

Daily Production Summary

Part #   Qty  Description               In Stock

58694     10   Cordless temp reader       25
45643      2   200hp magnetic pump        10
19365      5   3 speed electric drill     10
17443     20   20 lb box of pump clips   100
10344    100   48 ounce solvent bottle   250
```

Summary

In this chapter, you learned how to read and process report and log files. You developed a collection of scripts that processed these report and log files based on settings stored in an INI file and then created a summary report, consolidating the information gathered from the report and log files. As a result, you have demonstrated an understanding of how to apply VBScript to solving a real-world problem that would have involved a great deal more effort to solve using a more traditional programming language.

Chapter 19

Scheduling Script Execution

In this chapter, Molly will write a new script that she will then execute every 24 hours using the Windows Task Scheduler. This script, once executed, will be responsible for running each of the report and log analyzer scripts sequentially. As you go through this chapter, you will learn why Molly chose to create a scheduling script instead of simply setting up each of the report and log analyzer scripts as independent scheduled tasks. You will also learn how to work with the Scheduled Task Wizard.

Examining Scheduling VBScript Options

Now that Molly has finished writing and testing each of the report and log analyzer scripts, she needs to set up their automated execution. To accomplish this task, she plans on using the built-in Task Scheduler service. Molly has decided to use the Scheduled Task Wizard to define the execution schedule for report and log files.

Molly has learned that in order for her scripts to run with the appropriate security permissions and privileges when they execute, she will need to set up a special user account, which she calls a *service account*, and then associate that account with her scheduled tasks. Molly has already set up a new user account to be used to run any scripts that need to execute on an automated time schedule. She named this account `ScriptSchlr` and set it up as a local administrator account on the Windows 2000 Server where the order/inventory system resides.

Creating a Scheduled Task for Each Script

Molly has discovered that in order to set up the scheduled execution of each script individually, she will have to repeatedly run the Scheduled Task Wizard and associate each individual script to run using the `ScriptSchlr` account. Although not a difficult task to perform, Molly is concerned about the long-term maintenance of these scripts and of the `ScriptSchlr` account.

Even though she created the `ScriptSchlr` account with a password that does not expire, Molly knows that she will have to manually change its password at least once every six months in order to comply with the company's IT audit policy. This means that every six months, she will have to remember to not only change the `ScriptSchlr` account's password but also to go to the Scheduled Tasks folder and modify the scheduled task for each report and log script. This introduces the possibility that she may make a mistake and mistype the password for one or more scheduled tasks when modifying its schedule.

Creating an Intermediary Scheduling Script

To simplify things and to limit the potential for mishap as much as possible when she has to change the `ScriptSchlr` account's password, Molly has decided to create a new script called `MstrSched.vbs`. This script will take responsibility for sequentially running each of the report and log analyzer scripts, as depicted in Figure 19.1.

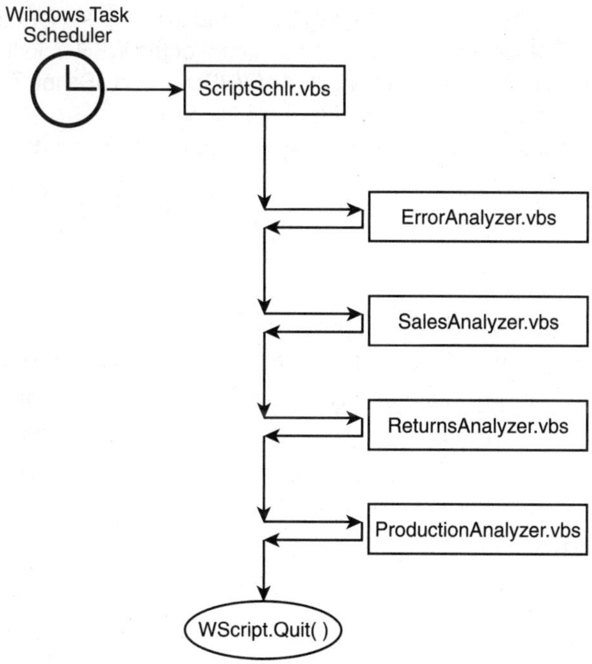

FIGURE 19.1 *Automating the execution of multiple scripts from a single VBScript*

This way, Molly only has to configure one scheduled task in order to set up the automated execution of all her report and log analyzer scripts, and she will only have to modify the account password for one scheduled task every six months.

Using the WshShell Object's Run() Method

After spending some time looking through the Windows Script Technologies help file, Molly came across the `Run()` method. This method belongs to the `WshShell` object and provides the ability to execute a program or script as a new process. It also provides the ability to wait on a child script run using the `Run()` method to finish executing before allowing the calling script to continue its execution.

NOTE

The Windows Script Technologies help file is a freely downloadable help file for the WSH (*Windows Script Host*). It provides a complete document of the WSH object model. In addition, it includes complete documentation of VBScript and JScript. To download a copy of the Windows Script Technologies help file, visit **www.microsoft.com/scripting** and look for a link called **Scripting Documentation Available for Download**.

Ensuring the sequential execution of each report and log analyzer script is a key requirement for Molly because it allows her to create one script that can schedule the execution of additional scripts sequentially, in order to ensure that only one child script runs at a time. By forcing the report and log analyzer scripts to run sequentially, Molly does not have to worry about any errors that would otherwise occur if two or more of the report and log analyzer scripts tried to access and write to the summary report at the same time.

NOTE

Detailed coverage of the `Run()` method is provided in the section "Working with the Windows Command Prompt" found in Chapter 13, "Scheduling Disk Maintenance."

Testing Her Hypothesis

In order to ensure that the Run() method will work as she thinks it should, Molly decides to perform a quick test and writes the following script.

```
'*************************************************************************
'Script Name: Script 19.1.vbs
'Author: Jerry Ford
'Created: 03/22/03
'Description: This script demonstrates the ability of the WshShell object's
'Run() method to sequentially control the execution of multiple child
'scripts.
'*************************************************************************


'Initialization Section

Option Explicit

On Error Resume Next

Dim WshShl

Set WshShl = WScript.CreateObject("WScript.Shell")


'Main Processing Section

WshShl.Run "Notepad", 1, True

WshShl.Run "Notepad", 1, True


'Terminate script execution
WScript.Quit()
```

The script is designed to call the Notepad application, pause for as long as it executes, resume execution by starting another instance of the Notepad, and then pause again until the Notepad application is closed. The VBScript statement that makes this process work is the following.

```
WshShl.Run "Notepad", 1, True
```

In addition to passing the name of the Notepad application as a parameter to the `Run()` method, two more parameters are passed. The first parameter is a numeric value that specifies the Windows style with which the Notepad application should be opened. By specifying this value as a `1`, the script will open Notepad in the exact same manner as if it were started from the Start menu. The second parameter passed to the script determines whether the script should wait on the Notepad application to finish running before resuming its own execution. By setting this value equal to `True`, Molly ensures the sequential execution of both instances of the Notepad application. Had she made the value of the second parameter equal to `False`, both instances of the Notepad application would have opened at the same time.

Monitoring Background Processes

When Molly executed her test script, she saw the first Notepad window appear. To verify that her VBScript was waiting in the background for the Notepad application to be closed, she opened the Windows Task Manager utility and verified that the script was still executing, as shown in Figure 19.2.

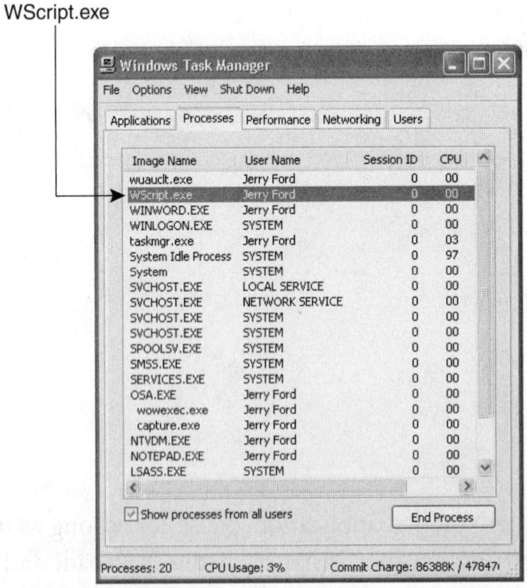

FIGURE 19.2 *Verifying that the VBScript is still executing as a background task*

Because she ran the script from the Windows desktop, it was processed by default using the `WScript.exe` execution host. Although the script itself does not appear in the list of active processes displayed by the Task Manager utility, the presence of an active `WScript.exe` execution host—when she knows that no other scripts are currently executing—is sufficient for her to infer that her test script is still running in the background. By leaving the Task Manager utility visible as she closes the first and second instances of the Notepad application, Molly is able to witness the termination of the test VBScript.

Setting Up an Intermediary Scheduling Script

Now that Molly is confident that she can use the `WshShell` object's `Run()` method to enforce the sequential execution of the report and log analyzer scripts, she begins work on developing the MstrSched.vbs script. To complete the development of this script, Molly will also have to learn how to work with a number of new built-in VBScript functions, as discussed in the following sections.

Creating Logic to Limit When the Script Can Execute

Molly plans to create a single script that will control the execution of both her report and log file analyzers and an archive management script that needs to be executed on the first day of each month. Molly plans to use the built-in VBScript `Day()` and `Date()` functions to ensure that the archive management script, which is named `ArchiveManager.vbs`, will only execute on the first day of each month. This way Molly can write a single script that can handle scheduling the execution of the `MstrSched.vbs` every day to run the report and log analyzer scripts, and still accommodate the monthly execution of the archive management script.

The syntax of the `Date()` function, which returns the current system date, is outlined below.

```
Date()
```

When executed, it returns the current system date in the form of mm/dd/yyyy, as demonstrated below.

```
strTodaysDate = Date()
MsgBox strTodaysDate
```

When executed, the previous VBScript statement displays a pop-up dialog box, as demonstrated in Figure 19.3.

FIGURE 19.3 *Using the* `Date()` *function to display the current system date*

One way to use the information returned by the `Date()` function is to determine whether or not a VBScript is being run on the first day of the month would be to parse out the value of the day field and determine whether it is equal to 1. An easier way to achieve this same result is to use the value returned by the `Date()` function as input to the `Day()` function. The `Day()` function returns a numeric value indicating the day of the month. The syntax for the `Day()` function is outlined below.

```
Day(Date)
```

`Date` represents any expression that specifies a date. Therefore, by wrapping up the `Date()` function inside the `Day()` function, as shown below, you can easily determine the current day of the month.

```
strTodaysDate = Day(Date())
```

When executed on the first day of the month, the value of `strTodaysDate` would be set equal to `1`. By testing the value of `strTodaysDate`, you can incorporate logic into a script that automatically terminates its execution if the day of the month is set to anything other than `1`.

Writing the MstrSched.vbs Script

The `MstrSched.vbs` script is very basic in its design. Given the script's relatively simple role and her tight project development schedule, Molly elected not to spend a lot of time on it or to give it too many bells and whistles. For example, she did not see the need to externalize its settings, nor did she add extra logic to subroutines that accept arguments in order to validate the receipt of any arguments or their validity.

The Initialization Section

The script's `Initialization Section`, shown below, enables the strict interpretation of variable names and error checking. This section also defines and instantiates the `WshShell` object.

```
Option Explicit
On Error Resume Next

Dim WshShl
Set WshShl = WScript.CreateObject("WScript.Shell")
```

The Main Processing Section

The `Main Processing Section`, shown below, begins with a series of four procedure calls to a subroutine named `RunScript()`. This subroutine accepts one argument, the name of a script to execute. Each of these four statements passes the `RunScript()` subroutine a different script name. Because the `MstrSched.vbs` script will be run daily, these four scripts will always be processed and their execution will occur sequentially. The next several lines in the `Main Processing Section` are designed to provide for the monthly execution of the `ArchiveManager.vbs` script. An `If` statement is used to execute the `Day()` and `Date()` VBScript functions in order to ensure that the `ArchiveManager.vbs` script will only be executed on the first day of the month. Finally, the last statement in this section uses the `WScript` object's `Quit()` method to terminate the script's execution.

```
RunScript("ErrorAnalyzer.vbs")
RunScript("SalesAnalyzer.vbs")
RunScript("ReturnsAnalyzer.vbs")
RunScript("ProductionAnalyzer.vbs")

If Day(date()) = 1 Then
  RunScript("ArchiveManager.vbs")
End If

'Terminate script execution
WScript.Quit()
```

The RunScript() Subroutine

The `RunScript()` subroutine, shown below, consists of three statements. The first statement identifies the name of the subroutine and defines the procedure's input argument. This argument represents the name of a report or log analyzer script and is used by the `Run()` method to specify the name of the script to be run. Each script run by this subroutine runs as a background task. In addition, this script will wait for each of the scripts that it calls to complete before returning processing control back to the statement that called it.

```
Sub RunScript(ScriptName)
  WshShl.Run ScriptName, 1, True
End Sub
```

The WriteToEventLog() Subroutine

The `WriteToEventLog()` subroutine, shown below, uses the `WshShell` object `LogEvent()` method to store a message event in the Windows application event log. This way Molly can verify the execution of the script by examining the system log, which she can do remotely from her Windows XP Professional desktop using the Event Viewer snap-in found in the Computer Management console.

```
Sub WriteToEventLog()
  WshShl.LogEvent 4, "Report and Log Analyzer Scheduler Script executing."
End Sub
```

NOTE

The Event Viewer snap-in found in the Computer Management console is started on Windows XP Professional by clicking on Start, right-clicking on My Computer, and selecting Manage from the context menu that appears. This opens the Computer Management console. To view the application log on a Windows 2000 Server for which you have the appropriate security rights and permissions, right-click on the Computer Management (Local) node at the top of the console tree and select Connect to another computer. Then supply the name or IP address of the other computer and click on OK. All that you have to do is expand the System Tools node, followed by the Event Viewer node, and then select the Application node to view the events stored in the remote computer's applications log.

The Fully Assembled Script

The entire VBScript is assembled below. When executed, it will run each of the report and log analyzer scripts sequentially. In addition, on the first day of each month it will run the archive management script.

```
'*************************************************************************
'Script Name: Script 19.1.vbs
'Author: Jerry Ford
'Created: 03/22/03
'Description: This script runs the report and log analyzer scripts,
'one at a time, waiting on each to complete before running the next script.
'*************************************************************************


'Initialization Section

Option Explicit
On Error Resume Next

Dim WshShl
Set WshShl = WScript.CreateObject("WScript.Shell")


'Main Processing Section

RunScript("ErrorAnalyzer.vbs")
RunScript("SalesAnalyzer.vbs")
RunScript("ReturnsAnalyzer.vbs")
RunScript("ProductionAnalyzer.vbs")

If Day(date()) = 1 Then
  RunScript("ArchiveManager.vbs")
End If

'Terminate script execution
WScript.Quit()
```

```
'Procedure Section

Sub RunScript(ScriptName)
  WshShl.Run ScriptName, 1, True
End Sub

Sub WriteToEventLog()
  WshShl.LogEvent 4, "Report and Log Analyzer Scheduler Script executing."
End Sub
```

Setting Up a Daily Automated Script Execution Schedule

Now that her script has been written, Molly needs to create a scheduled task to run it every morning, which she has decided to do at 4:00 A.M. The reports are generally ready for processing at midnight of each day and the nightly backup job that runs next on the server is typically finished at 2:00 A.M. Molly figures that by adding an additional two hours, she will be able to run her scripts without having to worry about whether the reports are ready or if the backup job is still processing.

Molly thought about creating another VBScript to set up the scheduled task for the `MstrSched.vbs` script. However, given that this is a one-time setup task, she decided that it was not worth the effort of writing another script just for this task. Instead, she will use the Scheduled Task Wizard as outlined in the following procedure.

1. Click on Start and then Control Panel. The Control Panel opens.
2. Click on Performance and Maintenance. The Performance and Maintenance folder opens.
3. Click on Scheduled Tasks. The Scheduled Tasks folder opens, as shown in Figure 19.4.

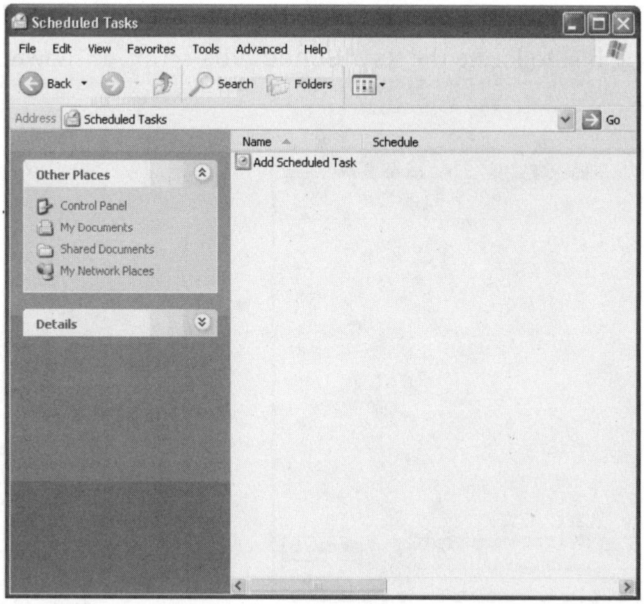

FIGURE 19.4 *The Scheduled Tasks folder provides a focal point for managing all scheduled tasks*

4. An icon is displayed for every currently scheduled task. To set up a new scheduled task, double-click on the Add Scheduled Task icon. The Scheduled Task Wizard starts. Click on Next.
5. The wizard prompts you to select a program for which you would like to set up an automated schedule, as shown in Figure 19.5.

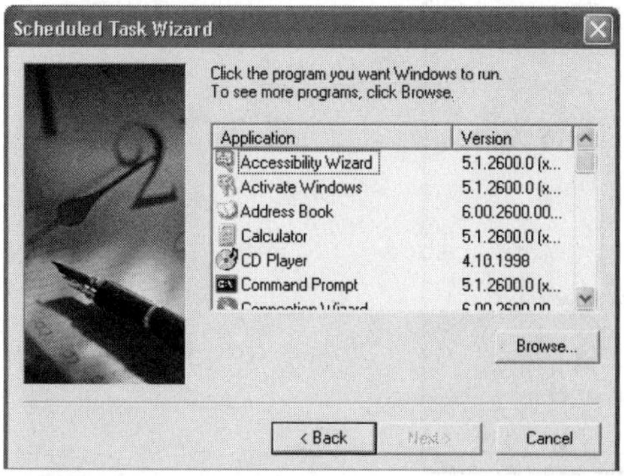

FIGURE 19.5 *The Scheduled Task Wizard automatically presents a list of applications whose execution can be automated*

6. Click on Browse. The Select Program to Schedule dialog box appears. Use this dialog box to locate the `MstrSched.vbs` script, as shown in Figure 19.6.

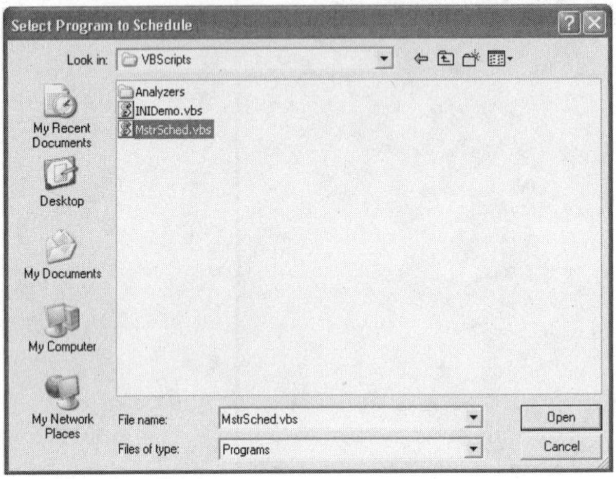

FIGURE 19.6 *Use the Select Program to Schedule dialog box to locate the VBScript that you wish to set up as a scheduled task*

7. Select your script and click on Open.
8. The wizard prompts you to supply the name for the new scheduled task and to select a type of schedule for running it, as shown in Figure 19.7. Select Daily and click on Next.

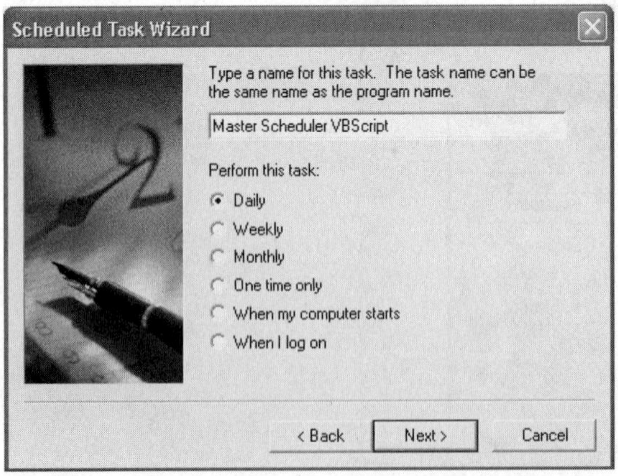

FIGURE 19.7 *The Scheduled Task Wizard assists you in setting up scheduled tasks using a variety of different schedules*

9. You are prompted to supply the specific time of day at which the scheduled task should run, as shown in Figure 19.8. Enter 4:00 P.M. in the Start Time field. Select the Every Day option located in the Perform this task section of the dialog box and then click on Next.

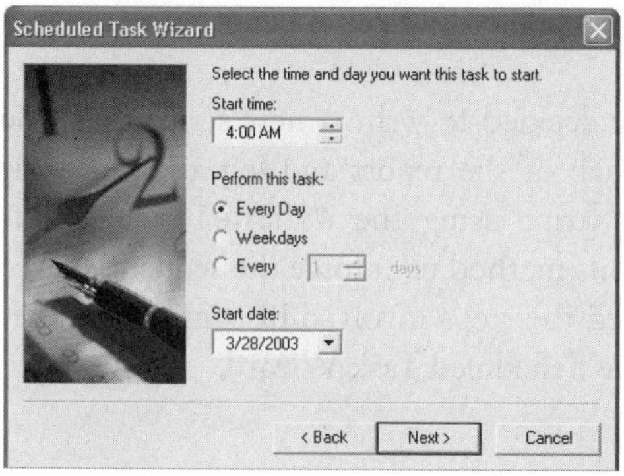

FIGURE 19.8 *The Scheduled Task Wizard requires that you specify a time of day for the execution of the scheduled task*

10. Next you are prompted to specify the name of a user account and its associated password, as shown in Figure 19.9. This scheduled task will use the user account's access privileges when executing your scripts. Molly would type `ScriptSchlr` in the username field and the account's password in the dialog box's two password fields.

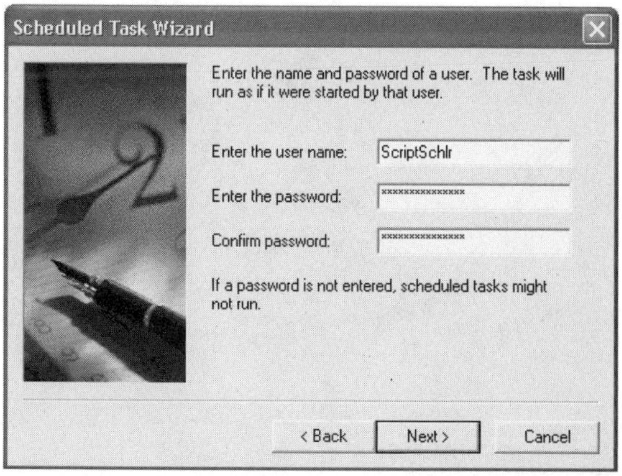

FIGURE 19.9 *Provide the name of a user account with sufficient security permissions and access rights to run your scripts*

11. The wizard announces that it has successfully created a new scheduled task. Click on Finish. The new scheduled task will now appear in the Scheduled Tasks folder.

Summary

This chapter explained why Molly decided to write a new script that would be responsible for the execution of each of the report and log analyzer scripts. It demonstrated how to create this script using the `WshShell` object's `Run()` method and explained how to use this method to enforce the sequential execution of scripts. This chapter also outlined the steps involved in configuring the automated execution of scripts using the Scheduled Task Wizard.

Chapter 20

Maintaining a 30-Day Summary Log Archive

In this chapter, you will learn how to use methods provided by the FileSystemObject and File objects. Using this information, you will develop a VBScript that maintains a 30-day summary log archive. In addition, you will learn detailed information about the WshShell object's LogEvent() method and the built-in VBScript Instr() function.

Managing Files with VBScript

The last script that Molly needs to write is one that will be scheduled to execute on the first day of each month. Its job will be to delete all summary report files stored in the D:\Order_Inventory\SummaryRpts folder on the Windows 2000 server where the order/inventory system is installed, as demonstrated in Figure 20.1.

When executed, the scripts will determine the current month and then delete all summary report files for the month that occurred two months ago. In other words, if the script was run on March 1, it would delete all summary report files for the month of January, leaving all of February's reports in place.

In addition to deleting old archive files, this script will record a message to the Windows application event log each time it is executed. It will also contain logic to prevent its accidental execution by only allowing its execution on the first day of each month.

Using the FileSystemObject

VBScript provides two different objects that have methods that can be used to delete files. The first is the FileSystemObject object's DeleteFile() method. This method provides you with the ability to delete one or more files at a time. The syntax for this method is shown below.

```
ObjectReference.DeleteFile ( FileName[, Kill])
```

ObjectReference is the variable representing an instance of the FileSystemObject. FileName is the complete name and path of the file to be deleted. Wildcard characters can be used to specify the deletion of more than one file.

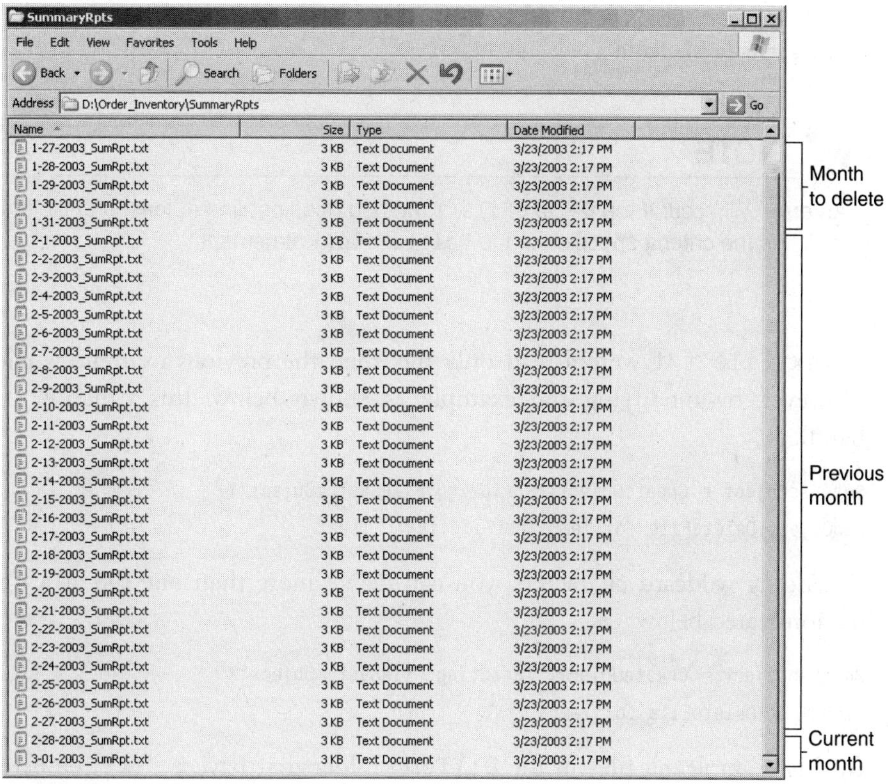

FIGURE 20.1 *The SummaryRpts folder is used to maintain an archived collection of at least one month's worth of summary reports*

`Force` is an optional parameter that allows for the deletion of read-only files when set equal to `True`.

NOTE

The `FileSystemObject` object also provides the ability to copy and move files using its `CopyFile()` and `DeleteFile()` methods.

The following VBScript statements demonstrate how to use the `DeleteFile()` method in order to delete a file named `TestFile.txt` located in `D:\Temp`.

```
Set FsoObject = CreateObject("Scripting.FileSystemObject")
FsoObject.DeleteFile "d:\Temp\TestFile.txt"
```

NOTE

An error will occur if the `DeleteFile()` method does not find at least one file that matches the criteria specified in the `DeleteFile()` statement.

If `TextFile.txt` were a read-only file, then the previous example would fail. However, by modifying the example as shown below, this situation can be handled.

```
Set FsoObject = CreateObject("Scripting.FileSystemObject")
FsoObject.DeleteFile "d:\Temp\TestFile.txt", True
```

By adding wildcard characters, you can delete more than one file at a time, as demonstrated below.

```
Set FsoObject = CreateObject("Scripting.FileSystemObject")
FsoObject.DeleteFile "d:\Temp\*.txt", True
```

In this example, all files in the `D:\Temp` folder that have a `.txt` file extension will be deleted.

Using the File Object

As an alternative to using methods belonging to the `FileSystemObject` object, you can use methods belonging to the `File` object. Using `File` object methods, you can directly administer individual files. These methods provide the ability to copy, move, and delete files, as outlined in Table 20.1.

Table 20.1 File Object Methods

Method	Description
`Copy()`	Copies an individual file or folder to a specified location
`Move()`	Moves an individual file or folder to a specified location
`Delete()`	Deletes the specified file or folder

NOTE

The `File` object's `Copy()`, `Move()`, and `Delete()` methods are capable of acting on both files and folders. As a result, it is important to be careful when working with these methods because it is easy, for example, to accidentally delete a subfolder located in the same folder as a file if both have the same name.

You can delete individual files using the `File` object's `Delete()` method. However, because this method only supports the deletion of one file at a time, you cannot use wildcard characters when specifying the name of the file to be deleted. The syntax of the `File` object's `Delete()` method is shown below.

```
ObjectReference.Delete( Force )
```

`ObjectReference` is the variable representing an instance of the `FileSystem Object`. `Force` is an option Boolean value that when set equal to `True` allows a read-only folder to be deleted.

NOTE

An error will occur if the `Delete()` method is unable to locate a matching file name (for example, if the specified file does not exist).

To use the `File` object's `Delete()` method, you first must instantiate the `FileSystemObject`, as shown below.

```
Set FsoObject = CreateObject("Scripting.FileSystemObject")
```

Next you need to use the `FileSystemObject` object's `GetFile()` method to retrieve a reference to the file that you plan to delete.

```
Set TargetFile = FsoObject.GetFile("d:\Temp\TestFile.txt")
```

Finally, you can delete the file.

```
TargetFile.Delete()
```

NOTE

The `FileSystemObject` object's `GetFile()` method has the following syntax:

```
ObjectReference.GetFile(FileName)
```

`ObjectReference` is the variable representing an instance of the `FileSystemObject`. `FileName` is the complete name and path of the file to be administered.

If the file passed to the `GetFile()` method is not found, an error will occur.

Other VBScript Language Elements Needed to Build the Archive Management Script

While thinking about how to develop the archive management script, Molly decided to use the `FileSystemObject` object's `DeleteFile()` method instead of the `File` object's `Delete()` method. Using the `DeleteFile()` method, she'll be able to delete summary reports on a month-by-month basis within a single `DeleteFile()` operation. Using the `Delete()` method, Molly would have to create a loop and iterate though a list of files stored in the `D:\Order_Inventory\SummaryRpts` folder looking for the file to delete.

Molly also wants to record a message in the Windows event log when the script runs so that she will have a record of its execution. She'll need to use the `WshShell` object's `LogEvent()` method. Additionally, she'll need to learn how to use the built-in VBScript `Instr()` function when executing the subroutine that determines which month's worth of files are to be deleted.

The WshShell Object's LogEvent() Method

For a time, Molly thought about creating a custom log file for her applications to which the scripts would continuously append messages as they were executed. She ultimately gave up on this idea as being too much work for too little gain and has instead decided to leverage the availability of the Windows application event log. To do this, she will have to use the `WshShell` object's `LogEvent()` method, which has the following syntax.

```
ObjectReference.LogEvent(intEventType, strMsg [,strComputer])
```

`ObjectReference` is the variable representing an instance of the `FileSystem Object`. `IntEventType` is a numeric value that specifies the event type. Table 20.2 provides a listing of the available event types. `StrMsg` represents the message to be recorded in the application event log, and `strComputer` is an optional parameter that specifies the name or IP address of another computer where the event should be sent. If omitted, the event is recorded locally.

Table 20.2 Windows Event Types

Value	Description
0	Specifies a successful event
1	Specifies an error event
2	Specifies a warning event
4	Specifies an informational event
8	Specifies a successful audit event
16	Specifies a failed audit event

NOTE

Windows NT, 2000, and XP all maintain application event logs. On Windows 98 and Me, application events are stored in `Wsh.log`, which resides in the same folder as the Windows system files (typically `C:\Windows`).

The following example demonstrates how to use the `LogEvent()` method to write a message to the application event log.

```
Set WshShl = WScript.CreateObject("WScript.Shell")
WshShl.LogEvent 1, "TestScript.vbs - Now executing"
```

The `LogEvent()` method returns a Boolean value of `True` when it successfully writes a message to the Windows application event log and a value of `False` when it fails to write the message, as demonstrated in the following example.

```
Set WshShl = WScript.CreateObject("WScript.Shell")
```

```
intAge = GetUserAge()
If intAge <= 18 Then
  WshShl.LogEvent 1, "Error - User not authorized to execute script"
Else
  WshShl.LogEvent 0, "Script now executing"
End If
Function GetUserAge()
  GetUserAge = InputBox("How old are you?")
End Function
```

In this example, the number entered by the user is checked to determine whether or not the script should execute. If the user is older than 18, the script is permitted to execute, otherwise it is not. A different message is recorded to the application event log based on the user's reported age.

The Built-in VBScript Instr() Function

One of the steps that Molly will need to perform in the archive management scripts is to determine which month's worth of summary reports to delete from the Windows 2000 server where the order\inventory system resides. To perform this task, she will need to leverage a number of different VBScript functions, including the `Instr()`, `Mid()`, and `Date()` functions. The `Mid()` function was previously introduced in Chapter 17 "Using Configuration Files to Control Script Execution" and the `Date()` function was introduced in Chapter 19 "Scheduling Script Execution". The `Instr()` function provides the ability to retrieve a numeric value representing the first occurrence of one string within another. Its syntax is outlined below.

```
InStr([StartPosition,] String1, String2[, CompType])
```

`StartPosition` is an option parameter that is used to specify the starting character position within `String1` where the search is to begin. `String1` represents the expression to be searched. `String2` represents the string to search for. `CompType` is an optional numeric value that specifies the type of comparison. A value of `0` specifies a binary comparison and a value of `1` specifies a text comparison. The value returned by the `Instr()` method varies based on multiple criteria, as outlined in Table 20.3.

Table 20.3 Instr() Return Values

Value	Condition
`0`	`String1` is zero length
`Null`	`String1` is null
`Null`	`String2` is null
`Start`	`String2` is zero length
`0`	`String2` not found in `String1`
`0`	`Start` is greater than the length of `String2`
Position where a match is found	`String2` found within `String1`

Writing the Archive Management Script

Molly is now familiar with everything that she needs to know in order to begin writing the archive management script. As with all her other scripts, she plans to follow a standard design, breaking the script down into three major sections and localizing objects and variable values whenever possible.

The Initialization Section

In the `Initialization Section`, shown below, Molly defines two string variables. The `strVerifyExecutionSchedule` variable will be used in the `Main Processing Section` to store a value indicating whether the script is permitted to run (for example, whether or not today is the first day of the month). The `strDeleteMonth` variable will be used to store a value representing the month's worth of summary report files to be deleted. This variable is used by multiple procedures in the script.

```
Option Explicit

Dim strVerifyExecutionSchedule, strDeleteMonth
```

The Main Processing Section

In the `Main Processing Section`, shown on the following page, Molly first calls a subroutine called `OkToRunToday()` to determine whether it's the first day of the month. If it is, the value returned is `Yes`. Next an `If...Then...Else` statement is set up that controls the execution of a number of procedures. If `strVerifyExecutionSchedule` indicates that today is the first day of the month, then the following procedures are called in the order shown below:

- **`MonthToDelete()`.** Determines which month's worth of summary report files should be deleted
- **`WriteToEventLog()`.** Writes a text string, passed to it as a variable, to the Windows application event log
- **`RemoveOldSummaryFiles()`.** Performs the actual deletion of old summary report files

If the script is not being run on the first day of the month, then the `WriteToEventLog()` subroutine is passed a text message indicating that the script cannot execute and the `WScript` object's `Quit()` method is executed to perform a controlled script termination.

```
strVerifyExecutionSchedule = OkToRunToday()


If strVerifyExecutionSchedule = "Yes" Then
  MonthToDelete()
  WriteToEventLog("Summary Report Archive Manager executing.")
  RemoveOldSummaryFiles()
Else
  WriteToEventLog("Summary Report Archive Manager execution " & _
    "terminated - invalid execution schedule.")
  WScript.Quit()
End If

'Terminate script execution
WScript.Quit()
```

The OkToRunToday() Subroutine

The `OkToRunToday()` subroutine, shown below, uses the built-in VBScript `Day()` and `Date()` functions (as demonstrated in the previous chapter) to determine whether the script is being executed on the first day of the month.

```
Function OkToRunToday()
```

```
    If Day(Date()) = 1 Then
      OkToRunToday = "Yes"
    End If

End Function
```

The MonthToDelete() Subroutine

The `MonthToDelete()` subroutine, shown below, is responsible for determining which month's worth of summary report files are to be deleted. It begins by defining two localized variables. The `intGetSlashPosition` variable is used to store a value indicating the location of the first backslash (`/`) character in the current date. The `strCurrentMonth` variable will be used to store a numeric value indicating the current month.

The value assigned to `intGetSlashPosition` is determined by using the `Instr()` function to search for the backslash (`/`) character in the date as retrieved by the `Date()` function. The value of `strCurrentMonth` is then determined using the `Mid()` function to parse out the month portion of the date (which is in the format of mm/dd/yyyy). The month value is parsed out by taking all the characters from the first character position until the occurrence of the first backslash (`/`) character (expressed as `intGetSlashPosition - 1`).

The value of `strDeleteMonth` is then determined by subtracting 2 from `strCurrentMonth`. If, for example, the current date is March 1, then the value of `strDeleteMonth` will be 1 (3 – 2 = 1). Two `If...Then` statements are then set up to adjust the value of `strDeleteMonth` in the event that the current month is either February or January. If the current month is February, then 2 – 2 will equal zero. Because the month that should be deleted in this instance is December, the first `If` statement checks to see if the value assigned to `strDeleteMonth` is 0 and changes its value to 12 if it is. Likewise, if the current month is January, the value of `strDeleteMonth` is adjusted to 11 (November).

```
Sub MonthToDelete()

  Dim intGetSlashPosition, strCurrentMonth

  intGetSlashPosition = Instr(Date(), "/")
```

```
    strCurrentMonth = Mid(Date(), 1, intGetSlashPosition - 1)

    strDeleteMonth = strCurrentMonth - 2

    If strDeleteMonth = 0 Then
      strDeleteMonth = "12"
    End If

    If strDeleteMonth = -1 Then
      strDeleteMonth = "11"
    End If

End Sub
```

The RemoveOldSummaryFiles() Subroutine

The `RemoveOldSummaryFiles()` subroutine, shown below, is responsible for deleting summary reports that are two months old from the `D:\Order_Inventory\SummaryRpts` summary report archive folder. It begins by setting up an instance of the `FileSystemObject` and defining a variable named `strSummaryRptPath`, which is then set to the location of the folder where the summary reports are stored.

The last statement in the subroutine uses the `FileSystemObject` object's `DeleteFile()` method to delete summary report files that are two months old. This is accomplished by appending together three pieces of information. The first piece of information is the path of the `SummaryRpts` folder. Next the numeric value of the current month is added, followed by `*_SumRpt.txt`. For example, if today was March 1, 2003, then the value passed to the `DeleteFile()` method would be `D:\Order_Inventory\SummaryRpts\01_SumRpt.txt`.

```
Sub RemoveOldSummaryFiles()

  Dim FsoObject, strSummaryRptPath
  strSummaryRptPath = "d:\Order_Inventory\SummaryRpts\"

  Set FsoObject = WScript.CreateObject("Scripting.FileSystemObject")
```

```
  FsoObject.DeleteFile strSummaryRptPath & strDeleteMonth & "*_SumRpt.txt"

End Sub
```

The WriteToEventLog() Subroutine

The `WriteToEventLog()` subroutine, shown below, sets up an instance of the `WshShell` object and then uses its `LogEvent()` method to write an informational message to the Windows application's event log.

```
Sub WriteToEventLog(strMessage)

  Dim WshShl

  Set WshShl = WScript.CreateObject("WScript.Shell")

  WshShl.LogEvent 4, strMessage

End Sub
```

The Fully Assembled Script

Once the archive management script shown below is fully assembled, Molly can place a copy of it in the `D:\VBScripts` folder on the Windows 2000 server where the order/inventory system resides and allow the `MstrSched.vbs` script developed in the previous chapter to automate its execution on a monthly basis.

```
'*************************************************************************
'Script Name: Script 20.1.vbs
'Author: Jerry Ford
'Created: 03/22/03
'Description: This script deletes all summary report files except for
'today's summary file and those of the previous month.
'*************************************************************************


'Initialization Section

Option Explicit
```

```
Dim strVerifyExecutionSchedule, strDeleteMonth


'Main Processing Section

strVerifyExecutionSchedule = OkToRunToday()

If strVerifyExecutionSchedule = "Yes" Then
  MonthToDelete()
  WriteToEventLog("Summary Report Archive Manager executing.")
  RemoveOldSummaryFiles()
Else
  WriteToEventLog("Summary Report Archive Manager execution " & _
    "terminated - invalid execution schedule.")
  WScript.Quit()
End If

'Terminate script execution
WScript.Quit()


'Procedure Section

Function OkToRunToday()

  If Day(Date()) = 1 Then
    OkToRunToday = "Yes"
  End If

End Function

Sub MonthToDelete()

  Dim intGetSlashPosition, strCurrentMonth

  intGetSlashPosition = Instr(Date(), "/")
```

```
    strCurrentMonth = Mid(Date(), 1, intGetSlashPosition - 1)

    strDeleteMonth = strCurrentMonth - 2

    If strDeleteMonth = 0 Then
      strDeleteMonth = "12"
    End If

    If strDeleteMonth = -1 Then
      strDeleteMonth = "11"
    End If

End Sub

Sub RemoveOldSummaryFiles()

    Dim FsoObject, strSummaryRptPath
    strSummaryRptPath = "d:\Order_Inventory\SummaryRpts\"

    Set FsoObject = WScript.CreateObject("Scripting.FileSystemObject")

    FsoObject.DeleteFile strSummaryRptPath & strDeleteMonth & "*_SumRpt.txt"

End Sub

Sub WriteToEventLog(strMessage)

    Dim WshShl

    Set WshShl = WScript.CreateObject("WScript.Shell")

    WshShl.LogEvent 4, strMessage

End Sub
```

Summary

In this chapter, you learned to use the VBScript `Instr()` function to search text strings for matching patterns. By combining this function with the `Mid()` and `Date()` functions, you can determine which group of files to delete when creating the archive management script. You also learned the ins and outs of file management, including how to delete one or more files. Finally, you learned about the `WshShell` object's `LogEvent()` method and how to use it to record messages in the Windows application event log.

PART IV

Professional Project 3

Project 3

Creating a Centralized Report Management Station

Project 3 Overview

This project expands on the previous project by incorporating the processing of reports from multiple order/inventory servers at Intuit Mechanical Tools. The primary focus of the project is the establishment of a centralized report management station where all order/inventory reports will be stored. As part of the process of managing the data stored on these reports, a new consolidated summary report will be developed. This consolidated report will consist of information retrieved from reports stored on each Windows 2000 server where the order/inventory system has been deployed.

This project will require the use of new FileSystemObject methods in order to manage moving and processing reports from the order/inventory servers to the centralized report management station. You will be introduced to numerous VBScript string functions that are required to parse information stored in the order/inventory reports. You will also learn how to develop a master scheduling script that will be responsible for controlling the execution of all the scripts that make up this project.

In addition to learning how to work with the previous VBScript resources, you will learn how to automate the execution of a number of tasks, including:

- Storing data in and retrieving it from the Windows registry
- Remotely administering files stored on network drives
- Creating both plain text and Microsoft Word-formatted reports
- Sending pop-up network messages that provide notification when the consolidated reports are available

Chapter 21

Project Case Study: Creating a Centralized Report Management Station

This chapter begins a new project case study. In this project, you'll observe as Molly Masterson develops a new centralized report management station for the order/inventory system at Intuit Mechanical Tools. Through the completion of this project, you will gain further experience in automating many of the tasks that were covered in the previous project. In addition, you will learn how to automate a number of new tasks, including:

- The storage and retrieval of configuration data in the Windows registry
- The remote administration of files stored on network drives
- The creation of text and Microsoft Word files
- The sending of notification pop-up messages over a network

Project Overview

It has been one month since Molly finished the development and deployment of her order/inventory report and log analyzer scripts. Since that time, an exciting new development has occurred at Intuit Mechanical Tools. Last week, the company was awarded a five-year contract with the local state government that will require it to almost double its production output. The first orders for this new contract will begin arriving in a week. Because this new contract was somewhat of a surprise, everyone at Intuit Mechanical Tools has to scramble in order to get things ready.

As a short-term solution to handling the increasing IT processing workload, the company has purchased a new Windows 2000 server and plans to install the order/inventory system on it. This server will then be used to handle all incoming sales and returns originating from the new government contract. Meanwhile, the current Windows 2000 server will continue to process all sales and returns from all current customers. At a later date (once more programmers have been hired), the company will work toward modifying the order/inventory system and consolidating all of the data managed from both the Windows 2000 servers. This means that a number of departments within Intuit Mechanical Tools will have to work harder in order to consolidate sales, returns, and production information from two different sources.

As a result of her success in completing her last project, the computer operations department has requested that Molly develop an automated process that will retrieve copies of the summary reports from both Windows 2000 servers and store them on a dedicated Windows 2000 Professional workstation located within the operations control center. In addition, the operations department would like for Molly to automate the processing of the summary reports from both servers and to create a single consolidated report, for which they would like to keep a rolling three-month archive.

Collecting Project Requirements

The first step that Molly took upon beginning this new project was to sit down with several members of the operations staff to determine exactly what they were looking for in regards to the creation of a consolidated summary report. At this meeting, she was asked to develop a daily report based on the following sample report that operations had manually created.

```
*******************************************************************************

Master Consolidated Summary report for 5/01/2003

*******************************************************************************

Errors:

Date      Time     Svr  Code Description
12:15:44  3/01/03  Sr2  001 Unable to access card reader on device wkstn442
14:00:14  3/01/03  Sr2  001 No inventory for part # 58692 - unable to fill order
                        39312
16:16:46  3/01/03  Sr2  003 Unable to print summary rpt on master printer (no
                        paper)
17:42:23  3/01/03  Sr1  002 Failure executing job # 434, sched 55 - code 0004534
18:19:19  3/01/03  Sr1  001 No inventory for part # 58655 - unable to fill order
                        39312
18:22:21  3/01/03  Sr1  001 Unable to access card reader on device wkstn113

-------------------------------------------------------------------------------

Sales summary:
```

```
Government:

Part # Qty  Description

58694  19   Cordless temp reader
45643   3   200hp magnetic pump
17443  15   20 lb box of pump clips
10344  35   48 ounce solvent bottle
19365   2   3 speed electric drill

Other Customers:

Part # Qty  Description

58694  23   Cordless temp reader
45643   2   200hp magnetic pump
17443  10   20 lb box of pump clips
10344  33   48 ounce solvent bottle
19365   5   3 speed electric drill

---------------------------------------------------------------------------

Return summary:

Government:

Part #  Qty Description

58694   2   Cordless temp reader
17443   7   20 lb box of pump clips
10344   4   48 ounce solvent bottle
45643   1   200hp magnetic pump
19365   1   3 speed electric drill
```

```
Other Customers:

Part # Qty  Description

58694    1   Cordless temp reader
17443    3   20 lb box of pump clips
10344    4   48 ounce solvent bottle
45643    3   200hp magnetic pump
19365    2   3 speed electric drill

-----------------------------------------------------------------------------

Daily Production Summary

Part #   Qty   Description                  In Stock

58694     20   Cordless temp reader           45
45643      4   200hp magnetic pump            20
19365     12   3 speed electric drill         20
17443     42   20 lb box of pump clips       200
10344    240   48 ounce solvent bottle       375
```

The report represents information extracted from the summary reports that will be generated on both Windows 2000 servers. The current Windows 2000 server is named Serv0001. The new server, which is still being configured, will be named Serv0002. The report itself is not substantially different from the summary reports already generated locally on the servers.

For starters, this new master consolidated summary report is still organized into four sections. The `Errors:` section now reports on errors from both Windows 2000 servers. A new field will need to be inserted that specifies the server from which the error was reported, in abbreviated form (Sr1 for Serv0001 and Sr2 for Serv0002).

The data presented in the `Sales summary:` and `Return summary:` sections is broken down into two sets of data. The first set of data lists government sales or returns collected from the summary reports on Serv0001, and the second set of data represents sales or returns data collected from the summary reports on the Serv0002 server for all other customers.

Finally, the information presented in the `Daily Production Summary` section presents totals collected from both servers.

Requirements Analysis

After meeting with the operations staff, Molly returned to her desk and wrote up a list of project requirements, which she then e-mailed to both her manager and the operations manager for approval. This list is shown below.

- Automate the collection of summary reports from both Serv0001 and Serv0002
- Read and process the summary reports from both servers and generate a master consolidated summary report
- Maintain a three-month archive of master consolidated reports on the Windows 2000 workstation located in the operations control center
- Log event messages to the Windows 2000 applications event log to facilitate the auditing and tracking of script activity
- Notify operations staff by means of a pop-up dialog box when the master consolidated summary report is available
- Create both a text and a Microsoft Word version of the master consolidated summary report
- Complete the development and testing of the project within 30 days

By requiring that both her manager and the operations manager confirm their acceptance of these requirements, Molly hopes to ensure that the new automation system she'll be developing will meet the needs of the operations department. In addition, by formalizing project requirements up front and getting everyone's approval, she can prevent feature creep (that is, the ad hoc addition of new requirements during the development of the project). Once approved, any changes to the project's requirements will have to be addressed at a later date. This will help to ensure that Molly does not miss her project deadline by having to provide for additional project requirements that she had not planned for.

Performing a High-Level Design

As part of her preliminary design and to help management and the operations staff better understand the overall scope of the project, Molly drew the sketch shown in Figure 21.1.

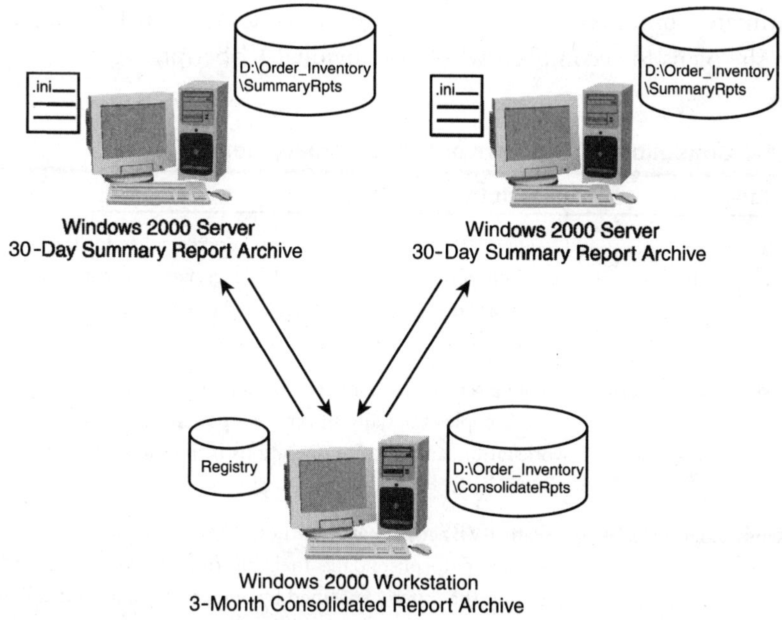

FIGURE 21.1 *An overview of the different components involved in developing a master consolidated reporting system*

As the sketch shows, Molly is planning on creating a centralized management workstation by copying the summary files from each Windows 2000 server and storing them on the Windows 2000 Professional workstation. The master consolidated summary reports will be stored on this workstation, as well.

For her own clarification, she depicted the INI files on each of the remote Windows servers where she stores VBScript reports and log analyzer configuration settings. Since everything is working well on the remote Windows 2000 servers, and for the sake of expediency, she plans to keep the INI files in place on the remote servers. However, she has decided to use the Windows 2000 registry on the Windows 2000 Professional workstation as the central repository for all the configuration settings for the scripts that she will develop as part of this new project.

Once she received formal approval of the project requirements that she had distributed and answered everyone's questions, Molly began work on a high-level design. Once again, she decided to use VBScript and the WSH and to tackle this project by developing a collection of small scripts, rather than trying to write one large all-inclusive program.

Molly ultimately produced the following list of tasks as shown in Table 21.1, each of which she plans to accomplish with an individual VBScript.

Table 21.1 Consolidated Order/inventory Summary Report Tasks

Type of Task	Description
Registry Setup	Create a VBScript that will create a registry key for the project and then populate that key with values, each of which stores a particular configuration setting for the scripts involved in this project
Remote Report Retrieval	Create a script that connects to each of the Windows 2000 servers, copies the daily summary reports to the Windows 2000 workstation, and notifies operations if the summary reports are not available
Report Consolidation	Create a VBScript that reads both of the summary reports generated each day, consolidates their information into a single report based on the criteria specified by operations, and notifies operations when the master consolidated report is ready
Archive Management	Create a VBScript that maintains a three-month archive of master consolidated summary reports and execute this script on the first day of each month in order to delete old report files

In addition to writing these scripts, Molly will need to set up their scheduled execution. Completion of this task will also include the one-time creation of a special service account on the Windows 2000 Professional workstation in order to facilitate the execution of scheduled tasks.

Creating the Registry Setup Script

Rather than embedding script settings within each VBScript or storing them in one or more INI files, Molly has decided to learn how to store them within the Windows registry. This way her scripts will run faster, because they will not have to perform any file I/O in order to retrieve their settings, and she won't have to manually edit her scripts and risk an accidental typo when modifying script settings. In fact, using the Regedt32 utility supplied with Windows 2000 or Windows XP, she'll be able to remotely modify registry settings for the scripts from the comfort of her own desktop, as demonstrated in Figure 21.2.

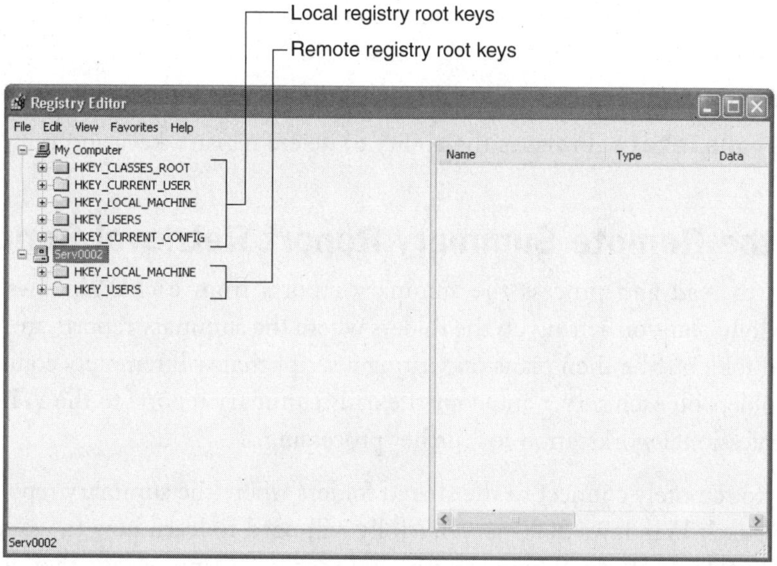

FIGURE 21.2 *Using the Regedt32 utility to remotely modify registry keys and values*

Molly is still in the process of determining exactly which types of configuration data she will externalize from her scripts and store within the Windows registry. She does know that she plans to create a key under the `HKEY_LOCAL_MACHINE` root key called `Intuit`. Under this key she will create a subkey called `VBScripts`, and within this subkey she will create one more key called `MstSumRpts`. Within the `MstSumRpts` subkey, she will store all the configuration settings for each of the VBScripts that will run on the Windows 2000 Professional workstation.

NOTE

For detailed information about the structure of the Registry and how it operates, refer to Chapter 22, "Developing the Setup Script."

In order to develop the setup script that will create the registry keys and store her script's configuration settings, Molly will need to learn how to work with the following `WshShell` object methods:

- **`RegWrite()`**. Provides the ability to create and change registry keys and values
- **`RegRead()`**. Provides the ability to retrieve registry keys and values
- **`RegDelete()`**. Provides the ability to delete registry keys and values

Creating the Remote Summary Report Retrieval Script

In order to read and process the summary reports from each Windows 2000 server, Molly plans on setting up the folders where the summary reports are stored as shared folders. She then plans on writing a script that will remotely connect to shared folders on each server and copy the daily summary reports to the Windows 2000 Professional workstation for further processing.

In order to remotely connect to the shared folders where the summary reports are stored on each Windows 2000 server, Molly will need to learn how to work with the `WshNetwork` object. This object provides access to properties that contain network information and to methods that allow you to connect to network drives and printers. In particular, Molly will have to learn how to work with the following `WshNetwork` object methods:

- **`MapNetworkDrive`.** Establishes a connection to a shared network drive or folder
- **`RemoveNetworkDrive`.** Disconnects a connection from a shared network drive or folder

Creating the Report Consolidation Script

The processing of the summary reports collected from the two Windows 2000 servers will be performed in much the same way that the report and log analyzer script processed the four report and log files described in Chapter 18, "Developing Script Log Analyzers." However, there are some differences. For one thing, Molly will have to add a new column to the `Errors:` section when writing the consolidated summary report in order to identify on which server each error occurred.

Another new requirement of the consolidated summary report is the accumulation of production inventory totals at the end of the report. This accumulation of totals will require the VBScript to match up line items based on matching part numbers, in order to calculate the total inventory on hand for each item.

In order to develop the VBScript that produces the consolidated summary report file, Molly will need to use each of the following `FileSystemObject` object methods:

- **`FileExists()`.** To validate whether a log or report file exists before trying to open it
- **`OpenTextFile()`.** To be able to work with the contents of the log or report file
- **`ReadLine()`.** To be able to read a line at a time from the INI file
- **`SkipLines()`.** To be able to skip header lines when reading files
- **`Close()`.** To close the INI file when done processing it
- **`WriteLine()`.** To be able to write a line of output to the summary file
- **`WriteBlankLines()`.** To be able to write blank lines and format the presentation of data in the summary file

Creating the Archive Management Script

The last VBScript that Molly will create for this project is one that manages three separate file archives, as outlined below.

- **`D:\Order_Inventory\Sr1_SummaryRpts`.** Stores a minimum of 90 days' worth of summary reports retrieved from Serv0001
- **`D:\Order_Inventory\Sr2_SummaryRpts`.** Stores a minimum of 90 days' worth of summary reports retrieved from Serv0002
- **`D:\Order_Inventory\ConsolidatedRpts`.** Stores a minimum of 90 days' worth of consolidated summary reports created from the individual summary reports retrieved from Serv0001 and Serv0002

Molly will use the Windows Task Scheduler service to automate the execution of this script on a monthly basis. Because the scheduling of this script is a one-time task that only needs to be performed on the Windows 2000 Professional workstation, Molly will manually set up its scheduled execution using the Scheduled Task Wizard.

In order to automate the execution of the archive management script, Molly will have to work with the following `FileSystemObject` object methods:

- **`FileExists()`.** To validate whether a log or report file exists before trying to open it

- **`MoveFile()`.** To move one or more files to an archive folder for a minimum one-month retention
- **`DeleteFile()`.** To delete one or more files stored in the archive folder after their 30-day retention period has passed

Molly also plans to provide this script with the ability to notify the operations staff when it has completed its execution and the consolidated summary report is ready for printing. Notification techniques implemented by this script will include the posting of messages to the Windows 2000 Professional application event log and the creation of pop-up messages on the Windows 2000 Professional workstation. In order to perform these two tasks, Molly will have to use the `WshShell` object's `LogEvent()` method and the Windows `Net Send` command.

Summary

In this chapter, you were introduced to a new project case study. You were provided with an overview of the information that Molly collected from the operations department, as well as the list of project requirements. A preliminary high-level design for the project was developed, and the major VBScript language constructs that will be required to develop each of the VBScripts that make up this project were briefly outlined and explained. In the four chapters that follow, you will get the chance to work on the development of all of the VBScripts.

Chapter 22

Developing a Setup Script

In this chapter, you will learn how to read, write, and modify data that is stored in the Windows registry. You will learn about the basic design of the registry and the structure that it uses to store data. You will then apply this information by developing a VBScript that creates a new registry key. The new key will store values containing configuration information for all the VBScripts developed by Molly for execution on the Windows 2000 Professional centralized management workstation.

Working with the Windows Registry

The Windows *registry* is a built-in database repository for configuration information on all Microsoft operating systems. It has been available since Windows 95. Microsoft and third-party hardware and software vendors use the Windows registry to store information about virtually every aspect of the computer, including the operating system itself.

By changing the contents of the registry, you can administer many aspects of a computer's operation, as well as the operation of its hardware and software. People work with the registry all the time, usually without even knowing. Most of the changes that users make to their desktops are stored in the registry. For example, you can modify the Windows screen saver settings manually from the Windows display dialog box or by making changes directly to the registry.

NOTE

To learn more about the registry keys and values involved in managing the Windows screen saver via the registry, refer to Chapter 11, "Customizing the Desktop."

The registry is highly reliable. As a result, most hardware and software developers have migrated data from their INI files into it. Likewise, you can leverage the power and convenience of the registry by using it as a central repository for all your VBScripts' configuration settings.

Examining the Registry Root Keys

The registry is organized into a hierarchical structure that closely resembles that of a file system. At the top of the hierarchy are five *root* or *parent* keys, which are also sometimes referred to as *hives*. Table 22.1 lists each of these root keys and provides a brief description of the types of information that they store.

Table 22.1 Registry Root Keys

Key	Short Name	Description
HKEY_CLASSES_ROOT	HKCR	Stores information regarding Windows file associations
HKEY_CURRENT_USER	HKCU	Stores information related to the user that is currently logged on to the computer
HKEY_LOCAL_MACHINE	HKLM	Stores information regarding global computer settings
HKEY_USERS	—	Stores information about all of the individuals that share the computer
HKEY_CURRENT_CONFIG	—	Stores information about the computer's current hardware configuration

Understanding How Data Is Stored

Data located in the registry is stored as *values*, which represent the name of an element to which data is associated. Values can be likened in many ways to files, which store data on the Windows file system. Values are organized within keys that act as a sort of folder or container. A registry *key* is a container that stores values or other registry keys. Data is stored in the registry using the following format:

```
Key : KeyType : Value
```

`Key` represents the fully qualified name of a registry key. `KeyType` specifies the type of data that the key stores. The registry stores a number of different types of data, as shown in Table 22.2. `Value` specifies the actual data that is to be stored.

Table 22.2 Registry Data Types

Data Type	Description
REG_NONE	Used to store an undefined data type
REG_BINARY	Used to store a binary value
REG_SZ	Used to store a string
REG_EXPAND_SZ	Used to store an expandable string, such as %COMPUTERNAME%
REG_MULTI_SZ	Used to store multiple strings
REG_LINK	A type reserved for use by Microsoft
REG_DWORD	Used to store a 32-bit integer
REG_DWORD_BIG_ENDIAN	Used to store a 32-bit integer in Big Endian format
REG_DWORD_LITTLE_ENDIAN	Used to store a 32-bit integer in Little Endian format
REG_QWORD	Used to store a 64-bit integer
REG_QWORD_LITTLE_ENDIAN	Used to store a 64-bit integer in Little Endian format
REG_RESOURCE_LIST	Used to store a list of device drivers

NOTE

Like every file and folder managed by the Windows NTFS file system, every Windows 2000 registry key and value is protected using security permissions. In order to read or modify a registry key or value, you must have the appropriate set of security permissions.

Manually Accessing Registry Data

The data stored in the Windows registry is often modified during the normal operation of the computer, with most people completely unaware that the changes that they are making are actually being stored in the registry. In addition, many of the Windows Control Panel applets, which are used to configure a wide variety of Windows functionality, are actually just user-friendly registry interfaces. The advantages to working with the Control Panel applets are that they hide the complexities of the registry and provide data validation, thus preventing invalid data from being added to the registry.

You may also directly view the contents of the Windows registry using the *Regedit* utility supplied with all Windows operating systems, demonstrated in Figure 22.1. Using Regedit you can view, add, modify, and delete registry keys and values.

Figure 22.1 shows the registry's five high-level root keys. The `HKEY_CURRENT_CONFIG` key has been expanded to display current Windows display settings, all of which are stored as string values (data type `REG_SZ`).

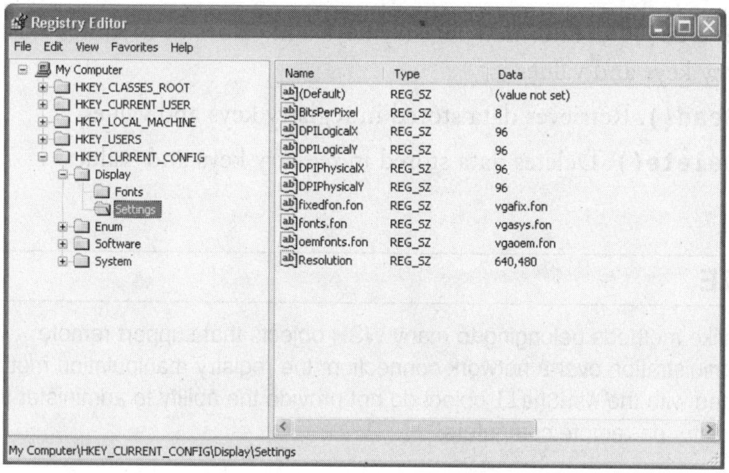

FIGURE 22.1 *Examining Windows display settings stored in the registry using the Regedit utility*

NOTE

If you are using Windows NT, 2000, or XP, then you also have the option of editing the registry using the *Regedt32* utility.

NOTE

Be extremely careful when directly editing the Windows registry using Regedit or Regedt32. Neither of these utilities provides an undo feature. Accidentally making a mistake when modifying the Windows registry can have potentially catastrophic effects on a computer, even rendering it inoperable. If you are not absolutely sure of the effects of making a particular change to the registry, then do not make it.

Using VBScript and the WSH to Programmatically Modify the Registry

The WSH provides access to the Windows registry via the `WshShell` object. Using methods belonging to this object, you can create VBScripts that can create, modify, and delete registry keys and values. The registry manipulation methods provided by the `WshShell` object are listed below.

- **`RegWrite()`**. Creates new registry keys and values or modifies existing registry keys and values
- **`RegRead()`**. Retrieves data stored in registry keys and values
- **`RegDelete()`**. Deletes data stored in registry keys and values

NOTE

Note that unlike methods belonging to many WSH objects that support remote resource administration over a network connection, the registry manipulation methods associated with the `WshShell` object do not provide the ability to administer the Windows registry on remote computers.

Using the RegWrite() Method

In order to work with any of the `WshShell` object's registry manipulation methods, you must first instantiate the `WshShell` object within your scripts. Once this is done you may use the `RegWrite()` method. This method provides the ability to write to the Windows registry. Specifically, it provides the ability to:

- Create a new registry key
- Add a value to a registry key and assign data to it
- Modify an existing value assignment

The `RegWrite()` method has the following syntax.

```
ObjectReference.RegWrite(Name, Value [, Type])
```

`ObjectReference` is the variable representing an instance of the `WshShell` object. `Name` specifies the key or value that is to be created or modified. `Value` specifies either the name of a new key, the name of a value to be added to an existing key, or the data to be assigned to an existing value. `Type` is an optional parameter that specifies a string value specifying the data type associated with a value.

When specifying a registry key, the value of `Name` must end with a backslash character. When specifying a registry value, the backslash character is omitted.

The `RegWrite()` method will automatically convert the `Value` parameter to a string or integer. When specified, the `Type` parameter identifies the data type to be used to store the data. Although the Windows registry is capable of storing numerous types of data, as shown in Table 22.2, the `RegWrite()` method only supports a subset of these methods, as listed below.

- REG_SZ
- REG_EXPAND_SZ
- REG_DWORD
- REG_BINARY

NOTE

The `REG_MULTI_SZ` data type is not supported by the `RegWrite()` method but is supported by the `RegRead()` method.

In order to use the `RegWrite()` method, all that you have to do is provide it with the name of a new registry key or value and specify its fully qualified location under one of the registry's five root keys.

TIP

Every registry key contains one default value, which by default has a data type of `REG_NONE`. If you wish you may change the data type and data assigned to the default value.

The following example demonstrates how to create a new registry key and value.

```
Set WshShl = WScript.CreateObject("WScript.Shell")
WshShl.RegWrite "HKCU\TestKey\EventLogging", "Enabled"
```

When executed, this example creates the key `HKCU\TestKey\` and adds a new value called `EventLogging`, which is then assigned the string `"Enabled"`, as shown in Figure 22.2.

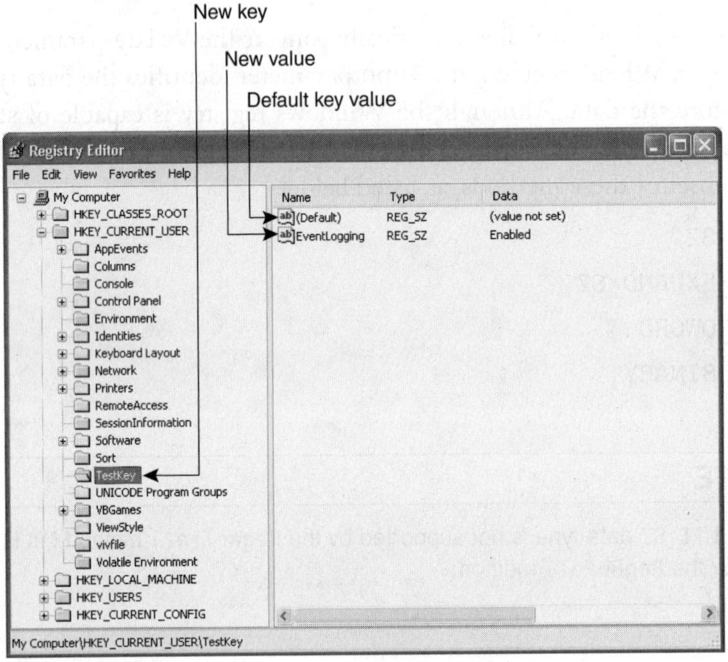

FIGURE 22.2 *Examining the new registry key and value*

You can use the `RegWrite()` method to modify an existing registry key or value, as demonstrated below.

```
Set WshShl = WScript.CreateObject("WScript.Shell")
WshShl.RegWrite "HKCU\TestKey\EventLogging", "Disabled"
```

In this example, the data assigned to the `EventLogging` value is set equal to `Disabled`. You can also change a key's default value, as demonstrated below.

```
Set WshShl = WScript.CreateObject("WScript.Shell")
WshShl.RegWrite "HKCU\TestKey\", "Author: Jerry Ford", "REG_SZ"
```

Note that in this example, no value name was supplied. As a result, the method assigned "Author: Jerry Ford" to the key's default value. The example also explicitly defined the value's data type as REG_SZ.

You may store any number of registry values under a single registry key. For example, the following VBScript statements can be used to store two additional values under the HKCU\TestKey\.

```
Set WshShl = WScript.CreateObject("WScript.Shell")
WshShl.RegWrite "HKCU\TestKey\DebugMode", "Disabled"
WshShl.RegWrite "HKCU\TestKey\NetworkNotification", "Enabled"
```

Figure 22.3 shows the status of the TestKey key and its associated values after running the previous example.

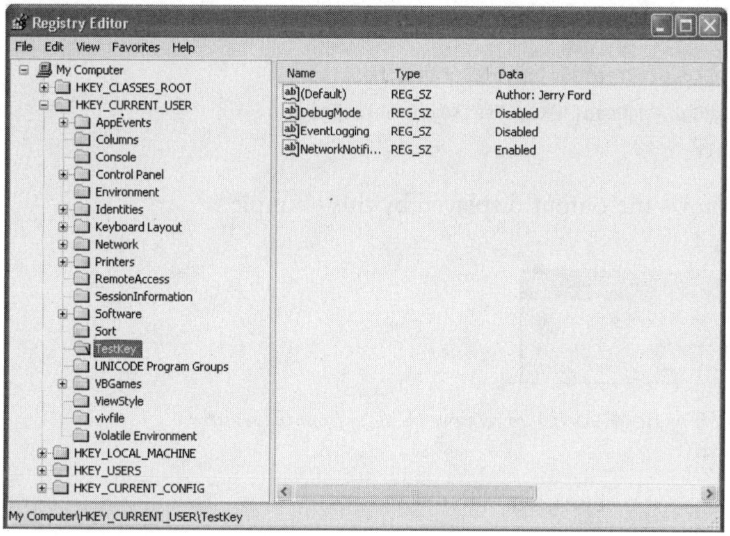

FIGURE 22.3 *Examining the new values assigned to the registry key*

Using the RegRead() Method

Once you have added new registry keys and values, you can programmatically retrieve them using the WshShell object's RegRead() method. This method has the following syntax:

```
ObjectReference.RegRead(Name)
```

`ObjectReference` is the variable representing an instance of the `WshShell` object. `Name` specifies the key or value that is to be retrieved.

The `RegRead()` method can be used to retrieve any of the following data types from the Windows registry:

- REG_BINARY
- REG_DWORD
- REG_EXPAND_SZ
- REG_MULTI_SZ
- REG_SZ

The following example demonstrates how to retrieve and display one of the registry values created by the previous examples.

```
Set WshShl = WScript.CreateObject("WScript.Shell")
strResult = WshShl.RegRead("HKCU\TestKey\EventLogging")
MsgBox strResult
```

Figure 22.4 shows the output displayed by this example.

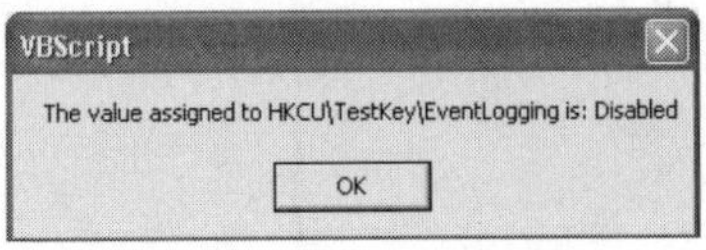

FIGURE 22.4 *Using* `RegRead()` *to retrieve the data from the registry*

If you perform a `RegRead()` operation and specify the name of a registry key instead of a value, then the method will return the default value assigned to the registry key, as demonstrated below.

```
Set WshShl = WScript.CreateObject("WScript.Shell")
strResult = WshShl.RegRead("HKCU\TestKey\")
MsgBox strResult
```

Using the RegDelete() Method

To delete a registry key or value, you will need to learn how to use the `RegDelete()` method. This method has the following syntax:

```
ObjectReference.RegDelete(Name)
```

`ObjectReference` is the variable representing an instance of the `WshShell` object. `Name` specifies the key or value that is to be deleted. If you specify a registry value, then that value is deleted. However, if you specify a key, the key and all values or subkeys stored underneath it are deleted.

The following example demonstrates how to delete a registry value.

```
Set WshShl = WScript.CreateObject("WScript.Shell")
WshShl.RegDelete "HKCU\TestKey\EventLogging"
```

Similarly, you can delete an entire key (along with all its subkeys and values) by specifying the fully qualified key name followed by the backslash character, as demonstrated below.

```
Set WshShl = WScript.CreateObject("WScript.Shell")
WshShl.RegDelete "HKCU\TestKey\"
```

Guarding against Registry Errors

If you specify a registry key or value that does not exist when using the `RegRead()` method, an error will occur, as demonstrated in Figure 22.5.

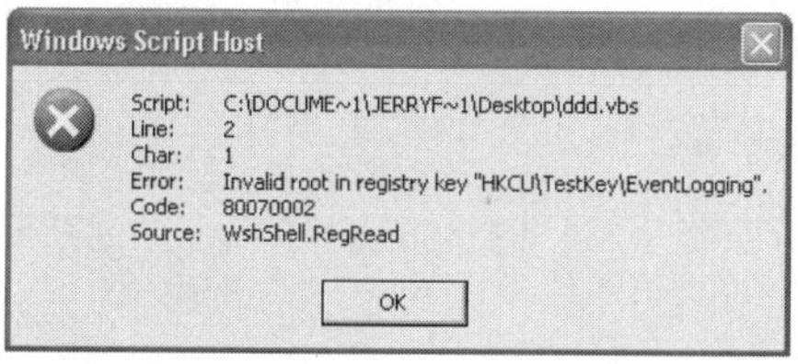

FIGURE 22.5 *An example of an error generated when a VBScript attempts to read a value that does not exist*

To prevent an error from terminating your script's execution, you can use the `On Error Resume Next` statement and then add logic to recover from the error.

For example, the following procedure demonstrates how to use the `Err` object to determine whether the execution of the `RegRead()` method was successful.

```
On Error Resume Next

Set WshShl = WScript.CreateObject("WScript.Shell")

strResult = WshShl.RegRead("HKCU\TestKey\EventLogging")

If Err <> 0 Then
  MsgBox "Add logic to proceed with a default setting and to log an event " & _
  "log message."
End If
```

If the `RegRead()` method is executed successfully, the example will silently end. However, if an error occurs (for example, the value does not exist), an error message is displayed.

NOTE

For more information on how to work with the `On Error Resume Next` statement and the `Err` object, refer to Chapter 6, "Data Collection, Notification, and Error Reporting."

The next example expands on the previous one. It demonstrates how to create a function in a VBScript that can be used to verify that a registry key or value exists before your script attempts to access its contents.

```
Set WshShl = WScript.CreateObject("WScript.Shell")

strRegKey = "HKCU\TestKey\EventLogging"

If RegKeyExists(strRegKey) = True Then
  strEvtLogStatus = WshShl.RegRead(strRegKey)
```

```
Else
 strEvtLogStatus = "Disabled"
  WshShl.LogEvent 4, "HKCU\TestKey\EventLogging not found - proceeding with " & _
    "default setting."
End If

Function RegKeyExists(RegKey)

  Dim strKeyToTest
  RegKeyExists = True

  On Error Resume Next

  strKeyToTest = WshShl.RegRead(RegKey)

  If Err <> 0 Then
    RegKeyExists = False
  End If

End Function
```

This example begins by instantiating the `WshShell` object. Then a variable named `strRegKey` is set equal to `HKCU\TestKey\EventLogging`. Next an `If` statement executes a function called `RegKeyExists()` and passes it the value of `strRegKey`. This function determines whether the registry key exists. If it does exist, a value of `True` is returned from the function and the value of a variable called `strEvtLogStatus` is set equal to the registry value by executing the `RegRead()` method. If the function does not return a value of `True`, then the value of `strEvtLogStatus` is set equal to a default setting. This allows the script to continue executing. An informational message is also written to the Windows application event log, as demonstrated in Figure 22.6.

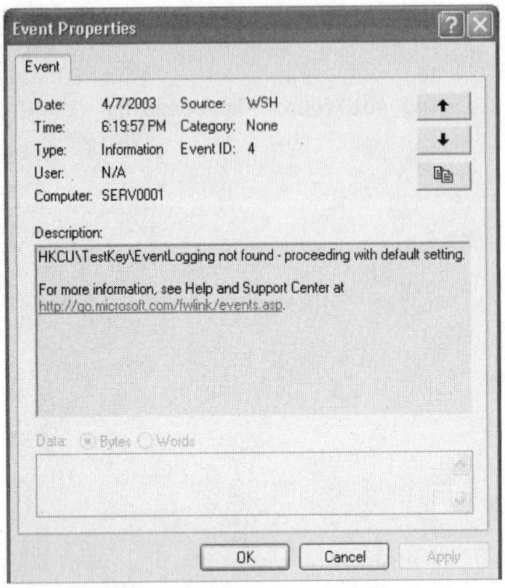

FIGURE 22.6 *Examining the format of the message written to the Windows application event log when an error occurs in the script*

The `RegKeyExist()` function accepts a single argument, the name of a registry key or value. It begins by defining a variable called `strKeyToTest`. Next it assigns a variable, named after the function, a default value of `True`.

> **NOTE**
>
> Functions return a result to their calling statements by assigning the value to be returned to a variable that has the same name as the function.

Next the `On Error Resume Next` statement is executed. By placing this statement inside the function, its scope is limited to the function. The next statement takes the `strKeyToTest` variable and assigns it the value returned by the `RegRead()` method. Then the default property of the `Err` object property is checked to determine whether an error occurred (whether the key or value exists). If an error did occur, then the value of `RegKeyExists` is set equal to `False`. If an error did not occur, then the value of `RegKeyExists` will remain `True` as set at the beginning of the function.

Creating the Setup Script

Molly is now ready to begin work on writing the first script for her new project. This VBScript setup script will be responsible for the one-time setup of registry entries to be used by the other scripts in her project. Specifically, this script will create a new registry key called HKLM\Software\Intuit\VBScripts\MstSumRpts\. In addition, it will create eight registry values located under that key. These values, as well as a description of their purpose and their initial settings, are listed in Table 22.3.

TIP

Molly can also use this script to reinitialize the registry values used by this project to their initial settings. In addition, by changing data that is associated with each setting in the script, she can reuse the script to later modify these values, thus saving herself the trouble of manually editing the registry.

Table 22.3 VBScript Project Registry Keys and Values

Key	Description	Value
EventLogging	A flag indicating whether events should be written to the Windows application event log	Enabled
DebugMode	A flag indicating whether intermediate results hould be displayed in pop-up dialog boxes during script execution	Disabled
NetworkNotification	A flag indicating whether network pop-up messages should be sent	Enabled
NtkNotifyList ASCK001	A list of user accounts to whom network pop-up messages should be sent	MJLF001
Win2000Svrs SERV0002	Names of the Windows 2000 servers where the order/inventory application is deployed	SERV0001

(continues)

Table 22.3 VBScript Project Registry Keys and Values (*continued*)

Key	Description	Value
SharedFolder	The name assigned to the shared folder on the Windows 2000 servers where the summary reports are stored	SumReports
RptArchive	The name of the folder on the Windows 2000 Professional workstation where the consolidated summary reports are to be stored	d:\Order_Inventory\LogFiles
RptFormat	A value of either Text or Word, indicating the file type of the consolidated summary report	Text

The Initialization Section

The script's `Initialization Section`, shown below, consists of just three statements. The first statement turns on the strict enforcement of variable naming. The second statement defines a variable for the `WshShell` object and a second variable that will be used in the `Main Processing Section` to determine if the script has permission to run. The last statement in this section initializes the `WshShell` object.

```
Option Explicit

Dim WshShl, IntResponse

Set WshShl = WScript.CreateObject("WScript.Shell")
```

The Main Processing Section

The `Main Processing Section`, shown below, begins by calling the `GetPermissionToRun()` function. It then uses an `If` statement to interrogate the value returned by this function to determine whether it is equal to 6 (that is, Molly clicked on `Yes` when prompted to allow the script to continue its execution).

If permission is given to execute, the script next calls the `CreateRegistryEntries()` subroutine eight times, passing it the name of a registry value and the data assigned to it. Since the `HKLM\Software\Intuit\VBScripts\MstSumRpts\` key will not exist on the first call to the `CreateRegistryEntries()`

subroutine, both the key and the stated value will be created. The remaining function calls will then store additional values under that key. Once all of the keys have been created, the script terminates its execution using the `WScript` object's `Quit()` method.

```
intResponse = GetPermissionToRun()


If intResponse = 6 Then
  CreateRegistryEntries
    "HKLM\Software\Intuit\VBScripts\MstSumRpts\EventLogging", "Enabled"
  CreateRegistryEntries
    "HKLM\Software\Intuit\VBScripts\MstSumRpts\DebugMode", "Disabled"
  CreateRegistryEntries
    "HKLM\Software\Intuit\VBScripts\MstSumRpts\NetworkNotification", "Enabled"
  CreateRegistryEntries
    "HKLM\Software\Intuit\VBScripts\MstSumRpts\NtkNotifiyList", "MJLF001
    ASCK001"
  CreateRegistryEntries
    "HKLM\Software\Intuit\VBScripts\MstSumRpts\Win2000Svrs",
    "SERV0001 SERV0002"
  CreateRegistryEntries
    "HKLM\Software\Intuit\VBScripts\MstSumRpts\SharedFolder", "SumReports"
  CreateRegistryEntries
    "HKLM\Software\Intuit\VBScripts\MstSumRpts\RptArchive",
    "d:\Order_Inventory\LogFiles"
  CreateRegistryEntries
    "HKLM\Software\Intuit\VBScripts\MstSumRpts\RptFormat", "Text"
End If


WScript.Quit()
```

The GetPermissionToRun() Function

The `GetPermissionToRun()` function uses the built-in VBScript `MsgBox()` function to display a prompt that gets confirmation before allowing the script to proceed further. If the `Yes` button is clicked, a value of 6 is returned to the calling statement. If the `No` button is clicked, a value of 7 is returned instead.

```
Function GetPermissionToRun()
```

```
  GetPermissionToRun = MsgBox("This script creates registry keys and " &_
    "values for the VBScripts that run on the Windows 2000 " & _
    "Professional centralized management workstation." & vbCrLf & vbCrLf & _
    "Do you wish to continue?", 4)

End Function
```

The CreateRegistryEntries() Subroutine

The `CreateRegistryEntries()` subroutine, shown below, accepts two input arguments. `Key_Value` stores the name of the registry key or value to be created and `Data` contains the actual data to be assigned. The `On Error Resume Next` statement is the first statement in the subroutine. It was added to allow the subroutine to continue executing if an error occurs when creating an individual registry key or value. Next the `WshShell` object's `RegWrite()` method is used to create the new key or value. Then the `Err` object's default property (the `Err.Number`) is checked to see if the write operation was successful. The `MsgBox()` function is used to display a confirmation stating whether the key was created or an error occurred.

```
Sub CreateRegistryEntries(Key_Value, Data)

  On Error Resume Next

  WshShl.RegWrite Key_Value, Data

  If Err <> 0 Then
    MsgBox "Error occurred writing " & Key_Value
  Else
    MsgBox Key_Value & " Created successfully."
  End If

End Sub
```

The Fully Assembled Script

The fully assembled VBScript is shown below. Once executed, it will create registry entries for the rest of the scripts that Molly needs to develop for this new project.

```
'*************************************************************************
'Script Name: Script 22.1.vbs
'Author: Jerry Ford
'Created: 04/05/03
'Description: This is the setup script for the Windows 2000 Professional
'centralized management workstation. It creates a registry key and assigns
'it a number of values which will be used by the VBScripts that run
'this computer.
'*************************************************************************

'Initialization Section

Option Explicit

Dim WshShl, IntResponse

Set WshShl = WScript.CreateObject("WScript.Shell")


'Main Processing Section

intResponse = GetPermissionToRun()

If intResponse = 6 Then
  CreateRegistryEntries
    "HKLM\Software\Intuit\VBScripts\MstSumRpts\EventLogging", "Enabled"
  CreateRegistryEntries
    "HKLM\Software\Intuit\VBScripts\MstSumRpts\DebugMode", "Disabled"
  CreateRegistryEntries
    "HKLM\Software\Intuit\VBScripts\MstSumRpts\NetworkNotification", "Enabled"
  CreateRegistryEntries
    "HKLM\Software\Intuit\VBScripts\MstSumRpts\NtkNotifiyList", "MJLF001
    ASCK001"
  CreateRegistryEntries
    "HKLM\Software\Intuit\VBScripts\MstSumRpts\Win2000Svrs",
    "SERV0001 SERV0002"
  CreateRegistryEntries
    "HKLM\Software\Intuit\VBScripts\MstSumRpts\SharedFolder", "SumReports"
```

```
  CreateRegistryEntries
    "HKLM\Software\Intuit\VBScripts\MstSumRpts\RptArchive",
    "d:\Order_Inventory\LogFiles"
  CreateRegistryEntries
    "HKLM\Software\Intuit\VBScripts\MstSumRpts\RptFormat", "Text"
End If

WScript.Quit()


'Procedure Section

Function GetPermissionToRun()

  GetPermissionToRun = MsgBox("This script creates registry keys and " & _
    "values for the VBScripts that run on the Windows 2000 Professional " & _
    "centralized management workstation." & vbCrLf & vbCrLf & _
    "Do you wish to continue?", 4)

End Function

Sub CreateRegistryEntries(Key_Value, Data)

  On Error Resume Next

  WshShl.RegWrite Key_Value, Data

  If Err <> 0 Then
    MsgBox "Error occurred writing " & Key_Value
  Else
    MsgBox Key_Value & " Created successfully."
  End If

End Sub
```

Figure 22.7 shows how the new `HKLM\Software\Intuit\VBScripts\MstRumRpts` key and its assigned values appear when viewed using the Regedit utility.

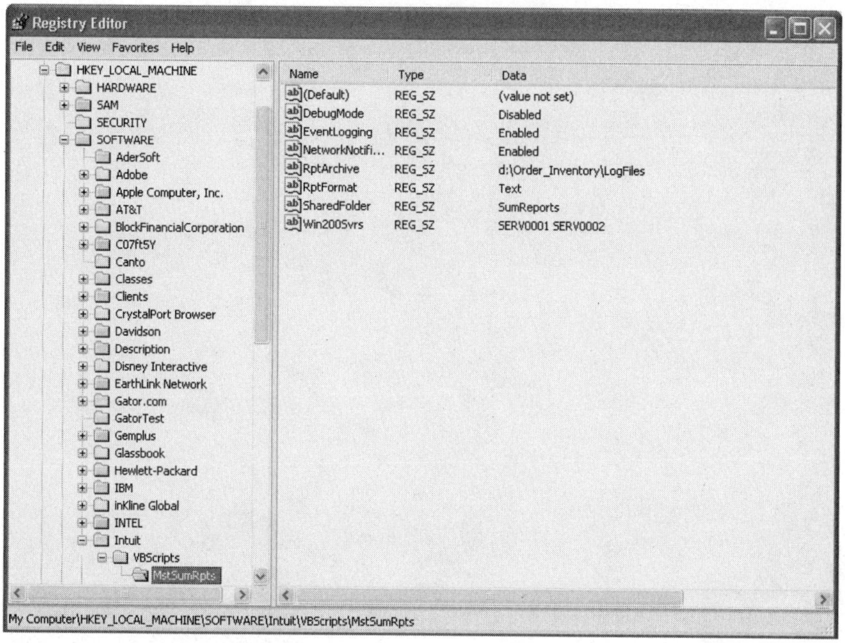

FIGURE 22.7 *Examining the registry key and values created by the setup script*

Summary

In this chapter, you learned how to work with the `WshShell` object's `RegRead()`, `RegWrite()`, and `RegDelete()` methods. You also learned about the registry's basic design and the types of data that it stores. You observed as Molly developed a VBScript that automated the setup of a registry key that stored multiple values. The values were then assigned data representing configuration settings that will be used by the VBScripts executing on the Windows 2000 Professional centralized management workstation.

Chapter 23

Collecting Remote Summary Reports

In this chapter, you will learn how to write VBScripts that can connect to network drives and then remotely administer files by copying, moving, and deleting them. Using this information, you will learn how to develop a script that collects the summary reports from the remote Windows 2000 servers at Intuit. As part of the development of this script, you will get the opportunity to work further with the Windows registry by retrieving the script's configuration settings.

Prerequisite Tasks

Before beginning work on her new project, Molly has a number of small tasks that she needs to accomplish. These tasks include:

- Creating a scheduling script to be used to set up the automated execution of the scripts that will make up this project.
- Creating a system account with administrative privileges to be used to set up the scheduled execution of the scheduling script. This will provide the project's scripts with the prerequisite security permissions that they will need to execute.
- Visiting both of the Windows 2000 servers and creating a network share for the `D:\Order_Inventory\SummaryRpts` folders in order to allow the report collection script to establish a remote network connection with these folders.

Creating a System Account

The first of the prerequisite tasks that Molly works on is the creation of a domain level system account. She arranged to have this account set up so that its password never changes. By setting this account up at the domain level, Molly ensures that it will have the security rights and permissions that are required to run her scripts on both the Windows 2000 servers and the Windows 2000 Professional workstation.

The name of the account that she created is `ScriptSchd`. Molly will associate this account with a scheduled task that she plans to set up on the Windows 2000

Professional workstation in order to set up the automated execution of her scheduling script.

Creating the Scheduler Script

Molly next creates the scheduling script that will manage the daily and monthly execution of the following VBScripts:

- The remote summary report
- The report consolidation script
- The archive management script

Molly created this new script, shown below, by copying and modifying the scheduling script that she developed for the previous project.

```
'*************************************************************************
'Script Name: Script 23.1.vbs
'Author: Jerry Ford
'Created: 04/10/03
'Description: This script runs the following list of scripts:
'      The Remote summary report collection script
'      The Report consolidation script
'      The Archive management script
'*************************************************************************


'Initialization Section

Option Explicit
On Error Resume Next

Dim WshShl
Set WshShl = WScript.CreateObject("WScript.Shell")


'Main Processing Section

RunScript("SumRptRetrieve.vbs")
RunScript("RptConsolidator.vbs")
```

```
RunScript("ArchiveMgr.vbs")

If Day(date()) = 1 Then
  RunScript("ArchiveMgr.vbs")
End If

'Terminate script execution
WScript.Quit()


'Procedure Section

Sub RunScript(ScriptName)
  WshShl.Run ScriptName, 1, True
End Sub

Sub WriteToEventLog()
  WshShl.LogEvent 4, "Master Scheduler Script executing."
End Sub
```

Creating the Network Folders

Next Molly visits both of the Windows 2000 servers and sets up the `d:\Order_Inventory\SumReports` folder as a shared folder. She grants the `ScriptSchd` account access to this new network folder, as outlined in the following procedure.

1. After logging on to a Windows 2000 server, Molly double-clicks on the My Computer icon. The My Computer dialog box opens.
2. She then double-clicks on the D: drive, followed by the Order_Inventory folder. The Order_Inventory folder opens, showing its contents.
3. Molly right-clicks on the `SummaryRpts` folder and selects the Sharing option from the menu that appears. This opens the folder's Properties dialog box.
4. She then selects the Share this folder option and enters **SumRpts** in the Share name field, as shown in Figure 23.1.

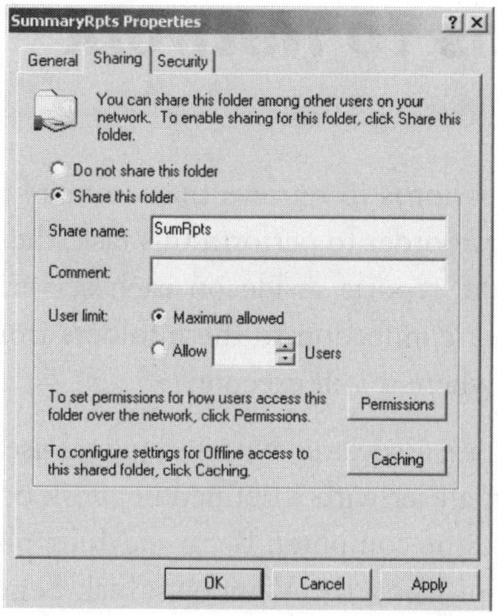

FIGURE 23.1 *Creating a network share for the* `SummaryRpts` *folder located on each of the Windows 2000 servers*

5. Next she clicks on the Permissions button. This displays the Permissions for SummaryRpts dialog box. From here, she can specify which users have remote access to the shared folder. She begins by selecting all currently defined accounts, one at a time, and clicking on Remove. She then clicks on Add and selects the `ScriptSchd` account from the list of domain accounts that are displayed.
6. Molly then clicks on OK three times to close all open dialog boxes.

At this point, the `SummaryRpts` folder is set up as a shared network folder to which only the `ScriptSchd` domain account has remote access.

NOTE

Molly could have also restricted both local and remote access to the `SummaryRpts` folder by configuring NTFS file permissions instead of or in addition to share level permissions.

Setting Up Connections to Network Drives and Folders

The basic purpose of the report retrieval script is to retrieve the summary report files from the two Windows 2000 servers. In order to perform this task, the script must have access to the folders where the reports reside on each server. This means that the script must have a network connection to these folders from the Windows 2000 Professional workstation where it will execute.

Unfortunately, network drive connections are associated with individual user profiles and are therefore only available when a user with a defined network drive or folder connection is currently logged on to the computer. Because Molly plans to execute the summary report retrieval script using the Windows Task Scheduler service at a time when no users are logged on to the computer, the script must take responsibility for establishing its own network connections to the shared folders on each Windows 2000 server.

Manually Setting Up Connections

The traditional way to connect to a remote network drive or folder is to create a drive mapping to it. A *mapped drive* is a logical network connection that makes a shared drive or folder look and act as if it were locally connected to the computer where the mapped connection is established.

NOTE

In order to map to a network drive or folder, you must be granted the appropriate level of access rights and permissions on the computer where the shared drive or folder exists.

The same steps are followed to manually set up either connection to a network drive or folder and can be performed from any number of Windows folders, including the Windows Explorer and My Computer folders. For example, the following procedure outlines the steps involved in creating a mapping to a remote folder called `SumReports` on a computer named `SERV0002`.

1. Click on Start and then My Computer. The My Computer folder appears.
2. Click on Tools and select the Map Network Drive menu option. The Map Network Drive dialog box appears.
3. Select a available drive letter from the Drive drop-down list.
4. Type **\\SERV0002\SumReports** in the Folder field, as demonstrated in Figure 23.2.

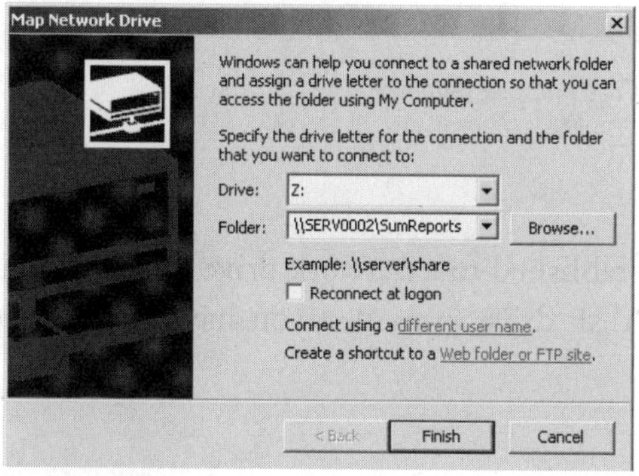

FIGURE 23.2 *Manually creating a mapped connection to a network folder*

5. To set up a persistent drive mapping that will be restored the next time you log on, make sure that the Reconnect at logon option is selected. Otherwise, clear this option.
6. Click on Finish. The Map Network Drive dialog box closes and is replaced by an Explorer window showing the contents of the network folder, as demonstrated in Figure 23.3.

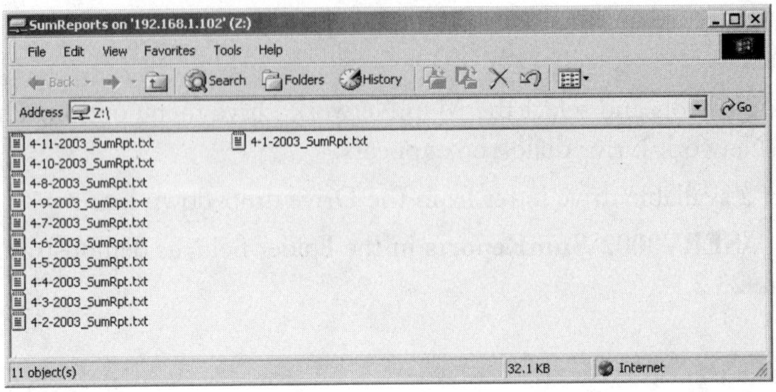

FIGURE 23.3 *Examining the contents of the mapped folder*

Once the mapped connection is established to a network drive or folder, you may work with it like any other local disk drive (provided you have the appropriate security access permissions).

Working with the WshNetwork Object

Because the report collection script will be run by the Task Scheduler service, Molly needs to equip it with the ability to establish its own network connections to each of the Windows 2000 servers' shared folders. To accomplish this, Molly will need to use methods associated with the `WshNetwork` object.

The `WshNetwork` object exposes a number of network-related resources on Microsoft networks. It provides access to several properties that can be used to collect network information. These properties are listed below.

- `ComputerName`
- `UserDomain`
- `UserName`

In addition to these methods, the `WshNetwork` object makes available a number of methods that provide the ability to work with network disk and printer resources. These methods include:

- `EnumNetworkDrives()`
- `EnumPrinterConnection()`
- `AddPrinterConnection()`

- `RemovePrinterConnection()`
- `SetDefaultPrinter()`
- `MapNetworkDrive()`
- `RemoveNetworkDrive()`

NOTE

To learn more about the properties and objects associated with the `WshNetwork` object, refer to Chapter 14, "Mapping Network Printers and Disks."

Mapping Drive Connections

In order to automate the establishment of a mapping to a network drive or folder, Molly needs to learn how to work with the `WshNetwork` object's `MapNetworkDrive()` method. The syntax of this method is outlined in Chapter 14. Once executed, the `MapNetworkDrive()` method sets up a network drive connection that allows a script to move, copy, create, and delete files and folders on the network drive or folder represented by the connection.

The following VBScript statements demonstrate how to establish a temporary connection to a network drive or folder.

```
Dim WshNtk
Set WshNtk = WScript.CreateObject("WScript.Network")
WshNtk.MapNetworkDrive "z:", "\\SERV0002\D"
```

First an instance of the `WshNetwork` object is set up. Then its `MapNetworkDrive()` method is executed, and it is passed a drive letter to be used in creating the mapping and the UNC path of the network drive or folder.

Disconnecting Drive Connections

For good form, Molly wants her script to explicitly disconnect its temporary network drive connections. To do this, she will need to use the `WshNetwork` object's `RemoveNetworkDrive()` method. The syntax of this method is outlined in Chapter 14.

An example of how to disconnect the drive mapping set up in the previous example is shown on the following page.

```
Dim WshNtk
Set WshNtk = WScript.CreateObject("WScript.Network")
WshNtk.RemoveNetworkDrive "z:"
```

As you can see, only the drive letter representing the network connection is required.

File Management

Administering files, locally or over a network, involves copying, moving, and deleting them. The WSH provides VBScript with the ability to administer files using methods belonging to the `FileSystemObject` object. The `FileSystemObject` object exposes the Windows file system, allowing your scripts to directly interact with and manage it. The `FileSystemObject` object also provides access to the `File` object, which provides additional methods for copying, moving, and deleting individual files.

Working with the FileSystemObject Object

In order to work with the `FileSystemObject` object, you must first instantiate it, as demonstrated below.

```
Set FsoObj = New WScript.CreateObject ("Scripting.FileSystemObject")
```

The `FileSystemObject` object provides direct access to methods that you can use to administer files. Some of these methods are listed below.

- **`CopyFile()`**. Provides the ability to copy one or more files to a different folder
- **`MoveFile()`**. Provides the ability to move one or more files to the specified folder
- **`DeleteFile()`**. Provides the ability to delete the specified file or files

Each of these methods allows you to manipulate one or more files at a time. They can be used to administer files on any drive to which the computer has a connection (provided that the appropriate level of security access is available). For more information about these methods, refer to Chapter 14.

Working with the File Object

In addition to the methods provided by the `FileSystemObject` object, you may use a number of methods provided by the `File` object when administering files, as listed below.

- **`Copy()`.** Provides the ability to copy a single file or folder
- **`Move()`.** Provides the ability to move a single file or folder
- **`Delete()`.** Provides the ability to delete the specified file or folder

One major difference between these three methods and the methods provided by the `FileSystemObject` object are that the `File` object's methods can only be used to work with one file at a time. Another difference is that the `File` object's methods can also be used to administer folders, whereas the `FileSystemObject` object provides an entirely different set of methods for working with folders.

In order to work with the `File` object, you must first set up an instance of the `FileSystemObject` object. Once this is done, you can use the `FileSystem Object` object's `GetFile` method to set up an instance of the `File` object, which will represent the file that you want to administer. You can then execute any of the `File` object's methods.

Of the three `File` object methods listed above, Molly needs to learn how to work with the `Copy()` method. Using this method, she plans to copy the summary report from both of the Windows 2000 servers each morning for processing on the Windows 2000 Professional workstation. This method has the following syntax:

```
ObjectReference.Copy(Target [, Overwrite])
```

`ObjectReference` is the variable representing an instance of the `File` object. `Target` specifies the destination file or folder that is to be copied. `Overwrite` is an optional parameter that, when set equal to `True`, forces an existing file or folder to be overwritten.

The following VBScript statements demonstrate how to use the `Copy()` method to copy a file called `TestFile.txt` located in the `D:\Temp` folder to a folder on a mapped network drive.

```
Set FsoObj = CreateObject("Scripting.FileSystemObject")
Set FileName = FsoObj.GetFile("d:\temp\TestFile.txt")
FileName.Copy "z:\Temp\TestFile.txt "
```

Developing the Report Collection Script

Molly is now ready to begin writing the summary report collection script. This script will be responsible for retrieving and storing local copies of the summary reports generated each morning on the Windows 2000 servers where the order/inventory system resides. This script will be executed by the scheduling script and will be immediately followed by a script that processes the reports that it retrieves.

The Initialization Section

Molly begins the script, like all her other scripts, with the `Option Explicit` statement in order to enforce the strict interpretation of variable names. Next, variables used throughout the script are defined, and the `WshNetwork`, `FileSystemObject`, and `WshShell` objects are instantiated. Finally, a constant is defined that will be used in all pop-up dialog boxes displayed by the script.

```
Option Explicit


Dim strEventLog, strDebug, strSvrList, strFolderList, strArchive
Dim WshNtk, FsoObj, WshShl, strSumRptFileName

Set WshNtk = WScript.CreateObject("WScript.Network")
Set FsoObj = CreateObject("Scripting.FileSystemObject")
Set WshShl = WScript.CreateObject("WScript.Shell")

Const cTitleBarMsg = "Summary Report Collection Script"
```

The Main Processing Section

In the `Main Processing Section`, shown on the following page, a series of subroutine and function calls control the overall execution of the script. The `SetDefaultSettings()` subroutine sets default configuration settings for the script. Then the `GetRegistrySettings()` subroutine retrieves script settings stored in the Windows registry, overriding matching default script settings. Next an `If` statement determines whether logging is enabled and writes a message to the Windows application event log if appropriate.

The MapNetworkDrive() function is executed twice, once for each Windows 2000 server. A drive letter and a UNC path is passed to the function each time. The UNC path is created by prepending the \\ characters to the name of one of the Windows 2000 servers, which is extracted from the variable strSvrList using either the Left() or Right() function, the backslash (\) character, and the name of the shared network folder on the Windows 2000 server (strFolderList).

```
SetDefaultSettings()

GetRegistrySettings()

If strEventLog = "Enabled" Then
  WriteToEventLog ("Summary Report Collection script now executing.")
End If

MapNetworkDrive "X:", "\\" & Left(strSvrList, 8) & "\" & strFolderList
MapNetworkDrive "Y:", "\\" & Right(strSvrList, 8) & "\" & strFolderList

strSumRptFileName = GetSummaryRptFileName()

CopyFolders "X:\" & strSumRptFileName, Left(strSvrList, 8)
CopyFolders "Y:\" & strSumRptFileName, Right(strSvrList, 8)

DisconnectNetworkDrive("X:")
DisconnectNetworkDrive("Y:")

If strEventLog = "Enabled" Then
  WriteToEventLog ("Summary Report Collection script finished executing.")
End If

TerminateScript()
```

The next statement in the Main Processing Section calls the GetSummaryRptFileName() function, which returns the name of the summary report to be retrieved. Then the CopyFolders() subroutine is called twice and passed the name of the file to be retrieved and the name of the server where the file resides.

Once both summary report files have been retrieved, the DisconnectNetwork-Drive() subroutine is executed twice in order to disconnect the previously established connections to the Windows 2000 server's shared network folders. If appropriate, another message is written to the Windows application event log and the `TerminateScript()` subroutine is executed in order to stop the scripts execution.

The SetDefaultSettings() Subroutine

The `SetDefaultSettings()` subroutine, shown below, defines default configuration settings for the script. These settings will be used to control the script's operation in the event that there is a problem accessing corresponding registry values.

```
Sub SetDefaultSettings()

  strEventLog = "Enabled"
  strDebug = "Disabled"
  strSvrList = "SERV0001 SERV0002"
  strFolderList = "SumReports"
  strArchive = "d:\Order_Inventrory\LogFiles"

  If strDebug = "Enabled" Then
    MsgBox "Default settings initialized: " & vbCrLf & vbCrLf & _
      "strEventLog" & vbTab & "=" & vbTab & strEventLog & vbCrLf & _
      "strDebug" & vbTab & vbTab & "=" & vbTab & strDebug & vbCrLf & _
      "strSvrList" & vbTab & vbTab & "=" & vbTab & strSvrList & vbCrLf & _
      "strFolderList" & vbTab & "=" & vbTab & strFolderList & vbCrLf & _
      "strArchive" & vbTab & "=" & vbTab & strArchive, , cTitleBarMsg
  End If

End Sub
```

If the script is being executed in debug mode (that is, the value of `strDebug` is equal to `Enabled`) then the VBScript `MsgBox()` function is used to display the value of each variable.

The GetRegistrySettings() Subroutine

The `GetRegistrySettings()` subroutine, shown on the next page, begins by executing the `On Error Resume Next` statement in order to prevent a problem in retrieving a configuration setting from the Windows registry from halting the script's execution. This will allow the script to proceed using a default setting if need be.

Next the subroutine attempts to read a registry value where one of the script's configuration settings is stored. The value of `Err.Number` (the default property of the `Err` object) is examined to determine whether an error occurred. If an error did occur and logging is enabled, a message is written to the Windows application event log and the value of `Err.Number` is reset to zero to clear out the error before the next registry value is read. The above process repeats itself until all the script's registry values have been processed.

```
Sub GetRegistrySettings()

  On Error Resume Next

  strEventLog = _
    WshShl.RegRead("HKLM\Software\Intuit\VBScripts\MstSumRpts\EventLogging")
  If Err <> 0 Then
    If strEventLog = "Enabled" Then
      WriteToEventLog ("Summary Report Collection script - Using " & _
        "default for strEventLog.")
      Err.Number = 0
    End If
  End If

  strDebug = WshShl.RegRead("HKLM\Software\Intuit\VBScripts\MstSumRpts\DebugMode")
  If Err <> 0 Then
    If strEventLog = "Enabled" Then
      WriteToEventLog ("Summary Report Collection script - Using " & _
        "default for strDebug.")
      Err.Number = 0
    End If
  End If

  strSvrList = _
    WshShl.RegRead("HKLM\Software\Intuit\VBScripts\MstSumRpts\Win2000Svrs")
  If Err <> 0 Then
    If strEventLog = "Enabled" Then
      WriteToEventLog ("Summary Report Collection script - Using " & _
```

```
        "default for strSvrList.")
      Err.Number = 0
    End If
  End If

  strFolderList = _
    WshShl.RegRead("HKLM\Software\Intuit\VBScripts\MstSumRpts\SharedFolder")
  If Err <> 0 Then
    If strEventLog = "Enabled" Then
      WriteToEventLog ("Summary Report Collection script - Using " & _
        "default for strFolderList.")
      Err.Number = 0
    End If
  End If

  strArchive = _
    WshShl.RegRead("HKLM\Software\Intuit\VBScripts\MstSumRpts\RptArchive")
  If Err <> 0 Then
  If strEventLog = "Enabled" Then
      WriteToEventLog ("Summary Report Collection script - Using " & _
        "default for strArchive.")
      Err.Number = 0
    End If
  End If

  If strDebug = "Enabled" Then
    MsgBox "Registry settings initialized: " & vbCrLf & vbCrLf & _
      "strEventLog" & vbTab & "=" & vbTab & strEventLog & vbCrLf & _
      "strDebug" & vbTab & vbTab & "=" & vbTab & strDebug & vbCrLf & _
      "strSvrList" & vbTab & vbTab & "=" & vbTab & strSvrList & vbCrLf & _
      "strFolderList" & vbTab & "=" & vbTab & strFolderList & vbCrLf & _
      "strArchive" & vbTab & "=" & vbTab & strArchive, , cTitleBarMsg
  End If

End Sub
```

Finally, if the script is being executed in debug mode, then the subroutine uses the VBScript `MsgBox()` function to display the value of each variable. Displaying variable values a second time assists Molly in tracking their contents as she develops the script. While she is developing and testing the script, she configures this value of `strDebug` to equal `Enabled`. Later, when she is done testing the script, she will change the value of this variable in the Windows registry to `Disabled`.

The MapNetworkDrive() Function

The `MapNetworkDrive()` function, shown below, accepts two arguments. The first argument is the drive letter to be used in setting up a network connection, and the second argument is the UNC path of one of the shared network folders residing on the Windows 2000 servers. Numerous intermediate results are displayed in pop-up dialog boxes as the function executes (if the script is run in debug mode).

The `FileSystemObject` object's `FileExists()` method is used to determine whether or not the network folder, specified as `strDrive`, is accessible (the network is not down, the folder exists, and so on). If the folder is accessible, another test is performed to determine whether or not the specified drive letter (`strLetter`) is in use. If it is then its connection is deleted in order to free up the drive letter for the script. However, if the network folder cannot be accessed when first tested, the `TerminateScript()` subroutine is called and the script terminates its execution.

```
Function MapNetworkDrive(strLetter, strDrive)

  If strDebug = "Enabled" Then
    MsgBox "strLetter = " & strLetter & vbCrLf & "strDrive = " & _
      strDrive, , cTitleBarMsg
  End If

  If FsoObj.DriveExists(strDrive) Then

    If strDebug = "Enabled" Then
      MsgBox strDrive & " exists", , cTitleBarMsg
    End If

    If FsoObj.DriveExists(strLetter) Then

      If strDebug = "Enabled" Then
        MsgBox "Deleting drive letter " & strLetter, , cTitleBarMsg
```

```
        End If

        WshNtk.RemoveNetworkDrive strLetter

      End If

      WshNtk.MapNetworkDrive strLetter, strDrive

    Else

      If strDebug = "Enabled" Then
        MsgBox strDrive & " does not exist", , cTitleBarMsg
      End If

      If strEventLog = "Enabled" Then
        WriteToEventLog "Summary Report Collection script - Unable to map " & _
        "to network drive " & strDrive
      End If
      TerminateScript()
    End If

End Function
```

Finally, the `WshNetwork` object's `MapNetworkDrive()` method is executed and passed a drive letter and the UNC path to a shared network folder.

The GetSummaryRptFileName() Function

The `GetSummaryRptFileName()` function, shown on the next page, determines the name of the current summary reports. It does so by completing a number of steps. First, the `Date()` function to get the current system date. Then the `Replace()` function is used to substitute all instances of the backslash (/) character, which is specified within the current date with the dash (-) character. Finally, the string value of `_SumRpt.txt` is appended to the end of the reformatted system date to arrive at the summary report's file name. This file name is returned to the statement that called this function by assigning its value to a variable that has the same name as the function.

```
Function GetSummaryRptFileName()

  GetSummaryRptFileName = Replace(Date(), "/", "-")

  GetSummaryRptFileName =  GetSummaryRptFileName & "_SumRpt.txt"

  If strDebug = "Enabled" Then
    MsgBox "Summary Report Files Name = " & GetSummaryRptFileName, , _
      cTitleBarMsg
  End If

End Function
```

The CopyFolders() Subroutine

The `CopyFolders()` subroutine, shown below, begins by determining whether or not the summary report is accessible. If it is not accessible, the script's execution is terminated by calling the `TerminateScript()` subroutine. If it is accessible, the `FileSystemObject` object's `GetFile()` method is used to instantiate an instance of the `File` object and create an association with a summary report (as specified by `strFileNameToCopy`).

```
Sub CopyFolders(strFileNameToCopy, strServerName)

  Dim strFileName

  If (FsoObj.FileExists(strFileNameToCopy)) Then
    If strDebug = "Enabled" Then
      MsgBox "File " & strFileNameToCopy & " found. Now copying...", , _
      cTitleBarMsg
    End If
  Else
    If strDebug = "Enabled" Then
      MsgBox "File " & strFileNameToCopy & " does not exist. Stopping " & _
      "script execution.", , cTitleBarMsg
    End If
    TerminateScript()
  End If
```

```
    Set strFileName = FsoObj.GetFile(strFileNameToCopy)

    strFileName.Copy (strArchive & "\" & strServerName & "_" & _
      Mid(strFileNameToCopy,4))
    If Err <> 0 Then
      If strEventLog = "Enabled" Then
        WriteToEventLog "Summary Report Collection script - Unable to copy " & _
          strFileNameToCopy
      End If
      If strDebug = "Enabled" Then
        MsgBox "Summary Report Collection script - Unable to copy " & _
          strFileNameToCopy, , cTitleBarMsg
      End If
      TerminateScript()
    End If

End Sub
```

Once instantiated, the `File` object's `Copy()` method is used to copy and rename the summary report to a local folder on the Windows 2000 Professional workstation. The value stored in `strArchive` specifies the folder where the summary report is to be stored. The name of the summary report is changed by appending the backslash (\) character, the value of `strServerName`, the underscore (_) character, and the value of `strFileNameToCopy` (less the drive letter specified in the first three characters of the `strFileNameToCopy`).

The DisconnectNetworkDrive() Subroutine

Once copies of both summary reports have been copied over to the Windows 2000 Professional workstation, the `DisconnectNetworkDrive()` subroutine is executed twice. The subroutine begins by executing the `On Error Resume Next` statement in order to prevent any problem that may occur when disconnecting a drive connection from halting the script's execution. Each time the subroutine is called, a different drive letter is passed to it, specifying the network connection to be disconnected.

```
Sub DisconnectNetworkDrive(strDriveLetter)

  On Error Resume Next
```

```
  If strDebug = "Enabled" Then
    MsgBox "Disconnecting " & strDriveLetter, , cTitleBarMsg
  End If

  WshNtk.RemoveNetworkDrive strDriveLetter
  If Err <> 0 Then
    If strDebug = "Enabled" Then
      MsgBox "Error occurred when disconnecting " & strDriveLetter, , _
        cTitleBarMsg
    End If
  End If

End Sub
```

The WriteToEventLog() Subroutine

The `WriteToEventLog()` subroutine accepts a single argument representing a message to be written to the Windows 2000 Professional workstation's application event log. It then writes this message as an informational event.

```
Sub WriteToEventLog(strMessage)

  WshShl.LogEvent 4, strMessage

End Sub
```

The TerminateScript() Subroutine

The `TerminateScript()` subroutine, shown below, displays a termination message in a pop-up dialog box, if the script is run in debug mode. It then executes the `WScript` object's `Quit()` method to halt the script's execution.

```
Sub TerminateScript()

  If strDebug = "Enabled" Then
    MsgBox "Script execution terminated.", , cTitleBarMsg
  End If
```

```
  WScript.Quit()

End Sub
```

The Fully Assembled Script

The fully assembled script is shown below. When executed, it will retrieve its configuration settings from the Windows registry, connect to the shared network folders located on each of the Window 2000 servers, and copy the current day's summary reports over to the Windows 2000 Professional workstation.

```
'*************************************************************************
'Script Name: Script 23.2.vbs
'Author: Jerry Ford
'Created: 04/11/03
'Description: This script copies files from remote servers to a central
'folder on a Windows 2000 Professional workstation.
'*************************************************************************

'Initialization Section

Option Explicit

Dim strEventLog, strDebug, strSvrList, strFolderList, strArchive
Dim WshNtk, FsoObj, WshShl, strSumRptFileName

Set WshNtk = WScript.CreateObject("WScript.Network")
Set FsoObj = CreateObject("Scripting.FileSystemObject")
Set WshShl = WScript.CreateObject("WScript.Shell")
Const cTitleBarMsg = "Summary Report Collection Script"


'Main Processing Section

SetDefaultSettings()
```

```
GetRegistrySettings()

If strEventLog = "Enabled" Then
  WriteToEventLog ("Summary Report Collection script now executing.")
End If

MapNetworkDrive "X:", "\\" & Left(strSvrList, 8) & "\" & strFolderList
MapNetworkDrive "Y:", "\\" & Right(strSvrList, 8) & "\" & strFolderList

strSumRptFileName = GetSummaryRptFileName()

CopyFolders "X:\" & strSumRptFileName, Left(strSvrList, 8)
CopyFolders "Y:\" & strSumRptFileName, Right(strSvrList, 8)

DisconnectNetworkDrive("X:")
DisconnectNetworkDrive("Y:")

If strEventLog = "Enabled" Then
  WriteToEventLog ("Summary Report Collection script finished executing.")
End If

TerminateScript()


'Procedure Section

Sub SetDefaultSettings()

  strEventLog = "Enabled"
  strDebug = "Disabled"
  strSvrList = "SERV0001 SERV0002"
  strFolderList = "SumReports"
  strArchive = "d:\Order_Inventrory\LogFiles"

  If strDebug = "Enabled" Then
    MsgBox "Default settings initialized: " & vbCrLf & vbCrLf & _
      "strEventLog" & vbTab & "=" & vbTab & strEventLog & vbCrLf & _
      "strDebug" & vbTab & vbTab & "=" & vbTab & strDebug & vbCrLf & _
```

```
        "strSvrList" & vbTab & vbTab & "=" & vbTab & strSvrList & vbCrLf & _
        "strFolderList" & vbTab & "=" & vbTab & strFolderList & vbCrLf & _
        "strArchive" & vbTab & "=" & vbTab & strArchive, , cTitleBarMsg
    End If

End Sub

Sub GetRegistrySettings()

  On Error Resume Next

  strEventLog = _
    WshShl.RegRead("HKLM\Software\Intuit\VBScripts\MstSumRpts\EventLogging")
  If Err <> 0 Then
    If strEventLog = "Enabled" Then
      WriteToEventLog ("Summary Report Collection script - Using " & _
        "default for strEventLog.")
      Err.Number = 0
    End If
  End If

  strDebug = WshShl.RegRead("HKLM\Software\Intuit\VBScripts\MstSumRpts\DebugMode")
  If Err <> 0 Then
    If strEventLog = "Enabled" Then
      WriteToEventLog ("Summary Report Collection script - Using " & _
        "default for strDebug.")
      Err.Number = 0
    End If
  End If

  strSvrList = _
    WshShl.RegRead("HKLM\Software\Intuit\VBScripts\MstSumRpts\Win2000Svrs")
  If Err <> 0 Then
    If strEventLog = "Enabled" Then
      WriteToEventLog ("Summary Report Collection script - Using " & _
        "default for strSvrList.")
      Err.Number = 0
    End If
```

```
  End If

  strFolderList = _
    WshShl.RegRead("HKLM\Software\Intuit\VBScripts\MstSumRpts\SharedFolder")
  If Err <> 0 Then
    If strEventLog = "Enabled" Then
      WriteToEventLog ("Summary Report Collection script - Using " & _
        "default for strFolderList.")
      Err.Number = 0
    End If
  End If

  strArchive = _
    WshShl.RegRead("HKLM\Software\Intuit\VBScripts\MstSumRpts\RptArchive")
  If Err <> 0 Then
  If strEventLog = "Enabled" Then
      WriteToEventLog ("Summary Report Collection script - Using " & _
        "default for strArchive.")
      Err.Number = 0
    End If
  End If

  If strDebug = "Enabled" Then
    MsgBox "Registry settings initialized: " & vbCrLf & vbCrLf & _
      "strEventLog" & vbTab & "=" & vbTab & strEventLog & vbCrLf & _
      "strDebug" & vbTab & vbTab & "=" & vbTab & strDebug & vbCrLf & _
      "strSvrList" & vbTab & vbTab & "=" & vbTab & strSvrList & vbCrLf & _
      "strFolderList" & vbTab & "=" & vbTab & strFolderList & vbCrLf & _
      "strArchive" & vbTab & "=" & vbTab & strArchive, , cTitleBarMsg
  End If

End Sub

Function MapNetworkDrive(strLetter, strDrive)

  If strDebug = "Enabled" Then
    MsgBox "strLetter = " & strLetter & vbCrLf & "strDrive = " & _
      strDrive, , cTitleBarMsg
```

```
    End If

    If FsoObj.DriveExists(strDrive) Then

      If strDebug = "Enabled" Then
        MsgBox strDrive & " exists", , cTitleBarMsg
      End If

      If FsoObj.DriveExists(strLetter) Then

        If strDebug = "Enabled" Then
           MsgBox "Deleting drive letter " & strLetter, , cTitleBarMsg
        End If

        WshNtk.RemoveNetworkDrive strLetter

      End If

      WshNtk.MapNetworkDrive strLetter, strDrive

    Else

      If strDebug = "Enabled" Then
        MsgBox strDrive & " does not exist", , cTitleBarMsg
      End If

      If strEventLog = "Enabled" Then
        WriteToEventLog "Summary Report Collection script - Unable to map " & _
        "to network drive " & strDrive
      End If
      TerminateScript()
    End If

  End Function

  Function GetSummaryRptFileName()

    GetSummaryRptFileName = Replace(Date(), "/", "-")
```

```
  GetSummaryRptFileName =  GetSummaryRptFileName & "_SumRpt.txt"

  If strDebug = "Enabled" Then
    MsgBox "Summary Report Files Name = " & GetSummaryRptFileName, , _
      cTitleBarMsg
  End If

End Function

Sub CopyFolders(strFileNameToCopy, strServerName)

  Dim strFileName

  If (FsoObj.FileExists(strFileNameToCopy)) Then
    If strDebug = "Enabled" Then
      MsgBox "File " & strFileNameToCopy & " found. Now copying...", , _
      cTitleBarMsg
    End If
  Else
    If strDebug = "Enabled" Then
      MsgBox "File " & strFileNameToCopy & " does not exist. Stopping " & _
      "script execution.", , cTitleBarMsg
    End If
    TerminateScript()
  End If

  Set strFileName = FsoObj.GetFile(strFileNameToCopy)

  strFileName.Copy (strArchive & "\" & strServerName & "_" & _
    Mid(strFileNameToCopy,4))
  If Err <> 0 Then
    If strEventLog = "Enabled" Then
      WriteToEventLog "Summary Report Collection script - Unable to copy " & _
        strFileNameToCopy
    End If
    If strDebug = "Enabled" Then
      MsgBox "Summary Report Collection script - Unable to copy " & _
```

```
        strFileNameToCopy, , cTitleBarMsg
      End If
      TerminateScript()
    End If

End Sub

Sub DisconnectNetworkDrive(strDriveLetter)

  On Error Resume Next

  If strDebug = "Enabled" Then
    MsgBox "Disconnecting " & strDriveLetter, , cTitleBarMsg
  End If

  WshNtk.RemoveNetworkDrive strDriveLetter
  If Err <> 0 Then
    If strDebug = "Enabled" Then
      MsgBox "Error occurred when disconnecting " & strDriveLetter, , _
        cTitleBarMsg
    End If
  End If

End Sub

Sub WriteToEventLog(strMessage)

  WshShl.LogEvent 4, strMessage

End Sub

Sub TerminateScript()

  If strDebug = "Enabled" Then
    MsgBox "Script execution terminated.", , cTitleBarMsg
  End If
```

```
  WScript.Quit()

End Sub
```

Figure 23.4 shows the summary report files once they have been copied over from each Windows 2000 server for the first time. They are stored on the Windows 2000 Professional workstation in `D:\Order_Inventory\LogFiles`. As you can see, each of the summary report file names has been modified to include the name of the server from which it was collected.

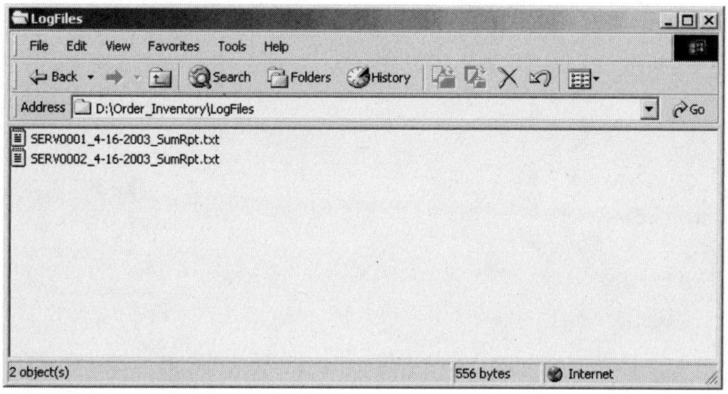

FIGURE 23.4 *Examining the summary report files after they have been copied over to the Windows 2000 Professional workstation*

Summary

This chapter showed you how to create VBScripts that can establish remote connections to shared network drives. You also learned how to copy, move, and delete network files. You observed as Molly developed a VBScript that collected remotely stored summary reports and stored them on the Windows 2000 Professional workstation for later processing. In the process, you strengthened your understanding of how to retrieve script settings stored in the Windows registry.

Chapter 24

Processing and Consolidating Report Data

In this chapter, you will learn how to develop a VBScript that reads and processes both of the summary report files collected from the SERV0001 and SERV0002 Windows 2000 servers. You will then learn how to create the consolidated summary report in either of two formats, text and Microsoft Word. Finally, you will learn how to develop a process that is capable of notifying selected operations staff members when the consolidated report is available.

Parsing String Contents

The script developed in this chapter will make heavy use of a number of VBScript functions that relate to parsing and manipulating the contents of strings. These functions will be used when reading and processing the two summary reports in order to identify and manipulate the data that is processed. You'll need to use these functions again later in the script when writing the consolidated summary report.

Indexing String Contents

One of the VBScript functions that will be used to develop this chapter's script is the `Split()` function. This function takes a string argument and builds a single dimension array made up of substrings extracted from the original string. This function will be used to process a registry value whose contents represent a list of usernames to whom network messages are to be sent. By splitting up this list of names into an array, you can then use a `For...Next` loop to iteratively process each username stored in the array. The `Split()` function has the following syntax:

```
Split(Expression [, Delimiter [, Count [, Compare]]])
```

`Expression` represents the string to be processed. `Delimiter` specifies an optional character that identifies substring boundaries. If omitted, the space character is assumed. `Count` is an optional parameter that can be used to limit the number of substrings retrieved, and `Compare` is an optional parameter that specifies the type of comparison to perform (specify a value of 0 to perform a binary comparison and a value of 1 to perform a text comparison).

For example, the following statements demonstrate how to use the `Split()` function. First, a string that stores a list of names, each separated by a space, is defined. Then the `Split()` function is used to create a single dimension array called `astrList` that stores each of these three names as array elements.

```
strList = "Mike Nick Mark"
astrList = Split(strList)
```

Removing Leading and Trailing Spaces

Another VBScript function that will be used in the script developed in this chapter is the `Trim()` function. This function retrieves a copy of a string without leading or trailing spaces and has the following syntax:

```
Trim(string)
```

`String` specifies the string to be processed by the function. The following example shows a statement that builds a string padded with a number of blank spaces. The statement is followed by a `MsgBox()` statement that uses the `Trim()` function to remove the extraneous blank spaces before it displays the contents of the string.

```
strList = "   Mike Nick Mark      "
MsgBox Trim(strList)
```

Converting a String to an Integer

Another VBScript function that will be useful in developing this chapter's VBScript is the `CInt()` function. This function retrieves an expression converted to an integer subtype. The syntax for this function is shown below.

```
CInt(Expression)
```

`Expression` represents a string expression. This function is useful when extracting numeric values from text strings, as demonstrated below.

```
strList = "There are 10 units on hand"
intCount = Cint(Mid(strList, 11,2))
```

In this example, a string is defined and then parsed using the `Mid()` function to extract the number of units on hand. While VBScript usually does a good job of converting values from one variant subtype to another, such as when you specify a mathematical operation, there are also times when it does not make the subtype adjustment correctly. Using the `Cint()` function, as shown above, you can explicitly convert a value to an integer subtype in order to ensure its correct interpretation.

Determining a String's Length

Another VBScript function that will be useful in developing this chapter's VBScript is the `Len()` function. This function retrieves the number of characters in a string or variable. The syntax for this function is listed below.

```
Len(string ¦ variable)
```

`String` represents a string whose length is to be calculated. In this chapter's VBScript, the `Len()` function will be used repeatedly to determine whether or not a blank line has been encountered within a report file (that is, a zero length string). For example, the following `If` statement demonstrates how to determine whether a variable has been assigned any data. If it has not been assigned data, its length will be equal to zero. In this example, an action is taken only when there is some data to process.

```
If Len(strText) > 0 Then
  ...
End If
```

Other VBScript Functions

This chapter will take advantage of a number of other VBScript functions when processing the summary reports and creating the consolidated summary report. These functions, listed below, have already been reviewed in earlier chapters.

- **`Mid()`.** Retrieves a subset of characters from a string
- **`Instr()`.** Retrieves the character position of the first occurrence of one string inside another
- **`Left()`.** Retrieves a subset of characters from the left side of a string
- **`Right()`.** Retrieves a subset of characters from the right side of a string

Working with the Word Object Model

This chapter's script will read two summary reports collected from the SERV0001 and SERV0002 Windows 2000 servers at Intuit. It will then process and combine the data found in these two reports to create a new consolidated summary report. This report will be available in two different formats, the standard text format presented in earlier examples and an optional Microsoft Word format. The Word version of the report may make it more convenient for many people at Intuit to view the report, which will be formatted using different fonts and selective character highlighting to make it more visually appealing than its plain text counterpart.

In order to write the Word version of the consolidated report, you will need to learn how to reference and work with the Word object model. At the top of the Word object model is the `Application` object. When Word is started, an instance of the `Application` object is automatically created. You can use properties and methods belonging to this object to access lower-level objects and collections in the Word object model. You can then use the properties and methods provided by these objects and collections to automate the creation of reports using Word. The following statement demonstrates how to instantiate Word from within a VBScript:

```
Set objMsWord = WScript.CreateObject("Word.Application")
```

This statement assigns a reference to the Word `Application` object in the form of a variable named `objMsWord`. In order to create the Word version of the consolidated summary report, you will need to learn how to work with the following Word objects:

- **`Documents`.** A collection representing all the currently opened instances of Word documents. This collection provides properties and methods required to create, open, save, and close files. The `Documents` collection is accessed using the `Application` object's `Documents` property.
- **`Document`.** An individual instance of a Word document. The `Document` object provides properties and methods required to create, open, save, and close files.
- **`Selection`.** Represents an instance of the currently open Windows pane. The `Selection` object is accessed using the `Application` object's `Selection` property. The `Selection` object is used when performing an action on a Word document, such as typing in text.
- **`Font`.** Provides access to properties that can be used to format the appearance of text within documents. The `Font` object is accessed using the `Selection` object's `Font` property.

Another useful `Application` object property is `ActiveDocument`, which retrieves a reference to the currently active Word document. The following example demonstrates how to use these objects and their properties and methods to create, write to, and save a Word file. The documentation for each statement used within the script is provided by comments embedded within the script itself.

```
'Define a variable to be used to store a reference to the Application object
Dim objWordDoc
'Instantiate Word and define the Application object reference
Set objWordDoc = WScript.CreateObject("Word.Application")

'Use the Documents collection's Add method to open a new empty Word document
objWordDoc.Documents.Add()

'Use the Font object's Name, Size and Bold properties to format text output
objWordDoc.Selection.Font.Name = "Arial"
objWordDoc.Selection.Font.Size = 12
objWordDoc.Selection.Font.Bold = True

'Use the Selection object's  Typetext() method to write a line of text
objWordDoc.Selection.Typetext("Report Header")

'Use the Selection object's TypeParagraph() method to insert two line feeds
objWordDoc.Selection.TypeParagraph
objWordDoc.Selection.TypeParagraph

'Use the Font object's Size and Bold property to format text output
objWordDoc.Selection.Font.Size = 10
objWordDoc.Selection.Font.Bold = False

'Use the Selection object's Typetext() and TypeParagraph() methods to write
'additional text
objWordDoc.Selection.Typetext("Line 1 of the report.")
objWordDoc.Selection.TypeParagraph
objWordDoc.Selection.Typetext("Line 2 of the report.")

'Use the Applications object's ActiveDocument property to reference the current
'document and then use the Document object's SaveAs() method to save the Word
```

```
'file
objWordDoc.ActiveDocument.SaveAs("c:\Temp\TextFile.doc")

'Use the document object's Close() method to close the Word document
objWordDoc.ActiveDocument.Close()

'Terminate the currently active instance of Word
objWordDoc.Quit()
```

NOTE

Because of the size and complexity of the Word object model, there is not enough room in this book to cover it in any greater depth. To learn more about Word's object model, check out **msdn.Microsoft.com/office**.

Developing a Network Messaging Procedure

One of the goals that Molly has for this script is to equip it with the ability to notify selected operations staff, in the form of a pop-up dialog box message, when the consolidated summary report is available. She thought about trying to display a pop-up message using the `MsgBox()` function on the Windows 2000 Professional workstation where the script executes. She discovered that this wouldn't work, because the script that creates the consolidation report runs in the background using the `WScript.exe` execution host. Therefore, even if she tries to use the `MsgBox()` function to display an interactive pop-up dialog box, the pop-up dialog box would not be displayed. Instead, the script would stop processing while it waited for the user to respond to the pop-up dialog box, which would never come, since the pop-up dialog box was not displayed.

After doing a little research, Molly came across the Windows `Net Send` command. This command provides the ability to send a text message over a network to a specified user or computer. The syntax of the `Net Send` command is shown below.

```
net send (name ¦ * ¦ /domain[:name] ¦ /users) message
```

`Name` represents the name of a user or computer to whom the message is to be sent. In order for the receiving user or computer to receive and display the pop-up message, the Windows messenger service must be running on his computer. In addition, the user must be logged on to his computer at the time that the message is sent. The asterisk (`*`) character can be used to send the message to all users within the domain or workgroup to which the sending computer is a member. The `/domain:name` parameter can be used to send the message to all names defined in the Windows domain. The `/users` parameter provides the ability to send the message to all users with an active network connection to the sending computer. `Message` represents the message text that is to be displayed in the pop-up dialog box.

In order to use the `Net Send` command from within a script, you need to use the `WshShell` object's `Run()` method, as demonstrated below.

```
Set WshShl = WScript.CreateObject("WScript.Shell")
strUser = "Jford"
strMsgTest = "This is a test!"
WshShl.Run "Net Send " & strUser & " " & strMsgTest
```

When executed, this example displays the pop-up dialog box shown in Figure 24.1 on the computer where the user whose username is `Jford` is currently logged on.

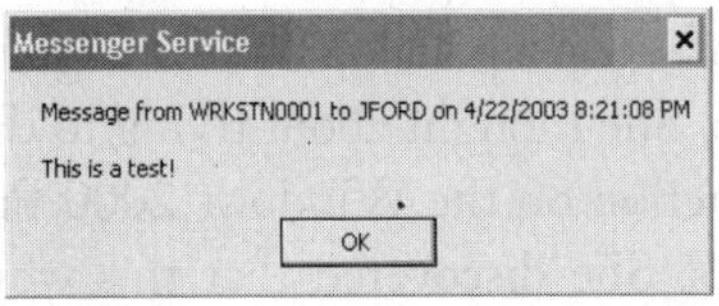

FIGURE 24.1 *Examining the contents of a network message created using the* `Net Send` *command*

Creating the Consolidation Report Script

The consolidated summary report creation script performs a number of different tasks. It reads and stores the contents of both summary reports into two separate arrays. Then it spins through both arrays, parsing out data to be used to create the consolidated summary report. This process involves numerous VBScript string-related functions. In addition to creating the standard text report, the script has the ability to create a Word version. Other script activities include retrieving configuration settings from the Windows registry, supporting a debug mode, logging application event messages, and sending network notification messages.

The Initialization Section

The script's `Initialization Section`, shown below, defines variables used globally throughout the script. In addition, it defines three dynamic arrays, which will be used to store the content of reports while they are being processed. A collection of constants and instances of the `WshShell` and `FileSystemObject` objects are also defined here.

```
Option Explicit

Dim strEventLog, strDebug, strSvrList, strArchive, strConsolFolder
Dim strRpt1, strRpt2, strConSolRptName, strRptFormat, strNetworkNotification

ReDim astrServ0001Array(0)
ReDim astrServ0002Array(0)
ReDim astrProductionArray(0)

Dim FsoObj, WshShl

Const cTitleBarMsg = "Consolidated Summary Report Creator"
Const cForReading = 1
Const cForWriting = 2
Const cForAppending = 8

Set WshShl = WScript.CreateObject("WScript.Shell")
Set FsoObj = CreateObject("Scripting.FileSystemObject")
```

The Main Processing Section

The script's `Main Processing Section`, shown below, consists of a series of procedure calls. The `SetDefaultSettings()` and `GetRegistrySettings()` subroutines are called to set up the script's configuration settings, as has been demonstrated in previous scripts. Messages are written to the Windows application event log by the `WriteToEventLog()` subroutine if event logging is enabled when the script starts executing. The IdentifyRptsToProcess() subroutine creates a variable that specifies the name of the current day's summary reports. The ReadSummaryReport() subroutine is then called twice and passed the name of a Windows 2000 server. This subroutine reads and then stores the contents of each summary report in an array.

The CreateConsolidatedTextReport() subroutine is then called in order to write the text version of the consolidated summary report. If appropriate, the CreateConsolidatedWordReport() subroutine is then executed in order to create a Word version of the report. If Network Notification is enabled, the NotifyOperationsStaff() subroutine is executed next. Finally, an optional message is written if the event logging is enabled and the script's execution is terminated by calling the TerminateScript() subroutine.

```
SetDefaultSettings()
GetRegistrySettings()

If strEventLog = "Enabled" Then
  WriteToEventLog("Consolidated Summary Report Creator executing.")
End If

IdentifyRptsToProcess()

ReadSummaryReport(Left(strSvrList, 8))
ReadSummaryReport(Right(strSvrList, 8))

CreateConsolidatedTextReport()

If strRptFormat = "Word" Then
  CreatConsolidatedWordReport()
End If

If strNetworkNotification = "Enabled" Then
  NotifyOperationsStaff()
End If

If strEventLog = "Enabled" Then
  WriteToEventLog("Consolidated Summary Report Creator finished.")
End If
```

```
TerminateScript()
```

The SetDefaultSettings() Subroutine

As demonstrated in previous scripts, the `SetDefaultSettings()` subroutine, shown below, establishes default configuration settings for the script.

```
Sub SetDefaultSettings()


  strEventLog = "Enabled"
  strDebug = "Disabled"
  strSvrList = "SERV0001 SERV0002"
  strArchive = "d:\Order_Inventrory\LogFiles"
  strRptFormat = "Text"
  strNetworkNotification = "Enabled"
  strConsolFolder = "d:\Order_Inventory\ConsolidatedRpts"

  If strDebug = "Enabled" Then
    MsgBox "Registry settings retrieved: " & vbCrLf & vbCrLf & _
     "strEventLog" & vbTab & "=" & vbTab & strEventLog & vbCrLf & _
     "strDebug" & vbTab & vbTab & "=" & vbTab & strDebug & vbCrLf & _
     "strSvrList" & vbTab & vbTab & "=" & vbTab & strSvrList & vbCrLf & _
     "strArchive" & vbTab & "=" & vbTab & strArchive & vbCrLf & _
     "strRptFormat" & vbTab & "=" & vbTab & strRptFormat & vbCrLf & _
     "strNetworkNotification" & vbTab & "=" & vbTab & strNetworkNotification & _
       vbCrLf & _
     "strConsolFolder" & vbTab & "=" & vbTab & strConsolFolder, , cTitleBarMsg
  End If

End Sub
```

The GetRegistrySettings() Subroutine

The `GetRegistrySettings()` subroutine, shown below, retrieves configuration settings from the Windows registry and logs messages in the Windows application event log if errors occur.

```
Sub GetRegistrySettings()
```

```
On Error Resume Next

strEventLog = _
  WshShl.RegRead("HKLM\Software\Intuit\VBScripts\MstSumRpts\EventLogging")
If Err <> 0 Then
  If strEventLog = "Enabled" Then
    WriteToEventLog ("Summary Report Collection script - Using default " & _
      "for strEventLog.")
    Err.Number = 0
  End If
End If

strDebug = WshShl.RegRead("HKLM\Software\Intuit\VBScripts\MstSumRpts\DebugMode")
If Err <> 0 Then
  If strEventLog = "Enabled" Then
    WriteToEventLog ("Summary Report Collection script - Using " & _
      "default for strDebug.")
    Err.Number = 0
  End If
End If

strSvrList = _
  WshShl.RegRead("HKLM\Software\Intuit\VBScripts\MstSumRpts\Win2000Svrs")
If Err <> 0 Then
  If strEventLog = "Enabled" Then
    WriteToEventLog ("Summary Report Collection script - Using " & _
      "default for strSvrList.")
    Err.Number = 0
  End If
End If

strArchive = _
  WshShl.RegRead("HKLM\Software\Intuit\VBScripts\MstSumRpts\RptArchive")
If Err <> 0 Then
If strEventLog = "Enabled" Then
    WriteToEventLog ("Summary Report Collection script - Using " & _
      "default for strArchive.")
```

```
      Err.Number = 0
    End If
  End If

  strRptFormat = _
    WshShl.RegRead("HKLM\Software\Intuit\VBScripts\MstSumRpts\RptFormat")
  If Err <> 0 Then
    If strEventLog = "Enabled" Then
      WriteToEventLog ("Summary Report Collection script - Using " & _
        "default for strRptFormat.")
      Err.Number = 0
    End If
  End If

  strNetworkNotification =
WshShl.RegRead("HKLM\Software\Intuit\VBScripts\MstSumRpts\NetworkNotification")
  If Err <> 0 Then
    If strEventLog = "Enabled" Then
      WriteToEventLog ("Summary Report Collection script - Using default for
strNetworkNotification.")
      Err.Number = 0
    End If
  End If

  strConsolFolder = _
    WshShl.RegRead("HKLM\Software\Intuit\VBScripts\MstSumRpts\ConsolFolder")
  If Err <> 0 Then
    If strEventLog = "Enabled" Then
      WriteToEventLog ("Summary Report Collection script - Using " & _
        "default for strConsolFolder.")
      Err.Number = 0
    End If
  End If

  If strDebug = "Enabled" Then
    MsgBox "Registry settings retrieved: " & vbCrLf & vbCrLf & _
     "strEventLog" & vbTab & "=" & vbTab & strEventLog & vbCrLf & _
     "strDebug" & vbTab & vbTab & "=" & vbTab & strDebug & vbCrLf & _
```

```
    "strSvrList" & vbTab & vbTab & "=" & vbTab & strSvrList & vbCrLf & _
    "strArchive" & vbTab & "=" & vbTab & strArchive & vbCrLf & _
    "strRptFormat" & vbTab & "=" & vbTab & strRptFormat & vbCrLf & _
    "strNetworkNotification" & vbTab & "=" & vbTab & strNetworkNotification & _
       vbCrLf & _
    "strConsolFolder" & vbTab & "=" & vbTab & strConsolFolder, , cTitleBarMsg
  End If

End Sub
```

The IdentifyRptsToProcess() Subroutine

The logic presented in the `IdentifyRptsToProcess()` subroutine has already been demonstrated numerous times in other VBScripts shown in this book. This subroutine is responsible for setting the value assigned to a variable that identifies the name of the current day's summary reports.

```
Sub IdentifyRptsToProcess()

  Dim strFileNameString

  strFileNameString = Replace(Date(), "/", "-")

  strConSolRptName = strConsolFolder & "\" & strFileNameString & _
    "_ConsolSumRpt.txt"

  strFileNameString = strFileNameString & "_SumRpt.txt"

  strRpt1 = strArchive & "\" & Left(strSvrList, 8) & "_" & strFileNameString
  strRpt2 = strArchive & "\" & Right(strSvrList, 8) & "_" & strFileNameString

  If strDebug = "Enabled" Then
    MsgBox "1st summary report to process = " & strRpt1 & vbCrLf & _
    "2nd summary report to process = " & strRpt2, , cTitleBarMsg
  End If

End Sub
```

The ReadSummaryReport() Subroutine

The `ReadSummaryReport()` subroutine, shown below, uses the `FileSystemObject` object's `FileExists()`, `OpenTextFile()`, `ReadLine()`, and `Close()` methods and a `Do...While` loop to process the appropriate summary report. The report to be processed is identified by an argument passed to the subroutine. The subroutine stores the contents of each report in an array called either `astrServ0001Array` or `astrServ0002Array`.

```
Sub ReadSummaryReport(strServerName)

  If strDebug = "Enabled" Then
    MsgBox "Server = " & strServerName, , cTitleBarMsg
  End If

  Dim strSourFile

  If strServerName = "SERV0001" then
    strSourFile = strRpt1
  Else
    strSourFile = strRpt2
  End If

  Dim FileRef, strRptLine

  Dim intArrayCounter, IntErrLevel
  intArrayCounter = 0

  If (FsoObj.FileExists(strSourFile)) Then
    Set FileRef = FsoObj.OpenTextFile(strSourFile, cForReading)
      Do Until FileRef.AtEndOfStream

        strRptLine = FileRef.ReadLine()

        If strServerName = "SERV0001" Then
          If Instr(1, intArrayCounter, "Date") <> 1 Then
            If Instr(1, intArrayCounter, "Part") <> 1 Then
              ReDim Preserve astrServ0001Array(intArrayCounter)
              astrServ0001Array(intArrayCounter) = strRptLine
```

```
                End If
              End If
            Else
              If Instr(1, intArrayCounter, "Date") <> 1 Then
                If Instr(1, intArrayCounter, "Part") <> 1 Then
                  ReDim Preserve astrServ0002Array(intArrayCounter)
                  astrServ0002Array(intArrayCounter) = strRptLine
                End If
              End If
            End If

            intArrayCounter = intArrayCounter + 1

          Loop
        FileRef.Close()

      Else
        WriteToEventLog("Consolidated Summary Report Creator - unable to open " & _
          strSourFile)
        TerminateScript()
      End If

    End Sub
```

The CreateConsolidatedTextReport() Subroutine

The `CreateConsolidatedTextReport()`, shown below, copies each summary report into an array and then creates the consolidated summary report by processing the contents of both arrays. It uses a variety of VBScript parsing functions to test, extract, and manipulate the contents of each line in each summary report before adding its data to the consolidated summary report.

```
Sub CreateConsolidatedTextReport()

  Dim intArrayCounter, OutPutFile, strMessage, strLocator
  Dim intQtyOne, intQtyTwo, intTotalQty, intSpacing, strMatch, strMatchlist
  Dim intInStockOne, intInStockTwo, intTotalInStock, intSpaces, intCounter2
  intArrayCounter = 0
```

```
  strLocator = "False"

  Set OutPutFile = FsoObj.OpenTextFile(strConSolRptName, 2, "True")

  If strDebug = "Enabled" Then
    MsgBox "Now creating to the Consolidated Summary Report"
  End If


  'Begin creating the consolidated summary report
  OutPutFile.WriteLine
"*****************************************************************************"
  OutPutFile.WriteBlankLines(1)
  OutPutFile.WriteLine "Master Consolidated Summary report for " & Date()
  OutPutFile.WriteBlankLines(1)
  OutPutFile.WriteLine
"*****************************************************************************"
  OutPutFile.WriteBlankLines(1)

  OutPutFile.WriteLine "Errors:"
  OutPutFile.WriteBlankLines(1)
  OutPutFile.WriteLine "Date      Time      Svr Code Description"

  'Process the Errors: section for the first server
  For Each intArrayCounter In astrServ0001Array

    If Instr(1, intArrayCounter, "Errors:") = 1 Then
      strLocator = "True"
    End If

    If strLocator = "True" Then
      If Instr(1, intArrayCounter, "Errors:") <> 1 Then
        If Instr(1, intArrayCounter, "Date      Time      Code Description") <> 1
Then
          If Instr(1, intArrayCounter, "-----") <> 1 Then
            If Len(intArrayCounter) > 0 Then
              intArrayCounter = Mid(intArrayCounter, 1, 17) & " Sr1 " & _
                Mid(intArrayCounter, 19)
```

```
              OutPutFile.WriteLine intArrayCounter
            End If
          Else
            Exit For
          End If
        End If
      End If
    End If

  Next

  intArrayCounter = 0
  strLocator = "False"

  'Process the Errors: section for the second server
  For Each intArrayCounter In astrServ0002Array

    If Instr(1, intArrayCounter, "Errors:") = 1 Then
      strLocator = "True"
    End If

    If strLocator = "True" Then
      If Instr(1, intArrayCounter, "Errors:") <> 1 Then
        If Instr(1, intArrayCounter, "Date      Time    Code Description") <> 1
Then
          If Instr(1, intArrayCounter, "-----") <> 1 Then
            If Len(intArrayCounter) > 0 Then
              intArrayCounter = Mid(intArrayCounter, 1, 17) & " Sr2 " & _
                Mid(intArrayCounter, 19)
              OutPutFile.WriteLine intArrayCounter
            End If
          Else
            Exit For
          End If
        End If
      End If
    End If
```

```
Next

OutPutFile.WriteBlankLines(1)
OutPutFile.WriteLine "-----------------------------------------------" & _
  "----------------------------"
OutPutFile.WriteBlankLines(1)

OutPutFile.WriteLine "Sales summary:"
OutPutFile.WriteBlankLines(1)
OutPutFile.WriteLine "Government:"
OutPutFile.WriteBlankLines(1)
OutPutFile.WriteLine "Part # Qty  Description"
OutPutFile.WriteBlankLines(1)

intArrayCounter = 0
strLocator = "False"

'Process the Sales summary: section for the first server
For Each intArrayCounter In astrServ0001Array

  If Instr(1, intArrayCounter, "Sales summary") = 1 Then
    strLocator = "True"
  End If

  If strLocator = "True" Then
    If Instr(1, intArrayCounter, "Sales summary:") <> 1 Then
      If Instr(1, intArrayCounter, "Part # Qty  Description") <> 1 Then
        If Instr(1, intArrayCounter, "-----") <> 1 Then
          If Len(intArrayCounter) > 0 Then
            intArrayCounter = Mid(intArrayCounter, 1, 17) & _
              Mid(intArrayCounter, 19)
            OutPutFile.WriteLine intArrayCounter
          End If
        Else
          Exit For
        End If
      End If
    End If
```

```
    End If

  Next

  OutPutFile.WriteBlankLines(1)
  OutPutFile.WriteLine "Other Customers:"
  OutPutFile.WriteBlankLines(1)
  OutPutFile.WriteLine "Part # Qty  Description"
  OutPutFile.WriteBlankLines(1)

  intArrayCounter = 0
  strLocator = "False"

  'Process the Sales summary: section for the second server
  For Each intArrayCounter In astrServ0002Array

    If Instr(1, intArrayCounter, "Sales summary:") = 1 Then
      strLocator = "True"
    End If

    If strLocator = "True" Then
      If Instr(1, intArrayCounter, "Sales summary:") <> 1 Then
        If Instr(1, intArrayCounter, "Part # Qty  Description") <> 1 Then
          If Instr(1, intArrayCounter, "-----") <> 1 Then
            If Len(intArrayCounter) > 0 Then
              intArrayCounter = Mid(intArrayCounter, 1, 17) & _
                Mid(intArrayCounter, 19)
              OutPutFile.WriteLine intArrayCounter
            End If
          Else
            Exit For
          End If
        End If
      End If
    End If

  Next
```

```
OutPutFile.WriteBlankLines(1)
OutPutFile.WriteLine "----------------------------------------------" & _
  "---------------------------"
OutPutFile.WriteBlankLines(1)

OutPutFile.WriteLine "Returns summary:"
OutPutFile.WriteBlankLines(1)
OutPutFile.WriteLine "Government:"
OutPutFile.WriteBlankLines(1)
OutPutFile.WriteLine "Part #  Qty Description"
OutPutFile.WriteBlankLines(1)

intArrayCounter = 0
strLocator = "False"

'Process the Return summary: section for the first server
For Each intArrayCounter In astrServ0001Array

  If Instr(1, intArrayCounter, "Return summary") = 1 Then
    strLocator = "True"
  End If

  If strLocator = "True" Then
    If Instr(1, intArrayCounter, "Return summary:") <> 1 Then
      If Instr(1, intArrayCounter, "Part #  Qty Description") <> 1 Then
        If Instr(1, intArrayCounter, "-----") <> 1 Then
          If Len(intArrayCounter) > 0 Then
            intArrayCounter = Mid(intArrayCounter, 1, 17) & _
              Mid(intArrayCounter, 19)
            OutPutFile.WriteLine intArrayCounter
          End If
        Else
          Exit For
        End If
      End If
    End If
  End If
```

```
Next

OutPutFile.WriteBlankLines(1)
OutPutFile.WriteLine "Other Customers:"
OutPutFile.WriteBlankLines(1)
OutPutFile.WriteLine "Part #  Qty Description"
OutPutFile.WriteBlankLines(1)

intArrayCounter = 0
strLocator = "False"

'Process the Return summary: section for the second server
For Each intArrayCounter In astrServ0002Array

  If Instr(1, intArrayCounter, "Return summary:") = 1 Then
    strLocator = "True"
  End If

  If strLocator = "True" Then
    If Instr(1, intArrayCounter, "Return summary:") <> 1 Then
      If Instr(1, intArrayCounter, "Part #  Qty Description") <> 1 Then
        If Instr(1, intArrayCounter, "-----") <> 1 Then
          If Len(intArrayCounter) > 0 Then
            intArrayCounter = Mid(intArrayCounter, 1, 17) & _
              Mid(intArrayCounter, 19)
            OutPutFile.WriteLine intArrayCounter
          End If
        Else
          Exit For
        End If
      End If
    End If
  End If

Next

OutPutFile.WriteBlankLines(1)
OutPutFile.WriteLine "---------------------------------------------" & _
```

```
    "--------------------------"
  OutPutFile.WriteBlankLines(1)

  OutPutFile.WriteLine "Daily Production Summary:"
  OutPutFile.WriteBlankLines(1)
  OutPutFile.WriteLine "Part #  Qty  Description              In Stock"
  OutPutFile.WriteBlankLines(1)

  intArrayCounter = 0
  strLocator = "False"
  intCounter2 = 0

  'Process the Daily Production Summary section for the first server
  For Each intArrayCounter In astrServ0001Array

    If Instr(1, intArrayCounter, "Daily Production Summary") = 1 Then
      strLocator = "True"
    End If

    If strLocator = "True" Then
      If Instr(1, intArrayCounter, "Daily Production Summary") <> 1 Then
        If Instr(1, intArrayCounter, "Part #  Qty  Description              In" & _
          "Stock") <> 1 Then
            If Len(intArrayCounter) > 0 Then

              ReDim Preserve astrProductionArray(intCounter2)
              astrProductionArray(intCounter2) = intArrayCounter
              intCounter2 = intCounter2 + 1

            End If
        End If
      End If
    End If

  Next

  intCounter2 = 0
```

```
intArrayCounter = 0
strLocator = "False"

'Process the Daily Production Summary section for the first server
For Each intArrayCounter In astrServ0002Array

  If Instr(1, intArrayCounter, "Daily Production Summary") = 1 Then
    strLocator = "True"
  End If

  If strLocator = "True" Then
    If Instr(1, intArrayCounter, "Daily Production Summary") <> 1 Then
      If Instr(1, intArrayCounter, "Part #  Qty  Description             In" & _
        "Stock") <> 1 Then
          If Len(intArrayCounter) > 0 Then

            intArrayCounter = Mid(intArrayCounter, 1, 17) & _
              Mid(intArrayCounter, 19)

            'Spin though astrProductionArray and determine if there are any
            'matching entries to process
            intCounter2 = 0
            strMatch = "False"
            For Each intCounter2 In astrProductionArray
              If Mid(intArrayCounter, 1, 5) = Mid(intCounter2, 1, 5) Then

                strMatch = "True"
                strMatchlist = strMatchList & " " & _
                  Mid(intArrayCounter, 1, 5)

                'Extract qty for both entries, add these values together and
                'write a single entry
                 intQtyOne = Mid(intArrayCounter, 9, 5)
                 intQtyOne = CInt(Trim(intQtyOne))
                 intQtyTwo = Mid(intCounter2, 9, 5)
                 intQtyTwo = CInt(Trim(intQtyTwo))
                 intTotalQty = intQtyOne + intQtyTwo
```

```
                intSpacing = Len(intTotalQty)
                intSpacing = 5 - intSpacing

                'Extract In Stock value for both entries, add these values
                'together and write a single entry
                intInStockOne = Mid(intArrayCounter, 39, 3)
                intInStockOne = CInt(Trim(intInStockOne))
                intInStockTwo = Mid(intCounter2, 40, 3)
                intInStockTwo = CInt(Trim(intInStockTwo))
                intTotalInStock = intInStockOne + intInStockTwo
                intSpaces = Len(intTotalInStock)
                intSpaces = 4 - intSpaces

                OutPutFile.WriteLine Mid(intArrayCounter, 1, 5) & "     " & _
                  intTotalQty & Space(intSpacing) & _
                  Mid(intArrayCounter, 14, 25) & Space(intSpaces) & _
                  intTotalInStock
              End If
            Next
            If strmatch <> "True" Then
              OutPutFile.Writeline intArrayCounter
            End If

          End If
        End If
      End If
    End If

  Next

  'Process non-duplicate production inventory data on the second server
  For Each intArrayCounter In astrProductionArray
    If Instr(1, strMatchList, Mid(intArrayCounter, 1 ,5)) = 0 Then
      OutPutFile.WriteLine intArrayCounter
    End If
  Next

  If strDebug = "Enabled" Then
```

```
    MsgBox "Done writing to the Summary Report"
  End If

  OutPutFile.Close()

End Sub
```

The CreateConsolidatedWordReport() Subroutine

The CreateConsolidatedWordReport() subroutine, shown below, creates a Word version of the consolidated summary report. To simplify the creation of this report, Molly decided that rather than recreating the report from scratch, she would set up a Do...Until loop and use it to copy the contents of the text version of the report into an array. This subroutine would then process the array using a For Each...Next loop and the methods and properties of the Word object model. To make the Word version of the consolidated summary report easier to read, Molly modified the Font object's Name, Size, and Bold properties each time the subroutine wrote a report header. She accomplished this by setting up a series of If statements that use the Instr() function to identify headers as the For Each...Next loop iterated through each line of the text version of the consolidated summary report.

```
Sub CreatConsolidatedWordReport()

  Dim objWordDoc, strSourFile, FileRef, strRptLine, intWordCounter
  Dim strFileNameString

  ReDim astrWordVersionArray(0)

  Set objWordDoc = WScript.CreateObject("Word.Application")

  Set FileRef = FsoObj.OpenTextFile(strConSolRptName, cForReading)

  strFileNameString = Replace(Date(), "/", "-")

  strConSolRptName = strConsolFolder & "\" & strFileNameString & _
  "_ConsolSumRpt.doc"
```

```
intWordCounter = 0

If strDebug = "Enabled" Then
  MsgBox "Writing the Word version of the consolidated summary report."
End If

'Read the entire report into an array
Do Until FileRef.AtEndOfStream

  strRptLine = FileRef.ReadLine()

  ReDim Preserve astrWordVersionArray(intWordCounter)
  astrWordVersionArray(intWordCounter) = strRptLine

  intWordCounter = intWordCounter + 1

Loop

FileRef.Close()

'Start creating the Word document
objWordDoc.Documents.Add()

objWordDoc.Selection.Font.Name = "Courier"
objWordDoc.Selection.Font.Size = 8
objWordDoc.Selection.Font.Bold = False

'Spin through the array, format and write the Word version of the report
For Each intWordCounter in astrWordVersionArray

  'Change Font properties for selected report headings
  If Instr(1,intWordCounter, "Master Consolidated Summary") Then

    objWordDoc.Selection.Font.Name = "Arial"
    objWordDoc.Selection.Font.Size = 12
    objWordDoc.Selection.Font.Bold = True

  End If
```

```
    If Instr(1,intWordCounter, "Errors:") Then
      objWordDoc.Selection.Font.Name = "Arial"
      objWordDoc.Selection.Font.Size = 10
      objWordDoc.Selection.Font.Bold = True
    End If

    If Instr(1,intWordCounter, "Sales summary:") Then
      objWordDoc.Selection.Font.Name = "Arial"
      objWordDoc.Selection.Font.Size = 10
      objWordDoc.Selection.Font.Bold = True
    End If

    If Instr(1,intWordCounter, "Returns summary:") Then
      objWordDoc.Selection.Font.Name = "Arial"
      objWordDoc.Selection.Font.Size = 10
      objWordDoc.Selection.Font.Bold = True
    End If

    If Instr(1,intWordCounter, "Daily Production Summary") Then
      objWordDoc.Selection.Font.Name = "Arial"
      objWordDoc.Selection.Font.Size = 10
      objWordDoc.Selection.Font.Bold = True
    End If

    'Write a line of the report
    objWordDoc.Selection.Typetext(intWordCounter)
    'Add a paragraph marker (.e.g. linefeed)
    objWordDoc.Selection.TypeParagraph

    'Reset default Font properties
    objWordDoc.Selection.Font.Name = "Courier"
    objWordDoc.Selection.Font.Size = 8
    objWordDoc.Selection.Font.Bold = False

  Next
```

```
    'Save the Word file
    objWordDoc.ActiveDocument.SaveAs(strConSolRptName)

    'Close the document
     objWordDoc.ActiveDocument.Close()

    'Exit Word
     objWordDoc.Quit()

End Sub
```

The NotifyOperationsStaff() Subroutine

The `NotifyOperationsStaff()` subroutine, shown below, uses the VBScript `Split()` functions to create an array containing the names of selected operations staff members who should be sent a network message indicating that the consolidated summary report is now available. A `For Each...Next` loop is then set up to spin through the array and send a message to each username using the `Net Send` command.

```
Sub NotifyOperationsStaff()

  On Error Resume Next

  Dim strUserName, strNtkNotifyList

  Dim astrNotifyArray

  strNtkNotifyList = "MJLF001 ASCK001"

  strNtkNotifyList = _
    WshShl.RegRead("HKLM\Software\Intuit\VBScripts\MstSumRpts\NtkNotifyList")
  If Err <> 0 Then
    If strEventLog = "Enabled" Then
      WriteToEventLog ("Summary Report Collection script - Using default " & _
        "for strNtkNotifyList.")
      Err.Number = 0
    End If
```

```
  End If

  astrNotifyArray = Split(strNtkNotifyList)

  For Each strUserName In astrNotifyArray
    WshShl.Run "Net Send " & strUserName & " " & "Order\Inventory " & _
      "consolidated report now available."
  Next

End Sub
```

The WriteToEventLog() Subroutine

As is the case with previous scripts, the `WriteToEventLog()` subroutine writes informational messages to the Windows application event log using a string passed to it as an argument.

```
Sub WriteToEventLog(strMessage)

  WshShl.LogEvent 4, strMessage

End Sub
```

The TerminateScript() Subroutine

The `TerminateScript()` subroutine, shown below, uses the `WScript` object's `Quit()` method to terminate the script's execution.

```
Sub TerminateScript()

  WScript.Quit()

End Sub
```

The Fully Assembled Script

The fully assembled VBScript is shown below. Molly will execute it as a background task on the Windows 2000 Professional workstation located in the operations command center. Depending on its registry configuration settings, it will create a text version and possibly a Word version of the consolidated summary report and then notify selected operations staff members of its availability.

```
'*************************************************************************
'Script Name: Script 24.1.vbs
'Author: Jerry Ford
'Created: 04/13/03
'Description: This script reads and processes the daily summary reports from
'both Windows 2000 Servers where the Order\Inventory system resides
'*************************************************************************

'Initialization Section

Option Explicit

Dim strEventLog, strDebug, strSvrList, strArchive, strConsolFolder
Dim strRpt1, strRpt2, strConSolRptName, strRptFormat, strNetworkNotification

ReDim astrServ0001Array(0)
ReDim astrServ0002Array(0)
ReDim astrProductionArray(0)

Dim FsoObj, WshShl

Const cTitleBarMsg = "Consolidated Summary Report Creator"
Const cForReading = 1
Const cForWriting = 2
Const cForAppending = 8

Set WshShl = WScript.CreateObject("WScript.Shell")
Set FsoObj = CreateObject("Scripting.FileSystemObject")


'Main Processing Section

SetDefaultSettings()
GetRegistrySettings()
```

```
If strEventLog = "Enabled" Then
  WriteToEventLog("Consolidated Summary Report Creator executing.")
End If

IdentifyRptsToProcess()

ReadSummaryReport(Left(strSvrList, 8))
ReadSummaryReport(Right(strSvrList, 8))

CreateConsolidatedTextReport()

If strRptFormat = "Word" Then
  CreatConsolidatedWordReport()
End If

If strNetworkNotification = "Enabled" Then
  NotifyOperationsStaff()
End If

If strEventLog = "Enabled" Then
  WriteToEventLog("Consolidated Summary Report Creator finished.")
End If

TerminateScript()


'Procedure Section

Sub SetDefaultSettings()

  strEventLog = "Enabled"
  strDebug = "Disabled"
  strSvrList = "SERV0001 SERV0002"
  strArchive = "d:\Order_Inventrory\LogFiles"
  strRptFormat = "Text"
  strNetworkNotification = "Enabled"
  strConsolFolder = "d:\Order_Inventory\ConsolidatedRpts"
```

```
  If strDebug = "Enabled" Then
    MsgBox "Registry settings retrieved: " & vbCrLf & vbCrLf & _
     "strEventLog" & vbTab & "=" & vbTab & strEventLog & vbCrLf & _
     "strDebug" & vbTab & vbTab & "=" & vbTab & strDebug & vbCrLf & _
     "strSvrList" & vbTab & vbTab & "=" & vbTab & strSvrList & vbCrLf & _
     "strArchive" & vbTab & "=" & vbTab & strArchive & vbCrLf & _
     "strRptFormat" & vbTab & "=" & vbTab & strRptFormat & vbCrLf & _
     "strNetworkNotification" & vbTab & "=" & vbTab & strNetworkNotification & _
     vbCrLf & _
     "strConsolFolder" & vbTab & "=" & vbTab & strConsolFolder, , cTitleBarMsg
  End If

End Sub

Sub GetRegistrySettings()

  On Error Resume Next

  strEventLog = _
    WshShl.RegRead("HKLM\Software\Intuit\VBScripts\MstSumRpts\EventLogging")
  If Err <> 0 Then
    If strEventLog = "Enabled" Then
      WriteToEventLog ("Summary Report Collection script - Using " & _
        "default for strEventLog.")
      Err.Number = 0
    End If
  End If

  strDebug = WshShl.RegRead("HKLM\Software\Intuit\VBScripts\MstSumRpts\DebugMode")
  If Err <> 0 Then
    If strEventLog = "Enabled" Then
      WriteToEventLog ("Summary Report Collection script - Using " & _
        "default for strDebug.")
      Err.Number = 0
    End If
  End If

  strSvrList = _
```

```
    WshShl.RegRead("HKLM\Software\Intuit\VBScripts\MstSumRpts\Win2000Svrs")
  If Err <> 0 Then
    If strEventLog = "Enabled" Then
      WriteToEventLog ("Summary Report Collection script - Using " & _
        "default for strSvrList.")
      Err.Number = 0
    End If
  End If

  strArchive = _
    WshShl.RegRead("HKLM\Software\Intuit\VBScripts\MstSumRpts\RptArchive")
  If Err <> 0 Then
  If strEventLog = "Enabled" Then
      WriteToEventLog ("Summary Report Collection script - Using " & _
        "default for strArchive.")
      Err.Number = 0
    End If
  End If

  strRptFormat = _
    WshShl.RegRead("HKLM\Software\Intuit\VBScripts\MstSumRpts\RptFormat")
  If Err <> 0 Then
    If strEventLog = "Enabled" Then
      WriteToEventLog ("Summary Report Collection script - Using " & _
        "default for strRptFormat.")
      Err.Number = 0
    End If
  End If

  strNetworkNotification =
WshShl.RegRead("HKLM\Software\Intuit\VBScripts\MstSumRpts\NetworkNotification")
  If Err <> 0 Then
    If strEventLog = "Enabled" Then
      WriteToEventLog ("Summary Report Collection script - Using default for
strNetworkNotification.")
      Err.Number = 0
    End If
  End If
```

```
  strConsolFolder = _
    WshShl.RegRead("HKLM\Software\Intuit\VBScripts\MstSumRpts\ConsolFolder")
  If Err <> 0 Then
    If strEventLog = "Enabled" Then
      WriteToEventLog ("Summary Report Collection script - Using " & _
        "default for strConsolFolder.")
      Err.Number = 0
    End If
  End If

  If strDebug = "Enabled" Then
    MsgBox "Registry settings retrieved: " & vbCrLf & vbCrLf & _
     "strEventLog" & vbTab & "=" & vbTab & strEventLog & vbCrLf & _
     "strDebug" & vbTab & vbTab & "=" & vbTab & strDebug & vbCrLf & _
     "strSvrList" & vbTab & vbTab & "=" & vbTab & strSvrList & vbCrLf & _
     "strArchive" & vbTab & "=" & vbTab & strArchive & vbCrLf & _
     "strRptFormat" & vbTab & "=" & vbTab & strRptFormat & vbCrLf & _
     "strNetworkNotification" & vbTab & "=" & vbTab & strNetworkNotification & _
     vbCrLf & _
     "strConsolFolder" & vbTab & "=" & vbTab & strConsolFolder, , cTitleBarMsg
  End If

End Sub

Sub IdentifyRptsToProcess()

  Dim strFileNameString

  strFileNameString = Replace(Date(), "/", "-")

  strConSolRptName = strConsolFolder & "\" & strFileNameString & _
    "_ConsolSumRpt.txt"

  strFileNameString = strFileNameString & "_SumRpt.txt"

  strRpt1 = strArchive & "\" & Left(strSvrList, 8) & "_" & strFileNameString
  strRpt2 = strArchive & "\" & Right(strSvrList, 8) & "_" & strFileNameString
```

```
  If strDebug = "Enabled" Then
    MsgBox "1st summary report to process = " & strRpt1 & vbCrLf & _
    "2nd summary report to process = " & strRpt2, , cTitleBarMsg
  End If

End Sub

Sub ReadSummaryReport(strServerName)

  If strDebug = "Enabled" Then
    MsgBox "Server = " & strServerName, , cTitleBarMsg
  End If

  Dim strSourFile

  If strServerName = "SERV0001" then
    strSourFile = strRpt1
  Else
    strSourFile = strRpt2
  End If

  Dim FileRef, strRptLine

  Dim intArrayCounter, IntErrLevel
  intArrayCounter = 0

  If (FsoObj.FileExists(strSourFile)) Then
    Set FileRef = FsoObj.OpenTextFile(strSourFile, cForReading)
      Do Until FileRef.AtEndOfStream

        strRptLine = FileRef.ReadLine()

        If strServerName = "SERV0001" Then
          If Instr(1, intArrayCounter, "Date") <> 1 Then
            If Instr(1, intArrayCounter, "Part") <> 1 Then
              ReDim Preserve astrServ0001Array(intArrayCounter)
              astrServ0001Array(intArrayCounter) = strRptLine
```

```
          End If
        End If
      Else
        If Instr(1, intArrayCounter, "Date") <> 1 Then
          If Instr(1, intArrayCounter, "Part") <> 1 Then
            ReDim Preserve astrServ0002Array(intArrayCounter)
            astrServ0002Array(intArrayCounter) = strRptLine
          End If
        End If
      End If

      intArrayCounter = intArrayCounter + 1

    Loop
  FileRef.Close()

Else
  WriteToEventLog("Consolidated Summary Report Creator - unable to open " & _
    strSourFile)
  TerminateScript()
End If

End Sub

Sub CreateConsolidatedTextReport()

  Dim intArrayCounter, OutPutFile, strMessage, strLocator
  Dim intQtyOne, intQtyTwo, intTotalQty, intSpacing, strMatch, strMatchlist
  Dim intInStockOne, intInStockTwo, intTotalInStock, intSpaces, intCounter2
  intArrayCounter = 0
  strLocator = "False"

  Set OutPutFile = FsoObj.OpenTextFile(strConSolRptName, 2, "True")

  If strDebug = "Enabled" Then
    MsgBox "Now creating to the Consolidated Summary Report"
  End If
```

```
  'Begin creating the consolidated summary report
  OutPutFile.WriteLine
"*****************************************************************************"
  OutPutFile.WriteBlankLines(1)
  OutPutFile.WriteLine "Master Consolidated Summary report for " & Date()
  OutPutFile.WriteBlankLines(1)
  OutPutFile.WriteLine
"*****************************************************************************"
  OutPutFile.WriteBlankLines(1)

  OutPutFile.WriteLine "Errors:"
  OutPutFile.WriteBlankLines(1)
  OutPutFile.WriteLine "Date     Time     Svr Code Description"

  'Process the Errors: section for the first server
  For Each intArrayCounter In astrServ0001Array

    If Instr(1, intArrayCounter, "Errors:") = 1 Then
      strLocator = "True"
    End If

    If strLocator = "True" Then
      If Instr(1, intArrayCounter, "Errors:") <> 1 Then
       If Instr(1, intArrayCounter, "Date     Time    Code Description") <> 1 Then
          If Instr(1, intArrayCounter, "-----") <> 1 Then
            If Len(intArrayCounter) > 0 Then
              intArrayCounter = Mid(intArrayCounter, 1, 17) & " Sr1 " & _
                Mid(intArrayCounter, 19)
              OutPutFile.WriteLine intArrayCounter
            End If
          Else
            Exit For
          End If
       End If
      End If
    End If
```

```
Next

intArrayCounter = 0
strLocator = "False"

'Process the Errors: section for the second server
For Each intArrayCounter In astrServ0002Array

  If Instr(1, intArrayCounter, "Errors:") = 1 Then
    strLocator = "True"
  End If

  If strLocator = "True" Then
    If Instr(1, intArrayCounter, "Errors:") <> 1 Then
      If Instr(1, intArrayCounter, "Date      Time     Code Description") <> 1
Then
        If Instr(1, intArrayCounter, "-----") <> 1 Then
          If Len(intArrayCounter) > 0 Then
            intArrayCounter = Mid(intArrayCounter, 1, 17) & " Sr2 " & _
              Mid(intArrayCounter, 19)
            OutPutFile.WriteLine intArrayCounter
          End If
        Else
          Exit For
        End If
      End If
    End If
  End If

Next

OutPutFile.WriteBlankLines(1)
OutPutFile.WriteLine "--------------------------------------------------" & _
  "---------------------------"
OutPutFile.WriteBlankLines(1)

OutPutFile.WriteLine "Sales summary:"
OutPutFile.WriteBlankLines(1)
```

```
OutPutFile.WriteLine "Government:"
OutPutFile.WriteBlankLines(1)
OutPutFile.WriteLine "Part # Qty  Description"
OutPutFile.WriteBlankLines(1)

intArrayCounter = 0
strLocator = "False"

'Process the Sales summary: section for the first server
For Each intArrayCounter In astrServ0001Array

  If Instr(1, intArrayCounter, "Sales summary") = 1 Then
    strLocator = "True"
  End If

  If strLocator = "True" Then
    If Instr(1, intArrayCounter, "Sales summary:") <> 1 Then
      If Instr(1, intArrayCounter, "Part # Qty  Description") <> 1 Then
        If Instr(1, intArrayCounter, "-----") <> 1 Then
          If Len(intArrayCounter) > 0 Then
            intArrayCounter = Mid(intArrayCounter, 1, 17) & _
              Mid(intArrayCounter, 19)
            OutPutFile.WriteLine intArrayCounter
          End If
        Else
          Exit For
        End If
      End If
    End If
  End If

Next

OutPutFile.WriteBlankLines(1)
OutPutFile.WriteLine "Other Customers:"
OutPutFile.WriteBlankLines(1)
OutPutFile.WriteLine "Part # Qty  Description"
OutPutFile.WriteBlankLines(1)
```

```
intArrayCounter = 0
strLocator = "False"

'Process the Sales summary: section for the second server
For Each intArrayCounter In astrServ0002Array

  If Instr(1, intArrayCounter, "Sales summary:") = 1 Then
    strLocator = "True"
  End If

  If strLocator = "True" Then
    If Instr(1, intArrayCounter, "Sales summary:") <> 1 Then
      If Instr(1, intArrayCounter, "Part # Qty  Description") <> 1 Then
        If Instr(1, intArrayCounter, "-----") <> 1 Then
          If Len(intArrayCounter) > 0 Then
            intArrayCounter = Mid(intArrayCounter, 1, 17) & _
              Mid(intArrayCounter, 19)
            OutPutFile.WriteLine intArrayCounter
          End If
        Else
          Exit For
        End If
      End If
    End If
  End If

Next

OutPutFile.WriteBlankLines(1)
OutPutFile.WriteLine "---------------------------------------------" & _
  "----------------------------"
OutPutFile.WriteBlankLines(1)

OutPutFile.WriteLine "Returns summary:"
OutPutFile.WriteBlankLines(1)
OutPutFile.WriteLine "Government:"
OutPutFile.WriteBlankLines(1)
```

```
OutPutFile.WriteLine "Part #  Qty Description"
OutPutFile.WriteBlankLines(1)

intArrayCounter = 0
strLocator = "False"

'Process the Return summary: section for the first server
For Each intArrayCounter In astrServ0001Array

  If Instr(1, intArrayCounter, "Return summary") = 1 Then
    strLocator = "True"
  End If

  If strLocator = "True" Then
    If Instr(1, intArrayCounter, "Return summary:") <> 1 Then
      If Instr(1, intArrayCounter, "Part #  Qty Description") <> 1 Then
        If Instr(1, intArrayCounter, "-----") <> 1 Then
          If Len(intArrayCounter) > 0 Then
            intArrayCounter = Mid(intArrayCounter, 1, 17) & _
              Mid(intArrayCounter, 19)
            OutPutFile.WriteLine intArrayCounter
          End If
        Else
          Exit For
        End If
      End If
    End If
  End If

Next

OutPutFile.WriteBlankLines(1)
OutPutFile.WriteLine "Other Customers:"
OutPutFile.WriteBlankLines(1)
OutPutFile.WriteLine "Part #  Qty Description"
OutPutFile.WriteBlankLines(1)

intArrayCounter = 0
```

```
strLocator = "False"

'Process the Return summary: section for the second server
For Each intArrayCounter In astrServ0002Array

  If Instr(1, intArrayCounter, "Return summary:") = 1 Then
    strLocator = "True"
  End If

  If strLocator = "True" Then
    If Instr(1, intArrayCounter, "Return summary:") <> 1 Then
      If Instr(1, intArrayCounter, "Part #  Qty Description") <> 1 Then
        If Instr(1, intArrayCounter, "-----") <> 1 Then
          If Len(intArrayCounter) > 0 Then
            intArrayCounter = Mid(intArrayCounter, 1, 17) & _
              Mid(intArrayCounter, 19)
            OutPutFile.WriteLine intArrayCounter
          End If
        Else
          Exit For
        End If
      End If
    End If
  End If

Next

OutPutFile.WriteBlankLines(1)
OutPutFile.WriteLine "---------------------------------------------" & _
  "---------------------------"
OutPutFile.WriteBlankLines(1)

OutPutFile.WriteLine "Daily Production Summary:"
OutPutFile.WriteBlankLines(1)
OutPutFile.WriteLine "Part #  Qty  Description             In Stock"
OutPutFile.WriteBlankLines(1)

intArrayCounter = 0
```

```
strLocator = "False"
intCounter2 = 0

'Process the Daily Production Summary section for the first server
For Each intArrayCounter In astrServ0001Array

  If Instr(1, intArrayCounter, "Daily Production Summary") = 1 Then
    strLocator = "True"
  End If

  If strLocator = "True" Then
    If Instr(1, intArrayCounter, "Daily Production Summary") <> 1 Then
      If Instr(1, intArrayCounter, "Part #  Qty  Description              In" & _
        " Stock") <> 1 Then
          If Len(intArrayCounter) > 0 Then

            ReDim Preserve astrProductionArray(intCounter2)
            astrProductionArray(intCounter2) = intArrayCounter
            intCounter2 = intCounter2 + 1

          End If
      End If
    End If
  End If

Next

intCounter2 = 0
intArrayCounter = 0
strLocator = "False"

'Process the Daily Production Summary section for the first server
For Each intArrayCounter In astrServ0002Array

  If Instr(1, intArrayCounter, "Daily Production Summary") = 1 Then
    strLocator = "True"
  End If
```

```
If strLocator = "True" Then
  If Instr(1, intArrayCounter, "Daily Production Summary") <> 1 Then
    If Instr(1, intArrayCounter, "Part #  Qty  Description              In" & _
       " Stock") <> 1 Then
        If Len(intArrayCounter) > 0 Then

          intArrayCounter = Mid(intArrayCounter, 1, 17) & _
            Mid(intArrayCounter, 19)

          'Spin though astrProductionArray and determine if there are any
          'matching entries to process
          intCounter2 = 0
          strMatch = "False"
          For Each intCounter2 In astrProductionArray
            If Mid(intArrayCounter, 1, 5) = Mid(intCounter2, 1, 5) Then

              strMatch = "True"
              strMatchlist = strMatchList & " " & _
                Mid(intArrayCounter, 1, 5)

              'Extract qty for both entries, add these values together and
              'write a single entry
               intQtyOne = Mid(intArrayCounter, 9, 5)
               intQtyOne = CInt(Trim(intQtyOne))
               intQtyTwo = Mid(intCounter2, 9, 5)
               intQtyTwo = CInt(Trim(intQtyTwo))
               intTotalQty = intQtyOne + intQtyTwo
               intSpacing = Len(intTotalQty)
               intSpacing = 5 - intSpacing

               'Extract In Stock value for both entries, add these values
               'together and write a single entry
               intInStockOne = Mid(intArrayCounter, 39, 3)
               intInStockOne = CInt(Trim(intInStockOne))
               intInStockTwo = Mid(intCounter2, 40, 3)
               intInStockTwo = CInt(Trim(intInStockTwo))
               intTotalInStock = intInStockOne + intInStockTwo
               intSpaces = Len(intTotalInStock)
```

```
                    intSpaces = 4 - intSpaces

                    OutPutFile.WriteLine Mid(intArrayCounter, 1, 5) & "    " & _
                      intTotalQty & Space(intSpacing) & _
                      Mid(intArrayCounter, 14, 25) & Space(intSpaces) & _
                      intTotalInStock
                  End If
                Next
                If strmatch <> "True" Then
                  OutPutFile.Writeline intArrayCounter
                End If

              End If
          End If
        End If
      End If

    Next

    'Process non-duplicate production inventory data on the second server
    For Each intArrayCounter In astrProductionArray
      If Instr(1, strMatchList, Mid(intArrayCounter, 1 ,5)) = 0 Then
        OutPutFile.WriteLine intArrayCounter
      End If
    Next

    If strDebug = "Enabled" Then
      MsgBox "Done writing to the Summary Report"
    End If

    OutPutFile.Close()

  End Sub

  Sub CreatConsolidatedWordReport()

    Dim objWordDoc, strSourFile, FileRef, strRptLine, intWordCounter
    Dim strFileNameString
```

```
ReDim astrWordVersionArray(0)

Set objWordDoc = WScript.CreateObject("Word.Application")

Set FileRef = FsoObj.OpenTextFile(strConSolRptName, cForReading)

strFileNameString = Replace(Date(), "/", "-")

strConSolRptName = strConsolFolder & "\" & strFileNameString & _
"_ConsolSumRpt.doc"

intWordCounter = 0

If strDebug = "Enabled" Then
  MsgBox "Writing the Word version of the consolidated summary report."
End If

'Read the entire report into an array
Do Until FileRef.AtEndOfStream

  strRptLine = FileRef.ReadLine()

  ReDim Preserve astrWordVersionArray(intWordCounter)
  astrWordVersionArray(intWordCounter) = strRptLine

  intWordCounter = intWordCounter + 1

Loop

FileRef.Close()

'Start creating the Word document
objWordDoc.Documents.Add()

objWordDoc.Selection.Font.Name = "Courier"
objWordDoc.Selection.Font.Size = 8
objWordDoc.Selection.Font.Bold = False
```

```
'Spin through the array, format and write the Word version of the report
 For Each intWordCounter in astrWordVersionArray

   'Change Font properties for selected report headings
   If Instr(1,intWordCounter, "Master Consolidated Summary") Then

     objWordDoc.Selection.Font.Name = "Arial"
     objWordDoc.Selection.Font.Size = 12
     objWordDoc.Selection.Font.Bold = True

   End If

   If Instr(1,intWordCounter, "Errors:") Then
     objWordDoc.Selection.Font.Name = "Arial"
     objWordDoc.Selection.Font.Size = 10
     objWordDoc.Selection.Font.Bold = True
   End If

   If Instr(1,intWordCounter, "Sales summary:") Then
     objWordDoc.Selection.Font.Name = "Arial"
     objWordDoc.Selection.Font.Size = 10
     objWordDoc.Selection.Font.Bold = True
   End If

   If Instr(1,intWordCounter, "Returns summary:") Then
     objWordDoc.Selection.Font.Name = "Arial"
     objWordDoc.Selection.Font.Size = 10
     objWordDoc.Selection.Font.Bold = True
   End If

   If Instr(1,intWordCounter, "Daily Production Summary") Then
     objWordDoc.Selection.Font.Name = "Arial"
     objWordDoc.Selection.Font.Size = 10
     objWordDoc.Selection.Font.Bold = True
   End If

   'Write a line of the report
```

```
    objWordDoc.Selection.Typetext(intWordCounter)

    'Add a paragraph marker (.e.g. linefeed)
    objWordDoc.Selection.TypeParagraph

    'Reset default Font properties
    objWordDoc.Selection.Font.Name = "Courier"
    objWordDoc.Selection.Font.Size = 8
    objWordDoc.Selection.Font.Bold = False

  Next

  'Save the Word file
  objWordDoc.ActiveDocument.SaveAs(strConSolRptName)

  'Close the document
   objWordDoc.ActiveDocument.Close()

  'Exit Word
   objWordDoc.Quit()

End Sub

Sub NotifyOperationsStaff()

  On Error Resume Next

  Dim strUserName, strNtkNotifyList

  Dim astrNotifyArray

  strNtkNotifyList = "MJLF001 ASCK001"

  strNtkNotifyList = _
    WshShl.RegRead("HKLM\Software\Intuit\VBScripts\MstSumRpts\NtkNotifyList")
  If Err <> 0 Then
    If strEventLog = "Enabled" Then
      WriteToEventLog ("Summary Report Collection script - Using " & _
```

```
        "default for strNtkNotifyList.")
      Err.Number = 0
    End If
  End If

  astrNotifyArray = Split(strNtkNotifyList)

  For Each strUserName In astrNotifyArray
    WshShl.Run "Net Send " & strUserName & " " & "Order\Inventory consolidated
report now available."
  Next

End Sub

Sub WriteToEventLog(strMessage)

  WshShl.LogEvent 4, strMessage

End Sub

Sub TerminateScript()

  WScript.Quit()

End Sub
```

Figure 24.2 shows a sample portion of the Word report created by the script. As you can see, by changing font properties, the report has been made easier to read.

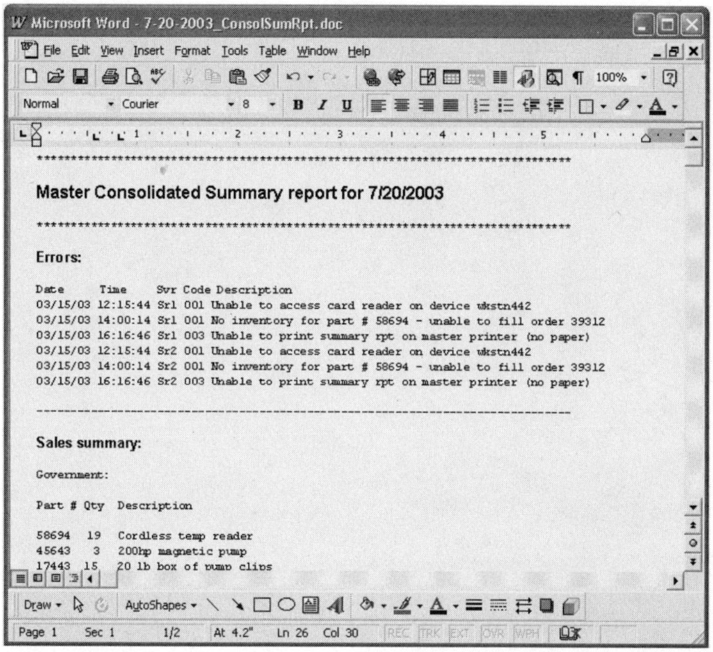

FIGURE 24.2 *Examining the Word version of the consolidated summary report*

Summary

In this chapter, you learned how to develop a VBScript that processes the summary reports collected from the two Windows 2000 servers that support Intuit's order/inventory system. You also learned how to work with the Word object model in order to develop a Word version of the consolidated report. In addition, you learned how to use the `Net Send` command to create a network notification process.

Chapter 25

Archive Management

In this chapter, you will copy and modify the archive management script developed in Chapter 20, "Maintaining a 30-Day Summary Log Archive," in order to develop a new script that maintains a three-month archive of reports on the Windows 2000 Professional workstation located in the Operations Command Center. This new script will then be executed on a monthly basis by the scheduling script developed in Chapter 23, "Collecting Remote Summary Reports."

Administering Report Files

The last script developed by Molly as part of this project is the archive management script. It will be executed on a scheduled basis on the first day of each month. Its job is to maintain three separate three-month archives on the Windows 2000 Professional workstation, as outlined in the following list.

- **`D:\Order_Inventory\Sr1_SummaryRpts`**. This folder will be used to store a minimum of 90 days' worth of summary reports created by the SERV0001 Windows 2000 server.
- **`D:\Order_Inventory\Sr2_SummaryRpts`**. This folder will be used to store a minimum of 90 days' worth of summary reports created by the SERV0002 Windows 2000 server.
- **`D:\Order_Inventory\ConsolidatedRpts`**. This folder will be used to store a minimum of 90 days' worth of consolidated reports created from information extracted from the summary reports copied over from SERV0001 and SERV0002.

Figure 25.1 shows the contents of the `d:\Order_Inventory` folders on the Windows 2000 Professional workstation. The `LogFiles` folder is used to temporarily store the summary report files copied over by the report retrieval script. The report consolidation script then reads the summary reports located in the `LogFiles` folder in order to create the consolidated reports, which are stored in the `ConsolidatedRpts` folder. When the archive management script executes, it copies the files stored in the `LogFiles` folder to either the `Sr1_SummaryRpts` or `Sr2_SummaryRpts` folders, as appropriate. Finally, the archive management script deletes any reports stored in the ConsolidatedRpts, Sr1_SummaryRpts, or Sr2_SummaryRpts folders that are more than three months old.

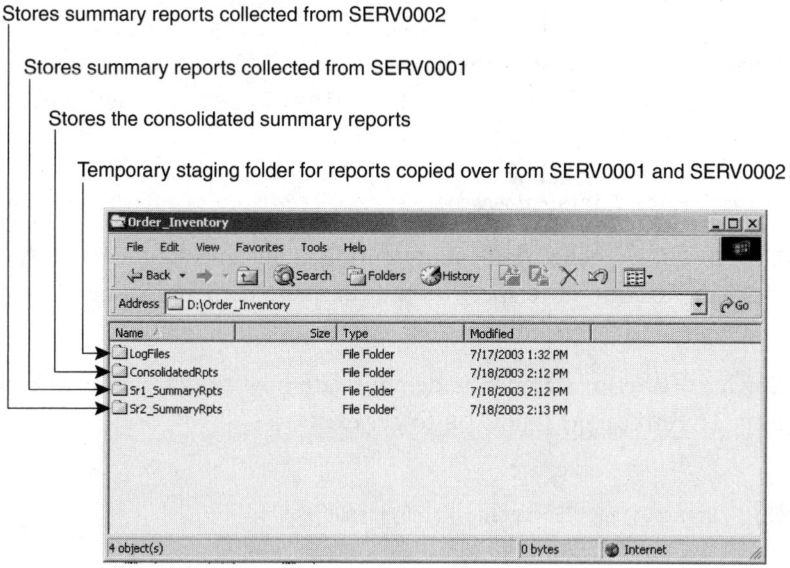

FIGURE 25.1 *Examining the folder structure used to manage and store reports on the Windows 2000 Professional workstation*

Working with Windows Folders and Files

In order to perform archive management tasks, Molly will need to work with the FileSystemObject object's DeleteFile() method again. The syntax for this method is provided in Chapter 20. In addition, she will need to learn how to work with a number of other methods belonging to the FileSystemObject. These methods include:

- **FolderExists()**. Provides the ability to determine whether or not a folder exists
- **CreateFolder()**. Provides the ability to create a new folder
- **MoveFile()**. Provides the ability to move one or more files to a specified folder

Determining Whether or Not a Folder Exists

In developing her script, Molly will need to determine whether certain folders exist before attempting to access their contents or store files in them. To perform this test, she plans to use the `FileSystemObject` object's `FolderExists()` method, which returns a Boolean value of `True` or `False` based on the existence of the specified folder. The syntax of the `FolderExists()` method is shown below.

```
ObjectReference.FolderExists(FolderName)
```

`ObjectReference` is the variable representing an instance of the `FileSystem-Object` object. `FolderName` specifies the complete path and name of the folder whose existence is to be tested.

The following VBScript statements demonstrate how to determine whether the `d:\Order_Inventory\LogFiles` folder exists.

```
Dim FsoObj
Set FsoObj = CreateObject("Scripting.FileSystemObject")

If (FsoObj.FolderExists(d:\Order_Inventory\LogFiles) = False) Then
  MsgBox "The specified folder does not exist."
Else
  MsgBox "The specified folder exists."
End If
```

Based on the results of the test, a script might perform any number of actions, including:

- Creating the folder if it does not already exist
- Saving a file in the folder
- Copying or moving a file into the folder
- Deleting the folder
- Examining the folder's contents

Creating a Folder

The first time the archive management script runs, the `Sr1_SummaryRpts` and `Sr2_SummaryRpts` folders will not exist. Rather than manually creating these two folders as she has done for other folders used by her scripts, Molly has decided to let the archive management script perform this task. In order to automate this task, Molly will need to use the `FileSystemObject` object's `CreateFolder()` method. The syntax for this method is outlined below.

```
ObjectReference.CreateFolder(FolderName)
```

`ObjectReference` is the variable representing an instance of the `FileSystemObject` object. `FolderName` specifies the name of the folder to be created.

NOTE

Always use the `FileSystemObject` object's `FolderExists()` method to determine that a folder does not already exist before attempting to create it. Otherwise, an error will occur.

Creating a folder is a straightforward task. First you must instantiate the `FileSystemObject`. Then you can check to make sure that the folder does not already exist using the `FolderExists()` method before finally using the `CreateFolder()` method, as demonstrated in the following example.

```
Dim FsoObj, strWorkingFolder
Set FsoObj = CreateObject("Scripting.FileSystemObject")

If (FsoObj.FolderExists("d:\Order_Inventory\ Sr1_SummaryRpts ") = false) Then
  Set strWorkingFolder = _
    FsoObj.CreateFolder("d:\Order_Inventory\ Sr1_SummaryRpts ")
End If
```

In this example, the script creates a folder called `Sr1_SummaryRpts` in the `D:\Order_Inventory` folder if the `Sr1_SummaryRpts` folder does not already exist.

TIP

You cannot use the `CreateFolder()` method to reinitialize an existing folder. If you attempt to do so, your script will receive an error. However, you can use the `DeleteFolder()` method to delete the folder and then recreate it again using the `CreateFolder()` method.

Moving Files between Staging and Archive Folders

The archive management script will need to be able to move files from the Log Files staging folder to the Sr1_SummaryRpts and Sr2_SummaryRpts archive folders. To perform this task, Molly will need to use the FileSystemObject object's MoveFile() method. This method has the following syntax:

```
ObjectReference.MoveFile (Source, Target )
```

ObjectReference is a variable representing an instance of the FileSystem-Object object. Source specifies the location of the file or files to be moved, and Target specifies the destination folder where the file or files are to be stored.

TIP

As an alternative to the FileSystemObject object's MoveFile() method, you could use the File object Move() method. However, this method only processes one file at a time, so in order to use it, you would have to set up a loop to process all of the files in the LogFiles folder.

The following VBScript statements demonstrate how to use the DeleteFile() method to move all the text files located in the d:\Order_Inventory\Log Files folder to the d:\Order_Inventory\ Sr1_SummaryRpts folder.

```
Dim FsoObj
Set FsoObj = CreateObject("Scripting.FileSystemObject")

Set FsoObj = CreateObject("Scripting.FileSystemObject")
FsoObj.MoveFile "d:\Order_Inventory\ LogFiles\*.txt", _
  "d:\Order_Inventory\Sr1_SummaryRpts "
```

Developing the Archive Management Script

Molly intends to copy and modify the archive management script that was presented in Chapter 20 when developing the archive management script for the Windows 2000 Professional workstation. In addition to the functionality already provided by that script, Molly intends to enable the script to support the following operations:

- Run in an optional debug mode
- Read configuration settings from the Windows registry
- Manage multiple log files
- Move log files between folders as part of the archive management process

The Initialization Section

The `Initialization Section`, shown below, begins with the `Option Explicit` statement in order to enforce script variable naming throughout the script. Next, it defines variables that are used globally. Then it defines a constant that specifies a text string to be used by all pop-up dialog boxes displayed by the script when run in debug mode. Finally, it instantiates the `FileSystemObject` and `WshShell` objects.

```
Option Explicit


Dim strVerifyExecutionSchedule, strDeleteMonth, strEventLog, strDebug
Dim strSvrList, strArchive, strSvr1Folder, strSvr2Folder, strConsolFolder
Dim FsoObj, WshShl


Const cTitleBarMsg = "Master Archive Management Script"


Set WshShl = WScript.CreateObject("WScript.Shell")
Set FsoObj = CreateObject("Scripting.FileSystemObject")
```

The Main Processing Section

The `Main Processing Section`, shown below, consists of a collection of subroutines and function calls. It begins by executing the `OkToRunToday()` function, which returns a value of `True` if the script is being executed on the first day of the month. The value returned by this function is assigned to the `strVerifyExecutionSchedule` variable, which is then tested to determine whether or not the script may execute. If its value is not set equal to `True`, a message is written to the Windows application event log and the `TerminateScript()` subroutine is run in order to halt the script's execution.

```
strVerifyExecutionSchedule = OkToRunToday()

If strVerifyExecutionSchedule = "True" Then
  SetDefaultSettings()
  GetRegistrySettings()
  If strEventLog = "Enabled" Then
    WriteToEventLog("Consolidated Summary Report Archive Manager executing.")
  End If
  MoveSummaryReports()
  MonthToDelete()
  RemoveOldReportFiles()
  If strEventLog = "Enabled" Then
    WriteToEventLog("Consolidated Summary Report Archive Manager finished.")
  End If
Else
  WriteToEventLog("Consolidated Summary Report Archive Manager execution" & _
    " terminated - invalid execution schedule.")
  TerminateScript()
End If

TerminateScript()
```

If the value assigned to the `strVerifyExecutionSchedule` variable is set equal to `True`, then the `SetDefaultSettings()` subroutine is called in order to establish default configuration settings. Next `GetRegistrySettings()` is executed. This subroutine extracts configuration settings stored in the Windows registry, overriding matching default configuration settings. If event logging is enabled, a message is then written to the Windows application event log specifying that the script is now running. Next the `MoveSummaryReports()` subroutine is executed. It copies summary reports from a staging folder to one of two archive folders for long-term storage. Then the `MonthToDelete()` subroutine runs and figures out which month's worth of summary and consolidated reports should be deleted. This information is then used by the `RemoveOldReportFiles()` subroutine, which performs the actual deletion of report files. Finally, another message is written to the Windows application event log if event logging is enabled and the script's execution is halted by calling the `TerminateScript()` subroutine.

The OkToRunToday() Subroutine

The `OkToRunToday()` subroutine, shown below, uses the VBScript `Day()` and `Date()` functions to determine if the script is being executed on the first day of the month. If it is, then the value of a variable named `OkToRunToday` is set equal to `True`.

```
Function OkToRunToday()

  If Day(Date()) = 1 Then
    OkToRunToday = "True"
  End If

  If strDebug = "Enabled" Then
    MsgBox "OkToRunToday = " & OkToRunToday
  End If

End Function
```

If debugging is enabled, the value of `OkToRunToday` is displayed using the VBScript `MsgBox()` function.

The SetDefaultSettings() Subroutine

The `SetDefaultSettings()` subroutine, shown below, sets default configuration settings for the script so that it can continue to execute in the event that it experiences a problem retrieving its configuration settings from its associated registry values. If debugging is enabled, the value of each variable modified by this subroutine is displayed in a pop-up dialog box.

```
Sub SetDefaultSettings()

  strEventLog = "Enabled"
  strDebug = "Disabled"
  strSvrList = "SERV0001 SERV0002"
  strArchive = "d:\Order_Inventrory\LogFiles"
  strSvr1Folder = "d:\Order_Inventory\Sr1_SummaryRpts"
  strSvr2Folder = "d:\Order_Inventory\Sr2_SummaryRpts"
  strConsolFolder = "d:\Order_Inventory\ConsolidatedRpts"
```

```
  If strDebug = "Enabled" Then
    MsgBox "Default settings initialized: " & vbCrLf & vbCrLf & _
      "strEventLog" & vbTab & "=" & vbTab & strEventLog & vbCrLf & _
      "strDebug" & vbTab & vbTab & "=" & vbTab & strDebug & vbCrLf & _
      "strSvrList" & vbTab & vbTab & "=" & vbTab & strSvrList & vbCrLf & _
      "strArchive" & vbTab & "=" & vbTab & strArchive & vbCrLf & _
      "strSvr1Folder " & vbTab & "=" & vbTab & strSvr1Folder & vbCrLf & _
      "strSvr2Folder" & vbTab & "=" & vbTab & strSvr2Folder & vbCrLf & _
      "strConsolFolder" & vbTab & "=" & vbTab & strConsolFolder, , cTitleBarMsg
  End If

End Sub
```

The GetRegistrySettings() Subroutine

The `GetRegistrySettings()` subroutine, shown below, begins by specifying the `On Error Resume Next` statement. This will ensure that this script's execution is not halted in the event of a problem retrieving registry values. As each registry value is read using the `WshShell` object's `RegRead()` method, the value of the `Err` object's default property (`Err.Number`) is checked to determine whether an error has occurred. If an error has occurred, a message is written to the Windows application event log and the value of `Err.Number` is reset to zero.

```
Sub GetRegistrySettings()

  On Error Resume Next

  strEventLog = _
    WshShl.RegRead("HKLM\Software\Intuit\VBScripts\MstSumRpts\EventLogging")
  If Err <> 0 Then
    If strEventLog = "Enabled" Then
      WriteToEventLog ("Summary Report Collection script - Using " & _
        "default for strEventLog.")
      Err.Number = 0
    End If
  End If

  strDebug = WshShl.RegRead("HKLM\Software\Intuit\VBScripts\MstSumRpts\DebugMode")
```

```
If Err <> 0 Then
  If strEventLog = "Enabled" Then
    WriteToEventLog ("Summary Report Collection script - Using " & _
      "default for strDebug.")
    Err.Number = 0
  End If
End If

strSvrList = _
  WshShl.RegRead("HKLM\Software\Intuit\VBScripts\MstSumRpts\Win2000Svrs")
If Err <> 0 Then
  If strEventLog = "Enabled" Then
    WriteToEventLog ("Summary Report Collection script - Using " & _
      "default for strSvrList.")
    Err.Number = 0
  End If
End If

strArchive = _
  WshShl.RegRead("HKLM\Software\Intuit\VBScripts\MstSumRpts\RptArchive")
If Err <> 0 Then
If strEventLog = "Enabled" Then
    WriteToEventLog ("Summary Report Collection script - Using " & _
      "default for strArchive.")
    Err.Number = 0
  End If
End If

strSvr1Folder = _
  WshShl.RegRead("HKLM\Software\Intuit\VBScripts\MstSumRpts\Svr1Folder")
If Err <> 0 Then
  If strEventLog = "Enabled" Then
    WriteToEventLog ("Summary Report Collection script - Using " & _
      "default for strSvr1Folder.")
    Err.Number = 0
  End If
End If
```

```
strSvr2Folder = _
  WshShl.RegRead("HKLM\Software\Intuit\VBScripts\MstSumRpts\Svr2Folder")
If Err <> 0 Then
  If strEventLog = "Enabled" Then
    WriteToEventLog ("Summary Report Collection script - Using " & _
      "default for strSvr2Folder.")
    Err.Number = 0
  End If
End If

strConsolFolder = _
  "WshShl.RegRead("HKLM\Software\Intuit\VBScripts\MstSumRpts\ConsolFolder")
If Err <> 0 Then
  If strEventLog = "Enabled" Then
    WriteToEventLog ("Summary Report Collection script - Using " & _
      "default for strConsolFolder.")
    Err.Number = 0
  End If
End If

If strDebug = "Enabled" Then
  MsgBox "Registry settings retrieved: " & vbCrLf & vbCrLf & _
   "strEventLog" & vbTab & "=" & vbTab & strEventLog & vbCrLf & _
   "strDebug" & vbTab & vbTab & "=" & vbTab & strDebug & vbCrLf & _
   "strSvrList" & vbTab & vbTab & "=" & vbTab & strSvrList & vbCrLf & _
   "strArchive" & vbTab & "=" & vbTab & strArchive & vbCrLf & _
   "strSvr1Folder " & vbTab & "=" & vbTab & strSvr1Folder & vbCrLf & _
   "strSvr2Folder" & vbTab & "=" & vbTab & strSvr2Folder & vbCrLf & _
   "strConsolFolder" & vbTab & "=" & vbTab & strConsolFolder, , cTitleBarMsg
End If

End Sub
```

The MoveSummaryReports() Subroutine

The `MoveSummaryReports()` subroutine, shown below, is responsible for moving the summary reports collected from the Windows 2000 servers (stored in the `LogFiles` staging folder on the Windows 2000 Professional workstation) to the

`Sr1_SummaryRpts` and `Sr2_SummaryRpts` archive folders. It begins by specifying a localized instance of the `On Error Resume Next` statement in order to prevent an error during one of the script's two move operations from terminating the script's execution. If debugging is enabled, a pop-up dialog box will display the name of each summary report as it is being processed.

```
Sub MoveSummaryReports()

  On Error Resume Next

  Dim strNewFolder1, strNewFolder2

  If strDebug = "Enabled" Then
    MsgBox "Moving......" & vbCrLf & vbCrLf & _
      strArchive & "\" & Left(strSvrList, 8) & "*.*" & vbCrLf & _
      strArchive & "\" & Right(strSvrList, 8) & "*.*"
  End If

  If (FsoObj.FolderExists(strArchive) = False) Then
     TerminateScript()
  Else
    If (FsoObj.FolderExists(strSvr1Folder) = False) Then
      Set strNewFolder1 = FsoObj.CreateFolder(strSvr1Folder)
    End If
    If (FsoObj.FolderExists(strSvr2Folder) = False) Then
      Set strNewFolder2 = FsoObj.CreateFolder(strSvr2Folder)
    End If
    FsoObj.MoveFile strArchive & "\" & Left(strSvrList, 8) & "*.*", _
      strSvr1Folder
    FsoObj.MoveFile strArchive & "\" & Right(strSvrList, 8) & "*.*", _
      strSvr2Folder
  End If

End Sub
```

Next the `FileSystemObject` object's `FolderExists()` method is used to verify that the `LogFiles` staging folder is accessible. If it is not, the `TerminateScript()` subroutine is called to halt the script's execution. Otherwise, the script uses the `FolderCreate()` method to create the `Sr1_SummaryRpts` and

Sr2_SummaryRpts archive folders if they do not exist (for example, if the script is running for the first time).

Finally, the FileSystemObject object's MoveFile() method is used to move the summary reports to the appropriate archive folder. The Left() and Right() functions are used to parse out the server name embedded in the strSvrList variable so that the subroutine will know to which archive folder to move the summary reports.

The MonthToDelete() Subroutine

The MonthToDelete() subroutine, shown below, is responsible for determining which month's worth of summary and consolidated report files is to be deleted. It begins by defining three variables. The intGetSlashPosition variable is used to store a value indicating the location of the first backslash (/) character in the current date. The strCurrentMonth variable will be used to store a numeric value indicating the current month.

The value assigned to intGetSlashPosition is determined by using the Instr() function to search for the backslash (/) character in the date as retrieved by the Date() function. The value of strCurrentMonth is then determined using the Mid() function to parse out the month portion of the date (which is in the format of mm/dd/yyyy). The month value is parsed out by taking all the characters from the first character position until the occurrence of the first backslash (/) character (expressed as intGetSlashPosition - 1).

The value of strDeleteMonth is then determined by subtracting 4 from strCurrentMonth. If, for example, the current date is June 1, then the value of strDeleteMonth will be 1 (5 – 4 = 1). Four If...Then statements are then set up to adjust the value of strDeleteMonth in the event that the current month is either January, February, March, or April. For example, if the current month is April, then 4 minus 4 will equal zero. Since the month that should be deleted in this instance is December, the first If statement checks to see if the value assigned to strDeleteMonth is 0 and changes its value to 12 if it is. Likewise, similar adjustments are made for the first three months of the year.

```
Sub MonthToDelete()

  Dim intGetSlashPosition, strCurrentMonth

  intGetSlashPosition = Instr(Date(), "/")
```

```
    strCurrentMonth = Mid(Date(), 1, intGetSlashPosition - 1)
    strDeleteMonth = strCurrentMonth - 4

    If strDeleteMonth = 0 Then
      strDeleteMonth = "12"
    End If

    If strDeleteMonth = -1 Then
      strDeleteMonth = "11"
    End If

    If strDeleteMonth = -2 Then
      strDeleteMonth = "10"
    End If

    If strDeleteMonth = -3 Then
      strDeleteMonth = "9"
    End If

    If strDebug = "Enabled" Then
      MsgBox "strDeleteMonth = " & strDeleteMonth
    End If

End Sub
```

The RemoveOldReportFiles() Subroutine

The `RemoveOldReportFiles()` subroutine, shown below, is responsible for deleting summary and consolidated reports more than three months old. It begins with the `On Error Resume Next` statement in order to prevent any errors that occur when deleting the files from halting the script's execution.

If debug mode is enabled, a pop-up dialog box is displayed, showing the string that the subroutine will use to identify which summary and consolidated reports it will delete. Next, the `DeleteFile()` method is used to delete the files. As you can see, the string that specifies which files are to be deleted is somewhat involved. It is assembled by specifying the name of the archive folder where the reports are stored (the `Sr1_SummaryRpts` or `Sr2_SummaryRpts` folders) and then appending the backslash (\) character, followed by the name of the files to be deleted.

The name indicating which files are to be deleted is established by performing the following steps:

1. Use the `Left()` and `Right()` functions to parse out the server names from the `strSvrList` variable.
2. Append the underscore (_) character.
3. Append the number of the month whose files are to be deleted (as specified by `strDeleteMonth`).
4. Append the `_SumRpt.txt` string. For example, the string required to delete all the summary reports for the month of January would be `d:\Order_Inventory\Summaryrpts\SERV0001_1_SumRpt.txt`.

```
Sub RemoveOldReportFiles()

  On Error Resume Next

  Dim strSummaryRptPath

  If strDebug = "Enabled" Then
    MsgBox "Deleting ......" & vbCrLf & vbCrLf & _
      strSvr1Folder & "\" & Left(strSvrList, 8) & "_" & strDeleteMonth & _
        "*_SumRpt.txt" & vbCrLf & _
      strSvr2Folder & "\" & Right(strSvrList, 8) & "_" & strDeleteMonth & _
      "*_SumRpt.txt" & vbCrLf & _
      strConsolFolder & "\" & strDeleteMonth & "*_ConsolSumRpt.txt"
  End If

  strSummaryRptPath = "d:\Order_Inventory\SummaryRpts\"

  FsoObj.DeleteFile strSvr1Folder & "\" & Left(strSvrList, 8) & "_" & _
    strDeleteMonth & "*_SumRpt.txt"
  FsoObj.DeleteFile strSvr2Folder & "\" & Right(strSvrList, 8) & "_" & _
    strDeleteMonth & "*_SumRpt.txt"
  FsoObj.DeleteFile strConsolFolder & "\" & strDeleteMonth & _
    "*_ConsolSumRpt.txt"

End Sub
```

The WriteToEventLog() Subroutine

The `WriteToEventLog()` subroutine, shown below, uses the `WshShell` object's `LogEvent()` method to write an informational message, passed to it as an argument, to the Windows application's event log.

```
Sub WriteToEventLog(strMessage)

  WshShl.LogEvent 4, strMessage

End Sub
```

The TerminateScript() Subroutine

The `TerminateScript()` subroutine, shown below, halts the script's execution using the `WScript` object's `Quit()` method.

```
Sub TerminateScript()

  WScript.Quit()

End Sub
```

The Fully Assembled Script

The fully assembled archive management script is shown below. It will be executed on the first day of each month and will maintain a three-month archive of summary reports collected from both Windows 2000 servers, as well as a three-month archive of consolidated summary reports.

```
'*************************************************************************
'Script Name: Script 25.1.vbs
'Author: Jerry Ford
'Created: 04/13/03
'Description: This script maintains a 90-day log archive of both summary
'and consolidated Order_Inventory reports
'*************************************************************************


'Initialization Section
```

```
Option Explicit

Dim strVerifyExecutionSchedule, strDeleteMonth, strEventLog, strDebug
Dim strSvrList, strArchive, strSvr1Folder, strSvr2Folder, strConsolFolder
Dim FsoObj, WshShl

Const cTitleBarMsg = "Master Archive Management Script"

Set WshShl = WScript.CreateObject("WScript.Shell")
Set FsoObj = CreateObject("Scripting.FileSystemObject")


'Main Processing Section

strVerifyExecutionSchedule = OkToRunToday()

If strVerifyExecutionSchedule = "True" Then
  SetDefaultSettings()
  GetRegistrySettings()
  If strEventLog = "Enabled" Then
    WriteToEventLog("Consolidated Summary Report Archive Manager executing.")
  End If
  MoveSummaryReports()
  MonthToDelete()
  RemoveOldReportFiles()
  If strEventLog = "Enabled" Then
    WriteToEventLog("Consolidated Summary Report Archive Manager finished.")
  End If
Else
  WriteToEventLog("Consolidated Summary Report Archive Manager execution" & _
    " terminated - invalid execution schedule.")
  TerminateScript()
End If

TerminateScript()
```

```
'Procedure Section

Function OkToRunToday()

  If Day(Date()) = 1 Then
    OkToRunToday = "True"
  End If

  If strDebug = "Enabled" Then
    MsgBox "OkToRunToday = " & OkToRunToday
  End If

End Function

Sub SetDefaultSettings()

  strEventLog = "Enabled"
  strDebug = "Disabled"
  strSvrList = "SERV0001 SERV0002"
  strArchive = "d:\Order_Inventrory\LogFiles"
  strSvr1Folder = "d:\Order_Inventory\Sr1_SummaryRpts"
  strSvr2Folder = "d:\Order_Inventory\Sr2_SummaryRpts"
  strConsolFolder = "d:\Order_Inventory\ConsolidatedRpts"


  If strDebug = "Enabled" Then
    MsgBox "Default settings initialized: " & vbCrLf & vbCrLf & _
     "strEventLog" & vbTab & "=" & vbTab & strEventLog & vbCrLf & _
     "strDebug" & vbTab & vbTab & "=" & vbTab & strDebug & vbCrLf & _
     "strSvrList" & vbTab & vbTab & "=" & vbTab & strSvrList & vbCrLf & _
     "strArchive" & vbTab & "=" & vbTab & strArchive & vbCrLf & _
     "strSvr1Folder " & vbTab & "=" & vbTab & strSvr1Folder & vbCrLf & _
     "strSvr2Folder" & vbTab & "=" & vbTab & strSvr2Folder & vbCrLf & _
     "strConsolFolder" & vbTab & "=" & vbTab & strConsolFolder, , cTitleBarMsg
  End If

End Sub
```

```
Sub GetRegistrySettings()

  On Error Resume Next

  strEventLog = _
    "WshShl.RegRead("HKLM\Software\Intuit\VBScripts\MstSumRpts\EventLogging")
  If Err <> 0 Then
    If strEventLog = "Enabled" Then
      WriteToEventLog ("Summary Report Collection script - Using " & _
        "default for strEventLog.")
      Err.Number = 0
    End If
  End If

  strDebug = WshShl.RegRead("HKLM\Software\Intuit\VBScripts\MstSumRpts\DebugMode")
  If Err <> 0 Then
    If strEventLog = "Enabled" Then
      WriteToEventLog ("Summary Report Collection script - Using " & _
        "default for strDebug.")
      Err.Number = 0
    End If
  End If

  strSvrList = _
    WshShl.RegRead("HKLM\Software\Intuit\VBScripts\MstSumRpts\Win2000Svrs")
  If Err <> 0 Then
    If strEventLog = "Enabled" Then
      WriteToEventLog ("Summary Report Collection script - Using " & _
        "default for strSvrList.")
      Err.Number = 0
    End If
  End If

  strArchive = _
    "WshShl.RegRead("HKLM\Software\Intuit\VBScripts\MstSumRpts\RptArchive")
  If Err <> 0 Then
  If strEventLog = "Enabled" Then
      WriteToEventLog ("Summary Report Collection script - Using " & _
```

```
      "default for strArchive.")
    Err.Number = 0
  End If
End If

strSvr1Folder = _
  WshShl.RegRead("HKLM\Software\Intuit\VBScripts\MstSumRpts\Svr1Folder")
If Err <> 0 Then
  If strEventLog = "Enabled" Then
    WriteToEventLog ("Summary Report Collection script - Using " & _
      "default for strSvr1Folder.")
    Err.Number = 0
  End If
End If

strSvr2Folder = _
  WshShl.RegRead("HKLM\Software\Intuit\VBScripts\MstSumRpts\Svr2Folder")
If Err <> 0 Then
  If strEventLog = "Enabled" Then
    WriteToEventLog ("Summary Report Collection script - Using " & _
      "default for strSvr2Folder.")
    Err.Number = 0
  End If
End If

strConsolFolder = _
  WshShl.RegRead("HKLM\Software\Intuit\VBScripts\MstSumRpts\ConsolFolder")
If Err <> 0 Then
  If strEventLog = "Enabled" Then
    WriteToEventLog ("Summary Report Collection script - Using " & _
      "default for strConsolFolder.")
    Err.Number = 0
  End If
End If

If strDebug = "Enabled" Then
  MsgBox "Registry settings retrieved: " & vbCrLf & vbCrLf & _
   "strEventLog" & vbTab & "=" & vbTab & strEventLog & vbCrLf & _
```

```
      "strDebug" & vbTab & vbTab & "=" & vbTab & strDebug & vbCrLf & _
      "strSvrList" & vbTab & vbTab & "=" & vbTab & strSvrList & vbCrLf & _
      "strArchive" & vbTab & "=" & vbTab & strArchive & vbCrLf & _
      "strSvr1Folder " & vbTab & "=" & vbTab & strSvr1Folder & vbCrLf & _
      "strSvr2Folder" & vbTab & "=" & vbTab & strSvr2Folder & vbCrLf & _
      "strConsolFolder" & vbTab & "=" & vbTab & strConsolFolder, , cTitleBarMsg
  End If

End Sub

Sub MoveSummaryReports()

  On Error Resume Next

  Dim strNewFolder1, strNewFolder2

  If strDebug = "Enabled" Then
    MsgBox "Moving......." & vbCrLf & vbCrLf & _
      strArchive & "\" & Left(strSvrList, 8) & "*.*" & vbCrLf & _
      strArchive & "\" & Right(strSvrList, 8) & "*.*"
  End If

  If (FsoObj.FolderExists(strArchive) = False) Then
     TerminateScript()
  Else
    If (FsoObj.FolderExists(strSvr1Folder) = False) Then
      Set strNewFolder1 = FsoObj.CreateFolder(strSvr1Folder)
    End If
    If (FsoObj.FolderExists(strSvr2Folder) = False) Then
      Set strNewFolder2 = FsoObj.CreateFolder(strSvr2Folder)
    End If
    FsoObj.MoveFile strArchive & "\" & Left(strSvrList, 8) & "*.*", _
      strSvr1Folder
    FsoObj.MoveFile strArchive & "\" & Right(strSvrList, 8) & "*.*", _
      strSvr2Folder
  End If

End Sub
```

```
Sub MonthToDelete()

  Dim intGetSlashPosition, strCurrentMonth

  intGetSlashPosition = Instr(Date(), "/")
  strCurrentMonth = Mid(Date(), 1, intGetSlashPosition - 1)
  strDeleteMonth = strCurrentMonth - 4

  If strDeleteMonth = 0 Then
    strDeleteMonth = "12"
  End If

  If strDeleteMonth = -1 Then
    strDeleteMonth = "11"
  End If

  If strDeleteMonth = -2 Then
    strDeleteMonth = "10"
  End If

  If strDeleteMonth = -3 Then
    strDeleteMonth = "9"
  End If

  If strDebug = "Enabled" Then
    MsgBox "strDeleteMonth = " & strDeleteMonth
  End If

End Sub

Sub RemoveOldReportFiles()

  On Error Resume Next

  Dim strSummaryRptPath

  If strDebug = "Enabled" Then
```

```
    MsgBox "Deleting ......" & vbCrLf & vbCrLf & _
      strSvr1Folder & "\" & Left(strSvrList, 8) & "_" & strDeleteMonth & _
        "*_SumRpt.txt" & vbCrLf & _
      strSvr2Folder & "\" & Right(strSvrList, 8) & "_" & strDeleteMonth & _
      "*_SumRpt.txt" & vbCrLf & _
      strConsolFolder & "\" & strDeleteMonth & "*_ConsolSumRpt.txt"
  End If

  strSummaryRptPath = "d:\Order_Inventory\SummaryRpts\"

  FsoObj.DeleteFile strSvr1Folder & "\" & Left(strSvrList, 8) & "_" & _
    strDeleteMonth & "*_SumRpt.txt"
  FsoObj.DeleteFile strSvr2Folder & "\" & Right(strSvrList, 8) & "_" & _
    strDeleteMonth & "*_SumRpt.txt"
  FsoObj.DeleteFile strConsolFolder & "\" & strDeleteMonth & _
    "*_ConsolSumRpt.txt"

End Sub

Sub WriteToEventLog(strMessage)

  WshShl.LogEvent 4, strMessage

End Sub

Sub TerminateScript()

  WScript.Quit()

End Sub
```

Summary

In this chapter, you learned how to create an archive management script that maintained three separate report archives, each of which stores a minimum of three months' worth of reports. In addition, you observed as Molly added debug logic to the script and adapted it to retrieve its configuration settings from the Windows registry.

PART V

Professional Project 4

Project 4

Reporting Application Summary Data via the Web

Project 4 Overview

In this final project, you will learn how to develop an order/inventory reporting Web site for Intuit Mechanical Tools. This project will involve moving consolidated summary reports to the corporate Web server. A three-month archive of the HTML reports will be maintained on the corporate Web server. In addition, copies of the Microsoft Word versions of these reports will be available for download.

This project will cover the development of the entire Web site. The site's HTML pages will include embedded VBScripts that manage the display and presentation of data, as well as the storage and retrieval of personalized configuration settings. In order to complete this project, you will also need to create a number of WSH-executed VBScripts. These scripts will:

- Create HTML pages that display the contents of individual reports
- Create an HTML page made up of links to each available HTML report page
- Copy the new HTML pages to the corporate Web server
- Remotely manage a three-month report archive on the Web server

The VBScripts that you will embed within the Web site's HTML pages will need to perform a number of tasks, including:

- Storing individual user settings in cookies
- Retrieving cookies from client computers
- Generating graphic effects on HTML pages
- Implementing browser redirection for visitors who have not yet specified their personalized configuration settings
- Performing form validation to ensure that the configuration settings specified by visitors are valid
- Using browser detection to validate that visitors are using a supported version of Internet Explorer

Chapter 26

Reporting Application Summary Data via the Web

This chapter defines a new project case study. Once again, this project centers around the continued efforts to improve the order/inventory process at Intuit Mechanical Tools. It has been a number of months since Molly completed her work on developing the summary report consolidation project. Things have gone very smoothly, and Molly has moved on to work on the development of other projects. In the meantime, several members of the operations management staff have been asking the company's IT staff to once again improve the order/inventory reporting process by providing browser-based reporting. This way, anyone within the company who has access to the corporate Intranet will be able to access the consolidated summary reports directly from a desktop.

Two new programmers have recently been hired at Intuit. They are Alexander Banks and William Carter. They both have a Visual Basic programming background and some experience with HTML. IT management thinks that assigning them to work on this project will help both of them to better understand the order/inventory system while also getting them some exposure and interaction with the operations staff.

As you work your way through this project, you will learn how to create interactive HTML pages by embedding VBScripts that leverage the power of Internet Explorer object models. You will also learn how to use VBScript and the WSH to create HTML files and provide dynamic content. In addition, you will learn how to automate a number of other tasks, including:

- How to use the `Folder` object to administer the contents of directories
- How to use VBScript to create cookies that store configuration settings on client computers
- How to enhance Web pages using VBScript to create graphic effects

Project Overview

Operations management would like to augment the reporting process by making consolidated summary reports available on the company's intranet so that they are readily accessible to everybody. This not only will make things convenient for many people within the company, but also will offload the responsibility now assigned to operations staff for collecting and distributing order/inventory consolidated summary reports.

Collecting Project Requirements

Alexander and William begin their work on this project by first meeting with Molly to learn about the work that she did on her two previous order/inventory reporting projects. Once they felt like they had a good understanding of how things worked, they went to talk with the company's Web master, Michael Barns, to discuss how to best go about the development of the project's Web site. After describing their assignment and talking it over with Michael, it was agreed that a new directory would be set up on the company Windows 2000 Web server called `d:\Intuit\OrderInventory\Reporting` and that Alexander and William would be granted full control over the folder and its contents. In addition, Michael instructed them to name their main HTML page `Default.html` so that he could set them up with their own URL, which he told them would be `http://Intuit.com/OrdInv/Default.html`. Using this model, Alexander and William can then create whatever file and folder structure they wish within the `d:\Intuit\OrderInventory\Reporting` directory in order to support the storage of the HTML and reporting files that will make up the order/inventory Reporting Web site.

Once they understood the existing reporting infrastructure as well as how they would organize the HTML files and report files on the company's Web server, Alexander and William's next step is to sit down with the operations management to collect detailed project requirements. During this meeting, they learn that the operations department is pleased with the current format of the consolidated summary report and no additional content is required. In addition, operations wants to continue to receive network notifications when the consolidated summary reports are created on the Windows 2000 Professional workstation. Therefore, no changes are required to the scripts that were written by Molly.

What the operations staff wants is to be able to access the daily consolidated summary report via Internet Explorer. After talking for a while, the operations management added another requirement. They want to be able to access a history of up to 90 days' worth of consolidated summary report files. Operations also wants to know if the report data could be presented in a tabular spreadsheet format instead of as a text file. They thought that such a format would make the report easier to review and analyze.

Finally, Alexander and William are asked if it would be possible to store the Microsoft Word versions of the consolidated archive reports and make them available for download. This way, individuals who still need a hard copy of the original report could download it instead of having to request one from operations.

Documenting Project Requirements

After meeting with the operations management staff, Alexander and William got together the next day to go over the information that they collected. They also asked Molly to sit in on this meeting in order to solicit her input. Together they assembled the following list of requirements from their meeting with operations management staff.

- Automate the distribution of consolidated summary reports to the corporate Web server
- Read and process each day's consolidated summary report and create an HTML version of the report in a table-based format
- Maintain a three-month archive of HTML consolidated summary reports on the corporate Web server and make those reports accessible online
- Make the Word versions of the consolidated summary reports available for download
- Complete the development and testing of the project within 30 days

Alexander, William, and Molly then discussed each of these requests to determine whether they were something that could be accomplished. They came to the conclusion that they could provide scripted solutions that would meet the requirements of each of these requests. Next, at Molly's suggestion, Alexander and William typed up this list of requirements and distributed them to both their manager and the operations management staff for approval.

Performing a High-Level Design

With an overall understanding of the current scripting environment and an approved requirements document, Alexander and William sit down and begin work on a preliminary high-level design. They decide upon a solution that would involve the use of VBScript in two different ways. First, using the WSH, they will develop a collection of VBScripts that would execute on the Windows 2000 Professional workstation, as depicted in Figure 26.1.

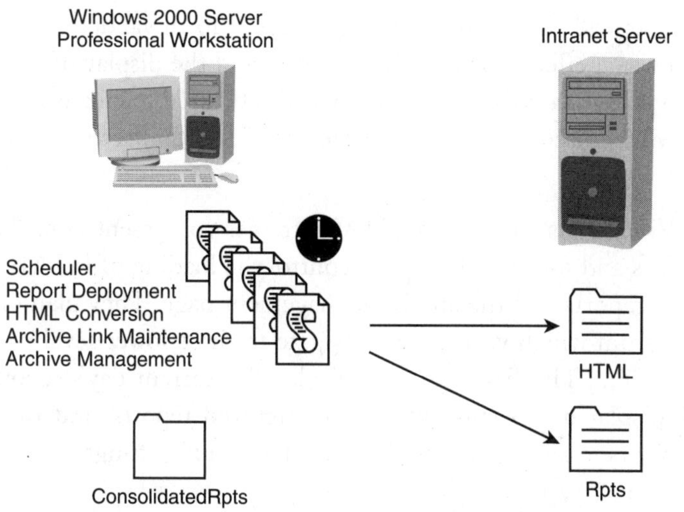

FIGURE 26.1 *VBScript and the WSH will be used behind the scenes to create HTML pages that display the consolidated summary reports*

The following collection of scripts will be created and executed on the Windows 2000 Professional workstation:

- **Scheduler**. This is a scheduling script that manages the sequential execution of the other three scripts that run on the Windows 2000 Professional workstation.
- **Report Deployment**. This script will create a network connection to the `d:\Intuit\OrderInventory\Reporting` folder on the company's Web server and copy over the HTML and Word report files.
- **HTML Conversion**. This script will create an HTML page that displays the current day's consolidated summary report in a table format.
- **Archive Link Maintenance**. This script will create an HTML page that lists links to each consolidated summary report stored in the summary report archive on the Web server.
- **Remote Archive Management**. This script will remotely administer the management of a three-month HTML page and Word report archive on the company's Web server.

In addition to the previous list of scripts, VBScripts will be embedded within the HTML pages that will make up the order/inventory Reporting Web site. These embedded VBScripts will control frame navigation and form validation and will provide enhanced visual effects such as link rollovers and the display of messages on the Internet Explorer status bar. VBScript will also be used to create and manage cookies that will be used to store customized configuration settings for users who visit the Web site.

Alexander and William plan on using HTML frames to present consolidated summary report files and to use VBScript to control the loading of HTML consolidated summary reports and the archive management page. They plan on creating a main page from which visitors can navigate to three lower-level pages as depicted in Figure 26.2. The first page will display the current day's report, the second page will display a collection of links to archived reports, and the third page will allow visitors to specify personalized configuration settings.

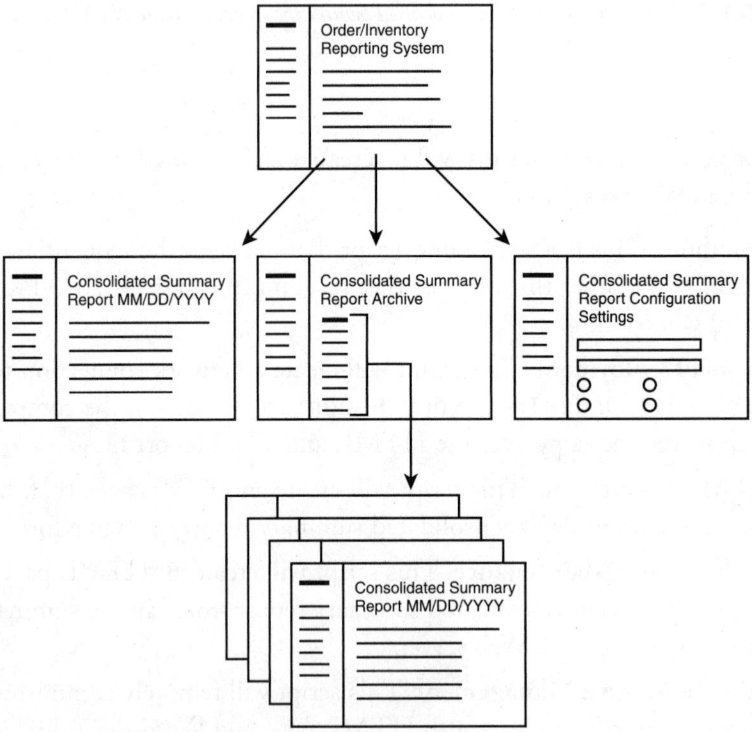

FIGURE 26.2 *VBScripts embedded within HTML pages will be used to control the navigation and presentation of information*

NOTE

A detailed breakdown of the HTML pages that will be created in support of this project and the precise location and roles of the embedded VBScripts is provided in Chapter 27, "Designing the Web Site."

Alexander and William decide that the best way to complete this project is to divide the work up, so each person will be responsible for completing specific tasks. Table 26.1 outlines the task assignments that they divided between themselves.

Table 26.1 HTML Reporting Tasks

Type of Task	Assigned To	Description
Prerequisite tasks	Alexander	Modify the scheduler script running on the Windows 2000 Professional workstation to run the Report Deployment and the Remote Archive Management scripts. Create registry entries on the Windows 2000 Professional workstation that will be used to control script execution.
Designing Web site	William	Determine the overall design of the Web site, including the links between the HTML pages, the content of each HTML page, and the design elements to be used on each HTML page.
Develop a home page	William	Create a home page using HTML frames. Embed VBScripts that add graphic effects, retrieve configuration settings stored in client-side cookies, provide frame control, and provide HTML links to subordinate HTML pages.
Create a Registration and Configuration Settings page	William	Create an HTML page that collects about information the users and their preferred Web site configuration settings and store this information on each visitor's computer using a cookie.

(continues)

Table 26.1 HTML Reporting Tasks (*continued*)

Type of Task	Assigned To	Description
Convert consolidated summary reports to HTML pages	Alexander	Create a script that converts the current day's consolidated summary report into an HTML page by embedding HTML tags within the new report and saving it as an HTML page.
Build Report Archive page	Alexander	Create a script that loops through the list of HTML consolidated summary reports and creates a page of links to all the reports currently stored in the archive folder.
Distribute HTML and Word files and perform archive management	Alexander	Create a script that establishes a network connection to the Web server, copies over HTML and Word files, and administers a three-month HTML and Word report archive.

Accomplishing Prerequisite Tasks

Alexander is responsible for performing the project's preliminary tasks, which include automating the scheduled execution of the WSH VBScripts that are part of this project and the creation of new registry entries. To facilitate the execution of the project's WSH-run VBScripts, Alexander has decided to modify the scheduler script developed by Molly for execution on the Windows 2000 Professional workstation (from Chapter 19, "Scheduling Script Execution") as shown below.

> **NOTE**
>
> By modifying the existing scheduler script, Alexander will remove a number of security obstacles. Molly has already set up the execution of this script to run using the `ScriptSchlr` account, which provides it with administrative level privileges. Alexander has already requested that Michael Barns, the company's Web master, provide this account with full access to the `d:\Intuit\OrderInventory\Reporting` folder on the company's Web server.

```
'*************************************************************************
'Script Name: Script 26.1.vbs
'Author: Jerry Ford
```

```
'Created: 04/25/03
'Description: This script runs scripts associated with the order/inventory
'reporting system
'*************************************************************************


'Initialization Section

Option Explicit

On Error Resume Next

Dim WshShl, intRcChk

Set WshShl = WScript.CreateObject("WScript.Shell")

intRcChk = 0

'Main Processing Section

RunScript("ErrorAnalyzer.vbs")
RunScript("SalesAnalyzer.vbs")
RunScript("ReturnsAnalyzer.vbs")
RunScript("ProductionAnalyzer.vbs")

'Three new sets of statements added to support web based reporting
intRcChk = RunScript("HTMLConvert.vbs")
If intRcChk > 0 Then
  NotifyOperationsStaff("HTMLConvert.vbs")
Else
  intRcChk = RunScript("ArchiveLinkMgr.vbs")
  If intRcChk > 0 Then
    NotifyOperationsStaff("ArchiveLinkMgr.vbs")
  Else
    intRcChk = RunScript("WebArchiveMgr.vbs")
    If intRcChk > 0 Then
      NotifyOperationsStaff("WebArchiveMgr.vbs")
    End If
```

```
  End If
End If

If Day(date()) = 1 Then
  RunScript("ArchiveManager.vbs")
End If

'Terminate script execution
TerminateScript()


'Procedure Section

Function RunScript(strScriptName)

 RunScript = WshShl.Run(ScriptName, 1, True)

End Function

Sub WriteToEventLog()

  WshShl.LogEvent 4, "Report and Log Analyzer Scheduler Script executing."

End Sub

Sub NotifyOperationsStaff(strFailedScript)

  Dim strUserName, strNtkNotifiyList

  Dim astrNotifyArray

  strNtkNotifiyList = _
    WshShl.RegRead("HKLM\Software\Intuit\VBScripts\MstSumRpts\NtkNotifiyList")

  astrNotifyArray = Split(strNtkNotifiyList)

  For Each strUserName In astrNotifyArray
    WshShl.Run "Net Send " & strUserName & " " & "Script " & _
```

```
        strFailedScript & " failed. " &_
        "Please notify The IT Dept."
    Next

End Sub

Sub TerminateScript()

    WScript.Quit()

End Sub
```

Alexander plans to add logic to each of the WSH-executed VBScripts that he is responsible for developing in order to return an error code indicating whether or not they ran successfully. In doing so, he provides the scheduling script with the ability to determine whether a problem occurred.

NOTE

VBScript can return a return code to a calling statement using the `WScript` object's `Quit()` method, as explained in Chapter 30, "Converting Reports to HMTL Documents."

Alexander chooses for the moment not to modify the manner in which the scheduler script's existing execution calls are made. Instead, he will explain to Molly what he has done and suggest that she retrofit her VBScripts to support the same functionality. However, he puts script return code checking in place for the scripts that he is developing. He does this by defining a variable called `intRcChk` and using it to store the value returned by the `RunScript` function. If a value greater than zero is returned, then an error has occurred within the called script, and the `NotifyOperationsStaff()` subroutine is called and passed the name of the script that failed.

To accommodate this new functionality, Alexander has to modify the `RunScript()` procedure by changing it from a subroutine to a function. He also modifies the procedure to return the return code supplied by each script that it execute.

Alexander also modifies the scheduling script by moving the `WScript.Quit()` statement into its own subroutine in order to improve the overall organization of the scheduling script. Finally, he adds the `NotifyOperationsStaff()` subroutine to the script, which he copies and pastes out of the VBScript that creates the consolidated summary report (from Chapter 24, "Processing and Consolidating Report Data"). Using this subroutine, the scheduling script can notify the operations staff of any errors that occur when processing his scripts. This will give the IT programming staff a chance to fix things before everyone comes in to work looking for the online copy of the consolidated summary reports.

Rather than develop a script to create a registry key and values for this new script, Alexander decides that since he only needs to create seven new registry values, it would be faster to create them manually using the `Regedt32` utility. Alexander creates a new registry subkey under `HKLM\Intuit\VBScript` called `WebRpting` to store each value for his new scripts, which are briefly explained below.

- **`HKLM\Intuit\VBScript\WebRpting\Debug`**. Specifies whether the script should display intermediate results in pop-up dialog boxes when executing (for example, when manually executed for troubleshooting purposes)
- **`HKLM\Intuit\VBScript\WebRpting\EventLogging`**. Specifies whether the script should write informational messages to the Windows application event log
- **`HKLM\Intuit\VBScript\WebRpting\ConSolRptLoc`**. Specifies the location of the folder on the Windows 2000 Professional workstation where copies of the consolidated summary reports are to be stored
- **`HKLM\Intuit\VBScript\WebRpting\HTMLFolder`**. Specifies the folder on the Windows 2000 Professional workstation where the HTML versions of the consolidated summary reports are to be stored
- **`HKLM\Intuit\VBScript\WebRpting\WebServer`**. Specifies the network name assigned to the company's Web server
- **`HKLM\Intuit\VBScript\WebRpting\Share_Rpts`**. Specifies the name of the shared folder on the company's Web server where copies of the Word versions of the consolidated summary reports are to be stored
- **`HKLM\Intuit\VBScript\WebRpting\Share_HTML`**. Specifies the name of the shared folder on the company's Web server where copies of the HTML versions of the consolidated summary reports are to be stored

NOTE

For more information about the Windows registry and how it works, refer to Chapter 22, "Developing a Setup Script."

Designing the Web Site

William is responsible for developing the HTML portion of this project and for its embedded VBScripts. As shown earlier in Figure 26.2, William plans to create a main page and to use HTML frames to control the presentation of data. Developing this Web site will require a basic understanding of HTML syntax as well as a working knowledge of frame design and implementation. An understanding of how to create and use HTML links to tie together HTML pages is also required.

Developing a Home Page

The main page or home page is the default page that all visitors will see when they open their Internet Explorer browser and type in **`http://Intuit.com/OrdInv/Default.html`**. In order to develop this HTML page, William will need to use a number of different development techniques, including:

- **Embedding VBScripts.** To provide graphic effects and process configuration settings stored in client-side cookies
- **Creating a Links page (left pane).** To create a Web page that defines links to the other HTML pages that will make up the Web site
- **Creating a Welcome page (right pane).** To provide visitors with a customized welcome message as well as instructions for using the Web site
- **Using redirection.** To redirect new visitors to the Registration and Configuration page before allowing them to access the rest of the Web site
- **Implementing browser detection.** To ensure that visitors are using a supported version of Internet Explorer
- **Reading cookies.** To retrieve user preferences and configuration settings established on the Web site's Registration and Configuration page

Creating the Registration and Configuration Page

The Registration and Configuration page will be used to collect the name of each visitor to the order/inventory Reporting Web site. In addition, it will allow visitors to specify personal preferences for things such as the background color of the links page and their preferred default page. In order to complete the development of this page, William will have to make use of:

- HTML forms
- VBScript form validation capabilities
- VBScript's ability to create and store cookies
- VBScript's ability to take control of the browser's status bar
- VBScript's ability to interact with visitors using pop-up dialog boxes

Converting Consolidated Summary Reports to HTML Pages

Alexander wants to develop the VBScript that creates an HTML version of the consolidated summary report based on the contents of the text version of the report. To do so, he will need to use a number of `FileSystemObject` object methods, including:

- **`FileExists()`**. Used to avoid errors by first validating that a file exists before trying to open it
- **`OpenTextFile()`**. Opens the specified file, allowing it to be further manipulated by other methods
- **`ReadLine()`**. Provides the ability to read a line of text in a file
- **`Close()`**. Closes a previously opened file
- **`WriteLine()`**. Provides the ability to write a line of text to the specified file
- **`WriteBlankLines()`**. Provides the ability to write a blank line in the specified file

In addition to these methods, Alexander will need a solid understanding of HTML syntax and will have to use this knowledge to insert HTML formatting tags within the HTML file generated by this script. Alexander will also need to use the `WshShell` object's `RegRead()` method to retrieve the script's configuration settings from the Windows registry.

Building the Report Archive Page

In addition to setting up the Archive Link Management script to retrieve its configuration settings from the Windows registry, Alexander will need to familiarize himself with the following objects, properties, and methods:

- **`GetFolder()`**. A `FileSystemObject` method that provides the ability to retrieve a reference to a specified folder
- **`Folder Object`**. Provides access to all the properties associated with a folder
- **`File Object`**. Provides access to all the properties associated with a file
- **`Files Collection`**. Provides access to all the files that reside in a specified folder
- **`Files Property`**. A property belonging to the `File` object that retrieves a reference to a `Files Collection`

In addition to these new objects, properties, and methods, Alexander will have to use the following `FileSystemObject` methods in order to generate the Archive Link Management HTML page:

- `OpenTextFile()`
- `Close()`
- `WriteLine()`
- `WriteBlankLines()`

Distributing HTML and Word Files and Performing Archive Management

In the final script of the project, Alexander will need to learn how to work with the `File` object's `Copy()` method in order to copy over the HTML and Word files from the Windows 2000 Professional workstation to the company's Web server. In addition, he will need to use the following `WshNetwork` methods to establish a network connection to the Web server and to break that connection when the script is done using it.

- `MapNetworkDrive()`
- `RemoveNetworkDrive()`

Specifically, Alexander will need to copy the HTML pages and Word files created on the Windows 2000 Professional workstation to the folders listed below on the Web server.

- **D:\Order_Inventory\HTML**. Stores a minimum of 90 days' worth of HTML reports containing Web-based versions of the consolidated summary reports
- **D:\Order_Inventory\Rpts**. Stores a minimum of 90 days' worth of Word reports containing the consolidated summary reports

Finally, to automate the execution of the archive management process, Alexander will have to use the following `FileSystemObject` object methods:

- `FileExists()`
- `DeleteFile()`

Summary

This chapter introduced you to the final case study in this book. An overview of the project assigned to Alexander and William was provided. This included the development of a list of project requirements. In addition, a high-level design was presented that outlined the overall plan for providing a Web-based reporting solution. This included the identification of each script that is to be developed, as well as the major VBScript language constructs that will be used in order to create each of these scripts. In the six chapters that follow, you will get the opportunity to see how Alexander and William tackle each of the tasks involved in completing this project.

Chapter 27

Designing the Web Site

In this chapter, William will provide a low-level design for the Order/Inventory Reporting Web site based on the high-level design outlined in the previous chapter. This will include the identification and placement of all interface elements and data content. It will also include the identification and placement of links that will support navigation between the pages that make up the Web site. In addition, William will determine what functionality he wants to add to each page on the Web site using VBScript and describe what each VBScript will provide.

A Quick Overview of the Order/Inventory Reporting Web Site

As explained in Chapter 26, "Project Case Study: Reporting Application Summary Data via the Corporate Intranet," Alexander and William plan to organize the Order/Inventory Reporting Web site into a collection of HTML pages. The site will have a Main page, which will serve as the default page for all visitors. From this page, visitors will be able to directly access the following three HTML pages:

- **The Daily Consolidated Summary Report page**. Displays the HTML version of the current day's consolidated summary report
- **The Reports Archive page**. Displays a list of links to HTML pages representing previous consolidated summary reports and provides access to downloadable copies of Microsoft Word versions of these reports
- **The Registration and Configuration Settings page**. Provides visitors with the ability to identify themselves to the Web site and to specify customization settings such as background colors and a default page

The content provided by the Web site's Main page and that of the Registration and Configuration Settings page will be static, meaning that it will be manually developed and updated by William as required. The content provided on the Daily Consolidated Summary Report page and the Reports Archive page will be dynamic, meaning that the content provided on these pages will be created by

WSH VBScripts each morning based on the information found on the consolidated summary reports.

> **NOTE**
>
> This chapter and the one that follows assume a basic understanding of HTML on the part of the reader. Therefore, only a brief explanation of the HTML involved in creating the HTML pages is presented in this book. If you feel that you need additional information about HTML and how to work with it, read *Learn HTML in a Weekend, 3rd Edition* by Steve Callihan (Premier Press, 2000).

The Web Site's Main Page

William has decided to use HTML frames as the key design element of the Order/Inventory Reporting Web site. He plans to organize the display of all content for this site by dividing the display into two separate frames, as demonstrated in Figure 27.1.

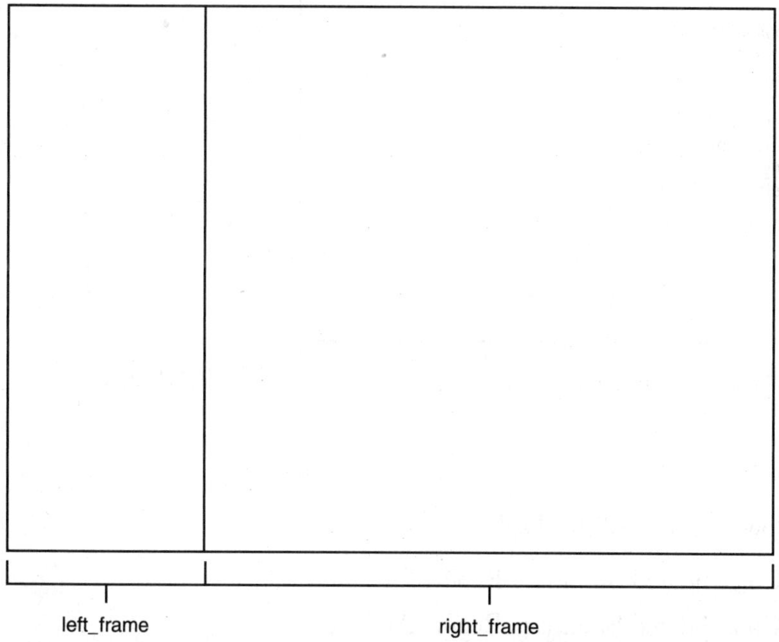

FIGURE 27.1 *Data presented at the Order/Inventory Reporting Web site will use frames*

The left frame will be called `left_frame` and will be used to display HTML links to each of the three HTML pages that can be directly accessed from the Main page. The right frame will be called `right_frame` and will be used to display the content provided by the Web site, including *links to* the reports, archives, and the Registration and Configuration Settings page.

Defining the Links Page

In order to display the list of links that is to be provided on the left-hand side of the display, William plans to create an HTML page called `Links.html` and to load this page into the `left_frame` frame of the `Default.html` page (the Web site's main page). An example of the content to be presented on the Links page is shown in Figure 27.2.

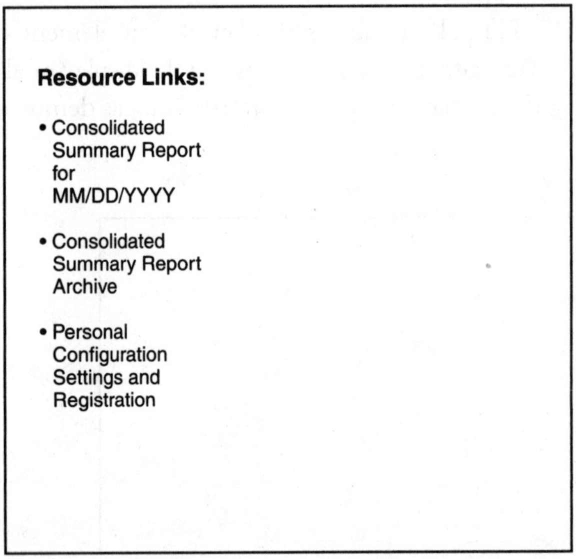

FIGURE 27.2 *The Links page provides navigation links to the other HTML pages*

The following links will be displayed:

- Consolidated Summary Report for Today
- Consolidated Summary Report Archive
- Personal Configuration Settings and Registration

Each of these links will be left-justified. In order to enhance the appearance of these links, William plans to embed a number of VBScripts on the Links page, which will provide the functionality outlined below.

- **Link rollovers**. Changes the color of a link as the mouse moves over and off of the link
- **Status bar messages**. Displays supplemental text messages in the status bar

William will add rollover effects that will turn the color of each link to red when the mouse is moved over it and blue when the mouse is moved off of the link. By implementing rollover effects in this manner, William will make it easier for visitors to identify which link currently has focus (which link will be opened if the left mouse button is clicked). In addition, William will display a message on the browser status bar describing the HTML page to which each link points whenever the visitor moves the pointer over it, thus providing the visitor with additional information without crowding the main display area.

Defining the Welcome Page

By default, all visitors will see the Welcome page displayed in the right frame when they visit the Order/Inventory Reporting Web site. The content to be provided on the page is shown in Figure 27.3 and will include basic information about the Web site as well as contact information for several departments, should visitors have any questions or concerns.

In addition to the text displayed on this seemingly simple HTML page, William plans to add a great deal of behind-the-scenes functionality in the form of embedded VBScripts, as outlined in the following list.

- **Cookie retrieval**. Retrieves information about visitors and their preferences from the client-side cache
- **Browser detection**. Determines what type of browser a visitor is using as well as its version number
- **Redirection**. Automatically loads different HTML pages based on browser type or user preferences

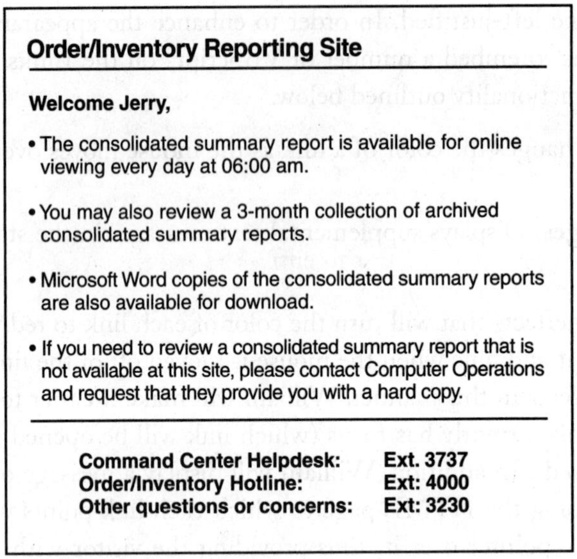
Order/Inventory Reporting Site
Welcome Jerry,
• The consolidated summary report is available for online viewing every day at 06:00 am.
• You may also review a 3-month collection of archived consolidated summary reports.
• Microsoft Word copies of the consolidated summary reports are also available for download.
• If you need to review a consolidated summary report that is not available at this site, please contact Computer Operations and request that they provide you with a hard copy.
Command Center Helpdesk: Ext. 3737
Order/Inventory Hotline: Ext: 4000
Other questions or concerns: Ext: 3230

FIGURE 27.3 *The Welcome page will serve as the default page and will greet visitors by name and provide general information about the Web site*

NOTE

A *cookie* represents a small amount of data that can be stored on visitors' computers when they visit your Web site. Using cookies, you can store information collected from the user and reuse that information the next time the visitor returns to your Web site in order to provide a personalized experience.

Each time a person visits the Order/Inventory Reporting site, the Welcome page will check to see whether their computer has a cookie from the Web site. If a cookie is found, it is retrieved and the data that it contains will be used to:

- Greet the visitor by name
- Set the Web site's color scheme
- Redirect the visitor to the preferred default page

Information stored in cookies is collected and saved on the Registration and Configuration Settings page. The first time users visit the Web site, they will not have a cookie. Therefore, their browsers will automatically be redirected to the Registration and Configuration Settings page. Once the visitor has supplied the information required on that page, a cookie is created and saved on the visitor's computer. Each visitor will have the option of returning to the Registration and Configuration Settings page in order to make modifications any time he wishes.

Visitors will be required to use Internet Explorer 5 or higher to use the Order/Inventory Reporting Web site. The Welcome page will automatically check the browser being used by each visitor to ensure that it meets this requirement. If the browser does not meet this requirement, the visitor's browser will be redirected to an HTML page that advises her of the requirement to use the appropriate browser.

Assembling the Main Page

Figure 27.4 shows how the Order/Inventory's Main page will look when loaded into the visitor's browser. As you can see, by implementing frames William provides a structure for consistently displaying content. He will also make considerable use of font size and highlighting in order to enhance the overall appearance of the Web site.

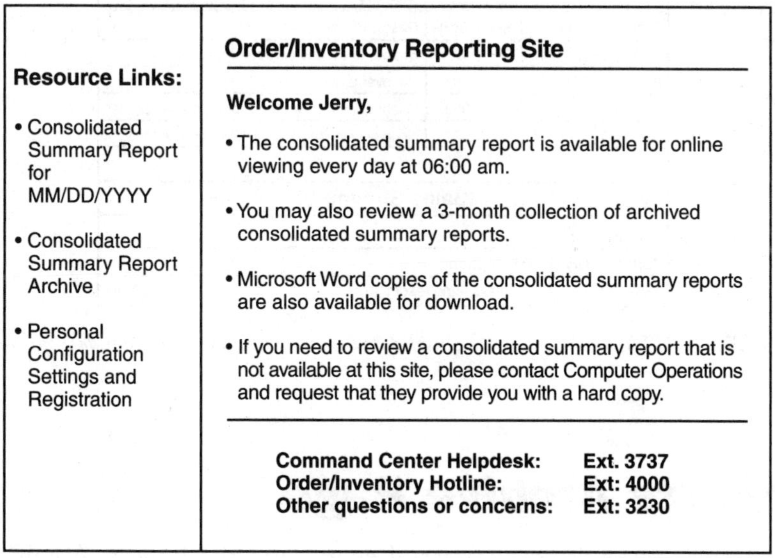
Resource Links:
• Consolidated Summary Report for MM/DD/YYYY
• Consolidated Summary Report Archive
• Personal Configuration Settings and Registration
Order/Inventory Reporting Site
Welcome Jerry,
• The consolidated summary report is available for online viewing every day at 06:00 am.
• You may also review a 3-month collection of archived consolidated summary reports.
• Microsoft Word copies of the consolidated summary reports are also available for download.
• If you need to review a consolidated summary report that is not available at this site, please contact Computer Operations and request that they provide you with a hard copy.
Command Center Helpdesk: Ext. 3737
Order/Inventory Hotline: Ext: 4000
Other questions or concerns: Ext: 3230

FIGURE 27.4 *The home page for the Order/Inventory Reporting system will serve as the Web site's default page*

The Daily Consolidated Summary Report Page

The Daily Consolidated Summary Report page, shown in the right-hand pane in Figure 27.5, is created each morning by a VBScript run on the Windows 2000 Professional workstation by the WSH. This HTML page uses HTML tables to display the contents of the current day's consolidated summary report in a spreadsheet-like format. Alexander is responsible for developing the automated creation of this HTML page each morning and for copying it to the `D:\Order_Inventory\HTML` folder on the company's Web server. Alexander will save this HTML page as `CurrentRpt.HTML`, overriding the previous day's consolidated summary report each morning with the current day's report.

All that William needs to do to integrate this HTML page into the Order/Inventory Web site is to make sure that he provides a static link to it on the Links page.

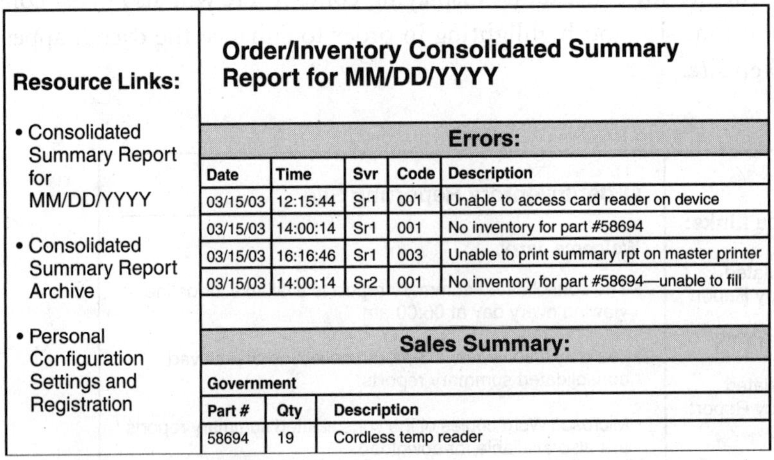
Resource Links:
• Consolidated Summary Report for MM/DD/YYYY
• Consolidated Summary Report Archive
• Personal Configuration Settings and Registration
Order/Inventory Consolidated Summary Report for MM/DD/YYYY
Errors:
Date | Time | Svr | Code | Description
03/15/03 | 12:15:44 | Sr1 | 001 | Unable to access card reader on device
03/15/03 | 14:00:14 | Sr1 | 001 | No inventory for part #58694
03/15/03 | 16:16:46 | Sr1 | 003 | Unable to print summary rpt on master printer
03/15/03 | 14:00:14 | Sr2 | 001 | No inventory for part #58694—unable to fill
Sales Summary:
Government
Part # | Qty | Description
58694 | 19 | Cordless temp reader

FIGURE 27.5 *The HTML version of the consolidated summary report will provide a spreadsheet-like view*

The Reports Archive Page

Like the Daily Consolidated Summary Report page, the Reports Archive page (shown in Figure 27.6) is created by a VBScript run by the WSH on the Windows 2000 Professional workstation. It provides access to a three-month archive of HTML versions of the consolidated summary reports. These reports will be organized by month and will be accessible by clicking on their links.

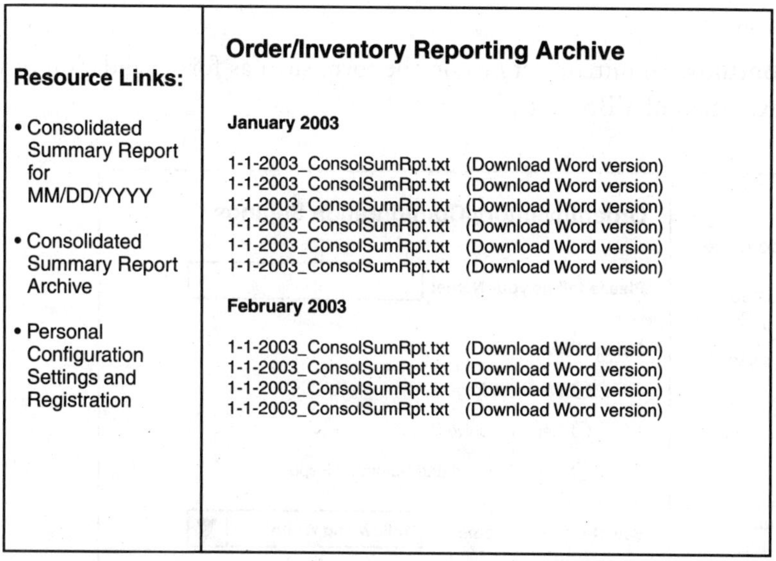

FIGURE 27.6 *The Reports Archive page provides links to the previous three months' worth of consolidated summary reports*

In addition to the HTML version of the consolidated summary reports, the Reports Archive page provides a link to Word versions of the reports. All that a visitor will have to do to download one of the Word versions of the report is to click on its link and then click on Yes when prompted to confirm the download.

The Registration and Configuration Settings Page

The Registration and Configuration Settings page, sketched out in Figure 27.7, will be created as an HTML form and will include a number of form elements, including:

- **Text fields**. To collect text string input

- **Radio buttons.** To provide a list of mutually exclusive choices from which visitors may select a single option
- **Drop-down lists.** To provide a predefined collection of options to select from
- **Buttons.** To initiate actions on the form such as form validation or the execution of VBScripts

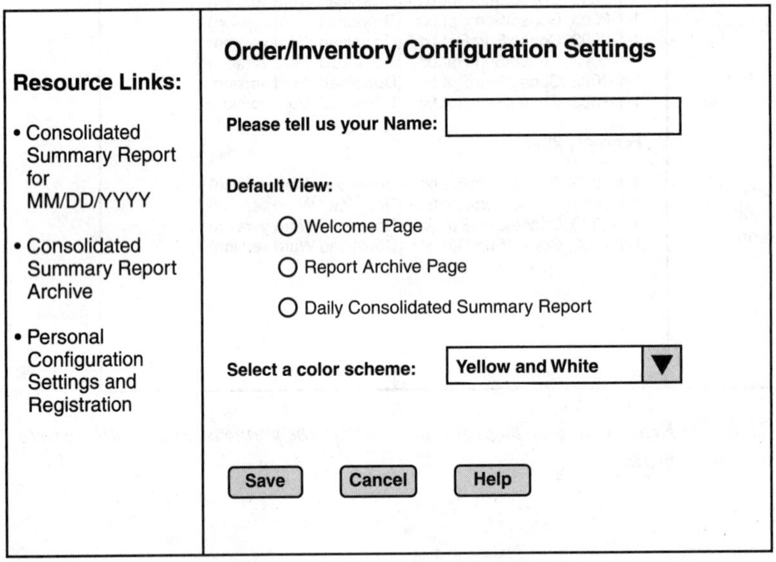

FIGURE 27.7 *The Registration and Configuration Settings page collects each visitor's name and personal preferences*

The form's text field will be used to collect the visitor's name. The collection of radio buttons will provide each visitor with the ability to specify a default page for the Web site. The drop-down list will provide the visitor with the ability to select from one of a number of predefined color schemes that will control the background color of the Links page. Finally, buttons will be used to initiate a number of script tasks, as outlined below.

- **Cookie creation.** Retrieves information about visitors and their preferences from the client-side cache
- **Form validation.** Determines what type of browser a visitor is using as well as its version number

- **Pop-up dialog box based confirmation**. Automatically loads different HTML pages based on browser type or user preferences
- **Pop-up dialog box based help**. Provides text-based help that explains the information required by each form element on the page

Summary

In this chapter, you observed as William outlined the content and format of each of the HTML pages that will make up the Order/Inventory Reporting Web site. This included defining the relationships and links among the HTML pages as well as the identification and placement of VBScripts within each of these HTML pages. The chapter also explained how these VBScripts will enhance the overall presentation of the Web site.

Chapter 28

Building the Web Site's Main Page

In this chapter, William begins work on creating the Order/Inventory Reporting Web site by creating the site's main or default page. The page will use an HTML frameset composed of two frames in order to display a menu of links on the left-hand side of the browser window and the content of the selected link in the right-hand frame. William will also embed a VBScript in the HTML page in order to add a series of graphic effects to the Web site. This script will perform such tasks as turning menu links into rollover links, retrieving configuration settings from client-side cache, and managing the content that is loaded into the right frame.

Working with Frames

The Order/Inventory Reporting Web site's main page is called `Default.html`. The HTML statements that make up this page are shown below. The page is divided into two frames. The first frame is called `left_frame`. It will automatically load an HTML page called `Links.html`. The second frame is called `right_frame` and will automatically load an HTML page called `Welcome.html`.

```
<HTML>

  <HEAD>
    <TITLE>Script 28.1 - Define a Frameset for the main web site page</TITLE>
  </HEAD>

  <FRAMESET COLS="175,*">
    <FRAME SRC="Links.html" NAME="left_frame" SCROLLING="no" FRAMEBORDER="1"
      NORESIZE>
    <FRAME SRC="Welcome.html" NAME="right_frame" SCROLLING="auto"
      FRAMEBORDER="1" NORESIZE>
  </FRAMESET>

</HTML>
```

The frames are created using the HTML <FRAMESET> and <FRAME> tags. The <FRAMESET> tags replace the <BODY> tags that are normally used to define an HTML page. The first frame is set up to be 175 pixels wide, and the rest of the available space is left for the frame on the right.

Building the Links.html Page

The `Links.html` page, which is automatically loaded into the `left_frame` frame of the `Default.html` page, provides a list of links to other pages on the Order/Inventory Reporting Web site. It is made up of HTML statements and a number of VBScript subroutines. The subroutines provide the `Links.html` page with the following features:

- The setting of the page's background color
- The creation of link rollover effects
- The posting of messages on the Internet Explorer status bar
- The loading of linked HTML pages into the `right_frame` frame

HTML for the Links.html Page

The HTML required to create the `Links.html` page is shown below. As you can see, it consists of a small collection of HTML tags. The key tags to focus on are the three link tags defined at the bottom of the HTML page. They define three links, named `DailyRpt`, `Archive`, and `Config`, and display text messages representing each link. Also note that the opening <FONT> tag sets the color of the text that will represent each link to blue.

```
<HTML>
  <HEAD>
    <TITLE>Script 28.2 - This page provides links to subordinate HTML pages</TITLE>
  </HEAD>

  <BODY>
    <BR>
    <H3>Resource Links:</H3><P><BR>
<DIV STYLE="color:blue;">
      <A NAME="DailyRpt"> Consolidated Summary Report for Today</A><P><BR>
```

```
      <A NAME="Archive"> Consolidated Summary Report Archive</A><P><BR>
      <A NAME="Config"> Personal Configuration Settings and Registration</A><P>
    </DIV>
  </BODY>
</HTML>
```

Adding VBScript to the HTML Page

Once the HTML page is defined, you can enhance it by embedding its VBScript. To embed a VBScript, you will need to add the following statements inside either the header or body section of the HTML page. The statements identify the beginning and ending of a VBScript.

```
<SCRIPT LANGUAGE="VBScript">
    <!-- Start hiding VBScript statements
      .
      .
      .
    ' End hiding VBScript statements -->
    </SCRIPT>
```

As you will see, the VBScript that is added to this HTML page will consist of a collection of subroutines. Each of these subroutines provides a distinct feature to the HTML page.

Setting the Default Background Color

The first subroutine embedded in the `Links.html` page is called `SetBackgroundColor()`. It executes when the `Links.html` page is loaded. This is accomplished by modifying the opening `<BODY>` tag, as shown below.

```
<BODY onLoad=SetBackgroundColor()>
```

This statement uses the browser's `onLoad` event to trigger the execution of the subroutine, which is shown below.

```
Sub SetBackgroundColor()
  If document.cookie <> "" Then
    astrCookieArray = Split(document.cookie,",")
    strColorScheme = astrCookieArray(2)
```

```
    document.bgColor = strColorScheme
  Else
    document.bgcolor = "yellow"
  End If
End Sub
```

The subroutine begins by checking the `document` object's `cookie` property to see if the visitor's computer has a cookie belonging to the Order/Inventory Web site. If the value assigned to `document.cookie` is not blank, then the VBScript `Split()` function is used to parse out the contents of the cookie into an array called `astrCookieArray`.

NOTE

The `document` object is exposed by the Internet Explorer browser object models. To learn more about the `document` object and its methods and properties, or any of the other browser-based objects, methods, and properties covered in this chapter, read Chapter 8, "VBScript and Internet Explorer."

The cookie created by the Order/Inventory Reporting Web site consists of three parts: storing the visitor's name, preferred default page, and preferred color scheme. Each of these pieces is loaded into the `astrCookieArray` array. The value stored in `astrCookieArray(2)` represents the visitor's preferred color scheme. The value stored in `astrCookieArray(2)` is then assigned to the `document` object's `bgcolor` property, thus changing the background color of the `Links.html` page. However, if a cookie from the Order/Inventory Reporting Web site is not found on the visitor's computer, the page's default background color of yellow is used.

NOTE

In Chapter 29, "Building the Registration and Configuration Settings Page," you will see that the `Config.html` page collects visitor configuration settings and stores them in client-side cache using a cookie.

Creating Link Rollover Effects

Next William modifies the HTML page by adding six new subroutines to the page's VBScript. These subroutines are shown below. As you can see, they are grouped into pairs. The first pair of subroutines creates the rollover effect for the `DailyRpt` link. The remaining pairs of subroutines manage the rollover effect for the `Links.html` page's other two links.

```
Sub DailyRpt_onMouseOver
  DailyRpt.style.color="red"
End Sub
Sub DailyRpt_onMouseOut
  DailyRpt.style.color="blue"
End Sub

Sub Archive_onMouseOver
  Archive.style.color="red"
End Sub
Sub Archive_onMouseOut
  Archive.style.color="blue"
End Sub

Sub Config_onMouseOver
  Config.style.color="red"
End Sub
Sub Config_onMouseOut
  Config.style.color="blue"
End Sub
```

The first subroutine in each pair is named by attaching the name of the link with which the subroutine is associated to the browser event that will trigger the subroutine executed. In this case, the first subroutine in each pair is the `onMouseOver` event. Whenever the visitor moves the pointer over the link associated with the subroutine, the subroutine changes the color of the text that represents the link to red.

The second subroutine in each pair changes the color of the link back to its initial blue color when the visitor moves the pointer off of its associated link. The result of the animation added by these six subroutines is that the links on the `Links.html` page dynamically change color to help the visitor identify the currently selected link.

Posting Messages on the Internet Explorer Status Bar

Once William has the rollover effects for the links working correctly, he modifies the subroutines that control them by adding logic that posts and clears messages on the Internet Explorer status bar whenever visitors move the pointer over one of the `Links.html` page's links. This trick is accomplished by modifying the `window` object's `status` property. For example, the following pair of subroutines shows how William modified the subroutines that respond to the `onMouseOver` and `onMouseOut` events for the `DailyRpt` link.

```
Sub DailyRpt_onMouseOver
  DailyRpt.style.color="red"
  window.status = "View today's consolidated summary report"
End Sub
Sub DailyRpt_onMouseOut
  DailyRpt.style.color="blue"
  window.status = ""
End Sub
```

As you can see, descriptive text is displayed when the `onMouseOver` event is triggered for the `DailyRpt` link. In similar fashion, the value of `window.status` is set equal to blank when the link's `onMouseOut` event is triggered.

Using VBScript to Control Frame Content

William's final task in creating the `Links.html` page is to create a collection of three subroutines that control the loading of other HTML pages in the `right_frame` frame of the `Default.html` page when visitors click on one of the `Links.html` page's links.

The first of these subroutines is called `DailyRpt_onClick()`. It executes when the visitor moves the pointer over the `DailyRpt` link and clicks on it. This subroutine uses a variable named `strFileNameString` to store the name of the current day's version of the consolidated summary report. Before writing the subroutine, William adds the following statement to define this variable at the beginning of the VBScript:

```
Dim strFileNameString
```

Next he creates the `DailyRpt_onClick()` subroutine, as shown below. The logic for this subroutine was borrowed from previous WSH-executed VBScripts and should look familiar by now. First William uses the `Date()` function to collect the current system date, and then he uses the `Replace()` function to replace all occurrences of the backslash (/) character with the dash (-) character. The string `ConsolRpt.html` is then appended to the end of `strFileNameString`. Finally, the subroutine loads the current day's HTML version of the summary report into the `right_frame` frame by assigning the value of the `strFileNameString` variable to `top.right_frame.location`. In the context of this HTML page, `top` is used to reference the parent frameset defined in `Default.HTML`, and `right_frame` identifies the frame where the HTML version of the consolidated summary report is to be loaded, as specified by the frame object's `location` property.

```
Sub DailyRpt_onClick
  strFileNameString = Replace(Date(), "/", "-")
  strFileNameString = strFileNameString & "_ConsolRpt.html"
  top.right_frame.location = "..\Rpts\" & strFileNameString
End Sub
```

NOTE

Note the use of `..\Rpts` to specify the location of the `Rpts` folder. When translated, `..\` tells the script that the location of the `Rpts` folder can be found by backing up to the parent folder of the current folder (from `D:\Intuit\OrderInventory\Reporting\HTML` to `D:\Intuit\OrderInventory\Reporting`) and then looking for the `Rpts` folder (`D:\Intuit\OrderInventory\Reporting\Rpts`).

The next two subroutines are much more straightforward than the previous subroutine. The `Archive_onClick()` subroutine, shown below, uses the `location` property to load the `archive.html` page, which contains a list of links to the HTML report archive on the corporate Web server.

```
Sub Archive_onClick
  top.right_frame.location="..\Rpts\Archive.html"
End Sub
```

Likewise, the `Config_onClick()` subroutine, shown below, loads the `Config.html` page, allowing visitors to specify their personal configuration preferences.

```
Sub Config_onClick
  top.right_frame.location="Config.html"
End Sub
```

Figure 28.1 shows how the `Links.html` page looks if loaded directly into the browser (when not loaded by `Default.html`).

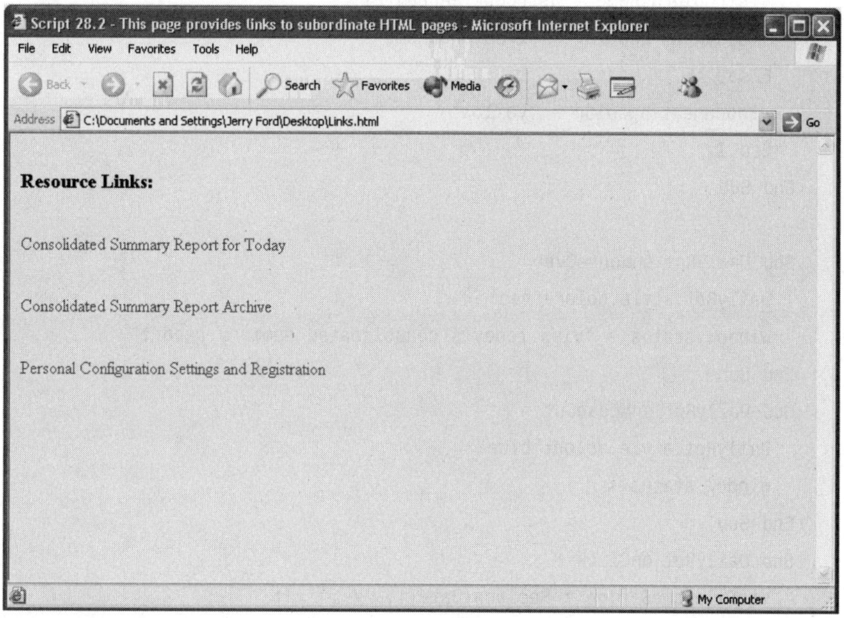

FIGURE 28.1 *The* `Links.html` *page provides access to the other pages on the Order/Inventory Reporting Web site*

The Fully Assembled Links.html Page

The fully assembled `Links.html` page is shown below. When loaded into the `left_frame` frame of the `Default.html` page, it provides a menu of links that allow the visitor to navigate the Order/Inventory Reporting Web site.

```
<HTML>
  <HEAD>
    <TITLE>Script 28.2 - This page provides links to subordinate HTML pages</TITLE>

    <SCRIPT LANGUAGE="VBScript">
    <!-- Start hiding VBScript statements
```

```
Dim strFileNameString

Sub SetBackgroundColor()
      If document.cookie <> "" Then
    astrCookieArray = Split(document.cookie,",")
    strColorScheme = astrCookieArray(2)
    document.bgColor = strColorScheme
  Else
    document.bgcolor = "yellow"
  End If
End Sub

Sub DailyRpt_onMouseOver
  DailyRpt.style.color="red"
  window.status = "View today's consolidated summary report"
End Sub
Sub DailyRpt_onMouseOut
  DailyRpt.style.color="blue"
  window.status = ""
End Sub
Sub DailyRpt_onClick
  strFileNameString = Replace(Date(), "/", "-")
  strFileNameString = strFileNameString & "_ConsolRpt.html"
  top.right_frame.location = "..\Rpts\" & strFileNameString
End Sub

Sub Archive_onMouseOver
  Archive.style.color="red"
  window.status = "View an archive of consolidated summary reports"
End Sub
Sub Archive_onMouseOut
  Archive.style.color="blue"
  window.status = ""
End Sub
Sub Archive_onClick
  top.right_frame.location="Archive.html"
End Sub
```

```
        Sub Config_onMouseOver
          Config.style.color="red"
          window.status = "Configure personal configuration settings"
        End Sub
        Sub Config_onMouseOut
          Config.style.color="blue"
          window.status = ""
        End Sub
        Sub Config_onClick
          top.right_frame.location="Config.html"
        End Sub

      ' End hiding VBScript statements -->
      </SCRIPT>
    </HEAD>

    <BODY onLoad=SetBackgroundColor()>
      <BR>
      <H3>Resource Links:</H3><P><BR>
      <DIV STYLE="color:blue;">
        <A NAME="DailyRpt"> Consolidated Summary Report for Today</A><P><BR>
        <A NAME="Archive"> Consolidated Summary Report Archive</A><P><BR>
        <A NAME="Config"> Personal Configuration Settings and Registration</A><P>
      </DIV>
    </BODY>
  </HTML>
```

Building the Welcome.html Page

The `Welcome.html` page is displayed by default in the `right_frame` frame on the `Default.html` page. However, each visitor has the option of configuring a different default page if they wish. This page provides basic information about the Order/Inventory Reporting Web site. In addition, it contains an embedded VBScript that provides a great deal of behind-the-scenes functionality, including:

- Detection of the type and version of browser being used to visit the Web site

- Redirection for visitors with browsers that are not Internet Explorer 5.0 or above
- Retrieval of configuration settings from client-side cache (from cookies)
- Redirection for first-time visitors to the Registration and Configuration Settings page

HTML for the Welcome.html Page

The HTML for the `Welcome.html` page is shown below. It uses standard HTML tags to organize and display informational content about the Web site.

```
<HTML>

  <HEAD>
    <TITLE>Script 28.1 - Order/Inventory Main Welcome Page</TITLE>
  </HEAD>

  <BODY>
    <HR>
    <UL>
      <LI>The consolidated summary report is available for online
          viewing every day at 06:00 am.</LI><P>
      <LI>You may also review a 3-month collection of archived
          consolidated summary reports.</LI><P>
      <LI>Microsoft Word copies of the consolidated summary reports
          are also available for download.</LI><P>
      <LI>If you need to review a consolidated summary report that is
          not available at this site, please contact Computer Operations
          and request that they provide you with a hard copy.</LI><P>
</UL>
    <HR>

    <B><PRE>
        Command Center Helpdesk:          Ext. 3737
        Order/Inventory Hotline:          Ext: 4000
        Other questions or concerns:      Ext: 3230
    </PRE></B>
  </BODY>
```

```
</HTML>
```

Figure 28.2 shows how the `Welcome.html` page looks when loaded directly into Internet Explorer.

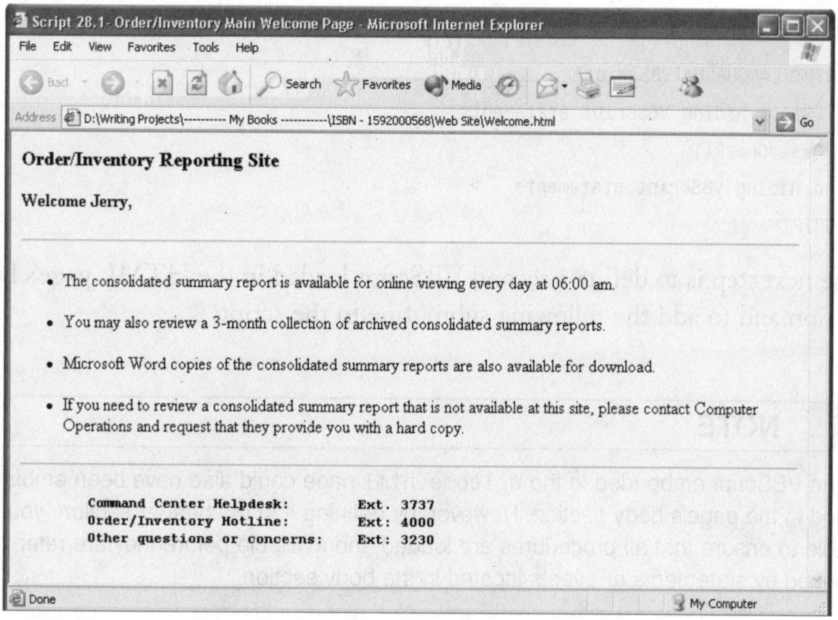

FIGURE 28.2 *The* `Welcome.html` *page greets visitors by name and provides information about the content available at the Order/Inventory Reporting Web site*

Redirection for Unsupported Browsers

Years ago, Intuit made Internet Explorer the company's standard browser. The IT staff at Intuit has done its best to ensure that all users at the company have upgraded their browsers to Internet Explorer 6.0. However, every so often somebody seems to pop up using an older version of Explorer.

William is developing the Order/Inventory Reporting Web site based on the assumption that all users will be using Internet Explorer version 5.0 or higher. However, to guard against the possibility that one or more employees at Intuit may still be using an older version of Internet Explorer, William has added a subroutine called `BrowserCheck()` to the `Welcome.html` page. This subroutine automatically redirects older browsers to an HTML page called `Browser.html`, where a message is displayed that advises visitors to upgrade to Internet Explorer 6.0 before accessing the Order/Inventory Reporting Web site.

The first step in setting up the `BrowserCheck()` subroutine is to define the following VBScript in the HTML page's BODY section. This script will then automatically execute the `BrowserCheck()` subroutine when the `Welcome.html` page is loaded.

```
<SCRIPT LANGUAGE="VBScript">
<!-- Start hiding VBScript statements
  BrowserCheck()
' End hiding VBScript statements -->
</SCRIPT>
```

The next step is to define a second VBScript loaded in the HTML page's header section and to add the following subroutine to the script:

NOTE

The VBScript embedded in the `Welcome.html` page could also have been embedded in the page's body section. However, by defining it in the header section, you are able to ensure that all procedures are loaded and available before they are referenced by statements or events located in the body section.

```
Sub BrowserCheck()

  browserName = navigator.appName

  If browserName = "Microsoft Internet Explorer" Then

    'Use the navigator appVersion property to collect information about
    'the visitor's Internet browser

    browserVersion = navigator.appVersion

    'The Instr() function searches a string for a specified set of characters
    findString = Instr(1, browserVersion, "MSIE")
```

```
    findString = findString + 5
    versionNumber = Mid(browserVersion, findString, 1)

    If versionNumber < 5 Then
      window.location = "Browser.html"
      End If
  Else
    window.location = "Browser.html"
  End If

End Sub
```

The `BrowserCheck()` subroutine begins by collecting the name of the browser being used to access the page by assigning the value of `navigator.appName` to a variable called `browserName`. Next an `If` statement is used to determine whether the `browserName` is equal to `Microsoft Internet Explorer`. If it is not, then the `right_frame` frame of the `Default.html` page is redirected to the `Browser.html` page using the `windows` object's `location` property. If the visitor is using an Internet Explorer browser the subroutine next checks to see what version is being used by assigning the value of `navigator.appVersion` to a variable called `browserVersion`. For example, the string assigned to `browserVersion` would look like `4.0 (compatible; MSIE 6.0; Windows NT 5.1; Q312461)` if the visitor was using an Internet Explorer version 6.0 browser.

Next the VBScript `Instr()` function is used to determine the location of the string `MSIE` within `browserVersion`. Once the starting character position of this string is ascertained, a value of 5 is added to it in order to calculate the position of the browser version number within the string. Next the `MID()` function is used to parse out the major version number in use. Then an `If` statement is used to determine whether the major version number is less than 5 (that is, Internet Explorer version 5.x). If it is less than 5, the `right_frame` frame of the `Default.html` page is redirected to add the `Browser.html`. Otherwise, no redirection action is taken.

Figure 28.3 shows how the Order/Inventory Reporting Web site will look when accessed by a visitor with an Internet Explorer 5.0 or higher browser.

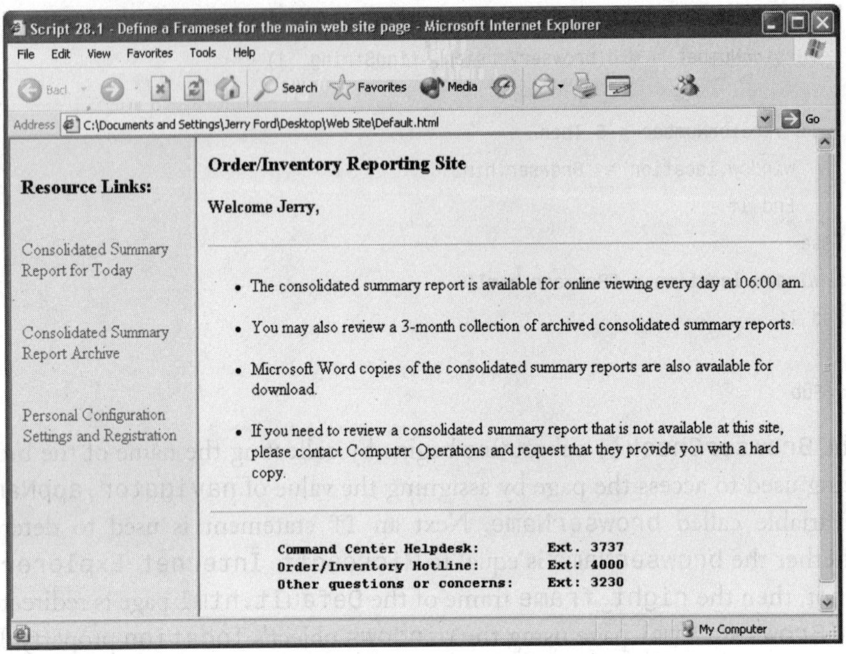
Script 28.1 - Define a Frameset for the main web site page - Microsoft Internet Explorer
File Edit View Favorites Tools Help
Search Favorites Media
Address C:\Documents and Settings\Jerry Ford\Desktop\Web Site\Default.html
Go
Resource Links:
Consolidated Summary Report for Today
Consolidated Summary Report Archive
Personal Configuration Settings and Registration
Order/Inventory Reporting Site
Welcome Jerry,
The consolidated summary report is available for online viewing every day at 06:00 am.
You may also review a 3-month collection of archived consolidated summary reports.
Microsoft Word copies of the consolidated summary reports are also available for download.
If you need to review a consolidated summary report that is not available at this site, please contact Computer Operations and request that they provide you with a hard copy.
Command Center Helpdesk: Ext. 3737
Order/Inventory Hotline: Ext: 4000
Other questions or concerns: Ext: 3230
My Computer

FIGURE 28.3 *By default, all visitors to the Order/Inventory Reporting Web site will see the* `Links.html` *and* `Welcome.html` *pages*

Retrieving a VBScript Cookie

The last task to perform in creating the `Welcome.html` page is to add logic that extracts visitor preferences from a cookie stored on their computers. This cookie is built and stored on the visitors' computers when they visit the site's Registration and Configuration Settings page. If a cookie for the Order/Inventory Reporting Web site is found on the visitor's computer, its contents are retrieved and parsed out. Otherwise, the `right_frame` frame on the `Default.html` page is redirected to the Registration and Configuration Settings page so that the visitor can choose configuration settings.

This process will be implemented as a subroutine called `Cookie_Check()`. The first step in setting up this process is to modify the VBScript located in the page's body section by inserting a call to the `Cookie_Check()` subroutine, as shown below.

```
<SCRIPT LANGUAGE="VBScript">
<!-- Start hiding VBScript statements
```

```
  BrowserCheck()
  Cookie_Check()
' End hiding VBScript statements -->
</SCRIPT>
```

Once this is done, you can add the code for the `Cookie_Check()` subroutine to the VBScript defined in the `Welcome.html` page's header section.

```
Dim strFileNameString
Function Cookie_Check()

  If document.cookie <> "" Then
    astrCookieArray = Split(document.cookie,",")
    strUserName = Mid(astrCookieArray(0), 8)
    strDefaultView = astrCookieArray(1)
    strColorScheme = astrCookieArray(2)

    If strDefaultView = "Archive" Then
      window.location = "Archive.html"
    End If
    If strDefaultView = "Welcome" Then
      document.write("<H3>Order/Inventory Reporting Site</H3><P>")
      document.write("<B>Welcome " & strUserName & ",</B><P>")
    End If
    If strDefaultView = "Daily" Then
      strFileNameString = Replace(Date(), "/", "-")
      strConSolRptName = strConsolFolder & "\" & strFileNameString & _
        "_ConsolSumRpt.txt"
      strFileNameString = strFileNameString & "_ConsolRpt.html"
      window.location = strFileNameString
    End If
  Else
    window.location = "Config.html"
  End If
End Function
```

To determine whether the visitor's computer has a cookie belonging to the Order/Inventory Reporting Web site, the subroutine begins by examining the value of the `document` object's `cookie` property. If it is blank, then the right_frame frame of the Default.html page is automatically redirected to the Config.html page. If the cookie is not blank, then the VBScript Split() function is used to assign the cookie contents to an array called astrCookieArray.

The first seven characters of the cookie specify its name and the equal sign. To extract the visitor's name from the cookie, the Mid() function assigns all the characters beginning at character position 8 of the first array element to a variable called strUserName. Next the visitor's preferred default page is extracted by assigning the value of astrCookieArray(1) to strDefaultView. Then the visitor's preferred color scheme is extracted and assigned to strColorScheme.

A series of three If statements then executes. The first If statement checks to see whether strDefaultView is equal to Archive. If it is, then the right_frame frame on the Default.html page is redirected to ..\Reports\Archive.html. From the visitor's point of view, it will look as if the Archive.html page was automatically loaded (the Welcome.html page is not displayed).

The second If statement checks to see whether strDefaultView is equal to Welcome. If it is, then a header message is written to the top of the Welcome.html page followed by a message that greets the user by name using the value stored in the strUserName variable. Once this is done, the rest of the content to be displayed on the Welcome.html page will be written as specified within its HTML tags.

Finally, the last If statement checks to see whether strDefaultView is equal to Daily. If it is, then the Config.html page is automatically loaded into the right_frame frame of the Default.html page.

The Fully Assembled Welcome.html Page

The fully assembled Welcome.html page is shown on the following page. When loaded into the right_frame frame of the Default.html page, the Welcome.html page greets the visitor by name and displays information about the Order/Inventory Reporting Web site. However, if this is the first time that the visitor has come to the Web site, the VBScript embedded in the Welcome.html page will redirect the visitor to the Config.html page. Finally, if the visitor is not using the correct version of Internet Explorer when accessing the Web site, a VBScript embedded within the Welcome.html page redirects the visitor to the

Browser.html page, where the visitor is advised which version of Internet Explorer to use when viewing the content provided by the Web site.

```
<HTML>
  <HEAD>
    <TITLE>Script 28.1 - Order/Inventory Main Welcome Page</TITLE>

    <SCRIPT LANGUAGE="VBScript">
    <!-- Start hiding VBScript statements

      Dim strFileNameString

      'Define a function to check for the cookie and use it in the
      'welcome message if found
      Function Cookie_Check()

        If document.cookie <> "" Then
          astrCookieArray = Split(document.cookie,",")
          strUserName = Mid(astrCookieArray(0), 8)
          strDefaultView = astrCookieArray(1)
          strColorScheme = astrCookieArray(2)

          If strDefaultView = "Archive" Then
            window.location = "..\Rpts\Archive.html"
          End If
          If strDefaultView = "Welcome" Then
            document.write("<H3>Order/Inventory Reporting Site</H3><P>")
            document.write("<B>Welcome " & strUserName & ",</B><P>")
          End If
          If strDefaultView = "Daily" Then
            strFileNameString = Replace(Date(), "/", "-")
            strConSolRptName = strConsolFolder & "\" & strFileNameString & _
              "_ConsolSumRpt.txt"
            strFileNameString = strFileNameString & "_ConsolRpt.html"
            window.location = strFileNameString
          End If
        Else
          window.location = "Config.html"
```

```
        End If
      End Function


      Sub BrowserCheck()

        browserName = navigator.appName

        If browserName = "Microsoft Internet Explorer" Then

          'Use the navigator appVersion property to collect information about
          'the visitor's Internet browser

          browserVersion = navigator.appVersion

          'The Instr() function searches a string for a specified set of charac-
ters
          findString = Instr(1, browserVersion, "MSIE")

            findString = findString + 5
            versionNumber = Mid(browserVersion, findString, 1)

            If versionNumber < 5 Then
              window.location = "Browser.html"
            End If
        Else
          window.location = "Browser.html"
        End If

      End Sub

    ' End hiding VBScript statements -->
    </SCRIPT>
  </HEAD>
  <BODY>

    <SCRIPT LANGUAGE="VBScript">
    <!-- Start hiding VBScript statements
```

```
    BrowserCheck()
    Cookie_Check()
  ' End hiding VBScript statements -->
  </SCRIPT>

  <HR>
  <UL>
    <LI>The consolidated summary report is available for online
        viewing every day at 06:00 am.</LI><P>
    <LI>You may also review a 3-month collection of archived
        consolidated summary reports.</LI><P>
    <LI>Microsoft Word copies of the consolidated summary reports
        are also available for download.</LI><P>
    <LI>If you need to review a consolidated summary report that is
        not available at this site, please contact Computer Operations
       and request that they provide you with a hard copy.</LI><P>
  </UL>
  <HR>

  <B><PRE>
      Command Center Helpdesk:         Ext. 3737
      Order/Inventory Hotline:         Ext: 4000
      Other questions or concerns:     Ext: 3230
  </PRE></B>

 </BODY>
</HTML>
```

Creating the Browser.html Page

The HTML that comprises the `browser.html` page, shown on the following page, is straightforward. It consists only of HTML tags and does not contain any embedded VBScripts. Its sole purpose is to advise visitors who are not using Internet Explorer version 5 or above to return using the proper browser, preferably Internet Explorer 6.0.

```
<HTML>

  <HEAD>
    <TITLE>This page is seen by visitors that are not using IE 5.0 or
above</TITLE>
  </HEAD>

  <BODY>

    <BR><BR><BR>

    <DIV STYLE="text-align:center;">
      <H3>Sorry, but to access the Order/Inventory Reporting web site
        you must use Internet Explorer version 5 or higher</H3>
    </DIV>

    <BR><BR>

    <DIV STYLE="text-align:center;">
      Please upgrade to Internet Explorer 6.0 or access this site from a
      different computer.
    </DIV>

  </BODY>

</HTML>
```

Figure 28.4 shows how the `browser.html` page is displayed when viewed by an earlier version of Internet Explorer.

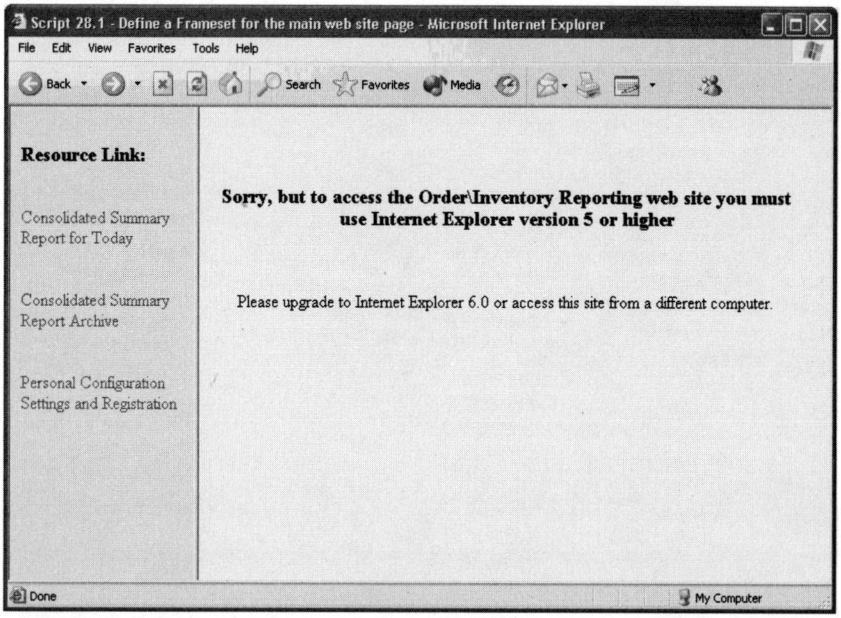

FIGURE 28.4 *The* `Browser.html` *page advises visitors to use Internet Explorer version 5.0 or higher*

Summary

In this chapter, you observed as William began work on the Order/Inventory Reporting Web site. Specifically, he developed the site's `Default.html` page using a frameset composed of two frames to display a menu of links and the content of the currently selected link. In addition to the HTML required to create the HTML pages, William embedded a number of VBScripts in order to add graphical effects to the Web site. VBScripts were also used to retrieve visitor configuration settings and to manage the loading of HTML pages into the frames.

Chapter 29

Building the Registration and Configuration Settings Page

In this chapter, William needs to develop an HTML page for the Reporting Web site that collects information about visitors and their configuration preferences. To accomplish this task, William will define an HTML form and use an embedded VBScript to validate its contents. Ultimately, the page will save each visitor's name and configuration preferences in a cookie stored locally on the visitors' computers.

Cookie Basics

Using global variables, you can store and reference values during the life of a script. However, these values are lost when the script ends, and they must be recreated the next time it runs. In order to build an interactive site and to provide a mechanism that allows visitors to specify personalized configuration settings, you need a way to store data that will outlive the lifetime of your scripts or a visitor's session at your Web site. One way to provide for *persistent storage* (the ability to reference data provided by visitors when they return to your Web site) is to use cookies.

A *cookie* is a text string that your Web site can store on visitors' computers. Cookies have been around since the early days of the Internet and were designed to provide a way of storing small amounts of data on visitors' computers. Today, powerful Web servers with back-end databases are capable of storing and retrieving enormous amounts of information about visitors, their preferences, and their actions. For a Web site like the Reporting Web site, where information is available for viewing but no actual data collection or processing is performed, using a back-end database to store a few pieces of information about visitors and their preferences is overkill. A much simpler solution is to use cookies.

Cookies provide an efficient means of storing all kinds of information. For example, using cookies you can:

- Store persistent data
- Provide a means of differentiating between visitors
- Provide a personalized experience
- Track user activity

- Store user preferences
- Store information about a user

A cookie is a text string that you can store in the browser's memory. By default, cookies expire when the visitor closes the browser. However, by setting an expiration date when you create a cookie, you can instruct the browser to retain your cookie. Browsers accommodate this request by saving a text copy of the cookie on their computer's local hard drive.

NOTE

Modern browsers provide users with the ability to block cookies. However, most users find it inconvenient or impractical to do so. It is important to understand that your scripts cannot actually store a cookie on the hard drives of the people that visit your Web site. Instead, you store the cookie in the browser's memory, and the browser decides whether or not to store the cookie on its computer's hard drive, based on browser configuration settings specified by its owner.

Cookie Storage

The way that cookies are stored on client computers depends on the type and version of the browser used to store the cookie, as well as the operating system being used to run the browser. For example, Netscape Communicator stores its cookies as text strings in one large text file located by default in `C:\Programs Files\Netscape\Users\`*`Username`*`\cookies.txt`. Internet Explorer, on the other hand, stores cookies as individual text files. On computers running Windows 95, 98, or Me, Internet Explorer stores cookie files by default in `C:\Windows\Cookies`. On computers running Windows 2000 or XP, Internet Explorer stores cookie text files by default in `C:\Documents and Settings\`*`Username`*`\Cookies`.

NOTE

A truly detailed discussion of cookies is beyond the scope of this book. If you are interested in learning more than the basics presented in this chapter, visit **http://www.cookiecentral.com**.

Internet Explorer is the browser used by employees at Intuit. This browser stores all its cookies as individual text files, as demonstrated in Figure 29.1.

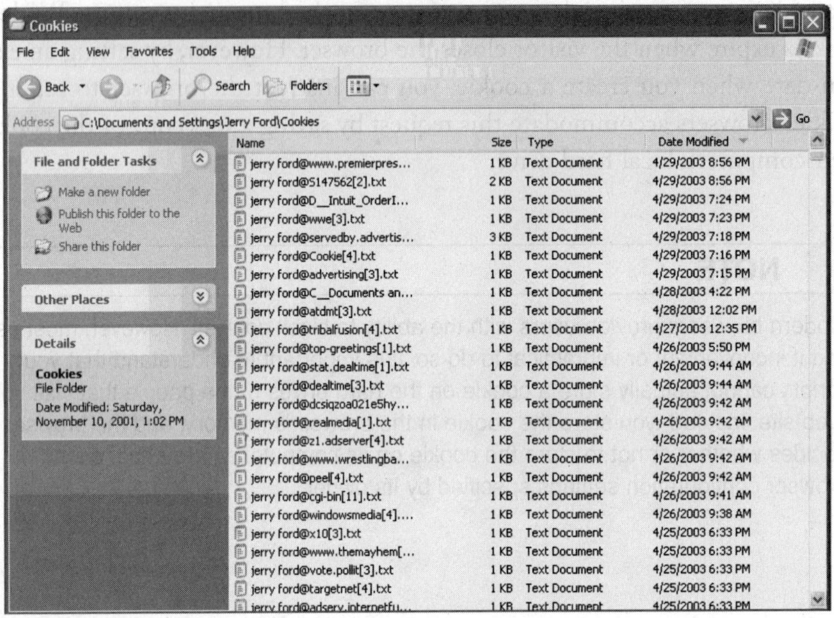

FIGURE 29.1 *Internet Explorer stores cookies as individual text files and associates them with specific individuals*

As you can see in Figure 29.1, Internet Explorer associates the visitor's username with each cookie when storing it. It does this to accommodate the possibility that multiple users may share the same computer. However, the usernames are never returned to the Web site that created the cookie; only the actual data stored in the cookie is returned (less the expiration date).

Cookies can be up to 4KB in size. All major browsers support cookies, including Netscape Communicator and Internet Explorer. Both of these browsers limit the number of cookies that can be stored on a computer to 300. The maximum number of cookies that a Web site can store on a visitor's computer is 20. In the event that either of these two thresholds is exceeded, the browser has to delete existing cookies to make room as new ones arrive. As a result of these limitations, cookies are limited to a collective maximum size of 1.2MB (per user) on any computer.

Cookies and Security

By default, cookies can only be accessed from the site that created them. This means that other Web sites will not be able to read your cookies off of a computer that has been used to visit your Web site. Likewise, you will only be able to retrieve cookies that your Web site was responsible for creating. Therefore, cookies can be seen as being somewhat secure. However, because cookies are stored as plain text files on client computers, they are freely visible to anyone with local access to them. This makes cookies inappropriate for storing sensitive pieces of information, such as credit card and social security numbers. Another limitation of cookies is that they are stored locally on the computer. If the visitor returns later to the Web site using another computer, there is no way to reassociate the data previously provided by the visitor. The data will have to be collected again if the user wants to reestablish her configuration settings.

Cookie Syntax

Your VBScripts can create and retrieve cookies using the `document` object's `cookie` property. Cookies consist of one or more parameters, each of which is separated by a semicolon (`;`). The syntax used to create cookies is shown below.

```
name=value [;expires=ExpDate] [;domain=DomName] [;path=PathName] [;secure]
```

`Name` specifies the name of the cookie. `Value` identifies the string of data to be stored by the cookie. `ExpDate` specifies a date that determines how long the cookie remains valid. `DomName` specifies an alternative host name from which the cookie may be accessed. `Path` specifies the top-level folder on the Web server from which cookies created by the Web server can be retrieved. `Secure` is a Boolean value that when set equal to `True` requires an `HTTPS` connection in order to create the cookie. Of all these parameters, only `name` and `value` are required when creating a cookie.

Creating and Retrieving a Simple Cookie

The following example demonstrates how to create a cookie named `VisitorName` and assign it a value of `Jerry`.

```
document.cookie = "VisitorName=Jerry"
```

Once created, the cookie can be retrieved, as shown below.

```
strVisitorName = document.cookie
```

If the visitor's computer does not have the cookie, an empty string is returned. In the previous example, the string that makes up the cookie is assigned to a variable called `strVisitorName`. Once the cookie is retrieved, you may use any of VBScript's string manipulation functions to parse out the data stored in the cookie.

Creating Persistent Cookies

Unless you explicitly specify an expiration date, your cookies will be deleted as soon as your visitors close their browsers. To make a cookie persistent, set its expiration date to a value that will last longer than the current browser session.

The following example demonstrates how to create a cookie that stores a visitor's name in a cookie that will persist for one year.

```
dtmExpDate = Weekdayname(DatePart("w",Date())) & ", "

dtmDayValue = DatePart("d",Date())

If Len(dtmDayValue) = 1 Then
  dtmDayValue = "0" & dtmDayValue
End If

dtmExpDate = dtmExpDate & dtmDayValue & "-" _
  & Monthname(DatePart("m",Date(),1) ) & "-" _
  & DatePart("yyyy",Date()) + 1 & " 00:00:00 GMT"

strCookie = "VisitorName=Jerry" & "; expires=" & dtmExpDate
```

The first statement creates a variable named `dtmExpDate` by retrieving the current date using the `Date()` function. It then uses the `DatePart()` function to extract a numeric value representing the day of the week. This value is then fed to the `Weekdayname()` function in order to determine the name of the current day of the week (in this example, the current day of the week is Friday). A `", "` string is then appended to the name of the day of the week.

The next statement retrieves a numeric value representing the current month using the `Date()` and `DatePart()` functions. The `Len()` function is then used to determine whether this value is one or two digits long. If it is just one digit long (the month is between January and September), a zero is appended to the front of it to create a two-digit value.

Next the value of `dtmExpDate` is modified by appending the two-digit month value to it followed by the "-" string and then the name of the current month (`Monthname(DatePart("m",Date(),1))`). Then another "-" string and a numeric value representing the next year (by adding 1 to the current year) is appended, followed by the " 00:00:00 GMT" string.

The end result is a cookie string that expires one year from the day that it is created. For example, if today is May 2, 2003, the cookie string would resolve to:

```
VisitorName=Jerry; expires=Friday, 02-May-2004 00:00:00 GMT
```

NOTE

The expiration date is not returned when you later retrieve the cookie's contents.

Specifying Valid Host Names

The domain parameter provides the ability to specify what host names on your site have access to your cookie. By default, the host name of the Web server that creates the cookies is automatically assigned. Using the `domain` parameter, you can allow other domains that belong to you to access your cookie. For example, if you created a cookie on a server at **http://www.intuitmechanical.com**, it would, by default, only be accessible from that site. However, if the company had a second site, such as **http://sales.intuitmechanical.com**, the cookie would not be accessible from this site. Using the `domain` parameter, you can make the cookie available on both sites, as demonstrated below. Note that the leading dot (in `.intuitmechanical.com`) is required.

```
document.cookie = "string=" & strCookieString & ";domain=.intuitmechanical.com"
```

NOTE

Because Intuit only has one Web server, William does not need to include this parameter when creating the Order/Inventory Reporting Web site's cookie.

Determining Which Folders Have Cookie Access

The browser's default behavior allows cookies to be accessed by pages located within the same folder as the page that created the cookie. The browser also allows the cookie to be accessed by any page that resides in subfolders of that folder. However, access from other folders on the Web server is automatically blocked.

For example, suppose the following folder structure was in place on the Intuit Web server:

- `\Intuit\OrderInventory\Reporting\HTML`
- `\Intuit\OrderInventory\Reporting\Rpts`
- `\Intuit\OrderInventory\Reporting\Rpts\May`
- `\Intuit\OrderInventory\Reporting\HTML\June`

If you had an HTML page located in the `\Intuit\OrderInventory\Reporting\Rpts` folder that created a cookie, that cookie would be accessible by other HTML pages located in that folder, as well as by HTML pages located in its two subfolders. However, the cookie would not be accessible from the `\Intuit\OrderInventory\Reporting\HTML` folder.

Using the `path` parameter, you can specify a higher-level folder from which the cookie should be accessible. For example, the following statement creates a cookie that can be accessed from any HTML page located in any folder on the Intuit Web site (or Web server).

```
document.cookie = "string=" & strCookieString & ";expires=" & dtmExpDate &
";path=/"
```

Requiring Secure Cookie Access

The final cookie parameter is the `secure` parameter. The `secure` parameter is a Boolean value that determines whether or not a cookie can be created when a secure protocol (such as `HTTPS`) is not being used. When set equal to `True`, the cookie is saved only if `HTTPS` is in use. When set to `False`, the cookie is saved regardless of whether `HTTP` or `HTTPS` is being used to connect to the Web site. For example, the following statement creates a cookie only if the visitor has established an `HTTPS` session to the Web site.

```
document.cookie = "string=" & strCookieString & ";expires=" & dtmExpDate & "; True"
```

Deleting Cookies

Deleting a cookie is a two-step process. First, you must create a new cookie string and set its value to null. Next, before saving the cookie, you must assign it an expiration date that is in the past. If you skip the first step and simply resave an existing cookie using an expired expiration date, your cookie will eventually be deleted (when the visitor closes the browser). However, if the visitor leaves your Web site and later returns without having closed his browser in the meantime, your cookie will still exist. By setting it equal to null and then saving it, you ensure that if the visitor returns without having first closed his browser, when you retrieve your cookie again, it will appear as if it was deleted (it will be returned a blank string).

Verifying Your Cookie's Creation

There are any number of reasons why your cookie might not get created on a visitor's computer. For example, the visitor may have configured his browser to reject cookies or to seek approval before storing one. The visitor may run software such as a personal firewall on his computer, which prohibits the collection of cookies. Regardless of the reasons, you cannot always count on your cookie being created as expected, especially when your Web site is connected to the Internet.

One way to verify that your cookie was created is to try and retrieve it immediately after creating it. If you can do this, then you'll know that you were successful in creating the cookie. If, however, you find that your cookie was not accepted, you'll need to take some type of action. For example, you might refuse to display any content except a message insisting that the visitor enable the acceptance of cookies on her browser. Alternatively, you might use default settings in place of user-specified settings in order to allow visitors to access your site without requiring them to supply you with any information. Fortunately for William, all employees' browsers at Intuit should have cookie acceptance enabled, eliminating the requirement of testing whether or not his cookies are created.

Collecting Information Using HTML Forms

The first step in creating a cookie for this project is to determine what information you wish to store in it. In the case of Intuit, William has decided to create an HTML form to collect information from visitors to the Web site. Once visitors have supplied the site's required configuration settings, a VBScript embedded within the HTML page will validate that the form has been correctly filled out and then save the visitor's personal configuration settings in a cookie. Figure 29.2 shows the HTML form that William will be creating.

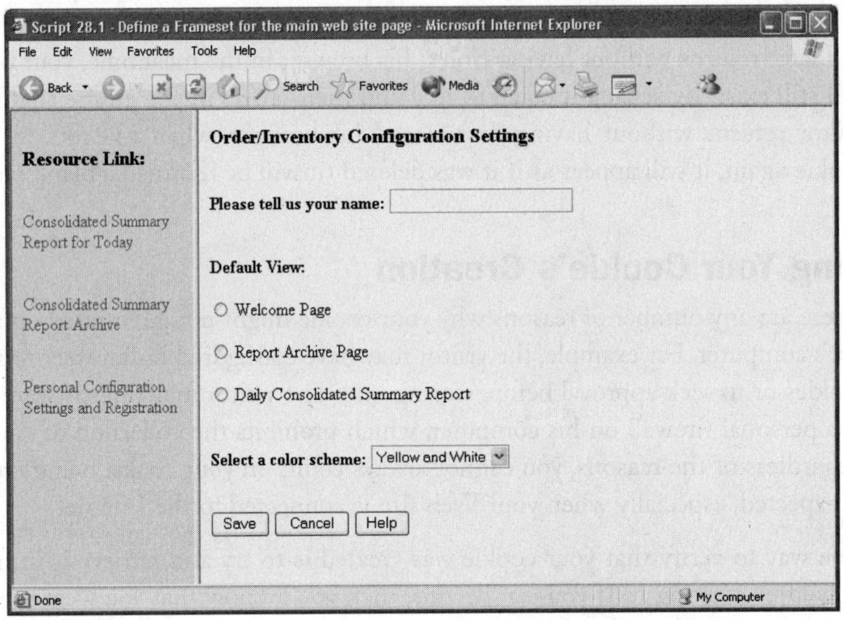

FIGURE 29.2 *Using a form to collect each visitor's name and personal preferences*

HTML for the Config.html Page

The HTML required to build this form is shown below. Note that each form element is assigned an explicit `Name` value in order to make it easy for the VBScript to access and validate the contents of individual form elements.

```
<HTML>
  <HEAD>
    <TITLE>Script 27.1 - The Order/Inventory Configuration Settings page</TITLE>
  </HEAD>

  <BODY>
```

```
    <H3>Order/Inventory Configuration Settings</H3>

    <BR>

    <FORM NAME="siteForm">
      <B>Please tell us your name:</B> <INPUT NAME="userName" TYPE="text" SIZE="25"
MAXLENGTH="40"><P><BR>
      <B>Default View:</B><P>
      <INPUT NAME="siteRadio" TYPE="radio" VALUE="Welcome"> Welcome Page<P>
      <INPUT NAME="siteRadio" TYPE="radio" VALUE="Archive"> Report Archive Page<P>
      <INPUT NAME="siteRadio" TYPE="radio" VALUE="Daily"> Daily Consolidated
Summary Report<P><BR>

      <P><B>Select a color scheme: </B>
      <SELECT NAME="siteList">
        <OPTION SELECTED VALUE="Yellow">Yellow and White
        <OPTION VALUE="LightBlue">Blue and White
        <OPTION VALUE="LightGreen">Green and White
        <OPTION VALUE="LightGrey">Grey and White
        <OPTION VALUE="Pink">Pink and White
      </SELECT></P><BR>

      <INPUT NAME="SaveButton" TYPE="button" VALUE=" Save ">
      <INPUT NAME="CancelButton" TYPE="reset" VALUE=" Cancel ">
      <INPUT NAME="HelpButton" TYPE="button" VALUE=" Help ">
    </FORM>
  </BODY>
</HTML>
```

The last form element on the HTML page defines a drop-down list. Figure 29.3 shows how the contents provided by this list will appear when visitors access them.

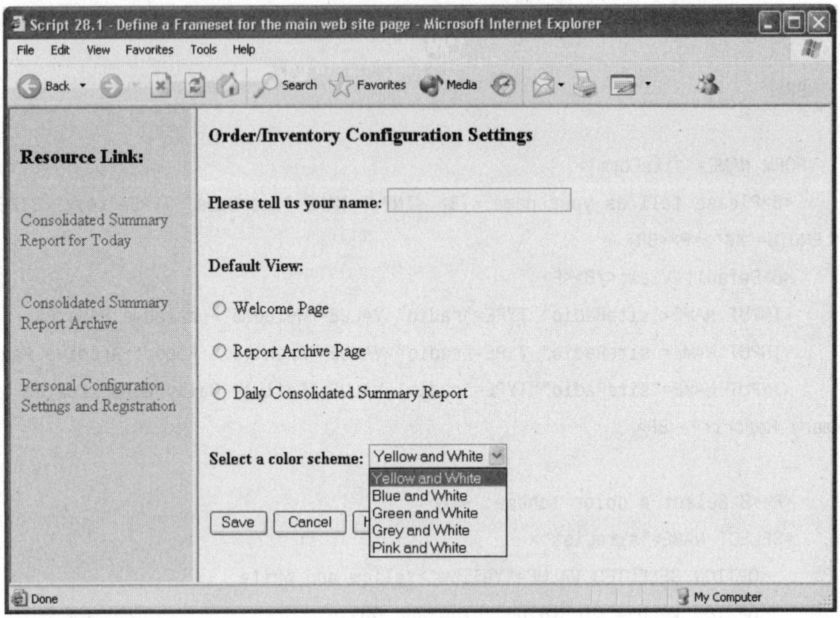

FIGURE 29.3 *Using a drop-down list to provide a list of choices without cluttering the display area*

Using VBScript to Process Form Contents

Once the form is created, you can begin work on the VBScript that will be embedded within it. This script will perform two main tasks. The first task is to validate that the form has been correctly filled out. The second task is to store the contents of the form in a cookie.

The form contains a button at the bottom of the HTML page named `SaveButton`. When clicked, the button should initiate a subroutine called `ProcessSettings()`, as shown below.

```
<INPUT NAME="SaveButton" TYPE="button" VALUE=" Save " onClick="ProcessSettings()">
```

The `ProcessSettings()` subroutine will examine each form element to ensure that the visitor has provided the required information.

Form Validation

To prepare the HTML page for its VBScript, William first embeds the opening and closing <SCRIPT> and </SCRIPT> tags in the page's header section. Next he defines the following variables and constants:

```
Option Explicit
Dim strRadioSelected, intCounter, strConfigSettings, strRadioSelection
Const cTitleBarMsg = "Order/Inventory Configuration Settings Help Page"
```

Once the above steps have been completed, William creates the `ProcessSettings()` function, as shown below.

```
Function ProcessSettings()

  If Len(document.siteForm.userName.value) < 1 Then
    MsgBox "You must provide your name to continue.", , cTitleBarMsg
    Exit Function
  End If

  strRadioSelected = "False"

  For intCounter = 0 To siteForm.siteRadio.length - 1
    If siteForm.siteRadio(intCounter).Checked = "True" Then
      strRadioSelection = siteForm.siteRadio(intCounter).value
      strRadioSelected = "True"
    End If
  Next

    If strRadioSelected = "False" Then
      MsgBox "You must specify your preferred default page.", , cTitleBarMsg
      Exit Function
    End If

    strConfigSettings = document.siteForm.userName.value &  "," & _
      strRadioSelection & "," & siteForm.siteList.value

    BakeTheCookie(strConfigSettings)

    top.left_frame.document.bgcolor = siteForm.siteList.value
```

```
    MsgBox " The following configuration settings have been saved:" & _
      vbCrLf & vbCrLf & _
      "Name = " & document.siteForm.userName.value & vbCrLf & _
      "Default View = " & strRadioSelection & vbCrLf & _
      "Color Scheme = " & siteForm.siteList.value, ,cTitleBarMsg

End Function
```

The function begins by determining whether or not the visitor entered his name in the form's text field (`document.siteForm.userName.value`). If a name was not supplied, the pop-up message shown in Figure 29.4 is displayed and the `Exit Function` statement is used to terminate the function's execution.

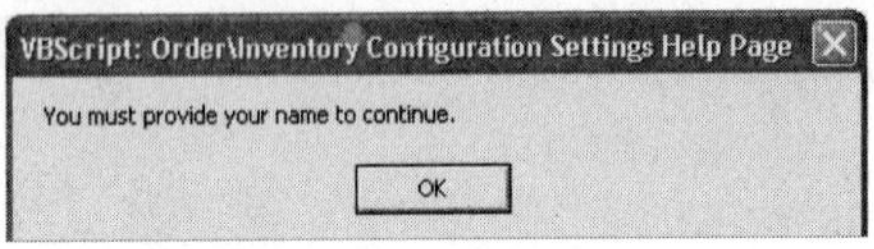

FIGURE 29.4 *Using pop-up dialog boxes to interact with visitors to ensure that they have provided required information*

If the visitor did supply his name, the function next checks to see if one of the three View options was selected by examining the value of `siteForm.siteRadio(intCounter).value`. If one of the radio buttons was selected, its value is then assigned to a variable called `strRadioSelection`. Otherwise, the pop-up dialog box shown in Figure 29.5 is displayed and the function stops executing.

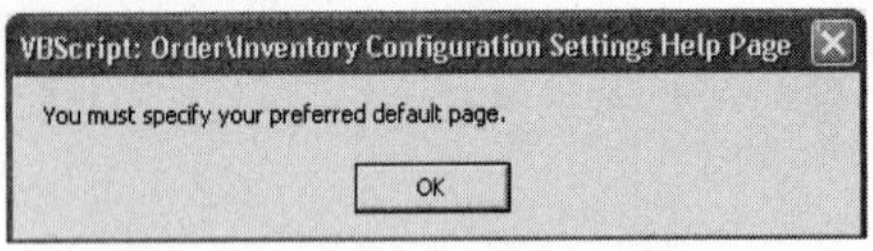

FIGURE 29.5 *If a radio button is not selected, a dialog box appears*

Finally, a string is created that contains the values specified by each of the form's elements. This string is then assigned to a variable called `strConfigSettings`. Next the `BakeTheCookie()` function is called and passed the string that was just created by the ProcessSettings() function. When control is returned from the BakeTheCookie() function, the value assigned to top.left_frame.document.bgcolor is set equal to the color specified to siteForm.siteList.value. The end result is that the background color displayed in the Default.html page's left_frame frame is immediately changed to reflect the visitor's preference. Lastly, a pop-up dialog box is displayed, informing the visitor that his configuration settings have been saved. Figure 29.6 shows the pop-up dialog box that is displayed when the visitor's settings are successfully collected.

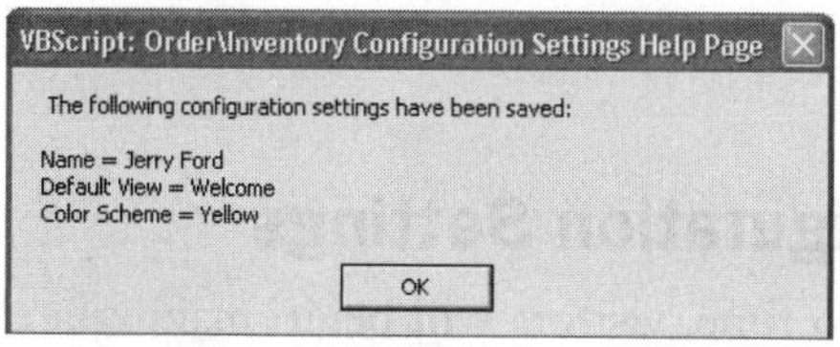

FIGURE 29.6 *Displaying the configuration settings specified by the visitor*

Baking a Cookie

The BakeTheCookie() function formats the test string that makes the cookie and then uses the document object's cookie property to save the cookie.

```
Function BakeTheCookie(strCookieString)

  Dim dtmExpDate, strCookie

  dtmExpDate = Weekdayname(DatePart("w",Date())) & ", " _
    & FormatDate(DatePart("d",Date())) & "-" _
    & Monthname(DatePart("m",Date(),1) + 1) & "-" _
    & DatePart("yyyy",Date()) _
    & " 00:00:00 GMT"
  strCookie = "string=" & strCookieString & ";expires=" & dtmExpDate
  document.cookie = strCookie
End Function
```

Formatting a Cookie Expiration Date

One additional function is required to complete the HTML page's embedded VBScript. It is named `FormatDate()`. Its job is to pad the beginning of the `dtmInputDate` with a zero if it is only one character long.

```
Function FormatDate(dtmInputDate)
  If Len(dtmInputDate) = 1 Then
    dtmInputDate = "0" & dtmInputDate
  End If
  FormatDate = dtmInputDate
End Function
```

Canceling a Change to Configuration Settings

William anticipates that from time to time, visitors will begin making a change on the Registration and Configuration Settings page, and after thinking about it, they'll decide not to save their changes. To help make things easier for these visitors, William has added the `CancelButton_onClick()` subroutine to the page's embedded VBScript.

```
Sub CancelButton_onClick()
  history.back()
End Sub
```

This function's name was created by appending `onClick` to the name assigned to the Cancel button. By naming the subroutine this way, William automatically associates it with the `CancelButton` button, thus facilitating its automatic execution when the button's `onClick` event occurs. Once executed, the subroutine uses the `history` object's `back()` method to reload the previously displayed URL back into the `right_frame` frame on the `Default.html` page.

Displaying Help

In order to help make the Registration and Configuration Settings page easier to work with, William has chosen to provide visitors with a help option. The idea is to provide visitors with instructions on how to properly complete the form when they click on the Help button. In order to provide this feature, William plans to use the VBScript `MsgBox()` function. But first, he must modify the `<INPUT>` tag associated with the button, as shown below.

```
<INPUT NAME="HelpButton" TYPE="button" VALUE=" Help " onClick="DisplayHelpDialog()">
```

William's modification causes the tag's `onClick` event to trigger the execution of the `DisplayHelpDialog()` subroutine, which is shown below.

```
Sub DisplayHelpDialog()
  MsgBox "All information collected by this form is required." & vbCrLf & _
    vbCrLf & vbCrLf & vbTab & "* Please tell us your name: " & _
    "- Enter your first and last name." & vbCrLf & vbCrLf & _
    vbTab & "* Default View: - Select the page that you want loaded " & _
    "by default when you visit this web site." & vbCrLf & vbCrLf & _
    vbTab & "* Select a color scheme: - Select your background and " & _
    "foreground color preferences." & vbCrLf & vbCrLf & _
    vbTab & "* Save - Click on this button to save your configuration" & _
    "settings." & vbCrLf & vbCrLf & vbTab & _
    "* Cancel - Click on this button to return to the previous page "& _
    "without saving your configuration changes." & vbCrLf & vbCrLf & _
    vbTab & "* Help - Displays this help message.", , cTitleBarMsg

End Sub
```

The `DisplayHelpDialog()` subroutine makes use of the `vbCrLf` and `vbTab` constants to improve the presentation of its content. When executed, this subroutine displays the pop-up dialog box shown in Figure 29.7.

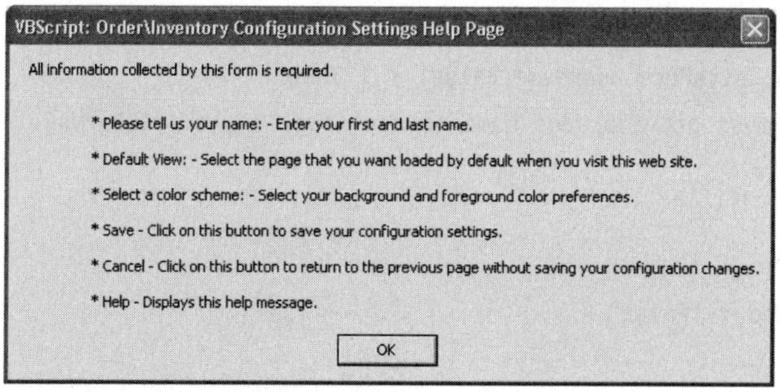

FIGURE 29.7 *Using the VBScript* `MsgBox()` *function to provide visitors with instructions on how to properly fill out the form*

The Fully Assembled Welcome.html Page

The fully assembled `Welcome.html` page is shown below. When loaded into the `right_frame` frame of the `Default.html` page, the `Welcome.html` page provides visitors to the Order/Inventory Reporting Web site with the ability to configure personal settings for the site. Using an embedded VBScript, the page will determine whether the form has been correctly filled out and, if appropriate, will store the visitor's configuration settings in a cookie.

```
<HTML>
  <HEAD>
    <TITLE>Script 27.1 - The Order/Inventory Configuration Settings page</TITLE>

    <SCRIPT LANGUAGE="VBScript">
    <!-- Start hiding VBScript statements

      Option Explicit

      Dim strRadioSelected, intCounter, strConfigSettings, strRadioSelection

      Const cTitleBarMsg = "Configuration Settings Help Page"

      Function ProcessSettings()

        If Len(document.siteForm.userName.value) < 1 Then
          MsgBox "You must provide your name to continue.", , cTitleBarMsg
          Exit Function
        End If

        strRadioSelected = "False"

        For intCounter = 0 To siteForm.siteRadio.length - 1
          If siteForm.siteRadio(intCounter).Checked = "True" Then
            strRadioSelection = siteForm.siteRadio(intCounter).value
            strRadioSelected = "True"
          End If
        Next
```

```
  If strRadioSelected = "False" Then
    MsgBox "You must specify your preferred default page.", , cTitleBarMsg
    Exit Function
  End If

  strConfigSettings = document.siteForm.userName.value &  "," & _
    strRadioSelection & "," & siteForm.siteList.value

  BakeTheCookie(strConfigSettings)

  top.left_frame.document.bgcolor = siteForm.siteList.value

  MsgBox "The following configuration settings have been saved:" & _
    vbCrLf & vbCrLf & _
    "Name = " & document.siteForm.userName.value & vbCrLf & _
    "Default View = " & strRadioSelection & vbCrLf & _
    "Color Scheme = " & siteForm.siteList.value, ,cTitleBarMsg

End Function

Sub DisplayHelpDialog()
  MsgBox "All information collected by this form is required." & _
    vbCrLf & vbCrLf & vbCrLf & _
    vbTab & "* Please tell us your name: - Enter your first and " & _
    "last name." & vbCrLf & vbCrLf  vbTab & _
    "* Default View: - Select the page that you want loaded by " & _
    "default when you visit this web site." & vbCrLf & vbCrLf & _
    vbTab & "* Select a color scheme: - Select your background " & _
    "and foreground color preferences." & vbCrLf & vbCrLf vbTab & _
    "* Save - Click on this button to save your configuration " & _
    "settings." & vbCrLf & vbCrLf & vbTab & _
    "* Cancel - Click on this button to return to the previous " & _
    "page without saving your configuration changes." & vbCrLf & _
    vbCrLf & vbTab & _
    "* Help - Displays this help message.", , cTitleBarMsg

End Sub
```

```
Sub CancelButton_onClick()
  history.back()
  End Sub

  Function BakeTheCookie(strCookieString)

    Dim dtmExpDate, strCookie

    dtmExpDate = Weekdayname(DatePart("w",Date())) & ", " _
             & FormatDate(DatePart("d",Date())) & "-" _
             & Monthname(DatePart("m",Date(),1) + 1) & "-" _
             & DatePart("yyyy",Date()) _
             & " 00:00:00 GMT"
    strCookie = "string=" & strCookieString & ";expires=" & dtmExpDate
    document.cookie = strCookie
  End Function

  Function FormatDate(dtmInputDate)
    If Len(dtmInputDate) = 1 Then
      dtmInputDate = "0" & rawDate
    End If
    FormatDate = dtmInputDate
  End Function

' End hiding VBScript statements -->
</SCRIPT>

</HEAD>

<BODY>

 <H3> Configuration Settings</H3>

 <BR>

 <FORM NAME="siteForm">
   <B>Please tell us your name:</B> <INPUT NAME="userName" TYPE="text"
```

```
            SIZE="25" MAXLENGTH="40"><P><BR>
        <B>Default View:</B><P>
        <INPUT NAME="siteRadio" TYPE="radio" VALUE="Welcome"> Welcome Page<P>
        <INPUT NAME="siteRadio" TYPE="radio" VALUE="Archive"> Report Archive Page<P>
        <INPUT NAME="siteRadio" TYPE="radio" VALUE="Daily"> Daily Consolidated
          Summary Report<P><BR>

        <P><B>Select a color scheme: </B>
        <SELECT NAME="siteList">
          <OPTION SELECTED VALUE="Yellow">Yellow and White
          <OPTION VALUE="LightBlue">Blue and White
          <OPTION VALUE="LightGreen">Green and White
          <OPTION VALUE="LightGrey">Grey and White
          <OPTION VALUE="Pink">Pink and White
        </SELECT></P><BR>

        <INPUT NAME="SaveButton" TYPE="button" VALUE=" Save "
          onClick="ProcessSettings()">
        <INPUT NAME="CancelButton" TYPE="reset" VALUE=" Cancel ">
        <INPUT NAME="HelpButton" TYPE="button" VALUE=" Help "
          onClick="DisplayHelpDialog()">
      </FORM>
    </BODY>
  </HTML>
```

Summary

In this chapter, you learned how to collect data from visitors to your Web site using an HTML form. You also learned how to work with various form elements, as well as how to use VBScript to validate form contents and ensure that visitors supply all required data. Once valid data is collected, you can save it for future reference using cookies. You do so by building a data string that includes an expiration date and then storing that string on the visitor's computer.

Chapter 30

Converting Reports to HTML Pages

In this chapter, Alexander will begin developing the first of the WSH VBScripts for the Order/Inventory reporting Web project. The purpose of this VBScript is to create an HTML page based on the contents of the current day's consolidated summary report. He will accomplish this task by opening the text-based version of the report file, reading it, and using its contents to create an output file that includes embedded HTML tags. The output file will then be saved as an HTML file.

Preparing to Create the HTML Conversion Script

Creating the HTML version of the consolidated summary report will not use any new VBScript or WSH functions or methods. It will use the same `FileSystemObject` I/O methods that you have seen in other chapters. The main difference is that the output file created by this chapter will include embedded HTML tags required to create a Web page. Therefore, you will use the `FileSystemObject` object's `WriteLine()` method extensively, as demonstrated below.

```
Dim FsoObj
Set FsoObj = CreateObject("Scripting.FileSystemObject")
Set strReportFile = FsoObj.OpenTextFile("D:\Temp\Test.HTML", 2, "True")
strReportFile.WriteLine("<HTML>")
strReportFile.WriteLine("  <HEAD>")
strReportFile.WriteLine("    <TITLE>Test HTML Page</TITLE>")
strReportFile.WriteLine("  </HEAD>")
strReportFile.WriteLine("  <BODY>")
strReportFile.WriteLine("  </BODY>")
strReportFile.WriteLine("</HTML>")
strReportFile.Close()
```

When executed, this example creates an HTML file called `Test.html` that has the following content:

```
<HTML>
  <HEAD>
```

```
    <TITLE>Test HTML Page</TITLE>
  </HEAD>
  <BODY>
  </BODY>
</HTML>
```

In order to create the HTML version of the consolidated summary report, the VBScript will have to make substantial use of parsing functions in order to identify and extract individual report elements. In previous chapters, this was accomplished using VBScript functions. However, as you will see, the more complicated parsing requirements required by this script will also require the use of the `RegExp` object and its properties.

> **NOTE**
>
> The `RegExp` object and its properties were introduced and demonstrated in Chapter 7, "VBScript Objects."

The last scripting element to be used in this chapter's script is the VBScript `Ubound()` object. This function retrieves the upper bound element for the specified array and will be used in conjunction with the `RegExp` object to process a portion of the current day's consolidated summary report.

> **NOTE**
>
> The VBScript `Ubound()` function was previously introduced in Chapter 5, "Arrays."

Creating the HTML Conversion Script

Alexander plans to provide all of the same basic functionality features that Molly provided in her VBScripts in her last project, including support for the Windows registry, a debugging mode, and event logging. The following sections detail the components of the HTML conversion script and provide an overview of their design and purpose.

The Initialization Section

The script's `Initialization Section`, shown below, begins by requiring strict variable interpretation. Next it defines all of the variables used globally by the script. It also defines variables that will be used to represent the `WshShell` and `FileSystemObject` objects, as well as an array called `astrErrors` that will be used to store the contents of each line of the report. Next a collection of constants is defined. Finally, a variable called `intReturnCode` is set equal to zero. This variable represents the return code value that the script will pass back to the script that executed it (the scheduling script). Setting the variable equal to zero in the `Initialization Section` ensures that unless the variable's value is explicitly changed during the execution of the script, a zero return code will be returned.

```
Option Explicit

Dim intReturnCode, strOutputFile, strReportFile, strSourceLine
Dim strSourceFile, strConsolTxtRpt, i, strFileNameString
Dim strEventLog, strDebug
Dim WshShl, FsoObj
Dim astrErrors

Set WshShl = WScript.CreateObject("WScript.Shell")
Set FsoObj = CreateObject("Scripting.FileSystemObject")

Const cForReading = 1
Const cForWriting = 2
Const cForAppending = 8
Const cTitleBarMsg = "HTML Report Conversion Script"

intReturnCode = 0
```

The Main Processing Section

Unlike the other scripts presented in this book, the `Main Processing Section` of this VBScript is very involved. It is made up of a combination of procedure calls, loops, and conditional tests that control the processing of the text version of the summary report and the creation of the new HTML version.

The Main Processing Section begins by calling the GetRegistrySettings() subroutine, which retrieves the script's configuration settings from the Windows registry, followed by the AssembleFileNames() subroutine, which builds two strings representing the names of the current day's report.

```
GetRegistrySettings()
AssembleFileNames()
```

Next, the current consolidated summary report file is opened for reading and an HTML file is created, as shown below.

```
Set strSourceFile = FsoObj.OpenTextFile(strConsolTxtRpt, cForReading)
Set strReportFile = FsoObj.OpenTextFile(strOutputFile, cForWriting , "True")
```

The next set of statements writes a message to the Windows application event log if event logging has been enabled for the script.

```
If strEventLog = "Enabled" Then
  WriteToEventLog("HTML Report Conversion Script now executing.")
End If
```

Likewise, the next several statements execute only if the script is being manually run in debug mode.

```
If strDebug = "Enabled" Then
  MsgBox "Beginning report development.", , cTitleBarMsg
End If
```

The next three statements set up a For...Next loop that skips through the headings of the daily consolidated summary report, as represented by strSourceFile.

```
For i = 0 to 8
   strSourceFile.SkipLine
Next
```

The next several statements call subroutines that write collections of HTML tags to the file.

```
WriteHeader()
BeginTableDefinition()
WriteTableHeader("Errors:")
WriteErrorsColHeadings()
```

Next, a `Do...Until` loop is used, as shown below, to iterate through the text version of the report until the first blank line is found (the end of the `Errors:` section of the report is reached). Upon each iteration of the loop, a line from the report is read and assigned to a variable called `strSourceLine`. The length of the string assigned to `strSourceLine` is then checked to see if it's zero (blank). If it is, the loop terminates; otherwise, contents of the string are loaded into an array using the `Split()` function and the `WriteErrorsData()` subroutine is called. This subroutine uses the contents of the array to write a line of data to the HTML page.

```
Do Until strSourceFile.AtEndOfStream
  strSourceLine = strSourceFile.ReadLine()
  If Len(strSourceLine) = 0 Then
    Exit Do
  Else
    astrErrors = Split(strSourceLine, " ", 5)
    WriteErrorsData()
  End If
Loop
```

NOTE

Note the use of the `Split()` function in the previous set of statements. It specifies a third parameter with a value of 5. This parameter limits the size of the array created by the `Split()` function to five elements. If you compare this statement to the output displayed on the HTML page created by this script, you will find that this matches up against the five columns of data displayed in the report, with the fifth column displaying a string representing all the remaining data from a line of the report after the fifth word (that is, the description).

Next, the `EndTableDefinition()` subroutine is called. This subroutine writes an HTML tag that marks the end of the `Errors:` table (`</Table>`).

```
EndTableDefinition()
```

The rest of the statements in the `Main Processing Section` write the remaining sections of the HTML file by repeating the same basic series of steps that you have seen thus far, making adjustments as necessary to specify appropriate end-of-section markers and to print the proper report headings.

```
BeginTableDefinition()

WriteTableHeader("Sales Summary:")
WriteTableSubHeader("Government:")
WriteSalesAndReturnsColHeadings()

For i = 0 to 7
   strSourceFile.SkipLine
Next

Do Until strSourceFile.AtEndOfStream
  strSourceLine = strSourceFile.ReadLine()
  If Len(strSourceLine) <> 0 Then
    If Instr(1, strSourceLine, "Other Customers:") Then
      Exit Do
    End If
    astrErrors = Split(strSourceLine, "  ", 3)
    WriteSalesAndReturnsData()
  End If
Loop

WriteTableSubHeader("Other Customers:")
WriteSalesAndReturnsColHeadings()

For i = 0 to 2
   strSourceFile.SkipLine
Next

Do Until strSourceFile.AtEndOfStream
  strSourceLine = strSourceFile.ReadLine()
  If Len(strSourceLine) <> 0 Then
    If Instr(1, strSourceLine, "----------") Then
      Exit Do
    End If
    astrErrors = Split(strSourceLine, "  ", 3)
    WriteSalesAndReturnsData()
  End If
Loop
```

```
EndTableDefinition()

BeginTableDefinition()

WriteTableHeader("Returns Summary:")
WriteTableSubHeader("Government:")
WriteSalesAndReturnsColHeadings()

For i = 0 to 6
   strSourceFile.SkipLine
Next

Do Until strSourceFile.AtEndOfStream
  strSourceLine = strSourceFile.ReadLine()
  If Len(strSourceLine) <> 0 Then
    If Instr(1, strSourceLine, "Other Customers:") Then
      Exit Do
    End If
    astrErrors = Split(strSourceLine, "  ", 3)
    WriteSalesAndReturnsData()
  End If
Loop

WriteTableSubHeader("Other Customers:")
WriteSalesAndReturnsColHeadings()

For i = 0 to 2
   strSourceFile.SkipLine
Next

Do Until strSourceFile.AtEndOfStream
  strSourceLine = strSourceFile.ReadLine()
  If Len(strSourceLine) <> 0 Then
    If Instr(1, strSourceLine, "----------") Then
      Exit Do
    End If
    astrErrors = Split(strSourceLine, "  ", 3)
```

```
    WriteSalesAndReturnsData()
  End If
Loop

EndTableDefinition()

BeginTableDefinition()

WriteTableHeader("Daily Production Summary:")
WriteProductionColHeadings()

For i = 0 to 4
   strSourceFile.SkipLine
Next
```

The last section of the daily consolidated summary report to be processed by the script is the `Daily Production Summary` section. Like before, a line of data from each row within this section is read into `strSourceLine`. However, rather than using the `Split()` function to parse out the contents of the report line, the `ParseProductionData()` subroutine is executed. The reason for this change is that the descriptive information inside this last section of the report is located in the middle of each row and does not have a predictable length. Therefore, it cannot simply be split into an array and be written out to the HTML page from there. More complicated parsing logic is required. Alexander developed the `ParseProductionData()` subroutine to parse out the data located in each row of this section of the report using the `RegExp` object and its methods and properties.

```
Do Until strSourceFile.AtEndOfStream
  strSourceLine = strSourceFile.ReadLine()
  ParseProductionData(strSourceLine)
  WriteProductionData()
Loop

strSourceFile.Close()

WriteFooter()

If strDebug = "Enabled" Then
```

```
    MsgBox "Report development completed.", , cTitleBarMsg
  End If

  If strEventLog = "Enabled" Then
    WriteToEventLog ("HTML Report Conversion Script finished executing.")
  End If
```

The last statement in the `Main Processing Section` calls the `TerminateScript()` subroutine and passes it the value stored in `intReturnCode`. This function uses the `WScript` object's `Quit()` method to terminate the script's execution and to pass the calling script a return code indicating whether this script experienced an error.

```
TerminateScript(intReturnCode)
```

The GetRegistrySettings() Subroutine

As you have seen in previous scripts, the `GetRegistrySettings()` subroutine, shown below, is responsible for retrieving the script's configuration settings from values stored in the Windows registry. In the event that an error occurs in retrieving any of the script's configuration settings, a message is posted to the Windows application event log and a value of 4 (representing a return code) is passed to the `TerminateScript()` subroutine.

```
Sub GetRegistrySettings()

  On Error Resume Next

  strEventLog = _
    WshShl.RegRead("HKLM\Software\Intuit\VBScripts\WebRpting\EventLogging")
  If Err <> 0 Then
    If strEventLog = "Enabled" Then
      WriteToEventLog ("HTML Report Conversion Script - Using default " & _
        "for strEventLog. RC = 4")
      TerminateScript(4)
    End If
  End If

  strDebug = WshShl.RegRead("HKLM\Software\Intuit\VBScripts\WebRpting\Debug")
```

```
    If Err <> 0 Then
      If strEventLog = "Enabled" Then
        WriteToEventLog ("HTML Report Conversion Script - Using default " & _
          "for strDebug. RC = 4")
        TerminateScript(4)
      End If
    End If

    strOutputFile = _
      WshShl.RegRead("HKLM\Software\Intuit\VBScripts\WebRpting\HTMLFolder")
    If Err <> 0 Then
      If strEventLog = "Enabled" Then
        WriteToEventLog ("HTML Report Conversion Script - Using default " & _
          "for strOutputFile. RC = 4")
        TerminateScript(4)
      End If
    End If

    strConsolTxtRpt = _
      WshShl.RegRead("HKLM\Software\Intuit\VBScripts\WebRpting\ConSolRptLoc")
    If Err <> 0 Then
    If strEventLog = "Enabled" Then
        WriteToEventLog ("HTML Report Conversion Script - Using default " & _
          "for strConsolTxtRpt. RC = 4")
        TerminateScript(4)
      End If
    End If

    If strDebug = "Enabled" Then
      MsgBox "Registry settings initialized: " & vbCrLf & vbCrLf & _
        "strEventLog" & vbTab & "=" & vbTab & strEventLog & vbCrLf & _
        "strDebug" & vbTab & vbTab & "=" & vbTab & strDebug & vbCrLf & _
        "strOutputFile" & vbTab & "=" & vbTab & strOutputFile & vbCrLf & _
        "strConsolTxtRpt" & vbTab & "=" & vbTab & strConsolTxtRpt & _
        vbCrLf, ,cTitleBarMsg
    End If

End Sub
```

The AssembleFileNames() Subroutine

The `AssembleFileNames()` subroutine, shown below, is responsible for determining the name of the current day's consolidated summary report, as well as for naming the new HTML version of the report.

```
Sub AssembleFileNames()

  strFileNameString = Replace(Date(), "/", "-")

  strConsolTxtRpt = strConsolTxtRpt & "\" & strFileNameString & _
    "_ConsolSumRpt.txt"

  If strDebug = "Enabled" Then
    MsgBox "strConsolTxtRpt = " & strConsolTxtRpt, , cTitleBarMsg
  End If

  strOutputFile = strOutputFile & "\" & strFileNameString & _
    "_ConsolSumRpt.html"

  If strDebug = "Enabled" Then
    MsgBox "strOutputFile = " & strOutputFile, , cTitleBarMsg
  End If

End Sub
```

The WriteHeader() Subroutine

The `WriteHeader()` subroutine, shown below, is responsible for writing a collection of HTML tags at the beginning of the HTML page. These HTML tags define basic page elements and specify the font type and size, as well as the manner in which the border of each table in the script is to be formatted.

```
Sub WriteHeader()
  strReportFile.WriteLine("<html>")
  strReportFile.WriteLine("  <head>")
  strReportFile.WriteLine("    <title>HTML Conversion Script</title>")
  strReportFile.WriteLine("    <style>")
  strReportFile.WriteLine("      TD { font-family:arial;")
```

```
    strReportFile.WriteLine("        font-size:11pt;")
    strReportFile.WriteLine("        border-top: thin ridge black;")
    strReportFile.WriteLine("        border-bottom: thin ridge black;")
    strReportFile.WriteLine("        border-right: thin ridge black;")
    strReportFile.WriteLine("        border-left: thin ridge black; }")
    strReportFile.WriteLine("     </style")
    strReportFile.WriteLine("   </head>")
    strReportFile.WriteLine("   <body>")
End Sub
```

The BeginTableDefinition() Subroutine

The `BeginTableDefinition()` subroutine, shown below, consists of a single statement. When called, it writes an opening `<TABLE>` tag to the HTML page.

```
Sub BeginTableDefinition()
    strReportFile.WriteLine("      <table width='100%' border='0' " & _
      "cellspacing='0' cellpadding='5'>")
End Sub
```

The WriteTableHeader() Subroutine

The `WriteTableHeader()` subroutine, shown below, is responsible for writing HTML tags that specify the format of a table on the HTML page.

```
Sub WriteTableHeader(strTableHeader)
    strReportFile.WriteLine("        <tr>")
    strReportFile.WriteLine("           <td colspan='5' style='background:purple; " & _
     "color:yellow;'>")
    strReportFile.WriteLine("           <center><b>" & strTableHeader & _
      "</b></center></td>")
    strReportFile.WriteLine("        </tr>")
End Sub
```

The WriteTableSubHeader() Subroutine

The `WriteTableSubHeader()` subroutine, shown on the following page, writes a string of text representing a section header in the report. The text that is written is passed to the subroutine as an argument.

```
Sub WriteTableSubHeader(strTableHeader)
  strReportFile.WriteLine("      <tr>")
  strReportFile.WriteLine("        <td colspan='3'>")
  strReportFile.WriteLine("        <b>" & strTableHeader & "</b></td>")
  strReportFile.WriteLine("      </tr>")
End Sub
```

The WriteErrorsColHeadings() Subroutine

The `WriteErrorsColHeadings()` subroutine, shown below, writes the column headings for the `Errors:` section of the report.

```
Sub WriteErrorsColHeadings()
  strReportFile.WriteLine("      <tr>")
  strReportFile.WriteLine("        <td><b>Date<b></td>")
  strReportFile.WriteLine("        <td><b>Time<b></td>")
  strReportFile.WriteLine("        <td><b>Svr<b></td>")
  strReportFile.WriteLine("        <td><b>Code<b></td>")
  strReportFile.WriteLine("        <td><b>Description<b></td>")
  strReportFile.WriteLine("      </tr>")
End Sub
```

The WriteErrorsData() Subroutine

The `WriteErrorsData()` subroutine, shown below, is responsible for writing a line of data to the `Errors:` section of the HTML page. It accomplishes this task by referencing the elements stored in the `astrErrors` arrays and writing them to the HTML file.

```
Sub WriteErrorsData()
  strReportFile.WriteLine("      <tr>")
  strReportFile.WriteLine("        <td>" & astrErrors(0) & "</td>")
  strReportFile.WriteLine("        <td>" & astrErrors(1) & "</td>")
  strReportFile.WriteLine("        <td>" & astrErrors(2) & "</td>")
  strReportFile.WriteLine("        <td>" & astrErrors(3) & "</td>")
  strReportFile.WriteLine("        <td>" & astrErrors(4) & "</td>")
  strReportFile.WriteLine("      </tr>")
End Sub
```

The WriteSalesAndReturnsColHeadings() Subroutine

The `WriteSalesAndReturnsColHeadings()` subroutine, shown below, is called to write the column headings for both the Sales Summary and Returns sections of the report.

```
Sub WriteSalesAndReturnsColHeadings()
  strReportFile.WriteLine("      <tr>")
  strReportFile.WriteLine("        <td><b>Part #</b></td>")
  strReportFile.WriteLine("        <td><b>Qty</b></td>")
  strReportFile.WriteLine("        <td><b>Description</b></td>")
  strReportFile.WriteLine("      </tr>")
End Sub
```

The WriteProductionColHeadings() Subroutine

The `WriteProductionColHeadings()` subroutine, shown below, is called to write the column headings for the Production section of the report.

```
Sub WriteProductionColHeadings()
  strReportFile.WriteLine("      <tr>")
  strReportFile.WriteLine("        <td><b>Part #</b></td>")
  strReportFile.WriteLine("        <td><b>Qty</b></td>")
  strReportFile.WriteLine("        <td><b>Description</b></td>")
  strReportFile.WriteLine("        <td><b>In Stock</b></td>")
  strReportFile.WriteLine("      </tr>")
End Sub
```

The WriteSalesAndReturnsData() Subroutine

The `WriteSalesAndReturnsData()` subroutine, shown below, writes a line of data to both the Sales and Returns sections of the report.

```
Sub WriteSalesAndReturnsData()
  strReportFile.WriteLine("      <tr>")
  strReportFile.WriteLine("        <td>" & astrErrors(0) & "</td>")
  strReportFile.WriteLine("        <td>" & astrErrors(1) & "</td>")
  strReportFile.WriteLine("        <td>" & astrErrors(2) & "</td>")
  strReportFile.WriteLine("      </tr>")
End Sub
```

The WriteProductionData() Subroutine

The `WriteProductionData()` subroutine, shown below, writes a line of data in the Production section of the report.

```
Sub WriteProductionData()
  strReportFile.WriteLine("      <tr>")
  strReportFile.WriteLine("        <td>" & astrErrors(0) & "</td>")
  strReportFile.WriteLine("        <td>" & astrErrors(1) & "</td>")
  strReportFile.WriteLine("        <td>" & astrErrors(2) & "</td>")
  strReportFile.WriteLine("        <td>" & astrErrors(3) & "</td>")
  strReportFile.WriteLine("      </tr>")
End Sub
```

The EndTableDefinition() Subroutine

The `EndTableDefinition()` subroutine, shown below, consists of a single statement. When called, it writes the closing `</TABLE>` tags to the HTML page.

```
Sub EndTableDefinition()
  strReportFile.WriteLine("    </table><p>")
End Sub
```

The WriteFooter() Subroutine

The `WriteFooter()` subroutine, shown below, writes the closing `</BODY>` and `</HTML>` tags to the end of the HTML page.

```
Sub WriteFooter()
  strReportFile.WriteLine("  </body>")
  strReportFile.WriteLine("</html>")
End Sub
```

The ParseProductionData() Subroutine

The `ParseProductionData()` subroutine, shown on the next page, replaces the `Split()` function used to parse out the rest of the report's data. This subroutine was developed because the data stored in the Production section of the report did not lend itself well to the built-in VBScript parsing functions. Instead, Alexander created this subroutine as a wrapper for a procedure that uses the properties associated with the `RegExp` object.

The subroutine begins by defining local variables for its own use. Next it instantiates an instance of the `RegExp` object. It then sets the `RegExp` object's `Pattern` property by assigning it a value of `" +"`, which, roughly translated, says to look for any instances of one or more consecutive spaces. Next, the value of the `RexExp` object's `Global` property is set equal to `True`, which causes the pattern search to apply to all matching occurrences within the search string.

The `Replace()` method is then used to replace any instances of one or more spaces within the string passed to the subroutine with a single space. Once all excess spaces have been removed, the `Split()` function is used to load the contents of the string into an array called `astrErrors`.

A `For...Each` loop is then used to iterate though the array. On its first iteration, it skips all processing because the value of `astrErrors` is not greater than one (it is equal to 0) and `astrErrors(0)` represents the first column of data in the Production section. Likewise, the second iteration of the loop does not result in any processing. From the third to the second-to-last iteration, the loop creates a single string and assigns it to a variable called `string2`. This string represents the descriptive information for each line in this section of the report. The value of `string2` is then assigned to `astrErrors(2)`, and the value of the last element of the array (`astrErrors(UBound(astrErrors))`) is assigned to `astrErrors(3)`.

When this subroutine terminates, the `astrErrors` array is fully loaded and ready to be written to the HTML page as a table entry.

```
Sub ParseProductionData(strQuote)
  Dim regExpObj, strStrippedString, intCounter, strString2, intArrayCounter
  Set regExpObj = New RegExp
  regExpObj.Pattern = " +"
  regExpObj.Global = True

  strStrippedString = RegExpObj.Replace(strQuote, " ")

  astrErrors = Split(strStrippedString, " ")

  intCounter = 0

  For Each intArrayCounter In astrErrors
```

```
      If intCounter > 1 Then
        If intCounter <> UBound(astrErrors) Then
          strString2 = strString2 & " " & intArrayCounter
        End If
      End If
      intCounter = intCounter + 1
    Next

    astrErrors(2) = strString2

    astrErrors(3) = astrErrors(UBound(astrErrors))

  End Sub
```

The WriteToEventLog() Subroutine

The `WriteToEventLog()` subroutine, shown below, writes an informational message passed to it as an argument to the Windows application event log using the `WshShell` object's `LogEvent()` method.

```
Sub WriteToEventLog(strMessage)

  WshShl.LogEvent 4, strMessage

End Sub
```

The TerminateScript() Subroutine

The `TerminateScript()` subroutine, shown below, is a modified version of the subroutine that you have seen in recent scripts. This subroutine uses the `WScript` object's `Quit()` method to terminate the script's execution and to pass a numeric value back to the script that called it, indicating whether or not the HTML conversion script ran successfully.

```
Sub TerminateScript(intRC)

  If strDebug = "Enabled" Then
    MsgBox "Script execution terminated.", , cTitleBarMsg
  End If
```

```
  WScript.Quit(intRC)

End Sub
```

The Fully Assembled Script

The fully assembled HTML conversion script is shown below. When it is executed, it automatically determines the name of the current day's consolidated summary report and then uses that file as input for creating a Web-based version of the report.

```
'*************************************************************************
'Script Name: Script 30.1.vbs
'Author: Jerry Ford
'Created: 05/03/03
'Description: This script converts the text version of the daily
'consolidated summary report to an HTML file
'*************************************************************************


'Initialization Section

Option Explicit

Dim intReturnCode, strOutputFile, strReportFile, strSourceLine
Dim strSourceFile, strConsolTxtRpt, i, strFileNameString
Dim strEventLog, strDebug
Dim WshShl, FsoObj
Dim astrErrors

Set WshShl = WScript.CreateObject("WScript.Shell")
Set FsoObj = CreateObject("Scripting.FileSystemObject")

Const cForReading = 1
Const cForWriting = 2
Const cForAppending = 8
```

```
Const cTitleBarMsg = "HTML Report Conversion Script"

intReturnCode = 0


'Main Processing Section

GetRegistrySettings()

AssembleFileNames()

Set strSourceFile = FsoObj.OpenTextFile(strConsolTxtRpt, cForReading)
Set strReportFile = FsoObj.OpenTextFile(strOutputFile, cForWriting , "True")

If strEventLog = "Enabled" Then
  WriteToEventLog("HTML Report Conversion Script now executing.")
End If

If strDebug = "Enabled" Then
  MsgBox "Beginning report development.", , cTitleBarMsg
End If

For i = 0 to 8
   strSourceFile.SkipLine
Next

WriteHeader()

BeginTableDefinition()

WriteTableHeader("Errors:")

WriteErrorsColHeadings()

Do Until strSourceFile.AtEndOfStream
  strSourceLine = strSourceFile.ReadLine()
  If Len(strSourceLine) = 0 Then
    Exit Do
```

```
  Else
    astrErrors = Split(strSourceLine, " ", 5)
    WriteErrorsData()
  End If
Loop

EndTableDefinition()

BeginTableDefinition()

WriteTableHeader("Sales Summary:")
WriteTableSubHeader("Government:")
WriteSalesAndReturnsColHeadings()

For i = 0 to 7
   strSourceFile.SkipLine
Next

Do Until strSourceFile.AtEndOfStream
  strSourceLine = strSourceFile.ReadLine()
  If Len(strSourceLine) <> 0 Then
    If Instr(1, strSourceLine, "Other Customers:") Then
      Exit Do
    End If
    astrErrors = Split(strSourceLine, "  ", 3)
    WriteSalesAndReturnsData()
  End If
Loop

WriteTableSubHeader("Other Customers:")
WriteSalesAndReturnsColHeadings()

For i = 0 to 2
   strSourceFile.SkipLine
Next

Do Until strSourceFile.AtEndOfStream
  strSourceLine = strSourceFile.ReadLine()
```

```
    If Len(strSourceLine) <> 0 Then
      If Instr(1, strSourceLine, "----------") Then
        Exit Do
      End If
      astrErrors = Split(strSourceLine, "  ", 3)
      WriteSalesAndReturnsData()
    End If
  Loop

  EndTableDefinition()

  BeginTableDefinition()

  WriteTableHeader("Returns Summary:")
  WriteTableSubHeader("Government:")
  WriteSalesAndReturnsColHeadings()

  For i = 0 to 6
     strSourceFile.SkipLine
  Next

  Do Until strSourceFile.AtEndOfStream
    strSourceLine = strSourceFile.ReadLine()
    If Len(strSourceLine) <> 0 Then
      If Instr(1, strSourceLine, "Other Customers:") Then
        Exit Do
      End If
      astrErrors = Split(strSourceLine, "  ", 3)
      WriteSalesAndReturnsData()
    End If
  Loop

  WriteTableSubHeader("Other Customers:")
  WriteSalesAndReturnsColHeadings()

  For i = 0 to 2
     strSourceFile.SkipLine
  Next
```

```
Do Until strSourceFile.AtEndOfStream
  strSourceLine = strSourceFile.ReadLine()
  If Len(strSourceLine) <> 0 Then
    If Instr(1, strSourceLine, "----------") Then
      Exit Do
    End If
    astrErrors = Split(strSourceLine, "  ", 3)
    WriteSalesAndReturnsData()
  End If
Loop

EndTableDefinition()

BeginTableDefinition()

WriteTableHeader("Daily Production Summary:")
WriteProductionColHeadings()

For i = 0 to 4
   strSourceFile.SkipLine
Next

Do Until strSourceFile.AtEndOfStream
  strSourceLine = strSourceFile.ReadLine()
  ParseProductionData(strSourceLine)
  WriteProductionData()
Loop

strSourceFile.Close()

WriteFooter()

If strDebug = "Enabled" Then
  MsgBox "Report development completed.", , cTitleBarMsg
End If

If strEventLog = "Enabled" Then
```

```
    WriteToEventLog ("HTML Report Conversion Script finished executing.")
  End If

  TerminateScript(intReturnCode)


  'Procedure Section

  Sub GetRegistrySettings()

    On Error Resume Next

    strEventLog = _
      WshShl.RegRead("HKLM\Software\Intuit\VBScripts\WebRpting\EventLogging")
    If Err <> 0 Then
      If strEventLog = "Enabled" Then
        WriteToEventLog ("HTML Report Conversion Script - Using default " & _
          "for strEventLog. RC = 4")
        TerminateScript(12)
      End If
    End If

    strDebug = WshShl.RegRead("HKLM\Software\Intuit\VBScripts\WebRpting\Debug")
    If Err <> 0 Then
      If strEventLog = "Enabled" Then
        WriteToEventLog ("HTML Report Conversion Script - Using default " & _
          "for strDebug. RC = 4")
        TerminateScript(4)
      End If
    End If

    strOutputFile = _
      WshShl.RegRead("HKLM\Software\Intuit\VBScripts\WebRpting\HTMLFolder")
    If Err <> 0 Then
      If strEventLog = "Enabled" Then
        WriteToEventLog ("HTML Report Conversion Script - Using default " & _
          "for strOutputFile. RC = 4")
        TerminateScript(4)
```

```
    End If
  End If

  strConsolTxtRpt = _
    WshShl.RegRead("HKLM\Software\Intuit\VBScripts\WebRpting\ConSolRptLoc")
  If Err <> 0 Then
  If strEventLog = "Enabled" Then
      WriteToEventLog ("HTML Report Conversion Script - Using default " & _
        "for strConsolTxtRpt. RC = 4")
      TerminateScript(4)
    End If
  End If

  If strDebug = "Enabled" Then
    MsgBox "Registry settings initialized: " & vbCrLf & vbCrLf & _
      "strEventLog" & vbTab & "=" & vbTab & strEventLog & vbCrLf & _
      "strDebug" & vbTab & vbTab & "=" & vbTab & strDebug & vbCrLf & _
      "strOutputFile" & vbTab & "=" & vbTab & strOutputFile & vbCrLf & _
      "strConsolTxtRpt" & vbTab & "=" & vbTab & strConsolTxtRpt & _
      vbCrLf, ,cTitleBarMsg
  End If

End Sub

Sub AssembleFileNames()

  strFileNameString = Replace(Date(), "/", "-")

  strConsolTxtRpt = strConsolTxtRpt & "\" & strFileNameString & _
    "_ConsolSumRpt.txt"

  If strDebug = "Enabled" Then
    MsgBox "strConsolTxtRpt = " & strConsolTxtRpt, , cTitleBarMsg
  End If

  strOutputFile = strOutputFile & "\" & strFileNameString & _
    "_ConsolSumRpt.html"
```

```
  If strDebug = "Enabled" Then
    MsgBox "strOutputFile = " & strOutputFile, , cTitleBarMsg
  End If

End Sub

Sub WriteHeader()
  strReportFile.WriteLine("<html>")
  strReportFile.WriteLine("  <head>")
  strReportFile.WriteLine("    <title>HTML Conversion Script</title>")
  strReportFile.WriteLine("    <style>")
  strReportFile.WriteLine("       TD { font-family:arial;")
  strReportFile.WriteLine("       font-size:11pt;")
  strReportFile.WriteLine("       border-top: thin ridge black;")
  strReportFile.WriteLine("       border-bottom: thin ridge black;")
  strReportFile.WriteLine("       border-right: thin ridge black;")
  strReportFile.WriteLine("       border-left: thin ridge black; }")
  strReportFile.WriteLine("    </style")
  strReportFile.WriteLine("  </head>")
  strReportFile.WriteLine("  <body>")
End Sub

Sub BeginTableDefinition()
  strReportFile.WriteLine("    <table width='100%' border='0' " & _
    "cellspacing='0' cellpadding='5'>")
End Sub

Sub WriteTableHeader(strTableHeader)
  strReportFile.WriteLine("      <tr>")
  strReportFile.WriteLine("        <td colspan='5' " & _
    "style='background:purple; color:yellow;'>")
  strReportFile.WriteLine("        <center><b>" & strTableHeader & _
    "</b></center></td>")
  strReportFile.WriteLine("      </tr>")
End Sub

Sub WriteTableSubHeader(strTableHeader)
  strReportFile.WriteLine("      <tr>")
```

```
  strReportFile.WriteLine("        <td colspan='3'>")
  strReportFile.WriteLine("        <b>" & strTableHeader & "</b></td>")
  strReportFile.WriteLine("      </tr>")
End Sub

Sub WriteErrorsColHeadings()
  strReportFile.WriteLine("      <tr>")
  strReportFile.WriteLine("        <td><b>Date<b></td>")
  strReportFile.WriteLine("        <td><b>Time<b></td>")
  strReportFile.WriteLine("        <td><b>Svr<b></td>")
  strReportFile.WriteLine("        <td><b>Code<b></td>")
  strReportFile.WriteLine("        <td><b>Description<b></td>")
  strReportFile.WriteLine("      </tr>")
End Sub

Sub WriteErrorsData()
  strReportFile.WriteLine("      <tr>")
  strReportFile.WriteLine("        <td>" & astrErrors(0) & "</td>")
  strReportFile.WriteLine("        <td>" & astrErrors(1) & "</td>")
  strReportFile.WriteLine("        <td>" & astrErrors(2) & "</td>")
  strReportFile.WriteLine("        <td>" & astrErrors(3) & "</td>")
  strReportFile.WriteLine("        <td>" & astrErrors(4) & "</td>")
  strReportFile.WriteLine("      </tr>")
End Sub

Sub WriteSalesAndReturnsColHeadings()
  strReportFile.WriteLine("      <tr>")
  strReportFile.WriteLine("        <td><b>Part #</b></td>")
  strReportFile.WriteLine("        <td><b>Qty</b></td>")
  strReportFile.WriteLine("        <td><b>Description</b></td>")
  strReportFile.WriteLine("      </tr>")
End Sub

Sub WriteProductionColHeadings()
  strReportFile.WriteLine("      <tr>")
  strReportFile.WriteLine("        <td><b>Part #</b></td>")
  strReportFile.WriteLine("        <td><b>Qty</b></td>")
  strReportFile.WriteLine("        <td><b>Description</b></td>")
```

```
  strReportFile.WriteLine("        <td><b>In Stock</b></td>")
  strReportFile.WriteLine("      </tr>")
End Sub

Sub WriteSalesAndReturnsData()
  strReportFile.WriteLine("      <tr>")
  strReportFile.WriteLine("        <td>" & astrErrors(0) & "</td>")
  strReportFile.WriteLine("        <td>" & astrErrors(1) & "</td>")
  strReportFile.WriteLine("        <td>" & astrErrors(2) & "</td>")
  strReportFile.WriteLine("      </tr>")
End Sub

Sub WriteProductionData()
  strReportFile.WriteLine("      <tr>")
  strReportFile.WriteLine("        <td>" & astrErrors(0) & "</td>")
  strReportFile.WriteLine("        <td>" & astrErrors(1) & "</td>")
  strReportFile.WriteLine("        <td>" & astrErrors(2) & "</td>")
  strReportFile.WriteLine("        <td>" & astrErrors(3) & "</td>")
  strReportFile.WriteLine("      </tr>")
End Sub

Sub EndTableDefinition()
  strReportFile.WriteLine("    </table><p>")
End Sub

Sub WriteFooter()
  strReportFile.WriteLine("  </body>")
  strReportFile.WriteLine("</html>")
End Sub

Sub ParseProductionData(strQuote)
  Dim regExpObj, strStrippedString, intCounter, strString2, intArrayCounter
  Set regExpObj = New RegExp
  regExpObj.Pattern = " +"
  regExpObj.Global = True

  strStrippedString = RegExpObj.Replace(strQuote, " ")
```

```
  astrErrors = Split(strStrippedString, " ")

  intCounter = 0

  For Each intArrayCounter In astrErrors

    If intCounter > 1 Then
      If intCounter <> UBound(astrErrors) Then
        strString2 = strString2 & " " & intArrayCounter
      End If
    End If
    intCounter = intCounter + 1
  Next

  astrErrors(2) = strString2

  astrErrors(3) = astrErrors(UBound(astrErrors))

End Sub

Sub WriteToEventLog(strMessage)

  WshShl.LogEvent 4, strMessage

End Sub

Sub TerminateScript(intRC)

  If strDebug = "Enabled" Then
    MsgBox "Script execution terminated.", , cTitleBarMsg
  End If

  WScript.Quit(intRC)

End Sub
```

The Automatically Generated HTML Page

When executed, the HTML conversion script reads and processes the current day's consolidated summary report and creates a matching HTML file. The following HTML file shows the output of such a file created by a typical day's execution of this script.

```
<html>
  <head>
    <title>HTML Conversion Script</title>
    <style>
      TD { font-family:arial;
      font-size:11pt;
      border-top: thin ridge black;
      border-bottom: thin ridge black;
      border-right: thin ridge black;
      border-left: thin ridge black; }
    </style
  </head>
  <body>
    <table width='100%' border='0' cellspacing='0' cellpadding='5'>
      <tr>
        <td colspan='5' style='background:purple; color:yellow;'>
        <center><b>Errors:</b></center></td>
      </tr>
      <tr>
        <td><b>Date<b></td>
        <td><b>Time<b></td>
        <td><b>Svr<b></td>
        <td><b>Code<b></td>
        <td><b>Description<b></td>
      </tr>
      <tr>
        <td>03/15/03</td>
        <td>12:15:44</td>
        <td>Sr1</td>
        <td>001</td>
```

```
    <td>Unable to access card reader on device wkstn442</td>
  </tr>
  <tr>
    <td>03/15/03</td>
    <td>14:00:14</td>
    <td>Sr1</td>
    <td>001</td>
    <td>No inventory for part # 58694 - unable to fill order 39312 </td>
  </tr>
  <tr>
    <td>03/15/03</td>
    <td>16:16:46</td>
    <td>Sr1</td>
    <td>003</td>
    <td>Unable to print summary rpt on master printer (no paper) </td>
  </tr>
  <tr>
    <td>03/15/03</td>
    <td>12:15:44</td>
    <td>Sr2</td>
    <td>001</td>
    <td>Unable to access card reader on device wkstn442</td>
  </tr>
  <tr>
    <td>03/15/03</td>
    <td>14:00:14</td>
    <td>Sr2</td>
    <td>001</td>
    <td>No inventory for part # 58694 - unable to fill order 39312 </td>
  </tr>
  <tr>
    <td>03/15/03</td>
    <td>16:16:46</td>
    <td>Sr2</td>
    <td>003</td>
    <td>Unable to print summary rpt on master printer (no paper) </td>
  </tr>
</table><p>
```

```
<table width='100%' border='0' cellspacing='0' cellpadding='5'>
  <tr>
    <td colspan='5' style='background:purple; color:yellow;'>
    <center><b>Sales Summary:</b></center></td>
  </tr>
  <tr>
    <td colspan='3'>
    <b>Government:</b></td>
  </tr>
  <tr>
    <td><b>Part #</b></td>
    <td><b>Qty</b></td>
    <td><b>Description</b></td>
  </tr>
  <tr>
    <td>58694</td>
    <td>19</td>
    <td> Cordless temp reader</td>
  </tr>
  <tr>
    <td>45643</td>
    <td> 3</td>
    <td> 200hp magnetic pump</td>
  </tr>
  <tr>
    <td>17443</td>
    <td>15</td>
    <td> 20 lb box of pump clips</td>
  </tr>
  <tr>
    <td>10344</td>
    <td>35</td>
    <td> 48 ounce solvent bottle</td>
  </tr>
  <tr>
    <td>19365</td>
    <td> 2</td>
    <td> 3 speed electric drill</td>
```

```
    </tr>
    <tr>
      <td colspan='3'>
      <b>Other Customers:</b></td>
    </tr>
    <tr>
      <td><b>Part #</b></td>
      <td><b>Qty</b></td>
      <td><b>Description</b></td>
    </tr>
    <tr>
      <td>58694</td>
      <td>19</td>
      <td> Cordless temp reader</td>
    </tr>
    <tr>
      <td>45643</td>
      <td> 3</td>
      <td> 200hp magnetic pump</td>
    </tr>
    <tr>
      <td>17443</td>
      <td>15</td>
      <td> 20 lb box of pump clips</td>
    </tr>
    <tr>
      <td>10344</td>
      <td>35</td>
      <td> 48 ounce solvent bottle</td>
    </tr>
    <tr>
      <td>19365</td>
      <td> 2</td>
      <td> 3 speed electric drill</td>
    </tr>
  </table><p>
  <table width='100%' border='0' cellspacing='0' cellpadding='5'>
    <tr>
```

```
  <td colspan='5' style='background:purple; color:yellow;'>
  <center><b>Returns Summary:</b></center></td>
</tr>
<tr>
  <td colspan='3'>
  <b>Government:</b></td>
</tr>
<tr>
  <td><b>Part #</b></td>
  <td><b>Qty</b></td>
  <td><b>Description</b></td>
</tr>
<tr>
  <td>58694</td>
  <td> 2</td>
  <td> Cordless temp reader</td>
</tr>
<tr>
  <td>17443</td>
  <td> 7</td>
  <td> 20 lb box of pump clips</td>
</tr>
<tr>
  <td>10344</td>
  <td> 4</td>
  <td> 48 ounce solvent bottle</td>
</tr>
<tr>
  <td>45643</td>
  <td> 1</td>
  <td> 200hp magnetic pump</td>
</tr>
<tr>
  <td>19365</td>
  <td> 1</td>
  <td> 3 speed electric drill</td>
</tr>
<tr>
```

```
    <td colspan='3'>
    <b>Other Customers:</b></td>
  </tr>
  <tr>
    <td><b>Part #</b></td>
    <td><b>Qty</b></td>
    <td><b>Description</b></td>
  </tr>
  <tr>
    <td>58694</td>
    <td> 2</td>
    <td> Cordless temp reader</td>
  </tr>
  <tr>
    <td>17443</td>
    <td> 7</td>
    <td> 20 lb box of pump clips</td>
  </tr>
  <tr>
    <td>10344</td>
    <td> 4</td>
    <td> 48 ounce solvent bottle</td>
  </tr>
  <tr>
    <td>45643</td>
    <td> 1</td>
    <td> 200hp magnetic pump</td>
  </tr>
  <tr>
    <td>19365</td>
    <td> 1</td>
    <td> 3 speed electric drill</td>
  </tr>
</table><p>
<table width='100%' border='0' cellspacing='0' cellpadding='5'>
  <tr>
    <td colspan='5' style='background:purple; color:yellow;'>
    <center><b>Daily Production Summary:</b></center></td>
```

```
</tr>
<tr>
  <td><b>Part #</b></td>
  <td><b>Qty</b></td>
  <td><b>Description</b></td>
  <td><b>In Stock</b></td>
</tr>
<tr>
  <td>58694</td>
  <td>20</td>
  <td> Cordless temp reader</td>
  <td>50</td>
</tr>
<tr>
  <td>45643</td>
  <td>4</td>
  <td> 200hp magnetic pump</td>
  <td>20</td>
</tr>
<tr>
  <td>19365</td>
  <td>10</td>
  <td> 3 speed electric drill</td>
  <td>20</td>
</tr>
<tr>
  <td>17443</td>
  <td>40</td>
  <td> 20 lb box of pump clips</td>
  <td>200</td>
</tr>
<tr>
  <td>10344</td>
  <td>200</td>
  <td> 48 ounce solvent bottle</td>
  <td>500</td>
</tr>
<tr>
```

```
      <td>99887</td>
      <td>1</td>
      <td> 48 ounce joint compound</td>
      <td>12</td>
    </tr>
    <tr>
      <td>33443</td>
      <td>3</td>
      <td> 5 speed hydro drill</td>
      <td>5</td>
    </tr>
    <tr>
      <td>12211</td>
      <td>3</td>
      <td> 3 speed water pump</td>
      <td>5</td>
    </tr>
  </body>
</html>
```

Figure 30.1 shows how the daily consolidated summary report will look when viewed as an HTML page displayed on the Order/Inventory Reporting Web site.

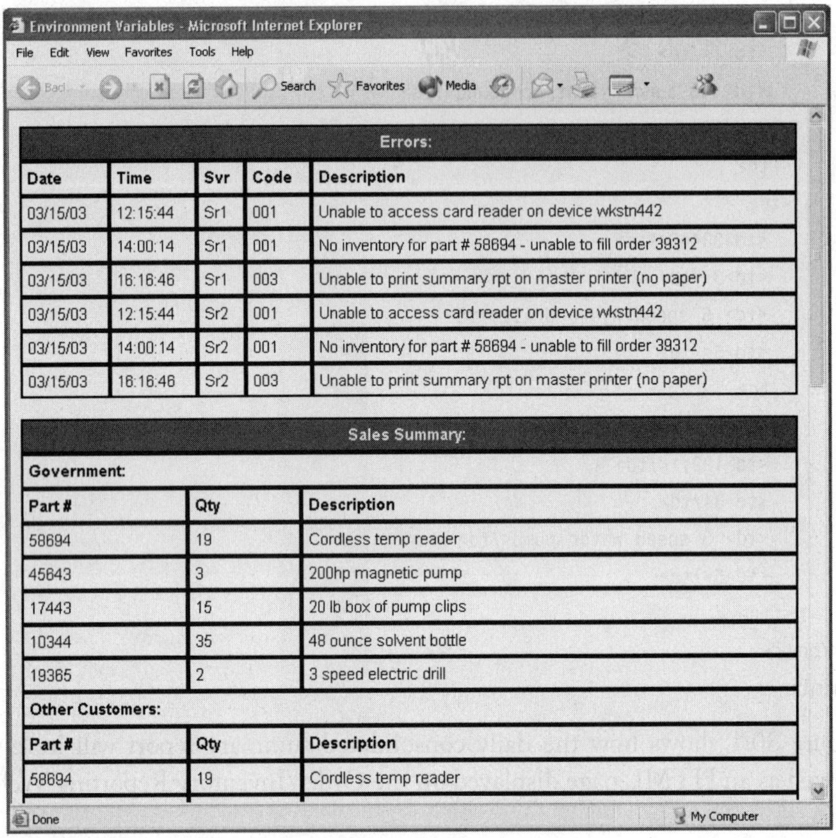

FIGURE 30.1 *Viewing the HTML version of the consolidated summary report*

Summary

In this chapter, you observed as Alexander created a text-to-HTML report conversion script. In creating this script, you learned how to embed HTML tags within VBScript-generated output files in order to automate the presentation of order/inventory data on the Order/Inventory Web site. This chapter also presented you with the opportunity to work with the `RegExp` object and its properties and methods.

Chapter 31

Building the Report Archive Page

In this chapter, Alexander will create a WSH-executed VBScript that creates an HTML page made up of links to all of the consolidated summary reports located in a report archive folder on the Intuit Web server. The report links will be organized and displayed by month. This page will also display a second set of links that provide visitors with the ability to view and download copies of the Microsoft Word versions of the consolidated summary reports.

Working with the Folder Object and the Files Collection

In order to develop the VBScript that will generate the Report Archive page, Alexander needs to learn how to work with both the `Folder` object and the `Files Collection`. To begin, he will need to establish a network connection to the shared folder on the Web server where the HTML versions of the consolidated summary reports are stored. Once this is done, he can use the `FileSystem Object` object's `GetFolder()` method to retrieve a reference to the shared folder. The syntax for the `GetFolder()` method is shown below.

```
ObjectReference.GetFolder(FolderName)
```

`ObjectReference` is the variable representing an instance of the `FileSystem Object`. `FolderName` specifies the name of the target folder.

> **NOTE**
>
> If the specified folder does not exist, the `GetFolder()` method will return an error. Consider using the `FolderExists()` method to first see whether the folder exists before attempting to use the `GetFolder()` method.

The reference set up by the `GetFolder()` method establishes a `Folder` object. Once established, your script can access all of the properties belonging to the `Folder` object. For example, the following VBScript statements demonstrate how to use the `GetFolder()` method to establish a reference to the `C:\Temp` folder on the local computer.

```
Set FsoObj = CreateObject("Scripting.FileSystemObject")
Set strTargetFile = FsoObj.GetFolder("c:\Temp")
MsgBox "Folder " & strTargetFile & " was last accessed on " & _
  strTargetFile.DateLastAccessed
```

Once the reference is established (by `strTargetFile`), the `Folder` object's `DateLastAccessed` property is displayed. Figure 31.1 shows the output displayed by this example.

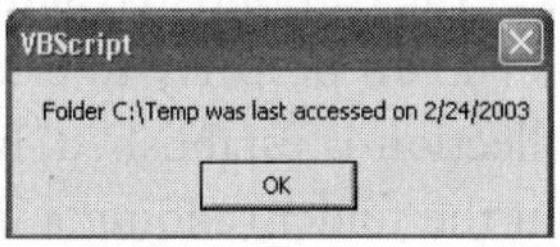

FIGURE 31.1 *Using the `Folder` object's properties to access information about a folder*

Once the `Folder` object has been established, you can use its `Files` property to retrieve a `Files Collection`. This collection will be made up of all the files that reside within the specified folder. For example, the following VBScript statements demonstrate how to list all of the files located within the `C:\Temp` folder found on the local computer.

```
Set FsoObj = CreateObject("Scripting.FileSystemObject")
Set strTargetFolder = FsoObj.GetFolder("c:\Temp")
Set strFileList = strTargetFolder.Files

For Each x in strFileList
  strDisplayList = strDisplayList & x & vbCrLf
Next

MsgBox strDisplayList
```

The `Files Collection` (represented by `strFileList`) is established by assigning the value stored in the `Folder` object's `Files` property (represented by `strTargetFolder.Files`) to a variable. Once established, a `For Each...Next` loop is set up to iterate through the collection of files and build a display string. Figure 31.2 demonstrates the output produced by this example.

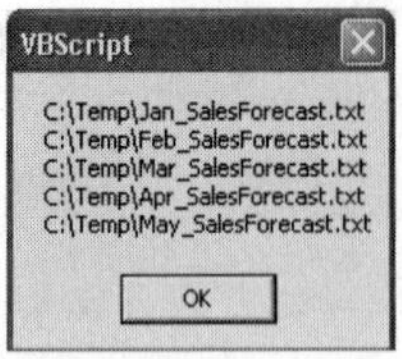

FIGURE 31.2 *By looping through the* `Files Collection`, *you can programmatically process all the files stored within a specified folder*

Alexander plans to use the `GetFolder()` method to set up a reference to the folder on the Web server where the HTML versions of the consolidated summary reports reside. He will then use the `Folder` object's `Files` property to establish a `Files Collection` for the folder. Once the collection is established, he can create a loop and use it to process each of the files in the folder (adding a link to the Report Archive page for each file in the collection).

Assembling the Report Archive Page

Alexander is now ready to begin work on the scripts that will automate the creation of the Report Archive page. As with his previous script, he plans to follow the organizational model developed by Molly. This will include providing support for a debug mode and for recording messages in the Windows application event log. Alexander will also add logic that provides a script return code.

The Initialization Section

The script's `Initialization Section`, shown below, begins by enforcing the strict interpretation of variable naming. It then defines all the variables used globally throughout the script and the `Main Processing Section`, including variables representing configuration settings—which will be extracted from the registry—and variables that represent the `FileSystemObject`, `WshNetwork`, and `WshShell` objects.

```
Option Explicit

Dim strSharedFolder, strSharedFiles, strWordList, strArchiveFile
Dim strWordFileName, intMonth, strMonth, intMonthStore
```

```
Dim strEventLog, strDebug, strHTMLFolder, strSharedRptFolder, strWebSvrName

Dim intReturnCode, intYearLoc, dtmYear

Const cForReading = 1
Const cForWriting = 2
Const cForAppending = 8
Const cTitleBarMsg = "Archive Link Maintenance Script"

Dim FsoObj, WshNtk, WshShl

Set FsoObj = CreateObject("Scripting.FileSystemObject")
Set WshNtk = WScript.CreateObject("WScript.Network")
Set WshShl = WScript.CreateObject("WScript.Shell")

intReturnCode = 0
intMonthStore = 0
```

Also defined is a collection of constants that specify file I/O options and the title bar message used in all pop-up dialog boxes created when the script is run in debug mode. Finally, the initial values are assigned to two variables. A zero is assigned to `intReturnCode`, representing the script's default return code. A zero is also assigned to `intMonthStore`. This variable is used in the `Main Processing Section` to determine when a new month-year subheading needs to be written on the HTML page.

The Main Processing Section

The script's `Main Processing Section`, shown on the following page, begins by calling the `GetRegistrySettings()` subroutine. This subroutine retrieves the script's configuration settings and provides it with information such as where to find the consolidated report archive and where to save the HTML file that it creates. Pop-up dialog boxes will display intermediate results using the `MsgBox()` function and will identify when key activities are occurring if the script is run in debug mode. Likewise, if event logging is enabled, informational messages will be recorded in the Windows application event log by the `WriteToEventLog` subroutine.

```
GetRegistrySettings()

If strEventLog = "Enabled" Then
  WriteToEventLog("Archive Link Maintenance Script now executing.")
End If

If strDebug = "Enabled" Then
  MsgBox "Beginning development of the archive list.", , cTitleBarMsg
End If

Set strArchiveFile = FsoObj.OpenTextFile(strHTMLFolder & "\Archive.html", _
  cForWriting , "True")

MapNetworkDrive "V:", "\\" & strWebSvrName & "\" & strSharedRptFolder

Set strSharedFolder = FsoObj.GetFolder("V:")

Set strSharedFiles = strSharedFolder.Files

WriteHeader()

WriteH3Heading()

For Each strWordList In strSharedFiles

  If Instr(1, strWordList.Name, ".doc") = 0 Then

    int1stDash = InStr(1, strWordList.Name, "-")
    intLengthOfMonth = int1stDash - 1
    intMonth = Left(strWordList.Name, intLengthOfMonth)

    If intMonth <> intMonthStore Then
      intYearLoc = Instr(1, strWordList.Name, "_")
      dtmYear = Mid(strWordList.Name, intYearLoc - 4, 4)

      intMonthStore = intMonth
      strMonth = MonthName(intMonth)
      strArchiveFile.WriteLine("<B><P>" & strMonth & " " & dtmYear & "</B><P>")
    End If
```

```
    strWordFileName = Replace(strWordList.Name, "html", "doc" )

    strArchiveFile.WriteLine("<A HREF=../" & "\Rpts\" & strWordList.Name & _
      ">" & strWordList.Name & "</A>" & " - " & "<A HREF=../" & "\Rpts\" & _
      strWordFileName & ">(Download Word Version) </A><BR>")
  End If

Next

DisconnectNetworkDrive("V:")

WriteFooter()

If strDebug = "Enabled" Then
  MsgBox "Archive list now completed.", , cTitleBarMsg
End If

If strEventLog = "Enabled" Then
  WriteToEventLog ("Archive Link Maintenance Script finished executing.")
End If

TerminateScript(intReturnCode)
```

The next activity performed in the `Main Processing Section` is instantiation of the variable representing the `Archive.html` file, which the script is creating. Next, the `MapNetworkDrive()` function is called to set up a network connection to the shared folder where HTML versions of the consolidated summary reports reside (on the Web server). Then the `GetFolder()` method is used to set up a working reference to the shared folder. Once this is done, a `Files Collection` is set up and associated with a variable called `strSharedFiles`.

At this point, writing the new HTML page can start. First, the `WriteHeader()` subroutine is called. This subroutine writes the HTML page's opening set of HTML tags. Then the `WriteH3Heading()` subroutine is called to write the page's main header. A `For Each...Next` loop is then used to process the files residing in the previously created `Files Collection`.

The loop begins by filtering out any files that have a `.doc` file extension, leaving only the HTML files for processing. The next three statements figure out the month with which the file is associated. The statements find the location of the first occurrence of the dash character within the file name, subtract 1, and then use the `Left()` function to set `intMonth` equal to the one- or two-character month value. The value of this variable is then compared to the value of `intMonthStore` (which is set equal to zero when the script first starts executing). If the values are different, the name of the month and the year in which the month occurs are written (in bold) to the HTML page as a section heading. In addition, the value of `intMonth` is set equal to the value of `intMonthStore`, thus ensuring that a new month-year header will be written if the loop later processes an HTML file that was created in a different month.

Next, the `Replace()` function is used to assign the name of the HTML page's corresponding Word report file and the `WriteLine()` method is used to write a string. The first portion of this string represents a link to the archive HTML file with which the link is associated. Its location is specified relative to the location of the script. The second portion of the string represents a link to the associated Word version of the archived report.

The `Main Processing Section` finishes up by calling the `DisconnectNetworkDrive()` subroutine, which breaks the mapped drive connection that the script set up in order to retrieve the `Files Collection`. Next the `WriteFooter()` subroutine is called in order to write the HTML page's closing HTML tags, and then the `TerminateScript()` procedure is executed.

The GetRegistrySettings() Subroutine

As with Alexander's previous script, the `GetRegistrySettings()` subroutine, shown below, retrieves the script's configuration settings from the Windows registry.

```
Sub GetRegistrySettings()

  On Error Resume Next

  strEventLog = _
    WshShl.RegRead("HKLM\Software\Intuit\VBScripts\WebRpting\EventLogging")
  If Err <> 0 Then
    If strEventLog = "Enabled" Then
      WriteToEventLog ("HTML Report Conversion Script - Using default " & _
        "for strEventLog. RC = 4")
```

```
    TerminateScript(12)
  End If
End If

strDebug = WshShl.RegRead("HKLM\Software\Intuit\VBScripts\WebRpting\Debug")
If Err <> 0 Then
  If strEventLog = "Enabled" Then
    WriteToEventLog ("HTML Report Conversion Script - Using default " & _
      "for strDebug. RC = 4")
    TerminateScript(12)
  End If
End If

strHTMLFolder = _
  WshShl.RegRead("HKLM\Software\Intuit\VBScripts\WebRpting\HTMLFolder")
If Err <> 0 Then
  If strEventLog = "Enabled" Then
    WriteToEventLog ("HTML Report Conversion Script - Using default " & _
      "for strHTMLFolder. RC = 4")
    TerminateScript(12)
  End If
End If

strSharedRptFolder = _
  WshShl.RegRead("HKLM\Software\Intuit\VBScripts\WebRpting\Share_Rpts")
If Err <> 0 Then
If strEventLog = "Enabled" Then
    WriteToEventLog ("HTML Report Conversion Script - Using default " & _
      "for strSharedRptFolder. RC = 4")
    TerminateScript(12)
  End If
End If

strWebSvrName = _
  WshShl.RegRead("HKLM\Software\Intuit\VBScripts\WebRpting\WebServer")
If Err <> 0 Then
If strEventLog = "Enabled" Then
    WriteToEventLog ("HTML Report Conversion Script - Using default " & _
```

```
          "for strWebSvrName. RC = 4")
        TerminateScript(12)
      End If
    End If

    If strDebug = "Enabled" Then
      MsgBox "Registry settings initialized: " & vbCrLf & vbCrLf & _
        "strEventLog" & vbTab & "=" & vbTab & strEventLog & vbCrLf & _
        "strDebug" & vbTab & vbTab & "=" & vbTab & strDebug & vbCrLf & _
        "strHTMLFolder" & vbTab & "=" & vbTab & strHTMLFolder & vbCrLf & _
        "strSharedRptFolder" & vbTab & "=" & vbTab & strSharedRptFolder & _
        vbCrLf & "strWebSvrName" & vbTab & "=" & vbTab & strWebSvrName & _
        vbCrLf, ,cTitleBarMsg
    End If

End Sub
```

The WriteHeader() Subroutine

The `WriteHeader()` subroutine, shown below, is responsible for writing the HTML page's open HTML tags and for specifying an opening `<FONT>` tag, which specifies the Courier font. This font was selected because it prints every character using a consistent character size, which will help provide for a consistent presentation of report data.

```
Sub WriteHeader()
  strArchiveFile.WriteLine("<HTML>")
  strArchiveFile.WriteLine("  <HEAD>")
  strArchiveFile.WriteLine("    <TITLE>Environment Variables</TITLE>")
  strArchiveFile.WriteLine("  </HEAD>")
  strArchiveFile.WriteLine("  <BODY>")
  strArchiveFile.WriteLine("    <FONT FACE='Courier'>")
End Sub
```

The WriteH3Heading() Subroutine

The `WriteH3Heading()` subroutine, shown on the following page, writes an `<H3>` level HTML heading to the HTML page, representing the page's title.

```
Sub WriteH3Heading()
  strArchiveFile.WriteLine("<H3>Order/Inventory Reporting Archive</H3><P>")
End Sub
```

The WriteFooter() Subroutine

The `WriteFooter()` subroutine, shown below, writes the HTML page's closing HTML tags, including a closing `</FONT>` tag.

```
Sub WriteFooter()
  strArchiveFile.WriteLine("    </FONT>")
  strArchiveFile.WriteLine("  </BODY>")
  strArchiveFile.WriteLine("</HTML>")
End Sub
```

The MapNetworkDrive() Function

The `MapNetworkDrive()` function, shown below, is responsible for establishing a network connection to the shared folder on the corporate Web server, where the archived copies of the HTML versions of the consolidated summary reports are stored.

```
Function MapNetworkDrive(strLetter, strDrive)

  If strDebug = "Enabled" Then
    MsgBox "strLetter = " & strLetter & vbCrLf & "strDrive = " & _
      strDrive, , cTitleBarMsg
  End If

  If FsoObj.DriveExists(strDrive) Then

    If strDebug = "Enabled" Then
      MsgBox strDrive & " exists", , cTitleBarMsg
    End If

    If FsoObj.DriveExists(strLetter) Then

      If strDebug = "Enabled" Then
         MsgBox "Deleting drive letter " & strLetter, , cTitleBarMsg
```

```
        End If

        WshNtk.RemoveNetworkDrive strLetter

      End If

      WshNtk.MapNetworkDrive strLetter, strDrive

    Else

      If strDebug = "Enabled" Then
        MsgBox strDrive & " does not exist", , cTitleBarMsg
      End If

      If strEventLog = "Enabled" Then
        WriteToEventLog "Summary Report Collection script - Unable to map " & _
        "to network drive " & strDrive
      End If
      TerminateScript(4)
    End If

  End Function
```

The drive letter to be used to set up the network connection and the path to the remote folder are passed to the function as arguments. The `FileSystemObject` object's `DriveExists()` method is used to determine whether or not the remote drive is available. If it is not available, the `TerminateScript()` subroutine is called and passed a value of 4, representing the script's return code. If the network drive is accessible, the function next checks to make sure that the specified drive letter is not already in use. If it is, its connection is disconnected using the `RemoveNetworkDrive()` method and the connection to the shared folder on the Web server is created using the `MapNetworkDrive()` method.

The DisconnectNetworkDrive() Subroutine

The `DisconnectNetworkDrive()` subroutine, shown on the next page, disconnects a network drive connection using the `WshNetwork` object's `RemoveNetworkDrive()` method. The connection to be terminated is specified by a variable called `strDriveLetter`, which is passed to the subroutine as an argument.

```
Sub DisconnectNetworkDrive(strDriveLetter)

  On Error Resume Next

  If strDebug = "Enabled" Then
    MsgBox "Disconnecting " & strDriveLetter, , cTitleBarMsg
  End If

  WshNtk.RemoveNetworkDrive strDriveLetter
  If Err <> 0 Then
    If strDebug = "Enabled" Then
      MsgBox "Error occurred when disconnecting " & strDriveLetter, , _
        cTitleBarMsg
    End If
  End If

End Sub
```

The WriteToEventLog() Subroutine

The `WriteToEventLog()` subroutine, shown below, writes a message which is passed to it as an argument to the Windows application event log.

```
Sub WriteToEventLog(strMessage)

  WshShl.LogEvent 4, strMessage

End Sub
```

The TerminateScript() Subroutine

The `TerminateScript()` subroutine, shown on the following page, uses the `WScript` object's `Quit()` method to halt the script's execution. In addition, it passes a script return code (indicating whether or not the script ran successfully) back to its calling script. This return code is passed to it as an argument called `intRC`, which is initially set equal to zero at the beginning of the script's execution.

```
Sub TerminateScript(intRC)

  If strDebug = "Enabled" Then
    MsgBox "Script execution terminated.", , cTitleBarMsg
  End If

  WScript.Quit(intRC)

End Sub
```

The Fully Assembled Script

The fully assembled script, shown below, creates the Report Archive page by connecting to the corporate Web server in order to collect a list of the currently available HTML consolidated summary report files. It then builds an HTML page by creating a link for each file that is found. A second set of links is added for the Word versions of the reports, allowing visitors to view and download formal copies of the reports.

```
'*************************************************************************
'Script Name: Script 31.1.vbs
'Author: Jerry Ford
'Created: 05/06/03
'Description: This script creates an HTML page that provides a list of
'links to old Order/Inventory consolidated reports.
'*************************************************************************

'Initialization Section

Option Explicit

Dim strSharedFolder, strSharedFiles, strWordList, strArchiveFile
Dim strWordFileName, intMonth, strMonth, intMonthStore

Dim strEventLog, strDebug, strHTMLFolder, strSharedRptFolder, strWebSvrName

Dim intReturnCode, intYearLoc, dtmYear
```

```
Const cForReading = 1
Const cForWriting = 2
Const cForAppending = 8
Const cTitleBarMsg = "Archive Link Maintenance Script"

Dim FsoObj, WshNtk, WshShl

Set FsoObj = CreateObject("Scripting.FileSystemObject")
Set WshNtk = WScript.CreateObject("WScript.Network")
Set WshShl = WScript.CreateObject("WScript.Shell")

intReturnCode = 0
intMonthStore = 0


'Main Processing Section

GetRegistrySettings()

If strEventLog = "Enabled" Then
  WriteToEventLog("Archive Link Maintenance Script now executing.")
End If

If strDebug = "Enabled" Then
  MsgBox "Beginning development of the archive list.", , cTitleBarMsg
End If

Set strArchiveFile = FsoObj.OpenTextFile(strHTMLFolder & "\Archive.html", _
  cForWriting , "True")

MapNetworkDrive "V:", "\\" & strWebSvrName & "\" & strSharedRptFolder

Set strSharedFolder = FsoObj.GetFolder("V:")

Set strSharedFiles = strSharedFolder.Files

WriteHeader()
```

```
WriteH3Heading()

For Each strWordList In strSharedFiles

  If Instr(1, strWordList.Name, ".doc") = 0 Then

    int1stDash = InStr(1, strWordList.Name, "-")
    intLengthOfMonth = int1stDash - 1
    intMonth = Left(strWordList.Name, intLengthOfMonth)

    If intMonth <> intMonthStore Then
      intYearLoc = Instr(1, strWordList.Name, "_")
      dtmYear = Mid(strWordList.Name, intYearLoc - 4, 4)

      intMonthStore = intMonth
      strMonth = MonthName(intMonth)
      strArchiveFile.WriteLine("<B><P>" & strMonth & " " & dtmYear & "</B><P>")
    End If

    strWordFileName = Replace(strWordList.Name, "html", "doc" )

    strArchiveFile.WriteLine("<A HREF=../" & "\Rpts\" & strWordList.Name & _
      ">" & strWordList.Name & "</A>" & " - " & "<A HREF=../" & "\Rpts\" & _
      strWordFileName & ">(Download Word Version) </A><BR>")
  End If

Next

DisconnectNetworkDrive("V:")

WriteFooter()

If strDebug = "Enabled" Then
  MsgBox "Archive list now completed.", , cTitleBarMsg
End If

If strEventLog = "Enabled" Then
  WriteToEventLog ("Archive Link Maintenance Script finished executing.")
```

```
End If

TerminateScript(intReturnCode)


'Procedure Section

Sub GetRegistrySettings()

  On Error Resume Next

  strEventLog = _
    WshShl.RegRead("HKLM\Software\Intuit\VBScripts\WebRpting\EventLogging")
  If Err <> 0 Then
    If strEventLog = "Enabled" Then
      WriteToEventLog ("HTML Report Conversion Script - Using default " & _
        "for strEventLog. RC = 4")
      TerminateScript(12)
    End If
  End If

  strDebug = WshShl.RegRead("HKLM\Software\Intuit\VBScripts\WebRpting\Debug")
  If Err <> 0 Then
    If strEventLog = "Enabled" Then
      WriteToEventLog ("HTML Report Conversion Script - Using default " & _
        "for strDebug. RC = 4")
      TerminateScript(12)
    End If
  End If

  strHTMLFolder = _
    WshShl.RegRead("HKLM\Software\Intuit\VBScripts\WebRpting\HTMLFolder")
  If Err <> 0 Then
    If strEventLog = "Enabled" Then
      WriteToEventLog ("HTML Report Conversion Script - Using default " & _
        "for strHTMLFolder. RC = 4")
      TerminateScript(12)
    End If
```

```
End If

strSharedRptFolder = _
  WshShl.RegRead("HKLM\Software\Intuit\VBScripts\WebRpting\Share_Rpts")
If Err <> 0 Then
If strEventLog = "Enabled" Then
    WriteToEventLog ("HTML Report Conversion Script - Using default " & _
      "for strSharedRptFolder. RC = 4")
    TerminateScript(12)
  End If
End If

strWebSvrName = _
  WshShl.RegRead("HKLM\Software\Intuit\VBScripts\WebRpting\WebServer")
If Err <> 0 Then
If strEventLog = "Enabled" Then
    WriteToEventLog ("HTML Report Conversion Script - Using default " & _
      "for strWebSvrName. RC = 4")
    TerminateScript(12)
  End If
End If


If strDebug = "Enabled" Then
  MsgBox "Registry settings initialized: " & vbCrLf & vbCrLf & _
    "strEventLog" & vbTab & "=" & vbTab & strEventLog & vbCrLf & _
    "strDebug" & vbTab & vbTab & "=" & vbTab & strDebug & vbCrLf & _
    "strHTMLFolder" & vbTab & "=" & vbTab & strHTMLFolder & vbCrLf & _
    "strSharedRptFolder" & vbTab & "=" & vbTab & strSharedRptFolder & _
    vbCrLf & "strWebSvrName" & vbTab & "=" & vbTab & strWebSvrName & _
    vbCrLf, ,cTitleBarMsg
End If

End Sub

Sub WriteHeader()
  strArchiveFile.WriteLine("<HTML>")
  strArchiveFile.WriteLine("  <HEAD>")
```

```
  strArchiveFile.WriteLine("    <TITLE>Environment Variables</TITLE>")
  strArchiveFile.WriteLine("  </HEAD>")
  strArchiveFile.WriteLine("  <BODY>")
  strArchiveFile.WriteLine("    <FONT FACE='Courier'>")
End Sub

Sub WriteH3Heading()
  strArchiveFile.WriteLine("<H3>Order/Inventory Reporting Archive</H3><P>")
End Sub

Sub WriteFooter()
  strArchiveFile.WriteLine("    </FONT>")
  strArchiveFile.WriteLine("  </BODY>")
  strArchiveFile.WriteLine("</HTML>")
End Sub

Function MapNetworkDrive(strLetter, strDrive)

  If strDebug = "Enabled" Then
    MsgBox "strLetter = " & strLetter & vbCrLf & "strDrive = " & _
      strDrive, , cTitleBarMsg
  End If

  If FsoObj.DriveExists(strDrive) Then

    If strDebug = "Enabled" Then
      MsgBox strDrive & " exists", , cTitleBarMsg
    End If

    If FsoObj.DriveExists(strLetter) Then

      If strDebug = "Enabled" Then
         MsgBox "Deleting drive letter " & strLetter, , cTitleBarMsg
      End If

      WshNtk.RemoveNetworkDrive strLetter

    End If
```

```
    WshNtk.MapNetworkDrive strLetter, strDrive

  Else

    If strDebug = "Enabled" Then
      MsgBox strDrive & " does not exist", , cTitleBarMsg
    End If

    If strEventLog = "Enabled" Then
      WriteToEventLog "Summary Report Collection script - Unable to map " & _
      "to network drive " & strDrive
    End If
    TerminateScript(4)
  End If

End Function

Sub DisconnectNetworkDrive(strDriveLetter)

  On Error Resume Next

  If strDebug = "Enabled" Then
    MsgBox "Disconnecting " & strDriveLetter, , cTitleBarMsg
  End If

  WshNtk.RemoveNetworkDrive strDriveLetter
  If Err <> 0 Then
    If strDebug = "Enabled" Then
      MsgBox "Error occurred when disconnecting " & strDriveLetter, , _
        cTitleBarMsg
    End If
  End If

End Sub


Sub WriteToEventLog(strMessage)
```

```
  WshShl.LogEvent 4, strMessage

End Sub

Sub TerminateScript(intRC)

  If strDebug = "Enabled" Then
    MsgBox "Script execution terminated.", , cTitleBarMsg
  End If

  WScript.Quit(intRC)

End Sub
```

The Content of the HTML File

The end result of executing this chapter's VBScript is the creation of an HTML page that contains links to all of the consolidated summary reports stored on the Web server. The following listing shows an example of an HTML page created by the VBScript. To make the example easier to view, all but the first three days' worth of entries for each month have been deleted.

```
<HTML>
  <HEAD>
    <TITLE>Environment Variables</TITLE>
  </HEAD>
  <BODY>
    <FONT FACE='Courier'>
<H3>Order/Inventory Reporting Archive</H3><P>
<B><P>May 2003</B><P>
        <A HREF=../\Rpts\5-1-2003_ConsolSumRpt.html>
            5-1-2003_ConsolSumRpt.html</A> -
        <A HREF=../\Rpts\5-1-2003_ConsolSumRpt.doc>
            (Download Word Version) </A><BR>
        <A HREF=../\Rpts\5-2-2003_ConsolSumRpt.html>
            5-2-2003_ConsolSumRpt.html</A> -
        <A HREF=../\Rpts\5-2-2003_ConsolSumRpt.doc>
```

```
        (Download Word Version) </A><BR>
    <A HREF=../\Rpts\5-3-2003_ConsolSumRpt.html>
        5-3-2003_ConsolSumRpt.html</A> -
    <A HREF=../\Rpts\5-3-2003_ConsolSumRpt.doc>
        (Download Word Version) </A><BR>
<B><P>June 2003</B><P>
    <A HREF=../\Rpts\6-1-2003_ConsolSumRpt.html>
        6-1-2003_ConsolSumRpt.html</A> -
    <A HREF=../\Rpts\6-1-2003_ConsolSumRpt.doc>
        (Download Word Version) </A><BR>
    <A HREF=../\Rpts\6-2-2003_ConsolSumRpt.html>
        6-2-2003_ConsolSumRpt.html</A> -
    <A HREF=../\Rpts\6-2-2003_ConsolSumRpt.doc>
        (Download Word Version) </A><BR>
    <A HREF=../\Rpts\6-3-2003_ConsolSumRpt.html>
        6-3-2003_ConsolSumRpt.html</A> -
    <A HREF=../\Rpts\6-3-2003_ConsolSumRpt.doc>
        (Download Word Version) </A><BR>
<B><P>July 2003</B><P>    <A HREF=../\Rpts\7-1-2003_ConsolSumRpt.html>
        7-1-2003_ConsolSumRpt.html</A> -
    <A HREF=../\Rpts\7-1-2003_ConsolSumRpt.doc>
        (Download Word Version) </A><BR>
    <A HREF=../\Rpts\7-2-2003_ConsolSumRpt.html>
        7-2-2003_ConsolSumRpt.html</A> -
    <A HREF=../\Rpts\7-2-2003_ConsolSumRpt.doc>
        (Download Word Version) </A><BR>
    <A HREF=../\Rpts\7-3-2003_ConsolSumRpt.html>
        7-3-2003_ConsolSumRpt.html</A> -
    <A HREF=../\Rpts\7-3-2003_ConsolSumRpt.doc>
        (Download Word Version) </A><BR>
<B><P>August 2003</B><P>
    <A HREF=../\Rpts\8-1-2003_ConsolSumRpt.html>
        8-1-2003_ConsolSumRpt.html</A> -
    <A HREF=../\Rpts\8-1-2003_ConsolSumRpt.doc>
        (Download Word Version) </A><BR>
    <A HREF=../\Rpts\8-2-2003_ConsolSumRpt.html>
        8-2-2003_ConsolSumRpt.html</A> -
    <A HREF=../\Rpts\8-2-2003_ConsolSumRpt.doc>
```

```
        (Download Word Version) </A><BR>
      <A HREF=../\Rpts\8-3-2003_ConsolSumRpt.html>
        8-3-2003_ConsolSumRpt.html</A> -
      <A HREF=../\Rpts\8-3-2003_ConsolSumRpt.doc>
        (Download Word Version) </A><BR>
    </FONT>
  </BODY>
</HTML>
```

On the first day of each month, the archive management script (which will be developed in the next chapter) clears out any reports older than three months old. As the month progresses, the size of the archive being maintained will expand to hold four months' worth of reports. As you can see, the report displays entries for May through August.

Figure 31.3 provides an example of how the Report Archive page will look when viewed from the Order/Inventory Reporting Web site. (Again, the size of the report has been reduced to make it easier to view.)

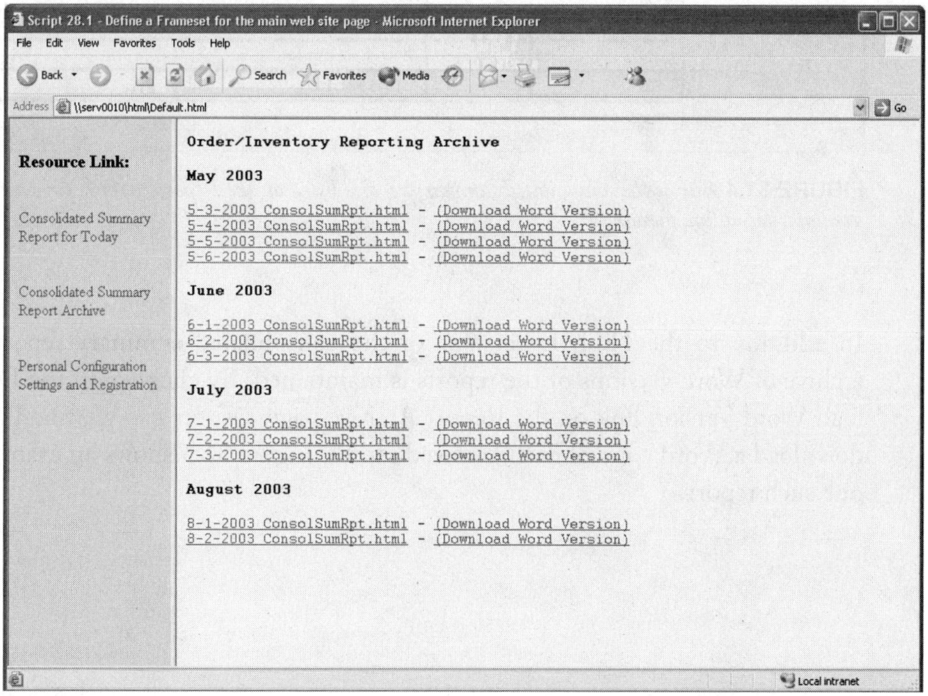

FIGURE 31.3 *Reviewing the collection of consolidated summary reports maintained on the corporate Web server*

Figure 31.4 shows an example of an archive consolidated summary report that has been selected for viewing from the Report Archive page.

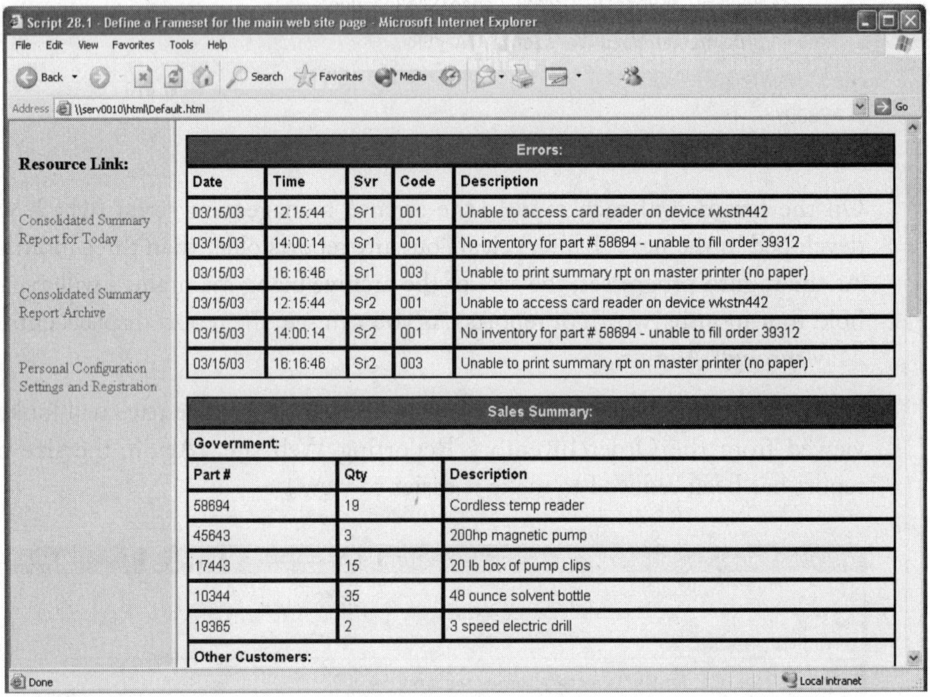

FIGURE 31.4 *Any of the consolidated summary reports listed on the Report Archive page are available for online viewing*

In addition to the HTML versions of the consolidated summary reports, an archive of Word versions of the reports is maintained. By clicking on the Download Word Version link on the Report Archive page, visitors can view and opt to download a Word copy of each archived report. Figure 31.5 shows an example of one such report.

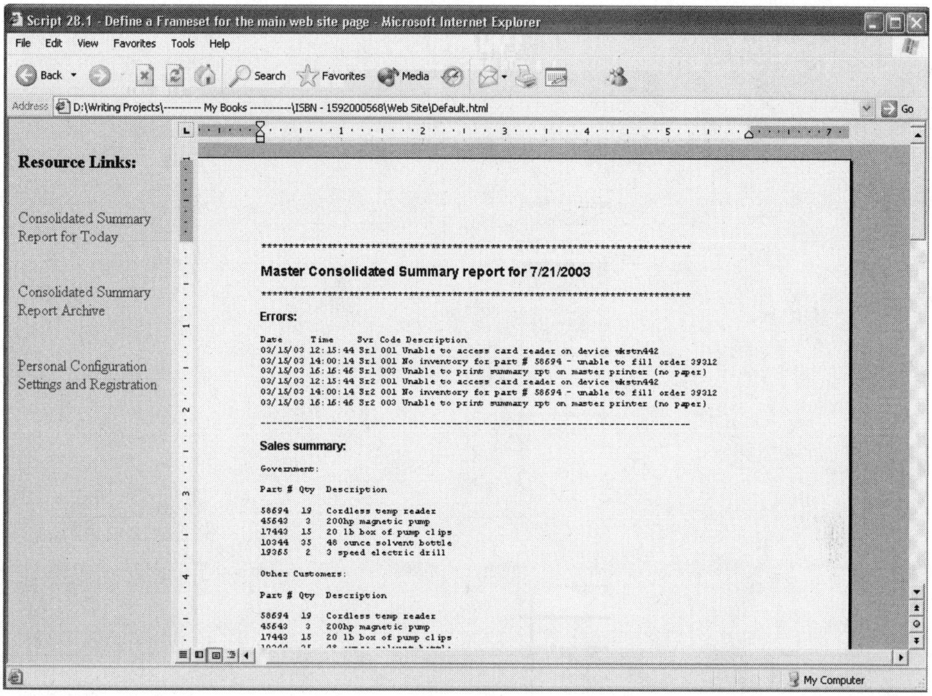

FIGURE 31.5 *Examining the Word version of an archived copy of one of the consolidated summary reports*

Summary

In this chapter, you observed as Alexander created a VBScript run by the WSH that built an HTML page. This page provided a list of links to each of the consolidated summary reports stored in an archive folder on the corporate Web server at Intuit. He also added links to the page that made copies of the Word versions of the consolidated summary reports available to visitors.

Chapter 32

Report Distribution and Remote Archive Management

This chapter represents the final script to be developed as part of the order/inventory reporting Web-based project. In this chapter, you will observe as Alexander creates a VBScript that copies HTML and Word files, as well as an updated copy of the `Archive.html` page, from the Windows 2000 Professional workstation to the corporate Web server. This script will also be used to trigger the remote execution of a small archive maintenance script, which will be started and remotely monitored from the Windows 2000 Professional workstation as it executes on the corporate Web server.

Implementing Remote Archive Management

The final tasks to be completed in the order/inventory reporting Web-based project is copying and moving files from the Windows 2000 Professional workstation to shared folders on the corporate Web server and the monthly maintenance of archive files stored in these folders. As he sat down and thought about how to complete these final two tasks, Alexander came up with three different ways of automating these activities. These options include:

- Using the Windows scheduler on the Windows 2000 Professional workstation to trigger the execution of a script on the workstation that establishes a network connection and performs archive maintenance
- Setting up a scheduled task on the corporate Web server that triggers a local script to perform archive maintenance
- Using the Windows scheduler on the Windows 2000 Professional workstation to copy an archive maintenance script to the Web server and trigger its execution using Remote WSH

Initially, Alexander was leaning toward the second option because it was the least complicated. This option eliminates the need for:

- Network connectivity
- The establishment of a remote network drive

- Workstation availability

However, Molly advised Alexander that he had better consult with the company's Web master before setting up a scheduled WSH VBScript on the corporate Web server. It turned out that Molly was correct. Michael Barns, the company's Web master, did not hesitate to tell Alexander that he was not permitted to use the server's scheduler service. Nor was Alexander allowed to store and run any VBScripts locally on the Web server.

Of the two remaining options, Alexander decided to go with the Remote WSH option because it would allow him to locally execute an archive maintenance script without having to store it on the Web server. Remote WSH provides the additional benefit of allowing monitoring of remotely executed scripts.

Introducing Remote WSH

Remote WSH provides the ability to initiate, monitor, react to, and even terminate a remotely executed script. Remote WSH is a new feature introduced by WSH version 5.6. The following requirements must be met in order to use it:

- Both the local and remote computers must support WSH version 5.6.
- Both the local and remote computers must be running Windows NT 4.0 Service Pack 3 or higher.
- Administrative privileges are required on the remote computer.

In addition to these requirements, Remote WSH must be enabled on the target computer. This is done by adding a value of Remote and assigning it a setting of 1 on the following registry key:

```
HKCU\Software\Microsoft\Windows Script Host\Settings\
```

NOTE

If you are attempting to use Remote WSH to execute a remote script on a computer running Windows XP Professional, you may have to first execute the following command on the workstation.

```
WScript -regserver
```

This command registers the `WScript.exe` execution host as a remote COM server.

Remote WSH Architecture

Remote WSH consists of several objects. These objects and their associated properties, methods, and events are shown in Figure 32.1.

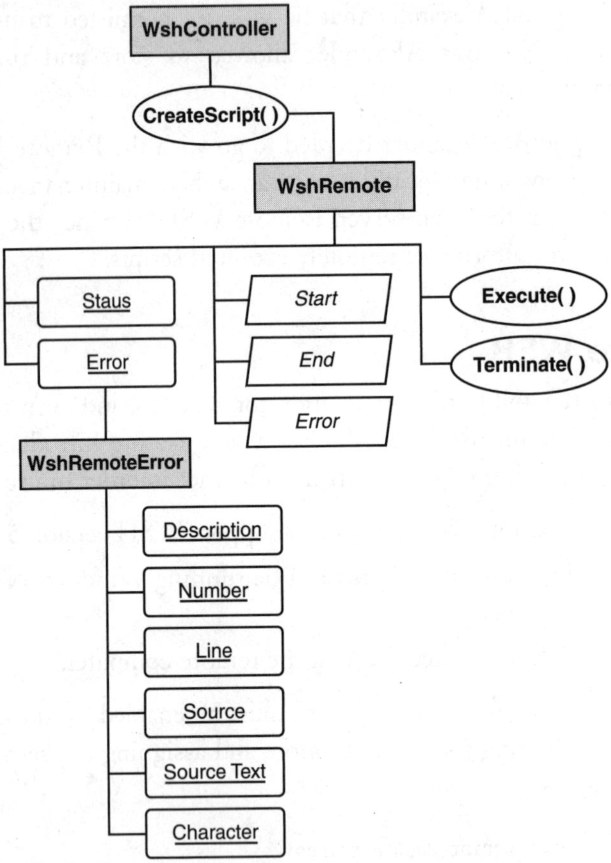

FIGURE 32.1 *The Remote WSH consists of three objects*

The topmost of these objects is the `WshController` object. The `WshController` object is instantiated as shown below.

```
Set WshControl = CreateObject("WshController")
```

The `WshController` object does not have any properties and only supports one method, `CreateScript()`. `CreateScript()` is used to create a `WshRemote` object (that is, to instantiate the `WshRemote` object). The syntax of the `CreateScript()` method is shown below.

```
ObjectReference.CreateScript(CommandLine,[ComputerName])
```

`ObjectReference` represents a variable reference to the `WshController` object. `CommandLine` is a string value that specifies the location of the script that is to be run remotely, as well as any switches that need to be included. The path to the script must be specified as it relates to its location from the local computer where the controlling script executes. `ComputerName` specifies the UNC name of the remote computer where the remote script will execute. If `ComputerName` is omitted, the remote script will run locally. For example, the following statement can be used to set up a `WshRemote` object reference called `RemoteScript` that will copy a script called `TestScript.vbs` to a computer called `SERV0010` and load it into a WSH process. However, the remote script does not begin to execute.

```
Set RemoteScript = WshControl.CreateScript(TestScript.vbs, SERV0010)
```

The `WshRemote` object (`RemoteScript`) represents the remote script and provides the ability to start, monitor, and terminate the remote script.

NOTE

The remote script is stored in memory on the remote computer. It is never written to the remote computer's hard disk drive and is deleted when its execution completes.

WshRemote Methods

The `WshRemote` object provides access to two methods. The `Execute()` method is used to trigger the remote execution of the script once it has been copied into memory on the remote computer. This method has the following syntax.

```
ObjectReference.Execute
```

`ObjectReference` specifies the variable reference to the `WshRemote` object. In order for the previously setup remote script to run on the remote computer, the following statement will have to be executed.

```
RemoteScript.Execute
```

The WshRemote object's second method is the Terminate() method. This method provides the ability to terminate a remote script. It has the following syntax.

```
ObjectReference.Terminate
```

ObjectReference specifies the variable reference to the WshRemote object. For example, to terminate the script that was set up to remotely execute in the previous example, the controlling script would have to execute the following statement.

```
RemoteScript.Terminate
```

WshRemote Events

As remote scripts execute, they can trigger up to three different events, which can be tracked by the controlling script. To set up the controlling script to handle events, you must use the WScript object's ConnectObject() method, which is used to connect an object's events with a function or subroutine that has a specified prefix. Remote WSH event procedures are established by assigning them a name made up of this prefix followed by the underscore character and the event name. The ConnectObject() method has the following syntax.

```
ObjectReference.ConnectObject(TargetObject, EventPrefix)
```

ObjectReference represents the WScript object. TargetObject specifies the name of the object to be connected to, and EventPrefix specifies a string value that will serve as the event's prefix. For example, the following statement enables the controlling script to trap events generated by the remote script using a prefix of RemoteScript_.

```
WScript.ConnectObject RemoteScript, "RemoteScript_"
```

Table 32.1 lists the three types of events that can be triggered by remote scripts.

Table 32.1 Events Triggered by Remote Scripts

Event	Description
Start	Triggered when the remote script begins executing
End	Triggered when the remote script stops executing
Error	Triggered if the remote script experiences an error

Using the previous example, you could establish an event handler for the remote script's `Start` event, as shown below.

```
Function RemoteScript_Start()
.
.
.
End Function
```

WshRemote Properties

If a remote script experiences an error, the `Error` event can be used to execute a procedure that processes error information provided by the `WshRemoteError` object. If an error occurs in a remote script, you can retrieve information about the error using the `WshRemote` object `Error` property. This property retrieves the `WshRemoteError` object, which provides access to a list of properties that provide information about the error. Table 32.2 lists each of the properties associated with the `WshRemoteError` object.

Table 32.2 Properties Associated with the WshRemote Error Object

Property	Description
`Description`	A description of error
`Number`	The numeric error code associated with the error
`Line`	The line number where the error occurred
`Source`	The object responsible for reporting the error
`SourceText`	The line of code that generated the error
`Character`	The character position in the line of code where the error occurred

NOTE

The technology behind the scenes that allows the `WshController` object to work is *DCOM,* which is short for *Distributed Component Object Model.* Using DCOM, the `WshController` object automatically handles all underlying communications between the controlling script and the remote script.

The `WshRemote` object's other property is the `Status` property, which provides the ability to track the status of a remotely executing script. The `Status` property represents the remote script's state as a numeric value. Table 32.3 lists and explains the different values that may be stored in the `Status` property.

Table 32.3 Remote Script Execution States

Value	Description
0	The remote script has not started executing yet.
1	The remote script is now executing.
2	The remote script has finished executing.

A Quick Remote WSH Example

In order to make sure that he had a working understanding of Remote WSH, Alexander decided to perform a quick test. First he wrote a VBScript that creates a small log file in the `c:\temp` folder of the computer upon which it is executed. He called this script `TestScript.vbs`. It is executed as a remote script. Then he created the following controlling script on the Windows 2000 Professional workstation and executed it.

```
Set wshController = CreateObject("WshController")
Set wshRemote = wshController.CreateScript("TestScript.vbs", "\\SERV0010")

WScript.ConnectObject wshRemote, "RemoteScript_"

wshRemote.Execute

Do Until wshRemote.Status = strExecutionComplete
  WScript.Sleep 2000
Loop

Sub RemoteScript_Start()
  MsgBox "Script TestScript.vbs is not executing."
End Sub
Sub RemoteScript_End()
  MsgBox "Script TestScript.vbs is finished."
End Sub
```

The controlling script begins by instantiating the `WshController` object. The script then copies a script called `TestScript.vbs` to a computer called `SERV0010` and creates an instance of the `WshRemote` object called `wshRemote` in order to interact with it. Next, the `ConnectObject()` method was used to define an event prefix in order to allow the controlling script to react to events generated by the remote script. Then the remote script was started using the `Execute()` method. The controller script then began a loop that checks every 2 seconds to see if the remote script has finished executing. Meanwhile, the controlling script's `RemoteScript_Start()` and `RemoteScript_End()` subroutines execute as the remote script starts and then finishes its execution.

Remote WSH Limitations

Remote WSH has a number of limitations that you must be aware of before working with it. First of all, it does not support the execution of any statements that generate a GUI interface. In other words, you cannot use the VBScript `MsgBox()` or `InputBox()` functions or the WSH `Echo()` and `Popup()` methods within scripts that will be remotely executed.

Remote WSH scripts are not able to access shared folders when they execute on the remote computer (using the credentials of the person that started them). In addition, Remote WSH does not provide a built-in mechanism for returning the script's output to the controlling script, leaving the responsibility for figuring out how to do so up to the script developer.

Creating the Final Script

Having reviewed the objects, methods, properties, and events that make up Remote WSH, Alexander is now ready to begin the development of the report distribution and remote archive management process. Alexander will complete this task by developing two scripts. The first script will be responsible for copying and moving files between the Windows 2000 Professional workstation and the Web server and for remotely running a second small archive maintenance script on the first day of each month. The archive maintenance script will manage the storage of a 3-month archive of report and HTML files on the corporate Web server.

The Initialization Section

The first script, referred to as the controlling script, begins by defining global variables, constants, and objects in its `Initialization Section`, as shown below. A value of zero is assigned to `intReturnCode`, which sets the script's default return code.

```
Option Explicit

Dim strEventLog, strDebug, strHTMLFolder, strSharedRptFolder, strWebSvrName
Dim strConSolRptLoc, strSharedHTMLFolder, strWordRpt, strHTMLRpt, intReturnCode
Dim strResults

Const cTitleBarMsg = "Remote Archive Management Script"
Const strExecutionComplete = 2

Dim FsoObj, WshNtk, WshShl

Set FsoObj = CreateObject("Scripting.FileSystemObject")
Set WshNtk = WScript.CreateObject("WScript.Network")
Set WshShl = WScript.CreateObject("WScript.Shell")

intReturnCode = 0
```

The Main Processing Section

The controlling script's `Main Processing Section`, shown on the following page, begins by calling the `GetRegistrySettings()` subroutine in order to retrieve its configuration settings from the Windows registry on the Windows 2000 Professional workstation. If debug mode and event logging are enabled, pop-up messages are displayed and written to the Windows application event log noting the script's execution status. Then the `MapNetworkDrive()` function is called twice and passed the drive letter and UNC name of the shared folders on the corporate Web server where the Reporting files reside.

Next, the `GetFileNames()` subroutine is called in order to determine the names of the HTML and Word files, representing the current day's consolidated summary reports that are to be copied over to the Web server. The `CopyAndMoveFiles()` subroutine then copies the current day's Word file and moves the current day's HTML files over. In addition, an updated copy of the

Archive.html page is moved over to the Web server. The DisconnectNetworkDrive() subroutine is then executed twice in order to delete the script's previously established network drive connections.

Next, the TimeToCleanArchive() function is executed in order to determine if it is time to remotely run the monthly archive maintenance script. If it is time, then the WshController object is instantiated. The CreateScript() method is then used to set up a WshRemote object reference and move the archive maintenance script, called RemoteArchiveMgr.vbs, to the Web server. The WScript object's ConnectObject() method is then run in order to allow the controller script to track events generated by the remote script. The WshRemote object's Execute() method is then used to start the remote script's execution. A Do...Until loop is set up that runs until the value of the WshRemote object's Status property is equal to strExecutionComplete (that is, 2). At that time, the TerminateScript() subroutine is called and the script's execution terminates.

```
GetRegistrySettings()


If strEventLog = "Enabled" Then
  WriteToEventLog("Remote Archive Management Script now executing.")
End If


If strDebug = "Enabled" Then
  MsgBox "Remote Archive Management Script now executing.", , cTitleBarMsg
End If


MapNetworkDrive "W:", "\\" & strWebSvrName & "\" & strSharedRptFolder
MapNetworkDrive "X:", "\\" & strWebSvrName & "\" & strSharedHTMLFolder

GetFileNames()

CopyAndMoveFiles()

DisconnectNetworkDrive("W:")
DisconnectNetworkDrive("X:")

If strDebug = "Enabled" Then
  MsgBox "Remote Archive Management Script now completed.", , cTitleBarMsg
```

```
End If

If strEventLog = "Enabled" Then
  WriteToEventLog ("Remote Archive Management Script finished executing.")
End If

strResults = TimeToCleanArchive()

If strResults = "Yes" Then

  Set wshController = CreateObject("WshController")
  Set wshRemote = wshController.CreateScript("RemoteArchiveMgr.vbs", "\\" & _
    strWebSvrName)

  WScript.ConnectObject wshRemote, "RemoteScript_"

  wshRemote.Execute

  Do Until wshRemote.Status = strExecutionComplete
            WScript.Sleep 2000
  Loop

End If

TerminateScript(intReturnCode)
```

The GetRegistrySettings() Subroutine

As you have already seen in numerous examples, the `GetRegistrySettings()` subroutine, shown below, is responsible for retrieving the script's configuration settings from the Windows registry.

```
Sub GetRegistrySettings()

  On Error Resume Next

  strEventLog = _
    WshShl.RegRead("HKLM\Software\Intuit\VBScripts\WebRpting\EventLogging")
```

```
If Err <> 0 Then
  If strEventLog = "Enabled" Then
    WriteToEventLog ("HTML Report Conversion Script - Using default " & _
      "for strEventLog. RC = 4")
    TerminateScript(12)
  End If
End If

strDebug = WshShl.RegRead("HKLM\Software\Intuit\VBScripts\WebRpting\Debug")
If Err <> 0 Then
  If strEventLog = "Enabled" Then
    WriteToEventLog ("HTML Report Conversion Script - Using default  & _
      "for strDebug. RC = 4")
    TerminateScript(12)
  End If
End If

strHTMLFolder = _
  WshShl.RegRead("HKLM\Software\Intuit\VBScripts\WebRpting\HTMLFolder")
If Err <> 0 Then
  If strEventLog = "Enabled" Then
    WriteToEventLog ("HTML Report Conversion Script - Using default " & _
      "for strHTMLFolder. RC = 4")
    TerminateScript(12)
  End If
End If

strConSolRptLoc = _
  "WshShl.RegRead("HKLM\Software\Intuit\VBScripts\WebRpting\ConSolRptLoc")
If Err <> 0 Then
If strEventLog = "Enabled" Then
    WriteToEventLog ("HTML Report Conversion Script - Using default " & _
      "for strConSolRptLoc. RC = 4")
    TerminateScript(12)
  End If
End If

strSharedRptFolder = _
```

```
  "WshShl.RegRead("HKLM\Software\Intuit\VBScripts\WebRpting\Share_Rpts")
If Err <> 0 Then
If strEventLog = "Enabled" Then
    WriteToEventLog ("HTML Report Conversion Script - Using default " & _
      "for strSharedRptFolder. RC = 4")
    TerminateScript(12)
  End If
End If

strSharedHTMLFolder = _
  "WshShl.RegRead("HKLM\Software\Intuit\VBScripts\WebRpting\Share_HTML")
If Err <> 0 Then
If strEventLog = "Enabled" Then
    WriteToEventLog ("HTML Report Conversion Script - Using default " & _
      "for strSharedHTMLFolder. RC = 4")
    TerminateScript(12)
  End If
End If

strWebSvrName = _
  WshShl.RegRead("HKLM\Software\Intuit\VBScripts\WebRpting\WebServer")
If Err <> 0 Then
If strEventLog = "Enabled" Then
    WriteToEventLog ("HTML Report Conversion Script - Using default " & _
      "for strWebSvrName. RC = 4")
    TerminateScript(12)
  End If
End If

If strDebug = "Enabled" Then
  MsgBox "Registry settings initialized: " & vbCrLf & vbCrLf & _
    "strEventLog" & vbTab & "=" & vbTab & strEventLog & vbCrLf & _
    "strDebug" & vbTab & vbTab & "=" & vbTab & strDebug & vbCrLf & _
    "strHTMLFolder" & vbTab & "=" & vbTab & strHTMLFolder & vbCrLf & _
    "strConSolRptLoc" & vbTab & "=" & vbTab & strConSolRptLoc & vbCrLf & _
    "strSharedRptFolder" & vbTab & "=" & vbTab & strSharedRptFolder & _
    "strSharedHTMLFolder" & vbTab & "=" & vbTab & strSharedHTMLFolder & _
    vbCrLf & "strWebSvrName" & vbTab & "=" & vbTab & strWebSvrName & _
```

```
      vbCrLf, ,cTitleBarMsg
  End If

End Sub
```

The MapNetworkDrive() Function

The `MapNetworkDrive()` function, shown below, is identical to the like-named function from the previous chapter. It accepts two arguments, a drive letter and the location of a shared network drive or folder, and creates a network drive connection.

```
Function MapNetworkDrive(strLetter, strDrive)

  If strDebug = "Enabled" Then
    MsgBox "strLetter = " & strLetter & vbCrLf & "strDrive = " & _
      strDrive, , cTitleBarMsg
  End If

  If FsoObj.DriveExists(strDrive) Then

    If strDebug = "Enabled" Then
      MsgBox strDrive & " exists", , cTitleBarMsg
    End If

    If FsoObj.DriveExists(strLetter) Then

      If strDebug = "Enabled" Then
         MsgBox "Deleting drive letter " & strLetter, , cTitleBarMsg
      End If

      WshNtk.RemoveNetworkDrive strLetter

    End If

    WshNtk.MapNetworkDrive strLetter, strDrive

  Else
```

```
    If strDebug = "Enabled" Then
      MsgBox strDrive & " does not exist", , cTitleBarMsg
    End If

    If strEventLog = "Enabled" Then
      WriteToEventLog "Summary Report Collection script - Unable to map " & _
       "to network drive " & strDrive
    End If
    TerminateScript(4)
  End If

End Function
```

The GetFileNames() Subroutine

The `GetFileNames()` subroutine, shown below, is responsible for ascertaining the names of the current day's Word and HTML versions of the consolidated summary reports, as has been demonstrated in previous chapters.

```
Sub GetFileNames()

  strHTMLRpt = Replace(Date(), "/", "-")

  strHTMLRpt = strHTMLRpt & "_ConsolSumRpt.html"

  strWordRpt = Replace(strHTMLRpt, "html", "doc")

  If strDebug = "Enabled" Then
    MsgBox "HTML Summary Report File Name = " & strHTMLRpt & vbCrLf & _
      "Word Summary Report File Name = " & strWordRpt, , cTitleBarMsg
  End If

End Sub
```

The CopyAndMoveFiles() Subroutine

The `CopyAndMoveFiles()` subroutine, shown in the following example, performs a series of three checks, using the `FileSystemObject` object's `File`

`Exists()` method to verify that the three files that it is to copy or move exist. If any of the files are not found, the `TerminateScript()` subroutine is called and passed a script return code value of 4. If all three files are found, then the `GetFile()` method is used to establish a reference to each of the three files, which are then copied or moved to the Web server using either the `File` object's `Move()` or `Copy()` methods. The `Err` object is checked after each move or copy operation to make sure that it was successful. If an error occurred during any of these operations, the `TerminateScript()` subroutine is called and passed a script return code of 8.

```
Sub CopyAndMoveFiles()

  Dim strFileName

  If (FsoObj.FileExists(strConSolRptLoc & "\" & strHTMLRpt)) = "False" Then
    If strDebug = "Enabled" Then
      MsgBox "File " & strHTMLRpt & " not found. Stopping " & _
      "script execution.", , cTitleBarMsg
    End If
    If strEventLog = "Enabled" Then
      WriteToEventLog "Remote Archive Management Script failed. Unable " & _
        "find file: " & strHTMLRpt
    End If
    TerminateScript(4)
  End If
  If (FsoObj.FileExists(strConSolRptLoc & "\" & strWordRpt)) = "False" Then
    If strDebug = "Enabled" Then
      MsgBox "File " & strWordRpt & " not found. Stopping " & _
      "script execution.", , cTitleBarMsg
    End If
    If strEventLog = "Enabled" Then
      WriteToEventLog "Remote Archive Management Script failed. Unable " & _
        "find file: " & strWordRpt
    End If
    TerminateScript(4)
  End If
  If (FsoObj.FileExists(strHTMLFolder & "\" & "Archive.html")) = "False" Then
    If strDebug = "Enabled" Then
```

```
      MsgBox "File Archive.html not found. Stopping " & _
      "script execution.", , cTitleBarMsg
    End If
    If strEventLog = "Enabled" Then
      WriteToEventLog "Remote Archive Management Script failed. Unable " & _
        "find file: Archive.html"
    End If
    TerminateScript(4)
  End If

  Set strFileName = FsoObj.GetFile(strConSolRptLoc & "\" & strHTMLRpt)
  strFileName.Move "W:\"
  If Err <> 0 Then
    If strEventLog = "Enabled" Then
      WriteToEventLog "Remote Archive Management Script failed moving " & _
        strHTMLRpt
    End If
    If strDebug = "Enabled" Then
      MsgBox "Remote Archive Management Script failed moving " & _
        strHTMLRpt, , cTitleBarMsg
    End If
    TerminateScript(8)
  End If

  Set strFileName = FsoObj.GetFile(strConSolRptLoc & "\" & strWordRpt)
  strFileName.Copy "W:\"
  If Err <> 0 Then
    If strEventLog = "Enabled" Then
      WriteToEventLog "Remote Archive Management Script failed copying " & _
        strWordRpt
    End If
    If strDebug = "Enabled" Then
      MsgBox "Remote Archive Management Script failed moving " & _
        strWordRpt, , cTitleBarMsg
    End If
    TerminateScript(8)
  End If
```

```
Set strFileName = FsoObj.GetFile("X:\Archive.html")
strFileName.Delete

Set strFileName = FsoObj.GetFile(strHTMLFolder & "\" & "Archive.html")
strFileName.Move "X:\"
If Err <> 0 Then
  If strEventLog = "Enabled" Then
    WriteToEventLog "Remote Archive Management Script failed moving " & _
      "Archive.html"
  End If
  If strDebug = "Enabled" Then
    MsgBox "Remote Archive Management Script failed moving " & _
      "Archive.html", , cTitleBarMsg
  End If
  TerminateScript(8)
End If

End Sub
```

The DisconnectNetworkDrive() Subroutine

As you have seen in previous chapters, the `DisconnectNetworkDrive()` subroutine, shown below, is responsible for disconnecting network drive connections previously set up by the `MapNetworkDrive()` Function.

```
Sub DisconnectNetworkDrive(strDriveLetter)

  On Error Resume Next

  If strDebug = "Enabled" Then
    MsgBox "Disconnecting " & strDriveLetter, , cTitleBarMsg
  End If

  WshNtk.RemoveNetworkDrive strDriveLetter
  If Err <> 0 Then
    If strDebug = "Enabled" Then
      MsgBox "Error occurred when disconnecting " & strDriveLetter, , _
        cTitleBarMsg
```

```
    End If
  End If

End Sub
```

The TimeToCleanArchive() Function

The `TimeToCleanArchive()` function, shown below, uses the `Date()` and `Day()` functions to determine whether the script is being executed on the first day of the month. It sets the value of `TimeToCleanArchive` equal to `Yes` if this is the case.

```
Function TimeToCleanArchive()

  If Day(Date()) = 1 Then
    TimeToCleanArchive = "Yes"
  End If

End Function
```

The RemoteScript_Start() Subroutine

The `RemoteScript_Start()` subroutine, shown below, is automatically executed when the remote script begins executing. It displays a notification message if the script is executing in debug mode and writes an informational message to the Windows 2000 Professional workstation's application event log if event logging is enabled.

```
Sub RemoteScript_Start()

  If strEventLog = "Enabled" Then
    WriteToEventLog("Remote Archive Management Script - started.")
  End If

  If strDebug = "Enabled" Then
    MsgBox "Remote Archive Management Script - started.", , cTitleBarMsg
  End If

End Sub
```

The RemoteScript_End() Subroutine

The `RemoteScript_End()` subroutine, shown below, executes when the remote script stops running. It displays a pop-up dialog box and records a message to the application event log, if appropriate.

```
Sub RemoteScript_End()


  If strEventLog = "Enabled" Then
    WriteToEventLog("Remote Archive Management Script - stopped.")
  End If

  If strDebug = "Enabled" Then
    MsgBox "Remote Archive Management Script - stopped.", , cTitleBarMsg
  End If

End Sub
```

The RemoteScript_Error() Subroutine

The `RemoteScript_Error()` subroutine, shown below, executes if the remote script experiences a error. It displays the values stored in `WshRemoteError` error properties when debug mode is enabled. It also records a message to the application event log if event logging is enabled.

```
Sub RemoteScript_Error()


  strErrorNo = Hex(wshRemote.Error.Number)
  strErrorNo = CStr(strErrorNo)

  If strEventLog = "Enabled" Then
    WriteToEventLog ("Error Number: " & strErrorNo & vbCrLf & _
      "Line Number:  " & wshRemote.Error.Line & vbCrLf & _
      "Description:  " & wshRemote.Error.Description)
  End If

  If strDebug = "Enabled" Then
    MsgBox "Error Number: " & strErrorNo & vbCrLf & _
      "Line Number:  " & wshRemote.Error.Line & vbCrLf & _
```

```
      "Description:  " & wshRemote.Error.Description
    End If

    wshRemote.Terminate()

End Sub
```

The WriteToEventLog() Subroutine

The `WriteToEventLog()` subroutine, shown below, writes an informational message, passed to it as an argument, to the Windows application event log.

```
Sub WriteToEventLog(strMessage)

  WshShl.LogEvent 4, strMessage

End Sub
```

The TerminateScript() Subroutine

The `TerminateScript()` subroutine, shown below, uses the `WScript` object's `Quit()` method to terminate the controlling script's execution and to pass a return code back to the calling script. The return code sent back to the calling script is passed to this subroutine as an argument.

```
Sub TerminateScript(intRC)

  If strDebug = "Enabled" Then
    MsgBox "Script execution terminated.", , cTitleBarMsg
  End If

  WScript.Quit(intRC)

End Sub
```

The Fully Assembled Script

The fully assembled report distribution and remote archive management script is shown below. When executed on the Windows 2000 Professional workstation in the computer operation's command center, it will establish a temporary network connection to the corporate Web server and copy over the HTML and Word files representing the current day's summary report files. An updated copy of the `Archive.html` page is moved over to the Web server as well. In addition, on the first day of each month, this script will remotely execute and monitor a remote WSH VBScript on the Web server, which will maintain a three-month archive of the HTML and Word files.

```
'*************************************************************************
'Script Name: Script 32.1.vbs
'Author: Jerry Ford
'Created: 05/09/03
'Description: This script moves the Archive.html page and the current day's
'HTML and Word consolidated summary reports to the corporate web server
'*************************************************************************

'Initialization Section

Option Explicit

Dim strEventLog, strDebug, strHTMLFolder, strSharedRptFolder, strWebSvrName
Dim strConSolRptLoc, strSharedHTMLFolder, strWordRpt, strHTMLRpt, intReturnCode
Dim strResults

Const cTitleBarMsg = "Remote Archive Management Script"
Const strExecutionComplete = 2

Dim FsoObj, WshNtk, WshShl

Set FsoObj = CreateObject("Scripting.FileSystemObject")
Set WshNtk = WScript.CreateObject("WScript.Network")
Set WshShl = WScript.CreateObject("WScript.Shell")

intReturnCode = 0


'Main Processing Section
```

```
GetRegistrySettings()

If strEventLog = "Enabled" Then
  WriteToEventLog("Remote Archive Management Script now executing.")
End If

If strDebug = "Enabled" Then
  MsgBox "Remote Archive Management Script now executing.", , cTitleBarMsg
End If

MapNetworkDrive "W:", "\\" & strWebSvrName & "\" & strSharedRptFolder
MapNetworkDrive "X:", "\\" & strWebSvrName & "\" & strSharedHTMLFolder

GetFileNames()

CopyAndMoveFiles()

DisconnectNetworkDrive("W:")
DisconnectNetworkDrive("X:")

If strDebug = "Enabled" Then
  MsgBox "Remote Archive Management Script now completed.", , cTitleBarMsg
End If

If strEventLog = "Enabled" Then
  WriteToEventLog ("Remote Archive Management Script finished executing.")
End If

strResults = TimeToCleanArchive()

If strResults = "Yes" Then

  Set wshController = CreateObject("WshController")
  Set wshRemote = wshController.CreateScript("RemoteArchiveMgr.vbs", "\\" & _
    strWebSvrName)
  WScript.ConnectObject wshRemote, "RemoteScript_"

  wshRemote.Execute
```

```
  Do Until wshRemote.Status = strExecutionComplete
        WScript.Sleep 2000
  Loop

End If

TerminateScript(intReturnCode)


'Procedure Section

Sub GetRegistrySettings()

  On Error Resume Next

  strEventLog = _
    WshShl.RegRead("HKLM\Software\Intuit\VBScripts\WebRpting\EventLogging")
  If Err <> 0 Then
    If strEventLog = "Enabled" Then
      WriteToEventLog ("HTML Report Conversion Script - Using default " & _
        "for strEventLog. RC = 4")
      TerminateScript(12)
    End If
  End If

  strDebug = WshShl.RegRead("HKLM\Software\Intuit\VBScripts\WebRpting\Debug")
  If Err <> 0 Then
    If strEventLog = "Enabled" Then
      WriteToEventLog ("HTML Report Conversion Script - Using default " & _
        "for strDebug. RC = 4")
      TerminateScript(12)
    End If
  End If

  strHTMLFolder = _
    "WshShl.RegRead("HKLM\Software\Intuit\VBScripts\WebRpting\HTMLFolder")
  If Err <> 0 Then
```

```
  If strEventLog = "Enabled" Then
    WriteToEventLog ("HTML Report Conversion Script - Using default " & _
      "for strHTMLFolder. RC = 4")
    TerminateScript(12)
  End If
End If

strConSolRptLoc = _
  WshShl.RegRead("HKLM\Software\Intuit\VBScripts\WebRpting\ConSolRptLoc")
If Err <> 0 Then
If strEventLog = "Enabled" Then
    WriteToEventLog ("HTML Report Conversion Script - Using default " & _
      "for strConSolRptLoc. RC = 4")
    TerminateScript(12)
  End If
End If

strSharedRptFolder = _
  WshShl.RegRead("HKLM\Software\Intuit\VBScripts\WebRpting\Share_Rpts")
If Err <> 0 Then
If strEventLog = "Enabled" Then
    WriteToEventLog ("HTML Report Conversion Script - Using default " & _
      "for strSharedRptFolder. RC = 4")
    TerminateScript(12)
  End If
End If

strSharedHTMLFolder = _
  WshShl.RegRead("HKLM\Software\Intuit\VBScripts\WebRpting\Share_HTML")
If Err <> 0 Then
If strEventLog = "Enabled" Then
    WriteToEventLog ("HTML Report Conversion Script - Using default " & _
      "for strSharedHTMLFolder. RC = 4")
    TerminateScript(12)
  End If
End If

strWebSvrName = _
```

```
    WshShl.RegRead("HKLM\Software\Intuit\VBScripts\WebRpting\WebServer")
  If Err <> 0 Then
  If strEventLog = "Enabled" Then
      WriteToEventLog ("HTML Report Conversion Script - Using default " & _
        "for strWebSvrName. RC = 4")
      TerminateScript(12)
    End If
  End If

  If strDebug = "Enabled" Then
    MsgBox "Registry settings initialized: " & vbCrLf & vbCrLf & _
      "strEventLog" & vbTab & "=" & vbTab & strEventLog & vbCrLf & _
      "strDebug" & vbTab & vbTab & "=" & vbTab & strDebug & vbCrLf & _
      "strHTMLFolder" & vbTab & "=" & vbTab & strHTMLFolder & vbCrLf & _
      "strConSolRptLoc" & vbTab & "=" & vbTab & strConSolRptLoc & vbCrLf & _
      "strSharedRptFolder" & vbTab & "=" & vbTab & strSharedRptFolder & _
      "strSharedHTMLFolder" & vbTab & "=" & vbTab & strSharedHTMLFolder & _
      vbCrLf & "strWebSvrName" & vbTab & "=" & vbTab & strWebSvrName & _
      vbCrLf, ,cTitleBarMsg
  End If

End Sub

Function MapNetworkDrive(strLetter, strDrive)

  If strDebug = "Enabled" Then
    MsgBox "strLetter = " & strLetter & vbCrLf & "strDrive = " & _
      strDrive, , cTitleBarMsg
  End If

  If FsoObj.DriveExists(strDrive) Then

    If strDebug = "Enabled" Then
      MsgBox strDrive & " exists", , cTitleBarMsg
    End If

    If FsoObj.DriveExists(strLetter) Then
```

```
        If strDebug = "Enabled" Then
          MsgBox "Deleting drive letter " & strLetter, , cTitleBarMsg
        End If

        WshNtk.RemoveNetworkDrive strLetter

      End If

      WshNtk.MapNetworkDrive strLetter, strDrive

    Else

      If strDebug = "Enabled" Then
        MsgBox strDrive & " does not exist", , cTitleBarMsg
      End If

      If strEventLog = "Enabled" Then
        WriteToEventLog "Summary Report Collection script - Unable to map " & _
        "to network drive " & strDrive
      End If
      TerminateScript(4)
    End If

  End Function

  Sub GetFileNames()

    strHTMLRpt = Replace(Date(), "/", "-")

    strHTMLRpt = strHTMLRpt & "_ConsolSumRpt.html"

    strWordRpt = Replace(strHTMLRpt, "html", "doc")

    If strDebug = "Enabled" Then
      MsgBox "HTML Summary Report File Name = " & strHTMLRpt & vbCrLf & _
        "Word Summary Report File Name = " & strWordRpt, , cTitleBarMsg
    End If
```

```
End Sub

Sub CopyAndMoveFiles()

  Dim strFileName

  If (FsoObj.FileExists(strConSolRptLoc & "\" & strHTMLRpt)) = "False" Then
    If strDebug = "Enabled" Then
      MsgBox "File " & strHTMLRpt & " not found. Stopping " & _
      "script execution.", , cTitleBarMsg
    End If
    If strEventLog = "Enabled" Then
      WriteToEventLog "Remote Archive Management Script failed. Unable " & _
        "find file: " & strHTMLRpt
    End If
    TerminateScript(4)
  End If
  If (FsoObj.FileExists(strConSolRptLoc & "\" & strWordRpt)) = "False" Then
    If strDebug = "Enabled" Then
      MsgBox "File " & strWordRpt & " not found. Stopping " & _
      "script execution.", , cTitleBarMsg
    End If
    If strEventLog = "Enabled" Then
      WriteToEventLog "Remote Archive Management Script failed. Unable " & _
        "find file: " & strWordRpt
    End If
    TerminateScript(4)
  End If
  If (FsoObj.FileExists(strHTMLFolder & "\" & "Archive.html")) = "False" Then
    If strDebug = "Enabled" Then
      MsgBox "File Archive.html not found. Stopping " & _
      "script execution.", , cTitleBarMsg
    End If
    If strEventLog = "Enabled" Then
      WriteToEventLog "Remote Archive Management Script failed. Unable " & _
        "find file: Archive.html"
    End If
    TerminateScript(4)
```

```
End If

Set strFileName = FsoObj.GetFile(strConSolRptLoc & "\" & strHTMLRpt)
strFileName.Move "W:\"
If Err <> 0 Then
  If strEventLog = "Enabled" Then
    WriteToEventLog "Remote Archive Management Script failed moving " & _
      strHTMLRpt
  End If
  If strDebug = "Enabled" Then
    MsgBox "Remote Archive Management Script failed moving " & _
      strHTMLRpt, , cTitleBarMsg
  End If
  TerminateScript(8)
End If

Set strFileName = FsoObj.GetFile(strConSolRptLoc & "\" & strWordRpt)
strFileName.Copy "W:\"
If Err <> 0 Then
  If strEventLog = "Enabled" Then
    WriteToEventLog "Remote Archive Management Script failed copying " & _
      strWordRpt
  End If
  If strDebug = "Enabled" Then
    MsgBox "Remote Archive Management Script failed moving " & _
      strWordRpt, , cTitleBarMsg
  End If
  TerminateScript(8)
End If

Set strFileName = FsoObj.GetFile("X:\Archive.html")
strFileName.Delete

Set strFileName = FsoObj.GetFile(strHTMLFolder & "\" & "Archive.html")
strFileName.Move "X:\"
If Err <> 0 Then
  If strEventLog = "Enabled" Then
    WriteToEventLog "Remote Archive Management Script failed moving " & _
```

```
        "Archive.html"
    End If
    If strDebug = "Enabled" Then
      MsgBox "Remote Archive Management Script failed moving " & _
        "Archive.html", , cTitleBarMsg
    End If
    TerminateScript(8)
  End If

End Sub

Sub DisconnectNetworkDrive(strDriveLetter)

  On Error Resume Next

  If strDebug = "Enabled" Then
    MsgBox "Disconnecting " & strDriveLetter, , cTitleBarMsg
  End If

  WshNtk.RemoveNetworkDrive strDriveLetter
  If Err <> 0 Then
    If strDebug = "Enabled" Then
      MsgBox "Error occurred when disconnecting " & strDriveLetter, , _
        cTitleBarMsg
    End If
  End If

End Sub

Function TimeToCleanArchive()

  If Day(Date()) = 1 Then
    TimeToCleanArchive = "Yes"
  End If

End Function

Sub RemoteScript_Start()
```

```
    If strEventLog = "Enabled" Then
      WriteToEventLog("Remote Archive Management Script - started.")
    End If

    If strDebug = "Enabled" Then
      MsgBox "Remote Archive Management Script - started.", , cTitleBarMsg
    End If

  End Sub

  Sub RemoteScript_End()

    If strEventLog = "Enabled" Then
      WriteToEventLog("Remote Archive Management Script - stopped.")
    End If

    If strDebug = "Enabled" Then
      MsgBox "Remote Archive Management Script - stopped.", , cTitleBarMsg
    End If

  End Sub

  Sub RemoteScript_Error()

    strErrorNo = Hex(wshRemote.Error.Number)
    strErrorNo = CStr(strErrorNo)

    If strEventLog = "Enabled" Then
      WriteToEventLog ("Error Number: " & strErrorNo & vbCrLf & _
        "Line Number:  " & wshRemote.Error.Line & vbCrLf & _
        "Description:  " & wshRemote.Error.Description)
    End If

    If strDebug = "Enabled" Then
      MsgBox "Error Number: " & strErrorNo & vbCrLf & _
        "Line Number:  " & wshRemote.Error.Line & vbCrLf & _
        "Description:  " & wshRemote.Error.Description
```

```
  End If

  wshRemote.Terminate()

End Sub

Sub WriteToEventLog(strMessage)

  WshShl.LogEvent 4, strMessage

End Sub

Sub TerminateScript(intRC)

  If strDebug = "Enabled" Then
    MsgBox "Script execution terminated.", , cTitleBarMsg
  End If

  WScript.Quit(intRC)

End Sub
```

Creating the Archive Maintenance Script

The previous VBScript executes an archive maintenance script, which is shown below. This is a relatively small script with limited functionality. It begins by defining the two variables that represent the month's worth of archive files to be deleted and the location of the folder on the Web server where the archived files reside.

Alexander was informed by Michael Burns, the corporate Web master, that he was not permitted to make modifications to the Windows registry on the corporate Web server. Therefore, he decided to hard code the location of the archive folder within the script. The script's `Main Processing Section` consists of just three statements. The first statement calls the `MonthToDelete()` subroutine, which determines which files are eligible for deletion from the archive. The second statement calls the `RemoveOldSummaryFiles()` subroutine, which performs the actual deletion of the files. The third statement uses the `WScript` object's `Quit()` method to terminate the script's execution. The logic presented in the `MonthToDelete()` and `RemoveOldSummaryFiles()` subroutines has already been covered several times in previous examples within this book.

```
'*************************************************************************
'Script Name: Script 32.2.vbs
'Author: Jerry Ford
'Created: 05/09/03
'Description: This script deletes HTML and Word versions of the
'consolidated summary reports that are older than 3 months old
'*************************************************************************


'Initialization Section

Option Explicit

Dim strDeleteMonth, strHTMLFolder

strHTMLFolder = "d:\Intuit\OrderInventory\Reporting\Rpts\"


'Main Processing Section

MonthToDelete()

RemoveOldSummaryFiles()

WScript.Quit()


'Procedure Section

Sub MonthToDelete()

   Dim intGetSlashPosition, strCurrentMonth

   intGetSlashPosition = Instr(Date(), "/")
```

```
    strCurrentMonth = Mid(Date(), 1, intGetSlashPosition - 1)
    strDeleteMonth = strCurrentMonth - 4

    If strDeleteMonth = 0 Then
      strDeleteMonth = "12"
    End If
    If strDeleteMonth = -1 Then
      strDeleteMonth = "11"
    End If
    If strDeleteMonth = -2 Then
      strDeleteMonth = "10"
    End If
    If strDeleteMonth = -3 Then
      strDeleteMonth = "9"
    End If

  End Sub

  Sub RemoveOldSummaryFiles()

    Dim FsoObject, strSummaryRptPath
    Set FsoObject = WScript.CreateObject("Scripting.FileSystemObject")

    FsoObject.DeleteFile strHTMLFolder & strDeleteMonth & "*"

  End Sub
```

Summary

In this chapter, you learned how to work with Remote WSH. This included a detailed examination of the `WshController`, `WshRemote`, and `WshRemoteError` objects and their methods and properties. You then learned how to apply Remote WSH to perform the remote file administration of the Word and HTML files on the Intuit corporate Web server. With the information presented in this chapter, you now have the background you need to develop scripts that can remotely administer any number of remote computers from a single Windows computer.

PART VI

Appendices

Appendix A

Windows XP Command Reference

This appendix provides an alphabetic command reference of Windows commands. This list of commands is based on the commands supported by the Windows XP Professional and Home Edition operating systems. Some of the commands listed here will not be supported by other Windows operating systems. Each Windows command is briefly described, and its syntax is explained in detail. For additional information on these commands, refer to the help system provided by your version of Windows.

Append

Enables programs to open files located in different folders as if they were stored in the current folder.

Syntax

```
append [;] [[drive:]path[;...]] [/x:{on ¦ off}][/path:{on ¦ off}] [/e]
```

Parameters

Parameter	Purpose
;	Clears the list of appended folders.
`[drive:]path`	Sets the drive, path, and folder to be appended.
`/x:{on ¦ off}`	Determines whether the MS-DOS subsystem searches appended folders when running programs. With `/x:on` the program performs the search, and with `/x:off` the program does not.
`/path:{on ¦ off}`	Determines whether a program should search appended folders, even when a path is provided along with the name of the file that the program is looking for. `/path:on` is the default.
`/e`	Creates an environment variable named APPEND and sets its value equal to the list of appended folders. The `/e` switch can only be used once after each time you restart your system.

Arp

A TCP/IP protocol command that displays and modifies the IP-to-MAC address translation tables used by the ARP (*Address Resolution Protocol*).

Syntax

```
arp -a [inet_addr] [-N [if_addr]]
arp -d inet_addr [if_addr]
arp - g [-N [if_addr]]
arp -s inet_addr ether_addr [if_addr]
```

Parameters

Parameter	Purpose
-a	Lists ARP entries.
-g	Lists ARP entries in the same manner as -a.
[inet_addr]	Identifies an IP address.
-N	Lists ARP entries for the network interface specified by *if_addr*.
[if_addr]	Identifies the IP address of the network interface whose address translation table should be modified. Otherwise, the first applicable interface will be used.
-d	Removes the entry specified by *inet_addr*.
-s	Adds a permanent entry in the ARP cache which associates the *inet_addr* IP address with the *ether_addr* MAC address.
ether_addr	Specifies a MAC address.

Assoc

Lists or changes file extension associations.

Syntax

```
assoc [.ext[=[filetype]]]
```

Parameters

Parameter	Purpose
None	Lists current file associations.
.ext	Specifies a specific file extension to list or modify.
[filetype]	Identifies a file type to be associated with the specified file extension.

At

Displays a listing of scheduled tasks (command, script, or program) and schedules the execution of new tasks.

Syntax

```
at [\\computername] [[id] [/delete] ¦ /delete [/yes]]

at [\\computername] time [/interactive] [/every:date[,...]
  ¦ /next:date[,...]] command
```

Parameters

Parameter	Purpose
None	Displays a listing of all scheduled tasks.
[\\computername]	Specifies a remote computer where the task is to be executed. If omitted, the command is scheduled locally.
Id	Identifies the ID number assigned to a scheduled command.
[/delete]	Terminates a scheduled command. If `id` is not present, all scheduled tasks are terminated.
[/yes]	Requires a confirmation before terminating a scheduled task.
time	Identifies the time to execute the task expressed as *hh*:mm on a 24-hour clock.
[/interactive]	Permits interaction with the desktop and the logged on user.
/every:*date*[,...]	Establishes a schedule for task execution based on specified days of the week or month. The date is specified as M, T, W, Th, F, S, Su or 1–31. Multiple dates are separated by commas. If omitted, the schedule is set to the current day.

Parameters (*continued*)

Parameter	Purpose
`/next:`*`date`*`[,...]`	Runs the task on the next occurrence of the day (M, T, W, Th, F, S, Su) or date (1–31). Multiple dates are separated by commas. If omitted, the schedule is set to the current day.
`command`	Specifies the task to execute.

Atmadm

Monitors connections and addresses and displays statistics for ATM (*asynchronous transfer mode*) networks.

Syntax

```
atmadm [-c][-a] [-s]
```

Parameters

Parameter	Purpose
`[-c]`	Lists information about the computer's established connections to the ATM network.
`[-a]`	Displays the registered ATM network service access point address for each ATM network interface on the computer.
`[-s]`	Provides statistical data for active ATM connections.

Attrib

Lists or modifies file attributes.

Syntax

```
attrib [+r¦-r] [+a¦-a] [+s¦-s] [+h¦-h] [[drive:][path] filename] [/s[/d]]
```

Parameters

Parameter	Purpose
`[+r]`	Specifies the read-only attribute.
`[-r]`	Clears the read-only attribute.
`[+a]`	Specifies the archive attribute.
`[-a]`	Clears the archive attribute.
`[+s]`	Identifies the file as a system file.
`[-s]`	Clears the system file attribute.
`[+h]`	Specifies the hidden file attribute.
`[-h]`	Clears the hidden file attribute.
`[[drive:][path] filename]`	Sets the drive, path, and file name to be processed.
`[/s]`	Applies changes to matching files in the current directory and all subdirectories.
`[/d]`	Processes directories.

Cacls

Displays or changes file ACLs (*access control lists*).

Syntax

```
cacls filename [/t] [/e] [/c] [/g user:perm] [/r user [...]]
  [/p user:perm [...]] [/d user [...]]
```

Parameters

Parameter	Purpose
filename	Displays a specified file's ACLs.
`[/t]`	Modifies the ACLs of specified files in the directory and its subdirectories.
`[/e]`	Edits an ACL rather than replacing it.
`[/c]`	Makes changes regardless of errors.

Parameters (*continued*)

Parameter	Purpose
`[/g user:perm]`	Sets specified user access rights including: n None r Read c Change f Full Control
`[/r user]`	Removes user access rights.
`[/p user:perm]`	Replaces user access rights, including: n None r Read c Change f Full Control
[/d *user*]	Denies user access.

Call

Calls a label or another script for execution as a procedure.

Syntax

```
call [drive:][path] filename [batch-parameters]
call :label [arguments]
```

Parameters

Parameter	Purpose
`[drive:][path] filename`	Sets the location and name of the script.
`[batch-parameters]`	Identifies the command-line information to be passed to the script.
`label`	Specifies a label within the script to jump.

Chcp

Displays or modifies the active console code page number.

Syntax

```
chcp [nnn]
```

Parameters

Parameter	Purpose
`None`	Displays the active console code page number.
[nnn]	Specifies one of the following code pages: 437 United States 850 Multilingual (Latin I) 852 Slavic (Latin II) 855 Cyrillic (Russian) 857 Turkish 860 Portuguese 861 Icelandic 863 Canadian-French 865 Nordic 866 Russian 869 Modern Greek

Chdir (Cd)

Displays the current directory name or changes the current directory.

Syntax

```
chdir [/d] [drive:][path] [..]
cd [/d] [drive:][path] [..]
```

Parameters

Parameter	Purpose
`None`	Displays the names of the current drive and directory.
`[/d]`	Changes the current drive and directory.
`[`*`drive:`*`][`*`path`*`]`	Changes to a specified drive and directory.
`[..]`	Changes the current directory to the parent directory.

Chkdsk

Displays disk status and corrects errors found on the specified disk.

Syntax

```
chkdsk [drive:][[path] filename] [/f] [/v] [/r] [/x] [/i] [/c] [/l[:size]]
```

Parameters

Parameter	Purpose
None	Displays disk status for the current drive.
[drive:]	Specifies the drive to be checked.
[*path*] *filename*	Specifies files to be checked for fragmentation.
[/f]	Repairs disk errors.
[/v]	Displays the name of each file that is processed.
[/r]	Finds bad sectors and attempts to recover lost data.
[/x]	NTFS only. Forces the volume dismount on NTFS volumes.
[/i]	NTFS only. Speeds up `chkdsk` by performing a less extensive check on NTFS volumes.
[/c]	NTFS only. Eliminates the checking of cycles inside folders on NTFS volumes.
/l[:*size*]	NTFS only. Displays or changes log file size on NTFS volumes.

Chkntfs

Displays or schedules the automatic system checking on FAT, FAT32, or NTFS volumes during system initialization.

Syntax

```
chkntfs volume: [...]
chkntfs [/d]
chkntfs [/t[:time]]
chkntfs [/x volume: [...]]
chkntfs [/c volume: [...]]
```

Parameters

Parameter	Purpose
volume:	Displays file system type of the specified volume.
/d	Restores default settings.
[/t]	Displays or modifies remaining time for automatic file checking.
[/x]	Prevents a specified volume from being checked during system initialization.
[/c]	Specifies that the volume be checked during system initialization.

Cipher

Displays or modifies folder and file encryption on NTFS volumes.

Syntax

```
cipher [/e¦ /d] [/s:dir] [/a] [/i] [/f] [/q] [/h] [/k] [/u] [/n]
  [pathname [...]] ¦ [/r:pathnamewithnoextn] ¦ [/w:pathname]
```

Parameters

Parameter	Purpose
None	Displays the current encryption status of the current folder and its contents.
[/e]	Encrypts the specified folders and turns on encryption for any files that may later be added to the folder.
[/d]	Decrypts the specified folders and turns off encryption for any files that may later be added to the folder.
[/s: *dir]*	Performs the specified operation on all folders and subfolders in the specified folder.
[/a]	Performs the specified operation on all specified files.
[/i]	Performs the specified operation even if errors occur.
[/f]	Encrypts or decrypts all specified objects regardless of their current encryption status.
[/q]	Limits reporting to essential information only.

Parameters (*continued*)

Parameter	Purpose
[/h]	Displays files with hidden or system attributes.
[/k]	Creates a new encryption key.
[/u]	Updates the encryption key.
[/n]	Prevents the updating of the encryption key.
[pathname]	Sets a folder, file, or pattern.
[/r:pathnamewithnoextn]	Creates a new recovery agent certificate and a new private key.

Cls

Clears the command console screen and displays the command prompt and cursor.

Syntax

```
cls
```

Cmd

Starts a new instance of the Windows shell.

Syntax

```
cmd [ [/c ¦ /k] [/s] [/q] [/d] [/a ¦ /u] [/t:fg] [/e: on ¦ off]
  [/f: on ¦ off] [/v: on ¦ off] string]
```

Parameters

Parameter	Purpose
[/c]	Exits the shell after executing the specified command.
[/k]	Executes the specified command and continues.
[/q]	Disables echoing.
[/d]	Prevents the execution of AutoRun commands.
[/a]	Formats output as ANSI characters.

(*continues*)

Parameters (*continued*)

Parameter	Purpose
[/u]	Formats output as Unicode characters.
[/t:*fg*]	Specifies foreground and background colors.
[/e: on | off]	Turns on support for command extensions.
[/f: on | off]	Turns on file and directory name completion.
[/v: on | off]	Turns on support for delayed variable expansion.
[string]	Sets the command to be executed.

Color

Sets console foreground and background colors. Returns ERRORLEVEL 1 if you try to set the foreground and background colors to the same value.

Syntax

```
color fb
```

Parameters

Parameter	Purpose
none	Restores default colors.
f	Sets the foreground color based on a hexadecimal value.
b	Sets the background color based on a hexadecimal value.
	Hexadecimal color assignments include:
	0 Black
	1 Blue
	2 Green
	3 Aqua
	4 Red
	5 Purple
	6 Yellow

Parameters (*continued*)

Parameter	Purpose
	7 White
	8 Gray
	9 Light blue
	A Light green
	B Light aqua
	C Light red
	D Light purple
	E Light yellow
	F Bright white

Comp

Performs a comparison of two files or two sets of files on a byte-by-byte basis.

Syntax

```
comp [data1] [data2] [/d] [/a] [/l] [/n=number] [/c]
```

Parameters

Parameter	Purpose
[data1]	Sets the path and file name of the first file or set of files.
[data2]	Sets the path and file name of the second file or set of files.
[/d]	Displays any differences using a decimal format.
[/a]	Displays any differences in character format.
[/l]	Displays line numbers where differences occur.
[/n=*number*]	Compares the specified *number* of lines in both files.
[/c]	Performs a case-insensitive comparison.

Compact

Displays and changes compression settings for files and folders on NTFS partitions.

Syntax

```
compact [/c¦/u] [/s[:dir]] [/a] [/i] [/f] [/q] [filename[...]]
```

Parameters

Parameter	Purpose
None	Displays information on the compression state for the current folder.
[/c]	Compresses the folder or file.
[/u]	Uncompresses the folder or file.
[/s:*dir*]	Specifies that all subfolders should be processed.
[/a]	Displays hidden or system files.
[/i]	Specifies that errors should be ignored.
[/f]	Forces the compression or uncompression of the folder or file.
[/q]	Limits reporting to essential information only.
[filename]	Sets the file or directory.

Convert

Converts FAT and FAT32 volumes to NTFS volumes.

Syntax

```
convert [volume] /fs:ntfs [/v] [/cvtarea:filename] [/nosecurity] [/x]
```

Parameters

Parameter	Purpose
volume	Identifies the driver letter to be converted.
/fs:ntfs	Converts the volume.
[/v]	Turns on verbose messaging.

Parameters (*continued*)

Parameter	Purpose
`[/cvtarea:`*`filename`*`]`	Specifies that the Master File table is to be written to an existing placeholder.
`[/nosecurity]`	Makes converted files and folders accessible to everyone.
`[/x]`	Dismounts the volume before converting.

Copy

Copies one or more files.

Syntax

```
copy [/d] [/v] [/n] [/y ¦ /-y] [/z] [/a ¦ /b] source [/a ¦ /b]
  [+ source [/a ¦ /b] [+ …]] [destination [/a ¦ /b]
```

Parameters

Parameter	Purpose
`[/d]`	Permits encrypted files to be copied and saved as decrypted files.
`[/v]`	Verifies the success of the copy operation.
`[/n]`	Uses a short file name as the destination file's new file name.
`[/y]`	Suppresses any confirmation prompts.
`[/-y]`	Displays confirmation prompts.
`[/z]`	Turns on a restartable mode before copying network files so that if network connectivity is lost, the `copy` operation will resume when connectivity is re-established.
`[/a]`	Identifies the file as an ASCII text file.
`[/b]`	Identifies the file as a binary file.
`source`	Specifies the file name of a file or set of files to be copied.
`destination`	Specifies the name and destination where the file is to be copied.

Country

Configures the MS-DOS subsystem so that it can use international dates, time, currency, case conversions, and decimal separators.

Syntax

```
country=xxx[,[yyy][,[drive:][path] filename]]
```

Parameters

Parameter	Purpose
xxx	Identifies the Country/Region code.
[yyy]	Identifies the Country/Region code page.
[*drive*:][*path*] *filename*	Sets the drive, path, and file name of the file that contains the Country/Region information.

Cprofile

Removes unnecessarily used space from profiles.

Syntax

```
cprofile [/l] [/i] [/v] [filelist]
cprofile [/ii] [/v] [filelist]
```

Parameters

Parameter	Purpose
[/l]	Cleans local profiles.
[/i]	Prompts before processing each profile.
[/v]	Displays detailed information about each action that is performed.
[filelist]	Displays a list of files from which user-specific file associations are removed.

Date

Displays or changes the current date.

Syntax

```
date [mm-dd-yy]
date [/t]
```

Parameters

Parameter	Purpose
[mm-dd-yy]	Specifies the date.
	mm must be 1–12
	dd must be 1–31
	yy must be 80–99 or 1980–2099
[/t]	Displays the date without prompting for a date change.

Debug

Starts the Debug program used to test MS-DOS executables.

Syntax

```
debug [[drive:][path] filename [parameters]]
```

Parameters

Parameter	Purpose
[*drive*:][*path*] *filename*	Specifies the drive, path, and file name of the executable file to text.
[parameters]	Command-line parameters required by the executable file.

Defrag

Reorganizes data stores on local volumes to improve storage and retrieval time.

Syntax

```
defrag volume [/a]
defrag volume [/a] [/v]
defrag volume [/v]
defrag volume [/f]
```

Parameters

Parameter	Purpose
volume	The driver letter to be defragmented.
[/a]	Displays an analysis report.
[/v]	Displays a verbose analysis.
[/f]	Forces defragmentation.

Del (Erase)

Deletes a file.

Syntax

```
del [drive:][path] filename [ ...] [/p] [/f] [/s] [/q] [/a[:attributes]]
erase [drive:][path] filename [ ...] [/p] [/f] [/s] [/q] [/a[:attributes]]
```

Parameters

Parameter	Purpose
[*drive*:][*path*] *filename*	Specifies the drive, path, and file name of the files to delete.
[/p]	Prompts for confirmation.
[/f]	Deletes read-only files.
[/s]	Deletes files in the current folder and its subfolders.
[/q]	Suppresses the confirmation prompts.
[/a]	Deletes files based on file attributes.

Dir

Displays a directory file listing.

Syntax

```
dir [drive:][path][filename] [...] [/p] [/q] [/w] [/d]
  [/a[[:]attributes]][/o[[:]sortorder]] [/t[[:]timefield]] [/s]
  [/b] [/l] [/n] [/x] [/c] [/4]
```

Parameters

Parameter	Purpose
None	Displays the disk's volume label, serial number, and a listing of its contents.
[*drive*:][*path*]	Specifies the drive and path for the folder to be displayed.
[*filename*]	Specifies a particular file to be displayed.
[/p]	Displays data a screen at a time.
[/q]	Displays information about file ownership.
[/w]	Displays the folder listing in multiple columns.
[/d]	Same as /w but sorts files by column.
/a[[:] *attributes*]	Limits the displays to directories and files that match supplied attributes. The following attributes can be used: h Hidden files s System files d Directories a Files ready to be archived r Read-only files -h Nonhidden files -s Nonsystem files -d Only display files -a Files without changes since the last backup

(continues)

Parameters (*continued*)

Parameter	Purpose
	-r Non-read-only files
/o [[:]*sortorder*]	Specifies the sort order used to display directory and file names. The following options can be used: n Alphabetically by name e Alphabetically by extension d By date and time s By size g Show folders before files -n Reverse alphabetical order by name -e Reverse alphabetical order by extension -d By reverse date and time -s By reverse size -g Show folders after files
/t [[:]timefield]	Determines the time field used to display or sorts the listing. Valid options: c Creation time a Last access time w Last written time
[/s]	Lists every occurrence of the specified file name.
[/b]	Lists each directory or file name.
[/l]	Displays unsorted lowercase folder and file names.
[/n]	Displays a long list format.
[/x]	Displays the short names.
[/c]	Displays the thousand separator (comma) when showing file sizes.
[/4]	Displays the date in a four-digit year format.

Diskcomp

Compares the contents of two floppy disks.

Syntax

```
diskcomp [drive1: [drive2:]]
```

Parameters

Parameter	Purpose
[drive1]	Identifies the location of the first disk.
[drive2]	Identifies the location of the second disk.

Diskcopy

Copies the contents of a source disk to a destination disk.

Syntax

```
diskcopy [drive1: [drive2:]] [/v]
```

Parameters

Parameter	Purpose
[drive1]	Identifies the location of the source disk.
[drive2]	Identifies the location of the destination disk.
[/v]	Verifies a successful copy operation.

Diskperf

Specifies the types of counters that can be used with the System Monitor.

Syntax

```
diskperf [-y[d¦v]¦-n[d¦v] [\\computername]
```

Parameters

Parameter	Purpose
None	Displays the status of performance counters.
[-y]	Specifies that the physical and logical disk performance counters should be started at system initialization.
[-yd]	Enables disk performance counters for physical drives at system initialization.
[-yv]	Enables disk performance counters for logical drives at system initialization.
[-n]	Prevents disk performance counters from starting at system initialization.
[-nd]	Disables physical drive disk performance counters at system initialization.
[-nv]	Disables logical drive disk performance counters at system initialization.
[\\computername]	Allows you to specify a network computer for viewing.

Doskey

Executes the Doskey program, which recalls commands and creates macros.

Syntax

```
doskey [/reinstall] ¦ [/listsize=size] ¦ [/macros:[all ¦ exename]]
  ¦ [/history] ¦ [/insert¦] ¦ [/overstrike] ¦ [/exename=exename]
  ¦ [/macrofile=filename] ¦ [macroname=[text]]
```

Parameters

Parameter	Purpose
[/reinstall]	Installs a new copy of Doskey.
[/listsize=*size*]	Sets the maximum number of commands contained in the history buffer.
[/macros]	Displays macros.
[all]	Displays macros for all executables.

Parameters (*continued*)

Parameter	Purpose
[exename]	Displays the specified executable's macro.
[/history]	Displays commands currently stored in memory.
[/insert ¦ /overstrike]	Specifies the insert mode.
[/exename=*exename*]	Identifies the program that will run the macro.
[/macrofile=*filename*]	Identifies the file that contains macros to be installed.
[macroname=[*text*]]	Creates a macro and assigns the commands set by *text*.

Dosonly

Prevents non-MS-DOS applications from being executed at COMMAND.COM.

Syntax

```
Dosonly
```

Driverquery

Displays device driver information.

Syntax

```
driverquery [/s computer] [/u domain\user /p password] [/fo table ¦ list ¦ csv]
[/nh] [/v] [/si]
```

Parameters

Parameter	Purpose
[/s *computer*]	Identifies the name of the computer or its IP address.
[/u domain\user /p password]	Executes the command using the supplied user's permissions.
[/fo table¦list¦csv]	Specifies the format in which returned results are to be displayed.

(continues)

Parameters (*continued*)

Parameter	Purpose
[/nh]	Prevents the displays of the heading when used with the /fo table option.
[/v]	Displays detailed information about drivers.
[/si]	Displays digital signature information.

Echo

Displays a message or enables and disables command echoing.

Syntax

```
echo [on ¦ off] [message]
```

Parameters

Parameter	Purpose
None	Displays the current echo setting.
on ¦ off	Turns command echoing on or off.
[*message*]	Specifies text to be displayed.

Echoconfig

Displays messages when processing the MS-DOS subsystem CONFIG.NT and AUTOEXEC.NT files during the initialization of the MS-DOS subsystem.

Syntax

```
echoconfig
```

Edit

Starts the MS-DOS editor.

Syntax

```
edit [[drive:][path] filename] [/b] [/g] [/h] [/nohi]
```

Parameters

Parameter	Purpose
[drive:][path] filename	Specifies the drive, path, and file name of a text file and creates it if it does not exist.
[/b]	Displays the MS-DOS editor with a black background and white foreground.
[/g]	Speeds up screen updating on a CGA monitor.
[/h]	Displays the number of lines that can be displayed on the monitor.
[/nohi]	Changes from a 16-color to an 8-color scheme.

Edlin

Starts a line-oriented ASCII text editor.

Syntax

```
edlin [drive:][path] filename [/b]
```

Parameters

Parameter	Purpose
[drive:][path] filename	Specifies the drive, path, and file name of an ASCII file.
[/b]	Instructs `edlin` to ignore the end-of-file characters.

Endlocal

Ends localization of environment changes in a script and restores environment variables to their previous values.

Syntax

```
Endlocal
```

Evntcmd

Displays SNMP (*Simple Network Management Protocol*) events.

Syntax

```
evntcmd [/s sysname][/v number] [/n] filename
```

Parameters

Parameter	Purpose
[/s *sysname*]	Sets the target system name.
[/v *number*]	Sets the level of messaging: 0=none; 10=detailed.
[/n]	Prevents the restart of the SNMP service when trap changes are received.
filename	Identifies a configuration file with information about which vent to trap.

Evntcreate

Provides administrators with the ability to post events to event logs.

Syntax

```
eventcreate [/s computer [/u domain\user [/p passwd]] [/l application
  ¦ system] ¦ [/so srcname] [/t error ¦ warning ¦ information ¦
  successaudit ¦ failureaudit] [/id event] [/d description]
```

Parameters

Parameter	Purpose
[/s]	Specifies the name of the target computer.
[/u]	Executes the command using the permission assigned to the specified user.
[/p]	Specifies the user's password.
[/l application ¦ system]	Specifies the target event log.
[/so srcname]	Sets the event source.

Parameters (*continued*)

Parameter	Purpose
`[/t error ¦ warning ¦ information ¦ successaudit ¦ failureaudit]`	Identifies the event type.
`[/id event]`	Sets the event type (between 1–65535).
`[/d description]`	Specifies an event description.

Evntquery

Displays events stored in event logs.

Syntax

```
Eventcreate[.vbs] [/s computer [/u domain\user [/p passwd]] [/fi filter]
  [/fo table ¦ list ¦ csv] [/r evtrange] [/nh] [/v] [/l [application]
  ¦ [system] ¦ [security] ["DNS server"] [userlog] [dirlogname] [*]]
```

Parameters

Parameter	Purpose
`[/s]`	Specifies the name of the target computer.
`[/u]`	Executes the command using the permission assigned to the specified user.
`[/p]`	Specifies the user's password.
`[/fi filter]`	Identifies the events to be included.
`[/fo table ¦ list ¦ csv]`	Specifies the format for the command output.
`[/r evtrange]`	Specifies the range of events to be displayed.
	`N` lists the n most recent events in the log.
	`-n` lists the n oldest event in the log.
	`n1-n2` list the events in the specified range.
`[/nh]`	Suppresses the display of column headers.

(*continues*)

Parameters (*continued*)

Parameter	Purpose
[/v]	Specifies verbose output.
[/l application ¦ system ¦ security]	Specifies the target event log.
["DNS server"]	Can be specified only if DNS is active on the target computer.
[*userlog*]	A user-defined log to be processed.
[*dirlogname*]	A directory log to be processed.
[*]	Specifies all logs.

Exit

Terminates a Windows shell session.

Syntax

```
exit [/b] [exitcode]
```

Parameters

Parameter	Purpose
[/br]	Exits the currently processing batch file.
exitcode	Sets an exit code number.

Expand

Uncompresses compressed files from distribution disks.

Syntax

```
expand [-r] source [destination]
expand -d source.cab [-f:files]
expand source.cab -f:files destination
```

Parameters

Parameter	Purpose
`[-r]`	Renames files as it expands them.
`-d`	Displays the list of files at the specified source location.
`[-f:`*`files`*`]`	Specifies the files in a .CAB file that are to be expanded.
`[destination]`	Specifies the location where files are to be expanded.

Fc

Compares two files and reports on their differences.

Syntax

```
fc [/a] [/b] [/c] [/l] [/lbn] [/n] [/t] [/u] [/w] [/nnnn]
  [drive1:][path1]filename1 [drive2:][path2]filename2
```

Parameters

Parameter	Purpose
`[/a]`	Displays the first and last lines for each set of differences.
`[/b]`	Performs a comparison of the files in binary mode.
`[/c]`	Ignores differences in case.
`[/l]`	Performs a comparison of the files in ASCII mode.
`[/lb`*`n]`*	Specifies the number of lines used by the internal line buffer. This value must be greater than or equal to the number of differing lines in the files being compared.
`[/n]`	Displays the line numbers.
`[/t]`	Prevents the expansion of tabs into spaces.
`[/u]`	Performs a comparison of the files as Unicode text files.
`[/w]`	Compresses white space during the comparison.

(continues)

Parameters (*continued*)

Parameter	Purpose
`[/nnnn]`	Sets the number of consecutive lines that must be matched before the two files are identified as resynchronized.
`[drive1:][path1]filename1`	Sets the drive, path, and file name of the first file.
`[drive2:][path2]filename2`	Sets the drive, path, and file name of the second file.

Fcbs

Sets a limit on the number of FCBs (*file control blocks*) that the MS-DOS subsystem accesses simultaneously.

Syntax

```
fcbs=x
```

Parameters

Parameter	Purpose
x	Sets the number of FCBs with a maximum setting of 255.

Files

Limits the number of files that the MS-DOS subsystem can open at one time.

Syntax

```
files=x
```

Parameters

Parameter	Purpose
x	Sets the number of files with a maximum setting of 255.

Find

Searches for a string of text in a file and displays any matches.

Syntax

```
find [/v] [/c] [/n] [/i] "string" [[drive:][path]filename[...]]
```

Parameters

Parameter	Purpose
[/v]	Displays lines that do not match the string.
[/c]	Displays a count of matching lines.
[/n]	Displays a line before each line.
[/i]	Performs a case-insensitive search.
"*string*"	Specifies the string to search for.
[*drive*:][*path*] *filename*	Specifies the drive, path, and file name of the file to be searched.

Findstr

Searches for strings in files using regular expressions.

Syntax

```
findstr [/b] [/e] [/l] [/r] [/s] [/i] [/x] [/v] [/n] [/m] [/o] [/p]
  [/offline] [/g:file] [/f:file] [/c:string] [/d:dirlist]
  [/a:color attribute] [strings] [[drive:][path] filename [...]]
```

Parameters

Parameter	Purpose
[/b]	Specifies that the match must occur at the beginning of a line.
[/c: *string]*	Uses the specified string as a literal search string.
[/e]	Specifies that the match must occur at the end of a line.
[/l]	Performs a literal search using the search string.

(continues)

Parameters (*continued*)

Parameter	Purpose
`[/r]`	Uses search strings as regular expressions.
[/s]	Searches for matches in the current folder and all subdirectories.
`[/I]`	Specifies a case-insensitive search.
`[/x]`	Prints lines that contain a match.
`[/v]`	Prints lines that do not contain a match.
`[/n]`	Prints the line number.
`[/m]`	Prints the file name where a match is found.
`[/o]`	Prints the seek offset before each match.
`[/p]`	Skips nonprintable characters.
`[offline]`	Causes a file with the offline attribute set to be processed.
`[/g` *`file]`*	Specifies a file that contains the search strings.
`[/f` *`file]`*	Specifies a file that contains a file list.
`[/d` *`dirlist]`*	Searches a comma-delimited list of folders.
`[/a` *`color attribute]`*	Specifies two-character hexadecimal color attributes.

Finger

Displays user information on a specified system running the Finger service.

Syntax

```
finger [-l] [user]@computer [...]
```

Parameters

Parameter	Purpose
`[-l]`	Provides information using a long list format.
`[User]`	Specifies a user. If omitted, information about all users is displayed.
`@computer`	Specifies the computer where the information is to be collected.

Flattemp

Enables or displays the use of flat temporary folders.

Syntax

```
flattemp [/query ¦ /enable ¦ /disable]
```

Parameters

Parameter	Purpose
[/query]	Displays the current setting for FLATTEMP.
[/enable]	Enables the use of temporary folders.
[/disable]	Disables the use of temporary folders.

For

Executes a command for each file in a set of files.

Syntax

```
for %%variable in (set) do command [command-parameters]
```

Parameters

Parameter	Purpose
%%variable	Specifies a parameter that the `for` command replaces with each text string in the specified `set` until all files have been processed.
(*set*)	Specifies files or text strings to process.
command	Specifies the command to be executed in each file in the `set`.
[command-parameters]	Provides parameters to be used by the specified command.

Forcedos

Starts a program using the MS-DOS subsystem.

Syntax

```
forcedos [/d directory] filename [parameters]
```

Parameters

Parameter	Purpose
[/d *directory*]	Sets the directory to be used by the specified program.
filename	Identifies the program to be started.
[parameters]	Provides parameters to be used by the specified program.

Format

Formats a disk.

Syntax

```
format volume [/fs:file-system] [/v:label] [/q] [/a:unitsize] [/c] [/x]
format volume [/v:label] [/q] [/f:size]
format volume [/v:label] [/q] [/t:tracks /n:sectors]
format volume [/v:label] [/q]
format volume [/q]
```

Parameters

Parameter	Purpose
volume:	Sets the mount point, volume, or drive to be formatted.
[/fs:*file-system*]	Specifies one of the following file systems: FAT, FAT32, or NTFS.
[/v:*label*]	Sets the volume label.
[/a:*unitsize*]	Sets the allocation unit size to use on FAT, FAT32, or NTFS volumes.
[/q]	Performs a quick format.

Parameters (*continued*)

Parameter	Purpose
[/f:*size*]	Specifies the size of the floppy disk.
[/t:*tracks*]	Specifies the number of tracks on the disk.
[/n:*sectors*]	Specifies the number of sectors per track.
[/c]	Specifies that files created on the new volume should be automatically compressed.
[/x]	Automatically dismounts a volume if required before formatting it.

Ftp

Transfers files to and from a computer running an FTP service.

Syntax

```
ftp [-v] [-d] [-i] [-n] [-g] [-s:filename] [-a] [-w:windowsize] [-A] [computer]
```

Parameters

Parameter	Purpose
[-v]	Prevents the display of remote server messages.
[-d]	Enables debugging.
[-i]	Prevents interactive prompting for multiple file transfers.
[-n]	Suppresses autologin upon the initial connection.
[-g]	Permits the use of wildcard characters in local file and path names.
[-s:*filename*]	Identifies a text file containing FTP commands that should be automatically executed when the FTP session starts.
[-a]	Uses any local interface to bind data connection.
[-w:*windowsize*]	Changes the default transfer buffer size from 4096 to a new value.
[-A]	Logs on as anonymnous.
[computer]	Specifies a remote computer to connect to.

Ftype

Displays or modifies file types used to associate file name extensions.

Syntax

```
Ftype [filetype[=[command]]]
```

Parameters

Parameter	Purpose
[filetype]	Specifies the file type you want to work with.
[command]	Specifies the open command that is used to open files of this type.

Getmac

Displays the MAC (*media access control*) address of network devices and lists network protocols assigned to each address.

Syntax

```
Getmac[.exe] [/s computer [/u domain\user] [/p passwd]] [/fo [table
  ¦ list ¦ csv] [/nh] [/v]
```

Parameters

Parameter	Purpose
[/s *computer*]	Identifies the target computer by name or IP address.
[/u *domain\user*]	Executes the command using the supplied user's permissions.
[/p *password*]	Specifies the user's password.
[/fo [table ¦ list ¦ csv]	Specifies the format in which returned results are to be displayed.
[/nh]	Suppresses the display of column headers.
[/v]	Specifies verbose output.

Goto

Instructs the shell to jump to a label in a script and begins processing commands starting with the next line.

Syntax

```
goto label
```

Parameters

Parameter	Purpose
label	Identifies the line in a script to which the shell should jump.

Gpresult

Displays Group Policy settings and Resultant Set of Policy on the target computer.

Syntax

```
gpresult [/s computer] [/u domain\user /p password] [/user trgtusername]
  [/scope [user ¦ computer]] [/v] [/z]
```

Parameters

Parameter	Purpose
[/s *computer*]	Identifies the target computer by name or IP address.
[/u *domain\user* /p *password*]	Executes the command using the supplied user's permissions.
[/user *trgtusername*]	Specifies the username whose Resultant Set of Policy is to be displayed.
[/scope [user ¦ computer]]	Provides either computer or user data.
[/v]	Specifies verbose output.
[/z]	Specifies all available information.

Gpupdate

Refreshes Group Policy settings.

Syntax

```
gpupdate [/target:computer ¦ user] [/force] [/wait:x] [/logoff] [/boot]
```

Parameters

Parameter	Purpose
`[/target:computer ¦ user]`	Specifies whether computer or user settings are processed.
`[/force]`	Applies all Group Policy settings.
`[/wait:x]`	Number of seconds to wait for the command to complete. 600 is default.
`[/logoff]`	Logs the user off after the command completes.
`[/boot]`	Restarts the computer after the command completes.

Graftabl

Instructs Windows to display the extended characters from a specified code page in full screen mode.

Syntax

```
graftabl [xxx] [/status]
```

Parameters

Parameter	Purpose
[xxx]	Specifies the code page. Valid options are: 437 United States 850 Multilingual (Latin I) 852 Slavic (Latin II) 855 Cyrillic (Russian) 857 Turkish 860 Portuguese

Parameters (*continued*)

Parameter	Purpose
	861 Icelandic 863 Canadian-French 865 Nordic 866 Russian 869 Modern Greek
`[/status]`	Identifies the currently selected code page.

Help

Provides online information about commands.

Syntax

```
help [command]
```

Parameters

Parameter	Purpose
[command]	Specifies the command.

Helpctr

Opens the Help and Support Center.

Syntax

```
helpctr [/url [URL]] [/mode [URL]] [/hidden] [/fromstarthelp]
```

Parameters

Parameter	Purpose
`[/url [URL]]`	Specifies the URL to be loaded when the Help and Support Center starts.
`[/mode [URL]]`	Specifies an XML definition file that controls the layout and text of the Help and Control Center.

(*continues*)

Parameters (*continued*)

Parameter	Purpose
`[/hidden]`	Starts the Help and Control Center but does not display its interface.
`[/fromstarthelp]`	Starts a new instance of the Help and Support Center.

Hostname

Displays the TCP/IP name of the computer.

Syntax

```
hostname
```

If

Supports conditional logic in scripts.

Syntax

```
if [not] errorlevel number command [else expression]
if [not] string1==string2 command [else expression]
if [not] exist filename command [else expression]
if [/i] string1 compare-op string2 command [else expression]
if cmdextversion number command [else expression]
if defined variable command [else expression]
```

Parameters

Parameter	Purpose
`[not]`	Reverses the test condition.
`errorlevel` *`number`*	Sets a true condition if the previous program returned an exit code equal to or greater than *`number`*.
`command`	Identifies a command that the shell is to execute if the preceding condition is satisfied.
`string1==string2`	Specifies a true condition when *`string1`* and *`string2`* are the same.

Parameters (*continued*)

Parameter	Purpose
`exist` *`filename`*	Specifies a true condition when a *`filename`* exists.
`compare-op`	Can be any of the following operators:
	`EQU` equal to
	`NEQ` not equal to
	`LSS` less than
	`LEQ` less than or equal to
	`GTR` greater than
	`GEQ` greater than or equal to
`[/i]`	Forces case-insensitive string comparisons.
`cmdextversion` *`number`*	Compares the internal version number associated with CMD.EXE to the specified number.
`defined` *`variable`*	Returns true if the environment variable is defined.
`[else expression]`	Specifies the command and any parameters that need to be passed to the command.

Ipconfig

A diagnostic command that displays and sets TCP/IP network configuration settings.

Syntax

```
ipconfig [/all [/renew [adapter]] [/release [adapter]] [/flushdns]
  [/displaydns] [/registerdns] [/showclassid adapter]
  [/setclassid adapter [classid]]
```

Parameters

Parameter	Purpose
None	Displays the IP address, subnet mask, and default gateway for each network interface.

(continues)

Parameters (*continued*)

Parameter	Purpose
`[/all]`	Produces all available configuration information.
`[/renew [`*`adapter`*`]]`	Submits a request to renew the DHCP configuration parameters.
`[/release [`*`adapter`*`]]`	Discards the current DHCP configuration.
`[/flushdns]`	Clears and resets DNS client cache.
`[/displaydns]`	Displays DNS client cache.
`[/registerdns]`	Registers DNS names and IP addresses for the computer.
`[/showclassid `*`adapter`*`]`	Displays the DHCP class ID for the specified network adapter.
`[/setclassid `*`adapter`*` [`*`classid`*`]]`	Configures the DHCP class ID for the specified network adapter.

Ipxroute

Displays and changes information about IPX (*International Packet Exchange*) routing tables.

Syntax

```
ipxroute servers [/type=x]
ipxroute ripout network
ipxroute resolve [guid ¦ name] [guid ¦ adapter]
ipxroute board=x [def] [gbr] [mbr] [remove=xxxx]
ipxroute config
```

Parameters

Parameter	Purpose
`servers [/type=`*`x`*`]`	Displays the SAP (Service Access Point) table.
`ripout `*`network`*	Determines whether *`network`* is accessible.
`resolve [guid ¦ name] [`*`guid`*` ¦ `*`adapter`*`]`	Resolves GUID to friendly name and vice versa.

Parameters (*continued*)

Parameter	Purpose
board=*x*	Identifies the network adapter to be queried.
[def]	Transmits data packets using the ALL ROUTES broadcast. When a packet is sent to a unique MAC address that is not listed in the routing table, it is sent to SINGLE ROUTES broadcast.
[gbr]	Transmits data packets using the ALL ROUTES broadcast. When a packet is sent to the broadcast address 255, it is sent to the SINGLE ROUTES broadcast.
[mbr]	Transmits data packets using the ALL ROUTES broadcast. When a packet is sent to a multicast address, it is sent to the SINGLE ROUTES broadcast.
[remove=*xxxx*]	Removes the specified address from the routing table.
config	Displays information about all IPX bindings.

Irftp

Sends and receives data over an infrared link.

Syntax

irftp [*drive*:\][[*path*]*filename*] [/h]

irftp /s

Parameters

Parameter	Purpose
[*drive:*] [[*path*]*filename*]	The drive, path, and file name to be transmitted.
/h	Specifies hidden mode, which prevents the display of the Wireless Link dialog box.
/s	Opens Wireless link properties.

Label

Creates, deletes, or modifies a disk's volume label.

Syntax

```
label [drive:][label]
label [/MP] [volume] [label]
```

Parameters

Parameter	Purpose
none	Instructs the shell to prompt you to change or delete the current label.
[drive:]	Specifies a disk.
[label]	Specifies a new volume label.
[/MP]	Specifies that the volume is a mount point or volume name.
[*volume*]	Sets the drive letter, volume name, or mount point.
[*label*]	Specifies a volume label.

Loadfix

Loads a program above the first 64KB of conventional memory and executes it.

Syntax

```
loadfix [drive:][path] filename
```

Parameters

Parameter	Purpose
[*drive*:][*path*]	Specifies the drive and path of the program.
filename	Specifies the program name.

Lodctr

Registers Performance counters and text for services and drivers.

Syntax

```
lodctr [\\computer] filename [/s:filename] [/r:filename]
```

Parameters

Parameter	Purpose
[*computer*] *filename*	Registers the Performance counters located in *filename* on the specified target computer.
[/s:*filename*]	Saves Performance counter settings to *filename*.
[/r:*filename*]	Restores Performance counter settings from *filename*.

Logman

Schedules performance counter and event trace log collections.

Syntax

```
logman [create [counter ¦ trace] collection] [start collection]
  [stop collection] [delete collection] [query collection ¦ providers]
  [update collection]
```

Parameters

Parameter	Purpose
[create [*counter* ¦ *trace*] *collection*]	Creates collection queries or trace collections.
[start *collection*]	Starts the specified collection query.
[stop *collection*]	Stops the specified collection query.
[delete *collection*]	Deletes the specified collection query.
[query *collection* ¦ providers]	*Collection* displays the specified collection's properties. Providers displays all registered providers.
[update *collection*]	Updates collection queries.

Lpq

A diagnostic utility that provides status information about a print queue on a computer running the LPD server.

Syntax

```
lpq -S server -P printer [-l]
```

Parameters

Parameter	Purpose
-S *server*	Specifies the computer name.
-P *printer*	Specifies the printer name.
[-l]	Provides for a detailed status.

Lpr

A utility used to submit a print file to a computer running an LPD server.

Syntax

```
lpr [-S server] -P printer [-C bannercontent] [-J jobname] [-o ¦ -ol]
  filename
```

Parameters

Parameter	Purpose
[-S *server*]	Specifies the computer name or IP address of the computer where the printer is located.
-P Printer	Specifies the printer name.
[-C *bannercontent*]	Specifies banner page content to print.
[-J *jobname*]	Specifies the print job name.
[-o ¦ =ol]	Specifies the file type. -o indicates a text file and -ol indicates a binary file.
filename	Specifies the file to be printed.

Mem

Displays information about memory usage of programs loaded into memory in the MS-DOS subsystem.

Syntax

```
mem [/program¦/debug¦/classify]
```

Parameters

Parameter	Purpose
None	Displays the MS-DOS subsystem memory status.
/program	Displays the status of programs loaded into memory. This switch is mutually exclusive with the other switches.
/debug	Displays the status of currently loaded programs and internal drivers. This switch is mutually exclusive with the other switches.
/classify	Displays the status of programs loaded into conventional memory and the upper memory area. This switch is mutually exclusive with the other switches.

Mkdir (md)

Creates a directory or subdirectory.

Syntax

```
mkdir [drive:]path
md [drive:]path
```

Parameters

Parameter	Purpose
[drive:]	Specifies the drive where the new folder is to be created.
path	Specifies the folder's name and path.

Mmc

Opens the MMC (*Microsoft Management Console*).

Syntax

```
mmc path\filename.msc [/a] [/64] [/32]
```

Parameters

Parameter	Purpose
path\filename.msc	Starts the MMC using an existing console.
[/a]	Opens an existing console in author mode.
[/64]	Opens the 64-bit MMC.
[/32]	Opens the 32-bit MMC.

More

Displays output one screen at a time.

Syntax

```
command name ¦ more [/c] [/p] [/s] [/tn] [+n]
more [[/c] [/p] [/s] [/tn] [+n]] < [drive:] [path] filename
more [/c] [/p] [/s] [/tn] [+n] [files]
```

Parameters

Parameter	Purpose
[*drive*:] [*path*] *filename*	Specifies a file to display.
command name	Specifies a command to execute and displays its output.
[/c]	Clears the screen.
[/p]	Expands form-feed characters.
[/s]	Removes multiple blank lines from the display.
[/t*n*]	Changes tabs to the specified number of spaces.
[+n]	Displays the file beginning on line *n*.
[files]	Specifies a collection of files to display.

Mountvol

Creates, deletes, or displays a volume mount point.

Syntax

```
mountvol [drive:]path VolumeName
mountvol [drive:]path /d
mountvol [drive:]path /L
mountvol drive: /s
```

Parameters

Parameter	Purpose
[drive:]path	Specifies an NTFS folder to contain the mount point.
VolumeName	Identifies the volume name that is the target of the mount point.
/d	Removes a volume mount point in the specified folder.
/L	Displays the mounted volume name in the specified folder.
/s	Mounts the EIF System Partition on the specified drive and an Itanium-based computer.

Move

Moves one or more files from one location to another, deleting it from its original location.

Syntax

```
move [/y ¦ /-y] [source] [target]
```

Parameters

Parameter	Purpose
[/y]	Suppresses confirmation prompts.
[/-y]	Enables confirmation prompts.
[source]	Specifies the location of the source files to be moved.
[target]	Specifies the destination location of the files.

Msinfo32

Displays information about the operating system, software, and hardware.

Syntax

```
Msinfo32 [/pch] [/nfo filename] [/report filename] [/computer system]
  [/showcategories] [/category categoryID] [/categories categoryID]
```

Parameters

Parameter	Purpose
`[/pch]`	Displays results using a history view.
`[/nfo filename]`	Saves results as an .nfo file.
`[/report filename]`	Saves results as a .txt file.
`[/computer system]`	Starts the System Information utility on the target computer.
`[/showcategories]`	Starts the System Information utility on the target computer using all available category IDs.
`[/category categoryID]`	Starts the System Information utility on the target computer using the specified category ID.
`[/categories categoryID]`	Starts the System Information utility on the target computer using the specified category ID or category IDs.

Nbtstat

Displays current TCP/IP connections and statistics using NetBIOS over TCP/IP.

Syntax

```
nbtstat [-a remotename] [-A IP address] [-c] [-n] [-r] [-R] [RR] [-s]
  [-S] [interval]
```

Parameters

Parameter	Purpose
[-a *remotename1*]	Displays a remote computer's name table using its name.
[-A *IP address*]	Displays a remote computer's name table using its IP address.
[-c]	Displays the contents of the NetBIOS name cache.
[-n]	Displays local NetBIOS names.
[-r]	Displays name-resolution statistics.
[-R]	Purges all names from the NetBIOS name cache and reloads the Lmhosts file.
[RR]	Releases and refreshes NetBIOS names.
[-s]	Attempts to display client and server sessions using host-names.
[-S]	Displays client and server sessions in the form of IP addresses.
[interval]	Displays statistics at the specified *interval* (in seconds).

Net accounts

Modifies the user accounts database and changes logon and password requirements.

Syntax

```
net accounts [/forcelogoff:{minutes ¦ no}] [/minpwlen:length]
  [/maxpwage:[days ¦ unlimited]] [/minpwage:days] [/uniquepw:number]
  [/domain]

net accounts [/sync] [/domain]
```

Parameters

Parameter	Purpose
None	Displays current domain, logon, and password settings.

(continues)

Parameters (*continued*)

Parameter	Purpose
`[/forcelogoff:{`*`minutes`*` ¦ no}]`	Specifies a number of minutes to wait before terminating a user session with a server when the user's logon time expires. `No` prevents a forced logoff.
`[/minpwlen:`*`length`*`]`	Sets the minimum password length.
`[/maxpwage:[`*`days`*` ¦ unlimited]]`	Sets a password expiration period.
`[/minpwage:`*`days`*`]`	Specifies a minimum number of days that must pass before users can change passwords.
`[/uniquepw:`*`number`*`]`	Establishes a password history requirement that prevents users from reusing a password for the specified number of times.
`[/`*`domain`*`]`	Specifies that the operation should occur on a domain controller instead of locally.
`[/sync]`	Causes the primary domain controller to synchronize with all the backup domain controllers.

Net computer

Adds or deletes computer accounts in the domain database.

Syntax

```
net computer \\computername [/add ¦ /del]
```

Parameters

Parameter	Purpose
`\\`*`computername`*	Specifies the computer to be added or deleted.
`[/add]`	Adds the computer.
`[/del]`	Deletes the computer.

Net config

Displays and changes configurable active services.

Syntax

```
net config [server ¦ workstation]
```

Parameters

Parameter	Purpose
[server]	Displays or changes the setting for the Server service.
[workstation]	Displays or changes the setting for the Workstation service.

Net continue

Reactivates a suspended service.

Syntax

```
net continue service
```

Parameters

Parameter	Purpose
service	Sets the server to reactivate.

Net file

Displays a list of all open shared files on a server and the number of file locks on each file.

Syntax

```
net file [id [/close]]
```

Parameters

Parameter	Purpose
`None`	Displays a list of the open files on a server.
`id`	Identifies the number of the file.
`[/close]`	Closes an open file and releases any locked records.

Net group

Adds, displays, or changes global groups on Windows domains.

Syntax

```
net group [groupname [/comment:"text"]] [/domain]
net group groupname {/add [/comment:"text"] ¦ /delete} [/domain]
net group groupname username[ ...] {/add ¦ /delete} [/domain]
```

Parameters

Parameter	Purpose
`None`	Displays a list of groups on the server.
`[groupname]`	Specifies a group name to add, expand, or delete.
`[/comment:"text"]`	Adds a comment for a new or existing group.
`[/domain]`	Performs the operation on the primary domain controller instead of locally.
`username``[ ...]`	Lists one or more usernames to be added or removed from a group.
`[/add]`	Adds a group or a username to a group.
`[/delete]`	Deletes a group or username from a group.

Net help

Lists network commands for which help is available and provides help for specified network commands.

Syntax

```
net help [command]
```

Parameters

Parameter	Purpose
None	Displays a list of network commands and topics for which help is available.
[command]	Specifies a command to retrieve help for.
{/help ¦ /?}	Displays syntax for the command.

Net helpmsg

Provides help with Windows error messages.

Syntax

```
net helpmsg message#
```

Parameters

Parameter	Purpose
message#	Specifies the four-digit number of the error message.

Net localgroup

Adds, displays, or modifies local groups.

Syntax

```
net localgroup [groupname [/comment:"text"]] [/domain]
net localgroup groupname {/add [/comment:"text"] ¦ /delete} [/domain]
net localgroup groupname name [ ...] {/add ¦ /delete} [/domain]
```

Parameters

Parameter	Purpose
None	Displays the name of the server and local groups on the server.
[groupname]	Specifies the name of the local group.
[/comment:"*text*"]	Adds or changes a comment for a new or existing group.
[/domain]	Performs the operation on the primary domain controller instead of locally.
name [...]	Lists one or more usernames or group names to be added or removed from a local group.
/add	Adds either a username or a global group to a local group.
/delete	Removes a username or group name from a local group.

Net name

Displays the list of computer names that will accept messages, or adds or removes a messaging name.

Syntax

```
net name [name [/add ¦ /delete]]
```

Parameters

Parameter	Purpose
None	Displays a list of names already in use.
[name]	Specifies a name to the computer.
[/add]	Adds a name to the computer.
[/delete]	Removes a name from the computer.

Net pause

Pauses active services.

Syntax

```
net pause service
```

Parameters

Parameter	Purpose
service	Name of the service.

Net print

Lists or manages print jobs and printer queues.

Syntax

```
net print \\computername\sharename
net print [\\computername] job# [/hold ¦ /release ¦ /delete]
```

Parameters

Parameter	Purpose
somputername	Specifies the name of the computer that manages the printer queue.
sharename	Specifies the name of the printer queue.
job#	Specifies the ID number assigned to a print job.
[/hold]	Places a print job on hold.
[/release]	Releases a print job from a hold status.
[/delete]	Deletes a print job.

Net send

Sends messages to users, computers, and messaging names.

Syntax

```
net send {name ¦ * ¦ /domain[:name] ¦ /users} message
```

Parameters

Parameter	Purpose
name	Specifies a username, computer name, or messaging name.
*	Sends a message to all names in the domain or your workgroup.
/domain[:*name*]	If *name* is not specified, it sends the message to all the names in the domain. If *name* is specified, the message is sent to all the names in the specified domain or workgroup.
/users	Sends a message to all users currently connected to the server.
message	Specifies the message text.

Net session

Lists or terminates sessions with clients connected to the computer.

Syntax

```
net session [\\computername] [/delete]
```

Parameters

Parameter	Purpose
None	Displays information about all active sessions.
[*computername*]	Identifies a specific network computer.
[/delete]	Terminates a session with *computername* and then closes all open files on the computer for the session.

Net share

Creates, deletes, and displays shared resources.

Syntax

```
net share [sharename]

net share [sharename=drive:path [/users:number ¦ /unlimited]
  [/remark:"text"]  [/cache: [manual ¦ automatic ¦ no]]

net share [sharename [/users:number ¦ unlimited] [/remark:"text"] "]
  [/cache: [manual ¦ automatic ¦ no]]

net share [[sharename ¦ drive:path] /delete]
```

Parameters

Parameter	Purpose
None	Displays information about all resources that are currently shared on the computer.
sharename	Specifies the name assigned to the shared resource.
drive:*path*	Specifies the absolute path of the folder to be shared.
/users:*number*	Limits the maximum number of users who can simultaneously access the share.
/unlimited	Allows unlimited simultaneous access to the share.
/remark:"*text*"	Adds a comment to the shared resource.
/cache:automatic	Enables offline cache and automatic reintegration.
/cache:manual	Enables offline cache with manual reintegration.
/cache:no	Advises that offline cache is not recommended.
/delete	Terminates the sharing of a resource.

Net start

Displays a list of started services. It is also used to start services.

Syntax

```
net start [service]
```

Parameters

Parameter	Purpose
None	Displays a list of active services.
[service]	Specifies the name of a service to start.

Netstat

Displays statistics for current TCP/IP connections.

Syntax

```
netstat [-a] [-e] [-n] [-o] [-p protocol] [-r] [-s] [interval]
```

Parameters

Parameter	Purpose
[-a]	Displays all connections.
[-e]	Displays Ethernet-related statistics.
[-n]	Displays IP addresses and port numbers in numerical form.
[-o]	Displays active TCP connections and shows the process ID for each connection.
[-p *protocol]*	Shows connections for the specified TCP/IP protocol.
[-r]	Displays the routing table.
[-s]	Displays information organized by protocol.
[interval]	Displays statistics at the specified *interval* (in seconds).

Net statistics

Displays log statistics for the local workstation service, server service, or any other services for which statistics are available.

Syntax

```
net statistics [workstation ¦ server]
```

Parameters

Parameter	Purpose
None	Displays a list of the active services that provide statistics.
[workstation]	Displays local workstation service statistics.
[server]	Displays local server service statistics.

Net stop

Terminates a network service.

Syntax

```
net stop service
```

Parameters

Parameter	Purpose
Service	Specifies any valid Windows NT or 2000 service.

Net time

Synchronizes the computer's internal clock with another computer's clock.

Syntax

```
net time [\\computername ¦ /domain[:domainname] ¦ /rtsdomain[:domainname]]
  [/set]

net time [\\computername] [/querysntp] ¦ [/setsntp[:ntp server list]]
```

Parameters

Parameter	Purpose
None	Displays the date and time as set on the computer designated as the network's time server.
`\\computername`	Specifies the name of a network server.
`/domain[:domainname]`	Specifies a domain to synchronize with.
`/rtsdomain[:domainname]`	Specifies a domain of the Reliable Time Server to synchronize with.
`/set`	Synchronize the computer's internal clock with the specified computer or domain.
`/querysntp`	Displays the name of the Network Time Protocol server.
`/setsntp[:ntp server list]`	Specifies a list of Network Time Protocol servers to be used using hostnames or IP addresses.

Net use

Displays information about network connections and connects a computer to network resources.

Syntax

```
net use [devicename ¦ *] [\\computername\sharename[\volume]]
  [password ¦ *]] [/user:[domainname\]username]
  [/user:[dotteddomainname\]username] [/user:[username@dotteddomainname]
  [.savecred] [/smartcard] [[/delete ¦ /persistent:[yes ¦ no]]]

net use devicename [/home[password ¦ *]] [/delete:{yes ¦ no}]

net use [/persistent:{yes ¦ no}]
```

Parameters

Parameter	Purpose
None	Displays a list of network connections.
[*devicename*]	Assigns a name to a new connection or specifies a device that is to be disconnected. For disk drives, use the D: through Z:, and for printers, use LPT1: through LPT3:.
[*computername**sharename*]	Specifies the name of the network computer and its shared resource.
[*volume*]	Specifies a server with a NetWare volume.
[*password*]	Specifies a password required to access the resource.
[*]	Specifies that you want to be prompted for the password.
[/user]	Specifies a different username to be used when making the connection.
[*domainname*]	Allows you to specify another domain.
[*username*]	Specifies the username to use when logging on.
[*dotteddomainname*]	The fully qualified DNS domain name.
[/delete]	Terminates a network connection.
[/persistent]	Allows you to define persistent connections that span system restarts.
[yes]	Restores the connection at next logon.
[no]	Doesn't restore the connection at next logon.

Net user

Displays user account information or adds and modifies user accounts.

Syntax

```
net user [username [password ¦ *] [options]] [/domain]
net user [username {password ¦ *} /add [options] [/domain][
net user [username [/delete] [/domain][
```

Parameters

Parameter	Purpose
`None`	Displays a list of user accounts on the local computer.
[username]	Specifies the account name to add, delete, change, or view.
[password]	Assigns a password to a new account or changes the password of an existing account.
`*`	Prompts for the password.
`[/domain]`	Performs the operation on the primary domain controller instead of locally.
`/add`	Adds a user account.
`[/delete]`	Deletes a user account.
[options]	Specifies any of the following options:
`/active:{no ¦ yes}`	Enables or disables the account.
/comment:"*text*"	Adds comments to an account.
/countrycode:*nnn*	Specifies the Country/Region codes to be used for help and error messages.
/expires:{*date* ¦ never}	Specifies the status of account expiration.
/fullname:"*name*"	Sets a user's full name rather than a username.
/homedir:*path*	Establishes the user's home directory.
`/passwordchg:{yes ¦ no}`	Determines whether the users can change their passwords.
`/passwordreq:{yes ¦ no}`	Specifies a password requirement.
/profilepath:[*path*]	Establishes the user's logon profile.
`/scriptpath:path`	Establishes the path for the user's logon script.
/times:{*times* ¦ all}	Defines time frames in which the user is permitted to use the computer. For example: W,8AM-5PM; F,8AM-1PM.
/usercomment:"*text*"	Determines whether an administrator can change or add to the user comment.
`/workstations:}` `{computername[,...] ¦ *`	Specifies up to eight workstations where the user is permitted to log on.

Net view

Displays a list of domains, computers, or resources being shared by a specified computer.

Syntax

```
net view [\\computername ¦ /domain[:domainname]]
net view /network:nw [\\computername]
```

Parameters

Parameter	Purpose
None	Displays a list of computers in the domain.
[*computername*]	Specifies a computer so that its resources can be viewed.
/domain[:*domainname*]	Specifies the domain that is to be viewed.
/network:nw	Displays servers on a Novell NetWare network.

Nslookup

Displays information from DNS (*Domain Name System*) name servers.

Syntax

```
nslookup [-option ...] [computer-to-find ¦ - [server]]
```

Parameters

Parameter	Purpose
[-option ...]	Specifies `nslookup` commands to be used as command-line options.
[computer-to-find]	Displays information for *computer-to-find* using the default DNS server.
[server]	Specifies a different DNS server to query.

Ntbackup

Provides a means for initiating backups from the command prompt.

Syntax

```
Ntbackup backup [systemstate] "@filename" /J  ["jobname"] [/P ["poolname"]]
  [/G ["guidname"]] [/T ["tapename"] [/N {"medianame"]] [/F ["filename"]]
  [/D ["description"] [/DS ["server"]] [/IS ["server"]]
  [/A] [/V: {yes ¦ no]] [/R: [yes ¦ no]] [/L: [f ¦ s ¦ n]]
  [/M backuptype]] [/RS: [yes ¦ no ]] [/HC: [on ¦ off]] [/SNAP: [on ¦ off]]
```

Parameters

Parameter	Purpose
backup	Specifies a backup operation is to be performed.
[systemstate]	Backs up system state data.
"@*filename*"	Identifies a backup selection file to be used.
/J ["*jobname*"]	Sets the job name to be listed in the job file.
[/P ["*poolname*"]]	Sets the media pool value.
[/G ["*guidname*"]]	Changes or adds a GUID.
[/T ["*tapename*"]	Changes or adds a tape name.
[/N {"*medianame*"]]	Sets a new tape name.
[/F ["*filename*"]]	Specifies the path and file name.
[/D ["*description*"]	Sets the label for a backup set.
[/DS ["*server*"]]	Backs up the directory service file on exchange servers.
[/IS ["*server*"]]	Backs up the Information Store file on exchange servers.
[/A]	Performs an append.
[/V: {yes ¦ no]]	Verifies the integrity of the backup.
[/R: [yes ¦ no]]	Limits access to its owner and administrators.
[/L: [f ¦ s ¦ n]]	Sets the log type (f = full, s = summary, n = no log is created).
[/M *backuptype*]]	Sets the backup type. Options are: daily, differential, and incremental.

Parameters (*continued*)

Parameter	Purpose
[/RS: [yes ¦ no]]	Backs up migrated data found on remote storage.
[/HC: [on ¦ off]]	Uses hardware compression if available on the tape drive.
[/SNAP: [on ¦ off]]	Specifies whether the backup is a volume shadow copy.

Ntcmdprompt

Runs CMD.EXE instead of COMMAND.COM after starting a TSR (*Terminate and Stay Resident*) program.

Syntax

```
ntcmdprompt
```

Path

Establishes a search path for executable files.

Syntax

```
path [[drive:]path[;...]] [%path%]
```

Parameters

Parameter	Purpose
None	Displays the current search path.
[*drive*:]*path*	Specifies a location to search.
;	If used as the only parameter, it clears all path settings.
[%path%]	Appends the current path to the new setting.

Pathping

A route-tracing command that combines the functionality of the `ping` and `tracert` commands.

Syntax

```
pathping [-n] [-h maximum_hops] [-g host-list] [-p period]
  [-q num_queries [-w timeout] [-T] [-R] target_name
```

Parameters

Parameter	Purpose
-n	Specifies not to resolve addresses to hostnames.
-h *maximum_hops*	Specifies a maximum number of hops when trying to reach the target.
-g *host-list*	Allows computers to be separated by intermediate gateways along *host-list*.
-p *period*	Specifies the time to wait (in milliseconds) between pings.
-q *num_queries*	Specifies the number of queries allowed for servers along the route.
-w *timeout*	Specifies the length of time to wait for a reply (in milliseconds).
-T	Includes a layer-2 priority tag to each ping packet that is sent to network devices along the route.
-R	Determines whether each network device on the route supports the RSVP (*Resource Reservation Setup Protocol*).
target_name	Specifies the destination target using either its hostname or its IP address.

Pause

Suspends processing of a script and prompts the user to press any key to continue.

Syntax

```
pause
```

Pbadmin

Administers phone books.

Syntax

```
Pbadmine.exe /N phonebook [/R regionfilepath\regionfilename]
  [/P datafilepath\datafilename]
```

```
Pbadmine.exe /I phonebook /R regionfilepath\regionfilename
Pbadmine.exe /I phonebook /R datafilepath\datailename
Pbadmine.exe /O phonebook computername username passwd
Pdadmine.exe /B phonebook
```

Parameters

Parameter	Purpose
None	Starts the Phone Book Administrator.
/N *phonebook*	Creates a new phone book.
[/R *regionfilepath\regionfilename*]	Sets the location and name of a region file to be used in an import operation.
[/P *datafilepath\datafilename*]	Sets the location and file name of a phone book file to be used in an import operation.
/I *phonebook*	Imports dates into a phone book. Sources include region and phone book files.
/O	Sets phone book options.
phonebook	Specifies the phone book's name
computername	Specifies the computer where the phone book is to be published.
username	Specifies the username that has FTP permissions over the phone book service on the target computer.
passwd	Specifies the user's password
/B *phonebook*	Publishes the phone book.

Pentnt

Looks for the floating-point division error in the Pentium chip, disables floating-point hardware, and turns on floating-point emulation if found.

Syntax

```
pentnt [-c] [-f] [-o]
```

Parameters

Parameter	Purpose
[-c]	Turns on conditional emulation.
[-f]	Turns on forced emulation.
[-o]	Turns off forced emulation and turns on floating-point hardware.

Perfmon

Opens the Performance console using the same settings found in the Windows NT 4.0 Performance Monitor utility.

Syntax

```
Perfmon.exe [filename] [/HTMLFILE:settingsfile]
```

Parameters

Parameter	Purpose
[filename]	Specifies the file name of an optional settings file.
[/HTMLFILE:settingsfile]	Specifies the name of converted files and the name of the Windows NT 4 settings file.

Ping

Tests connections with network devices on TCP/IP networks.

Syntax

```
ping [-t] [-a] [-n count] [-l length] [-f] [-i ttl] [-v tos] [-r count]
```

```
[-s count] [[-j computer-list] ¦ [-k computer-list]] [-w timeout]
 destination-list
```

Parameters

Parameter	Purpose
`[-t]`	Repeatedly pings the specified computer.
`[-a]`	Resolves IP addresses to computer names.
`[-n` *`count]`*	Sends the specified number of `ECHO` packets as defined by *`count`*.
`[-l` *`length]`*	Transmits `ECHO` packets of the specified *`length`*.
`[-f]`	Prevents packets from being fragmented by gateways.
`[-i` *`ttl]`*	Sets the `TTL` field to the specified *`ttl`* value.
`[-v` *`tos]`*	Sets the `TOS` field to the specified *`tos`* value.
`[-r` *`count]`*	Stores the route taken by outgoing packets and returning packets in the Record Route field.
`[-s` *`count]`*	Sets a timestamp for the number of hops as set by *`count`*.
`[-j` *`computer-list]`*	Routes packets by way of the list of computers specified by *`computer-list`* and permits consecutive computers to be separated by intermediate gateways.
`[-k` *`computer-list]`*	Routes packets by way of the list of computers specified by *`computer-list`* and prevents consecutive computers from being separated by intermediate gateways.
`[-w` *`timeout]`*	Specifies the time-out interval (in milliseconds).
`destination-list`	Specifies a list of target computers.

Popd

Changes to the directory stored by `pushd`.

Syntax

```
popd
```

Print

Displays the contents of a print queue or prints a text file.

Syntax

```
print [/d:device] [[drive:][path] filename[ ...]]
```

Parameters

Parameter	Purpose
None	Displays the print queue contents.
[/d:*device*]	Specifies a print device. Use LPT1, LPT2, and LPT3 or *servername**print_share*.
[*drive*:][*path*] *filename*	Specifies the drive, path, and file name of the file to be printed.

Prompt

Changes the command prompt.

Syntax

```
prompt [text]
```

Parameters

Parameter	Purpose
none	Resets the command prompt to its default setting.
[*text*]	Specifies the text to be displayed as the command prompt. In addition to text, you can also include the following: $q equals sign $$ dollar sign $t time $d date $p drive and path

Parameters (*continued*)

Parameter	Purpose	
	$v	Windows version number
	$n	Drive
	$g	Greater-than sign
	$l	Less-than sign
	$b	Pipe
	$_	Enter-linefeed
	$e	ANSI escape code (code 27)
	$h	Backspace
	$a &	Ampersand
	$c	Left parenthesis
	$f	Right parenthesis
	$s	Space
	$+	Zero or more plus sign (+) characters depending upon the depth of the pushd directory stack
	$m	Remote name associated with the current drive letter

Pushd

Records the name of the current directory for use by the popd command and then changes to the specified directory.

Syntax

```
pushd [path]
```

Parameters

Parameter	Purpose
[path]	Specifies a directory to set as the current directory.

Rasdial

Automates the RAS (*Remote Access Service*) client connection process.

Syntax

```
rasdial connectioname [username [passwd ¦ *]] [/domain:domain]
  [/phone:phonenumber] [/callback:callbacknumber]
  [/phonebook:phonebookpath] [/prefixsuffix]

rasdial [connectionname] /disconnect
```

Parameters

Parameter	Purpose
connectioname	Specifies the name given to the connection when it was set up.
[username [*passwd* ¦ *]]	Specifies a username and password with which to establish the connection.
[/domain:*domain*]	Identifies the domain where the user account resides.
[/phone:*phonenumber*]	Substitutes the specified phone number.
[/callback:*callbacknumber*]	Substitutes the specified call back number.
[/phonebook:*phonebookpath*]	Sets the path to the phone book file.
[/prefixsuffix]	Applies current TAPI location settings.

Rcp

Copies files between a Windows computer and a UNIX system.

Syntax

```
rcp [-a ¦ -b] [-h] [-r] [host] [.user:] [source] [host] [.user:]
  [path\destionation]
```

Parameters

Parameter	Purpose
`[-a]`	Specifies the use of the ASCII transfer mode.
`[-b]`	Specifies the use of the binary image transfer mode.
`[-h]`	Transfers files with hidden attributes on Windows computers.
`[-r]`	Copies the contents of all subdirectories to the destination server.
`[host]`	Specifies the target host computer.
`[.user:]`	Specifies the username.
`[source]`	Identifies the files to be copied.
`[path\destionation]`	Specifies the destination on the target computer where the files are to be copied.

Recover

Attempts to recover information from a damaged disk.

Syntax

```
recover [drive:][path] filename
```

Parameters

Parameter	Purpose
`[drive:][path] filename`	Identifies the drive, path, and file name of the file to be recovered.

Reg add

Displays, changes, or adds a registry subkey and value.

Syntax

```
reg add keyname [/v entry] [/ve] [/t type] [/s separator] [/d value] [/f]
```

Parameters

Parameter	Purpose
Keyname	Specifies the path to the subkey.
[/v *entry*]	Specifies the entry name to be added.
[/ve]	Adds the entry as a null value.
[/t *type*]	Sets the entry type (REG_SZ, REG_MULTI-SZ, REG_DWORD_BIG_ENDIAN, REG_DWORD, REG_BINA-RY, REG_DWORD_LITTLE_ENDIAN, REG_LINK, REG_FULL_RESOURCE_DESCRIPTOR AND REG_EXPAND_SZ).
[/s *separator*]	When using the REG_MULTI-SZ type, this parameter specifies the separator chapter that is to identify multiple pieces.
[/d *value*]	Specifies a value for a new registry entry.
[/f]	Adds a subkey or entry without requiring confirmation.

Reg compare

Compares two registry entries or subkeys.

Syntax

```
reg compare key1 key2 [/v entry] [/ve] [[/oa] ¦ [od] ¦ [/os] ¦ [/on]] [/s]
```

Parameters

Parameter	Purpose
key1	Specifies the path and name of the first entry or subkey.
key2	Specifies the path and name of the second entry or subkey.
[/v *entry*]	Compares a specific subkey entry.
[/ve]	Limits the comparison to entries without values.
[/oa]	Displays all differences and matches.
[od]	Displays only differences.
[/os]	Displays only matches.

Parameters (*continued*)

Parameter	Purpose
`[/on]`	Prevents the display of differences or matches.
`[/s]`	Performs a comparison of all entries and subkeys.

Reg copy

Copies registry entries.

Syntax

```
reg copy key1 key2 [/s] [/f]
```

Parameters

Parameter	Purpose
key1	Specifies the path and name of the first entry or subkey.
key2	Specifies the path and name of the second entry or subkey.
`[/s]`	Copies all entries and subkeys.
`[/f]`	Copies the subkey without requiring confirmation.

Reg delete

Deletes registry entries and subkeys.

Syntax

```
reg delete key [/v entry ¦ /ve ¦ /va] [/f]
```

Parameters

Parameter	Purpose
key	Specifies the path and name of the entry or subkey.
`[/v` *entry*`]`	Deletes a specific entry.
`[/ve]`	Only deletes entries with a null value.

(*continues*)

Parameters (*continued*)

Parameter	Purpose
`[/va]`	Deletes all entries on the subkey.
`[/f]`	Performs the deletion without requiring confirmation.

Reg export

Copies subkeys, entries, and values to an external file to allow them to be transferred to another computer.

Syntax

```
reg export key filename
```

Parameters

Parameter	Purpose
key	Specifies the path and name of the subkey.
filename	Specifies the name of the external file.

Reg import

Copies the subkeys, values, and entries from an external file into the registry.

Syntax

```
reg import filename
```

Parameters

Parameter	Purpose
filename	Specifies the name and path of the external file.

Reg load

Copies save entries and subkeys to a different registry subkey.

Syntax

```
reg load keyname filename
```

Parameters

Parameter	Purpose
keyname	Specifies the path to the subkey.
filename	Specifies the name and path of the file to be loaded.

Reg query

Displays child entries and subkeys for the specified subkey.

Syntax

```
reg query key [/v entry ¦ /ve] [/s]
```

Parameters

Parameter	Purpose
key	Specifies the path of the subkey.
[/v *entry*]	Gets the specified entry and its value.
[/ve]	Only returns entries with a null value.
[/s]	Gets all entries and subkeys in all tiers.

Reg restore

Restores saved registry subkeys and entries.

Syntax

```
reg restore key filename
```

Parameter

Parameter	Purpose
key	Specifies the path to the subkey.
filename	Specifies the name and path of the file that contains the entries and subkeys to be restored.

Reg save

Saves specified values, entries, and subkeys to a file.

Syntax

```
reg save key filename
```

Parameters

Parameter	Purpose
key	Specifies the path of the subkey.
filename	Specifies the name and path of the file that will be created.

Regsvr32

Registers .dll files with the registry.

Syntax

```
Regsvr32 [/u] [/s] [/n] [/I[:cmdline]] dllname
```

Parameters

Parameter	Purpose
[/u]	Unregisters server.
[/s]	Sets `regsvr32` to run silently in background mode.
[/n]	Prohibits the calling of `DllRegisterServer`.
[/I[:*cmdline*]]	Calls `DllInstall` and supplies the argument supplied by *`cmdline`* if present.
Dllname	Specifies the DLL to register.

Reg unload

Removes a portion of the registry that was previously loaded using the `reg load` command.

Syntax

```
reg unload key
```

Parameters

Parameter	Purpose
key	Specifies the path to the subkey.

Relog

Extracts performance counters from counter logs and converts the data into different formats, including text, comma-delimited text, and SQL.

Syntax

```
Relog [filename [filename …]] [-a] [-c path [path …]] [-cf filename]
  [-f [bin ¦ csv ¦ tsv ¦ SQL]] [-t value] [-o [outputfile ¦ DSNcouterlog]]
  [-b m/d/yyyy [[hh:]mm:]ss] [-e m/d/yyyy [[hh:]mm:]ss] [-config filename]
  [-q]
```

Parameters

Parameter	Purpose
[*filename* [*filename* …]]	Specifies the path and file name of one or more input files.
[-a]	Appends data from the input file.
[-c *path* [*path* …]]	Specifies the performance counter path to be logged.
[-cf *filename*]	Specifies the pathname of a text file that contains a list of counters to be added to the `relog` file.

(*continues*)

Parameters (*continued*)

Parameter	Purpose
`[-f [bin ¦ csv ¦ tsv ¦ SQL]]`	Sets the output files format (`bin` = binary, `csv` = text, `tsv` = comma-delimited text, and `sql` = SQL).
`[-t` *`value`*`]`	Specifies the collection interval.
`[-o [`*`outputfile`* `¦` *`DSNcouterlog`*`]]`	Sets the path for the output file or SQL database where counters are stored.
`[-b` *`m/d/yyyy`* `[[`*`hh`*`:]`*`mm`*`:]`*`ss`*`]`	Sets the start time for copying the first record from the input file.
`[-e` *`m/d/yyyy`* `[[`*`hh`*`:]`*`mm`*`:]`*`ss`*`]`	Sets the stop time for copying the last record from the input file.
`[-config` *`filename`*`]`	Sets the path of an optional settings file that supplies command-line parameters.
`[-q]`	Displays performance counters and time ranges for a specified input file.

Rem

Used to place comments in scripts.

Syntax

```
rem [comment]
```

Parameters

Parameter	Purpose
`[comment]`	A string of descriptive text information.

Rename (Ren)

Renames a file or group of files.

Syntax

```
rename [drive:][path] filename1 filename2
ren [drive:][path] filename1 filename2
```

Parameters

Parameter	Purpose
[*drive*:][*path*] *filename1*	Specifies the drive, path, and file name of the file to be renamed.
filename2	Specifies the new name for the file.

Replace

Replaces files in the destination directory with files that have the same name.

Syntax

```
replace [drive1:][path1] filename [drive2:][path2] [/a] [/p] [/r] [/w]

replace [drive1:][path1] filename [drive2:][path2] [/p] [/r] [/s] [/w]
  [/u]
```

Parameters

Parameter	Purpose
[*drive1*:][*path1*] *filename*	Specifies the drive, path, and file name of the source files.
[*drive2*:][*path2*]	Specifies the drive and path of the destination files.
[/a]	Adds files to the destination folder.
[/p]	Prompts for confirmation before a replacement is allowed.
[/r]	Permits the replacement of read-only files.

(continues)

Parameters (*continued*)

Parameter	Purpose
`[/w]`	Waits for you to insert a disk before beginning to look for the source files.
`[/s]`	Searches all subfolders in the destination folder and replaces matching files.
`[/u]`	Replaces files in the destination folder only if they are older than the files in the source folder.

Reset session

Resets a terminal server session.

Syntax

```
Reset session [sessionname ¦ sessionid] [/server:servername] [/v]
```

Parameters

Parameter	Purpose
[*sessionname*]	Name of the session to be reset.
[*sessionid*]	The session ID of the session to be reset.
[/server:*servername*]	Identifies the terminal sever where the session exists.
[/v]	Displays verbose information.

Rexec

Executes commands on remote computers that support the Rexec service.

Syntax

```
rexec computer [-l username] [-n] command
```

Parameters

Parameter	Purpose
computer	Specifies the remote computer.
[-l *username*]	Specifies a username on the remote computer.
[-n]	Redirects the input of REXEC to NULL.
command	Specifies the command to be executed.

Rmdir (Rd)

Deletes a folder.

Syntax

```
rmdir [drive:]path [/s] [/q]
rd [drive:]path [/s] [/q]
```

Parameters

Parameter	Purpose
[*drive*:]*path*	Specifies the drive and path of the folder to be deleted.
[/s]	Deletes the folder and its subfolders and their contents.
[/q]	Deletes folders without requiring confirmation.

Route

Configures routing tables.

Syntax

```
route [-f] [-p] [command [destination] [mask subnetmask] [gateway]
  [metric costmetric]] [if interface]]
```

Parameters

Parameter	Purpose
`[-f]`	Clears the routing tables of gateway entries.
`[-p]`	Makes routes persistent across system restarts.
`[command]`	Prints, adds, deletes, or changes the destination.
`[destination]`	Specifies the computer where the command will be sent.
`[mask` *`subnetmask]`*	Specifies a subnet mask for the route entry.
`[gateway]`	Specifies a gateway.
`[metric` *`costmetric]`*	Assigns an integer cost metric.
`[if` *`interface`*`]`	Specifies the interface index for the interface.

Rsh

Executes commands on remote computers that run the RSH service.

Syntax

```
rsh computer [-l username] [-n] command
```

Parameters

Parameter	Purpose
`computer`	Specifies the remote computer.
`[-l` *`username]`*	Specifies a username to use at the remote computer.
`[-n]`	Redirects the input of `Rsh` to `NULL`.
`command`	Specifies the command.

Runas

Permits the execution of specific tools and programs with different permissions than those provided by the user's current account.

Syntax

```
runas [/profile ¦ /noprofile] [/env] [/netonly] [/smartcard]
  [/showtrustlevels] [/trustlevel] /user:UserAccountName program
```

Parameters

Parameter	Purpose
/profile	Provides the name of the user's profile.
/noprofile	Prevents loading the user's profile.
/env	Replaces the user's local environment with the current network environment.
/netonly	Specifies that the user information is to be used for remote access.
[/smartcard]	Specifies that credentials are to be provided by a smartcard.
[/showtrustlevels]	Displays /trustlevel options.
[/trustlevel]	Sets the authorization level that is to be used to run the application.
/user:*UserAccountName*	Specifies the account with which to execute the program in the form of *user@domain* or *domain\user*.
program	Specifies the program or command to be executed by a specified account.

Set

Displays, changes, and deletes environment variables.

Syntax

```
Set [[/a [expression]] [/p [variable=]] string]
```

Parameters

Parameter	Purpose
`None`	Displays environment settings.
`[/a [`*`expression`*`]`	Sets *`string`* equal to a numerical expression.
`[/p]`	Sets a variable value equal to a line of input.
`variable`	Identifies the variable to set or modify.
`string`	Sets the value of the variable to *`string`*.

Setlocal

Initiates the localization of environment variables in a script.

Syntax

```
Setlocal [enableextension ¦ disableextensions] [enabledelayedexpansion
  ¦ disabledelayedexpansion]
```

Parameters

Parameter	Purpose
`[enableextension]`	Enables command extensions.
`[disableextensions]`	Disables command extensions.
`[enabledelayedexpansion]`	Enables delayed environment variable expansion.
`[disabledelayedexpansion]`	Disables delayed environment variable expansion.

Setver

Modifies the version number that the MS-DOS subsystem reports to executing programs.

Syntax

```
setver [drive:path] [filename n.nn]
setver [drive:path] [filename [/delete [/quiet]]
setver [drive:path]
```

Parameters

Parameter	Purpose
None	Displays the current version table.
[*drive*:*path*]	Specifies drive and path to SETVER.EXE.
[*filename*]	Specifies a program name to be added to the version table.
[*n.nn*]	Specifies the MS-DOS version that is reported to the specified program file.
[/delete]	Removes the version table entry for the specified program file.
[/quiet]	Hides deletion messages.

Sfc

Scans protected file systems and verifies their integrity.

Syntax

```
Sfc [/scannow] [/scanonce] [/scanboot] [/revert] [purgecache]
  [/cachesize=x]
```

Parameters

Parameter	Purpose
[/scannow]	Performs an immediate scan of all protected file systems.
[/scanonce]	Scans all protected file systems at one time.
[/scanboot]	Scans all protected file systems every time the computer is started.
[/revert]	Restores the scan to its default settings.
[purgecache]	Clears out Windows File Protection cache and performs an immediate scan.
[/cachesize=*x*]	Sets a maximum cache size in MB for Windows File Protection cache.

Shell

Specifies an alternative command interpreter to be used in place of the MS-DOS subsystem.

Syntax

```
shell=[[drive:]path] filename [parameters]
```

Parameters

Parameter	Purpose
`[[drive:]path] filename`	Specifies the drive, path, and file name of the alternative command interpreter.
`[parameters]`	Provides any command-line parameters required by the alternative command interpreter.

Shift

Shifts (changes) the position of replaceable parameters in a script.

Syntax

```
Shift /n
```

Parameters

Parameter	Purpose
`/n`	Identifies the argument where shifting should begin, where *n* is a value from 0 to 8.

Shutdown

Shuts down Windows XP and optionally restarts the computer or logs off the current user.

Syntax

```
shutdown [[-l ¦ -s ¦ -r ¦ -a]] [-f] -m[\\computer]] [-t xx] [-c "msg"]
  [-d[u][p]:xx:yy]
```

Parameters

Parameter	Purpose
[-l]	Logs the current user off.
[-s]	Shuts the local computer down.
[-r]	Restarts the computer once it has been shut down.
[-a]	Aborts the shutdown process.
[-f]	Forces the termination of active applications.
-m[\\computer]]	Allows for the specification of a remote computer.
[-t xx]	Specifies the amount of time to wait before the shutdown occurs.
[-c "msg"]	Displays a message in the System Shutdown dialog message area.
[-d[u][p]:xx:yy]	Lists a reason code for the shutdown (*u* = user code, *p* = planned shutdown code, *xx* = a major reason code with a value between 0 and 255, and *yy* = a minor reason code with a value of 0 to 65536).

Sort

Reads input and sorts it before writing it as output.

Syntax

```
sort [/r] [/+n] [/m kilobytes] [/l locale] [/rec characters]
  [[drive1:][path1]filename1] [/t [drive2:][path2]]
  [/o [drive3:][path3]filename3]
```

```
[command ¦] sort [/r] [/+n] [/m kilobytes] [/l locale] [/rec characters]
  [[drive1:][path1]filename1] [/t [drive2:][path2]] [/o
  [drive3:][path3]filename3]
```

Parameters

Parameter	Purpose
/r	Reverses the sort order.
/+*n*	Specifies the starting character position, *n*, where sort begins its comparison.

(continues)

Parameters (*continued*)

Parameter	Purpose
`/m` *`kilobytes`*	Specifies the allocation of memory for use by the `sort` command (in kilobytes).
`/l` *`locale`*	Changes the sort order of characters as defined by the default locale. The only available option is the "`C`" locale.
`/rec` *`characters`*	Sets the maximum number of characters that can be contained in a line on the input file (default is 4,096; maximum is 65,535).
`[`*`drive1:`*`][`*`path1`*`]`*`filename1`*	Specifies the location of the file to be sorted.
`/t [`*`drive2:`*`][`*`path2`*`]`	Specifies a path to a folder that the `sort` command can use for working storage when the data to be sorted cannot fit into memory.
`/o [`*`drive3:`*`][`*`path3`*`]` *`filename3`*	Specifies where a file's sorted input is to be stored.

Start

Opens a new command prompt window and executes the specified program, script, or command.

Syntax

```
start ["title"] [/d path] [/I] [/min] [/max] [/separate ¦ /shared]
  [/low ¦ /normal ¦ /high ¦ /realtime ¦ /abovenormal ¦ /belownormal]
  [/wait] [/b] [filename] [parms]
```

Parameters

Parameter	Purpose
`["`*`title`*`"]`	Displays the specified title in the command prompt title bar.
`[/d` *`path`*`]`	Specifies the path of the startup folder.
`[/I]`	Passes the environment settings of the CMD.exe startup environment to the command prompt window.

Parameters (*continued*)

Parameter	Purpose
`[/min]`	Minimizes the new window.
`[/max]`	Maximizes the new window.
`[/separate]`	Loads 16-bit applications into a separate memory space.
`[/shared]`	Loads 16-bit applications into a shared memory space.
`[/low]`	Runs the program and assigns it the idle priority.
`[/normal]`	Runs the program and assigns it the normal priority.
`[/high]`	Runs the program and assigns it the high priority.
`[/realtime]`	Runs the program and assigns it the real time priority.
`[/abovenormal]`	Runs the program and assigns it the above normal priority.
`[/belownormal]`	Runs the program and assigns it the below normal priority.
`[/wait]`	Runs the program and then waits for it to end.
`[/b]`	Starts an application without opening a command prompt window.
[*filename*]	Identifies the command or application to execute.
[*parms*]	Argument to be passed to the command or program.

Subst

Establishes an association between a path and a drive letter.

Syntax

```
subst [drive1: [drive2:]path]
subst drive1: /d
```

Parameters

Parameter	Purpose
None	Displays the names of any virtual drives.
[drive1:]	Specifies the virtual drive.
[drive2:]	Specifies the physical drive containing the specified path.

(*continues*)

Parameters (*continued*)

Parameter	Purpose
[path]	Specifies the path to be assigned to the virtual drive.
/d	Removes a virtual drive.

Systeminfo

Displays configuration information about a computer and its operating system and hardware.

Syntax

```
systeminfo[.exe] [/s computer [/u domain\user [/p passwd]]]
  [/fo [table ¦ list ¦ csv]] [/nh]
```

Parameters

Parameter	Purpose
[/s *computer*]	Specifies the target computer's name or IP address.
[/u *domain\user*]	Executes the command using the supplied user's permissions.
[/p *passwd*]	Specifies the user's password.
[/fo [table ¦ list ¦ csv]]	Specifies output format (table, list, or CSV).
[/nh]	Suppresses column headers.

Taskkill

Terminates tasks and processes.

Syntax

```
taskkill [/s computer] [/u domain\user [/p passwd]] [/fi filter]
  [/pid processid] ¦ [/im image] [/f] [/t]
```

Parameters

Parameter	Purpose
[/s *computer*]	Specifies the name or IP address of the target computer.
[/u *domain\user*]	Executes the command using the supplied user's permissions.
[/p *passwd*]	Specifies the user's password.
[/fi *filter*]	Specifies the type of process to terminate or not to terminate.
[/pid *processid*]	Specifies the process ID of the process to kill.
[/im *image*]	Specifies the image name of the process to kill.
[/f]	Forcefully terminates a process.
[/t]	Terminates all child processes of the parent process.

Tasklist

Lists applications and services, including their process ID.

Syntax

```
Tasklist[.exe] [/s computer] [/u domain\user [/p passwd]]
  [/fo [table ¦ list ¦ csv]] [/nh] [/fi filter] [/fi filter2 [ … ]]]
  [/m [module] ¦ /svc] /v]
```

Parameters

Parameter	Purpose
[/s *computer*]	Specifies the name or IP address of the target computer.
[/u *domain\user*]	Executes the command using the supplied user's permissions.
[/p *passwd*]	Specifies the user's password.
[/fo [table ¦ list ¦ csv]]	Specifies the format of the command's output.
[/nh]	Suppresses column headings.
[/fi filter]	Specifies the type of process to include or exclude from output.

(*continues*)

Parameters (*continued*)

Parameter	Purpose
`[/m [module]`	When specified, all processes using the module are listed, otherwise they are excluded.
`[/svc]`	Displays all available service information.
`[/v]`	Displays verbose output.

Tcmsetup

Configures the telephony client.

Syntax

```
tcmsetup [/q] [/x] /c server1 [server2 ... serverN]
tcmsetup [/q] /c /d
```

Parameters

Parameter	Purpose
`[/q]`	Prevents message box displays.
`[/x]`	Sets connection-oriented callbacks for heavy traffic networks with high pack-loss.
`/c`	Specifies client setup. Required parameter.
`server1`	Contains the remote server where the client will use TAPI service providers.
`[server2 ... serverN]`	Lists additional servers that are available to the client.
`/d`	Clears the list of remote servers and disables the telephony client.

Tftp

Transfers files between the local computer and a remote computer running the TFTP (*Trivial File Transfer Protocol*) service.

Syntax

```
tftp [-i] computer [get ¦ put] source [destination]
```

Parameters

Parameter	Purpose
[-I]	Sets binary image transfer mode.
computer	Specifies the local or remote computer.
[put]	Uploads files to the file *source* on the remote computer.
[get]	Downloads the file on the remote computer to the file *source* on the local computer.
source	Identifies the file to transfer.
[destination]	Identifies where to transfer the file.

Time

Displays system time or changes the computer's internal clock.

Syntax

```
time [/t] [hours:[minutes[:seconds[.hundredths]]] [A¦P]]
```

Parameters

Parameter	Purpose
None	Displays the computer's clock time and prompts for the new time.
[/t]	Displays current time without prompting to change the time.
[hours]	Sets the hour.
[minutes]	Sets the minutes.
[seconds]	Sets the seconds.
[hundredths]	Sets hundredths of a second.
[A¦P]	Sets A.M or P.M. for the 12-hour format.

Title

Places a message on the command console's title bar.

Syntax

```
title [string]
```

Parameters

Parameter	Purpose
[string]	Specifies the message text.

Tracerpt

Processes trace logs or data from event trace providers and creates reports.

Syntax

```
tracerpt [filename [filename ...]] [-o [filename]] [-report [filename]]
  [-rt session [session ...]] [-summary [filename]] [-config [filename]
```

Parameters

Parameter	Purpose
[*filename* [*filename* ...]]	Specifies the file name to be used during the event trace session.
[-o [*filename*]	Specifies a comma-delimited file.
[-report [*filename*]]	Sets the name of the output report file.
[-rt *session* [*session* ...]]	Gathers data from a realtime source.
[-summary [*filename*]]	Specifies the name of the output summary file.
[-config [*filename*]	Specifies the path of a settings file that supplies command-line arguments.

Tracert

A utility used to determine the route taken to a destination.

Syntax

```
tracert [-d] [-h maximum_hops] [-j computer-list] [-w timeout] target_name
```

Parameters

Parameter	Purpose
[-d]	Prevents the resolution of IP addresses to hostnames.
[-h *maximum_hops*]	Sets a maximum number of hops.
[-j *computer-list*]	Specifies a loose source route along *computer-list*.
[-w *timeout*]	Waits the specified number of milliseconds for each reply.
target_name	Identifies the target computer.

Tree

Provides a graphic view of the folder structure for the specified path or disk.

Syntax

```
tree [drive:][path] [/f] [/a]
```

Parameters

Parameter	Purpose
[*drive*:]	Identifies a drive that contains a disk whose directory structures should be displayed.
[*path*]	Identifies a folder whose directory structure is to be displayed.
[/f]	Displays the file names found in each directory.
[/a]	Sets the tree command to display text characters in place of graphic characters when identifying links to a subfolder.

Type

Displays the contents of a text file.

Syntax

```
type [drive:][path] filename
```

Parameters

Parameter	Purpose
[drive:][path] filename	Specifies the drive, path, and file name that is to be viewed.

Typeperf

Displays performance counter output to the console window or logs in to a file.

Syntax

```
typeperf [path [path …]] [-cf filename] [-f [csv ¦ tsv ¦ bin]]
  [-si interval] [-o filename] [-q [object]] [-qx [object]]
  [-sc samples] [-config filename] [-s computer]
```

Parameters

Parameter	Purpose
[*path* [*path* …]]	Specifies the path and name of the performance counter log that is to be used.
[-cf *filename*]	Specifies the filename of a file that lists counter paths that are to be monitored.
[-f [csv ¦ tsv ¦ bin]]	Specifies output format (csv = comma-delimited text file, tsv = tab-delimited text file, and bin = binary).
[-si *interval*]	Sets the time interval between collections in [mm:]ss format.
[-o *filename*]	Specifies an output file.
[-q [*object*]]	Displays counters that do not have instances.
[-qx [*object*]]	Displays counters with instances.

Parameters

Parameter	Purpose
[-sc *samples*]	Specifies the number of samples to be collected.
[-config *filename*]	Specifies the name of a file that contains command-line arguments.
[-s *computer*]	Specifies the target computer.

Unlodctr

Unloads performance counter names for services and device drivers from the registry.

Syntax

```
unlodctr [\\computer] drivername
```

Parameters

Parameter	Purpose
[\\computer]	Specifies the target computer.
drivername	Unloads the performance counter names for service and device driver *drivername*.

Ver

Displays the Windows version number.

Syntax

```
ver
```

Vol

Displays the serial number and disk volume label of the disk.

Syntax

```
vol [drive:]
```

Parameters

Parameter	Purpose
[drive:]	Specifies the drive whose information you want to display.

Vssadmin

Displays volume shadow copy backups and shadow copy writers.

Syntax

```
vssadmin list [shadows [/set= [shadow copy of GUID]] ¦ writers ¦ provides]
```

Parameter

Parameter	Purpose
List [shadows [/set= [*shadow copy of GUID*]]	Displays shadow copies for the shadow copy set.
[writers]	Displays information about installed shadow copy writers.
[provides]	Displays information about installed shadow copy providers.

W32tm

Diagnoses Windows Time problems.

Syntax

```
W32tm [/config [/computer] [[/update] [/manualpeerlist:list fo names]]
  [/syncfromflags:listofflags]] ¦ /monitor ¦ /ntpte ¦ /register ¦ resync
  [[:computer] [/nowait] ¦ [/rediscover]] ¦ [/tz ¦ /unregister]
```

Parameters

Parameter	Purpose
[/config [/*computer*] [[/update] [/manualpeerlist:*list fo names*]] [/syncfromflags:*listofflags*]	Changes time setting on the target computer.

Parameters

Parameter	Purpose
/monitor	Monitors the target computer.
/ntpte	Converts system time to a readable format.
/register	Registers execution as a service.
resync [[:*computer*] [/nowait] ¦ [/rediscover]]	Resynchronizes the clock at the first available opportunity.
[/tz]	Displays time zone information.
[/unregister]	Unregisters the services and any configuration date.

Xcopy

Copies folders and their contents, including files and subfolders.

Syntax

```
xcopy source [destination] [/w] [/p] [/c] [/v] [/q] [/f] [/l] [/d[:date]]
  [/u] [/i] [/s [/e]] [/t] [/k] [/r] [/h] [/a¦/m] [/n] [/o] [/x]
  [/exclude:file1[+[file2]][+[file3]] [/y ¦ /-y] [/z]
```

Parameters

Parameter	Purpose
source	Specifies location and name of the files to be copied.
[destination]	Specifies the destination of the copied files.
[/w]	Displays a confirmation message and waits for a reply.
[/p]	Prompts for confirmation before creating destination files.
[/c]	Ignores all errors.
[/v]	Verifies the success of each copy operation.
[/q]	Prevents the display of `xcopy` messages.
[/f]	Displays the file names being copied.

(*continues*)

Parameters (*continued*)

Parameter	Purpose
`[/l]`	Prevents command execution and displays a list of files that would have been copied.
`/d[:`*`date`*`]`	Copies source files that have been changed on or after *`date`*.
`[/u]`	Copies files from *`source`* if they also exist on *`destination`*.
`[/I]`	Creates the destination folder, if it does not exist, if *`source`* is a directory or contains wildcards.
`[/s]`	Copies directories and subdirectories as long as they contain files.
`[/e]`	Copies all subfolders.
`[/t]`	Copies the subdirectory structure and not the files.
`[/k]`	Copies read-only files to the destination where they will retain their read-only status.
`[/r]`	Overwrites read-only files.
`[/h]`	Copies files with hidden and system file attributes.
`[/a]`	Copies source files that have archive file attributes set.
`[/m]`	Copies source files that have archive file attributes set and then turns off archive file attributes.
`[/o]`	Copies file ownership and discretionary access control list data.
`[/x]`	Copies audit settings and system access control list data.
`[/n]`	Copies files using their NTFS short names.
`[/`*`exclude:file1`*`[+[`*`file2`*`]] [+[`*`file3`*`]]`	Excludes the files listed in specified files from being copied.
`[/y]`	Suppresses confirmation prompts when overwriting existing destination files.
`[/-y]`	Requires confirmation prompts before overwriting existing destination files.

Parameters (*continued*)

Parameter	Purpose
[/z]	Copies files to the network in restartable mode so that the copy operations will resume after failed connections are reestablished.

Appendix B

What's on the Companion Web Site

All of the scripts that you will see presented in this book are available for download at the book's companion Web site. To visit this Web site, open your Internet browser, type **http://www.premierpressbooks.com/downloads.asp** in the URL field, and press Enter. The Web site is shown in Figure B.1.

Some of the things that you will find at this Web site include:

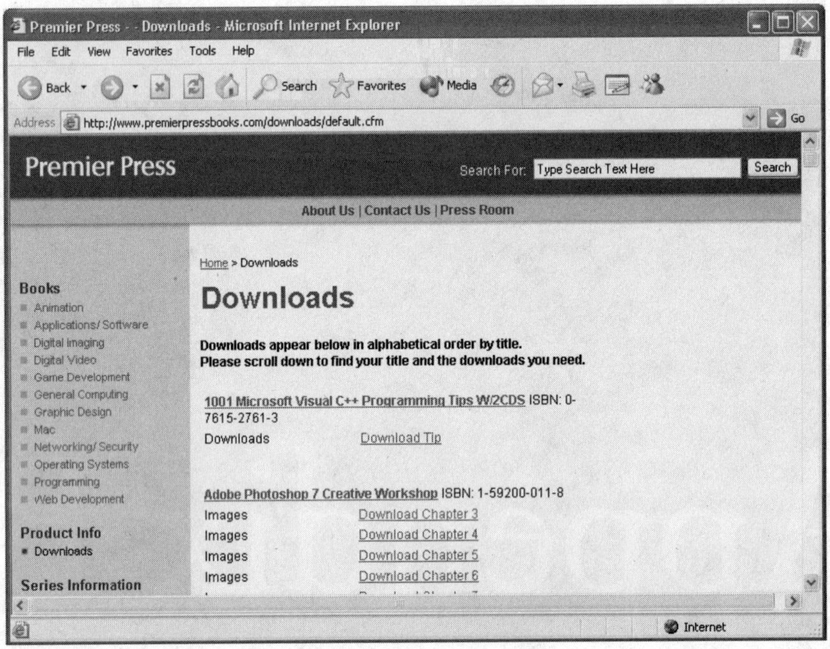

FIGURE B.1 *The Microsoft VBScript Professional Projects companion Web site*

- Access to download all the VBScripts presented in this book on a chapter-by-chapter basis
- Access to download all the VBScripts presented in this book as one large download

- Access to download sample VBScripts from other Premier Press books, including *Learn VBScript in a Weekend* and *Microsoft WSH and VBScript for the Absolute Beginner*

Index

Symbols

A

B

C

D

E

F

G

H

S

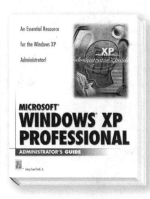

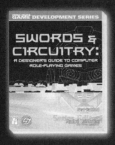